D1219117

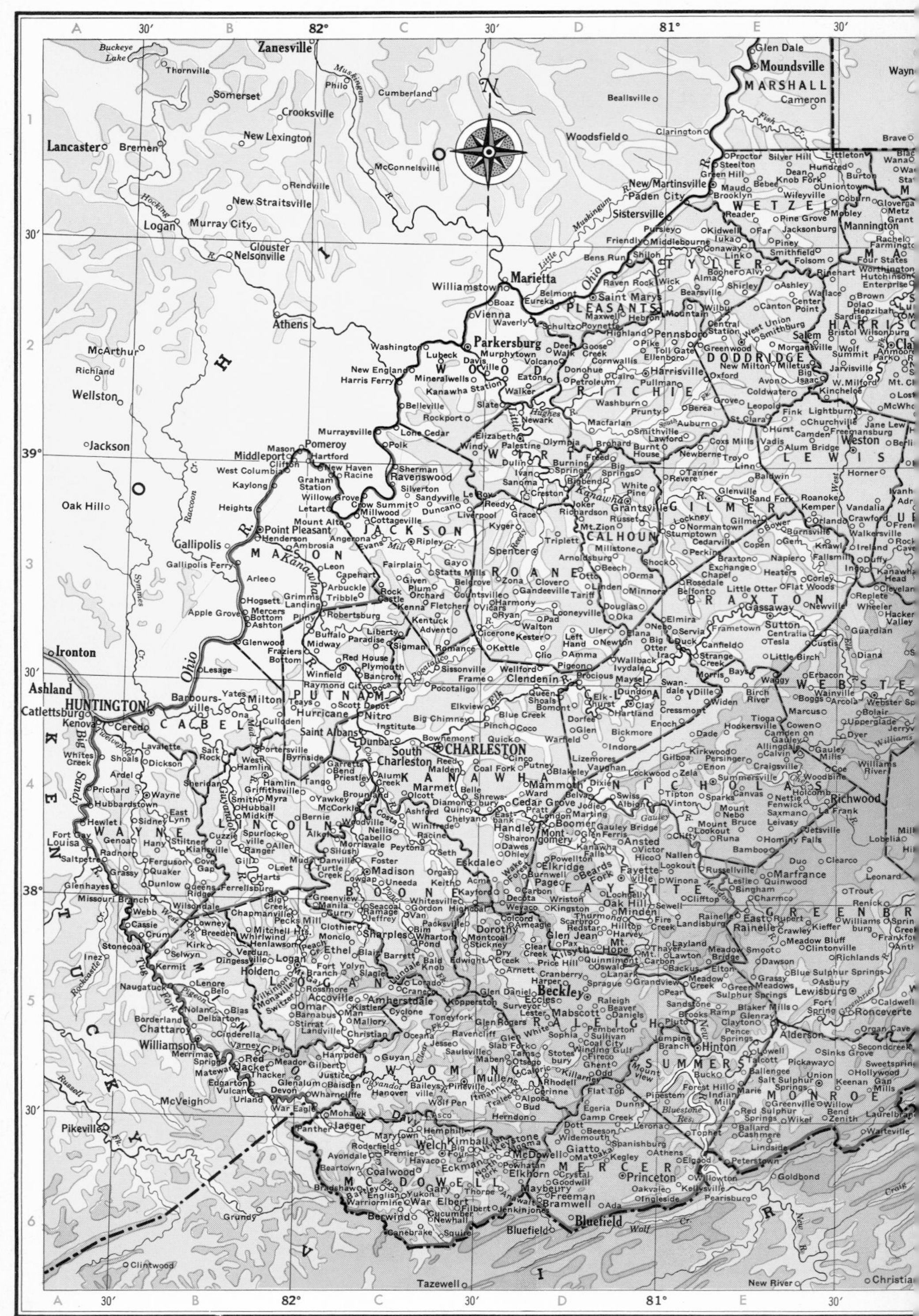

A
30′
B
82°
C
30′
D
81°
E
30′
1
2
3
4
5
6
39°
38°
N
O H I O
K E N T U C K Y
V I
MARSHALL
WETZEL
TYLER
PLEASANTS
WOOD
RITCHIE
DODDRIDGE
HARRISON
LEWIS
WIRT
CALHOUN
GILMER
JACKSON
MASON
ROANE
BRAXTON
CLAY
PUTNAM
CABELL
KANAWHA
NICHOLAS
WEBSTER
WAYNE
LINCOLN
BOONE
FAYETTE
GREENBRIER
LOGAN
MINGO
RALEIGH
WYOMING
SUMMERS
MONROE
MERCER
McDOWELL
Zanesville
Lancaster
Logan
Athens
Marietta
Parkersburg
Gallipolis
Point Pleasant
Ironton
Ashland
HUNTINGTON
CHARLESTON
South Charleston
Moundsville
New Martinsville
Sistersville
Saint Marys
Harrisville
Spencer
Ripley
Ravenswood
Clendenin
Madison
Williamson
Logan
Beckley
Oak Hill
Fayetteville
Hinton
Welch
Bluefield
Princeton
Lewisburg
Weston
Richwood
Pikeville
Tazewell
Ohio R.
Kanawha R.
Little Kanawha R.
Big Sandy R.
Tug Fork
Guyandot R.
Elk R.
Gauley R.
New R.
Bluestone Res.
Muskingum R.
Hocking R.

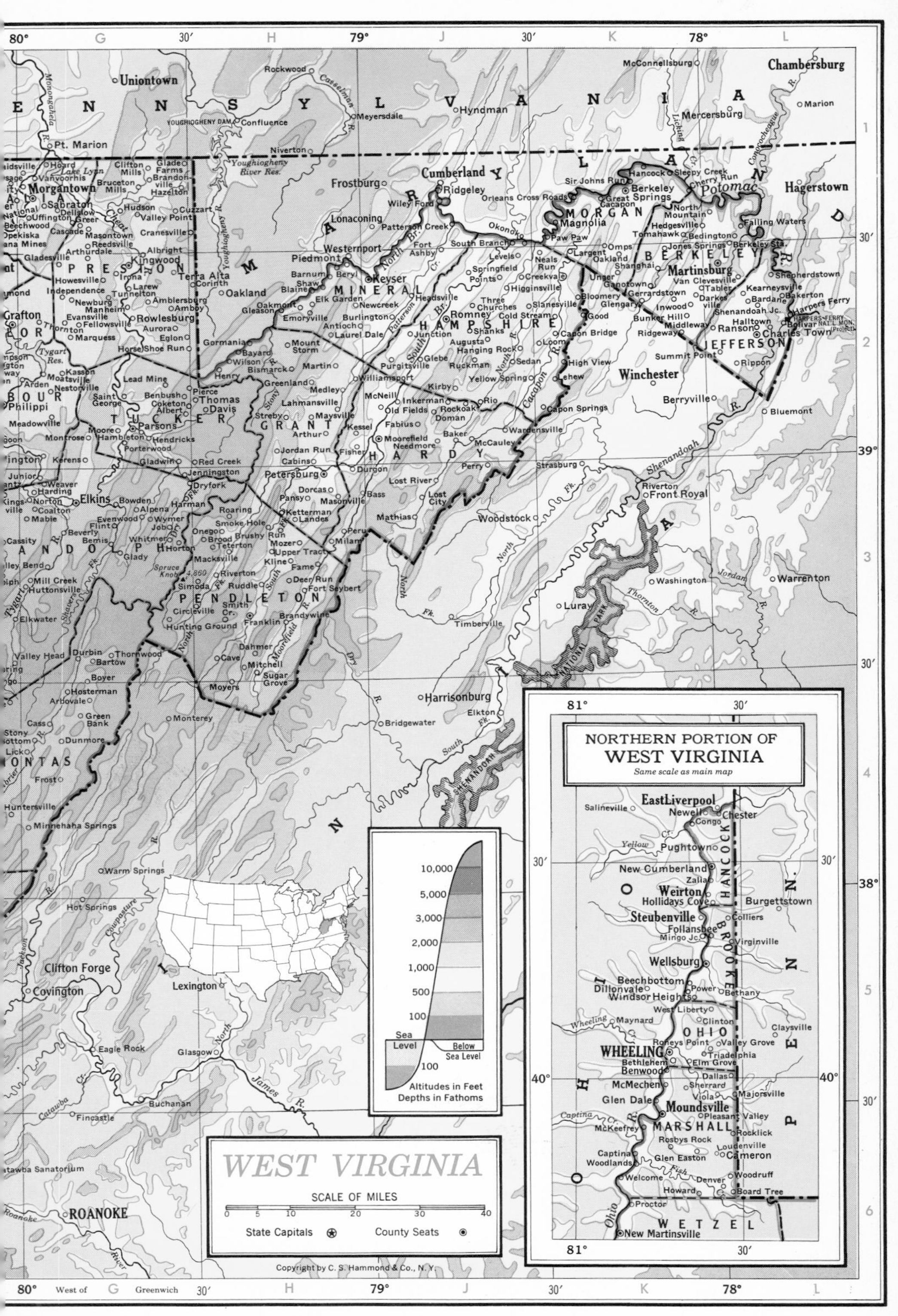

WEST VIRGINIA
SCALE OF MILES
0 5 10 20 30 40
State Capitals
County Seats
Altitudes in Feet
Depths in Fathoms
10,000
5,000
3,000
2,000
1,000
500
100
Sea Level
Below Sea Level
100
NORTHERN PORTION OF WEST VIRGINIA
Same scale as main map
Copyright by C. S. Hammond & Co., N. Y.
80° West of Greenwich
79°
78°
30′
39°
38°
40°
81°
G
H
J
K
L
1
2
3
4
5
6
PENNSYLVANIA
MARYLAND
VIRGINIA
OHIO
PENNSYLVANIA
PRESTON
MINERAL
HAMPSHIRE
MORGAN
BERKELEY
JEFFERSON
GRANT
HARDY
TUCKER
PENDLETON
HANCOCK
BROOKE
OHIO
MARSHALL
WETZEL
Uniontown
Chambersburg
Hagerstown
Cumberland
Morgantown
Martinsburg
Winchester
Charles Town
Harpers Ferry
Romney
Keyser
Petersburg
Moorefield
Franklin
Parsons
Kingwood
Elkins
Harrisonburg
Woodstock
Front Royal
Luray
Warrenton
Lexington
Clifton Forge
Covington
ROANOKE
Staunton
Wheeling
Weirton
Steubenville
Wellsburg
Moundsville
New Cumberland
East Liverpool
Chester
New Martinsville
Berkeley Springs
Frostburg
Westernport
Piedmont
Grafton
Thomas
Davis
Monterey
Warm Springs
Hot Springs
Potomac R.
Shenandoah R.
Youghiogheny River Res.
Ohio R.
James R.
Wheeling Cr.
Cheat R.
South Branch
SHENANDOAH NATIONAL PARK

West Virginia

the mountain state

CHARLES H. AMBLER
West Virginia University

FESTUS P. SUMMERS
West Virginia University

SECOND EDITION

PRENTICE-HALL, INC.
Englewood Cliffs, N.J.

Library of Congress
Catalog Card No.: 57-12033

Current printing (last digit):
12 11 10 9 8 7 6 5 4 3

PRINTED IN THE UNITED STATES OF AMERICA

95169

Preface

The authors are aware of the limitations of a single volume which attempts to cover the events of three and a half centuries. They hope, however, that this new edition of *West Virginia: The Mountain State* will meet the expectations and needs of both student and general reader. The availability of new material, mostly scholarly monographs, has necessitated not only the revision of the early chapters but also a recasting of the later ones. Consequently, that part of the 1940 volume covering the history of West Virginia since 1870 has been entirely rewritten. Chapters relating the political, social, and economic development of the state since 1940 have also been added. The present volume contains a number of illustrations not found in the 1940 work.

For helpful criticism, the authors wish to thank the following members of the West Virginia University faculty and staff: Dean Armand R. Collett, Professor Albert L. Sturm, and Associate Professor William D. Barns of the College of Arts and Sciences; Professor Maurice G. Brooks of the College of Agriculture; Professor Marlyn E. Lugar of the College of Law; Director John O. Knapp and Charles H. Hartley, former State Club Leader, of the Agricultural Extension Division; and Dr. John A. Caruso of the University Extension Division. For reading the chapter on military history, thanks go to Captain William E. Miller, the Assistant Adjutant General of West Virginia. The authors owe debts of gratitude to members of the library staff of West Virginia University for unfailing courtesy and cheerful responses to countless requests. Acknowledgments are also due the authors' secretaries, Mrs. Naomi Bennett and Mrs. Elizabeth Carnahan Lemon, whose skill and painstaking care expedited both the writing and the manufacture of the book. For errors which may have crept in, the authors ask the kind indulgence of their readers.

West Virginia University

C. H. A.
F. P. S.

Contents

Part One

Part Two

Part Three

Part One

Chapter I

Natural Features

LAND GRANT BOUNDARIES

BY A SECOND CHARTER, issued in 1609, the King of England granted to "The Treasurer and Company of Adventurers and Planters of the City of London, for the first Colony of Virginia," in absolute property, the lands extending from Point Comfort, along the seacoast, two hundred miles to the northward, and from the same point, along the coast, two hundred miles southward; and "up into the Land throughout from Sea to Sea, West and Northwest." This grant included parts of what are now North Carolina and Tennessee; all of Kentucky, Maryland, and Delaware; most of Pennsylvania; a part of New York; and all the remaining states to the west and the northwest to the Pacific Ocean. Subsequently this area was pared down by royal grants, and otherwise; but to that part now included in West Virginia, Virginia later strengthened her claims by conquest, by occupation, and by control.

GEOGRAPHIC INFLUENCES

Centrally located between lands lying on the Great Lakes on the one side and on the Atlantic Ocean on the other, West Virginia, in her beginnings, as today, was largely a product of conflicting forces striving to establish an equilibrium. In this she was not exceptional. As a noted teacher has well said, "Man's relations to his environment are infinitely more numerous and complex than those of the most highly organized plant or animal."[1] Consequently, the same authority concludes, "Man can no more be scientifically studied apart from the ground which he tills, or the lands

---

[1] E. C. Semple, *Influences of Geographic Environment* (New York, 1911), p. 2.

over which he travels, or the seas over which he trades, than polar bear or desert cactus can be understood apart from its habitat." If this conclusion is correct, it would be folly to overlook the geographic equation in human development anywhere.

There is no history aside from time and place. This is certainly true of West Virginia. A child of civil strife, her institutions, manners, and customs have been determined largely by environment. This was the determining factor in her exploration and settlement; later, it condemned her to an arrested development; and, today, through the utilization of natural resources, it is making her a part of one of the workshops of the world. But states, like individuals, do not live unto themselves. As a consequence, the historical background of West Virginia will be found in her geographic surroundings, as well as in her immediate environment. For this reason a general description of the region between the Great Lakes and seaboard Virginia will be helpful.

This area falls into four distinct and clearly defined sections. Beginning at the Atlantic and proceeding westward to the Fall Line—that granite ridge connecting Fredericksburg, Richmond, Petersburg, and other towns and cities to the north and the south—the first of these sections is a part of the Atlantic Coastal Plain known in Virginia and elsewhere as the "Tidewater." It is a low, sandy region, rarely more than two hundred feet in elevation, divided into the "Eastern Shore" and the "Western Shore" by the Chesapeake Bay. This majestic body of water is almost two hundred miles long, with an average width of about forty miles. Opposite its entrance, between Cape Charles on the north and Cape Henry on the south, is the James River, which extends far inland and on whose bank the first permanent English settlement in America was made. But the Chesapeake Bay receives still other rivers. Proceeding northward from the James there are the York, the Rappahannock, the Potomac, and smaller streams. For more than two hundred years these were the chief means of intercommunication for the numerous natural divisions of this section. They were navigable by large sailing vessels, and thus furnished the interior a means of intercourse with the outside world.

Immediately west of the Tidewater is a portion of the Appalachian Highland known as the "Piedmont Plateau," or simply the "Piedmont." In Virginia the outline of this section suggests a right triangle having the Blue Ridge Mountains for a hypotenuse. Its surface varies to the westward from rolling to hilly, finally becoming mountainous. Closely paralleling the Fall Line through this entire section and the uppermost reaches of the Tidewater is a narrow stretch of extremely poor land, a continuation of the Pine Barrens, more clearly marked to the southward. The soil of the Piedmont is mainly decomposed rocks of the Archean Age and contains gneiss, mica, granite, porphyry, and iron. It is well adapted to wheat, corn, fruits, and tobacco, and is well watered; several rivers, some of which are navigable for long stretches, extend across the entire area.

The section between the Blue Ridge and the top of the Allegheny Mountains, extending in northeasterly and southwesterly directions, is a part of the Appalachian Highland known as the "Appalachian Valley." It is sometimes referred to simply as the Valley. This area is broken here and there by intersecting lines of hills, that usually parallel surrounding mountains to form minor valleys. Many of these are unsurpassed for beauty of scenery and fertility of soil. The soil of this entire region is of limestone formation and is well adapted to grass, fruit, and wheat. Local rivers are the Shenandoah, the South Branch of the Potomac, two Cacapons, and the New; and, to the southwest, the Clinch and the Holston. The Potomac, the James, and the New cross the Appalachian Valley at right angles, forming gaps through which the early white explorer found access to the interior.

Most of the country between the top of the Alleghenies and Lake Erie is a part of the Allegheny Plateau. Of this section and that lying immediately to the west—the Central Lowland Plain or Prairie—which together comprise the north central portion of the United States, it is said, "Nowhere else, unless in western Europe, is there such a combination of fertile soil, fine climate, easy communication, and possibilities for manufacturing and commerce." The Ohio River flows through the middle of this section, gathering its numerous streams into one and pointing their common course westward. The effect has been to convert the Ohio into "a course of empire." East of this stream, the land surface rises gradually to the top of the Alleghenies; the intervening areas contain coal, gas, oil, and timber in large quantities. Westward, the ascent toward the Great Lakes is more gentle, but the intervening lands are rich in soil and natural resources. Rivers are comparatively few, and flow out to the Ohio rather than down to it.

EXTENT AND PHYSICAL SUBDIVISIONS

As already indicated, West Virginia occupies a central position in this vast expanse. The territory included in the state contains 24,282 square miles; and lies between 37° 12′ and 40° 38′ north latitude, and 77° 43′ and 82° 55′ west of Greenwich, its latitudinal and longitudinal dimensions being out of all proportion to its size. In other words, from one extreme to the other it extends 260 miles from east to west and 237 miles from north to south; it reaches farther north than Pittsburgh, farther south than Richmond, almost as far east as Baltimore, and farther west than Cleveland. Its altitude range is even greater, varying from 500 feet at the mouth of the Big Sandy to 4,860 feet on Spruce Knob, in Pendleton County. It declines thence to 247 feet at Harpers Ferry, the lowest point. When expressed in mean annual temperature, the range is greater still. The difference between the warmest and the coldest points is twenty degrees, which is equal to a latitudinal variation of almost 400 miles.

For purposes of more detailed description, this far-extended area will be divided into four distinct regions, or sections: the Ohio Valley, the Cumberland Plateau, the Allegheny Highland, and the Potomac section. The first of these embraces that area bounded on the north and west by the Ohio River, and on the south and east by an imaginary line running somewhat parallel thereto at a mean altitude of about 1,000 feet. It contains more than 8,000 square miles, in which rivers flow out to the Ohio through a succession of hills and valleys. Though the proportion of alluvial, or bottom, lands is greater here than that for the state as a whole, this is the region of hills, which are everywhere in sight and vary in elevation from a few hundred to more than 1,700 feet; the highest point, High Knob, in Braxton County, reaches 1,720 feet. The chief resources of this section are its fertile valleys and hilltops, and its oil, gas, salt and coal deposits.

The Cumberland Plateau is the northern continuation of the Cumberland Mountains. This area stretches entirely across West Virginia, from Kentucky to Pennsylvania, at a mean elevation of from 1,000 to 2,000 feet, and parallel with the Ohio Valley section. In the former the valleys assume canyon features, while the sharp broken sides of the hills indicate a plateau elevation, through which during the ages rivers have cut deep and narrow channels. Here, too, stream beds rise rapidly, sometimes producing falls, as in the Kanawha, the Tygart, the Coal, and other rivers, which throughout this part of their course are rugged and blocked by huge masses of stone, around which waters swirl and foam on their way to the sea. From the summits overlooking these picturesque scenes, vast tablelands and forest-covered hills extend in all directions, with here and there the low rim of a mountain ridge rising in dim outline, or perhaps a solitary peak some 3,000 feet in height. This section contains approximately 6,500 square miles and is well adapted to grazing.

The Allegheny Highland is the mountain section *par excellence*. Its area is approximately 6,000 square miles, and it extends in general northeasterly and southwesterly directions at an average width of about 50 miles. Here and there throughout this section are little mountain-walled prairies of great fertility, surrounded by summits, forests, and peaks of unexcelled beauty. It is because of the scenery of this section in particular that West Virginia has been called the "Mountain State." Here waters gather in wide, deep basins, and surrounding them are the long, symmetrical, parallel folds of the Alleghenies. Though strata are generally broken and tilted at almost any angle from horizontal to perpendicular, the roughhewn mountain walls of the other sections are not present, and the crests and slopes are not rugged. This section contains rich grazing and timber lands, and is famous for its mineral deposits. Here, too, the mythical water god resides. The lofty apex of the mountain region that connects the counties of Randolph, Pocahontas, and Pendleton is the source of many streams, among which are: the South Branch, the Cheat, the Tygart, the Elk, the Greenbrier, and the Jackson. One of these mingles its waters with those of the Potomac; four reach the sea by way of the Ohio and the Mississippi; and the sixth, the Jackson, finds an outlet by way of the historic James.

The Potomac section comprises that part of West Virginia lying east of the Alleghenies. The total area is about 3,500 square miles. It is one of the garden spots, as well as one of the beauty spots, of the state. Here, in season, luxuriant meadows, waving wheat fields, and heavily laden orchards contribute to human wants. Along the entire northern boundary of six counties—Grant, Mineral, Hampshire, Morgan, Berkeley, and Jefferson—the Potomac flows like a "flashing thread of silver," and from the south the Shenandoah divides Jefferson County into two unequal parts and joins the Potomac at Harpers Ferry. Fully 80 per cent of the land of both Berkeley and Jefferson counties is level or rolling, and rich bottom lands stretch across each of the eight counties of this section.

CLIMATE AND RAINFALL

West Virginia's varied topography is responsible for an equally varied climate and for copious rainfall. On the highest lands, the temperature may fall to thirty degrees below zero, and, in the lowlands, it sometimes reaches one hundred degrees above; the mean annual temperature is about fifty-six degrees Fahrenheit. Snows from three to four feet deep are not infrequent, and on the tops of high mountains they are sometimes six to seven feet, and even deeper. Where laurel beds and forests are dense, sheltering depressions of rocky soil, ice, and frozen ground remain throughout the year; and in mountainous regions, killing frosts may occur at any time, even in midsummer. Some summers are almost rainless, while others, the so-called "wet" years, are attended by more than the average rainfall, which is about forty-three inches annually. On the eastern side of the Alleghenies, the climate is different from that on the western side, and that of the plateau region between also has its distinctive qualities. Upon this summit, clouds from opposite seas meet and mingle their rains; and, when cold winds from the northwest encounter warm ones from the region of the Gulf of Mexico, the rainfall in the region west of the Alleghenies becomes torrential, contributing to floods in the Ohio and its tributaries. When these are augmented by waters from melting snows, as occurred in 1884, destructive inundations result. Nevertheless, according to the United States Weather Bureau, the sun shines about two hundred fifty days a year in West Virginia, and one hundred forty-seven of these days are cloudless.

The Ohio Valley, the Cumberland Plateau, and the Allegheny Highland sections of West Virginia are drained wholly by the Ohio River and its tributaries. The principal tributaries are the Monongahela, the Little Kanawha, the Kanawha, the Guyandot, and the Big Sandy rivers. Of these, the little Kanawha and the Guyandot alone lie wholly within the state. The Ohio is navigable from its mouth to Pittsburgh, and the Monongahela, thence south to its beginning at Fairmont. By the use of locks and dams the Little Kanawha is navigable from Parkersburg to Creston, Wirt County, and thence at favorable stages by light boats to Glenville and Burnsville. The Kanawha is navigable from its mouth to Montgomery, Fayette County, a distance of ninety miles.

NATURAL RESOURCES

In this day of scientific research, one is prone to go beyond existing conditions and their causes to determine something of the history of the latter. In the study of West Virginia, such research leads at once into the field of geology, which alone can tell the essential facts of prehistoric times. Fortunately, this book of knowledge is open so that he who wishes may read the story of the ages: the origins of coal, oil, gas, and sandstone. From its pages one may learn that West Virginia was once a part of the bed of an ancient sea, into which rivers poured mud, sand, and pebbles, depositing them under such conditions that they finally became sandstone. In the deeper parts of the sea, far from its shores, were many marine animals whose shells and skeletons were precipitated to the bottom, where pressure cemented them into limestone. These processes continued through the ages, the lands thus produced rising and falling meanwhile. Sometimes these movements were in a vertical fashion, at other times in a horizontal manner. Thus, when the lands affected attained a comparatively stable equilibrium, having in the meantime emerged from the sea, some surfaces were left as plateaus, while others became mountain ranges.[2]

Coal was formed in the same general way, but always at or near the water's surface. It is the product of successive periods when trees and other forms of vegetable life grew, fell, and were buried in the swamp and marsh lands, down through the Carboniferous Age of this part of the

[2] W. Va. Geological Survey, *Geology and Natural Resources of West Virginia* (1937).

world's history; each coal bed represents an ancient swamp, large or small, as the case may be. Following their formation, most of the coal beds seem to have submerged for varying periods of time, during which they were covered with sand and mud that eventually hardened into rock. In turn, these strata emerged, and other coal beds, together with their coverings of stone and shale, were formed after the manner of the first. In this way alone can the presence of several strata, one above the other at more or less irregular intervals, be explained.

Though less satisfactory in explaining the presence of oil- and gas-bearing strata, geology has nevertheless been a boon to oil and gas operators. The anticlinal theory, first perfected by Dr. I. C. White, lifted operations for these products from a game of chance to the plane of a more or less scientific enterprise. As a result, operators saved millions; production was stimulated to a point which gave West Virginia high rank among the leading oil- and gas-producing states of the Union; and the strata bearing these products were found to parallel somewhat closely the general northeasterly and southwesterly directions of the Allegheny Mountains, and were thought to owe their presence to the same agencies that produced these mountains and their associated ranges.

NATURAL WONDERS

It is also in geology that one finds explanations for still other phenomena, particularly those pertaining to rivers. The rugged gaps and towering canyons, scientists say, were formed while the earth's surface was attaining its present equilibrium. The emergence of the earth from its watery cover seems to have been very gradual; the Potomac, the South Branch, the New, and other rivers were thus permitted to cut beds across the rising surface. New River Canyon, which was formed in this manner, tells a story of an incessant struggle between an ever-present river and a constantly rising land surface that continued until the present equilibrium of the earth's surface was attained. A map of West Virginia by the state geological survey, under the direction of Dr. I. C. White, first published in 1899, was an epoch-making document in the state's subsequent development of industry, as well as in the study of her past.[3]

As already indicated, the Ohio River had a somewhat different origin. Before it developed, the rivers of what is now the Ohio Valley flowed north and northwest into lakes and possibly a sea. Then came a glacial

[3] This map was compiled by the late Professor Russell L. Morris, of West Virginia University, and has been republished from time to time with modifications. The last edition was in 1932. "A Relief Map of West Virginia" (1937), prepared by the West Virginia Geological Survey, was one of the most informative maps ever made of the state.

Seneca Rock and Seneca Caverns, Pendleton County

movement from the north, cutting off their outlets with a wall of ice and débris, and converting their upper courses into lakes. A more or less stationary period in the history of this age is believed to have fixed the Ohio at or near its present location. Subsequently, lakes lying in what is now West Virginia were drained dry, while those to the north remained in much the same locations they occupy today. It is at present easy to trace the extent of this glacial advance by the deposits of gravel which it left and by the fertility of the soil over which it extended.

In the struggle for adjustment, these and other conflicts of the elements produced additional natural wonders. In the northern and the eastern parts of the state are the "Hanging Rocks," of the South Branch River, in Hampshire County, which rise to a height of nearly three hundred feet; "The Trough," in Hampshire and Hardy counties, through which the South Branch rushes for a distance of seven miles between overhanging banks; the "Image Rocks," in Grant County, where the South Branch forces its way through Patterson Creek Mountain; the "Ice Mountain," in Hampshire County, a perpetual refrigerator; the "Lost River," in Hardy County, that dashes against a mountain and reappears two miles away to swell the current of the Great Cacapon; "Seneca Rock," in Pendleton County, that suggests the picturesque scenery of the Far West, and, near it, in the same county, "Seneca Caverns," bearing a striking resemblance to similar natural features in the Appalachian Valley; the "Blackwater Falls," in Tucker County, near Davis, that carry the waters of the Blackwater, a tributary of the Cheat, in a perpendicular column, sixty-five feet high, to trout-inhabited pools below; and, perhaps most remarkable of all these, "Canaan Valley," also in Tucker County, the bed of a prehistoric lake thirteen miles long and from three to five miles wide.

In the southern part of the state, striking natural features are probably less numerous, but they are none the less wonderful. In Fayette County, "Hawks Nest," or "Marshall's Pillar"—a towering precipice of rocks five hundred eighty-five feet high—overlooks New River; "Burning Rock," in Wyoming County, is a perpetual oven on which snow melts as quickly as it falls; in the same county, the "Roughs of the Guyan," a canyonlike feature of swirling rapids, terrorized raftsmen and boatmen in days gone by; in Mercer County, near Bluefield, "Pinnacle Rock" towers over Flat Top Mountain like the pillars of an ancient ruin; in the neighboring county of Monroe, "Peters Mountain" stretches in a straight and almost unbroken line for a distance of forty miles; and, in Greenbrier County, eight miles south of Lewisburg, is "Organ Cave," a fugitives' refuge, whose rock-ribbed sides give off musical strains when plied with stones and other hard substances.

Then, too, there are numerous mineral springs, some of which have long been famous both as health resorts and as social and political centers.

Prominent among these are: Berkeley Springs, in Morgan County, a favorite resort of health seekers in the formative days of the Union;[4] White Sulphur Springs, in Greenbrier County, a social and political center of the Old South during the ante bellum days of the last century and, at the present time, one of the most popular resorts in the United States; Old Sweet Springs, of Monroe County, long a favorite mecca of health seekers; and scores of others here and there—many of more than local fame and popularity.

Despite numerous signs of the presence of prehistoric lakes, West Virginia contains no important natural reservoirs. However, the increasing demands for electric power and flood control may restore some of her primitive beauty. In 1927, a dam was completed across the Cheat River, near the Pennsylvania-West Virginia line, and in such a position as to produce a body of slack water almost thirteen miles long. This body,

"Cheat Lake" near Morgantown

christened "Lake Lynn" but known locally as "Cheat Lake," lies almost entirely within West Virginia. Tygart River Reservoir Dam, near Grafton, was completed in 1938 and Bluestone Reservoir Dam, near Hinton, in 1948. With the completion of these and other projected reservoir dams, West Virginia will again become a land of lakes.

---

[4] This place was first known as "Warm Springs," then as "Bath." In 1748, George Washington spoke of it as "the famed Warm Springs."

Chapter II

The Aborigines

THE MOUND BUILDERS[1]

THE PREHISTORIC MOUNDS of the central and southern United States, "Western cousins of the Egyptian pyramids," are the repositories of America's greatest archaeological treasures. Scattered here and there throughout the Ohio and Mississippi valleys, from Canada to the Gulf of Mexico, are nearly one hundred thousand of these remains, which constitute the best record of the people who dwelt in these regions prior to the coming of the white man. Ohio alone contains almost ten thousand of them, more than thirty-five hundred of which have been explored. Among the mounds of the larger area are thousands of additional prehistoric remains, such as village sites, cemeteries, pictured rocks, and flint quarries.

These remains were sources of varied speculation on the part of explorers and early settlers west of the Alleghenies. In the absence of archaeological and other data, some inferred that they were the burial places of princes and rulers of an ancient civilization, possibly surpassing in grandeur and achievement that of the Ptolemies and the Belshazzars. Others attributed them to more modern times, and still others thought they were the work of the erratic De Soto, who penetrated the continent of North America in the early part of the sixteenth century in an effort to conquer it for Spain.

Scientific investigations dispelled all these theories and assigned the prehistoric mounds of the Ohio Valley to a culture possibly not so ancient as that of early Egypt or Babylon, and not so modern as the days of the Spanish conquerors. Although it is probable that some mounds in the Ohio Valley were built as late as the discovery of America, the num-

---

1 See Henry C. Shetrone, *Mound Builders* (New York, 1930); F. W. Hodge, "Handbook of American Indians," in Bureau of American Ethnology, *Bulletin No. 30*.

ber and character of those later discovered there left no doubt of the fact that they belonged to an earlier period. More disillusioning still was the discovery that these remains did not contain rich treasures of ancient princes. Consequently, the public, and even the scientists and historians, lost interest in them. It was not until well into the last century that efforts were revived to determine the origin and nature of these strange relics and their builders.

As a result of these activities, the cultural state attained by the Mound Builders has been fairly well defined. Their chief economic dependence

Grave Creek Mound

was agriculture, but they developed a primitive commerce, as well as skill in the fabrication of clays and copper. Certain fields, in the Middle West and elsewhere, attest to the activities of Mound Builder farmers. The fact that mounds built by them are the common repositories of grizzly bear teeth and volcanic glass, obtainable only in the Rocky Mountains; of copper, obtainable only in the region of the Great Lakes; and of shells and other relics of salt water origin, indicates that prehistoric America was crossed and recrossed by unsung Marco Polos, who traveled over plains, deserts, and mountains in search of articles of commerce. It is true that these articles might have passed from individual to individual or from tribe to tribe by gradual processes, but the exchange would indicate the existence of a commercial activity, however primitive.

What is probably more significant still is the fact that the Mound Builders knew how to weave hair and vegetable fibers into cloth, that was dyed in various colors and used for garments. Some of these articles were left in close proximity to sheets of copper and have, thus, been handed down to us in such excellent state of preservation that the process of manufacture can be determined, as well as the designs and colors of the cloth used.

West Virginia contains many of these mounds and other prehistoric remains. For the most part, they are located along the Ohio River and its tributary streams, but similar relics may be found also in the Eastern Panhandle and upon the plateaus of the Allegheny Mountains. As elsewhere, they are of various forms and sizes: circular and irregular enclosures, parallel lines of walls, elevated ways, basins and ditches, stone cairns, and other stone structures. The discovery of additional relics should not, therefore, arouse false expectations on the part of would-be archaeologists.

The great mound at Moundsville, near the mouth of Grave Creek, West Virginia, is one of the largest and most interesting of its kind in America. When first discovered by the white man, it was about two hundred ninety-five feet in diameter at the base and sixty-nine feet high, with a flat top sixty feet across. It was opened in 1838 by a tunnel, ten feet wide and seven feet high, which extended almost to its center, where two vaults were discovered. These contained human skeletons, copper bracelets, plates of mica, shell-beads, and other ornaments. Among the remains was a sculptured stone inscribed with characters resembling ancient alphabets, but the "Grave Creek Inscribed Stone" has been discredited.

Other large mounds are found here and there. The most important of these are in the Kanawha Valley, just west of Charleston. Some of these

South Charleston Mound

mounds were examined in 1883-1884 under the direction of the Smithsonian Institution. As a result, many informative disclosures were made. This was particularly true of a mound one hundred seventy-five feet in diameter at the base, and thirty-five feet high, located in present South Charleston. Because of their possible significance these discoveries will be recorded in the order in which they were made.

First, after the removal of a slight covering of earth, an irregular mass of large, rough, flat stones—some of which would have made a good load for two men—was encountered. Immediately under a wagonload or so of these stones, a stone vault, seven feet long and four feet deep, was discovered. In the bottom of this vault was a large and much decayed human skeleton, headless and accompanied only by a single rough spearhead. At a depth of six feet was found a second skeleton; it was apparently that of an adult of ordinary size and was also much decayed. At a depth of nine feet, in a mass of loose, dry earth, and surrounded by the remains of a bark coffin, a third skeleton was found, but it was in a much better state of preservation than those previously unearthed. Three or four feet deeper, there was found a walnut vault, about twelve feet square and eight feet deep. This contained five skeletons: one lay in the middle of the structure and the others surrounded it in such positions and conditions as to indicate that they were the remains of persons who had been buried alive.

It was at this point that the mound made its richest and most informing disclosures. The skeleton in the middle of the vault was of unusual size, "measuring seven feet six inches in length and nineteen inches between the shoulder sockets." It lay upon the back, head east, legs together, and arms by the sides. There were six heavy bracelets on each wrist; four other bracelets were found under the head, together with a spearhead of black flint, encased in a mass of mortarlike substance, which had evidently been wrapped in some sort of fabric. "On the breast was a copper gorget. In each hand were three spearheads of black flint, and others were about the head, knees and feet. Near the right hand were two hematite celts, and on the shoulders were three large and thick plates of mica. About the shoulders, waist, and thighs were numerous minute perforated shells and shell beads." Some of these relics were not unlike the ornaments and other devices used by the Cherokee Indians, and also those found in similar mounds in the state of Ohio.

Another mound examined at the same time and place and by the same parties was one hundred seventy-three feet in diameter and thirty-three feet high, but its contents were very unlike those just described. At a depth of four feet from the top, two human skeletons were found; however, from this point to a depth of twenty-four feet, nothing but hard clay of almost uniform consistency was unearthed. At this depth, the building material changed to a darker and softer substance, which continued for a distance of about seven feet and was mixed throughout with ashes, fragments of bark, and animal bones. At a depth of thirty-one feet, another human skeleton was found lying prostrate, head to the north, and surrounded by the remains of a bark coffin. In a circular fashion about these remains were ten other skeletons, extended horizontally, with their feet pointing toward the central one, but not quite touching it. A copper plate and shell beads were found with the central skeleton; shells, implements, ornaments, beads, and arrowheads accompanied those figures surrounding it to the north and east; but no implements or ornaments of any kind accompanied the remains lying to the west and south. It is doubtful whether any vault was used in this mound.

Smaller mounds in the same vicinity, excavated at the same time and subsequently, revealed a great variety of content. As a rule, they were of solid clay, but some contained strata of ashes and charcoal, while others were of more or less conglomerate materials. A few contained human skeletons buried near the top surface, but in most cases such remains were found at the bottom of the mound near the natural earth. A number of mounds seem to have been built over vaults dug in the earth after the manner of modern graves. A striking thing about the discoveries, suggesting no very fixed practices on the part of those responsible for them, was their lack of any kind of uniformity. Heads of skeletons lay to all points of the compass; some rested face downward, while others were face upward, and still others reclined on their sides; some had both arms extended at right angles to their bodies, while others had only one arm in this position. Some mounds contained ornaments, implements, and tools, such as those found in the larger mounds, and others contained few or no traces of such things. Generally, the remains indicated that they were from a common culture.

Different types of prehistoric remains are, also, interesting and informing. This is particularly true of circular enclosures and parallel walls, some of which repose on hilltops and suggest the possibility of use as fortifications and places of worship. Unlike primitive mounds, these structures are usually of stone, and external signs, such as tree growths and deposits of alluvium, indicate for some of those in West Virginia an age of from twenty-five to forty centuries.

One of these remains, located at Bens Run, in Tyler County, is among the most extensive of its kind in the United States. It consists of two parallel circular walls, about one hundred twenty feet apart, which enclose approximately four hundred acres of land. Two small mounds stand within this enclosure. Just south of these is a cross wall, running from side to side of the enclosure; and extending southward from it are two long, curved walls about three hundred feet apart, that parallel the outer walls but do not touch them.

On a hilltop to the southeast are mounds and other evidences of ancient burial grounds. In still another direction, there are two large platforms or roadways: one, one hundred ninety-two feet long by fourteen feet wide at its narrowest point; the other, one hundred feet long and thirty-five feet wide. These platforms are of flat stones placed edgewise; the stones were small enough for two persons to handle easily. Between them at one end is an artificial mound of dirt and stone, the summit of which carries large flat rocks placed in positions to indicate their use in religious ceremonies—possibly the worship of the great sun god.

These and other discoveries quickened efforts of archaeologists to determine who the Mound Builders were. They are now generally agreed that "Early man in America was a migrant, coming to this continent from Siberia as a hunter of big game sometime between 10,000 and 20,000 years ago," in the last stage of the Ice Age. The first culture is now known as the "Early Hunters." They are believed to have come to America in pursuit of big game, such as mastodons, giant sloths, wild pigs, and bison and to have become extinct with the passing of their food supply. They left few tangible remains and were followed between 5,000 and 7,000 years ago by the Archaic People who were of small to average stature, of slight, wiry build, and lived by hunting, fishing, and nature's bounty. Their domestic life centered about a fireplace built on the midden where they buried their dead in round graves. They made little use of pottery but were skilled in shell, bone, and flint work.

The Mound Builders, or Adena People, came into the Ohio Valley, perhaps from Mexico or Central America, about 2,000 years before the Christian Era. They had a highly developed society which adhered to well established ceremonial practices, and erected large communal public works, such as mounds, stone cairns, elevated ways, enclosures, parallel walls, and ditches. With their beans, squash, pumpkins, and sunflowers, they were the first agriculturists in the Ohio Valley; and with their grit-tempered pottery, woven cloth, mica sheets, and copper bracelets, pendants, finger rings, and plates, they were also its first industrialists. Generally, they cremated their dead and buried their remains, together with valuable artifacts, in small rectangular log tombs which were covered with low mounds. A selected few of the Adena dead, perhaps the leaders or rulers, were buried in the flesh, in large log tombs, over which earth mounds were erected. Large mounds, such as the "Mammoth Mound" at Moundsville, are believed to have been the result of successive burials of this kind. Like other prehistoric cultures, the Adena disappeared, and archaeologists have been unable to determine the cause. It may have been a plague, moral and social depravity, conquest, or inadequate food.

THE INDIANS[2]

Except for a few Tuscaroras along the Potomac, a few Shawnees at the mouth of the Kanawha, and the Delawares in what is now the Northern Panhandle, West Virginia was uninhabited by Indians when that region was first visited by white men. Along with those who may have remained of their cousins, the Mound Builders, the Indian inhabitants of the region are supposed to have abandoned present West Virginia about the middle of the seventeenth century. In so doing, they left unmistakable evidences of their previous occupation. Among other things, these consist of grooved axes, arrowheads, spearheads, and bell-shaped pestles—relics of a more nomadic culture than that of the Mound Builders. Such remains are to be found in almost every county of the state.

At the time of the coming of the white man, what is now West Virginia was a common hunting ground. As the land was surrounded on the north and the west by Indian tribes, with still other tribes living at no great distance, the statement is equivalent to saying that the territory was a common battleground. It was rich in game—deer, wild turkeys, and, in the earlier days, buffaloes. The region also contained numerous salt springs, which were sought alike by man and beast. It was in quest of salt springs and game animals which frequented them, that native tribes came into deadly combat with one another and, finally, with the white man.

This latter phase of the Indian history of West Virginia may be clarified by a brief review of the relations of the mother state with her untamed children of the forest. When the English established their first settlement at Jamestown, they encountered Indians belonging to many tribes, most of whom were confederated under a single chieftain, the Powhatan. It was his daughter, Pocahontas, who is reputed to have saved the life of Captain John Smith and who later married John Rolfe. Mixed descendants of this union still reside in England and America.

As long as the white man resided behind palisades and in his original settlement at Jamestown, his relations with the Indian were comparatively friendly and helpful. When this settlement broke up into plantations, following the introduction of tobacco culture on a large scale, the Indian was compelled to fight for his hunting grounds and the graves of his fathers. Each new advance of the white man—that immediately preceding 1622 or that in the days of Nathaniel Bacon, for example—brought a counterstroke which helped to make history. It is thus that the Great Massacre of 1622, the Massacre of 1644, and Bacon's Rebellion are ex-

---

[2] Shetrone, "The Indian in Ohio," in *Ohio Archaeological and Historical Quarterly,* Vol. XXVII, No. 3; *Harper's Atlas of American History;* Livingston Farrand, *Basis of American History 1500-1900* (New York, 1904).

plained. In each of these encounters, as in others, the Indian lost and was forced to yield additional territory.

These removals and concessions determined the Indian situation in West Virginia at the time of its exploration and settlement. To the north were the Delawares. Former residents of what is now eastern Pennsylvania, southern New York, and New Jersey, they had, after repeated stands in the intervening country, finally established themselves on the upper Ohio and the Allegheny, having meanwhile strengthened their tribe by accessions from the Munsee, the Mohican, and the Tuscarora stocks. Here they successfully withstood their traditional enemies, the Iroquois, and later opposed the English advance into the interior. Prominent among their leaders were White Eyes, a friend of the English; Killbuck, the alleged perpetrator of the Massacre of Fort Seybert; and Buckongahelas.

Outstanding among the Indian tribes were the Shawnees, the "aboriginal Arabs of America." Black Hoof, Cornstalk, Black Fish, Blue Jacket, and Tecumseh were noted among the chieftains who, in turn, terrorized the Virginia frontier. Perhaps no native tribe was a source of more anxiety and perplexity to English frontiersmen than were the Shawnees, a fact due largely to their unrelenting hostility and their ubiquitous presence. West of the Shawnees were the Miamis, whose chief town, Pickawillamy, and heroic chieftain, Little Turtle, were frequently mentioned in frontier annals. To the north, on the Sandusky and the Maumee rivers, lived the Wyandots, former Hurons, who had established themselves before the middle of the eighteenth century in what is now northern Ohio. These and smaller tribes, notably the Mingoes, who resided near the present site of Steubenville, acting singly or in federations, first made war among themselves, but finally directed their common efforts to withstand the advance of the English.

More remote, though possibly more important, were two other tribes, the Iroquois and the Cherokees, whose activities figured prominently in early local annals. When first known to Virginians, most of the Iroquois lived south of Lake Ontario in the present state of New York. At that time they were one of the strongest confederations of Indians in America. Their traditional friendship with the English was one of the determining influences in the conquest of the greater part of North America by the latter.

The Cherokees, traditional enemies of the Iroquois, resided in western North Carolina and eastern Tennessee. They had attained a comparatively high degree of civilization and were the outstanding tribe in their part of the country. They were generally friendly with the English, but their unrelenting warfare with the Iroquois was one of the things that helped to make the Trans-Allegheny a "no man's land," given over to savage warfare.

Anthropologically, the Ohio Valley Indians were interesting beings. They were characterized by swarthy complexion, reddish to brown in color and not red, as that term is generally used; their hair was straight and black with a bluish luster; their eyes were brown; and their faces were medium to broad in size and were marked by high cheek bones. In stature they compare favorably with the present-day inhabitants of this region, though the average varied among different tribes and localities. The giants and pigmies among them seem to have occurred no more frequently than among other peoples. Their heads were generally smaller than those of white men, and their foreheads were often low and receding; their hands and feet were not so large; but their chests and backs were stronger and were well developed, because of their active life in the open. As a whole, they seem to have attained a cultural status somewhere between that reached by the white man and the Negro.

Ethnologically, these Indians were even more interesting. Deeply religious, in that they were slaves to the power of magic, they developed no written language to preserve the names and the characteristics of the objects of their devotion and to describe their manner of worshipping them. Innately moral, in that they recognized many of the cardinal virtues, such as truth, honesty, and the sanctity of human life, they were, however, easy victims of circumstances; they abandoned moral standards on the slightest provocation. With a social and political order based upon kinship rather than upon territory, the tribe was the unit of government; but in emergencies tribes merged into federations. There were sharp lines between those who performed the social, civil, and military functions of the tribe. Among all Indians, filth, vermin, and intemperance kept living standards low, and thus rendered the natives susceptible to the diseases and vices of the white man.

Life centered in the villages, and Indian economy was of the most primitive sort. At the beginning of historic times, scores of wigwam villages dotted Indian lands to the north of what is now West Virginia. Here warriors prepared for the chase and for intertribal wars; here squaws, with the aid of shells and sticks, cultivated the surrounding land, ground corn in wooden mortars, dressed and cured meats, made skins into moccasins and other articles of clothing, and gathered wood from which they chiseled crude wooden household utensils. Like the Mound Builders, Indians living in and about western Virginia did not emerge from the Stone Age of human culture.

INDIAN TRAILS

Although Indians were practical geographers and astronomers, who were able in the darkest night to determine directions from the oak tree—its rough mossy side being always to the north—their paths, or trails, had nevertheless been determined for them largely by the buffalo. At the coming of the white man, many of these paths were deep gulleys, which had been traversed by man and beast for centuries. Almost without exceptions, they followed watersheds rather than watercourses. Passing generally east and west, from rivers to and across mountains, they crossed, recrossed, and were coterminous with one another, thus forming a network which, together with the fact that they were used from time to time by different tribes, makes it difficult—in some cases impossible—to determine either the names or the exact locations of the trails.

Although now almost entirely forgotten as such, Indian trails were the gateways through which explorers, traders, and settlers entered the lands embraced in present West Virginia and the surrounding territory. In most cases, these routes determined settlement sites, and they were for a long time the only means of intercommunication between the settlers and the regions whence they came. Despite the fact that the narrow, overhanging trails sometimes dislodged burdens and riders, these primitive highways were not impassable by pack horses. Freighted with salt, sugar, kettles, bar iron, nail bars, dry goods, glass, lead, and so on, these animals formed veritable caravans moving through the wilderness. In contrast with riders of that day who had to be constantly on the lookout for Indians, who persisted in using former trails for purposes of war and hunting, thousands of persons use these routes today, unconscious of the fact that they are passing over what have been for centuries main-traveled roads.

When the Virginians first penetrated the region beyond the Blue Ridge Mountains, they came upon the famous Warrior Path, which passed in general northeasterly and southwesterly directions. For a time this route was the main road between the Iroquois and the Cherokees; it was the route referred to in an act of the Virginia Assembly of 1722, which put into effect a treaty of that year with the Iroquois. Along and near this trail were many battlefields, of which that on the Potomac at or near Pack Horse Ford was famous. Here many conflicts are supposed to have taken place between aboriginal tribes and peoples. A branch of the Warrior Path passed by way of Cumberland Gap, through Kentucky to the mouth of the Scioto River, and then to Lake Erie at approximately the present site of Sandusky, Ohio.

Of all the Indian paths affecting West Virginia, the so-called "Seneca," or Shawnee Trail, was perhaps the most important.[3] Ascending the South

3 Maxwell, "The Seneca Trail," in *The West Virginia Review,* Vol. II, 393-395, 412; Carpenter, "West Virginia Buffalo Trails," in *The West Virginia Review,* Vol. VIII, 332-333, 348; James Veech, *Monongahela of Old* (Pittsburgh, 1858; 1892), Ch. 3; W. C. Dodrill, *Moccasin Tracks* (Charleston, W. Va., 1915), p. 48; Hu Maxwell, *History of Barbour County* (Morgantown, 1899), 179-180.

Branch of the Potomac, the North Fork of that stream, and Seneca Creek to Seneca Rock, it crossed the Alleghenies at or near the head of Cheat River. Then, by way of Cheat Mountain and Shavers Fork of Cheat River, it led almost direct to Elkins, where it branched north and south into what was perhaps formerly the Catawba Trail, which had been pushed westward with the advance of white settlements. Northward from Elkins, the Seneca Trail followed "Jim Shavers Ridge," and crossed over Laurel Hill and Indian Fork of Clover Run, to what is now Belington, Barbour County. Then, by Clover Run, it crossed Low Gap Hill, which it followed to the present site of Parsons. Near Parsons it crossed Holbert Run and then a level land to Yankee Drain. Then it passed almost direct to Stack House Run which it crossed about one-half mile east of Dugrad Hollow. Following this stream about three hundred rods, it turned up a hill, bearing east of Pole Ridge Hollow to the mouth of Horse Shoe Run. It proceeded along this stream about six miles to the Alexander Evans farm, from which it continued with the ridge between Lead Mine and Wolfe creeks. By way of Backbone Mountain over or near the present highway to Oakland, Maryland, it led to the source of the Youghiogheny River, where it intersected Nemacolin Path which it followed rather closely for some distance to "the Forks" of the Ohio River, where it continued with the general course of the Allegheny River to the land of the Senecas.

From Elkins, the southern branch of the Seneca Trail followed Tygart River past Beverly and Huttonsville to Mingo Flats. Then it turned west to the Little Kanawha River, along the waters of which it extended to the Ohio River. Another, possibly the main, branch of this trail continued direct from Mingo Flats to the Greenbrier River, and continued thence into North Carolina. That part of this route from Parsons to Bluefield, by way of Beverly, Huttonsville, Marlinton, and Lewisburg, was recently designated the "Seneca Trail," and is familiar as such to tourists.

The Dunmore, or "Pocahontas Trail," branched from the Seneca Trail at Seneca Rock, in Pendleton County, and followed the North Fork of the South Branch of the Potomac to the mouth of Dry Run. Then it crossed Snowy Mountain to what is now Crabbottom, Virginia, from which it followed Laurel Creek to the present Staunton-Parkersburg Pike, where it turned west and crossed the Alleghenies about thirty miles south of the main Seneca Trail. Near the headwaters of the Greenbrier River, the Pocahontas Trail divided into two branches: one continued by way of the Greenbrier River to and along the Kanawha River; and the other crossed Shavers Mountain to Shavers Fork of Cheat River, from which it crossed Cheat Mountain to Tygart River, where it intersected the Seneca Trail near Huttonsville. Then it followed a ridge road to trails connecting with those leading to the Little Kanawha River.

For the early settlers of the Monongahela Valley, the McCullough, or "Traders Trail," was the most important eastward outlet. After journeying from Pierpont's, over Cheat River, to Bruceton, in 1784, George Washington followed this trail for some distance, in his investigation of the portage possibilities between the eastern and western waters. From Winchester, past Wardensville and Moorefield, this trail intersected the main Seneca Trail near Old Fields. It then crossed the intervening mountains to Patterson Creek. Continuing by a branch of this stream, it scaled a spur of the Alleghenies, by way of Greenland Gap, to Mount Storm. Then it followed the general course of the Northwestern Turnpike, to the head of the Little Youghiogheny, with which stream and the Youghiogheny it continued to near the point where the Baltimore and Ohio Railroad crosses the latter. Then proceeding past Herrington and Murley Glades and Crab Orchard, it intersected the Pennsylvania-West Virginia line slightly east of the summit of Laurel Ridge. From this point, passing a little north of Morris Cross Roads, it crossed the Monongahela River into Greene County between the mouth of Cheat River and Neals Ferry.

Crossing the Allegheny Mountains into the Greenbrier Valley near Marlinton, the Kanawha, or "Buffalo Trail," followed Muddy Creek for some distance. Then it crossed branches of Meadow River, and continued over the general route of the present Midland Trail, past Ansted, over Gauley Mountain and down Gauley River, to what is now Belva, at the mouth of Twenty Mile Creek. From Twenty Mile Creek, this trail crossed a divide to Bell Creek and then another divide to Kellys Creek, from which it followed the general course of the Kanawha River to Malden and the mouth of Elk River, where it divided; one branch passed to the mouth of the Kanawha River, by way of Buffalo Ridge, and the other passed through Teays Valley, over or near the present route of the Chesapeake and Ohio Railroad into western Kentucky.

The most important outlet of the Monongahela Valley to the westward was the Warrior, or "Little Warrior Trail." Crossing the Ohio River at or near New Martinsville, it passed along Fishing and down Dunkard creeks, and crossed Cheat River at or near M'Farlands. It was over this route, probably more than any other, that Indian raiding parties, especially those from the Shawnee country, entered the Monongahela Valley.

Another outlet of the Monongahela Valley to the westward was the Scioto-Monongahela Trail. Connecting lower Shawnee Town with the mouth of the Little Kanawha River by way of the watershed between the Muskingum and the Ohio rivers, this trail passed by Neals Station, on or near the present site of Parkersburg, over the general course of what is now the Baltimore and Ohio Railroad, and along Dry Ridge to near the present site of West Union. Here it turned east to Middle Island Creek. Then it crossed to Ten Mile Creek and followed it and the Monongahela River into Pennsylvania near Morgantown.

Other important and somewhat clearly defined Indian trails included: the Little Kanawha Trail, a branch of the Scioto-Monongahela Trail, which followed the general course of the Little Kanawha River to Bulltown, near which it crossed into Elk Valley, and continued over the divide between the Elk and Gauley rivers to Webster Springs; Dunlaps Trail, which connected the present site of Lewisburg and Gap Mills, by way of Dunlaps, Second, and Indian creeks; and the "Horse Shoe," or North Branch Trail, which connected the headwaters of the Potomac, at or near Fairfax Stone, with Elkins, by way of Backbone Mountain, Lead Mine Run, Horse Shoe Run, and Tygart River.

INDIAN NAMES

Many proper names of Indian origin contributed to the beauty and effectiveness of the English language. Such names include Potomac, Cacapon, Opequon, Guyandot, and Shenandoah, "Daughter of the Stars." Some Indian names suggest close contact with nature; for example, Monongahela, "river of falling banks"; Ohio, or Ohi, "river of white caps," or "the white foaming waters"; and Elk, or Tiskelwah, "river of fat elk." These names and others of similar origin have meanings all their own. Unfortunately many of them, together with their meanings, have been lost, and some have been corrupted through modifications in spelling and in pronunciation.

Chapter III

Explorations and Early Settlements

THE QUEST FOR GOLD AND THE SOUTH SEA

BEFORE THE FIRST permanent English settlement was firmly established in Virginia, its promoters manifested an interest in westward explorations. Like others who had preceded them to America, these early explorers hoped to find wealth and a direct route to the "South Sea." It was in quest of these that Christopher Newport reached the falls of the James in 1607, and the following year penetrated the upper reaches of that stream to a distance of thirty miles inland from the present site of Richmond.[1]

That these initial successes were not followed up immediately was probably due to the fact that there were few persons of Admiral Newport's initiative among his immediate successors. Then, too, the work of founding a new colony under trying conditions taxed the Virginians to their utmost; thousands died in the attempt. Nevertheless, stories of the interior lingered in the memories of the colonists and were kept alive by natives, especially those interested in trade. Thus, in May, 1626, the governor and the council wrote the Privy Council, in England, that "discoveries by land . . . are of great hope both from the richness of the mountains and the possibilities of finding the passage to the South Sea." The same communication asked aid to accomplish these undertakings.

This request seems to have gone unheeded, for there is little more of record concerning the Virginia frontier before 1641. At that time, Cavaliers

[1] C. W. Alvord and Lee Bidgood, *First Explorations of the Trans-Allegheny* (Cleveland, 1912), p. 28.

were coming into the colony; in fact, another period of expansion had arrived. It was in response to this movement that parties petitioned the Burgesses for "leave and encouragement" to undertake discoveries southwest of the Appomattox River in the lands of the Occaneechi Indians. In March, 1643, their request was granted by an act which also granted, for a period of fourteen years, all the advantages that might arise from their discoveries, reserving only the usual one-fifth mineral royalty for the King of England.

But misfortunes and delays were impending. In 1644, an Indian massacre, inspired no doubt by the land-grabbing activities of the white man, took place in the James River settlements and resulted in the deaths of hundreds of persons. Nevertheless, the act of 1643 set a precedent for future legislation concerning the Virginia frontier. With the exception that subsequent adventurers were not to be excluded from newly discovered lands, later acts almost invariably granted original discoverers, for a period of fourteen years, first claims to all lands, including also a monopoly of the coveted Indian trade.

These delays and experiences were not without constructive results, leading as they did to greater protection for the frontier. To this end, accordingly, forts were established along the Fall Line, which separated the Tidewater from the Piedmont. In 1645, western approaches by way of the James, the Pamunkey, and the Chickahominy were thus secured; and in the following year, an outpost, later called "Fort Henry," was authorized at the falls of the Appomattox on the present site of Petersburg.[2]

For more than half a century these forts were strategic points in the defense of white settlements and in Indian relations. It was from these Virginia outposts that Abraham Wood, later referred to as the "Frontenac of Virginia"; William Byrd, the founder of Richmond; Cadwallader Jones, operating from the present site of Fredericksburg; and others took those initial steps which finally opened the Cherokee country and the Ohio Valley to trade with the English.

The immediate purpose of these outposts was defensive. On this point the act authorizing Fort Henry may be taken as typical legislation. After the need for defense and the impossibility of securing it at public expense had been recited, the fort, which had already been erected, was turned over to the control of an "undertaker," Captain Abraham Wood, to whom this same act granted six hundred acres of land adjoining, "for him and his heires for ever; with all houses and edifices belonging to the said Forte, . . . Provided that the said Capt. Wood do maintayne and keepe ten men constantly upon the said place for the terme of three

[2] Alvord and Bidgood, *First Explorations,* p. 29; P. A. Bruce, *Institutional History of Virginia* (New York, 1910), Vol. II, 97.

years, duringe which time he, the said Capt. Wood, is exempted from all publique taxes for himself and the said tenn persons."[3]

During the decades immediately following, the chief interest of the frontier continued to center in defense. About the time of Bacon's Rebellion, this problem became so serious that its solution had to be undertaken at public expense. To this end, an act of 1675 provided that five hundred men should be drawn from the mainland and the most secure parts of the country, and placed on the "heads of the rivers," or the Fall Line, and other places fronting upon the Indians. Under this act a number of new forts were established. Still later, 1691, mounted rangers were used—a lieutenant, eleven soldiers, and two Indians being stationed in frontier outposts to scout for enemy. At the same time, the Indian boundary was strictly defined.

Toward the beginning of the eighteenth century, when interest had shifted to the promotion of frontier settlements, a means of defense was sought in "cohabitations." An act of 1701, carrying this plan into effect, provided ample land grants for all such societies and declared that it would be inexpedient for any of them to enroll less than twenty-five fighting men. Meanwhile, all surveys of land for these societies were to be made at public expense, and for a term of years the inhabitants were to be exempt from the payment of quitrents and other public charges.

As a result of these arrangements, in the next generation, there developed in piedmont Virginia "the first truly American backwoods society with all its familiar activities: Indian trade, exploration, hunting, trapping; raising of hogs, cattle, and horses, which were branded and ran loose on the wild lands; pioneer farming, capitalistic engrossment, and exploitation of the wilderness." Of this frontier, Professor F. J. Turner has said:

> It was not long before cattle raisers from older settlements, learning from the traders of the fertile plains and peavine pastures of this land, followed the fur traders and erected scattered "cow-pens" or ranches beyond the line of plantations in the Piedmont. Even at the close of the seventeenth century, herds of wild horses and cattle ranged at the outskirts of the Virginia settlements, and were hunted by the planters, driven into pens, and branded somewhat after the manner of the later ranching on the Great Plains.[4]

Naturally, these activities were accompanied by speculations regarding regions to the westward. In 1648, Governor Berkeley was hearing strange stories of a great river beyond the mountains, of a gulf to the southward, and of red-capped Spaniards who visited the gulf "riding on asses." The

---

[3] Hening, *Statutes,* Vol. I, 326; F. J. Turner, *Frontier in American History* (New York, 1920), p. 84.

[4] Turner, *Frontier,* p. 88; P. A. Bruce, *Economic History of Virginia* (New York, 1895), Vol. I, 473-477.

following year, this information became more definite, and the natural inference was that the long-sought waterway to the "Sea of China" might yet become a reality. Moreover, the intervening mountains were still thought to contain minerals, possibly gold and silver.

It was in quest of these objectives that Captain Abraham Wood; Edward Bland, "Merchant"; Sackford Brewster and Elias Pennant, "Gentlemen"; their servants; and an Indian guide set off from Fort Henry (Petersburg), in August, 1650, through the lands of the Occaneechi Indians. Their route was that later known as the "Traders Path," or the Occaneechi Trail. This they followed to the falls of the Roanoke River, near where the Dan and the Staunton unite to form that stream. Here, after a five days' journey, they turned back to their starting point, having passed many Indian villages and encountered increasing signs of Indian hostility.

The results of this expedition were recorded by Bland in a pamphlet entitled "The Discovery of New Brittaine," published in London in 1651, where it aroused interest in the American frontier. A more important result of these discoveries was the conception which they gave Abraham Wood of the possibilities of the fur trade. At once he sent to London for guns, powder, shot, hatchets, kettles, and other articles to be used in barter with the Indians. Incidentally, his and Bland's representations are believed to have been factors in the growing interest of the English in the American frontier.

THE TRADE STIMULUS

Although Wood and others may have continued to make exploring and trading expeditions into frontier Virginia in the years immediately following 1650, further large-scale explorations of that section were forced to await the outcome of increased interest in the fur trade. Fortunately, this interest was not long in developing. In 1660, a committee of the English Privy Council was created for the purpose of fostering trade with the colonies. It was in pursuance of the policy evolved by this committee that the English, four years later, took New Amsterdam from the Dutch and changed its name to New York in honor of the Duke of York, a moving spirit in the new developments. A short time thereafter, cargoes of furs were reaching London from the former Dutch possessions; and, in 1670, the Hudson Bay Company was organized to participate in the American fur trade, with Sir William Berkeley, of Virginia, acting as its representative in America.

It was under these conditions that efforts were renewed to "find out the East Indian Sea," which was then believed to control the fur-trading situation in America. For this undertaking, Berkeley had at his command the services of Abraham Wood, at the time the most seasoned and experienced frontiersman in Virginia. Another possibility was William Byrd, who, like Wood, had been trained from his youth to endure the hardships of the frontier. Moreover, two hundred "gentlemen" of the colony were ready to undertake such an expedition. Thus encouraged, Berkeley was ready to lead the enterprise personally, and he prepared for an early start in the spring of 1670. Meanwhile, plans were made to overcome "all opposition, whether of the Spaniards or Indians," and the King was asked to sanction the undertaking. But the desired royal permission failed to arrive, and Berkeley hesitated to act without it.

There was then in Virginia a German physician, John Lederer, who possessed a bent for travel in strange lands and was willing to undertake the exploration of the Virginia wilds without a royal commission. Of this man's origin and early career there is no certain knowledge. He remained in the colony perhaps a year and a half (1669-1670), probably longer, during which time he made three exploring expeditions, at least two of which carried him to the top of the Blue Ridge Mountains at points near the headwaters of the Rappahannock. A third expedition proceeded almost due west from Fort Henry, by way of the Occaneechi Trail, to a tributary of the Roanoke, but did not reach the mountains. Lederer has, nevertheless, been proclaimed the "Hennepin of English explorers." However that may be, he was the first white man of record to gaze upon the Shenandoah Valley from the top of the Blue Ridge Mountains. Except for his contribution to the knowledge of Indian customs and to the geography of the Atlantic slope, his achievements were otherwise unimportant.

Governor Berkeley was not to be thwarted in his determination to find out "the ebbing and flowing of the Waters on the other side of the Mountains in order to the discovery of the South Sea." Again he turned to Abraham Wood, who, in 1671, fitted out an expedition instructed to accomplish this purpose. It consisted of Thomas Batts, Thomas Wood, and Robert Fallam, who, in company with one indentured servant and a faithful Appomattox Indian guide, left Fort Henry in September of that year. Fallam kept a journal of their experiences.

Under directions from Abraham Wood, this company proceeded almost due west to the headwaters of the Roanoke River. Thence, by way of the Staunton, a branch of the Roanoke, two of the party, Batts and Fallam, reached the Blue Ridge Mountains. Wood remained behind in an Indian town on account of illness. Traveling along the Staunton, then called the "Roanoke," Batts, Fallam, and their attendants crossed the Blue Ridge and descended into the Roanoke Valley to a Totero village near the present site of Roanoke, Virginia. Continuing by way of the Staunton, they reached the Alleghenies, which they crossed, and descended to waters flowing westward, now known as the New River.

After they had first taken formal possession in the name of the King of England, of all the lands drained by New River and its tributaries, they continued their journey for three days and are thought to have reached a point near the present boundary between Virginia and West Virginia. As their guides refused to go farther, they were forced to return; but they were not unconscious of the importance of their achievements. The glory of these was marred only by the discovery of signs of the former presence of white men on waters flowing to the westward, and by the subsequent discovery that the companion whom they had left behind had died in their absence.

Although little has been made of this expedition, it was significant in the annals of English explorations in America. Indeed, it seems to have resulted in the first recorded discovery of waters flowing into the Ohio River. This discovery contains all the settings and incidents for a story possessing the romance and splendor of those in which Parkman preserved the accomplishments of French contemporary explorers. Of its importance, an American historian said:

> It is one of the ironies of history that an event which redounds so much to the credit of Englishmen, and substantiates so completely the claims of the mother country to that particular territory for which she made war on her rival at such a cost of blood and money, is practically unknown and has even been frequently denied by historians. The names of Frontenac, Joliet, Marquette, and La Salle are familiar to every schoolboy, while those of their English competitors in exploration, who were in every respect their equals in daring and enterprise, have remained till this day in obscurity, almost in oblivion.[5]

Conditions leading to the Batts and Fallam expedition, together with the growing rivalry among fur traders stationed on the outposts of Virginia, inspired other ventures for the purpose of determining the extent and character of the interior. In the absence of confirming source materials, the number and personnel of these expeditions cannot be determined, but it is certain that the elder William Byrd, who operated from a fort located on the present site of Richmond, was not far behind Abraham Wood in venturing beyond the Blue Ridge Mountains. Indeed, he may have preceded him. Returning from their expedition of 1671, Batts and Fallam met Byrd, together with a "great company" of attendants, well beyond the Blue Ridge Mountains.

Apropos of his exploring expeditions, further statements about William Byrd, the founder of Richmond, are worth while. After Wood's death,

---

[5] Alvord and Bidgood, *First Explorations*, p. 20.

in 1680, Byrd was "the best informed man concerning western matters in the colony." His sources of information reached the remotest parts, even the upper Mississippi Valley, where the French were then making extensive explorations and discoveries, and were planning future settlements. As early as 1688, Byrd was apprehensive that the French activities in the Mississippi Valley would "result in cutting off the Virginia fur-trade." It is possible, and entirely probable, that later Virginia governors and explorers learned much from Byrd regarding the interior.

Following upon the heels of the Batts and Fallam expedition, James Needham and Gabriel Arthur (1673) entered upon an adventure of exploration and discovery that carried them by way of the Roanoke and the Yadkin rivers into what is now Tennessee. After enduring numerous hardships, Needham returned to Fort Henry, whence he had departed under directions from Abraham Wood; but Arthur tarried in the land of the Cherokees to learn their language and customs. While there, he participated in intertribal warfare, one expedition of which, he claimed, carried him into what is now Kentucky, and possibly into what is now West Virginia, even as far as the Ohio River.[6]

The Needham and Arthur expedition resulted in more than increased knowledge of the western country. First, and probably most important, the Cherokee trade, formerly monopolized by the Spaniards, was diverted to Virginia. In time this led to an alliance between the English and the Cherokees, which eliminated the Occaneechi as middlemen in the Virginia fur trade and brought about their expulsion from the Piedmont, together with other tribes pushed out from the Tidewater. Thus the way was paved for the settlement of the former section.

After these developments, interest in the fur trade lagged for a time. Bacon's Rebellion, with its accompanying antipathy for those engaged in the trade, may have been a depressing influence. Then, too, as already indicated, Abraham Wood died in 1680. It may be worth noting that about the same time Lord Shaftesbury, a moving spirit in England's effort to control the fur trade in America, went into exile. His death soon followed; and in the midst of subsequent wars to determine, first, the English succession, and then the Spanish succession—each of which events was reflected in the colonies—his purposes with reference to America were temporarily neglected.

Traders continued, however, to traverse piedmont Virginia, and some of them may have reached sections beyond the mountains. But, as already shown, the chief interest in the interior centered in defensive measures for existing settlements and in the fur trade. When an extension of the frontier was again considered, settlement therein was largely an indi-

---

[6] Alvord and Bidgood, *First Explorations,* pp. 79-89.

vidual enterprise. Luckily for those interested, the system of land grants for headrights—fifty acres for each imported person—had been all but abandoned. In lieu thereof, an act of 1705 legalized the growing practice of selling lands for cash, the usual price being from one to five shillings for fifty acres.

This practice, together with the lax methods of the local council, made possible the acquisition of large individual estates, some of which contained as many as five hundred thousand acres. It should be noted, however, that such grants were usually made on condition that their recipients settle upon the land a certain number of families within a fixed time. It was thus that "King" Carter, Robert Beverley, Benjamin Borden, and others acquired manorial estates in upland Virginia and west of the Blue Ridge Mountains.

SPOTSWOOD AND HIS KNIGHTS

In the midst of these events, Alexander Spotswood entered in 1710 upon the discharge of his duties as governor of Virginia. Although only twenty-eight years of age, he was rich in experience. Wounded in the Battle of Blenheim, he had risen to a command in the English Army. He was also a robust and vigorous character whose restless spirit was only slightly concealed under an air of dignity. Within a short time after his arrival he took steps to establish Indian missions, to encourage grape culture, to exterminate piracy, and to foster the smelting of iron. For this last-named service he was known as the "Tubal Cain of Virginia."[7]

To such a man the current ignorance regarding the Virginia frontier was intolerable. This was especially so since the French were then in possession of regions about the Great Lakes, from which they were reaping returns from trade, and since they had recently established themselves at Kaskaskia and on the lower Mississippi River. A reconnaissance, made in 1710, again revealed the fact that the Blue Ridge Mountains were not impassable, and Spotswood declared his intention to prove it personally. Thus sponsored, exploration became a popular pastime in Virginia. In August, 1716, Spotswood, accompanied by fifty mounted "gentlemen," with their Negro servants and Indian guides, set out to determine what lay beyond the mountains in the region of the upper Rappahannock.

This expedition was free from thrilling adventures. Proceeding by way of Swift Run Gap, it crossed the Blue Ridge into the valley of the Shenandoah. Then it proceeded direct to the west bank of that stream, then

[7] Leonidas Dodson, *Alexander Spotswood, Governor of Colonial Virginia, 1710-1722* (Philadelphia, 1932).

called the "Euphrates," where formal possession was taken of the surrounding country in the name of King George I of England. After Spotswood and his companions had celebrated this achievement by firing salutes and drinking toasts, they set out on their return. A band of rangers continued westward to the Warrior Path, then frequented by Iroquois, Cherokee, Shawnee, and other tribes. To commemorate the event, as well as to encourage other exploring expeditions, Spotswood gave each of his companions a golden horseshoe. Thus was instituted what later became known as the order of the "Knights of the Golden Horseshoe."

An unknown number of persons had preceded Spotswood beyond the Blue Ridge in the region of the Shenandoah Valley. In 1707, Louis Michel, "a Swiss Gentleman," made a map of the country about the junction of the Potomac rivers. Five years later, Baron Christopher de Graffenreid, prospecting for settlement sites for Swiss families which he, with the aid of Spotswood, was bringing to Virginia, visited that region and expressed himself as much pleased with the "possibility of mines." He was diverted from his plan to settle it by conflicting ownership claims of the proprietors of Maryland and the "Northern Neck."

PROFESSIONAL TRADERS

About 1725, professional traders took up the rôle of the explorer. To the southward, pioneers in this movement were Lachlan McGillivary and James Adair. The former established trade relations with the Creeks and married into that tribe, while the latter made trading expeditions to and long sojourns among Cherokees and Chickasaws.[8] These traders created a bond of union between the English and the Indians, which protected both against the machinations of the Spanish in Florida and the French on the Mississippi and in Canada.

For present purposes the most important of these traders was John Van Meter of New Jersey. As Adair was entering the Cherokee country, Van Meter, accompanied by a band of Delawares, visited the South Branch Valley. Following his return to New Jersey, he advised his friends and relatives to move to Virginia, where he assured them that they would find good lands.[9] But it was not until 1730 that his sons, John and Isaac,

[8] James Adair, *History of the American Indians* (London, 1775; reprinted Johnson City, Tenn., 1930).

[9] Samuel Kercheval, *A History of the Valley of Virginia* (Dayton, Va., 1902), p. 51; B. F. Vanmeter, *Genealogies and Sketches of Old Families* (Louisville, Ky., 1901).

acted on their father's advice. That year they patented forty thousand acres in "Old Frederick County" near present Winchester, which they the following year sold to Hans Yost Heydt, better known as Joist Hite.

FIRST SETTLEMENTS

Virginia lands were meantime attracting attention elsewhere. Shortly after the Van Meter visit, settlers began to make permanent homes along the Shenandoah, well up the Potomac on the south side, down the South Branch, and even on the headwaters of the James and the Greenbrier rivers. For the most part, these immigrants came from Pennsylvania and were an overflow from those German and Scotch-Irish pioneers who had established themselves upon the Pennsylvania frontier in the years immediately preceding. In the years following, they extended their settlements throughout the whole area between the Blue Ridge and the Alleghenies. Before the American Revolution, they were spilling over into regions to the east and the west and effectively cutting off the westward extension of institutions peculiar to eastern Virginia.

According to generally accepted tradition, the first settlement in present West Virginia was made by Morgan Morgan (November 1, 1688-November 17, 1766). The site of the Morgan settlement was on Mill Creek, near Bunker Hill in present Berkeley County. In 1924, it was marked by West Virginia with an appropriate monument which records the date of the settlement as 1726. However, as Morgan Morgan is now known to have been a coroner in Delaware from 1726 to 1729 inclusive, and as he did not purchase his Virginia lands until November, 1730, it is a reasonable assumption that he did not settle them before that year, or more probably early in 1731, which may therefore be accepted as a more authentic date than 1726 for that of his settlement in present West Virginia.

Almost simultaneously with the Morgan settlement, German families began to establish themselves along the south bank of the Potomac and in the valleys to the southward.[10] Their first settlement was at Mecklenburg, now Shepherdstown, West Virginia. Beginning in 1732, other families settled on Opequon, Back and Tuscarora creeks and the two Cacapon rivers. Among them were the Shepherds, Harpers, Foresters, Lemons, Mercers, Van Meters, Hites, and Van Swearingens. In 1732, Joist Hite and fifteen families cut their way through the wilderness from York, Pennsylvania, and settled near what is now Winchester. Two years later, other

[10] Kercheval, *Valley*, pp. 45-56; Alexander S. Withers, *Chronicles of Border Warfare* (Clarksburg, 1831), pp. 44-62; Oren F. Morton, *A History of Pendleton County*, (Franklin, W. Va., 1910), p. 31.

families came to the South Branch and made the first permanent settlement in what is now Hampshire County, West Virginia. By 1747, pioneers had crept up the South Branch into present Pendleton County, West Virginia, where settlements were made.

Contrary to accepted traditions the Van Metre, or Van Meter, brothers, John and Isaac, were not among the very first settlers of present West Virginia. It was not until 1744 that Isaac established himself permanently at Old Fields, an Indian village near present Moorefield, where he was visited by George Washington four years later, and killed in 1757 by Indians. About the same time, probably a little earlier, "John Van Metre first of Berkeley" made a permanent settlement in that county, and Henry Van Meter, eldest son of Isaac of Old Fields, settled on South Branch River in present Hardy County, near the Trough, where he, too, was visited by Washington in 1748.

Though the Scotch-Irish lived among the Germans, many of them made settlements farther up the Valley, in what are now Augusta and Rockbridge counties, Virginia.[11] In 1732, John Lewis, a pioneer among these adventurers, settled near the present site of Staunton. Four years later, Benjamin Borden secured from Governor Gooch a grant of five hundred thousand acres in the same region on condition that he settle one hundred families on it in ten years. To comply with this condition, Borden brought many immigrants to Virginia, among them being the Pattons, McDowells, Telfords, Whitleys, Alexanders, Moores, Archers, Stuarts, and Mulhollons.

Of those going west from this central settlement, the Harman, Ingles, and Draper families were pioneers. In 1748, they made a settlement in Drapers Meadows, near the present site of Blacksburg, Virginia, which was destroyed by Shawnees in 1755. The inhabitants were either murdered or carried into captivity.

The following year, 1749, the first recorded settlement west of the Alleghenies in what is now West Virginia was made near the present site of Marlinton by Jacob Marlin and Stephen Sewell. The best of friends in other respects, they could not agree on the subject of religion and, on that account, are said to have found it desirable "to live apart." Sewell took up his abode in a hollow sycamore tree that stood near their cabin. Here they were found in 1751 by Andrew Lewis, who had entered the region on a surveying expedition for the Greenbrier Company. Two years later, Andrew Culbertson made a settlement still farther west on Crumps Bottom, in Summers County, West Virginia. There were already several families living along streams flowing into Greenbrier River.

About the same time, settlers began to push over the Alleghenies from

---

[11] John L. Peyton, *History of Augusta County* (Staunton, 1882); Joseph A. Waddell, *Annals of Augusta County* (Richmond, 1882); Virgil A. Lewis, *A History of West Virginia* (Philadelphia, 1889), pp. 63-73.

the South Branch and the Potomac valleys. Among them were Robert Files and David Tygart, who, in 1753, built cabins within three miles of each other near the present town of Beverly, West Virginia. The first mentioned gave his name to Files Creek, the second to Tygart River. As these settlements were in exposed positions on or near the Seneca Trail, they did not become permanent. Files was murdered by Indians, but Tygart made his escape into the South Branch Valley.

A year later, the Eckarly brothers established themselves in Dunkard Bottom, in present Preston County, but they too were discovered by the ever-vigilant savage. Two were killed, and the third escaped only because of his absence from home when his cabin was attacked.

NEW COUNTIES

The frontier advance in Virginia called for accommodations in the form of local government. Land claims were to be proved and established; taxes were to be collected; and the need for an adequate and organized defense was ever present. In 1734, "Orange County" was created. It included all the lands of Virginia west of the Blue Ridge Mountains to the "uttermost limits" which embraced all of what is now West Virginia, Kentucky, Ohio, Indiana, Illinois, Michigan, Wisconsin, and a large part of Virginia.

Four years later, that part of Orange County west of the Blue Ridge was set apart and divided into the "District of Augusta" and the "District of Frederick," each of which was to become a county equal in power with the other counties of Virginia, when its population justified the appointment of justices of the peace and other officers. In keeping with this arrangement, "Frederick County" was created in 1743, with its seat of government at Winchester; and, two years later, Augusta became a county, with Staunton as its seat of government and, like Frederick, with a definite and restricted boundary.[12]

This left a large unorganized area, a sort of Indian country, which in time came to be called the "District of West Augusta." Before ten years had elapsed, however, it became necessary to reduce this district. In 1754, a new county, Hampshire, was created, which included most of the settlements on the South Branch River. No other counties were formed from the District of West Augusta until 1776, when it was further divided in a manner and for reasons to be noted later.

---

12 Robinson, "Virginia Counties," in Va. State Library, *Bulletin* (1916), pp. 64-96, 132, 188, 259.

HOWARD AND SALLING

Like other American pioneers, those who settled in the Appalachian Valley of Virginia were curious to know something of the lands beyond. It was to satisfy this wanderlust that John Howard petitioned the general assembly for permission "to go upon discoveries in the Lakes & River of Mississippi." The request was granted, and, in 1742, he, John Peter Salling (Salley), and others set out on an expedition of exploration and discovery.[13] Ascending the South Branch, they crossed the Alleghenies to New River. Descending this stream, the Coal, the Kanawha, the Ohio, and the Mississippi in turn, they, by the aid of a bullboat, reached New Orleans, where they were arrested.

After almost two years, Salling escaped and returned to Virginia, but Howard and his other companions were sent as prisoners to France. Nothing criminal appeared against them at their hearing in Paris; they were consequently discharged and proceeded to London. What became of them is not definitely known, but Salling kept a journal of his travels, which was later published and created much comment. It is not improbable that Peter Jefferson and Joshua Fry, each of whom knew Salling, got information from him for their celebrated map of Virginia, first published in 1751.

THE FAIRFAX LANDS

Meanwhile, the Virginia frontier was again attracting attention in the mother country. This was particularly true of the lands to the westward, between the Rappahannock and the Potomac rivers, where German families, as already indicated, were establishing themselves in permanent settlements. In 1669, Charles II granted this area, later known as the Northern Neck, to a group of court favorites who sold it to Lord Culpeper. From him it descended to Thomas, the sixth Lord Fairfax, who, in 1733, petitioned George II to assert his claims and ask that the government of Virginia be restrained from making grants therein. At that time Lord Fairfax planned to build up a feudal estate in America, from which he hoped to draw large returns annually in the form of quitrents. To determine his power to do this, suits were instituted, some of which—

---

13 See Salling, "Journal," in William M. Darlington, *Christopher Gist's Journals* (Pittsburgh, 1893), pp. 253-260. See also B. Frenow, *Ohio Valley in Colonial Days* (Albany, N. Y., 1890); Henry Howe, *Historical Collections of Virginia* (Charleston, S. C., 1845), p. 452.

notably that to which Joist Hite was a party—did not end until after the American Revolution.

In 1745, the Crown definitely conceded the Fairfax claims. As a result all the Northern Neck became the fee simple possession of Lord Fairfax, provided only that Crown grants to lands made therein prior to that date should be respected and confirmed. It was under these conditions that he entered upon the use of his heritage, one of the richest in America. The next year, 1746, Fairfax Stone was planted at the head fountain of the North Branch of the Potomac to mark the uttermost extent of the Fairfax lands.

Two years later, George Washington, a youth of sixteen years, went out with a party of surveyors of these lands and thus entered that school of experience from which he was later graduated with accomplishments which helped him to become the "Father of his Country." About the same time, Fairfax himself came to America and established a permanent home at Greenway Court, near Winchester, where he continued to reside as a bachelor until the end of the American Revolution, the results of which are said to have hastened his death.

Chapter IV

The French and Indian War

PRELIMINARIES

IN ITS LARGER PHASES, the French and Indian War, known in Europe as the "Seven Years' War," began in 1756 and resulted in a world-wide conflict. As such, it involved the future of India, the value of a recently formed alliance between the House of Hapsburg and the House of Bourbon, the fortunes of the rising state of Prussia, and the control of the high seas. These considerations account for the fact that hostilities were not formally declared in Europe until after they began in America. In the former quarter, new alliances were being formed and new possibilities were being considered.

In its narrower phase, the French and Indian War was a contest for the ownership of the Ohio Valley. It was also the culmination of a series of conflicts involving the possession of the Ohio Valley and a major part of North America. It will be recalled that three colonial wars—King William's, or the War of the English Succession, 1689-1697; Queen Anne's, or the War of the Spanish Succession, 1701-1713; and King George's, or the War of the Austrian Succession, 1744-1748—had preceded it, and that in each of these conflicts fighting had taken place in America. Locally, the French and Indian War began in 1754, when scouting bands encountered each other in the disputed area beyond the Alleghenies.

The French based their claims to the Ohio Valley largely on the alleged discoveries of La Salle, the fact that they were then in occupation of the Illinois country, and the activity of their traders. Since early in the eighteenth century they had maintained a more or less regular trade in farm products between their Illinois settlements and the lower Mississippi Valley. Their interest in the fur trade of the Ohio Valley was of older standing. Alarmed by the ever-increasing number of English traders coming into that coveted land and by reports to the effect that the English planned to take possession of it, the French resolved to assert their claims in a positive manner. For that purpose they sent out Celoron de Bienville (Blainville), who in 1749 planted leaden plates along the upper Ohio River and otherwise asserted the ownership claims of the French.

THE OHIO COMPANY

As the English claimed the Ohio Valley under the Virginia charter of 1609 and also because of the Batts and Fallam discovery of 1671 and the activities of their traders, they were at the same time preparing to assert their claims. The western boundary of Pennsylvania was then thought to be at or near the top of the Allegheny Mountains, and the initiative naturally fell to the Virginians. Through Thomas Cresap who then resided at Old Town, high on the Potomac River, and was in touch with the interior, leaders had been reminded of the need for and the advantages of action. The Ohio Company was accordingly organized in 1747 primarily for the purpose of making settlements.[1]

The moving spirit of the Ohio Company was Colonel Thomas Lee of Virginia. Among his associates were Lawrence and Augustine Washington, half brothers of George Washington; George Mason; and John Hanbury, a Quaker merchant residing in London, England. They and their associates petitioned for a grant in the vicinity of the Forks of the Ohio. After several hearings, their request was approved in England, and the governor and council in Virginia were ordered to make the grant. It was for 200,000 acres and was made on July 13, 1749, but on condition that the Ohio Company build a fort on the grant and settle it with one hundred families within seven years. Upon compliance with this condition, the company was to have an additional 300,000 acres, provided it settled three hundred more families within the next seven years.

Though these conditions were burdensome and perhaps unfriendly, the Ohio Company prepared for action. As participation in the Indian trade was then thought to be necessary, a supply of goods was ordered from Hanbury in London; a storehouse was built in 1749 at Wills Creek, on the present site of Cumberland, Maryland; and English traders were sent into the region of the upper Ohio. Moreover, in 1750 the company

[1] Kenneth P. Bailey, *The Ohio Company of Virginia and the Westward Movement* (Glendale, Calif., 1939), pp. 15-33.

employed Christopher Gist, then residing on the Yadkin River in North Carolina, to make an exploring expedition beyond the Allegheny Mountains and contact the natives with a view to assembling them for a conference.

As a road had not yet been made into the interior by way of waters flowing into the upper Potomac, Gist, setting out from Old Town on October 31, 1750, traveled almost due north to the Raystown Path in

LAN 1749 DV REGNE DE LOVIS XV ROY DE
FRANCE NOVS CELORON COMMANDANT DVN DE
TACHEMENT ENVOIE PAR MONSIEVER LE Mis DE LA
GALISSONIERE COMMANDANT GENERAL DE LA
NOVVELLE FRANCE POVR RETABLIR LA TRANQVILLITE
DANS QVELQVES VILLAGES SAUVAGES DE CES CANTONS
AVONS ENTERRE CETTE PLAQVE A L'ENTREE DE LA RIVIERE ET
SUR RIVE SEPTEN TRIONALE DE KANOUOUARA, QUI SE
DECHARGE A LEST DE LA RIVIERE OYO AUTREMENT
BELLE RIVIERE, CE 13 AOUT POVR MONVMENT DV RENOV-
VELLEMENT DE POSSESSION QVE NOVS AVONS PRIS DE LA DITTE
RIVIERE OYO ET DE TOVTES CELLES QVI Y TOMBENT
ET DE TOVTES LES TERRES DES DEVX COTES JVSQVE
AUX SOVRCES DES DITTES RIVIES VINSI QVE ONT
JOVY OV DV JOVIR LES PRECEDETNS ROYS DE FRANCE
ET QVILS SISONT MAINTENVS PAR LES ARMES ET
PAR LES TRAITTES SPECIALEMENT PAR CEVX DE
RISVVICK DVTRCHT ET DAIX LA CHPELLE

Facsimile of leaden plate buried at mouth of Wheeling Creek, August 13, 1749

Pennsylvania, which he followed across the mountains, through Loyalhanna to Shannopin's Town on the Allegheny about three miles from the Forks of the Ohio. Six days later Gist was at Logstown on the present site of Economy, Pennsylvania, where he found "a Parcel of reprobate traders," and learned that George Croghan, "prince of Pennsylvania traders," and Andrew Montour, son of the famous halfbreed, Madame Montour, had, only a few days before, left for the Indian country beyond the Ohio.[2]

Having disposed of his compass, the more effectively to conceal his real mission as the agent of a land company, Gist continued his journey as an envoy. At Muskingum, an Indian town, he came up with Croghan, who owned a trading post there. Accompanied by him, Montour, their em-

[2] *Christopher Gist's Journals* (Darlington ed.), pp. 32-41; Bailey, *Ohio Company,* pp. 85-100.

ployees, and a Negro boy, Gist then directed his course to Pickawillamy, the most important town of the Miamis. En route he visited Delaware, Shawnee, and Wyandot towns to invite their chiefs to the proposed conference. After a few days at Pickawillamy he set out for home.

On his return trip Gist first went to Shawnee Town, on the Ohio River, where he was given a reception. From this point he journeyed along the Ohio to within fifteen miles of the Falls, but he was forced to turn back because of increasing signs of Indian hostiles. His course then lay toward Kentucky River, which he crossed at or near the site of present Frankfort. Continuing by way of a route which may have crossed present Mercer County, West Virginia, he reached home in May, 1751. His report was not assuring. The Indian country beyond the Ohio was full of Pennsylvania traders; the French were arresting Englishmen and carrying them to Canada; and the French were making friends among the natives.

More disturbing still, the Ohio Company had encountered opposition at home in the person of John Robinson, Speaker of the House of Burgesses. In 1745, Robinson had received a grant of 100,000 acres on Greenbrier River in present West Virginia. Six years later, he, with the help of others, organized the Greenbrier Company for the purpose of developing and speculating in these lands. About the same time the Loyal Company was organized and given a grant of 800,000 acres on the southern frontiers of Virginia.

Though much space separated the Greenbrier grant from the Ohio Company's, the proprietors of the former were known to be unfriendly to the latter. Among other things they saw to it that Gist's request for a license as surveyor of the Ohio Company was for a time denied. Not to be outdone by it, they sent Thomas Walker into the interior on an exploring expedition. Going by way of the Warrior Path through Cumberland Gap, which he later named, Walker made extensive explorations in the present state of Kentucky. Returning, his course lay along the west side of the Allegheny Mountains to the Greenbrier Valley, where he inspected lands.

Following the death of Colonel Thomas Lee (1751) and of Lawrence Washington (1752), the reorganized Ohio Company was under the vigorous direction of the Mercers (John and his sons, George and James), George Mason, Richard Henry Lee, and George Washington. Moreover, Robert Dinwiddie was at this time made lieutenant governor of Virginia, and the Ohio Company seized the opportunity to make him a stockholder. Formerly, under the administration of Governor Gooch, its rivals had been favorites, but under the changed order, the situation was reversed.

Thus encouraged and reinforced, the Ohio Company decided to send Gist beyond the mountains on another journey of exploration. As the lands north of the Ohio were thought to be too distant and unprotected for its purposes, he was instructed to observe and examine lands on the south side in the vicinity of the Forks. Incidentally, he was to find the shortest and best route for a road between Wills Creek and the Monongahela River.

Gist's second journey occupied him from November 4, 1751 to March 29, 1752. Leaving Old Town in company with his son, he traveled through valleys and over mountains by a rather direct route to the site of present Brownsville, Pennsylvania, from which place he made detailed observations along a considerable stretch of the Monongahela River. His course was then directed toward the mouth of the Kanawha River through long stretches of present West Virginia.[3]

On his return trip, Gist engaged Thomas Cresap and Nemacolin, a friendly Delaware, to blaze a trail from Wills Creek to the Monongahela over a route indicated by him. The result was the "Nemacolin Trail," which lay along the route later followed by Braddock. It is now in part the National Road.

From this point, the affairs of the Ohio Company moved rapidly. As its representative, Gist was hustled off to Logstown where, on June 13, 1752, he, together with representatives of Pennsylvania and Virginia, and with Andrew Montour acting as interpreter, concluded the Treaty of Logstown. This document recognized Virginia's claims to land west of the Allegheny Mountains to the Ohio River and gave the Ohio Company permission to make the desired settlement and build a fort at or near the Forks. Most of the contracting Indians were Delaware and Shawnee chiefs, but Iroquois were present and recognized the "Right and title of his Majesty . . . to all the lands within the colony of Virginia," as granted in the 1744 Treaty of Lancaster.

About the same time, the Ohio Company built a larger storehouse at Wills Creek, which was, in fact, so commodious and secure as to serve in the ensuing wars as a fort. It became famous in the latter capacity. Originally it was intended as a base of deposits for another storehouse built in 1752 at the mouth of Red Stone Creek on the Monongahela River, from which it was planned to carry on an extensive Indian trade. Later this storehouse, too, was used as a place of refuge and as such came to be known as Red Stone Old Fort.

Shortly after the Treaty of Logstown, Gist was appointed surveyor of the Ohio Company. As he was thus assured of permanent employment, he took up his residence west of the mountains. For this purpose he chose in 1753 a beautiful site called "Gists," but now known as Mount Braddock. It is about half way between present Uniontown and Connellsville, Penn-

[3] *Christopher Gist's Journals,* p. 74; Bailey, *Ohio Company,* p. 99. Gist's route lay through present Marshall, Wetzel, Tyler, Ritchie, Wood, Wirt, Jackson, Putnam, and Mason counties.

sylvania, and not far from Brownsville and Fort Necessity. Early the following year he was joined by eleven other families who made settlements in the vicinity of his establishment.

It was at this juncture that the French announced their determination to dispute every foot of the English advance. Reasserting their claims to ownership as based upon the rights of occupation and discovery, they now redoubled their efforts to capture and deport English traders. They also induced Indians to disavow the Treaty of Logstown and declared their intention of building a chain of forts along the Ohio.[4] In keeping with this purpose, forts were started in 1753 at Presque Isle in Lake Erie near present Erie, at Le Boeuf on French Creek a short distance to the southward, and at Venango on the Allegheny River.

THE YOUNG COLONEL

Instead of meeting the French aggressions in kind, Dinwiddie decided to complain to the French commander in Canada "of the encroachments thus made, and of the injuries done the subjects of Great Britain, in violation of the laws of nations." Captain William Trent was first selected to carry this complaint. In midsummer, 1753, he proceeded all the way to Logstown on this mission, but turned back at that point without delivering his message; whereupon, Dinwiddie drafted George Washington, a young man of twenty-one years, who had already seen service on the frontier in the employ of Lord Fairfax. In making this selection, it did not, of course, occur to Dinwiddie that he was raising up a leader who would some day undo a part of the work which Dinwiddie, William Pitt, and young Washington himself were about to consummate.

On this mission, Washington left Williamsburg, Virginia, October 31, 1753, and went direct to Wills Creek, which he reached November 14.[5] Here he found Christopher Gist, who agreed to accompany him on the journey, the greatest perils of which came from the inclement weather, which swelled streams and made rafting, fording, and swimming perilous. Passing Gists, on the Youghiogheny, and Frasers, on Turtle Creek, they came to the Forks of the Ohio. Tarrying there long enough to appreciate the importance of this gateway to the West, they continued their journey to Logstown, where a powwow was held with the Indians with a view to

[4] Louis K. Koontz, *The Virginia Frontier*, 1754-1763 (Baltimore, 1925), pp. 39-40; Bailey, *Ohio Company*, p. 174; Charles H. Ambler, *George Washington and the West* (Chapel Hill, 1936), pp. 34-36.

[5] For details of this journey, see Washington, *Diaries* (Edited by Fitzpatrick), Vol. I, 43-65.

keeping them true to the agreements made at that place the year before. Then the party continued almost due north a distance of about sixty miles to Fort Le Boeuf, where Washington made complaint to Chevalier de St. Pierre, who received him cordially but made a flat denial of the facts and justice of his contentions.

The report that Washington took back to Virginia made clear the necessity for the use of force, if the colony would protect her interests on the frontier. In co-operation with the Ohio Company, Dinwiddie had already dispatched Captain Trent and a party of thirty-seven men to the Forks with instructions to build a fort at that point. Later in the same year, 1754, Washington followed with a company of one hundred fifty men, most of whom joined him in Frederick and Augusta counties.

Arriving at Wills Creek, Washington learned that Captain Trent had been diverted from his undertaking by the French, whose scouting parties were reported in possession of the lands about the upper Ohio. Undaunted, he continued into the interior, where this report was verified. In the neighborhood of what is now Uniontown, he and the French commander, Jumonville, held each other under surveillance for some time, but a skirmish followed in which Jumonville was killed. Although his conduct had not been free from suspicion, papers found on his person indicated Jumonville's friendly intentions. Complicating the situation, Washington later signed a paper stating that the French officer had been assassinated.

Following the Jumonville affair, the French descended in overwhelming numbers upon Washington and his command. Hard-pressed, he made a stand at Fort Necessity, in Great Meadows, where he defended himself during the entire day of July 3, 1754. Fearing that Washington might receive reinforcements, the French offered terms which were accepted. On the following day, the Virginians withdrew with the honors of war, but promised not to return to the Ohio Valley within the ensuing year to construct fortifications.

Knowledge of Washington's surrender at Fort Necessity produced consternation at Williamsburg, the capital of Virginia. Dinwiddie was for striking back at once, but temporarily the situation was hopeless. Wampum and "Spirit" were no longer tempting to coveted Indian allies, who first sulked in their tents and finally became hostile; sister, even neighboring, colonies were indifferent; and the assembly could agree upon no adequate plan of relief. Already Governor Dinwiddie had issued a proclamation allotting two hundred thousand acres of land along the Ohio for distribution among those who would serve against the French and Indians and who would settle these lands at once, but the offer was unavailing. Even fur traders were leaving the frontier, and few persons of any calling could be induced to enter it.

BRADDOCK'S DEFEAT

At this juncture, it was announced that the mother country would take a hand in military affairs in America. Although war had not been formally declared, a further postponement of hostilities was not desired. A short time thereafter, Sir Edward Braddock arrived in Virginia with two regiments of English Regulars. Thus a contest heretofore largely confined to Virginia became intercolonial and international. The local response was all that could be desired, and neighboring colonies prepared to join Virginia for a triumphal procession into the interior. The route selected was by way of the Potomac and the Nemacolin Trail, and the expedition was commanded by Regulars. Washington was not wholly satisfied with this arrangement, but he accompanied Braddock as an aide-de-camp.

Incidents of this expedition were as unusual as they were, at times, romantic, or even tragic. Near its destination, it moved like a conquering pageant, so grand as to draw from Washington the remark that he had never seen a more beautiful sight. It was at Cumberland that its leader for the first time looked upon Indians, saw their war dances, and heard their demoniacal yells that startled the night hours. It was here that his soldiers took advantage of the abandonment of the Indian maidens, who, led by their princess, Bright Lightning, threw themselves into the arms of the red-coated British, whose glorious dress completely captivated them. Nevertheless, their chieftains, under the leadership of "Jack, the Black Hunter," continued to follow in the trail of this strange retinue and to offer its succor, which Braddock alienated by his insistence upon discipline, and thus lost to his command men "any one of whom, in an Indian war, was equal to a whole company of British regulars."

On July 9, forty-two days after leaving Cumberland, this column reached the Monongahela, near the present site of Pittsburgh, where it encountered the French and Indians in a free-for-all contest. Soon British Regulars were in such a state of confusion that they shot down their companions in arms, mistaking them for Frenchmen. In the course of the encounter, four horses were shot from under General Braddock and two from under Washington, whose clothes were pierced by several bullets. Finally the general fell and was left to welter in his own blood, until two Virginians, whom he had disparaged because of their lack of military training, carried his body to safety. Seemingly unconcerned with his wounds and preoccupied with the incidents of a disaster which he could not understand, Braddock died four days later and was buried in the middle of a roadway—which then bore his name—while Washington read over his body the burial rites of the church. As has been well said: "Surely no more pitiful tale of the butchery of brave men, or of disaster following high hopes and great preparations was ever told."[6]

Although proud of the record of their own provincials who, under the direction of Washington, had been able to avert a complete disaster, Braddock's defeat drove terror into the hearts of Virginians everywhere. In a tone of helpless humility, Governor Dinwiddie implored his advisers and others to suggest some way to "retrieve the dishonor done to British arms"; and, in the name of the "Virginia forces that purchased immortal glory on the banks of the Monongahela," he asked the general assembly to take the necessary steps to preserve "the most valuable of all human treasures—religious and civil liberty." In response, the assembly voted forty thousand pounds for defense, and Washington was put in command of Virginia's forces on the frontier.

THE VIRGINIA FRONTIER

Meanwhile, settlers and traders alike were being pushed back over the mountains into the Shenandoah Valley and beyond the Blue Ridge. The "supplicating tears of the women" who accompanied them and the "moving petitions of the men" melted Washington into "deadly sorrow," and he stood ready to give himself "a willing sacrifice to the butchering enemy, provided that would contribute to the people's ease."[7] For a time it was feared that the English would be swept from the continent of North America.

Although adhering to the time-honored British policy of maintaining a stubborn and adequate defense, Washington constantly advised the necessity for offensive action in dealing with the French and Indians. He well knew that scattered forts, meagerly manned, could not avail to stop the stealthy incursions of a savage foe. He insisted, therefore, that "the cause" of their troubles, the French occupancy of Fort Duquesne, should be removed. To this end he made numerous suggestions and plans.

During all this time, only one aggressive movement was made by and through Virginia into the frontier. This was an expedition led by Major Andrew Lewis, the trusted friend and adviser of Washington, against the Shawnee towns on the Ohio. It left Fort Frederick, Augusta County, in February, 1756, and, passing down the New River and through Drapers Meadows, followed a route leading, in the general direction of the Big

[6] Koontz, *Virginia Frontier,* p. 70.

[7] Washington, *Writings* (Edited by Ford), Vol. I, 248-251; Koontz, *Virginia Frontier,* p. 75.

Sandy River, through a part of what is now West Virginia. Although it failed of military results, it is memorable as the first English military expedition to the waters of the Ohio south of Pittsburgh.

It must not be inferred that Virginia's frontier defense in the French and Indian War was impregnable. In 1756, the Indians, making successful attacks in what is now Hardy County, West Virginia, carried their depredations as far east as Martinsburg. In the same year, in the Battle of the Trough, they killed many settlers near the present site of Moorefield, and at the same time almost annihilated a military company under Captain John Mercer in Hampshire County. In 1758, under the leadership of Killbuck, a famous Delaware warrior, they attacked both Fort Seybert and Fort Upper Tract, in what is now Pendleton County; and, after killing or carrying away the occupants, they burned the forts. Accounts of minor assaults could be multiplied almost indefinitely.

Fortunately, a better day was ahead. William Pitt had assumed direction of affairs in England; and, under his influence, colonial differences were ironed out and gave way to co-operation, the British Navy became effective, and the tide of war in America began to turn in favor of the English. Following victories elsewhere, notably those at Louisburg and Fort Frontenac, preparations were made to attack Fort Duquesne. To this end, it was announced, General John Forbes was to lead a force of seven thousand men, including twelve hundred Scotch Highlanders and five thousand provincials, to retrieve the tragic failure of General Braddock. Disciplined in the school of adversity, Virginia and Pennsylvania reluctantly co-operated. The Virginians even gave up their favorite route of attack by way of Braddock's Road for another by way of Bedford and Fort Ligonier, in Pennsylvania. The result—the capture of Fort Duquesne by the English, November 25, 1758—broke the French power in the Ohio Valley and paved the way for a new order in America.

From their towns in the Illinois country, the French next appealed to the Cherokees, former allies of the English but now temporarily alienated. For months these Indians had waited at Winchester, eager to participate in the proposed attack upon Fort Duquesne, and had finally given up in despair. On their way home they fell into customary practices of pilfering, stealing horses, and marauding. Virginia frontiersmen, accustomed to regard no Indian as good but a dead one, killed some of these marauders. Thus the Indians were in a mood to listen to French suggestions of vengeance. The war which followed is known as the "Cherokee War."[8] It terminated in 1760 in a victory for the English, but not until the Indians had carried their murderous attacks throughout a large part of the region between the Blue Ridge and the Alleghenies.

---

[8] Koontz, *Virginia Frontier,* p. 92.

RESULTS

Already Quebec, the Gibraltar of America, had fallen, and soon thereafter peace was in process of negotiation. As a result, Manila and Cuba, captured by the English in the war, were returned to Spain, an ally of France, in exchange for Florida; and North America became British from the Atlantic to the Mississippi, with the exception of New Orleans, which, with all of Louisiana west of the Mississippi, went to Spain as an additional offset to her loss of Florida. All that remained to France of her former domain in America were two small islands, St. Pierre and Miquelon, near the mouth of the St. Lawrence River, together with some fishing privileges on the coast of Newfoundland. Incidentally, the English gained a foothold in India and increased their prowess upon the high seas, and thus made possible the birth of the British Empire, child of William Pitt.

Locally the most important result of the French and Indian War was the English occupation of the Ohio Valley. No sooner had Fort Duquesne fallen and been renamed "Fort Pitt," than traders and adventurers again pushed into the regions around the upper Ohio. Among them were many persons who had been on the frontier before, in western Pennsylvania and western Virginia, but in a very real way they were not the same persons. They were now experienced warriors with a degree of self-reliance and mental stature that made them almost invincible. Their opinions of British Regulars had also undergone a complete transformation. Thus schooled, the American frontiersman became a power for weal or woe in the new-born British Empire.

Their subsequent course was clearly indicated in the new and powerful advance of settlement that set in to the westward even before the formal cessation of hostilities. Homes on the South Branch were reoccupied, and venturesome characters again found their way across the Alleghenies. Among these was Thomas Decker, who, in 1758, led a party of settlers to the Monongahela, at the mouth of Decker's Creek, and made a settlement on the present site of Morgantown. The following year, this settlement was destroyed and its inhabitants were killed, but the reoccupation of the South Branch and the neighboring valleys was permanent. For the accommodation of their inhabitants, two towns, Romney and New Mecklenburg, now Shepherdstown, were laid out in 1762. In the same year, the burgesses established an agricultural and mechanical fair to be held twice a year in the latter for the purchase and sale of produce and supplies.

Chapter V

The Trans-Allegheny 1763-1775

PONTIAC'S CONSPIRACY

WITH THE TERMINATION of the French and Indian War in favor of the British, there were many persons in America who expected to make settlements in the Trans-Allegheny in the region of the upper Ohio. Would-be settlers thought of this region as a "Promised Land," coveted all the more because of the good reports—some from former residents—which reached them from time to time regarding it. Other would-be settlers had fought to win this land from the French and Indians and regarded it as belonging to the victors by the right of conquest. All remembered the proclamation of 1754 by Governor Dinwiddie, promising two hundred thousand acres along the Ohio to such persons as would serve in the impending war against the French and Indians and later settle upon grants.[1] Many were familiar also with the conditions under which companies had been formed in Virginia for the settlement of lands beyond the mountains. Thus it was that interested parties asked, "Why not resume the westward movement?"

Answers to this question were disappointing. First of all was the refusal of the Indians to give up their hunting grounds. Accustomed to a close association with his former allies, the French, whose *coureurs de bois* moved among his people—in some instances adopting their customs and intermarrying with them—the red man was reluctant to yield his lands to the "Long Knife," whose reputation for thoroughness, close bargaining,

[1] Koontz, *Virginia Frontier;* Robert Dinwiddie, "Official Records" in *Virginia Historical Society Collections*, 2 vols. (Richmond, 1883-1884), Vol. I, 96; Hening, *Statutes*, Vol. VII, 661-662.

and selfishness as a conqueror had preceded him. It was indeed a critical moment, which called for the best that was in the Indians.

As usual, such conditions brought forth a leader. On this occasion it was Pontiac, an Ottawa chieftain of rare qualities.[2] He was able to effect a unity of his kinsmen the like of which had never been seen before and has scarcely been equaled since. The Indians organized a resistance the formidableness of which lent credence to the conclusion that it was abetted; hence, the so-called "Conspiracy of Pontiac." From Mackinaw to Fort Pitt the British posts were attacked, and settlements were laid waste from northern New York to southern Virginia.

Instead of moving to the occupation of their Promised Land, the Virginians were called upon to defend it. The thousand militiamen summoned for this service came from Hampshire and adjoining counties and were under the command of Colonel Adam Stephen and Major Andrew Lewis, "both of whom were now officers of the best quality."

It was, however, Colonel Henry Bouquet who turned the tide against the Indians in this conflict. Advancing westward from Fort Ligonier, he on August 5, 1763 defeated them decisively at Bushy Run, about twenty miles southeast of Fort Pitt, in the most important Indian battle in the colony of Pennsylvania. In the autumn of 1764, Bouquet advanced from Fort Pitt into the Indian country beyond the Ohio as far as Muskingum River, where he surprised Indian hostiles and compelled them to sue for peace.[3]

THE INDIAN TRADE

Meanwhile, the mother country had reversed her policy regarding the occupation of the Trans-Allegheny. Perplexed by the Indian uprising of 1763, yet eager to make the most of the fur trade, she had made a temporary arrangement for the administration of the country west of the Alleghenies. This was embodied in the Royal Proclamation of 1763, which provided for the organization of three new royal provinces: Quebec, which was limited to the St. Lawrence Valley; East Florida; and West Florida. Previously, the management of Indian affairs in the intervening country had been intrusted to two superintendents: Sir William Johnson, for the district north of the Ohio; and Colonel John Stuart, for that to the southward. Colonial governors were forbidden to make land grants in these reserves, and settlers were ordered to withdraw.

---

[2] Francis Parkman, *Conspiracy of Pontiac* (Boston, 1913).

[3] Mary C. Darlington, *History of Colonel Henry Bouquet and the Western Frontier of Pennsylvania, 1747-1764* (c. 1920); Albert T. Volwiler, *George Croghan and the Westward Movement, 1741-7182* (Cleveland, 1926), p. 175.

Like other paper manifestoes, the Proclamation of 1763 was openly defied by immigrant homeseekers, who pushed into the forbidden land west of the Alleghenies. Of their movements in the years immediately following 1763, George Croghan, writing in 1766, said: "As soon as peace was made last year, contrary to our engagements, a number of our people came over the Great Mountain and settled at Redstone Creek upon the Monongahela, before they [the Indians] had given the country to the King, their Father." Of what was certainly the same movement, a letter from Winchester, Virginia, dated April 30, 1765, said: "The frontier Inhabitants of this Colony and Maryland, are removing fast over the Allegheny Mountains, in order to Settle and live there."[4] In varying numbers they continued to move into the transmontane country until it was completely occupied.

Chief interest in the western country now centered in the plans and activities of traders, some of whom hoped to make Fort Pitt an emporium of commerce surpassing in importance either Quebec or New Orleans. Individual traders had pushed into the interior before the Treaty of Paris (1763) was concluded. Now they planned to move in groups and to establish themselves permanently. Prominent among them was a company composed of John Baynton, Samuel Wharton, George Morgan, and others—often referred to as "Baynton, Wharton and Morgan." Their headquarters were in Philadelphia, where they had strong business alliances, mainly with Quakers. David Franks and Company, of the same city, but with connections predominantly Jewish, was a rival concern.

In 1765, under the direction of George Morgan, the Quaker group established a boatyard at Fort Pitt, from which were launched, in the course of a short time, sixty-five galley bateaux. With the exception of timbers, materials for these boats were carried all the way from Philadelphia on pack horses and wagons. Six hundred of the former were employed at one time by this one firm. Before the arrival of Daniel Boone in the "Dark and Bloody Land" as agent of Richard Henderson, these boats were being used to maintain commerce between the upper Ohio and the Illinois country. The number of men thus employed is said to have exceeded three hundred.[5]

Under the control of the British, the Indian trade of the Ohio Valley was disappointing. Returns were in no way commensurate with outlays, either those of the traders or those of the imperial government. The most successful French traders deserted the Illinois country; and some established themselves beyond the Mississippi in St. Louis, from which point they con-

[4] Neville B. Craig, *History of Pittsburgh* (Pittsburgh, 1917), p. 85; *Pa. Archives,* first series, Vol. IV, 217; Albert T. Volwiler, *George Croghan and the Westward Movement,* 1741-1782 (Cleveland, 1926), pp. 172-180.

[5] Clarence W. Alvord and Clarence E. Carter, *The Critical Period,* 1763-1765 (Springfield, Ill., 1915), pp. 311-314; Clarence W. Alvord, *The Mississippi Valley in British Politics,* 2 vols. (Cleveland, 1917), Vol. I, 301, 320; Volwiler, *Croghan,* 191, 198-203.

tinued to trade with their former friends and customers. Frontiersmen were unfriendly, seeing in the Indian trade instruments for their undoing, such as the rum, guns, and munitions of war that were freely dispensed. In Cumberland County, Pennsylvania, aggrieved settlers fell upon wagons carrying articles belonging to Baynton, Wharton and Morgan, dispersed those in charge, destroyed goods, and appropriated horses and wagons.

This failure was one of the determining influences in the subsequent history of the Trans-Allegheny, particularly that part of it now embraced in West Virginia. In an effort to recoup their losses, former traders became land jobbers and promoters of new colonies. Details of their intrigues constitute one of the most sordid, as well as one of the most informing, chapters in the history of American expansion. In the years immediately following 1765, they made for intercolonial rivalries and sectional prejudices; they stimulated immigration into the interior; and, finally, they almost succeeded in establishing a fourteenth colony within the territory of what is now West Virginia.

A NEW WESTWARD MOVEMENT

One of the most immediate and, in the long run, the most important effects of plans for occupying the Trans-Allegheny was a stimulated westward movement. Previously, immigrants had sought the West spasmodically and secretly. Virginia had no provisions for selling lands there, and, in going into the interior, settlers were violating the King's orders. Now, they turned their faces toward the upper Ohio Valley with a determination that could not be denied. It mattered not that Virginia continued to make no arrangements for their accommodations and that the Royal Proclamation of 1763 remained unrepealed. The immigrant movement into the interior assumed tidal proportions; from twenty-five thousand to thirty thousand persons established themselves on the upper Ohio and its tributaries before the Revolution. As a consequence, by 1770, this, the "First English-Speaking Trans-Appalachian Frontier" had taken on some of the aspects of an established and orderly community.

The conditions under which settlers came into this region lent interest to their movements and practices. The Scotch-Irish, interspersed with land speculators, a few Germans, and prospectors from the seaboard sections of Virginia, Maryland, and New Jersey, were the predominant element in this movement. Their characteristics and practices gave it color and momentum.[6] In the absence of land offices and surveyors, a tomahawk in a

[6] Roosevelt, *Winning of the West* (Sagamore series), Vol. I, 132-172; Withers, *Border Warfare,* pp. 191, 334, 373.

settler's hands sufficed to indicate the bounds of land claims. Thus were established the famous "tomahawk rights," which the frontiersmen themselves respected and Virginia later legalized. In crude log cabins, with the earth for floors and stone slabs or bark for roofs, the adventurers established "settlement rights." As a rule, these consisted of one hundred acres which could be extended to two hundred or more, in case no prior claims interfered.

For temporary subsistence, pioneers depended largely upon their prowess as hunters. The earliest settlers found a few buffaloes along the Ohio, but deer, wild turkeys, and other game were abundant throughout the Trans-Allegheny. Clad in typical frontier garb, leather breeches, moccasins, fur cap, and hunting shirt, and girded by a belt from which hung a hunting knife and a shot pouch—all homemade—the pioneer presented a unique appearance. In a short time he opened in the woods a patch, or clearing, on which he grew corn, wheat, flax, tobacco, and other products, even fruit. As his clearing was extended from year to year, and as opportunities offered, he was able to add domestic animals to his possessions and to approach a condition of living not unlike that to the eastward. Homespuns took the place of skins and the products of his cattle and sheep those of the chase. When he began to accumulate a surplus of agricultural products and animals, he thought of markets; but, as yet, schools and churches were far outside his plans.

Particulars of this movement throw light upon its character and extent. Learning that the Indian wars were ended, the Pringle brothers, John and Samuel, induced permanent settlers to join them in 1768 in the Buckhannon Valley, where, since 1764, they had lived in a hollow sycamore tree near the present site of Buckhannon. The new settlers came from the South Branch Valley, but the Pringles were deserters from the garrison at Fort Pitt. In 1764, John Simpson, a trapper, camped on a site on or near the present city of Clarksburg, and four years later, Zackquill Morgan made a permanent settlement on the present site of Morgantown. The next year, Ebenezer Zane and his two brothers established themselves permanently on the Ohio at Wheeling Creek; and several families, most of them from the South Branch Valley, settled near Clifton Mills and Bruceton, Preston County. In 1770, still other families settled on the Ohio River, among them the Tomlinsons, who stopped at the mouth of Grave Creek. Tomahawk rights in what later became Monongalia County increased from four in 1768, to twenty-two in 1769, and to ninety-two in 1770. When the county was formed (1776), there were nearly twelve hundred such claims within its bounds.

At the same time, a similar rapid expansion occurred in the region of the Greenbrier Valley. In 1769, Colonel John Stuart and others—among them Robert McClannahan, Thomas Renick, and William Hamilton—

established themselves there as permanent settlers. The same year, the Woods family settled near Peterstown. In the years immediately following, these settlers were joined by a dozen or more families, among them being the Manns, Millers, Alexanders, Nickels, Campbells, Dunsmores, Hokes, Lakes, Callaways, Sweeneys, Erskines, Grahams, and Hutchinsons.

About the same time, settlements began to push westward down the Kanawha River. Walter Kelley settled in 1773 at the mouth of Kelleys Creek, where he was killed by Indians. The next year, at the same place, William Morris made the first permanent settlement in the Kanawha Valley. Thomas Bullitt had meanwhile inspected lands at the mouth of Elk River, but it was not until May, 1775, that a survey was made. The tract thus pre-empted by Bullitt contained ten hundred and thirty acres and covered the site of Charleston. It was granted as compensation for services in the French and Indian War.

THE VIRGINIA-PENNSYLVANIA BOUNDARY

The first differences between Pennsylvania and Virginia frontiersmen were over trade. Following the 1744 Treaty of Lancaster, in which Iroquois relinquished to Virginia lands between the Allegheny Mountains and the Ohio River, and the Logstown Treaty of 1752, in which they gave the English exclusive trade rights in the upper Ohio Valley, Pennsylvania and Virgina traders in increasing numbers made the most of their opportunities. It mattered not that the Pennsylvanians were first in the field. What the Virginians lost in that they later tended to make good through asserting their claims to ownership of the trading country. When they prepared to use this method on a large scale, the resulting rivalry became bitter and disconcerting even in times of common danger.[7]

These differences were heightened by a boundary dispute which had its origin in the charters of the two colonies. Under her charter of 1609, Virginia claimed all the territory west of Maryland and south of Pennsylvania to the western boundary of the latter, then west and northwest to the Pacific Ocean. On the other hand, most interested parties, even the Virginians, agreed that the southern boundary of Pennsylvania extended westward five degrees, but there was no agreement as to the point of beginning. If this could be determined, then fixing the beginning point of the western boundary of Pennsylvania was only a matter of the correct use of compass and chain. There remained, however, the very important question of whether or not the resulting line should run due north or fol-

[7] N. B. Craig, ed., *The Olden Time Monthly Publication* (Pittsburgh, 1846-1848), Vol. I, 433-435; Crumrine, "The Boundary Controversy between Pennsylvania and Virginia," in *Annals of the Carnegie Museum*, Vol. I, 505-524.

low the meanders of the Delaware River at a distance of five degrees at every point on the line.

The crux of the resulting controversy was the control of the Forks of the Ohio, the trade center and the strategic focus for the upper Ohio Valley. Early in the French and Indian War, the Governor of Pennsylvania took possession of the disputed area, but her legislature, under the influence of Benjamin Franklin and the Pennsylvania traders, repudiated his claim and for a time refused to aid in its maintenance. On the other hand, the French and Indian War was brought on largely by the aggressiveness of Virginians. Because of the jealousies thus aroused, Pennsylvanians were able to poison the minds of the natives, and the French induced them to repudiate the Treaty of Logstown.

In the war which followed, the Pennsylvania-Virginia rivalries were temporarily pushed into the background. For a time the Proclamation of 1763 tended to keep them there; but as traders, largely Pennsylvanians, and, following the 1768 treaties of Hard Labour and Fort Stanwix, settlers, largely Virginians, again pushed into the upper Ohio Valley, colonial, factional, and personal rivalries and jealousies again became the order of the day in and about Fort Pitt, which had meanwhile been built at the Forks.

Relying largely upon their charter and a purchase claim concluded at Logstown in 1744, the Pennsylvanians prepared to assert their rights. In 1769, they opened a land office west of the mountains, and many settlements were made there. Under the helpful guidance of Arthur St. Clair, who owned large tracts of land in the Ligonier Valley and had taken up his residence there, they established in 1771 the county of Bedford, which included the Forks of the Ohio. County officials were designated, but surveyors engaged in 1767 in running the Mason and Dixon Line westward of Maryland were driven off by Indians. The resulting indications were that possession by the Pennsylvanians would count for the proverbial nine points in law.

Although thousands of Virginians were pushing into the disputed areas with the hope and expectation of acquiring lands either from Pennsylvania or from Virginia, and though George Washington was in favor of maintaining the English settlements then established along the road between Fort Cumberland and Fort Pitt,[8] Virginia officialdom moved slowly. On the other hand, the Vandalia promoters and the Indiana proprietors took alarm at the Pennsylvania activities and quickened their efforts to have their claims approved in England. Acting for them and for himself, George Croghan drove off Pennsylvania tax collectors and threatened them with death. To forestall the Penn proprietors, he at this time surveyed and sold a number of tracts to settlers.

[8] *Am. Hist. Rev.*, Vol. XLIV, 851; Ambler, *George Washington*, pp. 132-150.

Meanwhile it had fallen to the ever-active and resourceful Cresaps to look after their own and Virginia's interests. Since 1766, the Cresap settlement at Redstone Old Fort had given the Pennsylvanians much trouble. Under the leadership of Michael Cresap, the Virginians now formed an association to resist the Pennsylvania laws and officers. Under his direction they drafted a petition bearing nearly six hundred signatures, which asked Virginia to assume jurisdiction over the territory about the Forks of the Ohio.

About the same time, the Pennsylvanians took another step in defense of their claims. In February, 1773, they organized Westmoreland County, which included all of Pennsylvania west of the mountains. Hanna's Town, about thirty miles east of Fort Pitt, was designated as the county seat, and county officers were appointed.[9]

Fortunately perhaps for the Virginians, Lord Dunmore had meanwhile become their governor. His predecessor paid little attention to the alleged aggressions of the Pennsylvanians, but they, together with the fact that he, too, became interested in western lands, aroused Dunmore to action. With his approval a number of surveys were made in the Trans-Allegheny for veterans of the French and Indian War, including George Washington, and, in the summer of 1773, Dunmore visited Fort Pitt. He went to ascertain for himself whether or not he should make land grants in the upper Ohio Valley and thus check the "aspiring and encroaching spirit of the princely Proprietor [Penn]."

Accompanied by Colonel William Crawford, Dunmore reached Fort Pitt in August, 1773. He found there "upwards of ten thousand settlers" without magistrates to preserve order or militia to protect them against Indians. He reported that the people flocked about him and besought him to remedy their situation. It was on this trip that he met for the first time Captain John Connolly, a nephew of George Croghan, who became his loyal friend.

September 7, Dunmore was back in Williamsburg, and the results of his trip were soon forthcoming. In answer to the action of Pennsylvanians in creating the county of Westmoreland and to a petition from Virginians then settled near Fort Pitt, he and his council established on October 11, 1773 the District of West Augusta, which until then had no authoritative existence. But for a prohibitory statute, a new county would have been created. Instead, the jurisdiction of Augusta County was extended, and Connolly and Croghan were appointed justices of the peace.

In the course of the subsequent efforts of the "haughty and imperious" Connolly to extend the authority of the District of West Augusta over

---

[9] E. W. Hassler, *Old Westmoreland: A History of Western Pennsylvania during the Revolution* (Cleveland, 1900), pp. 5-9; Volwiler, *Croghan*, p. 307; James Veech, *The Monongahela of Old* (Pittsburgh, 1858; 1892), Ch. VIII.

Westmoreland County, Pennsylvania, he rebuilt Fort Pitt, renaming it "Fort Dunmore," and succeeded in twice getting into jail, thanks to the vigilance of Arthur St. Clair. In turn Connolly arrested Westmoreland justices. Civil war was prevented only by appeals to the governors concerned. But they were unable to agree, and thus the Virginia-Pennsylvania boundary controversy reached an impasse. Fortunately, the attention of the Virginians was diverted to Dunmore's War, which the Pennsylvanians accused them of provoking. The bitterness and suspicion thus aroused lingered for years and was partly responsible for the subsequent practice of recognizing the Mason and Dixon Line as the most convenient boundary between the North and the South.

Following Dunmore's War, the Virginia-Pennsylvania boundary controversy flared up again. In the summer of 1775, following Connolly's departure from the frontier and Governor Dunmore's flight from Virginia, it became so ominous that the Continental Congress asked the rival partisans to curb their tempers and desires until the struggle for a redress of their common grievances could be determined. All distrusted Connolly's dealings with the Indians. Accordingly another Indian conference was called, but on September 11, 1775, a few days before it met, a band of armed Virginians under Captain John Neville took possession of Fort Pitt.[10] With the Virginians in possession of the Forks, things dragged on in this fashion to 1779, when the two colonies agreed to appoint commissioners. In a spirit of compromise they agreed to extend the Mason and Dixon Line westward five degrees from its point of beginning as established by Mason and Dixon, and to accept the meridian passing through its most western point as the western boundary of Pennsylvania. This agreement was ratified by the legislatures of both states, but the location of the resulting line was not determined until 1784. In the interest of peace and accord, Virginia yielded her claims, but on condition that Pennsylvania would validate the land claims already patented. As most of the settlers in southwest Pennsylvania, prior to 1784, came from Virginia and held their land titles from her, this arrangement solved what would otherwise have been another cause of dissension.

DUNMORE'S WAR

As was to be expected, extension of the Virginia frontier into the Trans-Allegheny met with resistance from the natives. It mattered not that they had previously ceded their lands in formal treaties; these were forgotten,

---

10 *Amer. Archives,* fourth series, Vol. III, 717, 723; *Penn. Archives,* first series, Vol. IV, 659.

since in the presence of the white man in the rôle of a settler, the Indian was always uncomfortable. Unfortunate encounters occurred with increasing frequency, and barbarities were committed by both the whites and the savages.[11] About 1773, the latter were carrying murdering and pillaging expeditions into the heart of Virginia, and threatening establishments in the Clinch and Holston valleys. In the course of these raids, among the fiercest and bloodiest in the annals of savage warfare, settlements were laid waste; men and women were murdered in cold blood; infants were dashed to death against trees and stones; and men, women, and children alike were carried into captivity to become the sires and dames of a generation of half-breeds, some of whom showed flights of genius, whereas others outdid the savages in barbarity.

Evidently a crisis was at hand in the relations between the white man and the red man in North America. Had it been marked by a greater degree of love and forbearance and less of the spirit of power, the outcome might have contributed to a new order of things in the world. Instead of the Ohio Valley becoming a melting pot for European peoples, it might have become an assimilating ground of two races. Traditions are replete with the possibilities of such an event. Instead, frontiersmen, driven to extremes by the excesses of savagery, increased their supplies of ammunition, polished their guns, picked their flints, and otherwise made ready for their part in a struggle for the extermination of their enemies. The savages were equally determined and aggressive.

In April, 1774, Governor Dunmore called upon Virginia militiamen to protect the frontier settlements. About the same time, he sent his agent, John Connolly, to Fort Pitt. Appalled at the conditions which he found there in the relations between the frontiersmen and the Indians, Connolly issued a letter in which he advised the frontiersmen to defend themselves. Along the upper Ohio in the vicinity of Fort Fincastle (Wheeling), this letter was accepted as a declaration of hostilities, and residents and sojourners prepared to conduct themselves accordingly. In panic, noncombatants fled across the Monongahela, "more than a thousand passing over in one day," while able-bodied men prepared for war.

The command of volunteers was first offered to George Rogers Clark, a sojourner on his way to Kentucky, but it was finally given to Michael Cresap, a recent immigrant from Maryland, who accepted the responsibility with reluctance. The encounter which followed is known as "Cresap's War."

Another border incident had meanwhile precipitated war on a large

[11] See R. G. Thwaites and L. P. Kellogg, *Documentary History of Dunmore's War* (Madison, Wis., 1905); Withers, *Border Warfare,* pp. 134-187; Clarence W. Alvord, *The Mississippi Valley in British Politics,* 2 vols. (Cleveland, 1917), Vol. II, 188-190.

scale. This was the murder of Logan's family. This gruesome incident took place on April 30, 1774, at a grogshop kept by Joshua Baker on the Virginia side of the Ohio River opposite the mouth of Yellow Creek. It so incensed the Mingo chieftain, Logan, who had lived at peace with the white man, but had become addicted to the use of intoxicants, that he went on the warpath and took many braves with him.

The conflict that ensued is known as "Dunmore's War." It was of short duration. Following closely upon the heels of a punitive expedition led by Major Angus McDonald, Lord Dunmore himself led an army of about twelve hundred men, most of whom had enlisted in the counties of Frederick, Berkeley, and Hampshire, by way of the Monongahela to Fort Pitt. The plan was to unite his forces at some point below with another army of about equal strength which General Andrew Lewis had collected at Camp Union, now Lewisburg, and was leading into the interior by way of the Kanawha River.

Descending the Ohio about the middle of September, 1774, Dunmore reached the mouth of the Hocking River, where he halted, erected a fort, and awaited word from General Lewis. Hearing nothing and knowing that the general was able to care for himself, Dunmore continued westward toward the Indian villages on or near the present site of Chillicothe, Ohio, but he had not gone far before he was overtaken by a messenger who bore information of the defeat of the Indians in a battle at the mouth of the Kanawha.

The Battle of Point Pleasant was of more than passing importance. It has been referred to as "The First Battle of the American Revolution," but it was more important on another score. By breaking the force of the savage's power in the Ohio Valley, it taught him to respect the American colonists, particularly the Virginians, and thus prevented a possible early and general alliance of the Indians of that region with the British. The consequence of such an alliance might have proved injurious, even fatal, to the Patriot cause in the American Revolution.

This battle gave the Indians of the Trans-Allegheny a rare opportunity to display their best qualities of bravery and leadership. At strategic moments in its progress during the whole day of October 10, 1774, the voice of their commander, Cornstalk, could be heard above the din of battle, cheering his braves and urging them on to the best that was in them. He well knew that a crisis was at hand in the affairs of the red man. If he could conquer General Lewis and then surprise and defeat Dunmore, as planned, he could retain the Indian hunting grounds. Otherwise everything was lost. At times in the contest he outgeneraled his opponents and was on the point of crushing them.

It must have been with sad hearts, therefore, that Cornstalk and his companions gave up the contest and stole from the battlefield in the dead of night. It was of small consequence that they could bury their dead and carry their wounded with them. Having failed to defeat one army of white men, Cornstalk knew it would be folly to hold out against two, and he advised peace on the terms of the conquerors. To those who opposed, he submitted the alternative of killing their wives and children and fighting until victory had been attained or the last Indian had perished in combat. Instead, the Indians chose peace.

The treaty by which this peace was concluded was made at Camp Charlotte, in the heart of the Indian country, and was only a preliminary understanding pending final negotiations, which were to have been resumed the following year. Temporarily, the Indians agreed to return all prisoners; to make good all stolen property; to regard the Ohio River as their southern boundary, even for hunting excursions; to permit boats to pass unmolested; and to give hostages until the outcome of future arrangements regarding trade and other matters could be determined.

As in fighting, so in peace the Indian gave evidences of the best that was in him. This was notably true of Logan, or John Shikellamy. Although he did not participate in the Battle of Point Pleasant, his presence was desired at the peace negotiations as an evidence of good faith, for it was well known that he had had a part in murderous raids in his search for vengeance. Noticing Logan's absence, Lord Dunmore sent his interpreter, John Gibson, to bring him to the conference; but Logan refused to go. Instead, he sent Dunmore a letter, the content of which is a fine example of Indian eloquence. Although modified from time to time, this speech has come down to us in these words:

> I appeal to any white man to say if he ever entered Logan's cabin hungry, and he gave him not meat; if ever he came cold and naked, and he clothed him not. During the last long and bloody war, Logan remained quiet in his cabin, an advocate of peace. Such was my love for the whites that my countrymen pointed as they passed and said, "Logan is the friend of white men." I had ever thought to have lived with you, but for the injuries of one man, Colonel Cresap, who the last spring, in cold blood, and unprovoked, murdered all the relatives of Logan, not even sparing my women and children. There runs not a drop of my blood in the veins of any living creature. This called upon me for revenge. I have sought it; I have killed many; I have fully glutted my revenge. For my country, I rejoice at the beams of peace. But do not harbor the thought that mine is the joy of fear. Logan never felt fear. He will never turn on his heel to save his life. Who is there to mourn for Logan? Not one.

At once, Logan's so-called speech became popular; later, it was recited in schools and churches and found its way into the leading newspapers of America and England. In his *Notes on Virginia,* Thomas Jefferson paid it high tribute and subsequently attempted to prove the truthfulness of the references to Colonel Cresap.[12] As a result, the genuineness of the speech itself was attacked. Its authorship was attributed to John Gibson, to Simon Girty, and even to the "fertile brain of Thomas Jefferson," but scholars now generally agree that the speech was, in substance, the product of Logan's mind.

The possibilities of the situation seem to confirm these conclusions. They recall the fact that Logan was a half-breed of unusual parts and experiences, who numbered among his friends and acquaintances Christian missionaries and men of position and influence. They were not able to fix upon Colonel Cresap responsibility for the murder of Logan's family, but they did not question Logan's sincerity in thinking Cresap guilty of that heinous crime.

Despite their victory at Point Pleasant and the subsequent Indian concessions, other results of Dunmore's War were keenly disappointing to Virginia frontiersmen. They felt that the temporary peace was premature and that more important concessions should have been made. The general colonial situation and the contemporaneous meeting of the First Continental Congress complicated this situation and gave it an imperial aspect. The feeling incident thereto found expression in an address drafted at Fort Gower, November 5, 1774, by retiring soldiers and officers.

Although declaring loyalty to King George and respect for and confidence in Governor Dunmore, the "Fort Gower Address" expressed concern in the events then taking place in Boston and Philadelphia and the resolve of its authors to use "arms . . . for no other purpose than the honor of America and Virginia."[13] These sentiments place it in a class with the "Mecklenburg Declaration," issued almost six months later. Moreover, the tone of the former document, together with its contents and the conditions under which it was drafted, add to the significance and importance of the Battle of Point Pleasant.

WASHINGTON'S LANDS

A member of that motley band of land grabbers which was largely responsible for Dunmore's War, George Washington visited the Ohio Valley in 1770. He came to locate lands for himself and others and not to

[12] In answer to Jefferson, John J. Jacob, who had married Cresap's widow, wrote *A Biographical Sketch of the Life of the Late Captain Michael Cresap,* published in 1826 at Cumberland, Md. See also Jefferson, *Notes,* appendix; Joseph Doddridge, *Notes on the Settlement and Indian Wars of the Western Parts of Virginia and Pennsylvania from 1763 to 1783* (Ritenour and Lindsey ed.), pp. 293-307; Withers, *Border Warfare,* pp. 148-150.

[13] Thwaites and Kellogg, *Dunmore's War,* pp. 191, 311; *Amer. Archives,* fourth series, Vol. I, 962-963; Withers, *Border Warfare,* p. 179.

survey them, as has been claimed ever since. Following the 1768 treaties of Fort Stanwix and Hard Labour, lands lying south of the Ohio in present West Virginia were taken rapidly. To avoid conflicting claims and to get good lands, Washington, accompanied by his faithful friend and physician, Dr. James Craik, and attendants, directed his course to the mouth of the Kanawha River.

On this, his fifth journey to the Trans-Allegheny, Washington left Mount Vernon October 5, 1770 on horseback. Going by way of Leesburg, Fort Necessity, and historic Braddock Field, in twelve days he reached Fort Pitt, about three hundred miles inland. Accompanied by George Croghan, he then went to Logstown, from which place he descended the Ohio in a canoe. At the mouth of the Kanawha he saw many buffaloes and "a Couple of Birds in size between a Swan and a Goose." He noted also the passage of a canoe laden with sheep for the Illinois country.

After marking trees to indicate the beginnings of proposed surveys, Washington ascended the Kanawha a distance of about nine miles. He then set out on his return trip up the Ohio. Except for a meeting with Kiashuta, an Indian chief on a hunting trip, the homeward journey along the Ohio was uneventful. Kiashuta entertained him in Indian fashion and gave him information regarding the Ohio and Kanawha valleys.

As a result of this journey and subsequent surveys, most of which were made by Colonel Crawford, Washington obtained patents for tracts of land in present West Virginia west of the Alleghenies, aggregating about 34,000 acres.[14] A tract of 10,990 acres on the south side of the Kanawha River in present Mason County extended almost to the mouth of that river. Other tracts were near present Saint Albans and Nitro, Kanawha County. A tract of 250 acres embracing the "Burning Spring" at present Malden, Kanawha County, was owned jointly by Washington and General Andrew Lewis. Other lands selected by Washington at this time in present West Virginia west of the mountains were a tract of 587 acres at Round Bottom, a short distance below present Moundsville; one of 2,314 acres at Washington Bottom, about ten miles below the mouth of Little Kanawha River; a tract of 2,448 acres on the site of Ravenswood; and one of 4,395 acres a short distance below at Millwood.

After Washington's death these lands, including lots in Berkeley Springs, then Bath, and a tract near by, were inherited by his nieces and nephews. About the middle of the eighteenth century his brothers, Charles and Samuel, had settled beyond the Blue Ridge Mountains in present Jefferson

---

14 Ambler, *George Washington,* pp. 173-174; Roy B. Cook, *Washington's Western Lands* (Strasburg, Va., 1930), pp. 37-113. Washington owned lands also in Kentucky and Ohio, and three tracts in Pennsylvania—one at Perryopolis, another at Canonsburg, and a tract of 238 acres embracing the site of Fort Necessity.

County, West Virginia—Samuel at "Harewood," and Charles at "Happy Retreat," which after 1833 was called "Mordington." Here they reared large families, members of which, like their fathers and their distinguished

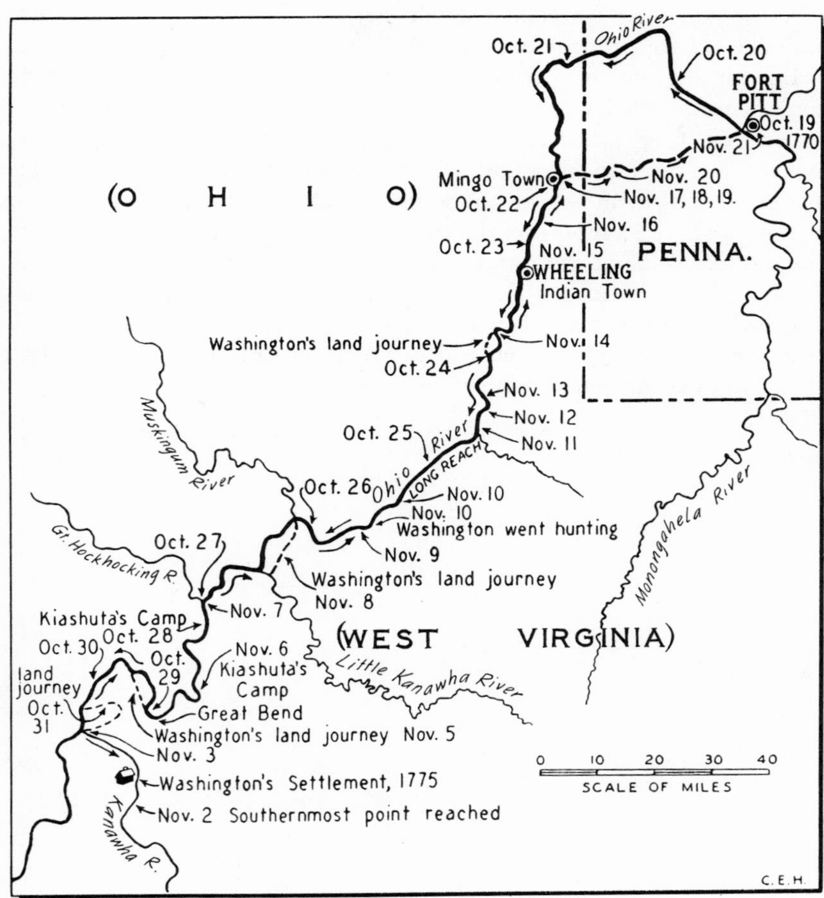

Washington's Ohio River journey, 1770, and settlement, 1775

uncle, caught the spirit of the West, so that they became pioneers and carried the Washington family name across the continent.

In the spring of 1774, Washington planned to establish a permanent settlement on his 10,990 acre tract on the Kanawha. In a characteristic manner, he neglected no detail of his proposed settlement. From his lands at present Perryopolis, Pennsylvania, tools and supplies were to be sent down the Ohio, where lands were to be cleared, cabins built, and fruit trees planted. In keeping with plans formerly proposed by his half brother, Lawrence Washington, for settling the Ohio Company's lands, Washington first planned to use Palatine Germans for his proposed settlement. When this proved impractical, he bought English and Irish redemptioners, who, despite their temporary servile status, were encouraged to expect ultimate self-government and religious liberty.

But for the Indian uprisings resulting in Dunmore's War, Washington's plan for establishing a settlement on the Kanawha would have been carried out in 1774. Instead, it was abandoned until the following spring, when it was put into effect under the supervision of James Cleveland. The site of his settlement was on the south side of the Kanawha River, about ten miles above its mouth in the then county of Fincastle. In April, 1776, the assessed value of the improvements made there was £1100 15s 7½d, or about $5,000.[15] But for the fact that the servants had refused to work and had run away, the value might have been more. Resumption of Indian hostilities in 1777 put an end to this enterprise, and two years later the buildings, fourteen in number, were burned.

---

15 Ambler, *George Washington*, pp. 156-158; Cook, *Washington's Western Lands*, pp. 47-50.

Chapter VI

The Revolution

TREATY OF PITTSBURGH, 1775

THE EARLY DEVELOPMENTS of the Revolution in Virginia greatly incensed her western inhabitants. Disappointed because of the results of Dunmore's War, their spirits were raised to the fighting point when they learned that Governor Dunmore had called off the negotiations then pending with neighboring Indian tribes, and was permitting the return of hostages. Nor was his decision to abandon Forts Dunmore (Pitt), Blair (Randolph), and Fincastle (Henry) more cordially received. Temporarily forgetting their differences, the westerners reoccupied Fort Dunmore, renaming it Fort Pitt; they organized committees of safety; and, probably more significant still, they petitioned both the Virginia Assembly and the Continental Congress, setting forth their situation and asking for aid and guidance. As they could not hold Fort Blair, it was temporarily abandoned. Later it was rebuilt and named "Fort Randolph."

Both the Continental Congress and the Virginia Assembly resolved to complete the pending negotiations with the Indians and to do everything in their power to enlist their friendship and neutrality. In pursuance of this purpose, Virginia sent among the Indians Captain James Wood, instructed to negotiate a permanent peace. He met with success, and, as a result, "the largest Indian delegation ever seen at this frontier post," Fort Pitt, assembled in September, 1775. Among them were "Ottawa and Wyandot from the neighborhood of Detroit; Mingo, Shawnee, and Delaware from the Ohio Valley; and Seneca from the upper Allegheny." A satisfactory treaty of peace, neutrality, and friendship was concluded.[1]

In its effects upon the frontier and the Revolution, the Treaty of Pittsburgh can hardly be overestimated; it clinched the results of the Battle of

[1] For a text of the treaty negotiations, see Reuben G. Thwaites and Louise P. Kellogg, *Revolution on the Upper Ohio, 1775-1777* (Madison, Wis., 1908), pp. 25-127.

Point Pleasant. Although the effects were temporary, the border was spared an immediate visitation of savage barbarities, and given time to build forts and otherwise to prepare for trying days ahead. Meanwhile, Scotch-Irish frontiersmen and their neighbors rushed to the aid of the Continental Army and gave it a driving power and an enthusiasm that contributed much to its ultimate success. Within a week after the first call of the Continental Congress for riflemen reached Virginia, Captain Hugh Stephenson, of Shepherdstown, and Captain Daniel Morgan, from near Winchester, each enlisted a company and set out for Boston. They left Shepherdstown in July, 1775, and reached their destination the following month.[2] They were the first troops from south of the Potomac to join the Continental Army.

CONTRIBUTIONS TO INDEPENDENCE

This was not, however, western Virginia's only contribution to the armies of the Revolution. She answered nine other calls, always contributing her quota or a large part of it. She was represented on most of its important battlefields, notably those of Quebec, Saratoga, Cowpens, and King's Mountain. Among her leaders who achieved distinction were: Major Generals Horatio Gates and Charles Lee, Brigadier General Adam Stephen, Colonels Hugh Stephenson and William Darke, and Captains Henry Bedinger and Abraham Shepherd. Competent authorities assert that the bones of more Revolutionary soldiers repose in the soil of West Virginia than in any state other than the original thirteen.

The contributions of West Virginia to the cause of independence were not confined to soldiers and officers. She supplied also wagons, food, clothing, and other articles. For example, under a requisition made in 1780, Berkeley County contributed seventy-one suits of clothes and seventy-one head of cattle, and Greenbrier sent eight suits and eight head of cattle. The collection and transportation of these materials, together with the mobilization and demobilization of soldiers, created centers of activity here and there, notably in the Valley. Shepherdstown became a hive of activity.

It was in defense of the frontier that the inhabitants of northwest Virginia made their greatest contribution to the success of the Revolution. In 1777, their territory, together with that immediately to the northward, became a "back door" for the enemy.[3] The British ministry had resolved to

---

2 Danske Dandridge, *Historic Shepherdstown* (Charlottesville, 1910), Ch. 8; Washington, *Writings* (edited by Sparks), Vol. IV, 124.

3 Reuben G. Thwaites and Louise P. Kellogg, *Frontier Defense on the Upper Ohio, 1777-1778* (Madison, Wis., 1912), Introduction, x-xii.

terminate the war at once, and to that end General Howe and General Burgoyne were ordered to cut the colonies in two by a joint movement by way of the Hudson River and Lake Champlain. In aid of this movement, no resource was to be neglected. Already General Hamilton, stationed at Detroit, had concluded a military alliance with neighboring Indian tribes and was sowing seeds of dissension among others and among wavering Patriots throughout the border. William Pitt protested the use of savages against England's revolting subjects, but King George professed to see in them a "Providential" means of "curbing rebellion and restoring the Constitution."

It was to withstand this threatened aggression that the Continental Congress sent General Edward Hand to command the forces at Fort Pitt. He arrived in June, 1777. A former residence at the Forks had familiarized him with some of his problems. Accordingly, he at once made it clear that he would regard all persons abetting the existing bitterness between Pennsylvanians and Virginians, because of their boundary dispute and other differences, as "dangerous and disaffected to the American Cause." At the same time he called upon Colonel David Shepherd, lieutenant of Ohio County, and others, for aid. They were warned of the importance of maintaining peace with the Indians, but confidence was expressed in their ability to deal with the situation in the event such a peace could not be preserved.

The response to General Hand's request was all that could have been desired. Old forts were restored; new ones were built;[4] and every community, however small, contributed of its man power and subsistence to defend them. Moreover, a counterstroke against Detroit was planned. Like Washington at that time, many frontiersmen were convinced that their perilous situation could be relieved only by removing "the cause," the British occupation of Detroit. To that end, volunteers representing every settlement in northwest Virginia assembled at Point Pleasant under their numerous captains.

RESUMPTION OF BORDER WARFARE

This condition gave rise to an unfortunate incident which brought its own reward. Impelled by the growing demand within his own and neighboring tribes for war against the Patriots, Cornstalk, a Shawnee chieftain and reputed friend of the Virginians, visited Fort Randolph to give warning of the impending danger. Unfortunately, about the time of his ar-

[4] For a list of forts, together with a description of each, see W. Va. Dept. of Archives and History, *Biennial Report* (1906), pp. 217-250.

rival, fatal encounters took place between Indians and individuals of the military companies then gathering to participate in the proposed Detroit expedition. As Cornstalk's conduct had not always been above suspicion, he was accordingly seized and held as a hostage. His murder a few days later, although unauthorized, could not be explained to the satisfaction of the Indians, and undoubtedly contributed to the intensity and fierceness of the conflict that followed.[5]

About the time of Cornstalk's murder, in the autumn of 1777, Wyandots, Mingoes, and a few Shawnees and Delawares made an attack upon Fort Henry which would have made a general resumption of Indian hostilities inevitable. On the other hand, it may be accepted as proof of the timeliness and sincerity of Cornstalk's friendship. About two hundred warriors participated in the attack, which was conducted with all the arts and ruses of savage warfare.

Many traditions, some of them of doubtful origin, are associated with this attack. One is that it was led by Simon Girty, but Girty had not yet deserted the Patriot cause and did not do so until the following spring. Another tradition is the oft-repeated story regarding Major Samuel McCulloch. In trying to bring aid to the besieged from Short Creek, he is said to have been intercepted and almost surrounded, the only escape left to him being by way of the precipice overhanging Wheeling Creek at the top of the hill over which the National Road now descends into Wheeling. This precipice he is supposed to have successfully descended on horseback; today a monument at "McCulloch's Leap" marks the site of his alleged accomplishment. That Major McCulloch descended a precipice at or near Fort Henry, there seems to be little doubt; but that it was this particular precipice or at this particular time, the present writers have no positive proof.

Whatever its origin and the incidents of its beginnings, there is no mistaking the fact that savage warfare was again the order of the day in the Trans-Allegheny. It needed no formal declaration. Following the attack upon Fort Henry, county militia from both Pennsylvania and Virginia began to arrive at Fort Pitt for garrison duty in the outlying posts. Among the reinforcements sent to the relief of Fort Henry was a band of militia from Hampshire County, whose inhabitants had long been free from Indian attacks. Arriving at Fort Henry in the waiting period preceding the attack, they became restless, and forty-six of their number, under the command of Captain William Forman, started on a scouting expedition down the Ohio. In McMechen's Narrows, about halfway between what are now Wheeling and Moundsville, they were surprised in a native am-

[5] Thwaites and Kellogg, *Dunmore's War*, pp. 432-433, and *Frontier Defense*, Introduction, xii, pp. 157-163, 175-177, 233-237; Withers, *Border Warfare*, pp. 211-214; Doddridge, *Notes* (Ritenour and Lindsey ed.), Ch. 28.

Fort Henry, Wheeling, 1777

bush, and twenty-one of them were killed. This event is known in border history as the "Forman Massacre."

As a result of these developments, the proposed expedition against Detroit was abandoned. Instead, General Hand contented himself with making more secure his defense, with organizing and provisioning the militia, and with training and disciplining his numerous captains and colonels of militia, whose mastery of frontier warfare had not fitted them for the most effective organized efforts. To this end an expedition into the Indian country to the north of the Ohio was deemed necessary. With a small force collected from the counties of western Pennsylvania and Virginia, in February, 1778, General Hand set out on the expedition, the first to be made into the Indian country following the outbreak of the Revolution. Floods and other obstacles intervened, however, and he did not go farther than Beaver Creek, where two Indian camps, inhabited chiefly by squaws, were raided, and the "Squaw Campaign" ended in ridicule. In disgust, General Hand resigned and retired.

The next important Indian attack, that of 1778, was made to avenge the death of Cornstalk. In pursuit of this purpose, in May of that year, about two hundred Indians attacked Fort Randolph, which they besieged for a week. Finally, despairing of success, they moved up the Kanawha toward the Greenbrier settlements, which were probably saved from complete destruction by two white messengers, John Pryor and Philip Hammond, sent out from Fort Randolph by its commander, Captain William McKee, and disguised as Indians—their make-up being the work of Nonhelema, the "Grenadier Squaw," a sister of Cornstalk, who, despite the recent murder of her brother and other relatives by the whites, had remained friendly to the Patriots and continued to reside at Fort Randolph.[6]

The inhabitants of the Greenbrier country were saved from these vengeance seekers only after desperate struggles. The decisive action took place at Fort Donnally, near the present site of Frankford, Greenbrier County. Historians agree that this was "one of the most thrilling episodes in the annals of border warfare." The final victory of the whites was recognized as a "second Point Pleasant." The fact that Indians never again invaded the New River country in considerable numbers, is proof of its importance.

With the beginning of these and the numerous contemporaneous attacks upon the Virginia frontier, its inhabitants deserted their homes and betook themselves to forts and blockhouses. Henceforth, "forting" became the normal condition of living on the Virginia frontier. Heretofore, in

[6] Withers, *Border Warfare,* pp. 176, 242; Louise P. Kellogg, *Frontier Advance on the Upper Ohio, 1778-1779* (Madison, Wis., 1916), pp. 16, 64-65, 68-69, 98. Cornstalk's daughter, Aracoma, married Boling Baker and, as the ruler of a small area, resided with him for many years on the present site of Logan, Logan County, W. Va., George T. Swain, *History of Logan County* (Logan, W. Va., 1927), pp. 4-12.

the frontiersman's calendar, winter had usually stood for peace, but the frontier knew no peace during the years of the mid-Revolution. In their palisaded enclosures, men, women, and children were prisoners. In some places agriculture and other activities were continued, but always with an eye to the necessity for defense. In other words, all slept with one eye open and one hand on a gun.

Fort Donnally, Greenbrier County

These conditions were pregnant with incidents of national and international importance. One of these "worthy of a place among the hero tales of American history" was the journey of Captain George Gibson, of the Virginia militia, and Lieutenant William Linn (1776-1777) down the Ohio and the Mississippi to New Orleans and their return to Fort Henry with nine thousand pounds of gunpowder. Prior to this, the British had boasted of the alleged inability of the revolting colonists to sustain themselves, because of their inability to make or to secure this coveted commodity. Leaving Gibson behind to deceive the Spaniards, who were trying to appear neutral, Lieutenant Linn, with the aid of forty-three men and several barges, was able to execute the feat described. His timely arrival was probably the determining factor in the successful defense of Fort Henry and other neighboring forts and stockades.

Here, as elsewhere, the Patriots did not fight alone. The Fates seemed to be with them. In New Orleans, Gibson and Linn met Oliver Pollock, an American sympathizer and unofficial agent of Virginia. It was through his resourcefulness that they were able to accomplish the object of their mission and to elude the Spanish guards. He probably worked also in co-operation with friends of the Americans at Kaskaskia, who met Linn at the mouth of the Ohio and gave him the necessary aid and assistance to escape his pursuers.

GEORGE ROGERS CLARK AND THE ILLINOIS

A more spectacular and probably more important event was the expedition of George Rogers Clark into the Illinois and his capture of Kaskaskia and Vincennes. In the boldness of its conception, and the brilliancy and success of its execution, this exploit has few parallels in American history. A brief review of accompanying events and conditions will suffice to show the accuracy of this statement. With aid from the Continental Congress and the militia, General Hand, as already stated, had failed even to launch his proposed expedition against Detroit. Later, an invasion of the Indian country beyond the Ohio had resulted in pitiful failure; almost every Indian tribe north of the Ohio was hostile; many persons on the frontier were deserting the Patriot cause; and General Hamilton was breathing threats of death for all who persisted in defying the authority of King George. Clark was able, nevertheless, to capture Kaskaskia without the loss of a man or the discharge of a gun. Afterwards, he recaptured Vincennes and sent General Hamilton a prisoner of war to Richmond, Virginia. The hero of this romance was then in his twenty-fourth year.[7]

Clark has been justly praised for his accomplishment, and numerous claims have been made regarding its importance and consequences; but too little has been said of those men who helped make it possible. A history of West Virginia, however brief, cannot overlook the fact that most of Clark's men came from counties of western Virginia, some from what is now the "Mountain State." Accompanying him were four captains—John Montgomery, William Harrod, Leonard Helm, and Joseph Bowman—and about one hundred seventy-five others who "in their buckskin clothes and coonskin caps," as described by a recent biographer of Clark, "no doubt made a rough-looking lot; but history hardly records a braver."

THE LOYALISTS

Not all the frontiersmen of the Trans-Allegheny were Patriots. Early in the conflict with the mother country, Captain John Connolly, Governor

[7] James A. James, *The Life of George Rogers Clark* (Chicago, 1928), Chs. 6-8; Kellogg, *Frontier Advance,* pp. 17, 25, 232-233, 258-259; T. Bodley, *George Rogers Clark* (Boston, 1926), Chs. 5-6.

Dunmore's agent at Fort Pitt, conceived the possibility of separating the northern colonies from the southern by a military movement directed against the upper Ohio from Detroit. If successful there, he planned to join Governor Dunmore in the east by way of Braddock's Road and the Potomac River. Although this was not a wholly impracticable or impossible undertaking, the "Connolly Plot" failed largely because of the absence of local support, but there were those on the frontier who sympathized with the purpose of the scheme.

Later, following the resumption of Indian hostilities along the border and Governor Hamilton's threats of death and destruction for all who remained in rebellion, the Loyalists developed greater strength. As a rule, Hamilton's threats were tempered with promises of mercy for all returning prodigals, some of whom were doubtless attracted by promises of extensive land grants and other material considerations. To all, the outcome of the pending struggle was uncertain: to some, its possible consequences were appalling; to others, they were attractive. As always under such conditions, some frontiersmen wavered, while others openly allied themselves with the enemy. Among the latter were Captain Alexander McKee, Simon Girty, Matthew Elliott, Robert Surphlitt, and John Higgins, who reached Detroit in May, 1778. About the same time, George Morgan, John Campbell, and even General Hand were suspected and accused of defection.[8]

The Loyalist movement did not stop with those in high places, but included hundreds of the inhabitants of both Pennsylvania and Virginia. General Hand thought the devil had possessed them, and Colonel Zackquill Morgan enlisted five hundred men to put down the "frantic scene of mischief." An unfortunate incident connected with his efforts resulted in the death of a Loyalist named Higginson, or Hickson, who fell from a boat while crossing Cheat River and was drowned. Colonel Morgan was accused of having pushed him into the water, and was indicted, tried, and acquitted. Among the numerous captures made by Morgan, some persons were found who had sworn allegiance to the King of England and were expecting new leaders from Fort Pitt.[9]

With other threatened invasions by the British and the return of events and conditions which indicated failure for the Americans, additional Loyalists appeared from time to time in the Trans-Allegheny, but the only other formidable manifestation of sympathy for the British occurred east of the Alleghenies, in the region now included in Hardy, Grant, and Pendleton counties and a part of Hampshire. The participants were largely Germans led by John Brake. Their disloyalty took the form of refusals to take oaths of allegiance to the government of Virginia, to enlist for serv-

8 Thwaites and Kellogg, *Frontier Defense,* Introduction, xvi, pp. 184-186.

9 James M. Callahan, *A History of West Virginia* (Chicago, 1923), Vol. I, 85; Virgil A. Lewis, *A History of West Virginia* (Philadelphia, 1889), pp. 139-144.

ice against the British, and to pay taxes. Finally, growing bolder because of lenient treatment, they elected John Claypole, a Scotsman, as their captain, and prepared to join the British. This was going too far, and General Daniel Morgan, hero of the Cowpens, who happened to be near, collected four hundred militia and marched against them. As a result, they were defeated and begged for mercy, but not before several of them had been killed. Later, some of them joined the Patriot Army.

NEW COUNTIES

The Revolution was not far advanced before Pennsylvania and Virginia resumed disconcerting disputes over their common boundary line. The bitterness engendered thereby was heightened by the activities and intrigues of land jobbers and by proposals for the formation of new states in the disputed area. To assert her authority, as well as to accommodate settlers and prospective settlers, Virginia, in 1776, divided the District of West Augusta into Ohio, Monongalia, and Yohogania counties and established seats of government for each. That famous district was thus eliminated, except as a state senatorial district, for which purpose it continued to be used for some years thereafter.[10]

The creation of additional counties by the state of Virginia is not without significance. In 1770, Botetourt was formed from Augusta and made to include all territory west of the Alleghenies and south of the District of West Augusta. In 1772, Fincastle was created out of territory belonging to Botetourt and included all the present state of Kentucky and West Virginia south of the New and Kanawha rivers; but, in 1776, Fincastle County was entirely eliminated and the territory formerly embraced therein became Montgomery, Washington, and Kentucky counties. The first-named included all of what is now West Virginia south of New and Kanawha rivers. From this territory Greenbrier County was formed in 1778; Berkeley, formed from Frederick, preceded it by five years.

WESTSYLVANIA AND FRANKLIN

Closely allied with the formation of new counties in the Trans-Allegheny was a new state movement which may also have been associated in sentiment and perhaps otherwise with the Vandalia project (see Chapter

[10] M. P. Robinson, "Virginia Counties," in Va. State Library, *Bulletin*, Vol. IX, Nos. 1-3. See also Callahan, *History*, Vol. I, 92-93; Lewis, *History*, Part II.

VII). In 1776, inhabitants of the District of West Augusta petitioned the Continental Congress to establish that district as a separate state to be known as "Westsylvania"—"the fourteenth Link in the American Chain."[11] The plan to form the new state had its origin in the mind of David Rogers, a member of the Virginia Assembly, but it was endorsed by others. Arguments in favor of the proposed state throw light upon conditions. Contending that "no Country or People can be Either rich, flourishing, happy or free . . . whilst annexed to or dependent on any Province, whose seat of government is those of Pennsylvania & Virginia, four or five hundred miles distant, and separated by a vast, extensive & almost impassible Tract of Mountains," Rogers and his associates asserted, furthermore, that they would not suffer themselves to be "arbitrarily deprived and robbed of those Lands & that Country to which by the Laws of Nature & of Nations they are entitled as first Occupants."

Another new state movement of this period involved lands now included in part in West Virginia. This project was the creation of Colonel Arthur Campbell and his associates, and was known as the "Franklin" or "Washington County movement." It embraced most of southwestern Virginia, the southeastern part of Kentucky, the eastern half of Tennessee, a part of Georgia and Alabama, and all of what is now Mercer County and a part of what is now Summers County, West Virginia. The authorities made it clear that Virginia would not sanction such a movement insofar as it affected her territory, and it came to an end.

THE FRONTIER RETREAT

In the midst of this planning and scheming, military events were taking place on the border. In 1778, General Lachlan McIntosh succeeded General Hand in the command at Fort Pitt and led a successful attack upon Indians north of the Ohio, which carried him to the Tuscarawas and the Muskingum rivers, on the latter of which he built Fort Laurens. The next year he was succeeded by General Daniel Brodhead, who commanded successful expeditions against Indians on the upper Allegheny and the Muskingum rivers, but his inordinate ambition spread dissension throughout the whole frontier and abetted the scores of persons then turning Loyalist. As a result, General Washington turned to Colonel George Rogers Clark, an officer of Virginia, but he, too, was prevented from carrying out the proposed expedition against Detroit. Clark's failure was due largely to rivalries and jealousies between Pennsylvanians and Virginians and to

[11] Turner, "Western State Making in the Revolutionary Era," in *Am. Hist. Rev.*, Vol. I, 70-87, 251-269.

the severity of the winter of 1779-1780, one of the worst in the annals of the West.

As a result, most of the military advantages previously gained by the Patriots were lost in what has been fittingly described as the "Frontier Retreat on the Ohio." Following the ruthless murder of their chieftain, White Eyes, a tried and trusted friend of the English, the Delawares declared war in 1781 and formally joined the British. For some time they and their confederates had been making hostile incursions along the border, even as far as Morgantown. After a hasty attack upon the Delawares, in which some of their towns on and near the Muskingum were destroyed, General Brodhead was relieved by General William Irvine, the fourth and last commander at Fort Pitt in the period of active hostilities, but Colonel George Rogers Clark continued to be the moving spirit of the Patriot cause in the West.

Conditions being unfavorable, Clark soon gave up in despair. The reasons have been described by a discerning historian in these words.

> With all the Indian nations arrayed in complete hostility, with the army of defense honeycombed with dishonesty and intrigue, with disorder and discontent rife among the inhabitants, even the Herculean efforts of Clark were insufficient to restore the morale of the frontier. After the departure of his troops, the forces of disintegration reigned supreme and the defeat which the British could not accomplish was nearly achieved by the lack of integrity and virtue on the part of the officers stationed on the frontier.[12]

Under these conditions a second attack upon Fort Henry, sometimes referred to as "the last battle of the Revolution," was planned and executed on September 10, 1782. Whatever may be said of its historical sequence, it was a fierce and trying ordeal. Led by Joseph Brant—the attacking party of Indians and English included almost three hundred warriors who demanded unconditional surrender. When this was refused, they attacked with stones and logs which were used as battering rams. After these proved unavailing, the attackers resorted to an improvised wooden cannon, which did more harm to them than to the besieged. Disgusted, the assailants left the fort, but not before a number of them had paid the price of their folly with their lives.

It was in this second attack upon Fort Henry that Elizabeth Zane, sister of Colonel Ebenezer Zane, won an enviable place among American Revolutionary heroines. An unverified tradition says that she, under fire, carried a supply of gunpowder from her brother's residence for the use of the besieged in the fort. It is true that the fort was not far away, but it was far enough to expose her in passing to a volley of lead, which she

---

[12] Louise P. Kellogg, *Frontier Retreat on the Upper Ohio,* 1779-1781 (Madison, Wis., 1917), pp. 34-35, 37, 136-137, 399-401.

escaped without harm to the admiration of the enemy and future generations.

Another heroine story of this period is that of Mrs. John Bozarth, who resided on Dunkard Creek, in Monongalia County, near present Core. In April, 1779, she defended her log cabin against an attack, in which she killed three Indians with an ax. The attack was so sudden and unexpected that the Bozarth children were playing undisturbed in the yard. Knowing that they could easily dispatch them, the Indians attacked the cabin, but were met by its daring defender and slain one by one. Unable to gain admission, the remaining Indians turned upon the children and murdered them in sight of their mother.

Another somewhat typical heroine story of this period tells much regarding the purposes and potentialities of the characters involved. In September, 1779, Mrs. John Pauley, formerly Margaret Hanley, set out from the Greenbrier section with her family in a party of relatives and neighbors to locate lands in Kentucky. On horseback with their children and necessary household articles, Mrs. Pauley led the party, while the men, guns in hand, followed with the cattle. On the third day out, the party was surprised by Indians near the mouth of East River. In the attack which followed the women were knocked unconscious; their children were dashed to death against trees; and the men were either murdered or forced to flee for their lives.

Mrs. John Pauley, together with her sister-in-law, Mrs. James Pauley, was spared, only to be carried into captivity. As "Yellow Gold," she was adopted by Chief White Bark and lived unmolested in his family for five years. Only once in this time was her life in danger. That was to satisfy White Bark's desire for vengeance for the death of his son, Wabapusite, a bold and daring warrior, who was killed by whites in 1782 while he was on a raiding expedition in Kentucky. Two years later Mrs. Pauley was ransomed and returned to her home in the Greenbrier settlements. About a year later she married Michael Erskine, and five children were born to them. The youngest of these children, Jane Erskine, married Hugh Caperton, father of Allen T. Caperton, who, from March 4, 1875 until his death on July 26, 1876, was a United States Senator from West Virginia. John Pauley, Jr., born shortly after his mother's captivity and ransomed with her, later successfully engaged in the fur trade on the upper Missouri River.

Already the Moravian Indians, Christian converts residing on the Tuscarawas River about forty miles north of Wheeling, had fallen victims to the upper and nether millstones of savage barbarity. Moving from the Susquehanna River under direction of David Zeisberger and John Heckewelder, Christian missionaries whose accomplishments have never been duly appreciated, these Indians had established themselves on the Tuscarawas River in 1772, where they built a number of towns, among them Gnadenhütten and Schönbrunn, which had become refuges for Indians bent upon mischief. On the other hand, the Indians and their Tory leaders accused the missionaries of friendship for the Americans and of keeping them informed of hostile military movements. Both contentions were true. It is now known that Zeisberger and Heckewelder were General Brodhead's most dependable sources of information regarding impending Indian attacks, and that they, on more than one occasion, saved frontier outposts from surprises and consequent destruction. They also admitted, however, their inability to keep hostiles from lodging with them. As a result, the mission settlements were first laid waste by a detachment under General Brodhead, which began the destruction that was completed in the same year, 1781, when the settlements were attacked by a band of two hundred fifty Indians, mostly Wyandots, led by Matthew Elliott. The leaders of the Moravians were carried to Detroit, and some never returned.[13]

Soon thereafter the condition of Virginians everywhere became desperate. The British attacked eastern Virginia; the capital was abandoned; and Benedict Arnold, now in the service of the British, spread destruction along the banks of the James. As on the frontier, it was a condition calling for sacrifices. They were made in a spirit which explains the ultimate success of the common cause. One example will suffice: Mrs. William Lewis, of Augusta County, in sending her remaining sons, of seventeen, fifteen, and thirteen years, to join Washington—the others being already with him —is reported to have said, "Go, my children. I spare not my youngest, my fair-haired boy, the comfort of my declining years." When this incident was related to General Washington, he is said to have exclaimed: "Leave me but a banner to plant upon the mountains of Augusta, and I will rally around me the men who will lift our bleeding country from the dust, and set her free!"

Other traditions of similar origin testify abundantly to the patriotism of western Virginians in the Revolution. This is especially true of the Presbyterians, who, almost without exception, were Whigs of the firmest and most unconquerable spirit. Intimate contacts had familiarized General Washington with their traits; he is said to have expressed a willingness, other resources having failed, to "repair with a single standard to West Augusta, and there rally a band of patriots who would meet the enemy at the Blue Ridge, and there establish the boundary of a free empire in the West." Betraying his Fabian qualities, Washington let drop still other expressions of confidence in the inhabitants of western Virginia. Perhaps

[13] Withers, *Border Warfare,* pp. 313-327; Joseph Doddridge, *Notes on the Settlement and Indian Wars . . .* (Wellsburg, Va., 1824), pp. 188-204; Samuel Kercheval, *A History of the Valley of Virginia* (Winchester, 1833), pp. 206-226.

the most authentic of these was that to his secretary, Colonel Joseph Reed, in which Washington said: "We must retire to Augusta County, Virginia. Numbers will be obliged to repair to us for safety; and we must try what we can do in carrying on a predatory war; and if overpowered we must cross the Allegheny Mountains."[14]

[14] R. Hughes, *George Washington,* Vol. II (New York, 1928), 552.

Chapter VII

Indiana and Vandalia

PRELUDE

FROM BEGINNING TO END of the English explorations and settlements in the Trans-Allegheny, land jobbing and colony building consumed much time and energy of promoters. Among their proposals were "Indiana" and "Vandalia," whose annals constitute an interesting and informing, if not always creditable, chapter in American history. The Indiana project had a bearing upon the Declaration of Independence and the Articles of Confederation. It was also a factor in making the Federal Constitution and in its subsequent amendment. Vandalia was a grandiose and somewhat unique colonizing experiment involving large stakes and many personal and sectional loyalties and interests.[1]

HARD LABOUR AND FORT STANWIX

Despite the efforts then being made to establish the Indian trade on a permanent and profitable basis in the Ohio Valley to the exclusion of permanent settlements, and in keeping with the King's Proclamation of 1763 for that and other purposes, persons supposedly interested in trade only, notably George Croghan and William Trent, were however planning to establish a colony north of the Ohio and east of the Mississippi rivers in the region of the Illinois country. After enlarging the circle of their trader associates so as to include among others the firm of Baynton, Wharton and Morgan of Philadelphia, these promoters petitioned the King for

[1] See Thomas P. Abernethy, *Western Lands and the American Revolution* (New York, 1937); Max Saville, *George Morgan, Colony Builder* (New York, 1932); Alvord, *Mississippi Valley;* Volwiler, *Croghan;* Bailey, *Ohio Company;* and Charles A. Hanna, *Wilderness Trail,* 2 vols. (New York, 1911).

a grant, on which to establish a colony. Their request received the support of Benjamin Franklin, but it met opposition in Lord Hillsborough, president of the Board of Trade for the colonies, who indicated, however, that he might favor a similar proposal in the Trans-Allegheny east of the Ohio River.[2]

By this time, the trading enterprises in the Ohio Valley had all but collapsed, and Fort Pitt was on the point of being abandoned. To meet this situation and its possibilities, the Crown was forced to change its policy with respect to the Ohio Valley. In defiance of the Proclamation of 1763, settlers were then pushing beyond the Alleghenies in large numbers. To have restricted them might have led to independent action on the part of jobbers and promoters who, together with the defiant settlers, claimed that the coveted lands belonged to them by the right of conquest and the law of nature.

To avoid the consequences of such claims, but without formally rescinding the Proclamation of 1763, Colonel John Stuart, superintendent of Indian affairs in the Southern District with headquarters at Charleston, South Carolina, was instructed to negotiate for a new and more westward boundary between the English settlements and the Indian lands. Acting upon these instructions, Stuart concluded in 1768 the Treaty of Hard Labour, in which the Cherokees gave up claims to lands in present West Virginia. In the Treaty of Lochaber, negotiated by Stuart in 1770, this cession was enlarged so as to include the eastern portion of the present state of Kentucky.

In keeping with the same purpose and policy, Sir William Johnson concluded on November 5, 1768 the Treaty of Fort Stanwix, in which Iroquois and other interested Indians relinquished all claims to lands lying south of present Kittanning, Pennsylvania, between the Allegheny Mountains and the Ohio River to the Tennessee River. This vast area was thus opened to white settlement. Its northern stretches were soon occupied. But present concern will be with certain "Despoiled Traders" in their efforts to recoup themselves and incidentally promote a new colony.

Two days before they signed the Treaty of Fort Stanwix, Indians, in keeping with their promise of 1765, ceded to the "Sufferers of 1763" a tract of 2,862 square miles embracing all of present West Virginia north of the Little Kanawha River and west of the Monongahela River (see accompanying map).[3] The agreement by which this cession was made, was an integral part of the Treaty of Fort Stanwix, and, as set forth therein, the cession was for the sole and express use and benefit of the

---

2 Abernethy, *Western Lands,* pp. 30, 33, 45; Alvord, *Mississippi Valley,* Vol. II, 123; Bailey, *Ohio Company,* pp. 241-244.

3 Saville, *George Morgan,* pp. 78-79; Alvord, *Mississippi Valley,* Vol. II, 62-65; Bailey, *Ohio Company,* p. 236.

Sufferers of 1763. Moreover, the validity of the larger grant was conditional upon the King's acceptance of the smaller for the purpose for which it was made. As the losses of the aggrieved traders aggregated £85,916, this sum was the price offered for this land grant which was named "Indiana" and as such found a place on maps of that day.

As the method of securing this grant is somewhat typical of American land jobbing, it is on that account interesting and informing. Weeks before the date set for the opening of negotiations at Fort Stanwix, Sam-

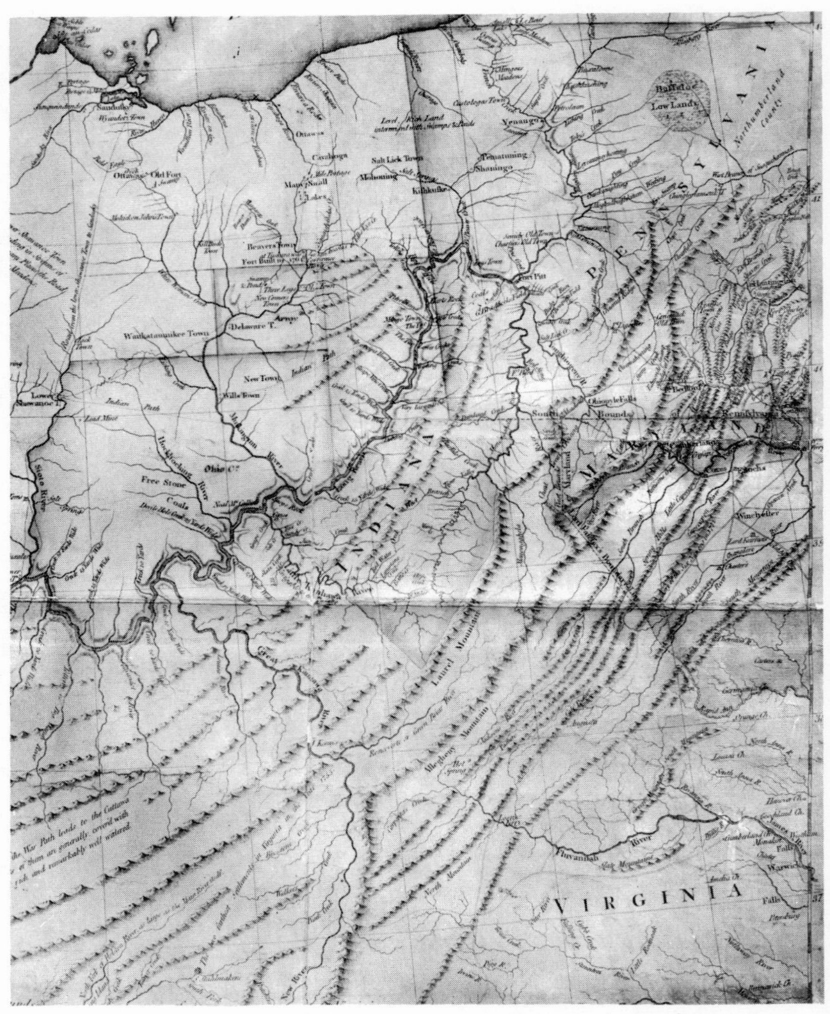

Section of Thomas Hutchin's map of 1778 showing Indiana

uel Wharton and William Trent, representing the despoiled traders, visited Sir William Johnson in his home in the Mohawk Valley. When things had been arranged to their satisfaction, they moved into Indian villages, where chiefs were plied with liquor and presents and reminded of their rights and duties in the matter of the desired reparations.

When the contents of the Treaty of Fort Stanwix became known, Virginia challenged it with ominous determination. It mattered not that Thomas Walker of Virginia had signed the treaty as a witness. Virginia then claimed the Trans-Allegheny on the basis of her charter of 1609, also as the result of several Indian cessions and because of actual possession.

At the same time, the Treaty of Fort Stanwix was meeting with a half-hearted opposition in England. Lord Hillsborough had not yet given final approval of his suggested colony west of the Alleghenies and south of the Ohio River, and on that account he looked upon the Fort Stanwix negotiation as premature, if not illegal. He therefore asked Johnson by what authority he had fixed a boundary in Indian territory not under his jurisdiction and by what leave he ignored the property rights of others, evidently the Virginians. In reply Johnson reminded Hillsborough of Walker's presence at the negotiations and of the terms and conditions of the larger land grant to the King. More subtle still, he assured Hillsborough that, in case the negotiations were not acceptable, they could be undone.

THE GRAND OHIO COMPANY

Johnson and his associates had no intention, however, of retracing their steps. Already they had sent Samuel Wharton to London to look after their interests. To his great surprise and delight he learned that the Indiana grant did not require royal confirmation to make it valid. As Indiana was thus a fact beyond the reach of its critics, Wharton soon lost sight of it and became engrossed in promoting a colony in the Trans-Allegheny south of the Ohio River.

For this purpose the "Grand Ohio Company," known in America as the "Vandalia Company" and in England as the "Walpole Company," was organized in the spring of 1769. Its shareholders included Thomas and Richard Walpole, George Grenville, and Thomas Pownall, together with Benjamin Franklin, Joseph Galloway, Joseph Wharton, Sir William Johnson, George Croghan, William Trent, and other Americans. In June, 1769, the Grand Ohio Company petitioned the King for permission to purchase 2,400,000 acres, but on the suggestion of Lord Hillsborough the proposal was enlarged so as to include enough territory to make a formidable colony to be called "Vandalia," in honor of the Queen who, it was claimed, had descended from an ancient Vandal line.[4]

Though only a few of the Indiana shareholders were members of the Vandalia Company, their grant was included within the proposed colony. By a skillful use of shares Wharton induced George Mercer, agent of the

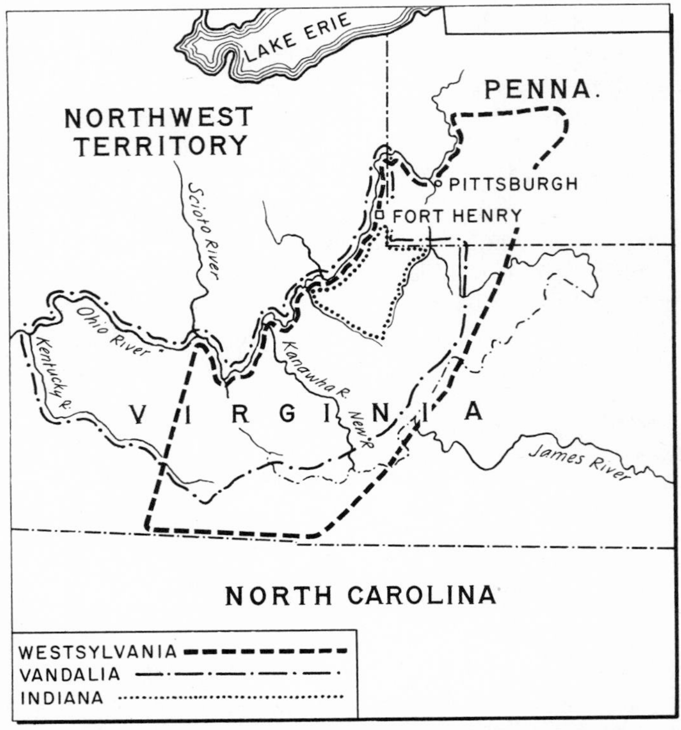

Trans-Allegheny land and colonization projects, 1768-1781

Ohio Company of 1747, to unite its interests with those of Vandalia, but the Virginia members of the Ohio Company repudiated the arrangement. Meanwhile Wharton had made friends for Vandalia in high places. Accordingly, his project was on August 14, 1772 accepted by the King in Council who gave directions for the preparation of the papers needed to make it effective.[5] As these papers were in 1774 about to pass under the Great Seal of the Realm, reports from the disturbed conditions in America so changed the situation in England as to prevent action. Thus and thus

[4] Alvord, *Mississippi Valley,* Vol. II, 120, 200.

[5] Saville, *George Morgan,* p. 81; Bailey, *Ohio Company,* pp. 260-265; Kate M. Rowland, *The Life of George Mason* (New York, 1892), Vol. I, 157; Shaw Livermore, *Early American Land Companies* (New York, 1939), pp. 119-122.

only was prevented the formation of a new colony out of territory most of which is now embraced in West Virginia.

GEORGE MASON BESTS GEORGE MORGAN

With the failure of Vandalia, the Indiana proprietors took steps in the summer of 1775 to separate it from that project. For that purpose George Morgan and William Trent buried the hatchet and sought the advice of Benjamin Franklin, mentor of the Indiana and Vandalia claimants. In keeping with this, a meeting of the Sufferers of 1763 was held on September 21, 1775, at Pittsburgh. The Whartons and others interested primarily in Vandalia failed to attend, but a majority of the Indiana shareholders were present and bent upon independent action. This plan provided for surveys to determine the bounds of their grant, for a plan of procedure with respect to alleged squatters, and for a land office at Fort Pitt. At the same time, Virginians, notably William Grayson, were made members of the Indiana Company, and Virginia's jurisdiction over it was recognized.[6]

For a time the Whartons and their associates did not go along with the Indiana program, but finally they agreed to vest technical ownership of the Vandalia Company in a committee and its administration in the officers of the Indiana Company. In January, 1776, both factions adopted "Articles of Agreement" which were to serve as a sort of constitution. Morgan was then named as secretary of the proposed land office and as receiver-general for the company. A short time thereafter, he opened a land office at Fort Pitt and made ready to reclaim from alleged squatters all lands belonging to his company.

Apprised of these plans and purposes, the Virginia Convention, then in session, sought to defeat Morgan's plans. The discussions incident thereto passed in review many phases of the Indiana claims, as well as Virginia's claims to lands west of the Alleghenies. As the Continental Congress was then considering a declaration of independence which, if made good, would put the colonies on their own, the situation called for action. On June 24, 1776, the Virginia Convention resolved, therefore, that,

> all persons actually settled on any of the said lands ought to hold the same without paying any pecuniary or other consideration whatever to any private person or persons (pretending to derive title from Indian deeds and purchases) until . . . the validity of the title under such Indian deeds or purchases shall have been considered and determined on by the Legislature of this country . . . and that no purchases of

---

[6] Abernethy, *Western Lands*, p. 144.

lands within the chartered limits of Virginia shall be made under any pretense whatever, from any Indian tribe or nation, without the approbation of the Legislature.[7]

Meanwhile Virginia delegates in Congress had concerned themselves with Morgan's plans and activities. Jointly they waited upon Thomas Wharton to ask by what authority Morgan acted and whether Wharton and his associates knew that Virginia had bought the lands in question in the Treaty of Lancaster of 1744, or whether they knew of the Virginia law of 1754, which forbade land purchases from Indians by private individuals. Wharton had not heard of any of these things and was for a time greatly perplexed, but he refused to desert the Indiana project. Instead he sought to prevent the registration of its deed at Pittsburgh.

Action on the part of Virginia was evidently imperative. In keeping with her implied purpose, as previously stated on June 24, she resolved to determine for herself the validity of the Indiana claim. For this purpose she appointed commissioners who went to Pittsburgh in the spring of 1777 to take testimony. Morgan and others appeared at the hearings, and the commissioners were able to collect much evidence which was, however, indecisive and on the whole unfavorable to Virginia.

Though the developments tended to favor them, the Indiana proprietors became alarmed at Virginia's activity and persistence with respect to their claims. By means of a memorial which went into every detail of the subject, they therefore asked the Virginia General Assembly to submit its case to "any impartial court." Instead, Virginia invited the claimants to present their case at the bar of her general assembly. With some misgiving the offer was accepted, and William Trent was chosen to make the presentation.[8] Virginia was represented by George Mason.

Mason and Trent presented their case with great ability and in much detail, but the odds were against Trent. In Virginia, under her independent status, he was, in fact, only a foreigner. Exultant in her newfound sovereignty and eager to make the most of it for her subjects in areas toward which they had cast longing eyes for almost a generation, her general assembly on June 9, 1779 resolved that,

the deed from the Six United Nations of Indians, bearing date on the third day of November, 1768, for certain lands between the Allegheny Mountains and the River Ohio, above the mouth of the Little Kanawha Creek . . . to . . . a certain William Trent . . . as well as all other deeds which have been or shall be made . . . by any Indian nation or nations, for lands within the limits of the charter and territory of Virginia as aforesaid, to or for the use of any private person or persons shall be and the same are hereby declared utterly void, and of no effect.

---

[7] Kate Mason Rowland, *The Life of George Mason* (New York, 1892), Vol. I, 224; Saville, *George Morgan*, p. 91; Bailey, *Ohio Company*, p. 270.

[8] Saville, *George Morgan*, p. 93.

The same year, the Virginia General Assembly enacted Mason's land-office bill and a twin measure for settling outstanding claims to unpatented lands, but the Indiana and Vandalia claimants profited from neither. Each of these acts was designed in the interest of individual settlers who had already established themselves, and they took no cognizance of land jobbers and colony promoters. Under these acts surveys made prior to January 24, 1778 by accredited surveyors were validated. As these laws were general in their application, nothing was said about the Indiana and Vandalia claims.

VIRGINIA ASSERTS HER RIGHTS

Thwarted at every turn by Virginia, the Indiana claimants next turned to the Confederation Congress which was then engaged in a discussion of "Western Lands." Moreover, a new government under the Articles of Confederation was on the point of being launched. As many persons, even those in the inner circle, thought this government would automatically supersede the British Crown in American affairs, the consequences of its formation were fraught with many possibilities. Accordingly, the American wing of the Vandalia Company revived its claim and joined it with the Indiana claim in an effort to stop Virginia and salvage what they could.

In pursuit of these plans and purposes, William Trent presented on September 14, 1779 a memorial in behalf of the Vandalia proprietors.[9] Again he reviewed the history of their claims, but more to the point was an assertion to the effect that the territory in dispute was then a part of the United States and not exclusively a part of Virginia. He asked, therefore, that Vandalia be established as originally planned and proposed. If that were done, he guaranteed protection to squatters and promised to pay the United States the amount originally promised the Crown for the Vandalia cession.

On the same day, George Morgan presented the Indiana claims. On the whole he accepted Trent's arguments and proposals, but he went further. Fresh from his failures at the Virginia capital and doubtless chagrined by them, he explained his treatment there as purposely designed to thwart Congress in any action that it might take with respect to Western Lands or to determine justice, either in the acquisition of public or private property.

From this point, the Indiana and Vandalia controversies, particularly

[9] Congress, *Journals,* Vol. XV, 1063; Saville, *George Morgan,* pp. 96-97.

the former, developed into a struggle between Congress and Virginia. In reply to Trent and Morgan, Virginia delegates in Congress submitted a "Statement of Facts," in which they drew a distinction between jurisdiction of the lands in dispute and the merits of the controversy regarding them. Moreover, this statement flatly repudiated the jurisdiction of Congress over the Western Lands, but the committee to which the matter had been referred, recommended ". . . to the State of Virginia, and every other State in similar circumstances, to suspend the sale, grant, or settlement of any land unappropriated at the time of the declaration of independence, until the conclusion of the war."

As the Virginia General Assembly had denied the Indiana appeal by narrow margins, the majority faction now sought to safeguard the state's interest by getting behind her delegates in Congress. For this purpose it directed that a remonstrance be sent to Congress, "asserting the rights of this Commonwealth to its own territory." This paper was drafted by Mason and, though it may not have been presented, is evidence of the attitude of Virginia toward the jurisdiction of Congress. Among other things, it pointed to the possibility of "an intolerable despotism" in the event that Congress should assume "a jurisdiction . . . not only unwarranted by, but expressly contrary to the fundamental principles of the Confederation." This remonstrance asserted also that the United States had no territory, but "in right of some one individual state in the Union," and that under the proposed Articles of Confederation, "no state could be deprived of territory for the benefit of the United States."

Following this presentation, the debate on Western Lands occupied Congress during most of the ensuing year. Throughout this debate, the landless states, led by Maryland, a number of whose citizens were themselves interested in Western Lands, insisted that they should be ceded to the United States. Largely as a result of this stand, Congress on September 6, 1780 asked the landholding states to cede their claims. At the same time, it assured them that, in possession of the United States, these lands would constitute a common fund; that all Indian titles to individuals would be voided.

Though Trent continued to protest against the Virginia land offices, they were opened, and to his surprise, on January 2, 1781, Virginia agreed to cede her claim to lands "North-West of the River Ohio to the Congress of the United States." Compliance with the agreement was conditional, however, upon the willingness of Congress to erect and admit new states, republican in form, out of the ceded territory; to compensate Virginia for her expenditures incident to its conquest; to make certain land grants to her Revolutionary soldiers; to reserve the remaining lands as a "common fund for the use and benefit of such of the United American States, as have become or shall become members of the confederation"; and to void all Indian or royal grants or sales to private individuals or persons within the ceded territory. Most important of all, "the remaining territory of Virginia" on the south side of the river Ohio was to be guaranteed to her.[10]

On March 1, 1781, following the Virginia land cessions, the Articles of Confederation went into effect. In the face of Virginia's dominant influence and her recent assertions, Morgan, who had become a citizen of New Jersey, was baffled, but on advice of Benjamin Franklin, Thomas Paine, and others, decided to carry his case to the Confederation Congress. Accordingly, he asked New Jersey to sponsor his case. Under the influence of Sir William Franklin and others interested in the Indiana claims, Morgan's request was readily granted, and, "as the Guardian of the Subjects of New Jersey," her legislators instructed her delegates in Congress to apply to that body for a court of inquiry to determine the validity of the Indiana and the Vandalia claims.[11] Despite Virginia's opposition, this request was granted, and the matter was referred to the "Committee on Western Lands."

To the surprise and chagrin of Virginians, the committee report held the grants to the Despoiled Traders valid, "according to the then usage and custom of purchasing lands from the Indians." As the grants upon which these claims were based were made with the approval of the King and the knowledge and consent of New York and Virginia, the committee recommended therefore that Congress confirm to all such persons as were then citizens of the United States, their respective shares to such lands, provided they are "finally ceded or adjudged to the United States." The committee recommended furthermore that the Virginia cession be declined and that she be asked to cede all her lands beyond a "reasonable western boundary."[12]

In the same manner, the committee recognized the validity of the grant to form a colony to be "called Vandalia, lying on the back of Virginia, from the Allegheny Mountains west to the river." It was stated also that this grant had been agreed to by the King and Council, and "completed all to affixing the seals and passing the usual forms of office." As so large a grant to private individuals was thought to be "incompatible with the interests, government and policy of these United States," the committee recommended that Congress reimburse such Vandalia claimants as were then citizens of the United States for their purchase money and other expenditures, provided they and the states concerned ceded their claims to the United States.

Relying on that part of Article IX of the Articles of Confederation,

---

[10] Virginia, *Revised Code* (1819), Vol. I, 39; Hening, *Statutes*, Vol. X, 564-566.

[11] Saville, *George Morgan*, pp. 101-102.

[12] Congress, *Journals*, Vol. XXII, 228-229.

which provided "that no state shall be deprived of territory for the benefit of the United States," and also that judges and commissioners adjudging disputes between states, as a congressional court, should take an oath "well and truly to hear and determine the matter in question, according to the best of his judgment, without favor, affection, or hope of reward," on April 18, 1782, Arthur Lee of the Virginia delegation moved,

> That previous to any determination in Congress, relative to the cessions of the western lands, the name of each member present be called over by the secretary, that on such call, each member do declare upon his honour, whether he is, or is not personally interested directly or indirectly in the claims of any company or companies, which have petitioned against the territorial rights of any one of the states, by whom such cessions have been made, and that such declaration be entered on the journals.

Unwilling to face the searching inquisition of this resolution, the matter was on May 6 postponed indefinitely.

Meanwhile the Virginia General Assembly had appointed a committee of distinguished persons to prepare a statement of her position for presentation to Congress. Because of his familiarity with the matter, Mason was chosen to prepare this statement, which again went into every phase of the Indiana and Vandalia controversy. In conclusion, Congress was reminded of Virginia's good faith in entering the Confederation and of the fact that the proposals then being made to dismember her, if successful, would most certainly result in a dissolution of the Federal Compact.[13]

In the face of such a declaration, among the first of the kind made by Virginia, the Confederation was in danger. Fortunately the spirit of compromise was then in the ascendancy. In response thereto, Congress indicated on September 13, 1783 the conditions upon which it would accept the Virginia land cession. The following month, Virginia revised her proposal by omitting references to the disputed lands south of the Ohio River and accepting a commission as a means of determining her claims resulting from the conquest of the Northwest Territory. Otherwise the proposal was the same as that made on January 2, 1781. Though it was not wholly acceptable to Congress, it was accepted on March 1, 1784. Thus Virginia came into undisputed ownership of the lands between the Allegheny Mountains and the Ohio River embracing a large part of present West Virginia.

Though Congress had thus relinquished its claims to these lands, Morgan still looked to it for reparations for the Sufferers of 1763. For that purpose he again approached the matter through the sovereign state of New Jersey, which again authorized him to present his grievances in the name of his newly adopted state. The resulting memorial asked Congress, in conformity with Article IX of the Articles of Confederation, to hear

[13] Rowland, *Mason,* Vol. II, 23.

and judge the case of New Jersey against Virginia on its merits. Again the power and influence of Virginia triumphed, and the matter was dropped.

INDIANA AND THE CONSTITUTION

Following the ratification of the Federal Constitution, George Morgan carried the Indiana case to the Supreme Court. For that purpose he employed Benjamin H. Morgan, a distinguished Philadelphia attorney, who on August 11, 1792 brought a suit, styled "William Grayson *et al. v.* the Commonwealth of Virginia—a Bill in Equity." The attorney general of Virginia was summoned to appear in her behalf, but he refused to attend. Instead, the Virginia General Assembly denied the jurisdiction of the court in the matter and directed "the executive to pursue such measures in this case, as may seem most conducive to the interest, honor, and dignity of the Commonwealth."

Pursuant to this resolution, action was begun in Congress for the adoption of an amendment to the constitution which would embody in the fundamental law the Virginia ideas of state sovereignty. In this the Virginians had the support of Georgians aggrieved by the results of "Chisolm *v.* Georgia," in which judgment had been rendered against the latter. The proposed amendment became in 1798 the Eleventh to the constitution of the United States, which forbids a citizen to sue a state. Upon the adoption of this amendment, Morgan's case was dismissed by the Federal court for lack of jurisdiction. Thus ends the story of Indiana. Following acceptance by Congress of the Virginia land cession, little was said about Vandalia.

Chapter VIII

Border Warfare

THE SETTING

AS IN 1763, the Treaty of Paris of 1783 did not end Indian wars on the Virginia frontier.[1] An immigrant movement of unprecedented size was then under way, and as usual, under the resulting stress the natives were concerned about their hunting grounds and the graves of their fathers. Following the Virginia land cession to the Confederation Congress and its acceptance, that body prepared to make the most of its newly acquired possession. Among other things, it planned to pay debts incurred in behalf of American independence. In due time it planned also to erect republican states west of the Ohio River.

For these purposes, treaties were made with Iroquois and other tribes; a system of rectangular surveys was authorized under the Ordinance of 1785; and finally the famous Ordinance for the Government of the Northwest Territory was enacted. Though this document has attracted much attention because of its bill of rights and its provisions for new states, its chief importance for present purposes lies in the fact that it was enacted at the request of and to pave the way for prospective settlers. On April 7, 1788, the first permanent settlement in Ohio was made at Marietta. About the same time, land surveyors were at work in the vicinity of present Steubenville, Ohio. Aroused by these activities, Indians, true to form under such provocations, forgot their treaties and took to the warpath. For more than half a decade thereafter they terrorized the Virginia frontier, carrying death and destruction in their paths.

Encouraged by the British who continued to occupy American posts about the Great Lakes, mainly in the region of present Detroit, Michigan,

[1] See Withers, *Chronicles of Border Warfare* (Thwaites ed., 1895); Wills De Hass, *History of the Early Settlement and Indian Wars of Western Virginia* (Wheeling, 1851); Lucullus V. McWhorter, *The Border Settlers of Northwestern Virginia from 1768 to 1795* (Hamilton, Ohio, 1915); Doddridge, *Notes on the Settlement and Indian Wars* (Ritenour and Lindsay ed.).

and to supply Indians with firearms and firewater, the savages had already committed scores of depredations in present West Virginia. Among these were the murder of the Cunningham children in 1785, on Cunningham Run in Harrison County, and the capture of Mrs. Edward Cunningham, who was carried into captivity; the murder in the same year of Edward Doolin, one of the founders of present New Martinsville; and the murder of the Crow sisters, Elizabeth, Susan, and Catharine, on a branch of Wheeling Creek. The following year, the Indians carried their murdering and pillaging expeditions into the Monongahela and Kanawha valleys with results too gruesome to relate.

Under these conditions, forting again became the order of the day on the Virginia frontier. New forts were built and private residences again took the form of blockhouses. Thus forced to cover, frontiersmen looked to a strong national government for help and deliverance. Dunmore's War had been marked by unwholesome rivalries and jealousies between Virginians and Pennsylvanians, and the success of the American Revolution had at times been endangered by conflicting claims of land jobbers and Indian traders. As George Washington had been able to overcome these handicaps and carry his country to independence, residents of present West Virginia, among them a large number of Revolutionary soldiers, looked to him, as President of the United States, to deliver them from an unbearable situation. More than anything else perhaps this explains the fact that almost to a man they favored in 1788 the ratification of the Federal Constitution.

WASHINGTON TAKES A HAND

As Washington understood the aggressiveness of the white man, when tempted by the spirit of adventure, new lands, and opportunities for trade, he determined to deal with the Indian situation with the olive branch. Among other things he advised his childish wards to be good, and he offered rewards of $500 each for the arrest of whites who perpetrated outrages upon them. On the whole, he agreed with Edmund Pendleton that "the plan of annual presents . . . unaccompanied by other measures, is not the best mode of treating ignorant savages."

With the arrival of settlers and the clinking of surveyors' chains in the Northwest Territory, Indians repudiated their treaties made with the whites just following the Revolution as fraudulent and void, and again went on the warpath. Washington was therefore forced to deal with them in their own way. Early in 1790, he sent General Josiah Harmar among them, but he met with indifferent success. The following year, he sent

Governor Arthur St. Clair into the Northwest, but his inglorious defeat moved the Indians to bolder acts of defiance. Then Washington sent General Anthony (Mad Anthony) Wayne to deal with the situation. After some months of preparation, Wayne defeated the Indians decisively in 1794 at the Battle of Fallen Timber. Then followed the Treaty of Greenville, in which Indians ceded to the United States the larger part of the present state of Ohio.

Meanwhile, hostile Indians in large numbers continued to visit the Virginia frontier. On August 27, 1790, they destroyed Fort Tackett (Coal Fort), on or near the site of present St. Albans, West Virginia, and carried Mrs. Lewis Tackett and her son, Lewis, Jr., into captivity. At the same time others escaped capture and possible death by fleeing to Fort Lee at Clendenin, now Charleston, West Virginia. In 1790, a resident of Monongalia County, in asking to be excused from jury service, made affidavit that "Indians have killed or tuck six of my neighbors and in justice to my family I cannot leave them." The last hostiles in the Monongahela Valley were held captives at present Fairmont in 1795. Their presence there was of wide interest and attracted men, women, and children alike over a radius of about twenty-five miles, who rode on horseback to see the "dreaded savages."

More than is appreciated, Virginia frontiersmen were responsible for the outcome of Indian wars carried on under Washington's direction in the country beyond the Ohio River. Almost every family in northwest Virginia and southwest Pennsylvania gave one or more members for either regular or militia duty. Had the Indians developed leadership comparable to that of Pontiac and Cornstalk, the struggle might have been longer and more bitterly contested. Usually the whites were the aggressors. As such they sometimes outdid savages in barbarity. These and other pertinent facts are best told through their actors.

THE MORGANS

A half score or more Morgans had a part in post-Revolutionary Indian wars on the Virginia frontier. Of all these, the "Indian Fighter," David Morgan (May 12, 1721-May 8, 1813), third son of Morgan Morgan, first settler of West Virginia, left the most unusual and interesting record.[2] Together with members of the Prickett, Ice, Hall, Cochran, Hayes, Cunningham, Hartley, Barnes, Haymond, and Springer families, he settled

[2] Colonel Morgan Morgan Monument Commission, *Report* (Charleston, W. Va., 1924), pp. 70-83; Withers, *Border Warfare,* pp. 276-279; Sylvester Myers, *History of West Virginia,* 2 vols. (New Martinsville, W. Va., 1915), Vol. I, 209-214.

near present Fairmont, just before the American Revolution. When in 1774 the Indians began to menace them, these families built Pricketts Fort on the Monongahela River about five miles below present Fairmont. Morgan lived on the opposite or west side of the river about a mile from the fort.

Though he fought Indians as long as there were any to fight, the encounter which, more than any other, placed David Morgan in the class of border heroes, took place in 1779 at his home. Returning from Pricketts Fort he found two Indians pilfering his place and menacing the lives of his children. In the combat which followed, Morgan shot one of the Indians. The other one he dispatched with a knife after a desperate hand-to-hand encounter. Tradition has it that he skinned these Indians and tanned their hides. One hundred years later, when these killings were commemorated by the erection of a monument on the site of their enactment, descendants exhibited a shot pouch and saddle skirt which they claimed were made from the skin of one of the Indians dispatched by David Morgan. The binding of a book now reposing in the library of the Iliff School of Theology, Denver, Colorado, is said to have been made from the same material.

In or about 1745, David Morgan married Sarah Stephens, who bore him eight children, five boys and three girls. Four of his sons, Morgan, James, Evan, and Zackquill, served in the American Revolutionary Army under Captain William Haymond, who also resided near present Fairmont, Marion County, West Virginia, and was also David Morgan's Revolutionary captain. Like their father, his sons continued to fight Indians until long after the Revolutionary War. Together with their younger brother, Stephen, and their sisters, Elizabeth who married Abraham Lowe, Sarah who married Abraham Burris, and Catherine who married Major James West, they left a numerous progeny which includes leaders in many parts of the United States. Among these was Ephraim F. Morgan, great great-grandson of David Morgan, who was from 1921 to 1925 governor of West Virginia.

Levi, Morgan ("Spy Mod"), and James Morgan, sons of Colonel Zackquill Morgan, founder of Morgantown, were also noted scouts and Indian fighters. In the period of the Indian incursions into northwestern Virginia following the Revolution, they built a fort on the site of present New Martinsville, from which they, with little assistance from others, turned back more than one hostile band bent upon attacking settlers in the Monongahela Valley. Levi Morgan (1766-1826) was a scout in the ill-fated St. Clair expedition of 1791, and his brothers, James and Morgan, were regulars. Levi Morgan's Indian killings are said to have aggregated almost a hundred. Like the Indians themselves, he attacked without warning and killed without mercy.

Of the many stories about Levi Morgan's Indian adventures, that enacted on Buffalo Creek in present Marion County, West Virginia, is most frequently recalled. While skinning a wolf that he had caught in a trap, three Indians suddenly came upon him. After a game of hide and seek with trees and saplings as their screens, Morgan shot one of the Indians, but, when he went to reload his gun, he discovered to his horror that his powder had escaped from his horn.

In the foot race which followed, Morgan was pursued by one of the other Indians. To distract him, he threw his gun into his path but to no avail. Then he used his shot pouch and coat in the same manner, but his pursuer kept on. Upon reaching the crest of a hill, Morgan called in a loud voice, "Come on, come on; here is one, hurry up." The ruse worked and the Indian retraced his steps, but Morgan had lost his gun, his shot pouch, and his coat. Some years later, he met the Indian and learned that he still had his gun. Morgan bantered him for a friendly foot race. As the Indian lost, he insisted that he must have his gun back and recovered it.

At the instance of Aaron (Uncle Aaron) Morgan, for years a unique member of the West Virginia Legislature residing at Porters Falls, Wetzel County, West Virginia, a monument was erected in 1909 to the memory of Levi Morgan. It mattered not that he had spent his declining years in Kentucky and died there. The unveiling of a monument to his memory at New Martinsville, Wetzel County, was an event of more than local interest. It attracted guests not only from West Virginia and vicinity, but from far-off Oregon where many of the descendants of Colonel Zackquill Morgan and David Morgan had established themselves in the days of the covered wagon.

THE POE BROTHERS

Andrew Poe (1742-1823) and Adam Poe (1748-1838) were born in Frederick County, Maryland.[3] About 1763 Andrew settled on Harmans Creek in Washington County, Pennsylvania, about twelve miles from the Ohio River, where in 1769 he was joined by his brother, Adam. Here in a school of thrilling adventure, they became backwoodsmen in every sense of the word: alert, shrewd, courageous, and "determined to contest inch by inch with the savages their right to the soil and their privilege to live." The Poes were known also for their immense size.

In the summer of 1781, the Poe brothers had an opportunity to prove

[3] De Hass, *Indian Wars*, pp. 365-372; Withers, *Border Warfare*, pp. 362-364; Doddridge, *Notes*, pp. 232-237; Kercheval, *Valley*, pp. 240-243.

their prowess and win an undying place in border annals. While scouting for Indians, Andrew located two resting by the side of the Ohio River near the mouth of Tomlinsons Run, about six miles north of present New Cumberland, West Virginia. One of the Indians, named Big Foot, was of monstrous size. Creeping to within twenty feet of them, Poe took aim at Big Foot's breast and pulled the trigger, but his gun "flashed."

Instantly both of the Indians were on their feet in a mood for mortal combat. Equally eager for a fray and undaunted by the odds against him, Poe leaped upon Big Foot with such force as to knock him down and stun him. In doing so, he pulled down the smaller Indian, and for a time the three had it rough and tumble. Then the smaller Indian was able to escape Poe's grasp, but he did not flee. Instead he tried to scalp him. Finally Poe escaped Big Foot and grabbed a gun, with which he dispatched the smaller Indian.

By this time the larger Indian was on his feet. A desperate hand-to-hand encounter followed. In the course of this struggle the participants, due to the slippery condition of the river bank, slid into the water. The fight continued, however, until they were carried beyond their depth. Seeing that Big Foot could outswim him, Andrew Poe turned and swam to the shore, only to be pursued by his antagonist with murderous intent. In the encounter which continued, Big Foot was shot by Adam Poe, who came to the rescue. Mortally wounded but unwilling to surrender his scalp to the white man, Big Foot pushed himself into the stream and soon his lifeless body sank out of sight in its current.

LEWIS WETZEL

Lewis Wetzel (1763-1808), "the Boone of Northwestern Virginia," was the son of John Wetzel, a German, who with his five sons, Martin, George, John, Jacob, and Lewis, and his two daughters, Susan and Christiana, settled in 1772 on Wheeling Creek in present Ohio County, West Virginia, about fourteen miles from the Ohio River. All the Wetzels were hunters and Indian fighters, but Lewis was the most reckless and daring.[4] In his frontier environment he grew to manhood, a bold, wary, active person without a superior in his favorite avocation, Indian fighting. Of him it has been said, "No man on the western frontier was more dreaded by the enemy and none did more to beat them back into the heart of the forest."

While yet a youth, Lewis Wetzel had several encounters with Indians,

---

[4] Clarence B. Allman, *The Life and Times of Lewis Wetzel* (Nippanee, Ind., 1939); Withers, *Border Warfare*, pp. 125, 161-163, 338-339; Doddridge, *Notes*, pp. 229-232; De Hass, *Indian Wars*, pp. 344-364; Kercheval, *Valley*, pp. 238-239.

in one of which his brother, George, was killed. These experiences developed in him an undying hatred for the entire Indian race. The exact number of scalps taken by him is not known, but it is known that his desire for scalps was never satisfied. As with Jesse Hughes, this led Wetzel to murder Indians in times of peace. For such an act he was arrested at Marietta, Ohio, but he escaped confinement, only to become a greater hero than ever among his neighbors in Ohio County, Virginia.

Lewis Wetzel owed his prowess largely to his fleetness of foot and his ability to load his gun and shoot it as he ran. One of his favorite tricks was to persuade a band of Indians to follow him, thus separating them. When this was accomplished to his satisfaction, he would turn quickly and shoot the foremost pursuer. Then, reloading as he ran, he would turn quickly and shoot the next nearest Indian in a like manner. He could imitate the birds and beasts of the forest and was thus able to decoy Indians to their undoing. He was an artist in dodging behind trees and saplings when necessity occurred. He died at Natchez, Mississippi, the hero and idol of a generation of backwoodsmen.

JESSE HUGHES

What Lewis Wetzel, the Poe brothers, and the Morgans, David and Levi, were to northwestern Virginia, Jesse Hughes (1750?-1829) was to the more central portions of present West Virginia.[5] About 1771, following his marriage to Miss Grace Tanner, he settled on the site of an old Shawnee village near present Jane Lew, Lewis County. Here at the mouth of Jesses Run, he built a cabin which he used as a base for hunting and scouting trips into the surrounding areas. He was a soldier in Dunmore's War and his subsequent scouting activities carried him to Pricketts Fort and to points on the Ohio River.

Because of his bad temper and his undying enmity for Indians, Jesse was not a good leader, but he was a master scout. As described by McWhorter in his *Border Settlers,* Jesse was tall and slender. His countenance was hard, stern, and piercing, and his eyes were cold, fierce, and as penetrating and restless as those of "the mountain panther," or like a rattlesnake's. He could see at night as well as a wild animal, and "He was of an irritable, vindictive, and suspicious nature, and his hatred, when aroused, knew no bounds."

Like other Virginia frontiersmen, notably Daniel Boone and Levi Mor-

---

[5] Lucullus V. McWhorter, *The Border Settlers of Northwestern Virginia from 1768 to 1795* (Hamilton, Ohio, 1915) devotes a number of chapters almost entirely to Jesse Hughes. See also Withers, *Border Warfare,* pp. 137, 246, 288, 377-380, 410.

gan, when there were no more Indians to kill and game to catch, Jesse Hughes answered the call of the West. After selling his lands on Hackers Creek, he moved to a site near Vincennes in present Indiana, but, like other mountaineers, he found the swamp lands of the Wabash Valley unhealthy. Instead of going farther West, as did others, he returned to Virginia. During the remaining years of his life, he lived in present Jackson County, West Virginia. He was buried at Ravenswood.

ANNE BAILEY

Anne Bailey, "the White Squaw of the Kanawha," is an outstanding character of this period of Indian warfare. Her acts and alleged acts bulk large in the traditions of the Kanawha Valley.[6] She is thought to have been born in Liverpool, England, and to have come about 1761 to Virginia, where she resided for a time near Staunton. Soon after her arrival, she married Richard Trotter, who was killed in the Battle of Point Pleasant.

Immediately upon learning of her husband's death, Anne became "Mad Anne" and, clothing herself in the garb of the frontiersman, set out for vengeance. She became a noted scout and carried messages in the Kanawha Valley. After the Indian wars, she resumed her civilian life and customs, having meanwhile married John Bailey. She resided most of the remainder of her life in Gallipolis, Ohio, where she died in 1825. Her grave is in the West Virginia State Park at Point Pleasant.

OTHER FIGHTERS

Scores of other fighters had a part in pushing the Virginia frontier westward and withstanding resulting Indian attacks. In the region of Fort Henry (Wheeling) Captain Samuel Brady (1758-1796) was notably effective. He saved the lives of many settlers, among them Jenny Stoops, and was known throughout a large area as a resourceful and effective benefactor and defender. He was buried at West Liberty, Ohio County.

Captain William Lowther (1742-1814) was to the Hackers Creek settlements in the central part of present Trans-Allegheny West Virginia what Samuel Brady was to the region about Fort Henry. Lowther was also a justice of the peace for the District of West Augusta, and the first sheriff of both Harrison and Wood counties. His descendants are legion.

---

[6] Virgil A. Lewis, *Life and Times of Anne Bailey* (Charleston, W. Va., 1891).

Among other frontiersmen who distinguished themselves in this period as Indian fighters were John Cutright (1754-1850), a resident of Buckhannon Valley; Jacob Westfall (1755-1835), who built Westfall Fort in Randolph County; George Jackson (1757-1831), who witnessed the surrender of Lord Cornwallis, and left numerous descendants in present West Virginia; and John Hacker (1743-1821), who accompanied George Rogers Clark on his 1778 expedition into the Northwest Territory.

Chapter IX

Post-Revolutionary Days to 1800

A NEW IMMIGRANT MOVEMENT

DURING the closing days of the Revolution and those immediately following, an immigrant tide, surpassed in size only by a similar movement into Kentucky, pushed into northwestern Virginia. Eager to escape oppressive taxes, the evils of an unsound currency, the exactions of creditors, and the consequent prevailing annoyances from lawyers and courts, many persons sought these refuges to begin life anew under different conditions. Some of them were also seeking retreats in which to escape the odium of having been Loyalists. As a result of these movements, the total population of the Trans-Allegheny rose to one hundred twenty-five thousand in 1790, at least twenty thousand of whom lived in what is now West Virginia.

Among those going into Kentucky at this time was Abraham Lincoln, grandfather of a future President of the United States; and the Hanks family, from which Nancy Hanks, mother of President Lincoln, descended. The Lincoln family emigrated from the Valley of Virginia, as did also the Hanks family; but, before going west, the Hankses are said to have sojourned in a log cabin near what is now Mikes Run, Mineral County, West Virginia. Here, it is claimed, Nancy Hanks was born. In 1929, a commission, acting for West Virginia, designated the site of her supposed birthplace, and six years later it was marked by a monument.[1]

As already indicated, immigrants established themselves in northwest Virginia while the Revolutionary War was in progress. In 1778, Thomas

[1] W. Va. Legislature, *Hand Book and Manual* (1929) pp. 793-810. A Hanks cabin was on the present Doll farm, on the east side of New Creek Mountain.

Ingles and his family located in Wrights Valley near the present site of Bluefield, though they later moved to Burkes Garden. In 1780, the Davidson and the Bailey families settled on a branch of the Bluestone, a tributary to New River; and, in the same year, John Toney established himself at the mouth of East River. Two years later, Captain George Pearis founded Pearisburg on lands formerly entered by William Ingles; and, the next year, Christian Peters established a home at Peterstown, Monroe County. About the same time, many Revolutionary soldiers, together with some Hessians and Tories, made settlements at intervening points, as well as at certain sites farther removed toward the Big Sandy River.

Among those pioneers coming after the Revolution was George Chapman. In 1783, he located and entered one thousand acres, including the present site of New Cumberland. In 1784, Henry Flesher made the first permanent settlement, in what is now Weston. In the same year, Henry McWhorter settled in Harrison County. He later moved to Jane Lew, where he continued to reside for thirty-seven years. In 1785, Captain James Neal erected a blockhouse near the site of Parkersburg. In that year, Joseph Woods and four Scottish families laid out a town on the site of Belleville, Wood County; and, two years later, Isaac Williams settled on the south side of the Ohio opposite Fort Harmar, where Williamstown, then Williamston, stands.

Because of repeated Indian attacks, settlements on the upper Kanawha and lower New River were checked somewhat. George Clendenin, of

Fort Lee, 1788-1795, named for Governor Henry (Light Horse Harry) Lee

Greenbrier County, purchased in 1787 the Bullitt lands at the mouth of Elk River and in April, 1788, erected Fort Lee on a site now included in Charleston, which dates its beginnings from Clendenin's activities. At the time there were only four other settlements or posts on the Kanawha—one at its mouth (Point Pleasant); Tacketts at the mouth of Coal River, on the site of present Saint Albans; John Morris's about twenty miles above Coal River; and another at present Cedar Grove. About ten persons resided in each of these places. By 1791, the twenty-mile stretch between the mouth of Elk River and the mouth of Kelleys Creek was "all inhabited."[2]

None of the settlers who came into the Kanawha Valley at this time left a more abiding impression than did Daniel Boone, whose resourcefulness as a hunter and Indian fighter had already done much to make it possible for white men to reside in Kentucky, then known as the "Dark and Bloody Land." Among other things, he had blazed the Wilderness Trail by way of Cumberland Gap, and had participated in laying the foundations of its government. But through his own negligence and the fraudulent acts of others, Boone lost his holdings in Kentucky, and, in 1788, he moved to Kanawha County, Virginia. His first settlement was near Point Pleasant. In 1791, he settled near present Charleston and about that time was elected to the general assembly to represent Kanawha County.

Boone was first of all a hunter.[3] Clad in the typical garb of the frontiersman and with no other luggage than his tomahawk and "Old Isaac," his favorite bear trap, he made excursions far and near in pursuit of beavers, otters, foxes, and raccoons. Single trips netted a hundred or more pelts. As civilization tended to displace primitive conditions in the Kanawha Valley, Boone, in a characteristic way, became restless and longed for an environment more suited to his tastes as a frontiersman. In 1795, he left the Kanawha Valley and soon thereafter found a retreat on Femme Osage Creek in Missouri, where he died September 26, 1830, at the age of eighty-six.

The rapid growth of population in Trans-Allegheny Virginia in the post-Revolutionary days necessitated the incorporation of towns and the formation of counties. Not satisfied with this organization, except as a means to an end, Kentuckians agitated the formation of a new state, a movement in which they were successful in 1792. Temporarily all proposals for new states in northwest Virginia were abandoned; the inhabitants of that region contented themselves with other arrangements. The towns incorporated for their convenience, together with the date of incorporation and the present location, were: 1782, Lewisburg in Green-

---

[2] John P. Hale, *Trans-Allegheny Pioneers* (Cincinnati, 1886; Charleston, 1931), p. 275; Lewis, *Anne Bailey,* Ch. 9; *Charleston* (W. Va.) *Daily News,* June 4, 1939.

[3] R. G. Thwaites, *Daniel Boone* (New York, 1913), pp. 211-223; Hale, *Trans-Allegheny Pioneers,* pp. 279, 299.

Daniel Boone alone in the wilderness

brier County; 1785, Clarksburg in Harrison, and Morgantown in Monongalia counties; 1786, Charles Town in Jefferson County; 1787, Frankfort in Mineral, Middletown in Berkeley, West Liberty in Ohio, and Watson in Hampshire counties. Counties formed in this period, together with their names and the counties from which they were taken and the date of formation, were: Harrison, from Monongalia, 1784; Hardy, from Hampshire, 1786; Randolph, from Harrison, 1787; Pendleton, from Augusta, Rockingham, Hardy, and Bath, 1788; and Kanawha, from Greenbrier and Montgomery, 1788.

PIONEER CHURCHES AND MINISTERS

From their earliest beginnings, the inhabitants of present West Virginia were deeply religious. There is ground for belief that a Presbyterian congregation was organized within her bounds before the date generally accepted as that of her first settlement.[4] Be that as it may, a church building was "set up" in 1734 by Quakers at near-by Hopewell on Opequon Creek. In 1767, Quakers built a meetinghouse on the east side of Bear Garden Mountain, and other Quaker congregations were at that time holding regular services in their residences, some of which were built for that purpose.

In 1735, William Hoge came from Elk River, Delaware, settled on Opequon Creek, and built a Presbyterian meetinghouse on his own lands, and land deeds of that year refer also to a Presbyterian meetinghouse at the Big Spring on Cedar Creek. That same year the Rev. William Williams was given permission to erect two church edifices, one on his own land and one on lands of Morgan Bryan. These two preaching places were later known as "Bullskin" and "Tuscarora." After 1736, all four of these churches were visited regularly by ministers from the Donegal Presbytery.[5]

Meanwhile, Moravian missionaries had visited the South Branch Valley. Leonard Schnell and John Brandmueller were there in 1749 and found "whole families clothed in Indian fashion."

After the Quakers and the Presbyterians, the Baptists were first and

---

[4] September 19, 1719, "the people of Potomoke, in Virginia" requested the Synod of Philadelphia, for "an able gospel minister to settle amongst them." The following year Reverend Daniel McGill reported to the Synod that he had visited Potomoke, "remained some months and put the people into church order." If this congregation was at or near Shepherdstown, as now believed, it indicates an earlier settlement in present West Virginia than the one made by Morgan Morgan. See Church Minutes, Witherspoon Building, Philadelphia.

[5] Donegal Presbytery, *Minutes;* William H. Foote, *Sketches of Virginia* (Philadelphia, 1856); James R. Graham, *Planting of Presbyterianism in the Northern Neck of Virginia* (Winchester, Va., 1904).

most active[6] They were in Gerrardstown in present Berkeley County as early as 1743. About that time, they became associated with Presbyterians in the joint ownership of church properties in the Shenandoah and South Branch valleys. In 1764, they formed the Ketocton Regular Baptist Association, which served an area extending from King George County in eastern Virginia to the Monongahela River, a distance of two hundred miles.

The ministerial activities of these sects were arrested somewhat by the French and Indian and the Revolutionary wars, the westward migrations, and the absence of institutions of learning, but well before the end of the eighteenth century, ministers made their appearance in the Trans-Allegheny. As elsewhere in Virginia, their work was aided by the epoch-making act of her general assembly in 1785, which disestablished the Protestant Episcopal Church as the state-supported church, and legalized religious liberty.[7] This act was an incentive to dissenting sects everywhere in Virginia. Aided by the spirit out of which it grew, Francis Asbury and other dissenting preachers organized congregations in many parts of that state, even in the Trans-Allegheny.

After the separation in 1784 of the Methodists from the Church of England, Asbury, together with Rev. Thomas Coke, became superintendent of the Methodists in America.[8] As such, Asbury entered upon an active ministry which in the course of a few years carried him into many parts of the United States. Under his direction, congregations were organized in Trans-Allegheny Virginia, and church edifices were built. In 1786, Rehoboth Church, near Union, Monroe County, was "raised." It was dedicated two years later by Asbury, who visited it at other times. This building is said to be the oldest structure of its denomination west of the Alleghenies.

Other denominations, notably the Baptist, were active in the Trans-Allegheny. In 1773, they organized a congregation at present Bridgeport, Harrison County, West Virginia, and on November 5, 1775 Rev. John Corbly organized a Baptist congregation in the Forks of Cheat, near Stewartstown, in what the next year became Monongalia County. Two years later, under the ministry of John Alderson, Baptist congregations were organized in present Monroe County, West Virginia, which became a center of influence of that denomination.

Because of the policy of the Presbyterians of using only trained ministers, they were not so aggressive as other denominations, notably the Methodists and the Baptists, in carrying the gospel beyond the Allegheny

---

6 Robert B. Semple, *Rise and Progress of the Baptists in Virginia* (Richmond, 1810).

7 H. J. Eckenrode, *Separation of Church and State in Virginia* (Richmond, 1910); Bishop William Meade, *Old Churches, Ministers, and Families of Virginia,* 2 vols. (Philadelphia, 1857).

8 Asbury, *Journal* . . . from August 7, 1771, to December 7, 1815, 3 vols.

Mountains. This was true despite the fact that a large element of the Virginia frontier population, particularly the Scotch-Irish, inclined to that faith. In 1783, however, Rev. John McCue of the Hanover Presbytery, organized three congregations in Greenbrier County, at Lewisburg, Spring Creek, and Good Hope. He served them until 1794, when he was succeeded by Rev. Benjamin Grigsby, under whose direction the "Old Stone

Old Stone Church, Lewisburg, Greenbrier County

Church," now standing, was erected in 1796 at Lewisburg. Following his departure that year, there was no regular Presbyterian minister in the Greenbrier field until 1808, when Lexington Presbytery sent Rev. John McElhenney to serve it as a missionary. Meanwhile Presbyterian congregations had been organized elsewhere in the Trans-Allegheny.[9] Those organized about 1790 at Elm Grove and West Liberty in Ohio County had in fact become centers of influence.

Stimulated by competition, the deposed Protestant Episcopal Church, though disdaining evangelical methods, sent missionaries into the Trans-Allegheny. Its congregation organized at Wellsburg about 1792 by Rev. Joseph Doddridge was a center of influence which reached well into Pennsylvania and even into Ohio.

Neither the Lutherans nor the Catholics were aggressive beyond the Alleghenies. Activities of the former were determined largely by the nor-

[9] Rose W. Frye, *Recollections of the Rev. John McElhenney* (Richmond, 1893); *The West Virginia News* (Ronceverte), June 16, 1938.

mal expansion of German settlements, and the Catholics were handicapped by having few members among the Virginia population, either east or west of the mountains. Virginians residing along and near the Potomac who adhered to that sect were visited from time to time by priests from Maryland, who regarded the "Virginia Side" as a "land of danger." According to an eminent Catholic historian, John Gilmary Shea, "Father Fambrack of Frederick, Maryland, visited it [the Virginia side] only by night and slept by his horse, ready to mount and put him at full speed at the slightest warning."

THE FAIRFAX LANDS

The Federal Government had scarcely been launched before the subject of Virginia land titles again came to the fore. Lord Fairfax, to whom the remaining "waste and ungranted lands" of the Northern Neck were awarded early in the century, died in 1781 without issue, after assigning his lands to a relative, Denny Martin, on condition that he assume the Fairfax title. By an act of 1779 creating a general land office to regulate the sale of waste and unappropriated lands and to abolish "servile, feudal, and precarious" tenure within its jurisdiction, the Virginia General Assembly declared null and void the Fairfax title and authorized the sale of all lands formerly held thereunder in the same way that other such lands were sold by the state.

Subsequently, the Treaty of 1783—recognizing American independence and safeguarding the rights of Loyalists—subjected this course to questionable legality, as did also the fact that Virginia had recognized the validity of the Fairfax grant. Nevertheless, she proceeded to grant patents to unsold lands formerly owned by Fairfax, and to prevent the collection of quitrents on those previously sold by him. As a result, in 1791, Martin, assignee of Lord Fairfax, instituted suit to determine his rights. The action took the form of an ejectment proceeding against one David Hunter, who occupied lands under a patent issued in 1788 by the state of Virginia.

For a time, the Martin ejectment suit aroused much interest, involving, as it did, the right and title to other lands, the interpretation of the Treaty of 1783, and the practical application of the Constitution of the United States. The outcome of the long-drawn-out suit between Joist Hite and Fairfax, instituted in 1749 and terminated in 1786, was still a subject of current comment and satisfaction. It validated titles to lands granted directly by the King, or his agent, prior to the taking over of the Northern Neck by its feudal proprietor. But the joy thus occasioned was neutralized somewhat by warnings from George Mason and Patrick Henry to the effect that many land titles would be subjected to double taxation in the event that Virginia ratified the Federal Constitution.

Under the circumstances, the decision of the Virginia District Court at Winchester, in 1794, sustaining the validity of Martin's claims and ordering the ejectment of Hunter, was a keen disappointment and was generally resented. Later, after John Marshall and a group of associates, including his brother James, had acquired title to the "waste and ungranted land" of the former Fairfax estate—Hunter appealed the decision of the Winchester court to the Virginia Court of Appeals, which, in 1810, reversed the lower court's decision. In 1813, in the famous case of "Martin *v.* Hunter's Lessee," the whole matter was reviewed by the United States Supreme Court which, three years later, sustained the decision of the Winchester court.

MARKETS AND TRANSPORTATION

Post-Revolutionary inhabitants of western Virginia were much concerned with markets. Surpluses of agricultural products were accumulating, but without markets they were valueless, except as a means of subsistence. Many shippers were using flatboats and other craft, but this practice restricted opportunities to those residing along the larger streams and did not solve the problem of a means of returning home; for it was a laborious undertaking to navigate a boat of any kind against the currents of the Ohio and the Mississippi, even with the additional aid of sails.[10]

The commerce thus carried on, over the Ohio and thence to the Mississippi, was, however, considerable. It was with the hope of controlling it to his own advantage that James Wilkinson, "the most finished rascal in American annals," entered into secret understandings with the Spanish. This defection spread to many settlers, among them James Robertson, founder of settlements on the Cumberland River; John Sevier, hero of the Watauga settlements; and others interested in trade, commerce and problems of defense.

To them the Jay-Gardoqui Treaty, being considered by the Confederation Congress in 1786, was especially objectionable, because it would have surrendered, in return for certain commercial privileges of chief benefit to New England, the right of Americans to navigate the Mississippi River for twenty-five years. Unable to secure redress by negotiation, some frontiersmen would have dismembered the Union in order to obtain better trade and commercial opportunities.

---

[10] Charles H. Ambler, *History of Transportation in the Ohio Valley* (Glendale, Calif., 1932), pp. 17-31; Archer W. Hulbert, *The Ohio River, Course of Empire* (New York, 1906), pp. 226-249.

Fortunately, necessity was again a stimulus to invention. From the time of the first settlements on the Ohio, there were those who had tried to use mechanical devices to navigate it. Disappointed in the outcome of their experiments, their endeavors were now turning to the possibilities of

James Rumsey

steam. The proposed steamboat, on which men had labored for years, promised a fabulous private fortune for its inventor and incalculable benefit for the public. As a result, would-be inventors were busy in almost every state of the Union. Prominent among those working on and near the Ohio were Edward West, John Fitch, and James Rumsey.

At the close of the Revolution, Rumsey was in Shepherdstown, Virginia, contemplating the possibilities of improved water transportation. Shortly thereafter, and with no other tools than those found in a blacksmith's shop, he built a "mechanical boat," which made four miles against the current of the Potomac, in an exhibition at Bath, (West) Virginia. General Washington was present and witnessed Rumsey's achievement, which he commended and subsequently referred to repeatedly. It was through Washington's intercession that the Virginia Assembly, the following year, 1785, granted Rumsey and his heirs, for a term of ten years, the sole and exclusive right to navigate Virginia waters with boats "constructed upon a model that will greatly facilitate navigation against the current of rapid rivers."[11] The same year, Maryland granted Rumsey a similar privilege.

Whatever the merits of Rumsey's invention, little practical good came of it. A "war of pamphlets" followed between him and John Fitch, his outstanding rival inventor, in which Fitch denied the practicability of Rumsey's invention and claimed priority for himself for a boat completed in 1786. Both died before their dreams were realized, Rumsey in London, where he was buried in St. Margaret's Churchyard near Westminster Abbey, and Fitch in Kentucky, where his remains were interred at Bardstown, on the banks of the Ohio.

WASHINGTON AND INTERNAL IMPROVEMENTS

It was in the midst of these dynamic conditions that George Washington again visited the Ohio Valley. He had just relinquished command of the Continental Army and retired to his estate at Mount Vernon to live in seclusion, some thought, and to receive and enjoy the respect of those who already regarded him as the "Father of His Country." Again the frontier called him. He had large realty interests there, but more important than these were his patriotic purposes. Realizing that the interior might be occupied by a population largely foreign, with no predilection for the original states, Washington was convinced of the necessity of binding the West to the East by ties of interest.

Starting from his home, September 1, 1784, two days after General Lafayette had completed a two weeks' visit with him, Washington traveled by Leesburg and Snickers Gap to the Shenandoah and thence, by Charles Town, Back Creek, Bath, and Old Town, to Cumberland. Refreshing his memory on the way with scenes and incidents that must have seemed somewhat legendary in view of all that had happened since 1753-1755, he retraced Braddock's Road to Simpsons, near Connellsville. Then he proceeded to his lands on Millers Run, near Washington, Pennsylvania.

[11] Hening, *Statutes*, Vol. XI, 502; Ella May Turner, *James Rumsey* (Scottdale, Pa., 1930), pp. 9-25.

After a few days in Washington, he went to Beeson Town, now Uniontown, where he engaged an attorney to aid in ousting Scotch-Irish squatters who had settled on his lands. This done, he set out for home.[12]

Washington's decision to return through Trans-Allegheny Virginia was probably due to information to the effect that the newly established bound-

Washington's trans-Allegheny journey, 1784

ary between Pennsylvania and Virginia left his lands in the former state. This was not only disappointing to him, but it interfered with plans, then maturing in his mind, for connecting the eastern and western waters by means of canals within the bounds of Virginia.

From what is now Point Marion, Pennsylvania, the return route led by way of Pierponts, a few miles east of Morgantown, where, September 24, 1784, Washington met and conferred with Zackquill Morgan, founder of Morgantown. From there, he followed the "New Road" eastward, over Laurel Hill, to Bruceton. From this point, by traveling in a southeast direction, he reached the North Branch of the Potomac River, having meanwhile crossed the "Yough" at or near the present site of Webster Switch, on the Baltimore and Ohio Railroad. From the North Branch, he continued in a direction south of east to the upper waters of the South Branch

12 Washington, *Diaries,* Vol. II, 279-328; Ambler, *George Washington and the West,* pp. 175-187.

and thence, through Brocks Gap, to Rockingham Court House, whence he went direct to Mount Vernon.

Immediately upon his return home, Washington submitted to Governor Harrison plans and suggestions for connecting the navigable waters of the Potomac River with those of the Monongahela. These plans were accompanied by comments upon the diffusion and the importance of the inland navigation of the United States. Despite possible opposition from residents of eastern Pennsylvania, who objected to any plan for internal improvement which would tend to divert the products of western Pennsylvania to Baltimore, he favored a route by way of the Potomac River, Wills Creek, and the Youghiogheny River. In case Pennsylvania interests attempted to thwart the enterprise, Washington assured Governor Harrison that there were then in western Pennsylvania one hundred thousand persons ready to join in a movement looking to the dismemberment of that state.

It was under these conditions that Virginia launched her first comprehensive plan for internal improvements. All subsequent plans were but modifications of the one adopted in 1785. It contemplated joining the eastern and western waters by artificial waterways, all of which were to be connected by a system of roads and turnpikes. In support of this program, Washington visited the general assembly, which responded to his suggestion by creating the James River and the Potomac companies, of which Washington became first president.[13] Already, the assembly had authorized a state road from Winchester to Morgantown, by way of Romney. This route was opened in 1786, and a road was then legalized to connect Lewisburg and Warm Springs. A state road from Lewisburg to the Falls of the Kanawha, authorized in 1785, was completed the following year; and, the next year, a wagon road was authorized for the purpose of connecting the Falls of the Kanawha with Lexington, Kentucky. About the same time, a branch was extended from the Winchester-Romney-Morgantown Road to Clarksburg, from which point (1789) a road was marked to the mouth of the Little Kanawha.

THE FEDERAL CONSTITUTION

The attitude of the inhabitants of western Virginia toward this document can be best understood from a review of the debates of the ratifying convention. Patrick Henry, the most effective of the Anti-Federalists,

13 Washington, *Diaries,* Vol. II, 376-377; Wayland F. Dunaway, "History of the James River and Kanawha Company," in Columbia University, *Studies,* Vol. CIV, No. 2 (New York, 1922).

warned the inhabitants of Trans-Allegheny Virginia that holders of former Fairfax lands and those granted to the Indiana, the Vandalia, and the Ohio companies might be dispossessed. They were warned, also, against the dangers of establishing a government under which other states would have the power to barter the free navigation of the Mississippi River, as had been attempted in the Jay-Gardoqui Treaty. Finally, they were told that these same states under the leadership of land jobbers, new-state promoters, and proponents of selfish internal improvement interests might otherwise combine to produce the undoing of Virginia. In the event of possible interstate warfare, it was pointed out that the position of the border might become especially trying.

On the other hand, Federalists assured the inhabitants of Trans-Allegheny Virginia that they could expect to secure the free navigation of the Mississippi and a much-desired protection from Indian attacks and from internal enemies only from a government strong enough and respectable enough to secure and maintain those coveted things. Questions regarding the tenure of the former Fairfax and other lands were dismissed by the Federalists as chimerical. Interested parties were assured that Virginia had retained enough of her sovereign power to ensure her continued control over internal matters. Moreover, it was pointed out that America's prestige among the nations of the world, to say nothing of her credit both at home and abroad, demanded ratification.

To a frontier population interested primarily in protection against a savage foe, the free navigation of the Mississippi River, and the removal of the British from the Northwest Territory, these arguments were convincing. This trend of opinion is plainly revealed in the vote on ratification. All the Valley of Virginia now embraced in West Virginia, together with the Trans-Allegheny, except the region south of the Kanawha and a small divided area along the Monongahela River, voted "yes"; whereas the remainder of Trans-Allegheny Virginia, including all Kentucky except a small district in and about Louisville, voted "no."

As yet, there were few persons residing south of the Kanawha, and their interests tended to harmonize with those of Kentucky, which was already mapping out a course of its own. This, probably more than any other factor, accounts for the vote of Kentucky, as well as that of the region south of the Kanawha. At the time, these sections were more interested in the navigation of the Mississippi than they were in their defense against the Indian.

It would be a mistake, however, to conclude that the attitude of any part of Virginia toward the ratification of the Federal Constitution was determined wholly by her Convention of 1788. Each important section of the state then had its own traditions and interests which, after all, were determining factors. This was true of northwest Virginia, despite the fact that it had also been settled only recently. Among its traditions was an active anti-British sentiment which found expression in the fight for independence and in counterattacks against the Indian. It may be recalled also that Revolutionary soldiers, particularly those of the Continental Army, generally favored the ratification of the Constitution. At this time, the Cincinnati, an organization of officers of the Revolutionary Army, through which Washington worked for ratification, was strong along the upper Potomac and in the Trans-Allegheny; and northwest Virginia had no established traditions which fostered the type of particularism known to eastern Virginia.

For some time following the launching of the Federal Government, the counties of northwest Virginia, together with those of the Valley, sent Federalists to the general assembly and to Congress. In both bodies, these representatives acted as strict partisans. They supported most of Hamilton's plans for putting the Federal Government into operation. In the general assembly, they endorsed the assumption of the state debts by the Federal Government, a proposal which to many Virginians was the most objectionable feature of the Hamilton program. In Congress, the Virginia Federalists accepted Hamilton's proposals with little hesitation and opposed the election of Thomas Jefferson to the presidency in 1800-1801.[14]

The loyalty of a large part of Trans-Allegheny Virginia to the new Federal régime was given the acid test in the Whiskey Insurrection of 1794-1795. A Federal law of 1791, levying a tax of four pence per gallon on all distilled spirits, had, from the first, been resented by the Scotch-Irish "Whiskey Boys" of southwest Pennsylvania, and by others of the same section. Whiskey, the chief article taxed, was to them a satisfactory form of consumption for corn and rye. What was more important, it was a good form in which to market them, as it represented great value in small bulk. Moreover, it was a product of honest toil and belonged to its producers, as they thought, by the laws of nature. Hence, their opposition to taxing it took the form of insurrection. At this stage of their resentment, they attacked Federal revenue officers, one of whom was located in Morgantown, Virginia. But Virginians did not join them in their opposition to the excise laws. Instead, they aided Governor Lee in a military demonstration to enforce them, despite the fact that they had esteemed brands of rye of their own, notably "Old Monongahela."

THE TREND TO STATE RIGHTS

The year 1795 marked an important turning point in Trans-Allegheny Virginia history. Having defeated the Indians the year before in the battle

[14] Charles H. Ambler, *Sectionalism in Virginia,* 1776-1861 (Chicago, 1910), pp. 61-100.

of Fallen Timbers, General Wayne concluded the Treaty of Greenville, which brought peace to the border and opened to immediate settlement the southern and eastern portions of the present state of Ohio. By the Jay Treaty of 1794, the British gave up all forts heretofore occupied by them in the Northwest Territory; and, the following year, the Spanish conceded the right to navigate the Mississippi River and, temporarily, the privilege to deposit American goods at New Orleans. This privilege could be withdrawn, however, at any time after three years.

In northwestern Virginia, the results of these changes manifested themselves in many ways, but in none more strikingly than in politics. Both in Congress and in the general assembly, Federalists tended to give way to Republicans, as the followers of Thomas Jefferson were then called. In 1795, George Jackson, an anti-excise man, was elected to Congress by a comfortable majority, although he had failed of election two years before by a margin of six votes. It was not until the tariff and internal improvements became issues, more than twenty years later, that Federalists were again elected to Congress from Trans-Allegheny Virginia. Meanwhile, strict-construction Republicans replaced liberal Federalists in the general assembly; most of the counties west of the Alleghenies either favored Virginia's determined stand for state rights in 1798 or were divided in their opposition to it. Under the leadership of John George Jackson, son of George Jackson and brother-in-law of James Madison, the party of Jefferson and Madison all but supplanted the party of Washington and Marshall.

POPULATION GROWTH AND MOVEMENTS

The trend to state rights was accompanied by a rapid growth in population. It was at this time that settlers first entered the Big Sandy Valley in considerable numbers. The uncertainty of land titles, caused by overlapping and conflicting claims, had retarded permanent settlements, but now the whole region south of the Kanawha literally "swarmed with surveyors and speculators." Robert Morris, assignee of William Cary Nicholas, was offering eight million acres for sale and settlement in that section. It was during this period, also, that Joseph Ruffner, who had previously purchased a tract of land which included the famous Salines, near Malden, moved from the Shenandoah Valley to Charleston, on the Kanawha. Choice lands in intervening places and to the north were being rapidly taken; immigrants on their way west were making mention of the "beautiful plantations" and "large fields of corn and grane" that dotted the hillsides all the way from Morgantown to Wheeling. As a result, the population of the counties now embraced in West Virginia increased from approximately fifty-five thousand, in 1790, to more than seventy-eight thousand, in 1800, almost thirty-five thousand of whom lived west of the Alleghenies.

There were those in the East who feared that this movement to the West would drain the former section of its best blood and eventuate in the dismemberment of the Union. Fortunately, Union-saving influences were at work in individual attachments and initiative, and these were supplemented by agencies of government. Outstanding among such agencies supplied by Congress was a regular mail service on the Ohio between Wheeling and Cincinnati, first established in 1794. In 1796, Congress increased these facilities by a route which extended from Wheeling to Limestone (Maysville) by way of Zanesville and Chillicothe over "Zanes Trace."

At the same time, Virginia was responding to the needs and demands of her western inhabitants. In 1797, Brooke County was created from Ohio County; in 1798, Wood County was formed from Harrison and a part of Kanawha; and, in 1799, Monroe was formed from Greenbrier and a part of Botetourt. In this same period, also, the following towns, together with the date of action and the name of the county in which each is now located, were incorporated: 1790, Beverly, in Randolph, and Smithfield, in Harrison; 1791, Wellsburg, in Brooke, and Darkesville, in Berkeley; 1794, Charleston, in Kanawha, Franklin, in Pendleton, and Point Pleasant, in Mason; 1795, Vienna, in Wood, and Wheeling, in Ohio; 1796, Pleasantsville, in Monongalia; and in 1798, Smithfield, in Berkeley. During these years, new roads were authorized; several ferries were established; and provision was made for clearing rivers of snags and other obstructions so as to make them navigable for flatboats and canoes.

Chapter X

From State Rights to Nationalism 1800-1829

THE LOUISIANA PURCHASE

AT THE OPENING of the nineteenth century, the right of Americans to navigate the Mississippi River was again a topic of discussion in Trans-Allegheny Virginia, as elsewhere in the Ohio Valley.[1] The period during which goods might be deposited at New Orleans had expired; Spain had refused to extend it and was threatening to deny that privilege entirely. Without such a concession, the navigation of the Mississippi was valueless to American frontiersmen. Accordingly, they were insisting that the Federal Government secure this right for them. Because of the disturbed condition of Europe, they feared that either France or England might acquire Louisiana and be even more exacting with them than Spain had been. In the event of such a contingency, they asserted, the loss to the frontier would be incalculable. To prevent any possibility of loss, they were willing to arm themselves, to descend the Mississippi, to take New Orleans, and to hold it for their own use and that of their country.

The purchase of Louisiana by the United States made unnecessary the execution of these intentions. This opportunity came unexpectedly. Spain secretly transferred the territory to France; but Napoleon, realizing that he might not be able to hold it, offered to sell the land to the United States,

[1] Ambler, *Transportation in the Ohio Valley,* pp. 71-72.

to prevent England from getting it. Unable to find authority in the Constitution under which to accept the offer, Jefferson, a strict constructionist, decided to make the purchase and to amend the Constitution afterwards. The West, which had stood by him on the Virginia and Kentucky Resolutions of 1798, would hardly have permitted any other course. At once, his popularity in that section increased; Trans-Allegheny Virginia became state rights or Republican. However, some of the counties in the upper Ohio Valley and along the Potomac, including those now in West Virginia, continued to oppose Jefferson politically and carried their opposition well into the administration of James Madison.

Among the many results of the purchase of Louisiana affecting western Virginia was a greatly stimulated commercial activity. Keelboats, flatboats, barges, arks, and other such devices came into use in large numbers; but the craft which then gave greatest promise of service to the interior were ships, brigs, and schooners. In the early nineties of the preceding century, at least one such vessel was built at or near Pittsburgh, and descended thence to the high seas. Beginning about 1800, others were built; following 1803, their number increased, together with their capacity. For the most part they were owned by farmers and merchants who used them to transport their products to New Orleans. Here both cargoes and vessels were sold, the latter going on to the high seas. But for the inadequate credit conditions then existing in the Ohio Valley, the undependable navigation of the Ohio River, the Embargo and Nonintercourse acts, and finally the advent of the steamboat on western waters, this form of transportation might have assumed large proportions.

BURR AND BLENNERHASSETT

Among the numerous persons finding homes along the Ohio on Virginia soil, about the beginning of the nineteenth century, was one Harman Blennerhassett, an eccentric Irishman, who, together with his wife, daughter of the lieutenant governor of the Isle of Man and Blennerhassett's own niece, had recently immigrated to America.[2] After a journey down the Ohio in a keelboat and an enjoyable winter in social intercourse at Marietta (1797), he purchased an island in the Ohio about two miles below Parkersburg, then Newport. In this decision he seems to have been influenced by a desire to own Negro slaves, but he wished also to be near the intelligent and educated officers of the American Army, then stationed at Belpré and Marietta, Ohio.

[2] William H. Safford, *Life of Harman Blennerhassett* (Chillicothe, O., 1850) and *Blennerhasset Papers* (Cincinnati, 1864); Alvaro F. Gibbens, *Historic Blennerhassett* (Charleston, 1925).

For the frontier, the residence built by Blennerhassett on his island estate was little short of palatial. The halls were light, airy, and elegant; and the furnishings consisted of gay-colored carpets, splendid mirrors, classic pictures, and rich tapestries. There was a library which contained some of the rarest books then to be found either in Europe or in America. Behind

Harman Blennerhassett

the mansion, after the fashion then familiar in the South and later found in increasing numbers in western Virginia and in Kentucky, were the slave quarters.

It was in this "tempting Eden" that Aaron Burr sojourned for a time, while planning his ill-fated expedition to the Southwest, the exact purpose of which has never been determined.[3] Having encountered a debacle in politics, as a result of which he killed Alexander Hamilton, Burr was

[3] Walter F. McCaleb, *Aaron Burr Conspiracy* (New York, 1903); Edward Channing, *The Jeffersonian System 1801-1811* (New York, 1906), pp. 155-168.

seeking to rehabilitate himself in that section of the United States where his deed was most approved and where the political party with which he had been affiliated was strongest. His plans seem to have been indefinite and doubtless would have been modified to suit any opportunity.

In any event, force was considered necessary to assure even a small measure of success, and, to that end, Blennerhassett's energies and means were enlisted in the work of recruiting and equipping soldiers for the proposed undertaking. While the latter worked in and about Marietta, Ohio, Burr was active in Tennessee and elsewhere. The two finally joined each other at the mouth of the Cumberland River, whence, with the aid of thirteen boats and about a hundred men, they descended the Ohio and the Mississippi to a point near Natchez, where the party dispersed to avoid the arrest of its leaders. After wandering in the wilderness about a month, Burr was apprehended and carried to Richmond, Virginia, where he was held to answer a charge of high treason. Meanwhile, Blennerhassett had also been arrested and was held under a similar charge.

The legal proceedings that followed constitute one of the choice comedies of American justice and politics.[4] After being detained for some time, during which Burr was given the liberties of Richmond and was wined and dined by its leading Federalists, he was arraigned there before Chief Justice Marshall, a political enemy of Jefferson who earnestly sought the conviction of Burr. Some of the prosecuting witnesses came from the vicinity of Blennerhassett's home, but not one of them, to say nothing of the necessary two, could testify as an eyewitness to an overt treasonable act on the part of Burr. As this evidence is necessary for conviction under the Constitution, he was allowed to go free, to the great delight of the Federalists. Both he and Blennerhassett were held on other charges, but neither was ever brought to trial. Blennerhassett was ruined, however, and his dream of a sylvan paradise was shattered; he died in abject poverty. Yet the story of his life still lives among the traditions of Parkersburg and its environs.

THE COMING OF THE STEAMBOAT

In the midst of the Burr trial, an event of the greatest consequence to American commerce and to the commerce of the world took place. For the Ohio Valley, it was one of the most important incidents in the annals of that territory. It was the practical application of steam to water transportation, first achieved by Robert Fulton with his "Clermont," on the Hudson, in 1807. Two years later, he and his associates had the Ohio sur-

[4] Thomas Carpenter, *The Trial of Aaron Burr,* 3 vols. (Washington, 1807).

veyed, with a view to the use of their invention on that river; and, in 1811, their agent, Nicholas J. Roosevelt, completed, at Pittsburgh, the "New Orleans," the first practical steamboat built on the inland waters of America.

Although this boat descended the Ohio and the Mississippi successfully and entered a profitable trade between New Orleans and Natchez, the practicability of steam navigation on the inland rivers was not thus established. There remained to be determined whether or not steamboats could be operated with profit against the swifter and more uncertain currents of the Ohio, the upper Mississippi, and the numerous tributaries of each. Under favorable but abnormal conditions, the "Enterprise," a small boat of forty-five tons, ran from New Orleans to Louisville in forty-five days; but there were still doubts about the practicability of steam navigation under normal conditions.

Fortunately, these misgivings were soon dispelled when a boat named the "Washington" was built at Wheeling, Virginia, in 1817, by George White, under the direction of Captain Henry M. Shreve, an outstanding character among the early steamboatmen on the Ohio and the Mississippi. Under Shreve's command, the "Washington" made the run from New Orleans to Louisville in twenty-five days, under normal conditions. The event was heralded with delight throughout the Ohio Valley; Louisville celebrated it with a public dinner in honor of Captain Shreve, who took advantage of the occasion to predict that the running time of steamboats between New Orleans and Louisville would be reduced from twenty-five to ten days. He lived to see it reduced to five.

In Trans-Allegheny Virginia the results of the application of steam to navigation were numerous and far reaching. In less than ten years, sternwheelers and other specially designed craft ascended the Kanawha to Charleston, and the Monongahela to Morgantown. In a short time thereafter, smaller streams including even the Elk, a tributary of the Kanawha, were being successfully navigated; and boatyards were established in almost every town and city along the Ohio River. Moreover, timbermen found employment in supplying boat-building materials, chiefly gunwhales, which were hewed from native trees and floated downstream to boatyards.

THE WAR OF 1812

In the War of 1812, western Virginia made a creditable record. Ardently Republican and motivated by a desire for vengeance because of Indian atrocities, the inhabitants of that region early espoused the cause of free trade and sailor's rights. When the call to arms came, they were not outdone by any of the "War Hawks."[5] In all, fifty-two companies were enrolled, wholly or in part, and each of sixteen counties supplied at least one major and one colonel. Following the surrender of General Hull at Detroit, western Virginia was asked to raise a brigade of its own. In response, more than a thousand men enlisted, and, after a short rendezvous at Point Pleasant, under the command of General Joel Leftwich, they joined General Harrison in northern Ohio.

When eastern Virginia was invaded in 1814, volunteers from the western counties hurried to the rescue in large numbers. Their conduct was long remembered in the East. Referring to it in the Constitutional Convention of 1829-1830, Charles F. Mercer said:

> At the cry of invasion and danger from the East, every man of the West, from the summit of the Blue Ridge, to the shores of the Ohio, capable of bearing arms, mounted his knapsack and turned his face from home. . . . In a fortnight, 15,000 men were mustered in sight of the Capitol. . . . In one morning a thousand of them were discharged as supernumeraries. On their return home, they met the eagles of the West, still sweeping their flight to the East.

TRANSPORTATION AND ENTERTAINMENT

Following the Treaty of Ghent, which ended the War of 1812, western Virginia, together with other sections of the interior, entered upon a new era in its development. Outstanding among the factors making for progress in the upper Ohio Valley was the completion of the Cumberland, or National, Road to Wheeling, in 1818. At once, the stagecoach tended to displace the Conestoga wagon and similar vehicles, as a means of conveyance to and from the West. In a short time, James Reeside, later known as the "Land Admiral"—who numbered among his friends General Jackson, Henry Clay, Thomas Hart Benton, John J. Crittenden, and others equally distinguished—was operating over the route his famous line of stages, organized in relays.[6] Although only a short section of this road was in Virginia, its close proximity to her northern boundary throughout a distance of more than two hundred miles caused its influence to be felt almost as much as in the states through which it passed for longer distances.

Simultaneously, other routes of travel leading for long distances through territory now embraced in West Virginia were functioning in a manner equally spectacular. By 1808, cattle drivers from Ohio and Kentucky were

[5] W. Va. Dept. of Archives and History, *Third Biennial Report* (1911), pp. 142-185.

[6] Thomas B. Searight, *The Old Pike* (Uniontown, Pa., 1894), pp. 16, 107-116; Archer B. Hulbert, *The Cumberland Road* (Cleveland, O., 1904), Ch. 4.

passing over the Kanawha route in search of eastern markets for such of their hogs, sheep, and cattle as survived the attacks of bears and wolves en route. By 1826, the number of hogs passing this way annually was estimated at sixty thousand, while going to the West, at the same time, might have been seen immigrants, slave coffles, and wagons of all descriptions. Meanwhile, less important intermediary routes were passing to and fro their burdens of human beings, carriages, and livestock. This was notably true of what later became the Northwestern Turnpike.

The following description of the traffic going by way of the Kanawha route in 1829 is from the pen of a contemporary:

> During the past year the roads passing through Charleston have been crowded with travel of every sort. There was the seeker for health passing from the mountains; the adventurer, who after years of absence, was returning to the home of his infancy; the emigrant from the sand hills and red clay of eastern Virginia wending his way to the land of promise far toward the setting sun, gladly changing the country of herrings and chinquopins for one not flowing with milk and honey but producing abundantly of the more substantial enjoyments of "hog and hominy"; the farmer and the speculator with their herds of swine, horses and mules, in defiance of the tariff phobia and anti-hog resolutions of Georgia and South Carolina, passing onward to the gold region, wisely calculating that their brethren of the South will exchange their "yellow dirt" for the good cheer which they bring them and find it more comfortable to live upon bacon than hasty resolutions and *paper manifestoes;* the demon in human form, the dealer in bones and sinew, driving hundreds of his "fellow worms," clanking the chains of their servitude, through the free air of our valley, and destined to send back to us from the banks of the Mississippi the sugar and the cotton of that soil moistened with sweat and blood—all these and more we have seen passing in review before us in the course of a few months.[7]

All along these routes of travel, "entertainment" became a regular and profitable business. Inns, ordinaries, hostelries, taverns, and, toward the twenties, a few hotels were established by county courts, which fixed rates for bed and board, together with prices of beverages. Some of these taverns and inns were also health resorts. An example is that at the White Sulphur Springs, frequented by rheumatics since the days of the Revolution. By the twenties, the resort had become a famous social and political center, visited by cotton planters, politicians, and tourists. Soon Red Sulphur Springs, Old Sweet Springs, and Salt Sulphur Springs, all in Monroe County, became formidable rivals of the White Sulphur, particularly with those seeking the restoration of their health; and taverns and inns offering first-class "entertainment" were to be found at more or less regular intervals on all main-traveled routes and on the less-frequented lateral roads and turnpikes.

[7] Ambler, *Transportation,* Ch. 5; James M. Callahan, *Semi-Centennial History of West Virginia* (Charleston, W. Va., 1913), p. 100; Wm. A. MacCorkle, *The White Sulphur Springs* (Charleston, W. Va., 1924); *Kanawha Register* (Charleston, Va.), February 5, 1830.

Ordinaries and hostelries on their dangling, rattling signboards announced "Entertainment for Man and Beast" and keepers catered to hog and cattle drivers. One of these signs read:

> Daniel Ruffner has opened a place of private entertainment at his commodious residence one and one-half miles from Charleston on the road leading thence to Lewisburg. His pastures are extensive, and corn abundant. He will therefore be able to accommodate the cattle and hog merchants. For travelers on horseback or in carriages he will be able to furnish good stables well equipped with all kinds of provender for horses.[8]

BANKS AND BANKING

In the period immediately following the War of 1812, the greatest economic need of western Virginia was credit and banking facilities. In their absence it was almost impossible to carry on business and to accommodate the thousands of travelers who were then passing through that section annually. At the time there were only two banks in all Virginia, and they were located in Richmond. Along with the banks of neighboring states, they too had suspended specie payment. Thus, western Virginia was left without a medium of exchange, except coin, which was too scarce to be a factor. It was under these conditions that private citizens established unincorporated banks. These issued notes without legal authorization, in somewhat the same way that distillers later made "moonshine." Like the liquor, the notes served a need, however, and consequently circulated freely, as determined by the reputation of their respective producers.

Knowing that this condition could not continue and that the east would probably insist upon retaining its banking monopoly, interested parties in the western counties launched a reform movement that had in view a redistribution of representation in the general assembly and an extension of suffrage to nonfreeholders. Their purpose was to control the general assembly so that they could give themselves banks and other things long denied them by the conservative east. To further this end, a convention was called, to meet in Staunton, in August, 1816.[9] It was at this juncture that Thomas Jefferson wrote his famous letter to Samuel Kercheval, of Winchester, again espousing the cause of reform in the state government. The assembly remained deaf to all such suggestions; but, in 1817, it estab-

[8] *Kanawha Western Virginian and Kanawha County Gazette,* November 1, 1826; *Western Virginian,* July 2, 1828, and October 29, 1828.

[9] George T. Starnes, *Branch Banking in Virginia* (New York, 1931), Chs. 2-3; *Niles Weekly Register,* Vol. XI, 17-24; Charles H. Ambler, *Thomas Ritchie, a Study in Virginia Politics* (Richmond, 1913), pp. 66-68.

lished two banks beyond the mountains: one at Winchester, the other at Wheeling.[10] Moreover, these banks were allowed to establish branches in neighboring towns, and the agitation for reform ceased temporarily.

INDUSTRY

The growth of industry was the impelling force back of the demand for banks. At the same time it laid the basis for a new order of things in western Virginia. Along the Kanawha the chief interest centered in salt making, which was put on a paying basis about 1808 by the "Ruffner Brothers," David and Joseph. After much experimenting with deep borings and improved casings, they made available satisfactory quantities of brine of superior quality, and made it possible to produce almost unlimited quantities of salt at reduced prices. As a result, "Kanawha salt" came into general use throughout a large section of the Ohio Valley. It was especially prized for curing and preserving meats, and for domestic uses.

Attracted by these conditions and opportunities, numerous competitors entered the saltmaking industry. By 1814, a stretch six and one-half miles long, the "Salines," on the Kanawha above Charleston, was given over to saltmaking. The substitution of coal for wood as fuel for the furnaces stimulated production, which had risen from almost nothing, in 1808, to more than six hundred thousand bushels annually, in 1814, and gave employment to from two thousand to twenty-five hundred persons, who built and operated boats, dug coal, made barrels, and performed the numerous other services necessary to keep the various saltmaking establishments in operation. Negro slaves were among those thus employed. Some slaves were owned by saltmakers, and others were engaged by the year under contract between their masters and their employers.

With a limited market and no protection from outside importations by way of the Great Lakes and the Mississippi River, competition among salt producers threatened the future of their industry. The price fell from five to two dollars per bushel, and producers were on the verge of insolvency. To avert these and other possible calamities, in 1817, producers pooled their interests in the form of a trust, operative as of January 1, 1818. Un-

---

10 The bank at Wheeling was named the "Northwestern Bank of Virginia," and that at Winchester the "Bank of the Valley of Virginia." The capital stock of each was to be not less than $400,000, nor more than $600,000. The directors of the former were authorized to establish branches at Wellsburg, Morgantown, and Clarksburg, while those of the latter were authorized to establish a branch in one of the counties of Jefferson, Berkeley, Hardy, or Hampshire. Starnes, *Banking,* p. 62; Va. General Assembly, *Acts* (1817), Chs. 49, 55-68; *Niles Weekly Register,* Vol. XI, 336.

der this arrangement, each producer placed the control of his establishment in the hands of a board of directors and such officers as it might elect. These allotted quotas to individual producers, fixed prices, regulated the time and amount of all shipments, and apportioned monthly dividends. This monopoly, one of the first in the United States and certainly one of the first of importance in the Ohio Valley, aroused resentment. Finally, complaints regarding it reached the Federal Government, which ordered an investigation. Nevertheless, Kanawha salt producers continued to act more or less co-operatively. With one accord, they sponsored a protective tariff and otherwise demonstrated their approval of the American System.[11]

Meanwhile, other factors were stimulating industry. Outstanding among them was the introduction of an improved breed of sheep, the Merino.[12] In a few years, counties of northwest Virginia contained thousands of these animals; their wool product was being extensively fabricated in the numerous woolen mills which then appeared in every town of that section, and in the carding and weaving plants which came to occupy a prominent place at the country crossroads, to say nothing of that used in the home with the aid of domestic devices.

Among other factors for this new industrial order were the improvement of steam navigation; the War of 1812, with its numerous demands; and the completion of roads and turnpikes, notably the Cumberland, or National, Road. Under the impetus of such forces, the iron industry continued to prosper in Monongalia and in neighboring counties to the eastward. The Jackson Iron Works on Cheat River was known far and near for the fine quality of its products.[13] Toward the end of this period, Wheeling had four iron foundries, four woolen and cotton mills, four steam engine plants, two paper mills, four sawmills, and eight glass plants. Wellsburg had two glass plants, one paper mill, one woolen factory, and two potteries. Moreover, both Wellsburg and Wheeling were centers of large flour-milling industries, whose total product reached almost three hundred thousand barrels annually, more than half of which was sold on the lower Mississippi and in the West Indies.[14]

---

[11] See Charleston (W. Va.) *Gazette,* July 25, 1920, for copy of original contract; *Congressional Debates,* Vol. VII, 127, 131, 136, and Vol. VIII, Part 3, 3314, 3469; M. F. Maury and William Fontaine, *Resources of West Virginia* (Wheeling, 1876).

[12] Beall, "Sheep and Wool," in Maury and Fontaine, *Resources,* Ch. 6; Henry S. Randall, *Fine Wool Sheep Husbandry* (New York, 1863).

[13] Samuel T. Wiley, *History of Monongalia County* (Kingwood, 1883), pp. 254-259, and *History of Preston County* (Kingwood, 1882); James M. Callahan, *History of West Virginia,* 3 vols. (Chicago, 1923), Vol. I, 135, 142, 155, 231-232, and *Semi-Centennial History of West Virginia,* pp. 49, 51, 60, 65, 67-68, 81, 118.

[14] For a review of the Wheeling industries of about 1815, see Wheeling *Intelligencer,* April 12, 1879.

THE TARIFF AND INTERNAL IMPROVEMENTS

The potency of these and possibly still other factors in changing western Virginia from particularism to nationalism is seen in the attitude of that section toward the tariff. The extreme northwest counties cast the only vote given by Virginia for the protective tariff of 1824. In 1828, Virginia gave three votes for the "Tariff of Abominations"; these votes were cast, however, by representatives from an area suggesting, in its extent and boundaries, the present state of West Virginia. Residents of this area sent delegates to the famous Harrisburg Convention of 1827, called in the interest of the protective tariff, and they petitioned Congress to retain protective duties on woolens and salt. The duty on salt was urged because it was being brought to New Orleans as ballast for ships and distributed along the Mississippi and the Ohio by steamboats; while the tariff on woolens was asked to preserve the sheep-raising and woolen industries against British competition.

The attitude of western Virginia on the subject of internal improvements was even more suggestive of a reversion to nationalism. With the completion of the Cumberland Road, and the subsequent success of New York and Ohio in constructing extensive internal improvements, western Virginia began to petition Congress and the assembly for appropriations for roads and canals. The sectional character of the vote of Virginia upon congressional proposals affecting internal improvements suggests that already described in connection with the tariff. After the Federal Survey Bill became a law (1824), western Virginia was literally overrun by surveyors and others engaged in locating routes for proposed roads and canals. About the same time, the newly organized Baltimore and Ohio Railroad Company was requesting a right of way across Virginia for its proposed lines, a route by way of the Potomac, the Shenandoah, and the Kanawha rivers being preferred. The result was a generally awakened interest in internal improvements that put upon the Federal Government main reliance for financial aid.

This tendency was manifested most strongly in the presidential election of 1828.[15] In this contest, a majority of Trans-Allegheny Virginia counties voted for John Q. Adams, while the vote in most of the other counties of western Virginia was closely divided between Adams and his victorious rival, General Jackson. Adams' inaugural address, with its statements to the effect that he would lay low the mountains and the hills and exalt the valleys by a comprehensive system of internal improve-

---

15 For maps showing the votes, by counties, of the elections of 1824 and 1828, see Ambler, *Sectionalism*, pp. 130-134.

ments, although ridiculed elsewhere, had been believed in western Virginia. So strong was the resulting Adams sentiment in that quarter that William C. Rives, a critic of the nationalistic tendencies, accused his opponents of using "political engineering" and "topographical arguments" to smother out Jackson majorities in western Virginia.

Chapter XI

The Constitutional Convention of 1829-1830

GEOGRAPHIC SECTIONS

DURING THE THREE DECADES immediately preceding 1830, Trans-Allegheny Virginia was comparatively prosperous. It became a land of newspapers; transportation facilities became increasingly adequate; and thousands of persons crossed it annually to and from the east. As a result, a white population of less than 40,000 in 1800 trebled by 1830, and Negro slaves showed an even greater percentage increase. Nine counties became sixteen, and two score or more towns were either newly incorporated or received new charters. In the decade ending 1810, the new counties formed in Trans-Allegheny Virginia, together with those from which they were taken, were: Mason, from Kanawha, 1804; and Cabell, from Mason, 1809. To these were added before 1820: Tyler, from Ohio, 1814; Lewis, from Harrison and Randolph, 1816; Preston, from Monongalia and Randolph, 1818; and Nicholas, from Greenbrier, Kanawha, and Randolph, in the same year. During the next decade, only one new county, Logan (1824), was formed. It was created out of parts of Cabell, Giles, Tazewell, and Kanawha.

To the east between the Alleghenies and the Blue Ridge and including southwestern Virginia and the Eastern Panhandle of West Virginia, popularly known as "the Valley," were twenty-four other counties. In

1830, these contained a total white population in excess of 150,000, and a total Negro population of more than 40,000. For some time their delegates and senators in the general assembly had voted with those from the Trans-Allegheny. As indicated elsewhere, the Shenandoah Valley and its environs had been strongly Federalist during most of the life of that party; and now sheep raising, together with increasing activity in iron smelting and, in the extreme southwest, in saltmaking, tended to make the entire Valley nationalistic, after the manner of the Trans-Allegheny. New counties in this area, now a part of West Virginia, were: Jefferson, taken from Berkeley, 1801; Morgan, from Berkeley and Hampshire, 1820; and Pocahontas, from Bath, Pendleton, Randolph, and Greenbrier, 1821.

Farther east, including both the Piedmont and the Tidewater, were sixty-seven other counties, with a total white population of approximately 375,000 and a Negro population, including 40,000 freemen, of 457,000. The basis of the economic life for both sections was agriculture, the income from which was supplemented by returns from the domestic slave trade. Danville, Norfolk, and Alexandria were centers of this traffic.[1] But the counties of the upper Piedmont did not contain many Negroes and had economic interests not unlike the counties west of the mountains. In the assembly, both delegates and senators from the former tended to vote with those from the Valley and the Trans-Allegheny. This tended to maintain a fairly even political balance between the two grand sections, the transmontane and the cismontane.

Under these conditions, the counties in the Trans-Allegheny made no complaint of their treatment by the east. Except for desired internal improvements, they had been able to get about what they wanted. Following 1810, a redistribution of state senators, together with the creation of new counties, each of which was entitled to two delegates in the lower house of the assembly, left little to be desired on the score of representation for the time being and for some time in the future. As late as 1830 the Trans-Allegheny had a larger representation in the house of delegates than its white population would have warranted on a basis of equal representation for equal numbers.

Under normal conditions, eastern Virginia would, in all probability, have continued to make concessions to western Virginia in representation and in suffrage; but, the Tidewater and the Piedmont were overtaken by an economic depression that tended to blind their leadership. As usual in such circumstances, the impotency thus induced was accompanied by elements of distrust, which can best be understood in the light of economic causes. Former tobacco lands were being given over to broom sedge and pines; during a short period immediately preceding 1829, land values declined from $206,000,000 to $90,000,000, and exports fell from $8,000,000

[1] Frederic Bancroft, *Slave-Trading in the Old South* (Baltimore, 1931).

to almost $3,000,000. Meanwhile, John Randolph was threatening to run away from his Negroes and predicting that deer and wild turkeys would soon be as plentiful in the environs of Williamsburg as they then were in the wilds of Kentucky; Madison could not secure a loan from the United States Bank; Jefferson mortgaged his home to pay debts incurred by the financial failures of friends; and James Monroe became dependent upon relatives. It mattered not that some inhabitants traced their undoing to the protective tariff, while others found it in emigration to the South and the West. The crisis was real, and it embarrassed everyone and complicated everything.

ANOTHER REFORM MOVEMENT

It was under these conditions that the comparatively prosperous counties of western Virginia joined in agitation for reform in their state and local governments. The Valley was especially interested in a redistribution of representation. On the other hand, the Trans-Allegheny was chiefly interested in extending suffrage and in reforming local institutions, particularly the county government. Its industrial population was increasing rapidly and asked the suffrage as a drawing card to other immigrants. Moreover, the system of close corporations, under which the county government was conducted, was galling to an intelligent and ambitious population, composed mostly of newcomers.

In its early stages, this movement met with favor in all sections. In 1824, several counties in the east, acting independently of the general assembly, polled their voters on the question of a constitutional convention and gave majorities for it;[2] Jefferson again came from retirement to advocate reform; and both Thomas Ritchie, of the Richmond *Enquirer,* and John Hampden Pleasants, of the Richmond *Whig,* endorsed it editorially. The advisability of reform was debated favorably in Richmond; and petitions came from all parts of the east, asking for a new constitution. Under this pressure, the house of delegates (1824-1825) passed a bill authorizing a vote of the people upon the question, but it failed to pass the more conservative senate.

In the years immediately following 1825, the reform movement in Virginia became largely a contest between nationalism and state rights, or particularism. By an analysis of the vote of the general assembly of 1828 to submit a proposal calling a constitutional convention, the editor of the

---

[2] Richmond *Enquirer,* May 16, 1824; *Niles Weekly Register,* Vol. XXVI, 117, 179.

Winchester *Republican* showed that ninety-nine of the one hundred twenty-six state rights men in that body had voted against it. In the course of the debate that followed, Benjamin Watkins Leigh asserted that the convention had been called "to overthrow the doctrine of state rights," and he observed, furthermore, that when "the Federal Government points a road along the Valley, or along the foot of the Blue Ridge, or across the country at the head of Tidewater—state rights fall or tremble at the very sight of the tremendous undertaking."[3]

The referendum on the constitutional convention, taken in 1828, resulted in 21,896 votes for, to 16,646 against. An analysis of this vote shows the large, populous counties of the Valley—along the Potomac, and in the northwest—together with a few of the larger counties of the Piedmont's foothills and the old Federalist stronghold, Accomac County, voting "yes." The remaining counties opposed, in varying degrees. For instance, the Tidewater, other than the Eastern Shore, was all but unanimous in the negative; the Piedmont was almost equally divided; and, in the Trans-Allegheny, approximately one fourth of the votes polled were "no." A belt of counties extending along the whole southern and southwestern portion of what is now West Virginia gave negative majorities.

ORGANIZATION AND PERSONNEL OF THE CONVENTION

Although the constitutional convention had been endorsed by a majority of the voting population, it was with much difficulty that the general assembly called it. After weeks of debate it was decided that each of the twenty-four senatorial districts, into which the state was then divided, would be allowed to elect four delegates. Theoretically, this was a concession to the reformers. Practically, however, it meant their defeat, because the senate was then elected upon a basis of white population as determined by the census of 1810; but no restriction, either as to the office which the delegates held or the place of their residence, was imposed upon the voters in their selections.

This liberal arrangement, together with the importance of the occasion, enabled the voters to make good selections; and they did. Among the delegates chosen by districts east of the mountains were two ex-Presidents of the United States, James Madison and James Monroe; the Chief Justice of the United States Supreme Court, John Marshall; the

[3] *Niles Weekly Register,* Vol. XXXVI, 65; Va. Con. Conv. *Debates* (1829-1830), p. 154.

Governor, William B. Giles; two United States Senators, John Tyler and Littleton W. Tazewell; a number of Representatives in Congress, of whom the most prominent were John Randolph, Charles F. Mercer, and Philip P. Barbour; and judges and lawyers of more than local prominence. Outstanding among the delegates from that part of the Valley now embraced in Virginia were: Samuel McDowell Moore, Chapman Johnson, and Briscoe G. Baldwin. Delegates from the Trans-Allegheny included Alexander Campbell and Philip Doddridge, of Brooke County; Edwin S. Duncan, of Harrison County; Eugenius M. Wilson and Charles S. Morgan, of Monongalia County; and Lewis Summers, of Kanawha County.

While friends on the outside were calling attention to the far-reaching importance of the approaching deliberations and were reminding delegates of the fact that the "eyes of the world were upon them," the convention organized in Richmond, October 5, 1829, in the presence of distinguished visitors from many parts of the United States and from abroad, who had come to drink of Virginia's eloquence at its fountain head. James Monroe was made president; secretaries and reporters were designated; and the convention then adjourned while four of its committees—each composed of one delegate from each of the twenty-four districts—on the Bill of Rights and the legislative, executive, and judicial departments of the government, respectively, prepared reports as a basis of discussion.

The first important contest of the convention came in the committee on the Bill of Rights. The eastern delegates were for passing this matter by until later in the deliberations and finally carried a recommendation to that effect. From the beginning, the western delegates opposed this course. Instead they wished to begin where the framers of 1776 had left off. To this end, they insisted upon rewriting the Bill of Rights. Those favoring this course claimed that a new bill of rights should contain a declaration for equal representation for equal numbers of people, and for free white manhood suffrage. Speaking later of their failure in this matter, Alexander Campbell said:

> So anxious were some gentlemen here to put to sea, that when we called for the compass and the pilot, they exclaimed: Never mind, we will get the compass and the pilot when we get to port. We are now a thousand miles from land. Gentlemen are making fine speeches upon the elements of the ocean, and now and then upon the art of sailing. It will be well if the *rari nantes in gurgite vasto,* apply not to us.[4]

Meanwhile, the committee on the legislative department was having difficulty in making a report. The reformers controlled twelve of its twenty-four members, and the conservatives eleven, while Madison, the

[4] Va. Con. Conv., *Debates* (1829-1830), p. 117.

twenty-fourth member, refused to concede the extreme demands of either side. Reformers, like Doddridge, stood out for the white basis of representation in both houses and for a general extension of suffrage. On the other hand, the conservatives desired a basis for both houses to be determined by a compound ratio of white population and direct taxes. Madison favored the white basis for one house, but opposed it for both. As a result, the committee finally recommended that "in the apportionment of representation in the House of Delegates regard should be had to the white population exclusively," and said nothing about a basis for the senate, which was left to be determined by the convention. It also recommended an extension of suffrage.

CONVENTION DEBATES

In its first stages, the debate that followed on the basis of representation took a theoretical turn. The reformers tended to adhere to "eternal truths" and "natural rights." In support of these fundamentals, they reverted to John Locke and John Milton and had much to say about a state of nature in its supposed connection with the origins of governmental institutions. Thus fortified, they demanded the creation of a government under which the people could rule by majority votes. A few delegates from counties east of the Blue Ridge agreed with these contentions, notably Robert B. Taylor, of Norfolk, who, because of protests from his constituents, was forced to leave the convention before it completed its deliberations.

Although there was not unanimity in the conservative ranks—older heads, such as Madison, Monroe, Marshall, and Randolph, tending to concede some of the demands of the westerners and opposing all attempts to depart from the Bill of Rights *in toto;* and younger leaders, such as Benjamin Watkins Leigh and Abel P. Upshur, conceding nothing—the conservatives generally agreed in denying the requests of the reformers. Denouncing the Bill of Rights as a compilation of "metaphysical subtleties," the extremists in the conservative ranks defended the rights of property, as such, to a representation in the law-making bodies of the state. Upshur insisted that this was particularly true in Virginia, where one great section of the state, the cismontane, possessed a "peculiar" property that might be subjected to unjust taxation and even fanatical assault from the other section, the transmontane. Admitting the possibility of separating property and people as policy-determining factors in government, Leigh believed it would be inexpedient to do so; he insisted that, as soon as the separation was felt, property would either purchase people or they would destroy property. Therefore, he warned against the folly of establishing a government whose constitution contained germs of anarchy and corruption.[5]

To these contentions, delegates from the western counties replied that property, of whatever kind, had intrinsic qualities which had always enabled it to protect itself, and that added power, expressly conferred, had always operated to deprive individuals of their rights and liberties. Admitting, for argument's sake, the desirability of providing for two majorities—a majority of numbers and a majority of property—Campbell insisted that this would necessitate the consideration of still other majorities: namely, those of intellect, physical strength, scientific skill, and general literature, which he maintained were as dear to some men as the possession of Negro slaves was to others.

With increasing references to such subjects as taxation and Negro slavery, the convention debates took a practical turn. As already indicated, the chief differences between eastern and western Virginia were those separating particularists and nationalists. Taking the "exactions of the federal government and the state government together," Leigh doubted "whether there is a people on earth more heavily taxed than the slaveholding planters of Virginia." He, therefore, opposed the white basis of representation because, if adopted, it would cause representation to "rise in the Mountains, and overflow and drown the Lowlands; while *taxation,* rising in the Lowlands, and reversing the course of nature, will flow to the Mountains, and there spend, if not waste its fertilizing streams, over every narrow valley and deep glen."

Although admitting that they did not pay as much taxes as did the easterners, the westerners denied any intention on their part to impose upon the former by collecting from them oppressive and unjust taxes for the purpose of building roads west of the Blue Ridge Mountains. Reminding the east of the fact that the internal improvement projects of the west were a legacy from "the fathers," and that later legislatures had kept them alive by promises made only to be broken, to the great detriment of the whole state, the reformers tried to quiet the suspicions of their opponents by assuring them that Negro slavery was increasing in the west and that this might be expected to continue until the economic unity of Virginia had been effected.

Scorning all statements to the effect that the western counties would become slaveholding to a degree sufficient to affect their attitude toward the east, Upshur analyzed the situation in these words: "There exists in

---

5 Ambler, *Sectionalism,* pp. 152-153; Va. Con. Conv., *Debates* (1829-1830), p. 156.

a great portion of the west, a rooted antipathy to this species of population; the habits of the people are strongly opposed to it. With them, personal industry, and a reliance on personal exertion, is the order of society. They know how little slave labor is worth; while their feelings as free men forbid them to work by the side of a slave. And besides, Sir, their vicinity to non-slave-holding States, must forever render this sort of property precarious and insecure."[6]

Realizing the force of the arguments of their opponents, some of the westerners were willing to accord slave-holders constitutional guarantees for the protection of their property, provided the white basis were conceded. But the conservatives spurned all suggestions of "paper guarantees." Barbour was unwilling to accept any arrangement which the west had both the interest and the power to violate. Upshur insisted that there could be no guarantee for the protection of slave property in any government other than that which came from the possession of political power by its owners.

The convention next proceeded to discuss suffrage. In support of white manhood suffrage, the reformers quoted Jefferson and demanded their natural right. Other features of their arguments were more practical. For instance, mention was made of the fact that Virginia was then the only state in the Union adhering to freehold suffrage and that the recent exodus of whites was due, in a measure, to their inability to participate in their own government. Asserting that the time was near at hand "when not only Virginia, but all the Southern States, must be essentially military!"—Morgan, of Monongalia County, believed it expedient to call forth "every free white human being and to unite them in the same common interest and government."

In answer to these arguments, the east had ready replies. John Randolph denied that Jefferson was an authority on any subject, unless it be the mechanism of a plow. Voicing a protest against the rising tide of Jacksonian democracy, others asserted that an extension of suffrage had always preceded democratic revolution, toward which they professed to believe that the United States were then drifting. However, their general attitude was probably best expressed by Leigh, who classed white manhood suffrage with other plagues: the Hessian fly, the varioloid, the influenza, the smallpox, and the circuit court system, which had arisen in the North and later spread to the South above the Fall Line in the great rivers.[7]

---

[6] Va. Con. Conv., *Debates* (1829-1830), p. 76.

[7] Va. Con. Conv., *Debates* (1829-1830), p. 407.

THE NEW CONSTITUTION

But for the willingness of the delegates from the districts in the upper Piedmont, together with a solitary delegate from west of the Blue Ridge —Cooke, of Frederick County—to compromise their differences, this argument might have continued indefinitely. As finally agreed upon, no "principle" for future apportionments of representation in either house of the assembly was adopted. Instead, a plan was approved for a senate of thirty-two members and a house of one hundred thirty-four delegates. These were allotted arbitrarily, nineteen senators to the cismontane section, and thirteen to the transmontane; whereas the Tidewater was given thirty-six delegates, the Piedmont forty-two, the Valley twenty-five, and the Trans-Allegheny thirty-one. Reapportionments were provided for in 1841 and at intervals of ten years thereafter, providing they were concurred in by two thirds of each house, and the senators never exceeded thirty-six nor the delegates one hundred fifty.

Other proposals, some of them compromises, included the following: suffrage was extended to leaseholders and housekeepers under requirements that excluded more than thirty thousand white men of legal age; the executive power was vested in a governor, elected by joint ballot of the assembly for a term of three years; although reduced in size and in powers, the executive council was retained; judges of the higher courts were to be elected by a joint ballot of the assembly; and justices of the peace remained appointive by the executive, as did sheriffs. There was no provision for future amendments to the constitution. The vote on the completed document was: 55 ayes to 40 nays. Cooke was the only delegate from west of the Blue Ridge to vote "yes," and Stanard the only one from east of that divide to vote "no."

DISMEMBERMENT SUGGESTED

While these results were being worked out, the possible dismemberment of the state was being discussed generally. There were few issues of the Richmond *Enquirer* for December, 1829, that did not mention the possibility of the western delegates retiring to make a constitution of their own. Later, Doddridge admitted that they had contemplated such a course. On the other hand, the preservation of the united Commonwealth was only a second wish with Leigh; and Morris, of Hanover County, warned the westerners that they could not emancipate the slaves of Virginia or even impose a tax upon them without causing a sword to be unsheathed that would "be red with blood before it found the scabbard." Older heads were more conservative and considerate of consequences. They saw in the forceful separation of Virginia the initial step in a movement that would result in the dismemberment of the Union, a result which they deplored.

Nevertheless, the Trans-Allegheny could not accept the constitution finally determined upon. It had entered the reform movement with no grievance on the score of representation. Now it found itself bound hand and foot for an indefinite time. Worse still, it was on the point of being deserted by its ally, the Valley, which had been the aggressor during the entire affair. It mattered not that the Valley delegates, with one exception, had voted to disapprove the work of the convention. There was no denying the fact that the Valley was comparatively satisfied with the results and that the Trans-Allegheny would have to fight alone in the future, against greater odds than in the past.

Under the circumstances, the first thought of the Trans-Allegheny people was of immediate dismemberment.[8] To this end, a writer in the Wheeling *Gazette* for April 6, 1830, suggested that the west call a convention of its own and that it appoint commissioners empowered to treat with the "eastern nabobs for a division of the state—peacefully if we can, forcefully if we must." Already, citizens of Ohio County, in mass meeting assembled, had resolved, "That a constitution characterized by and composed of such ingredients is unfit for the government of a free people"; and others were declaring that, in the event such a constitution were ratified, they would propose, for the next alternative, separation—which, it was claimed, would not be impossible, provided "the people of the West willed it."

For a time, however, milder councils prevailed, and the Trans-Allegheny directed its energies to efforts to defeat the ratification of the proposed new fundamental law. In the popular referendum which followed, some of its counties cast almost their entire vote against ratification. Out of a total of 646, Ohio County gave only 3 votes for ratification; Brooke gave no vote for it; and Harrison gave only 8 in a total of 1,128. In fact, no county in what is now West Virginia west of the Alleghenies gave a majority, or anything approaching it, for ratification. On the other hand, the Valley was more evenly divided. All of its counties approved though by small

---

[8] Wheeling *Gazette,* March 12, 1830; Richmond *Compiler,* March 12, 1830; Richmond *Enquirer,* March 23, 1830, March 26, 1830, and April 2, 1830.

majorities. The counties east of the Blue Ridge were as unanimous in their approval as those west of the Alleghenies were in their disapproval. Madison County, in the Piedmont, gave 256 votes for ratification and none against it. The total vote was 26,055 for, to 15,566 against.

As soon as this result was announced the inhabitants of the Trans-Allegheny resumed agitation for dismemberment. Some of them favored attaching themselves to Maryland or to Pennsylvania. Such was the purport of a series of articles written by "Senex," which appeared in many newspapers. In the absence of provisions for amending the new constitution, and confronted by what seemed an end to reform, "Senex" desired separate statehood for the Trans-Allegheny as a means of self-preservation. Such an eventuality, he thought, would be followed by a large inflow of capital and immigrants, both of which had previously tended to avoid that section. Incidentally, it was not as "patriots of Virginia" but as "patriots of America" that the editor of the Wheeling *Compiler* favored dismemberment and separate statehood.[9]

The willingness of contemporaries in the Valley to see the counties of the northwest go their way shows a cleavage that helps to explain the later movement culminating in the formation of West Virginia as a separate state in the Union, leaving to the mother state most of the Valley and all the counties of the southwest. Otherwise the eastern boundary of West Virginia might have been the Blue Ridge Mountains. Apropos of this point, the following from the Winchester *Republican* for December 3, 1830, is informing:

> The Virginia Legislature will convene Monday. . . . Matters of great moment will come before it, and the discussions will be as interesting as those of the late convention. The preservation of the state, we believe, will depend upon this Legislature. Dispute the claims of the Trans-Allegheny counties to what they may deem a proper share of the fund for internal improvements and *a division of the state must follow*—not immediately perhaps, but the signal will be given for the rising of the clans, and *they will rise*. It is not worth while now to speculate on the mode and manner in which the government will be opposed. Sufficient unto the day is the evil thereof. But a crisis is approaching. The northern counties demand to be separated from the state with a view to attaching themselves to Maryland or Pennsylvania; the southwestern counties go for a division of the state into two commonwealths. Should the latter be effected, what will be our condition in the Valley? Infinitely worse than the present. The mere dependency of a government whose interest and whose trade would all go westward, we would be taxed without receiving any equivalent; and instead of being chastened with whips, we would be scourged with scorpions. Of the

---

[9] *Kanawha Banner* (Charleston), September 17, 1830, October 1, 1830, October 8, 1830, and November 15, 1830.

two projects spoken of, that which would be least injurious to the Valley and the state at large, would be to part with the northwestern counties. Let them go. Let us get clear of this disaffected population. Then prosecute the improvements called for in the southwest, and that portion of our state, deprived of its northern allies, would give up its desire for a separation.

Chapter XII

Sectional Strife 1830-1850

NEGRO SLAVERY

BEFORE THE ECHOES of her Constitutional Convention of 1829-1830 had ceased to be heard, Virginia was rent by another sectional controversy which assumed threatening aspects. Negro slavery was the subject of discussion, and the proposals made for dealing with it ranged all the way from immediate abolition to an unqualified endorsement of the institution as a positive good. In the face of the silence heretofore maintained on the subject, the frankness and freedom used on this occasion astounded and confounded the members of the assembly, as well as their neighbors both in the North and in the South.[1]

This controversy was precipitated by the Nat Turner Insurrection, which occurred in Southampton County, Virginia, August 22-23, 1831, and resulted in the death of sixty-one white persons, most of them women and children. When the general assembly of 1831-1832 met, it was flooded with petitions from all sections of the state, asking that action be taken regarding the slave and Negro problems. Some of these petitions requested that the state undertake the immediate emancipation of all slaves and that all freedmen be deported, others asked for Federal aid to accomplish these ends, and still others urged that a plan for gradual emancipation and deportation be provided.

Fearing that discussion might abet the Abolitionist movement, then

[1] See Thomas R. Dew, *Review of the Debates on the Abolition of Slavery in the Virginia Legislature of 1831-1832* (Richmond, 1832); Harrison, "A Review of the Speech of Thomas Marshall in the Virginia Assembly of 1831-1832," in *American Quarterly Review,* December, 1832; *African Repository,* March, 1833; T. M. Whitfield, *Slavery Agitation in Virginia, 1829-1832* (Baltimore, 1930).

just beginning in the North, and that it might also complicate local conditions, leaders of the slaveholding interests tried in vain to maintain silence and indifference toward their "peculiar" institution. But silence was no longer golden. All realized that slavery was at the bottom of the differences between eastern and western Virginia and that inaction on the subject meant dismemberment of the Commonwealth, if not immediately, certainly in the future. Moreover, the possibility of other insurrections had to be considered. Those desiring silence would probably have prevailed, had it not been for an editorial from the pen of Thomas Ritchie, editor of the Richmond *Enquirer,* in which he said:

> It is possible from what we learn that the committee on the colored population will report some plan for getting rid of the people of color. But is this all that can be done? Are we forever to suffer the greatest evil which can scourge our land, not only to remain but to increase within its domains? "We may shut our eyes and avert our faces, if you please," writes an eloquent South Carolinian; "but there it is, the black and gnawing evil at our doors—and meet the question we must at no distant day." God only knows what it is the part of wise men to do on that momentous and appalling subject. Of this I am sure, that the difference, nothing short of frightful, between all that exists on one side of the Potomac and all on the other side, is owing to that cause alone. The disease is deep rooted—it is at the heart's core—it is consuming and has all along been consuming our vitals, . . . something must be done.[2]

Soon thereafter, Thomas Jefferson Randolph, grandson of Thomas Jefferson and a member of the assembly, revived the postnati plan of his illustrious grandfather for dealing with the situation. As modified, it contemplated the gradual emancipation of every slave within the Commonwealth: the males, born after July 4, 1840, at the age of twenty-one; and the females, born after the same date, at the age of eighteen.

Again the slaveholding interests tried to prevent consideration of any proposals having for their purpose the freeing of the Negroes. To this end, they moved that "it is inexpedient for the present to make any legislative enactments for the abolition of slavery"; but William B. Preston, of Montgomery County, countered with a resolution of diametrically opposite purport, which became the subject of the long-drawn-out debate which followed.

Although only two years had intervened since representatives from western Virginia had spoken indulgently of Negro slavery and had even predicted its westward extension, they now regarded such an eventuality as the greatest calamity that could befall them and expressed fear lest the state laws against the domestic slave trade should force them to become slave owners in spite of themselves. By comparing eastern Virginia with western Virginia and with free states, those favoring abolition professed to see their economic salvation in the accomplishment of their desires. The

[2] Richmond *Enquirer,* January 7, 1832.

effects of slavery upon Virginia were depicted by Thomas Marshall in these words: "All the chief glories of Virginia style have faded; gone is the massive coach with its stately *attelage* of four or six; shut is the benevolent hall door; . . . the watering places no longer blaze with the rich but decent pomp of Virginians; and the cities rarely bear witness of her generous expense." His opinion of the possible effect of Negro slavery upon other inhabitants may be gathered from the following, spoken at the same time: "It [slavery] is ruinous to the whites; it retards improvements, roots out our industrious population, banishes the yeomanry from the country, and deprives the spinner, the weaver, the smith, the shoemaker, and the carpenter of employment and support."[3]

In favor of the postnati plan of emancipation, the westerners asserted that there could be no property rights in the unborn and that an act declaring them free did not infringe the rights of private property. Others admitted the validity of such rights, but insisted that a sacrifice should be made for the common good. On this point, James McDowell, of Rockbridge County, said: "Private property, which a state allows to be held by its citizens, must consist with the general end for which the state is created; the power to correct an evil tendency is inherent in all government, and the exercise of such a power is no infringement of private rights."

A few westerners based their opposition to Negro slavery upon the principles of the Declaration of Independence. One of the most eloquent efforts of this kind was that of McDowell, in which he said:

> You may place the slave where you please, you may dry up to the utmost the fountains of his feelings, the spring of his thought—you may close upon his mind the avenue to knowledge and cloud it over with artificial night—you may yoke him to your labor as an ox which liveth only to work and worketh only to live—you may put him under any process, which, without destroying his value as a slave, will debase and crush him as rational being—you may do this and the idea that he was born to be free will survive all. It is allied to his hope of immortality—it is the ethical part of his nature which oppression cannot reach—it is the torch lit up in his soul by the hand of the Deity and never meant to be extinguished by the hand of man.

In reply to these and similar arguments, the easterners denied that Negro slavery was responsible for the "gullied hillsides" and the "turned out fields" then to be seen almost everywhere east of the Blue Ridge.[4] Such spectacles, they insisted, had appeared only after the planters and their Negroes had deserted these lands to build new commonwealths in the South and the Southwest. They claimed that scientific agriculture, then just in its beginnings, would reclaim the slaveholding east, whose population had not fled from the alleged evils of Negro slavery. In proof

---

[3] *Amer. Quart. Rev.* (December, 1832), 395.

[4] For a summary of the arguments, see Whitfield, *Slavery Agitation*.

of this contention, easterners pointed to the fact that most of the former inhabitants of eastern Virginia were then to be found in the South.

Defenders of Negro slavery opposed the postnati plan of abolition on the ground of impracticability. They asserted that it would increase the demand for slaves and thus increase slave prices. Under such a stimulus, it was affirmed, the African slave trade would be revived. Moreover, the Abolitionists were reminded of the fact that "the fathers" had considered this very plan and discarded it, both before slavery had fastened itself upon the state, and after there was a sincere desire to be rid of it.

Admitting that slavery was "a mildew which had blighted . . . every region it had touched from the creation of the world," other easterners, nevertheless, opposed its abolition, except under certain conditions. Outstanding among these were: (1) the immediate removal of all freedmen from the state; (2) provisions safeguarding the rights of private property; and (3) no taking of any slave from his owner without his consent and without compensation. As a rule, the ones imposing the conditions opposed the postnati plan of emancipation, because it deprived slave owners of the child-bearing power of their female slaves, "an item of chief consideration in their sale and purchase."

A notable tendency of this debate—of importance later—was a disposition on the part of proslavery men to sneer at westerners and to make invidious comparisons. They were called the "Rufus Kings of the South"; both Charles J. Faulkner and William B. Preston were ridiculed for comparing the Abolition movement to "a great political revolution" and to "the generous efforts of the Parisian patriots of 1789"; and George W. Summers was an object of suspicion because of his loyalty to the principles of the Declaration of Independence. He was the "Byron of the West, walking on the mountain tops and gazing on the desolation which burns in the plains below."

What chafed the westerners most were implications drawn from questions then asked by the east, such as: "When our aged mothers shall call in vain for protection from their slaughtered sons, will they [westerners] be found leading or mingling with the savage foe?" Equally disconcerting were statements to the effect that in case abolition had diffused itself through the mountains of Virginia, the only alternative left to the east was dismemberment, because it was only in this way that the horrors of another Saint Bartholomew's Day could be averted.

To make matters worse for those desiring intrastate comity, proslavery Virginia began to defend its "peculiar" institution from the pages of history, from the teachings of Christianity, and from the writings of economists. In its initial phases, this was primarily the work of Thomas R. Dew, of William and Mary College, a trained political scientist recently graduated from a German university, where he had been taught that the inequality of men was fundamental in all social organizations of the highest order. These teachings were set forth by him in a powerful essay entitled "A Review of the Debates in the Virginia Legislature of 1831-32," in which he also pointed out the "insuperable" difficulties of any plan of emancipation and deportation, and deprecated the possibility of successful slave insurrections.

Those attempting to answer Dew, whether from western Virginia or elsewhere, were as voices crying in the wilderness. At any rate, this was the experience of Jesse Burton Harrison, of Lynchburg. His review of the arguments made in the Virginia Assembly of 1831-1832, intended as an answer to the ultra position taken by proslavery leaders, attracted little or no attention even in western Virginia and was published anonymously. Nor did President Madison's answer to Dew receive a more respectful and effective consideration. Although steadfastly refusing to become Abolitionists of the Garrison type, the antislavery advocates of western Virginia steadily declined in numbers. Between the "devil and the deep blue sea," they continued, however, to advocate reforms in state and county governments and to strengthen their attachment to the Union.

SLAVERY AND THE CHURCH

Although the merits and demerits of Negro slavery continued to be debated privately and publicly in both eastern and western Virginia, another clash between the sections was avoided until 1844, when the subject came up in conferences of the Methodist Episcopal Church.[5] The Baltimore, Pittsburgh, and other conferences of that denomination, which included portions of Virginia, forbade ministers to own Negroes; but, on the other hand, the state laws of both Maryland and Virginia permitted them to own this species of property and forbade manumissions. Thus, when a minister came into possession of slaves involuntarily, as some did by inheritance and otherwise, he was in the embarrassing position of violating state laws in case he freed them, and of violating church law in case he did not. The General Conference of 1840 had tried to solve this anomaly by an order permitting ministers to own slave property where state laws did not allow emancipation or permit the liberated slave to enjoy freedom; but the Baltimore Conference refused to accept this decision and suspended one of its ministers, John A. Harding, for failure to comply with its resolution forbidding ministers to own slaves.

The debate in the General Conference of 1844, to which Harding ap-

[5] John N. Norwood, *Schism in the Methodist Episcopal Church* (Alfred, N. Y., 1923); Methodist Episcopal Church General Conference, *Debates* (1844), pp. 28 ff.

pealed for reinstatement, brought into the open the gulf separating eastern and western Virginia. Harding was represented on this occasion by William A. Smith, of the Virginia Conference, an ardent pro-Southern advocate. In defense of his client, he pointed to the fact that the highest church law, that of the General Conference, permitted ministers to own slaves. He, therefore, insisted that the action of the Baltimore Conference suspending Harding was ultra-Abolitionist and asked that it be rescinded. Furthermore, he warned the church not to endanger its spiritual life by becoming embroiled in politics and charged Abolitionists with having killed the African Colonization Society. Finally, he admitted that slavery was a great evil, but he considered it beyond control, "yet not necessarily a sin." He added: "We must then quietly submit to a necessity, which we cannot control or remedy, endeavoring to carry the gospel of salvation to both master and slave."

In reply to this argument, John A. Collins, of the Baltimore Conference, admitted that abolition had killed gradual emancipation and Negro colonization, as planned by the African Colonization Society, but he denied the justice of the contention regarding the relation of ministers of the Christian religion to Negro slavery. The following excerpts from his argument expressed the attitude of a large part of the Border, certainly most of what is now West Virginia, on that subject: "We are just where we always were, standing as a breakwater to pro-slavery in the South and the waves of abolition in the North. . . . We will not combine with the enemies of the African either in the North or in the South. . . . Abolition shall not make us pro-slavery."

The appeal was decided against Harding after his case became complicated with a similar one involving Bishop James O. Andrew, of Georgia. As a result, the Methodist Episcopal Church divided into northern and southern communions; the line of division, as originally agreed upon, paralleled closely, for a part of its course, the eastern and southern boundary of present West Virginia. Lawsuits involving the possession of church property and other matters followed; as a result, most of West Virginia, together with a large part of the Border, had until 1939 two Methodist Episcopal Churches. Other churches divided, also, notably the Baptist and the Presbyterian, and for a time maintained separate communions.

THE RUFFNER PAMPHLET

While this agitation was in progress, Henry Ruffner, Samuel McDowell Moore, John Letcher, and other members of the Franklin Society of Lexington, Virginia, were debating phases of Negro slavery. As a result of their deliberations, Ruffner, a slaveholder, appealed to "the People of West Virginia" in an "Address," in which he summarized the evils of Negro slavery and asked for remedial action.[6] Among other things, he charged slavery with responsibility for keeping immigrants out of Virginia, for crippling her commerce, agriculture, and industry, for imposing hurtful social ideals upon her, and for retarding education generally. Ruffner's remedy was gradual emancipation west of the Blue Ridge Mountains, provided it could be worked out in such a manner as not to disturb property rights, and to make the freedmen industrious, intelligent, and religious beings. Of its reception, Ruffner later said: "The valley . . . objected to our movement as ill-timed while northern abolition was raging. . . . West of the Alleghenies the pamphlet was better received; but in East Virginia some papers denounced it as abolitionist."

INTERNAL IMPROVEMENTS

Meanwhile, sectional rivalry over internal improvements had not abated.[7] In the opening years of this period, western Virginia was literally alive with proposals for the construction of roads, turnpikes, canals, and railroads; and the general assembly, for the corresponding years, was flooded with petitions asking the incorporation of internal improvement companies and appropriations for the proposed undertakings. The fact that neighboring states completed internal improvement systems, while Virginia effected little other than planning, was a constant source of dissatisfaction in her western counties. This was particularly true of the failure to connect the waters of the James River with those of the Kanawha by means of a canal, and also of the indifference, at times approaching hostility, which she showed toward the Chesapeake and Ohio Canal, then in process of construction. Realizing that they could expect little from their own state, the westerners naturally looked to the Federal Government for relief and became increasingly dissatisfied with their general assembly.

An irritant conducive to the latter attitude was the opposition of the general assembly to plans of private corporations, which seemed to offer a solution for the internal improvement problems of the western counties.

---

[6] The full title of this pamphlet was "Address to the People of West Virginia delivered at Lexington, Virginia, in 1847." It was reprinted in Wheeling, 1862, and in Bridgewater, Virginia, 1932.

[7] See I. F. Boughter, *Internal Improvements in Northwestern Virginia* (Ph.D. dissertation, University of Pittsburgh, 1930, MS.); Dunaway, "History of the James River and Kanawha Company," in Columbia University, *Studies,* Vol. CIV, No. 2.

For instance, the Baltimore and Ohio Company desired a franchise to extend its lines through Virginia to the Ohio River, by way of the Valley and the Kanawha River. Still hoping to provide some means of improved transportation that would keep the western counties and the lower Ohio Valley tributary to Richmond and Norfolk, instead of to Baltimore and Philadelphia, the assembly refused this permission and decided to keep the tracks of the Baltimore and Ohio Company as far north as possible.

As eastern Virginia, under the influence of John C. Calhoun and his henchmen, was already thinking of a united South, based upon the institution of Negro slavery, some enterprises in the west received favor. This was particularly true of the Wheeling Bridge. After repeated efforts on the part of Virginia to have Congress build the proposed bridge, it was completed on October 30, 1849 as a private enterprise. While Wheeling celebrated the formal opening of the bridge, Pennsylvania prepared to destroy the object of the rejoicing. Indeed, she alleged that it was a nuisance, injurious to the commerce of the Ohio and to the internal improvements of western Pennsylvania, and asked the Federal Supreme Court to order its removal.

After a thorough investigation, the Court ordered the Wheeling Bridge removed or so altered as not to interfere with navigation; and its owners were given until February, 1853, to comply with the order. Never daunted, Wheeling appealed to Congress, asking that the bridge be designated a post road and that the boats using the waters under it be required to adjust their smokestacks to suit existing conditions. This request was granted in July, 1852, and little more was heard about the Wheeling Bridge until it was blown down by a storm in 1854, when Pittsburgh again made a fruitless effort to prevent its being rebuilt.

Meanwhile, and for reasons already indicated, liberal appropriations were being made for the construction of roads and turnpikes in the western counties, but it was hard for their inhabitants to content themselves with these improvements, when they wanted canals and railroads instead. It was with state aid that the James River and Kanawha Turnpike —with a branch to Guyandotte, on the Ohio—was extended from Charleston to the "Mouth of Sandy" in the early thirties. The stretch between Lewisburg and Charleston had been previously completed, also with state aid, in the late twenties. At once, Guyandotte became an important river terminus, and the overland route by way of the Kanawha grew in favor with cattle and hog drivers passing to and from the eastern markets. It also became a favorite mail and passenger route between the East and the West. The time between Richmond and Guyandotte in 1837, was four and one-half days; and hotels, inns, and hostelries along the way grew in numbers and in attractiveness.

The most important road built in western Virginia at this time was the Northwestern Turnpike, connecting Winchester and Parkersburg.[8] Suggested by Washington as early as 1784 as an all-Virginia route between the East and the West, its completion had been delayed by bad engineering and poor financing. After the completion of the Cumberland Road to Wheeling, interest in the Virginia route was revived and

Sketched by J. H. Diss Debar

The first coach made in Virginia to be used in travel between Winchester and the Ohio River

kept alive with indifferent results until 1831, when the Virginia General Assembly reorganized the company in charge of its construction and authorized it to borrow $125,000 on the credit of the state. More important still, the engineer in charge was given power to determine its location.

The chief engineer of the Northwestern Turnpike was Charles B. Shaw, who was directed by Colonel Claudius Crozet, a French artillery officer who had served with Napoleon and was then the chief engineer of Virginia. It was due largely to their skill and engineering ability that this highway was completed when it was, and that it became a popular thoroughfare. Ignoring those sectional differences which cursed West Virginia from her earliest history, they chose a route passing by Romney, Burlington, Aurora, Fellowsville, Grafton, Clarksburg, West Union, and Pennsboro, over the best grades possible. From the Virginia line to Parkersburg, all of the route, except eight and one-half miles in Maryland, was

[8] Callahan, *History,* Vol. I, 184-186; Boughter, *Internal Improvements;* Colonel William Couper, *Claudius Crozet* (Charlottesville, Va., 1936), pp. 73-91.

in Virginia. At a total cost of $400,000, it was completed in 1838, and at once took rank among the main-traveled routes between the East and the West.

The Staunton and Parkersburg Turnpike, first authorized in 1824, but not completed to Parkersburg until 1847, was an important factor in the development of central northwest Virginia. Connecting the points indicated by its name, this road passed by Monterey, Beverly, Buckhannon, and Weston. From its inception, the state insisted that the counties through which it passed should bear a part of the cost of construction—a fact which delayed its completion and led finally to the use of lotteries as a means of raising assigned quotas.

Other internal improvements of this period affecting western Virginia were: the Baltimore and Ohio Railroad, completed to Cumberland, Maryland, in 1842; the slackwater improvement of the Monongahela River, extended to Brownsville, Pennsylvania, in 1844; and the Chesapeake and Ohio Canal, completed to Cumberland, Maryland, in 1850, but opened to use through a part of its course at an earlier date. Meanwhile, main highways were being connected into one vast system by a network of roads and lesser turnpikes. All were more or less tributary to the Ohio River, which then came into its own in a somewhat spectacular manner, in this, the heyday of its passenger packet.

POPULATION AND NEW COUNTIES

More significant still was the rapid increase in the white and a corresponding decrease in the slave populations of Trans-Allegheny Virginia. In the decades between 1820 and 1850, the whites increased from almost 177,000 to more than 302,000, whereas the increase in the Negroes was only five per cent for the first decade and eleven per cent for the second. This growth necessitated the formation of new counties,[9] which were created more frequently than formerly, when each county had been entitled to two delegates in the lower house of the general assembly. The counties formed are an index to population movements of the period. For the most part they were either on or near the newly opened turnpikes, or on or near navigable waters. In the decade from 1830 to 1840, only five were formed, namely: in 1831, Jackson, from Mason, Kanawha, and Wood; in the same year, Fayette, from Logan, Greenbrier, Nicholas, and Kanawha; in 1835, Marshall, from Ohio; in 1836, Braxton, from Lewis, Kanawha, Nicholas,

[9] For historical sketches of West Virginia counties, see Lewis, *History of West Virginia*, pp. 436-735. For a description, as of 1876, see Maury and Fontaine, *Resources of West Virginia*.

and Randolph; and, in 1837, Mercer, from Giles and Tazewell. In the next decade, fourteen new counties were formed. They, together with the counties from which the area of each was taken and the date of formation, were: 1842, Marion, from Monongalia and Harrison; in the same year, Wayne, from Cabell; 1843, Ritchie, from Harrison, Lewis, and Wood; in the same year, Barbour, from Harrison, Lewis, and Randolph; 1844, Taylor, from Harrison, Barbour, and Marion; 1845, Gilmer, from Lewis and Kanawha; in the same year, Doddridge, from Harrison, Tyler, Ritchie, and Lewis; 1846, Wetzel, from Tyler; 1847, Boone, from Kanawha, Cabell, and Logan; 1848, Hancock, from Brooke; in the same year, Wirt, from Wood and Jackson; also in that year, Putnam, from Kanawha, Cabell, and Mason; in 1850, Raleigh, from Fayette; and, in the same year, Wyoming, from Logan.

EDUCATION

Meanwhile, the long-standing differences between eastern and western Virginia on the subject of education were tending to reach a climax.[10] Ever since Thomas Jefferson had proposed a state-wide system of free public schools, these sections had differed on this subject. The east tended to favor higher education, while the west desired that of a more elementary character. It was largely through votes of the western counties that the general assembly, in 1810, created a permanent "Literary Fund." When the state prepared to use the proceeds of this fund, the differences between the east and the west became pronounced. The former section tried to get the largest possible share for a proposed university, while the latter insisted that the entire proceeds should be used to aid in the establishment of a more adequate free public school system. The result was a compromise, by which $45,000 was set aside annually for the education of poor white children.

With only occasional complaints from the western section, this arrangement continued until about 1840, when it was subjected to a vigorous attack. When, by the use of statistics, Governor Campbell showed that illiteracy was increasing, Virginians, regardless of their place of residence, began an agitation for reform. The movement centered in the west where a number of educational conventions were held in the years immediately following.

Of all these gatherings, the one held in Clarksburg, Harrison County, September 8-9, 1841, was perhaps the most important. It was attended by

[10] Charles H. Ambler, *A History of Education in West Virginia* (Huntington, W. Va., 1951).

leaders from many of the western counties and from neighboring states, who listened to addresses on the benefits of the free public school and on plans for adapting it to local needs and conditions. Among the resolutions adopted was one urging the use of proceeds from the sale of public lands, recently allotted the state, for the support of internal improvements and free public schools. Other prominent citizens sent communications. That from Judge Edwin S. Duncan, of Harrison County, was typical. In part, it said:

> A splendid university has been endowed accessible only to the sons of the wealthy planters of the eastern part of the state and to the southern states. I have heard of only two students attending it from the northwest. The resources of the Literary Fund are frittered away in the endowment of an institution whose tendencies are essentially aristocratic and beneficial only to the very rich. . . . The men of small farms are left to their own means for the education of their children. They cannot send them to the University, and they are prohibited, if they would, from joining in the scramble for the annual donation to the poor [which is scattered in the] ostentatious manner of a nabob who throws small change among the paupers and cries "catch who can."[11]

Following this convention, northwest Virginia gave a varied account of itself on the subject of education, but it always opposed any form of state support for the university. Students from that section refused to attend this or any eastern institution even when given appointments exempting them from tuition and other fees. Out of a total resident enrollment of one hundred thirty-four in the university in 1844-1845, scarcely more than a dozen students were from counties west of the Alleghenies. Meanwhile, members of the general assembly from these counties were helping to defeat a proposal to establish a chair of agriculture and an agricultural experiment station at the university, and were insisting that the revenue from the sale of forfeited lands—the chief source of income for the Literary Fund—be returned to the counties where the lands lay, to be used there to maintain free public schools.

[11] U. S. Commissioner of Education, *Report* (1899-1900), Vol. I, 435.

Chapter XIII

Pioneering in Literature and Education

CRADLE BOOKS

WEST VIRGINIA'S literary background is somewhat unusual. Within its boundaries were enacted some of the most thrilling and heroic deeds and adventures of American pioneer life. Accounts of these experiences were handed down from generation to generation by word of mouth, enriching the folk songs and tales imported from foreign lands. Meanwhile, explorers and adventurers wrote journals and diaries which added a feature of reality to this rich and, as yet, not wholly exploited heritage. Among these journalistic writings were those of Thomas Batts, John Peter Salling (Salley), Thomas Walker, Christopher Gist, George Washington, Francis Asbury, and the numerous travelers who passed down the Ohio River and through western Virginia in the last decade of the eighteenth and the first decades of the nineteenth century.[1]

Although not so well known as were the writings of some of the authors mentioned in the above paragraph, West Virginia incunabula, or "cradle books," are not without interest. *A Short Treatise on the Application of Steam,* by James Rumsey, was perhaps the first of these works. The first edition of this pamphlet appeared in 1787, the place of publication being given as "somewhere in Virginia." The following year, it was reprinted in Philadelphia. This work, together with another by the same

1 For more or less detailed bibliographies, see Virgil A. Lewis, *Hand Book of West Virginia* (Charleston, 1904), pp. 133-173; Callahan, *History of West Virginia,* Vol. I, Chs. 19, 37; Mary M. Atkeson, *A Study of the Literature of West Virginia* (Columbus, Ohio, 1921); Ella Mae Turner, *Stories and Verse of West Virginia* (Hagerstown, Md., 1923); Warren Wood, *Representative Authors of West Virginia* (Ravenswood, W.Va., 1926).

author, entitled *A Plan Wherein the Power of Steam is Fully Shown,* printed in Berkeley County, Virginia, 1788, was attacked by John Fitch in a "war of pamphlets" between Fitch and Rumsey over the priority of their respective inventions.

Christian Panoply; Containing an Apology for the Bible in a Series of Letters Addressed to Thomas Paine (Shepherdstown, 1797), by R. Watson, D.D., F.R.S., Lord Bishop of Landaff, etc., was the first book published in what is now West Virginia. It was a modest volume in calf, and was accompanied by "An Address to Scoffers at Religion," by the same author, and by "A Brief View of the Historical Evidences of Christianity," by William Paley, M.A., Archdeacon of Carlyle. The "Address" by Watson was popularly referred to as "Watson's Reply to Tom Paine."

Although it was neither written nor published in western Virginia, *A Short Narrative of the Sufferings of Mary Kinnan* (Elizabethtown, New Jersey, 1795) has been classed among West Virginia cradle books. It was only a pamphlet, the romantic setting for which was laid at Elkwater, on Tygart River. In 1791, after witnessing the murder of her husband and child, Mrs. Kinnan was taken captive by marauding Shawnees and carried to their villages north of the Ohio, where she was detained until 1794, when she made her escape. Despite the fact that the story of her experiences is said to have been spoiled in the writing, the work became popular. First, and even second, editions are now considered rare possessions.

JOURNALS AND HISTORIES

Colonel John Stuart's *Memoirs of Indian Wars and Other Occurrences,* written at Lewisburg in 1799, but not published until 1832, has been pronounced "indispensable." Stuart commanded a company in the battle of Point Pleasant and was among the most prominent pioneers in the Greenbrier Valley. He was the first clerk of the court of Greenbrier County and was not related to John Stuart, Indian agent for the British government in the region south of the Ohio River.

The *Journal of the Lewis and Clark Expedition* (Pittsburgh, 1807), by Patrick Gass, was of more than general interest to West Virginians. For a long time its author lived in Wellsburg, where he died, in 1871, at the age of ninety-nine. As the earliest available account of the Lewis and Clark expedition, the Gass *Journal* was eagerly received. In 1808, it was reprinted in London, England, and, later, in Philadelphia, where it went through three printings: the first in 1810, another in 1811, and still another in 1812. In *Life and Times of Patrick Gass* (Wellsburg, 1859), John G. Jacob, an editor of note, preserved important incidents in the life of Gass, who was already famous as the last surviving member of the Lewis and Clark expedition.

The historical and other works of the Rev. Joseph Doddridge appeared in the first quarter of the nineteenth century. The most important of his historical writings was his *Notes on the Settlement and Indian Wars in the Western Parts of Virginia and Pennsylvania from 1763 to 1783, Inclusive* (Wheeling, 1824), usually referred to as Doddridge's *Notes.* It was published in one volume, and was later characterized by Theodore Roosevelt as "the most valuable book we have on old-time frontier ways and customs." Others have been equally appreciative, and, as a consequence, the *Notes* have been used extensively. In *Logan, the Last of the Race of Shikellimus, Chief of the Cayuga Nation* (Buffalo Creek, Virginia, 1823), Doddridge attempted to immortalize a historic Indian character.

Doddridge, minister and physician, was born October 14, 1769, in Friends Cove, Bedford County, Pennsylvania, and died November 9, 1826, at his home in Wellsburg, Virginia.[2] Before he was four years of age, his father moved from Bedford County to southwest Pennsylvania, where Joseph, together with his brother Philip—who became a distinguished lawyer—and his sisters, Ann and Ruth, grew up amidst most primitive surroundings. Nevertheless, Joseph's views of life were "just and liberal, drawn as they were from the Bible, general experience and observation." As he was also a keen observer, had a tenacious memory, and was an accomplished scholar, he was well qualified for his greatest service, that of depicting the life, manners, and customs of the Virginia-Pennsylvania frontier.

Doddridge had many other interests; his *Treatise on the Culture of Bees* (Wellsburg, 1813) was the first scientific publication in what is now West Virginia. In his *Logan,* previously mentioned, he agreed with Thomas Jefferson in attributing to "Colonel" Michael Cresap chief responsibility for the murder of the family of Logan. This charge was too much for John J. Jacob, a Revolutionary soldier of Hampshire County, Virginia, who had married Cresap's widow and knew the facts. Accordingly, Jacob answered the charge in a *Biographical Sketch of the Late Michael Cresap.*[3]

Chronicles of Border Warfare (Clarksburg, 1831), by Alexander Scott Withers, was the most important historical work of this period. Although based upon tradition rather than documentary sources, it was favorably received by the general public and by historians as well. Fortunately, most of the traditions upon which it was based were authentic. Thus it became

---

[2] For a biographical sketch, see Narcissa Doddridge, "Memoir of the Reverend Joseph Doddridge," in Doddridge, *Notes* (Ritenour and Lindsey, ed.), pp. 243-272.

[3] The first edition of this work was printed in Cumberland, Md., 1826. It was reprinted at Cincinnati, 1866.

a useful repository of information regarding the Trans-Allegheny frontier. The composite character of the work contributed to its merit; Withers drew upon the historical writings and materials of Hugh Paul Taylor,[4] Judge Edwin S. Duncan, Noah Zane, John Hacker, and others.

From a pencil sketch by J. H. Diss Debar

Alexander Scott Withers

Perhaps more than anything else, *Chronicles of Border Warfare* inspired Lyman C. Draper to his career as collector of documentary source materials pertaining to the American frontier. Shortly after the *Chronicles*

[4] Hugh Paul Taylor was "the precursor . . . of the school of historic gleaners." Over the signature "Son of Cornstalk," he published a series of articles covering the forty years immediately prior to the close of the Revolution. These appeared in *The Fincastle Mirror,* and had to do with life and happenings on the Virginia frontier. See Withers, *Border Warfare* (edited by Thwaites), "Memoir of the Author," p. ix.

appeared, Draper took up the self-imposed task of collecting sources of information needed to correct and amplify its lurid stories, as well as the tales found in Doddridge's *Notes*. He succeeded well in the means to the end, though the end itself was never attained, but the Library of the Wisconsin Historical Society became the beneficiary of his activities.

Although only indirectly responsible for historical interest in his contemporaries, Alexander Scott Withers is worthy of more than passing mention. Draper thought he deserved "to have his name and memory perpetuated as a public benefactor." Withers was born October 12, 1792, at Green Meadows, Fauquier County, Virginia. He was descended on his father's side from English ancestry. "His mother was the daughter of Thomas Chinn and Jannet Scott—the latter a native of Scotland and a first cousin of Sir Walter Scott." From childhood, Withers was a lover of books and knowledge. To his last days, he read the Greek and Latin classics in the originals. He was trained for law, but, because of diffidence in public speaking, he abandoned the bar, after a brief period of practice.

In 1827, in pursuit of a long-cherished desire to go west, Withers settled near Clarksburg, Virginia, now West Virginia. After the publication of the *Chronicles,* from which he realized little or nothing in a financial way, he moved to Missouri. He returned to western Virginia in a short time and established himself as an agriculturist in Lewis County, in the neighborhood of Weston. Later, he moved to the town of Weston, where he resided until 1861, when he removed with the family of his eldest daughter, wife of Thomas Tavenner, to their home near Parkersburg, Virginia. He died near Parkersburg, January 23, 1865, after a brief illness.[5]

What the *Chronicles of Border Warfare* was to Trans-Allegheny Virginia, a *History of the Valley of Virginia* (Winchester, 1833), by Samuel Kercheval, was to the lower Shenandoah Valley. Like Withers, Kercheval wrote mostly from verbal tradition rather than from documentary evidence; but, since he was of mature years when he wrote and enjoyed a reputation for truthfulness and sound judgment, his *History of the Valley* has been generally accepted as authentic. It has been quoted extensively and frequently, and recently was republished in a fourth edition.

Other ante bellum writings included: *Sketches of Virginia, Historical and Biographical* (1850), by William H. Foote, then pastor of the Presbyterian Church in Romney, Hampshire County; the *Life of Harman Blennerhassett* (1850), by Judge William E. Safford who, ten years later, edited the *Blennerhassett Papers;* and a *History of the Early Settlement and Indian Wars of Northwestern Virginia* (1851), by Wills De Hass, a local chronicler of more than ordinary merit.

Meanwhile, still other historical writings of more or less local background and interest had appeared. These included Henry Howe's *Vir-*

[5] Withers, *Border Warfare,* "Memoir of the Author," p. x.

ginia: Its History and Antiquities (1845); Robert R. Howisson's *History of Virginia* (1848); Thomas A. Morris's *Sketches of Western Methodism* (1852); William Meade's *Old Churches, Preachers, and Families of Virginia* (1857); and Charles Campbell's *History of the Colony and Ancient Dominion of Virginia* (1860), regarded by authorities as the best history of Virginia published prior to her dismemberment in 1863. Another chronicle of interest was James Moore's *The Captives of Abb's Valley* (1840), an account of an Indian massacre that occurred in 1784 near the present eastern boundary of Mercer County, West Virginia.

POETRY AND PROSE

The West Virginia environment has always inspired writers of poetry, but at no time was the quality of their productions better than in the second and third generations following the American Revolution. A romantic background was then passing into tradition; a varied scenery, dotted here and there with sites of historic interest, inspired the poetic muse; expert singers of ballads were still abroad in the land; and long winter evenings before the open fires inspired the emotions.

A chronicler of the life and customs of this changing order, Joseph Doddridge preserved also something of its sentiments. His "A Dirge" had its inspiration in the death of General Washington and was written on the first anniversary of the general's birthday following his death. In his "An Elegy on the Family Vault," Doddridge rather successfully imitated Gray's "Elegy." His other poetical works were largely hymns and songs.

Among other poets of this period who either resided in western Virginia or drew their inspiration from local experiences was Margaret Agnew Blennerhassett, widow of Harman Blennerhassett, whose *Widow of the Rock and Other Poems, by a Lady* (1824), included "The Deserted Isle," a portrayal of its author's experiences on Blennerhassett Island. Seven years later, Thomas S. Lees, Wheeling, published *Musings of Carol,* a series of poems, some of which pictured the beauties of the Ohio River. Possibly best of all the local antebellum poems were those of Philip Pendleton Cooke, first published in *Froissart Ballads and Other Poems.* Among these was "Florence Vane," one of the most popular love songs in the English language.

Conditions productive of poetry were perhaps even more favorable to the preservation and growth of ballads and folk songs. Scores of rhymes and jingles came into existence and were handed down from person to person during these decades. Among the best folk songs were "The Battle of Point Pleasant," long a local favorite; and "New Hope, or the

Rescue: a Tale of the Great Kanawha," sometimes referred to also as "Young Kate" or "The Allens."

Writers of prose were quite as original as were writers of poetry. Among the former was Mrs. Anne (Newport) Royall, who resided for a time at Old Sweet Springs and at Charleston. In the twenties, she published *Sketches of History, Life and Manners in the United States,* data for which was drawn from the Kanawha Valley. Shortly thereafter, she moved to Washington, D.C., where she founded *Paul Pry,* a newspaper, the name of which was soon changed to *The Huntress.* If not the first, Mrs. Royall was among the first women newspaper editors in the United States.[6]

Other contemporary prose writers included Stephen T. Mitchell, author of "The Rambles and Reveries of Franklin Fanciful, Barrister," and "Reflections and Notes on the Battle of Point Pleasant," each of which appeared in the *Spirit of the Old Dominion* (Richmond, 1827). Some years later, Philip Pendleton Kennedy, under the *nom de plume* "The Clerk of Oxenford," published *The Blackwater Chronicle,* consisting of notes and stories depicting life and customs in the Virginia mountains. They were illustrated by pen pictures of unusual merit, the work of David Hunter Strother, or "Port Crayon."

The writings of Alexander Campbell were published in fifty-two volumes, which included *The Christian System; Living Oracles; New Testament, with Notes and Introduction; and Lectures on the Pentateuch.* All were written at Bethany. Writings of a similar character included the Rev. James Sarin's *Sermons* (Wheeling, 1822), the first book published in that city; and, the next year, in the same place, Thomas Vincent's *Christ's Certain and Sudden Appearing to Judgment.*

EARLY NEWSPAPERS AND EDITORS

The first newspaper in what is now West Virginia[7] was perhaps the *Potomac Guardian and Berkeley Advertiser,* established at Shepherdstown in 1790 by Nathaniel Willis, grandfather of the later distinguished writer, N. P. Willis. Before the century ended, the *Gazette* was being published regularly at Martinsburg by the same editor, but no other newspapers of importance appeared before the nineteenth century.

In 1808, the Eastern Panhandle added to its meager press publications the *Farmer's Repository,* the first agricultural journal published in Virginia west of the Blue Ridge Mountains. It was published at Charles

[6] Sara H. Porter, *Life and Times of Anne Royall* (Cedar Rapids, 1909).

[7] Callahan, *History,* Vol. I, Ch. 19; Douglas C. McMurtrie, *Beginnings of Printing in West Virginia* (Charleston, 1941).

Town until 1827, when it was merged with the *Virginia Free Press* of the same city, edited and owned by J. S. Gallaher and H. N. Gallaher. Other newspapers published there in this period, in the order of their establishment, were: the *American Eagle, Virginia Monitor, Journal,* Shepherdstown *Gazette, Ladies' Garland,* and the *Potomac Pioneer.* Hampshire and Hardy counties did not have a newspaper until 1830, when William Harper established the *Hampshire and Hardy Intelligencer,* which was soon changed to the *South Branch Intelligencer,* under which name it continued to appear for two generations.

The first newspaper published west of the Alleghenies in northwest Virginia was the *Monongalia Gazette and Morgantown Advertiser,* the first number of which appeared in 1803, in Morgantown. It was followed in time by other papers published in the same place, namely, the Morgantown *Gazette,* 1810, the Morgantown *Spectator,* 1815, and, after 1820, by a half dozen other newspapers. The *Bystander,* first published in 1810, seems to have been Clarksburg's first newspaper. In 1816, the *Western Virginian* was established there and was followed by the *Republican Compiler,* 1817; the *Independent Virginian,* 1819; the *Gazette,* 1822; the *Rattlesnake,* 1822; and others. The first newspaper published in Wheeling was the *Repository,* which appeared in 1807. Following it closely were the *Times,* the *Gazette,* the *Telegraph,* and the *Virginian.* On the Ohio above Wheeling, the Charles Town *Gazette* was established in 1814, but it was succeeded by the Wellsburg *Gazette* (new series), in 1822. The older series of that publication was then in its three hundred twelfth number.

On the Kanawha, journalism developed more slowly and seems to have had its impetus in the times and conditions already described in this chapter. The first newspaper for that section was probably the *Spectator,* published in Charleston, in 1818, by Herbert P. Gaines. It was followed in less than a year by the *Patriot,* published in the same place and by the same editor, but this periodical was also short-lived. From 1820 to 1829, newspapers were published intermittently in Charleston by one Mason Campbell, who finally gave way to the Laidleys. For about a year, they published the *Western Virginian,* which was succeeded, in 1830, by the *Kanawha Banner.* After four years, this publication was replaced by the *Kanawha Patriot,* a Whig paper. Meanwhile, in 1820, Joseph C. Waggoner had commenced in Lewisburg, Greenbrier County, the publication of the *Palladium and Pacific Monitor,* which he continued for about ten years.

With the rapid growth of population in Trans-Allegheny Virginia during the twenties and thirties of the nineteenth century, additional newspaper press facilities became imperative. Many new counties were formed in the decades immediately following; railroad towns came into existence; and highways continued to be frequented by the traveling public. These dynamic conditions stimulated good writing, and the creation of new counties with their legal publications and official notices made the profession a profitable one.

Not all the newly established newspapers of the forties and fifties were mere dependents upon courthouse favors. Under the editorship of Enos W. Newton, a New England gentleman of culture and ability, the *Kanawha Republican,* founded at Charleston in 1842, assumed the tone and size of a metropolitan daily. In 1852, the *Intelligencer* was established at Wheeling; later, under the editorship of Archibald W. Campbell, it became one of the leading dailies of the upper Ohio Valley. Other contemporary editors of note, together with their newspapers, were: James W. Beller of the Charles Town *Spirit of Jefferson;* Daniel H. Polsley of the *Western Transcript,* Wellsburg; and John G. Jacob of the Wellsburg *Herald,* long the "Nestor of the Press" in the Northern Panhandle of West Virginia.

ELEMENTARY SCHOOLS

The first community school in present West Virginia is believed to have been at Old Fields, near Moorefield in present Hardy County. In 1748 a party, of which George Washington was a member, began to survey there near "the School House." Five years later a schoolmaster was employed in nearby Romney. When the Greenbrier settlement was destroyed that year, a schoolmaster was among the persons killed. In 1762 both a German and an English school were taught in present Shepherdstown.[8] There was thus considerable school sentiment in present West Virginia before the Revolution. Disestablishment of the state church (1785), shifting responsibility for the education of children of the indigent poor from it to the state, made action on its part imperative.

To meet this responsibility the general assembly authorized in 1796 the voters to elect three aldermen from "the most honest and able men" in each county of the state. Upon authorization of the county court, the aldermen were required to divide the county into districts. Then the householders of each district were authorized to assemble in mass meeting and establish their school. But few aldermen were elected and few, if any, schools were established under the proposed aldermanic system. Jefferson later explained the failure as follows: "The members of the courts are the wealthy members of the counties; and as the expenses of the schools are to be defrayed by a contribution proportioned to the aggregate of other taxes which everyone pays, they considered it as a plan to educate the poor at the expense of the rich."[9]

[8] Ambler, *History of Education,* p. 3.

[9] Thomas Jefferson, *Writings* (Definitive ed.), XIV, 413.

The aldermanic system having failed to accomplish its purpose, the 1809 general assembly authorized the establishment of a permanent literary fund, but the income was not expected to provide immediate relief. Enthusiasm for "the Fund" became somewhat general, however, and the general assembly, in 1816, diverted to it about $1,200,000 repayments of funds lent by Virginia to the United States to finance the War of 1812. In 1818, $45,000 of the income was allotted for annual distribution for the education of poor children.[10]

The new social and political forces of the thirties of the nineteenth century subjected educational conditions to severe tests. The most disconcerting of these was the fact, set forth by Governor Campbell in 1838, that illiteracy, already appalling, was increasing.

In response to the resulting memorials, an act of 1846 gave school commissioners, holding office under the act of 1817, authority to supplement the state aid for the poor by local taxes. The application of the law was, however, fettered by much red tape in the form of petitions and referenda, and thus made impracticable. Free public schools were established in Kanawha and in Ohio and in Jefferson counties; but the essential features of the older systems were preserved elsewhere. Funds continued to be administered as doles to the poor, and "old fields" continued to be good enough sites for school buildings.

Instruction was, as a rule, poor and limited to "readin', 'ritin', and 'rithmetic." While masters were selected almost solely with reference to their ability "to keep order," some of them were rare personalities. In Kanawha County, the books in most common use as texts were the Bible, Pike's *Arithmetic,* the *Elementary Speller,* Murray's *Geography,* and Murray's *Grammar.* In Marion County, about the same time, the only textbooks used were the *United States Speller* and the New Testament; while, in Hampshire County, the books used in addition to these were the *English Reader* and an arithmetic. Boys and girls built the schoolhouse fires and swept the building; wood, the fuel in common use, was supplied by the patrons, as a community enterprise.

SECONDARY SCHOOLS AND COLLEGES

In the later antebellum days, secondary education in northwest Virginia was on a comparatively high plane. In fact, that region has since been described as "a land of academies." In a partial list of secondary institutions established there prior to 1861, a chronicler included fifty-three.[11]

[10] Ambler, *History of Education,* pp. 18-33.

[11] Lewis, *Hand Book,* pp. 93-96; Callahan, *History,* Vol. I, 281-292.

Although he admitted that some of these institutions were operated on a small scale, he described others as the "beacon lights of education." These fitted young men for pursuit of the classics in William and Mary, Princeton, Harvard, Yale, and similar institutions. More significant still, perhaps, the benefits of these academies were not restricted to residents; some of them enrolled students from many states of the Union.

Brooke Academy was the oldest institution of its kind in Trans-Allegheny Virginia on the Ohio south of Pittsburgh. It was incorporated in 1800, twenty-two years after it first began to offer instruction. In 1843, it had an enrollment of one hundred students, and, nine years later, it was merged into Meade Collegiate Institute.

Randolph Academy at Clarksburg was, however, the oldest regularly incorporated secondary school in Virginia west of the Alleghenies. Under more favorable conditions it might have become to Trans-Allegheny Virginia what William and Mary was to the East, a semipublicly maintained institution of the highest order. Indeed, such a thing seems to have been contemplated in its charter, which set aside surveyor's fees, formerly allotted to William and Mary College, for its maintenance. Its first board of trustees included in its membership Edmund Randolph, Benjamin Harrison, George Mason, and Patrick Henry.

Outstanding among similar institutions were: the Potomac Academy, the seat of the Romney Literary Society, one of the oldest organizations of its kind in western Virginia; the Northwestern Academy, at Clarksburg, of which Gordon Battelle was the first principal; Preston Academy, which began work in the early forties under the direction of Alexander Martin, first president of the West Virginia University; and Lewisburg Academy, incorporated in 1812, and for forty-eight years under the direction of the Rev. John McElhenney. In 1858, Marshall Academy, "for a quarter of a century the most famous institution of learning in western Virginia," became Marshall College.

Of all such institutions, the Lancastrian Academy, later Linsly Institute, was unique. It was founded at Wheeling, in 1814, from the proceeds of a bequest from Noah Linsly on condition that it use the Lancastrian method of instruction. This was more objective than the methods in current use and was carried on by the aid of "monitors," student assistants. It is claimed that this was the first institution chartered in an American slave state for the free education of the poor.

The excellent work done in these academies led to a demand for educational institutions of a higher order. In 1838, the Reverend Joshua Bradley founded Rector College, at Pruntytown, which was incorporated as the "Western Virginia Educational Society," and received state aid in the form of free scholarships. From the beginning, it was under Baptist control. In 1850, it employed two teachers and enrolled one hundred students.

Bethany College, founded at Bethany in 1840 by Alexander Campbell, is the oldest existing institution of college rank in West Virginia. From the first, it was under the control of the Christians, or Disciples of Christ. For the site of this institution, its founder and first president chose a place "entirely rural" and "detached from all external society." In 1850, it employed five teachers and enrolled one hundred thirty students. Its income, however, did not exceed seven thousand five hundred dollars annually.

LIBRARIES

From the earliest days, many settlers in northwest Virginia were interested in books. Private libraries were not large; generally they included the Bible, a catechism, and a few books of a more literary character, preferably such works as Vergil's *Aeneid* and Homer's *Iliad*. These were read and reread, and many of the more sagacious among the pioneer settlers were able to repeat from memory book after book of the Bible. Closely associated with these small libraries were collections of Indian relics, mounted animals and birds, and other curios of local origin.

Meanwhile, private and institutional libraries became of increasing interest and importance. In most cases, the books were the property of incorporated literary societies, which functioned in conjunction with educational institutions or as private and individual agencies. Between 1830 and 1860, a dozen or more such "reading circles" were incorporated. Perhaps the most useful public library was at Lewisburg, established in 1831 for the use of the State Supreme Court, which sat there ninety days in each year to hear appeals from inferior courts west of the Blue Ridge Mountains. Another library of importance was that of Bethany College. It was built around the private libraries of Alexander Campbell and his father. For a long time, it was the largest library in Trans-Allegheny Virginia.

Chapter XIV

Ante Bellum Days

1850-1860

POLITICS AND THE REFORM MOVEMENT

AS THE CONSTITUTION of 1830 gave the general assembly power "after the year 1841, and at intervals thereafter of not less than ten years, . . . two-thirds of each House concurring, to make re-apportionments of Delegates and Senators, throughout the Commonwealth," western Virginia earnestly awaited the earliest opportunity for redress of her standing grievance in representation. As the appointed time approached, there was scarcely a newspaper in the Trans-Allegheny that did not condemn editorially that arrangement by which the transmontane section, with a total white population of 271,000, had only ten senators and fifty-six delegates in the general assembly, whereas the cismontane, with a white population of 269,000, had nineteen senators and seventy-eight delegates in that body.

The assembly of 1841-1842 referred the subject of representation to a special committee, whose majority report favored a reapportionment on a suffrage basis and not on the white basis desired by the west. A minority report adhered, however, to the mixed basis of white population and property. As a result of the discussion that followed, the matter was postponed indefinitely, whereupon fifty delegates for the western counties made a formal protest which was spread upon the Journal of the house.

Despairing of desired results, the editor of the *Kanawha Republican* urged the advantages of separate statehood for western Virginia and advised the east not to oppose the move, which, if successful, would increase the power of the South in the Federal Congress, as the proposed new state, "Appalachia," would have two senators of pro-Southern sympathies.[1] Some friends of the plan, however, considered statehood impossible so long as John Tyler was President; his alleged haste in dispatching Federal troops to Rhode Island to be used in putting down Dorr's Rebellion was regarded as indicative of the possible outcome of any movement having for its purpose the dismemberment of Virginia.

Leaders in the Trans-Allegheny accordingly turned their efforts to another constitutional convention. To this end, delegates from ten counties of northwest Virginia met at Clarksburg, in May, 1842, and adopted resolutions asking that a poll be taken in the western counties on that subject. In August of the same year, delegates from twenty counties met in Lewisburg and, after listening to animated addresses, adopted resolutions asking the general assembly to determine the opinion of the voters of the state on the question of a constitutional convention called for the purpose of equalizing representation on the white basis.

But for the fact that "politics make strange bed fellows," eastern and western Virginia might have reached the parting of the ways a decade or more before the Civil War. This step seems to have been checked, however, by the formation of new political alliances bent more upon winning elections than upon achieving reform. Accordingly, the "Richmond Junto" drew close to the famous "Tenth Legion" of the Valley in a Democratic party alliance that catered to the west under a slogan that lauded the Union. Incidentally, western Virginia received benefits and concessions which caused it to forget former grievances.

An enumeration of some of the political and other concessions made to the west through these political alignments will serve to indicate something of their soothing effects. In 1845, James McDowell, of the Tenth Legion, was made governor; and, at the same time, Isaac Samuels Pennybacker, a resident of the Valley, became a United States Senator. More significant still, the Baltimore and Ohio Company was given permission to extend its lines from Cumberland to Wheeling through Virginia territory to the Ohio River provided it did not touch that stream "at any point further south than the mouth of Fish Creek," in Wetzel County. This was also a period of activity in the construction of state roads and in the formation of new counties in the Trans-Allegheny, and concessions were made to that section in the matter of free schools. Although only three companies and a small detachment from what is now West Virginia saw service in the Mexican War, a resident of Jefferson County, Colonel John Francis Hamtramck, commanded the Virginia troops in that conflict.[2]

---

[1] *Kanawha Republican,* June 18, 1842.

[2] Colonel Hamtramck served with distinction in the War of 1812. Among other residents of West Virginia who served with him in the Mexican War were Thomas J. ("Stonewall") Jackson, Jesse Lee Reno, E. W. McComas, and John W. Rowan.

Thus it was that in the forties eastern Virginia was able to defeat repeated proposals looking to a constitutional convention. Finally, when the east saw that it could control the reform movement, it resolved to have a convention, but under such conditions as would leave no question about its control. As authorized, the convention consisted of one hundred thirty-five delegates, each of whom represented approximately 13,151 white inhabitants and $7,000.24 in state taxes. This apportionment gave the east seventy-six delegates, and the west, fifty-nine; whereas, an apportionment on the white basis only would have given the east sixty-one delegates, and the west, seventy-four.

Northwest Virginia might have accepted these arrangements had they been the result of an understanding between political high priests in the interests of spoils, party harmony, and the Union; but developments in national affairs made such a course impossible. Threatened with the loss of benefits from the Mexican War, in 1850, Mississippi called a convention to meet at Nashville, Tennessee, to weigh the value of the Union and take such action as conditions required. In fact, talk of secession was at that time current throughout the South. What was more alarming still, it was being seriously considered in eastern Virginia, where influential newspapers were boldly proclaiming the death of the major political parties, and individuals were rededicating themselves to a "confederation of equals" and reaffirming their devotion to the Virginia Resolutions of 1798. Consequently, northwest Virginia was again compelled to take a position between the extremes of abolition on the one side and of proslavery on the other. As usual under such circumstances, she returned to fundamentals and rededicated herself to the Union.

When the time came for electing delegates to the proposed convention of 1850-1851, eastern and western Virginia were as far apart as they had been at any time in their history. In the east numerous state rights associations had endorsed secession and reform in the same resolutions. Moreover, Judge Beverly Tucker, professor of constitutional and common law in William and Mary College, had addressed the Nashville Convention in the interest of secession and the formation of a "Southern Confederacy." Instead of two political parties sparring for spoils and willing to compromise their differences, these developments revealed a North and a South of irreconcilable tendencies. Under the circumstances, western Virginia, epitomizing the North, elected a solid delegation favorable to the white basis of representation and prepared to fight as never before. Except for a solitary delegate—Henry A. Wise, of Accomac County—the east was equally committed to the mixed basis.

THE REFORM CONVENTION

When the "Reform Convention" met in Richmond, October 14, 1850, census data were not available, and it adjourned to meet again January 6, 1851. Meanwhile, the "Compromise of 1850" was effected, bringing a temporary calm between the forces of slavery and freedom in the United States, and political parties again resumed the rôles of conciliators within their own ranks. Nevertheless, eastern and western Virginia contended bitterly when the convention resumed its session, the bone of contention being the basis of representation in the general assembly. With slightly more emphasis upon the subject of Negro slavery, the arguments used repeated for the most part those of 1829-1830, and need not be reproduced here even in summary.

In the absence of older heads, such as those who guided the Convention of 1829-1830, the Convention of 1850-1851 was more than once on the point of disbanding. On May 10, 1851, it adjourned for a day, not knowing what the next day would bring forth. In time, however, a compromise was agreed upon, under which representation in the house of delegates was apportioned on the white basis of the census of 1850, and that for the senate was fixed arbitrarily, the east receiving thirty, and the west, twenty senators. The feature of the new constitution which made this plan acceptable to the west was a provision which gave the general assembly power to reapportion representation in both the house and the senate upon the white basis in 1865 and, in the event it did not do so, required the governor to submit the question of the white and the mixed basis to a popular referendum.

For these concessions, the east exacted constitutional guarantees which, in turn, became as much a source of dissatisfaction in the northwest as the basis of representation had been. These provisions required true and actual value assessments of all property, except slaves. On each slave over twelve years of age, a tax might be assessed equivalent to that on land valued at $300, whereas slaves under twelve years of age were to be exempt from taxation. Thus, while the western farmer was being taxed on the full value of his livestock, regardless of its age, the slave owner paid nothing on his young Negroes and paid on a fixed value below the average market price on Negroes of marketable age and quality.

As slave prices advanced, these discriminations became more objectionable. The westerners had escaped their "political degradation," but at the price of an unfair tax. Moreover, the constitutional provision forbidding the assembly to pledge the credit of the state to defray the obligations of any company or corporation was a deathblow to internal improvement schemes in the west, as was also the provision prohibiting lotteries for any purpose, even for raising church funds.

Although somewhat belated, other provisions of the new constitution were in line with modern tendencies and were little controverted. Suffrage was extended to all white males over twenty-one years of age; multiple voting was abolished, although the viva-voce method was retained; the office of governor and lieutenant governor were made elective by popular vote, as were also those of members of the judiciary—even the justices of the peace—and the sheriff and other county officers, such as the county clerk, the circuit clerk, and the commonwealth's attorney; the governor's term was extended from three to four years; jurors were to be paid for their services and summoned regularly instead of from the loungers who happened to be within reach of the sheriff on the opening day of court; annual sessions of the assembly gave way to biennial, of ninety days' duration; and special legislation in matters pertaining to divorce, lotteries, religious bodies, changes in the names of individuals, and the disposal of personal estates was forbidden; a growing tendency to create new counties wherever desired was restricted by a provision which prohibited the formation of any county of less than six hundred square miles in area, or the reduction of an existing county below that limit; and a capitation tax equivalent to that paid on land valued at $200 was levied on every voter, one half of which was set aside for the support of schools.

Despite a provision forbidding the emancipation of any slave or any descendant of a slave, the constitution of 1851 was progressive, and the body that made it was consequently called the "Reform Convention." Always able to force their extreme contentions, the easterners, nevertheless, refrained from doing so. The price might have been the disruption of the Democratic party, which was laying plans for another period of state and national rule. Even the Union was at stake. Under the circumstances, ratification was effected with little or no opposition. The vote was 75,748 for, to 11,063 against with most of the latter coming from counties in the east which hesitated to accept the compromises on representation.

INTERNAL IMPROVEMENTS

The completion of the Baltimore and Ohio Railroad from Cumberland to Wheeling, by way of Grafton and Fairmont, December 24, 1852, did much to reconcile northwest Virginia to its new constitution. This "marriage of the East and the West" by the first continuous railroad between the Atlantic Ocean and the Ohio River was a red-letter day in the history of Wheeling. On January 12, 1853, Wheeling celebrated with appropriate oratory and military display. Locally, the city was believed to have taken another, possibly a decisive, step in the struggle with Pittsburgh for commercial ascendancy on the upper Ohio.

At once, points along the route of this road, notably Grafton and Fairmont, became important industrial centers, but the most noticeable of immediate effects was a stimulated traffic on the Ohio River. Before the completion of the railroad to Wheeling, the famous "Union line of packets" had been organized to operate between that city and Louisville, in an effort to give the South the unbroken line of intercommunication between the East and the West long desired by Calhoun and others. Most of the capital stock of the company operating these boats was owned in slave territory, and Southerners delighted to find on the boats, as well as on the trains of the Baltimore and Ohio Railroad, an atmosphere "delightfully Southern." Until the Baltimore and Ohio Company effected through connections with cities in the Middle West, by means of a ferry at Benwood, these packets did a profitable business; soon thereafter they were, however, forced to seek trade elsewhere.

The completion of the Northwestern Virginia Railroad from Grafton to Parkersburg (1857), now a part of the Baltimore and Ohio system, was also an event of importance in northwest Virginia. It opened up a stretch of country about one hundred miles long, which soon became a rich oil- and timber-producing section, and it made Parkersburg an important river center.

These successes revived interest in other internal improvement schemes in the Trans-Allegheny. Chief interest centered in the proposed Covington and Ohio Railroad, which was projected as a means of connecting the James River with the Ohio, by way of the Kanawha. The advantages of such an improvement were amply set forth at an internal improvement convention which met at White Sulphur Springs in 1854. Among other things, it would offer a means of accommodating the Kanawha Valley commerce and of diverting traffic from the northwest to Richmond and Norfolk. In support of the enterprise, the Richmond *Enquirer* said:

> It will be observed that two-fifths of the whole Trans-Allegheny region is wholly isolated, that it has no connection with the northern frontier except a precarious one up the Ohio and none with eastern Virginia. Yet this very region is the seat of a large portion of the military strength of the state, containing, as it does, a majority of the white population. *It is as if we had a citadel filled with men and out-works feebly manned, with no connection from one to the other.* The Covington and Ohio Railroad will pass through the heart of this region and will, when finished, pour its strength either upon the Seaboard by way of Staunton and Richmond or upon the northern frontier by way of Staunton and Harper's Ferry.[3]

[3] Richmond *Enquirer,* August, 10, 1855; Ambler, *Sectionalism,* p. 312.

Like other Virginia enterprises of similar character, the Covington and Ohio Railroad was forced to run the gamut of sectional opposition. In the first place, the James River and Kanawha Canal Company claimed a right of way closely paralleling that over which it was proposed to build the railroad. Then there were many Virginians who feared that such a road would divert traffic from Virginia to Baltimore by way of the Shenandoah Valley. These favored, instead, a road by way of the Kanawha and the New rivers to some point on the Virginia and Tennessee Railroad, the eastern terminus of which was Richmond. On the other hand, the inhabitants of northwest Virginia, now enjoying the benefits of the Baltimore and Ohio Railroad, built at private expense, refused to tax themselves to aid an enterprise that would not benefit them directly. As a result of an alliance between these and other interests, the general assembly (1855-1856) refused to aid the Covington and Ohio Railroad, and its construction was delayed.

Under conditions then developing in the country at large, this was too important an enterprise to be defeated by rivalries and jealousies. The Kansas-Nebraska Bill and the Dred Scott decision were tending to break down political parties and to array the South and the North against each other. In fact, secession was again being considered as a possibility in both sections. In such an eventuality, the control of the Border was strategic. Hence it was necessary for the South, and for Virginia in particular, to make ready. Under this stimulus, the Virginia Assembly (1857-1858) appropriated $800,000 to aid the completion of the Covington and Ohio Railroad and authorized branch lines.

The next legislature was even more liberal toward this enterprise and appropriated $2,500,000 for it, a portion of which was spent in grading that part of the proposed roadbed which lay between Charleston and the "Mouth of Sandy." Meanwhile, William Ballard Preston had been in France as the special agent of Virginia to negotiate for the establishment of a steamship line between Norfolk and Nantes. The possibilities of the situation were received with enthusiasm everywhere, even in the Trans-Allegheny, where the *Kanawha Valley Star* said: "It is in the power of this Legislature in five years to build up cities and fleets, and an immense commerce both home and foreign."[4]

But the exigencies of the times seemed to call for a more certain transportation than that provided by the railroad, which was as yet in an experimental stage in the Ohio Valley. To this end, interest was revived in the completion of the James River and Kanawha Canal, then described as a "gaping wound in the heart of the Commonwealth." Its completion was urged on the ground that a continuous canal would afford the only means whereby heavy freight, lumber, building stones, and coal, could be

[4] January 19, 1858; Ambler, *Sectionalism*, p. 316.

transported to the sea. As a result of this agitation, the general assembly (1859-1860) authorized the James River and Kanawha Canal Company to borrow $2,500,000 and vested the entire control of its affairs in its own stockholders. It was in anticipation of this latter action that arrangements were made for the transfer of the property of the company to certain French interests which owned lands along the route of the proposed canal. These interests organized the Virginia Canal Company, agreed to complete a continuous waterway from the James to the Ohio, and proposed to maintain a regular steamship line between Virginia and France.[5]

A revival of interest in internal improvements naturally attracted attention to the Kanawha River. As then planned, the Covington and Ohio Railroad was to leave that stream near Charleston and extend, thence, directly to the "Mouth of Sandy" over a route paralleling closely that now followed by the Chesapeake and Ohio Railroad. The sluice and dam improvements on the Kanawha maintained only three and one-half feet of navigable water. This was entirely inadequate for the accommodation of the numerous craft then engaged in the transportation of cannel coal from mines which had been opened near Charleston, about 1850, following reports made by W. B. Rogers, of the University of Virginia. Accordingly, interested parties united in demanding relief. But nothing came of their requests, and, as eastern and northwest Virginia approached the parting of the ways, residents of the Kanawha Valley joined those from other sections in accusing the eastern counties of retarding the development of the entire state to the injury of all concerned.

SOCIAL AND ECONOMIC CONDITIONS

These charges were not without foundation. It was at this time that cattle and hog drivers ceased to pass through northwest Virginia going to and from eastern markets. Travelers also deserted its picturesque highways for the railroads, only two of which, the Baltimore and Ohio and the Northwestern Virginia, had as yet penetrated its hills. Among local effects, "entertainment" became a losing business, and turnpikes and state roads fell into decay.

This decline naturally extended to industry. In the early fifties, the Ohio Salt Company secured a monopoly of the salt produced in the Ohio Valley. As its supplies came largely from Meigs County, Ohio, and Mason County, Virginia, the more inaccessible supplies on the Kanawha were

---

[5] James River and Kanawha Canal Company, *Twenty-fourth Annual Report,* p. 449; Dunaway, *James River and Kanawha Company.*

left to play a rôle in a "vanishing industry."[6] The period witnessed, also, failures among the iron makers of northwest Virginia; and the sawmills, and spinning and weaving devices in use in that section decreased in number. Except for the discovery of petroleum, first found in large quantities in the vicinity of Parkersburg in 1860, and for the stimulating influence of the Baltimore and Ohio Railroad, conditions in Trans-Allegheny Virginia in the decade immediately preceding the Civil War were anything but encouraging.

Nevertheless, the decade witnessed an increase of almost 75,000 in population in present West Virginia. The greatest gains were in counties along the Baltimore and Ohio Railroad and along navigable rivers; but the most significant shift was in the slave population, which declined from 20,500, in 1850, to less than 18,000, in 1860. During the same period, the number of free Negro residents increased from slightly more than 2,000 to almost 3,000.[7]

The results of these population changes manifested themselves most directly in the rise of new towns and in the formation of new counties. Of the former, more than a score were incorporated; among them were: St. Marys, 1851; Ravenswood and Harpers Ferry, 1852; Benwood, Kingwood, and Fetterman, 1853; Piedmont, Mason City, Mannington, and Grafton, 1856; and Rowlesburg and Spencer, 1858. Meanwhile, seven new counties were formed. In 1851, Pleasants, one of the smallest counties in the state, was created from parts of Wood, Tyler, and Ritchie. In the same year, Upshur was formed from parts of Randolph, Barbour, and Lewis. No additional counties were created until 1856, when Calhoun was formed from Gilmer, Roane, and Kanawha; Roane, from Gilmer; and Tucker, from Randolph. In 1858, McDowell was formed from Tazewell, and Clay, from Braxton and Nicholas. Two years later, Webster was created from parts of Nicholas, Braxton, and Randolph.

JOHN BROWN AT HARPERS FERRY

To this land of comparatively steady habits, the first information of a slave insurrection at Harpers Ferry, October 16, 1859, had the effect of a fire bell in the night. The possibilities of such insurrections had been contemplated indifferently for years; the chief concern had always been for neighbors and relatives in the East and the South. In due time, rumor

[6] Wheeling *Intelligencer,* December 27, 1854; Isaac Lippincott, "Early Salt Trade in the Ohio Valley," in *Journal of Political Economy,* Vol. XX, 1029.

[7] Callahan, *History of West Virginia,* Vol. I, 576-578; Charles H. Ambler, *Francis H. Pierpont, Union War Governor of Virginia and Father of West Virginia* (Chapel Hill, 1937), pp. 402-403.

gave way to the fact that one John Brown, of Ossawatomie, and twenty-two followers—three of them his sons, and five of them Negroes—had attacked the United States Arsenal at Harpers Ferry in an effort to incite a slave insurrection and to put an end to slavery in America. More disconcerting was the confirmed report that persons of means and influence in the North had abetted this undertaking and that they were trying to

Harpers Ferry

make a hero of its leader. Accordingly, West Virginians generally rejoiced in his apprehension and his subsequent execution, December 2, 1859.

The far-reaching results of this fanatical and ill-advised blow at slavery were not, however, appreciated locally, where Brown was regarded as "just another fanatic." Stories of his stoical bearing during his trial and execution made little appeal and, for that and other obvious reasons, he was not considered a martyr. Had his attempt been made a few months earlier, it would perhaps have been a determining influence in the gubernatorial election which resulted in the choice of John Letcher, a former opponent of Negro slavery. Despite the efforts of Henry A. Wise, the retiring governor, to capitalize the incident for political purposes, by the time of the presidential election of 1860 West Virginians had resumed their usual composure. This condition was fostered by the absence of adequate means of intercommunication and by the fact that the leading political parties, even the "Black Republican" party, condemned the so-called insurrection as a "lawless invasion" and as one of "the gravest crimes." It remained for later historians and poets to immortalize the scene of this insurrection and the name of its leader.

PARTY POLITICS

True to their traditions, West Virginians of the decade immediately preceding the Civil War took an active part in party politics. Most leaders were either Democrats or Whigs. The Democrats prided themselves upon their loyalty to the Union and their devotion to the interests of the common people; whereas the Whigs prided themselves upon their conservative traditions, but conceded nothing to their opponents in loyalty to the Union. Toward the end of the period, most Whigs became either Constitutional Unionists or Democrats. Few members of either of the old parties

John Brown's Fort at Harpers Ferry. John Brown and his followers, when attacked by U.S. Marines, made their last stand in this building, the fire-engine house of the U.S. Arsenal

affiliated with the Know-Nothings, or Americans, an ephemeral nativist party of the fifties; and, until well after 1860, there were few prominent Republicans.

Outstanding among the Whigs was George W. Summers, of Kanawha County. Before 1850, he had served two terms in Congress as a Representative, and, in that year, he was elected a delegate to the Reform Convention. The following year he was the unsuccessful nominee of his party for governor, and shortly thereafter he became judge of the circuit court. Nevertheless, he continued to be prominent politically and, in 1861, was regarded by President Lincoln as a pivotal character. To the surprise of many and possibly to his own political undoing, in the war which followed he became a neutral.

On the other hand, Summers's outstanding local contemporary, Waitman T. Willey, of Monongalia County, reflecting possibly the difference between northern and southern Trans-Allegheny Virginia, became an ardent Union man. He, too, had been a delegate to the Reform Convention and was a defeated candidate for the lieutenant governorship. He was an effective orator and organizer, and during the fifties of the nineteenth century was the official head of the local Sons of Temperance.

Other Whigs were: General John J. Jackson, of Wood County; John S. Carlile, of Harrison County; Chester D. Hubbard, of Ohio County; and Francis H. Pierpont, of Marion County—all of whom, without exception, cast their lots with the Union in the Civil War.[8]

Prominent among the Democrats was Joseph Johnson, of Harrison County. Prior to 1850, he served a number of terms as a Representative in Congress, and, that year, was elected a delegate to the Reform Convention. The following year, he was elected governor of Virginia. He was the first person to reach that coveted position by popular vote, and the only person so honored from Trans-Allegheny Virginia. Later, he cast his lot with the Confederacy, as did also Charles J. Faulkner, of Berkeley County, who, after Johnson, was perhaps the outstanding Democrat in present West Virginia. Faulkner was a member of the Reform Convention and a Representative in Congress from 1851 to 1859, when he became United States Minister to France. Other prominent Democrats were William G. Brown of Preston County, Sherrard Clemens of Ohio County, and Albert Gallatin Jenkins of Cabell County—all of whom, except Jenkins, supported the Union.

Making acceptance of the Compromise of 1850 a test of party loyalty, as well as of devotion to the Union, Democrats continued to adhere to the party of Jackson and Polk and to receive the spoils of office, which included internal improvements, as a reward for party loyalty. Such con-

[8] For biographical sketches of these and other contemporaneous leaders, see George W. Atkinson and Alvaro F. Gibbens, *Prominent Men of West Virginia* (Wheeling, 1890).

siderations brought to them the governorship in 1851. Four years later, and as a reward for his espousal of their cause in the Reform Convention, they were instrumental in raising Henry A. Wise, of the Eastern Shore, to that position; the United States Senatorship went to James M. Mason, of the Valley; while the westerners received minor political rewards as the price of party loyalty. As a result, James Buchanan received the largest vote ever given in western Virginia before 1856, to any Democratic candidate for President.

THE PRESIDENTIAL ELECTION OF 1860

But there were trying days ahead for party men in Virginia, as elsewhere. As throughout the nation, the Dred Scott decision tended to divide Democrats into two hostile camps, an eastern and a western taking the place of a southern and a northern. In 1859, the western Democrats were able to make John Letcher governor, 4,500 of his 5,569 majority coming from two congressional districts in the extreme northwestern part of the state. From the beginning of the canvass to the end, the western leaders spoke with enthusiasm of Letcher's conservatism, of his love for the Union, and of his former alleged hostility to Negro slavery. On the other hand, eastern editors denounced him as an Abolitionist and a Free Soiler who in "the darkest hour of the South was found encouraging the abolitionist sentiments of the Ruffner Pamphlet." After his election, the Richmond *Whig* commended him to a "Black Republican" convention meeting in Wheeling, as a presidential possibility, saying: "His majority comes from that neighborhood, and his Ruffner antecedents entitle him to the consideration of a convention proposed to be held where his friends reside."[9]

With her western counties controlling, or thinking they controlled, the state administration, Virginia entered the presidential contest of 1860. The candidates were: Bell, of the Constitutional Union party, which appealed to former Whigs and conservatives generally; Douglas, a Democrat, running on a platform of loyalty to the Union and to the principles of squatter sovereignty, as expressed in the Democratic platform of 1856; Lincoln, the candidate of the Republican party, standing on a platform opposing the extension of slavery and camouflaging the hostility of the North to its existence in the South by planks on internal improvements and public lands; and Breckenridge, a Democrat, favoring Federal pro-

---

[9] Ambler, *Sectionalism*, pp. 322-325; Richmond *Whig*, June 7, 1859; Henry T. Shanks, *The Secession Movement in Virginia, 1847-1861* (Richmond, 1934), pp. 56-62.

tection of slavery in the territories, as set forth by the highest authority in the land through the Dred Scott decision.

The results of this contest did not, however, run true to precedent. Although Bell received the electoral vote, Breckenridge was a close second. He was less than 500 votes behind in a total for the two of almost 150,000 and won a minority of the electors. For the most part, former Whigs tended to support Bell, while former Democratic strongholds stuck to Breckenridge. This was true even in the northwest, where Breckenridge, a resident of Kentucky, was defended as a Union man, a friend of Letcher and Buchanan, an advocate of state rights, and, most important of all, the candidate of the regular party organization. Douglas received a few more than 16,000 votes, most of them from counties in the Valley and along the Ohio River. Lincoln's vote of almost 2,000 came largely from the Panhandle.[10]

[10] *Tribune Almanac* (1861), p. 30; Ambler, *Sectionalism,* p. 330; Edward C. Smith, *The Borderland in the Civil War* (New York, 1927), p. 62; James C. McGregor, *The Disruption of Virginia* (New York, 1922), pp. 88-89; and Shanks, *Secession Movement,* pp. 110-120.

Part Two

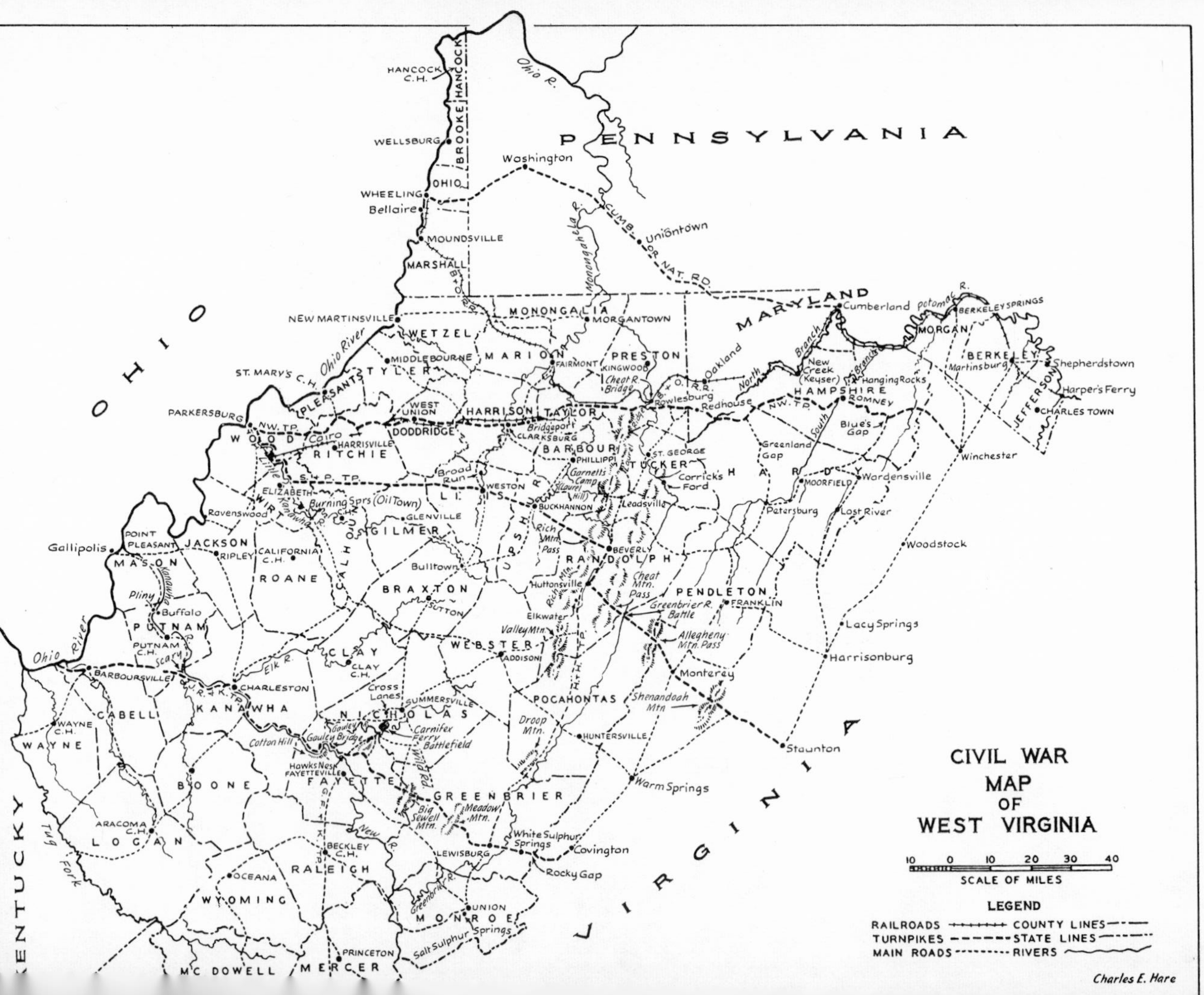

CIVIL WAR
MAP
OF
WEST VIRGINIA
10 0 10 20 30 40
SCALE OF MILES
LEGEND
RAILROADS
TURNPIKES
MAIN ROADS
COUNTY LINES
STATE LINES
RIVERS
Charles E. Hare
PENNSYLVANIA
OHIO
MARYLAND
VIRGINIA
KENTUCKY
Ohio R.
Ohio River
Washington
Uniontown
CUMB. OR NAT. RD.
Monongahela R.
HANCOCK C.H.
HANCOCK
BROOKE
WELLSBURG
OHIO
WHEELING
Bellaire
MOUNDSVILLE
MARSHALL
B+O R.R.
NEW MARTINSVILLE
WETZEL
MONONGALIA
MORGANTOWN
MARION
FAIRMONT
PRESTON
KINGWOOD
Cheat R. Bridge
Oakland
B+O R.R.
Rowlesburg
Redhouse
North Branch
Cumberland
Potomac R.
BERKELEY SPRINGS
MORGAN
BERKELEY
Martinsburg
Shepherdstown
Harper's Ferry
JEFFERSON
CHARLES TOWN
New Creek (Keyser)
Hanging Rocks
HAMPSHIRE
ROMNEY
NW. TP.
South Branch
Blue's Gap
Greenland Gap
Winchester
HARDY
MOORFIELD
Wardensville
Petersburg
Lost River
Woodstock
ST. MARY'S C.H.
MIDDLEBOURNE
TYLER
PLEASANTS
WEST UNION
DODDRIDGE
HARRISON
TAYLOR
Bridgeport
CLARKSBURG
BARBOUR
PHILLIPPI
ST. GEORGE
TUCKER
Corrick's Ford
PARKERSBURG
NW. TP.
WOOD
Cairo
HARRISVILLE
RITCHIE
Little Kanawha R.
S.H.P. TP.
ELIZABETH
WIRT
Broad Run
WESTON
LEWIS
Garnett's Camp
Laurel Hill
Leadsville
BUCKHANNON
UPSHUR
Ravenswood
Burning Sprs (Oil Town)
C.H.
CALHOUN
GLENVILLE
GILMER
Rich Mtn. Pass
BEVERLY
RANDOLPH
Gallipolis
POINT PLEASANT
MASON
JACKSON
RIPLEY
CALIFORNIA C.H.
ROANE
Bulltown
Huttonsville
Cheat Mtn. Pass
Rich Mtn.
PENDLETON
FRANKLIN
Greenbrier R. Battle
Kanawha
Pliny
Buffalo
PUTNAM
PUTNAM C.H.
Scary
BRAXTON
SUTTON
Elkwater
Valley Mtn.
Allegheny Mtn. Pass
Lacy Springs
Harrisonburg
Ohio River
BARBOURSVILLE
Elk R.
CLAY
CLAY C.H.
WEBSTER
ADDISON
H.T.K. TP.
Monterey
CHARLESTON
J.R.+K. TP.
Cross Lanes
SUMMERSVILLE
NICHOLAS
POCAHONTAS
Shenandoah Mtn.
CABELL
KANAWHA
Gauley
Carnifex Ferry Battlefield
Droop Mtn.
HUNTERSVILLE
Staunton
WAYNE C.H.
WAYNE
Cotton Hill
Gauley Bridge
Wild Rd.
Hawks Nest
FAYETTEVILLE
FAYETTE
BOONE
GREENBRIER
Warm Springs
Big Sewell Mtn.
Meadow Mtn.
ARACOMA C.H.
LOGAN
New R.
White Sulphur Springs
Covington
Tug Fork
BECKLEY C.H.
RALEIGH
LEWISBURG
Rocky Gap
OCEANA
WYOMING
Greenbrier R.
UNION
MONROE
Salt Sulphur Springs
PRINCETON
MC DOWELL
MERCER

Chapter XV

Virginia and Secession

LINCOLN AND THE SOUTH

EVENTS FOLLOWING 1850, notably the Kansas-Nebraska Act, the Dred Scott decision, and John Brown's attack upon Harpers Ferry, quickened the disintegrating influences then operating throughout the United States. Most alarming of the resulting consequences was the breakdown of the national Democratic and Whig parties into sectional parties, each with a basis in economic and sentimental differences. In the presidential election of 1856, a new Republican party, with John C. Frémont, the Pathfinder, as its standard-bearer, polled 114 electoral votes, all of them, except those from Oregon, California, Iowa, and Minnesota, from states north of the Ohio River and the Mason and Dixon line.

With the ultimate triumph of this party, which was generally conceded, the consequences were unmistakable. Among other things, the Dred Scott decision would be rescinded and there would be no security for minority rights in slave property. More than anything else the possibilities tended to solidify the South, including eastern Virginia. Alleging that the "government of the Fathers" would, in the event of such a triumph, cease to serve the purposes of its founders, Southerners everywhere had declared their intention to abandon that government, "peacefully, if they could, but forcefully, if they must."

For their purposes John C. Calhoun had evolved a remedy, secession, which was only a technical assertion of the right of revolution. As in 1832, his native state, South Carolina, had accepted this remedy and was ready and eager to follow it to its logical conclusion. On December 20, 1860, about six weeks after the election of Abraham Lincoln and with that as her chief provocation, she accordingly attempted to terminate her connection with the Federal Union by an act of secession. Shortly thereafter she was followed by six other states, Georgia, Florida, Alabama, Mississippi,

Louisiana, and Texas, who joined her in the formation of a government for the Confederated States of America, with its capital at Montgomery, Alabama.

Through the help of the newspaper press, Virginians had meanwhile concerned themselves with the possibilities of Lincoln's election. Under the leadership of the Richmond *Enquirer,* dominated by Henry A. Wise, a small but powerful group of editors and leaders insisted that the Union was already terminated. On the other hand, the Richmond *Whig,* spokesman of the Constitutional Union party and other conservative elements in Virginia, declared that she would not join the Cotton States because of the constitutional election of Abraham Lincoln or any other man to the presidency.

Except in the northwest, most Virginians admitted the right of secession under sufficient provocation. There was, however, almost unanimous accord in denying to the Federal Government the right to coerce a state in any event. Moreover, these conceptions of state rights were inextricably tied up with a consciousness of common interest with the Cotton States, which were largely Virginian in their origins and had kept in close touch with her through common traditions and the domestic slave trade. Thus an attack upon either state rights or Negro slavery was almost certain to produce defensive action.[1] As a precautionary measure the Calhoun followers in Virginia set their hearts upon an extra session of the general assembly and upon a convention of the people.

While the Valley adhered to a conservative middle course, in Trans-Allegheny Virginia the secession of the Cotton States was generally regarded as the work of hotheads and was resented accordingly in resolutions suggestive of those adopted in 1832 and again in 1850. Generally residents of northwest Virginia regarded the guarantees under the Federal Constitution as sufficient protection for property of whatsoever kind and accepted the Dred Scott decision as final. Their chief concern was for their own safety and security. Few persons in the northwest cared for Negroes, other than to be rid of them.

When knowledge of the proposed secession of the Cotton States first reached northwest Virginia, its inhabitants expressed their disapproval in mass meetings. One of the first of these was held in Preston County, on November 12, 1860. Other meetings followed in rapid succession. The following resolutions, adopted January 1, 1861, by "the largest and most enthusiastic" gathering ever assembled in Wood County, are typical of those adopted elsewhere:

> Resolved, That the doctrine of Secession of a State has no warrant in the Constitution, and that such doctrine would be fatal to the Union, and all the purposes of

[1] Bancroft, *Slave-Trading in the Old South,* pp. 88-120, 237-240.

its creation; and, in the judgment of this meeting, secession is revolution. . . . We are deeply impressed with the conviction that our national prosperity depends on preserving the Union as it is; and we see nothing in the election of Abraham Lincoln to the Presidency of the United States . . . affording any just or reasonable cause for the abandonment of what we regard as the best Government ever yet devised by the wisdom and patriotism of men. That the result of calling a Convention to consider what position Virginia shall assume in the revolutionary movements of South Carolina, will be the means of precipitating the State into a connection fatal to her credit, her prosperity, and the happiness of her people.[2]

Simultaneously, other counties were speaking in a language equally unmistakable. After listening to an address by Sherrard Clemens, their Representative in Congress, residents of Ohio County deprecated the possibility of the secession of Virginia and alleged that such a course would place her in the position of a border frontier. January 5, 1861, "workingmen" of the same county declared their unwillingness to be bound by the acts of any convention, the purpose of which was to alter the relation of Virginia to the Government of the United States. About the same time residents of Tyler County declared themselves as favorable to "striking West Virginia from Eastern Virginia and forming a State independent of the South and firm to the Union," in the event Virginia attempted to secede from it.

Equally significant and expressive were protests from individual leaders. Among these was a statement by Waitman T. Willey, of Monongalia County. In a letter to the *Western Virginia Guard* (Clarksburg), dated December 26, 1860, he opposed the secession of the Cotton States as illegal and contrary to good policy. Regarding the threatened secession of Virginia, he expressed himself as believing that such a course would place her at the "tag-end" of an insurrectionary government and expose her western counties to devastation and ruin. As the Republican party was then menaced by factional differences, Willey thought its rule would be temporary and harmless. In any event, he relied upon Lincoln's Whig traditions to make him "a conservative Chief Magistrate . . . faithful to the Constitution." He could not, therefore, see in his election a sufficient provocation for drastic action on the part of any state. Indeed, he regarded such a course as sheer folly, since it deprived a seceding state of her share in the common treasure and the public domain as well.

Many voters of the northwest were Jackson rather than Calhoun Democrats. Because of their traditional conservatism and party regularity they had voted for Breckenridge in 1860. In doing so they had followed the leadership of Henry A. Wise, who, more than any other east Virginian, was the mentor of the northwest. Veiling his real purposes under a

[2] Wheeling *Intelligencer*, January 4, 1861; Virgil A. Lewis, *How West Virginia Was Made* (Charleston, 1909), p. 26.

declaration of intention to "fight in the Union," Wise was signally effective. As understood by his loyal followers, his plan offered a possibility of a redress of grievances and also of the preservation of the Union.[3] In 1861, as in 1832, however, leaders in northwest Virginia would have hanged South Carolina traitors "higher than Haman."

THE GENERAL ASSEMBLY

In the face of protests such as those made by Willey and the general disapproval of the northwest, to which Governor Letcher owed his election, he convened the Virginia General Assembly in extra session on January 7, 1861. Before the election of Lincoln, he had promised the president of the James River and Kanawha Company to convene the assembly for the purpose of considering the company's offer to sell the canal to a French concern. Moreover, ninety-four members had petitioned him on November 7, 1860, to convene it on the first Monday in December to meet the crisis produced by the election of Lincoln. Instead Letcher compromised by selecting January 7, 1861.

In this course Letcher, a Douglas Democrat, was motivated by honest and constructive purposes. Both at home and in neighboring states he was deservedly popular, and, as governor of Virginia he was in a strategic position in a crisis. Though leaders in all sections of the state, even the northwest, were not opposed to a state convention, he opposed it as unnecessary and unwise. Following Brown's attack upon Harpers Ferry, he had recommended that Virginia take the lead in bringing about a convention of all the states, authorized to compromise their differences. True to his western Virginia traditions, Letcher placed blame for the existing impasse upon Abolitionists and Fire-eaters alike. If they could only be induced to compromise, he believed that the Union could be preserved.

But the convening of the assembly came too close to Lincoln's election for immediate consideration of Letcher's recommendations. Indicative of what could happen under sufficient provocation, it occupied itself instead with plans for war. As stated by a correspondent for the Wheeling *Intelligencer,* "The great aim, even among most of its Western members, appears to be to hurry things and *precipitate* the crisis."[4] Under the spell of such purposes the assembly, by unanimous votes, denied the right of the Federal Government to coerce a state and adopted plans for reorganiz-

---

3 Shanks, *Secession Movement,* p. 125; Barton H. Wise, *Life of Henry A. Wise* (New York, 1899), pp. 267-268.

4 Wheeling *Intelligencer,* January 14, 1861.

ing the state militia. Each house resolved also that Virginia would go along with the Cotton States in case war followed the failure to redress their grievances.

Continuing to ignore the governor's recommendations, on January 14 the assembly authorized a convention to meet in Richmond on February 13. Election of delegates was set for February 4, at which time the voters were to determine for themselves whether or not important decisions of the proposed convention would be final. This, the "reference" referendum, was a concession to the opposition, particularly the northwest, as was also the decision to choose delegates on the population rather than on the "mixed" basis of representation. It was indicated also that attention would be given to reforms in the state government.

Ignoring these concessions, the northwest condemned the assembly action as precipitate. Echoing the Richmond *Whig,* the legislators were in fact nicknamed "precipitators." Considering the short time allowed for the choice of delegates, the inclemency of the season, and the difficulties of intercommunication, this designation was not without foundation in fact. Moreover, the authorization was condemned as undemocratic. The conventions of 1829-30 and 1850-51 had each been authorized by the voters.

Already the fears of the northwest with respect to the assembly had been prophetically expressed by John J. Davis, of Harrison County. From numerous articles published in the newspapers, he was convinced that the assembly would be induced to call a convention, ostensibly to determine "what course Virginia shall pursue," but for the real purpose of carrying her out of the Union. By "dexterous and never tiring" trickery and "wirepulling," he expected "the movers of this scheme," first, to build up a majority in the convention favorable to disunion. This accomplished, they would then proceed, by the use of vigilance committees and methods familiar to Jacobins, to work upon public opinion by exciting to action "the worst and most depraved portion" of the population. In the event of such a consummation, he feared that Virginia would be "dragged out of the Union" against the wishes of her conservative and representative citizens.[5]

It was almost two weeks before the assembly gave attention to Letcher's recommendations for the preservation of the Union. In keeping therewith, it invited all of the states, including the seceding ones, to appoint delegates to a conference to meet in Washington, February 4, in what later became known as the "Peace Conference." Five delegates, including John Tyler and George W. Summers, were named to represent Virginia, and the Crittenden compromise was suggested as a basis of action. At the same time, commissioners were sent to President Buchanan and the seceding states to ask that they each refrain from "any and all acts calculated

[5] Granville D. Hall, *The Rending of Virginia* (Chicago, 1902), p. 144.

to produce a collision of arms between the states and the Government of the United States."

THE SECESSION CONVENTION

On the face of the returns, the result of the election for delegates to the convention was an overwhelming victory for the Unionists. The "reference" proposal carried by about 55,000 votes in a total of slightly more than 145,000; and the Unionist strength in the state at large was estimated at around 50,000.[6] Seward, Lincoln, and others in high places were apprised of these results and were assured that Virginia would not join "the Gulf Confederacy."

After these gusts of enthusiasm had given place to reflection, it revealed that the triumph of the Unionists was not so complete as was at first estimated. On this point the Richmond *Whig* agreed that the results proved only that Virginia was opposed to precipitate action and that she expected assurances for the preservation of her constitutional rights in the Union. There was also hope of influencing Congress which was then considering various compromise proposals.

Additional reflections revealed that the convention was divided into three groups or factions. In the order of their size and importance, there were first, the moderates, consisting of about seventy delegates, who came largely from the Valley, the upper Piedmont, and from Potomac counties. Then there was a group of about fifty Unionist delegates coming largely from Trans-Allegheny and Valley counties. They were led by George W. Summers and Alexander H. H. Stuart, upon whom Lincoln depended to keep Virginia in the Union. Finally there was a small but ardent secessionist group, for the most part protégés of John C. Calhoun, who came from the Piedmont and the Tidewater. Like the corresponding elements and factions in the country at large, the two smaller groups were uncompromising, but the balance of power rested with the moderates who were for the most part not unqualifiedly for either the Union or secession.

On the whole, the convention organization was favorable to the Unionists and was so reported and understood throughout Virginia and the country at large. Its most important committee, that on Federal Relations, was composed of ten moderates, seven Unionists, and four secessionists. John J. Janney, of Loudoun County, an ardent Unionist, was, on the nomination of George W. Summers, made chairman of the convention;

[6] Smith, *Borderland,* pp. 109-110; Shanks, *Secession Movement,* pp. 151-157; Beverly B. Munford, *Virginia's Attitude Toward Slavery and Secession* (New York, 1910), p. 256.

but, instead of proceeding at once to the business before it, the convention was "entertained" with speeches which dealt for the most part with Virginia's contributions to the Union and with various phases of coercion and secession.

Among the speeches made in this period was that by Waitman T. Willey, a Unionist, of Monongalia County, delivered on March 4 from a prepared manuscript. Although admitting that the South had grievances which should be redressed, Willey quoted from a letter of James Madison, written in 1832 to deny the legality of secession. Furthermore, he quoted resolutions of both South Carolina and Mississippi to show that they had not always accepted the secession doctrine which, Willey claimed, had its origin in the infamous Hartford Convention.

During the next several days the advantages were decidedly with the secessionists. Appeals of visiting commissioners from the Cotton States made a profound impression throughout Virginia, and the long-awaited Peace Conference report proved disappointing. The failure of Congress and the country at large to rally to this Virginia-sponsored effort to preserve the Union was followed at once by Lincoln's inaugural address which declared his intention "to hold, occupy, and possess the property and places belonging to the Government."

Reactions to these developments were spontaneous and emphatically dissenting.[7] Even the conservative Richmond *Whig* indicated that coercion would be met by "the stern resistance of an united South," and the radical Richmond *Enquirer* proclaimed war at hand. Secessionist meetings again became the order of the day in several centers east of the mountains, and Southerners, passing through Virginia from the Federal capital to cast their lots with the seceding states, added fuel to the burning embers. As a result the secessionists made a number of recruits, but their effort to carry Virginia out of the Union at this time was defeated decisively.

The ability of the moderates and Unionists to weather this storm of particularism was a demonstration of their strength. In the first place the former group realized that Virginia was not prepared for war. Moreover, it was then generally understood among the leaders that "the hideous Chimpanzee from Illinois" was only a figurehead, and that William H. Seward would be President in everything but name. Even before the inauguration, Seward had encouraged Virginians to believe that Lincoln would follow a conciliatory course toward the seceding states.

The moderates were able therefore to control the Committee on Federal Relations, which made a preliminary report on March 9, and a supplemental report ten days later. Though somewhat vague and indefinite with respect to the alleged right of secession, these reports definitely condemned the use of force by the Federal Government for any purpose

[7] Shanks, *Secession Movement*, pp. 174-176.

against a state. The supplemental report recommended that a conference of the Border States and a national convention be called at once. The assumption was that Virginia was willing to await the outcome of their deliberations, and thus the secessionists were again outgeneraled and defeated.

In despair the secessionists temporarily gave up their fight. Meanwhile the moderates placed their hopes in Seward. If he could prevent aggressive action on the part of the President, it was generally conceded that war would be averted; but instead of adjourning the convention in the midst of this triumph, as Lincoln requested, they kept it in session to deal with possible contingencies. Seemingly it did not occur to the moderates that they might lose control.

Toward the end of March, this smug security was disturbed by rumors to the effect that the President intended to relieve Fort Sumter and that Seward could control him no longer, if indeed he had ever controlled him. Again the state rights sentiment ran high throughout eastern Virginia, and a number of leaders and newspapers of that section joined the secessionists. Because of concern over these developments, Lincoln on April 3 sent for George W. Summers, but Summers found it impracticable to leave Richmond at that time and sent John B. Baldwin to confer with Lincoln in his place. Two days later, in a sentence of unmistakable meaning, Baldwin reported the President as having said, "You have come too late."

From this point the Virginia secessionists gained ground rapidly. Though they failed on April 4 by a vote of 45 to 85 to pass a secession ordinance, their policy of delay and filibustering was being crowned with success. From a control which Baldwin, on April 4, considered so absolute as to make unnecessary the adjournment of the convention, the moderates, only a few days later, did not dare to adjourn for fear that the radical assembly, which was still in session, would authorize another convention to meet at once. Under the changed situation, the convention had in fact ceased to be representative.

Taking advantage of this shift in public opinion, which he was quick to detect, Wise, toward the end of March, sponsored an invitation to certain selected men, drawn almost entirely from eastern counties, to meet in Richmond on April 16 for the purpose of consulting with "the friends of Southern rights." Many of the faithful were thus on hand by April 15, when they threatened to disband the convention and would probably have done so but for the opposition of Marshall Ambler, a secessionist. The next day the "Spontaneous Southern Rights" assembly met behind closed doors in a hall by itself, but close enough to that of the regular convention to permit of free access from one to the other.

Meanwhile the venerable Edmund Ruffin and Roger A. Pryor, each of whom had spent much time in "firing the Virginia heart" in county meetings ever since Lincoln's election, had gone to South Carolina to do what they could to precipitate the secession of Virginia from that strategic angle. In a speech at Charleston on April 10, Pryor urged the Confederates to fire on Fort Sumter, and told them that "just so certain as tomorrow's sun will rise upon us, just so certain will Virginia be a member of the Southern Confederacy. We will put her in, if you but strike a blow."[8] Two days later, as a member of the "Palmetto Guards," Ruffin fired the first shot.

The firing upon Fort Sumter produced panic in Richmond. Among the many descriptions of the scenes enacted there at that time, the following from the pen of an eyewitness and a member of the convention, Robert Y. Conrad, is one of the best:

> Yesterday as soon as the news came of the capture of Fort Sumter, there was a great parade of mobocracy and military in the streets, a park of artillery was taken and placed on the public square, just before the Capitol, and one hundred guns fired in honour of the disgrace of our own national flag, the governor was serenaded by a procession with palmetto banners, in front of his own house, and then the doors of the Capitol were forced, and the flag of the Confederated Southern States hoisted on the roof of the Capitol, just over the Hall in which we sit. The rejoicings, with procession, torches, fire works, bonfires, music were kept up until midnight. . . .
>
> The worst of this matter is that men of standing and influence, including some members of the Convention, openly countenance all these proceedings and avow the purpose to establish a provisional revolutionary government, and other regular authorities. I understand several highly respectable men harangued them to this effect. A few days will determine whether this attempt will be persevered in.[9]

It was in the midst of such conditions that on April 15 Lincoln called for 75,000 troops to be used to enforce the laws of the United States. As a consequence a secession ordinance could have been approved at once, but the secessionists, now in control of the situation, chose to do more "heart firing," and to hear the "friends of Southern rights" who were then rapidly rallying to the scene of action.

With the stage thus set, Wise appeared on April 16 before the convention. According to accounts by eyewitnesses, he drew "a pistol from his bosom and laid it before him, and proceeded to harangue the body in the most violent and denunciatory manner." He concluded by taking his watch from his pocket and "with glaring eyes and bated breath, declared that events were then transpiring which caused a hush to come over his soul. At such an hour, he said, Harper's Ferry and its armory were in possession of Virginia soldiers; at another period the Federal Navy Yard and property at Norfolk were seized by troops of the state."

Wise and his friends had taken responsibility for this course in the re-

---

[8] Shanks, *Secession Movement,* p. 198; Mrs. Roger A. Pryor, *Reminiscences of Peace and War* (New York, 1924), p. 120; New York *Tribune,* April 15, 1861.

[9] *Conrad Papers,* in Virginia State Library, Richmond.

fusal of Governor Letcher to act. They regarded war as inevitable and under the circumstances considered it a patriotic duty to safeguard Virginia. Wise has been criticized for his part in this matter, but the manner of taking Virginia out of the Union was only an incident. Public opinion demanded it, and, in all probability, had the convention refused, another convention would have been called at once, if not by the regular assembly, certainly by the "selected friends of Southern rights."

The following day the convention adopted an ordinance of secession. The vote was 88 for, to 55 against. The ordinance was to be effective when ratified by the people in their regular spring election, which fell that year on May 23. This ordinance repealed the acts by which Virginia had ratified the Federal Constitution and the amendments thereto, and declared that document no longer binding upon her and her citizens and subjects. It also declared dissolved "the Union between the State of Virginia and the other States under the Constitution" and reclaimed "all the rights of sovereignty which belong and appertain to a free and independent State."[10]

Virginians residing east of the Alleghenies generally approved the action of the convention on secession. Without waiting for the results of the promised referendum, it proceeded therefore to put the state in a condition of defense. For that purpose Colonel Robert E. Lee was named by Governor Letcher to command the military and naval forces of the state and, on the same day, April 19, Jefferson Davis, President of the Provisional Government of the Confederate States, was notified of Virginia's desire to enter "an alliance, offensive and defensive," with them. On April 23 a committee, of which ex-President John Tyler was chairman, reported such a treaty, which was approved by Virginia the following day. On April 29, five persons were elected to represent her in the Confederate Congress, and on May 7, she was formally admitted to its councils. Early in June, 1861, the capital of the newly formed Confederacy was moved from Montgomery, Alabama, to Richmond, Virginia.

---

[10] For copy of the secession ordinance, see Lewis, *How West Virginia Was Made,* p. 14.

Chapter XVI

The Reorganized Government

SECESSION AFTERMATHS

OF THE 47 DELEGATES from what is now West Virginia in the Virginia Secession Convention, 32 voted against secession, 11 for it, and 4 did not vote. Two of those who did not vote later signed the ordinance, as did also two of those who had voted in the negative. The number of those favoring secession was therefore 15.[1] With these, Lincoln's call for troops to be used to coerce the seceding states, rather than the theoretical right of secession, was the determining factor. Having repeatedly declared against the right of coercion, they refused to back down when put to the test. Political alliances, social influences, and the like were also important factors.

Most of the delegates from present West Virginia who voted against secession lingered in Richmond two to three days awaiting "a more happy

[1] Those voting against the ordinance were: Edward M. Armstrong, George W. Berlin, Caleb Boggess, William G. Brown, John S. Burdett, James Burley, Benjamin W. Byrne, John S. Carlile, Sherrard Clemens, C. B. Conrad, James H. Couch, Alpheus F. Haymond, Chester D. Hubbard, John J. Jackson, William McComas, James C. McGrew, Henry H. Masters, Logan Osburn, Spicer Patrick, Edmund Pendleton, George McC. Porter, Samuel Price, David Pugh, Marshall M. Dent, Ephraim B. Hall, Allen C. Hammond, James W. Hoge, Burwell Spurlock, Chapman J. Stuart, George W. Summers, Campbell Tarr, and Waitman T. Willey—thirty-two in all.

Those voting for the ordinance were: Allen T. Caperton, John Echols, Napoleon B. French, James Lawson, Johnson Orick, Henry L. Gillispie, Cyrus Hall, Leonard S. Hall, John N. Hughes, Samuel Woods, and Franklin P. Turner—eleven in all.

Those not voting were: Thomas Maslin, Benjamin Wilson, Alfred M. Barbour, and Paul McNeil, but the two last named later signed the seccession ordinance.

George W. Berlin and Alpheus F. Haymond voted against secession, but later cast their lots with the Confederacy.

See Lewis, *How West Virginia Was Made,* pp. 29-30; and Shanks, *Secession Movement in Virginia,* pp. 204-207. The official documents may be found in W. Va. Legislature, *Hand Book and Manual* (1917), pp. 259-260; W. Va. Department of Archives and History, *Second Biennial Report* (Lewis, 1908), pp. 158-160.

turn of events." When this did not come, a number of them, variously estimated at from twelve to twenty, met in the room of Sherrard Clemens in the Powhatan Hotel, where they concluded that their presence in Richmond was no longer desired and that it might be dangerous to themselves. They resolved, therefore, to return to their constituents and to do everything in their power to thwart the rising tide of secession. By some, the dismemberment of the Commonwealth was considered possible and desirable.

After being joined by Waitman T. Willey and William G. Brown, neither of whom attended the conference in the Powhatan Hotel, a number of delegates from the northwest left Richmond early Sunday morning, April 21, 1861. They had received passports from Governor Letcher and departed without being molested. At Alexandria one or two experienced slight demonstrations of disapproval, and, because of precautions for the defense of the Federal capital, only one or two were able to reach Washington. Others went to Manassas Junction, whence they reached their homes either by way of Staunton or Winchester.

West of the mountains the returning delegates were greeted with enthusiasm, and some of them took advantage of their welcome to speak freely. Without exception their speeches reflected uncertainties and misgivings. This was true of that by Willey at Fairmont, where he denounced not only the secessionists but also President Lincoln. Laboring under the erroneous belief that the President had refused to receive a delegation of Unionists sent by the convention to ask delay in relief of Fort Sumter, Willey accused him of having precipitated civil war. It was at this time and place that he first gave expression to his "triple treason" doctrine, according to which he claimed that it was then possible for a citizen of Virginia to commit treason against the Federal Government, against the state of Virginia, and against the Southern Confederacy.[2]

The returning delegates found a new state movement well under way. Shortly after casting his vote against the secession ordinance, John S. Carlile, of Harrison County, had left Richmond to take charge of a Unionist movement in the northwest. If conditions favored, he was already committed to a new state. He was the moving spirit in a convention held at Clarksburg, April 22, but "conventions" and mass meetings were then the order of the day in the northwest.

Because of its program the Clarksburg Convention will receive more than passing mention. Under the direction of Carlile it adopted a "Preamble and Resolutions" which recommended, among other things, that "the people in each and all of the counties comprising Northwestern Virginia," appoint no less than five of "their wisest, best, and discreetest men,

[2] Charles H. Ambler, *Waitman Thomas Willey* (Huntington, W. Va., 1954), p. 43.

to meet in Convention on the 13th day of May next, to consult and determine upon such action as the people of Northwestern Virginia should take in the present fearful emergency." This proposal was accompanied by an "Address," which condemned the secession of Virginia as "contrary to the expectation of a large majority of the people of the state," and as a breach of plighted faith. It also expressed regret at her precipitate action in levying war against the United States and adhering to their enemies.

This program came in the nick of time, for every regular civilian organization in the northwest was rapidly disintegrating and assuming a militant air; public officials were resigning their posts; bands of armed men were traversing the public highways in search of such advantages as suited their respective purposes; and farmers, mechanics, and businessmen left their labor to swell the groups congregating here and there to discuss "the situation." In fact, the feeling of disquiet and distrust was so general and intense as to overshadow the usual order of society. Roads were picketed in every direction; the peaceful yeomanry, not yet aroused to the exigencies of the situation, stood aghast; and everyone, despairing of police protection, was preparing to protect his life and liberty.[3]

Under such conditions the Clarksburg "Preamble and Resolutions" were seized upon with avidity. The *Western Virginia Guard* (Clarksburg), in an extra, printed them in full, and through voluntary expressmen, mounted on horseback, copies of "the Guard Extra" were hastened to Weston, Kingwood, Morgantown, and other near-by points. Copies were also sent along the railroad westward to Wheeling and Parkersburg and eastward to Martinsburg and along the Potomac.

Though the Clarksburg program and address were concerned primarily with the secession ordinance and plans for the future, delegates from the northwest carried away from Richmond grievances which they could not forget. Encouraged to expect reforms in the state government, they brought the subject up at what seemed to be an opportune time, only to have their proposals brushed aside as comparatively unimportant. Insistence upon a hearing brought charges of demagoguery and of a desire to trade submission in Federal matters for reforms in the state government. As interest in Federal relations tended to supersede everything else, the honesty of their purposes and the seriousness of their needs were thus underestimated.

Under the circumstances, the attitude of the secessionists can be understood. In the first place they expected the northwest to go along in any event. With them the "Virginia doctrines" had long been first. Besides, the Covington and Ohio Railroad was then being pushed to completion over a route now occupied by the Chesapeake and Ohio. Then, too, both in

[3] Ambler, *Pierpont*, p. 82.

the general assembly and in the early stages of the convention, the northwest had concurred in declarations regarding state rights and against coercion, and since the Reform Convention of 1850-1851 it had supplied its full share of state officers. Moreover, tried and trusted political leaders and representatives of leading families had assured their friends in the east that, in a crisis, "the northwest will be with you to a man." The action of the southwest in accepting secession seemed to confirm this prediction.[4] In the face of such things, to suspect the northwest was to charge it with ingratitude and disloyalty, unpardonable sins among politicians. However, a number of leaders suspected the worst and were willing to allow the northwest to go its way, even if that entailed dismemberment of the Commonwealth.

THE FIRST WHEELING CONVENTION

(May 13-15, 1861)

The convention authorized at Clarksburg, April 22, and formally called by the Wheeling *Intelligencer* five days later, met in Washington Hall, Wheeling, on May 13. Ever since it has been known as the "First Wheeling Convention."[5] It was composed of 436 "delegates," 162 of whom were from the Panhandle. The delegates represented 27 counties, all of which, except Frederick, are now a part of West Virginia. Ignoring the Clarksburg authorization and the *Intelligencer* call, most of the delegates were elected irregularly and did not claim constituent powers.

With Major William B. Zinn of Preston County presiding, the delegates first engaged in a spirited debate to determine the character of their gathering. Some claimed that it was a mass meeting, while others insisted that it was a regularly constituted and authorized convention, as planned and intended by the Clarksburg Convention. Following this indecisive debate, John W. Moss of Wood County was elected president. Later, with flags flying and the delegates and onlookers singing *The Star-Spangled Banner,* the convention endorsed the Clarksburg Address and condemned the Virginia Secession Ordinance as treason.

Led by Carlile, a majority of the delegates favored proclaiming a new state at once. It mattered not that the proposed state would be in the Union, but not formally a part of it. Nor did the provision of the Federal

[4] The vote of the southwest was 18 for secession, to 3 against. See Shanks, *Secession Movement,* p. 205.

[5] For the "Proceedings" of this convention, see Lewis, *How West Virginia Was Made,* pp. 35-76.

constitution which forbade the formation of new states within the bounds of existing states without their consent give great concern. According to Carlile, Vermont, Kentucky, and Tennessee afforded precedents for the proposed new state; and, recalling the decision in Luther *v.* Borden, he believed that Congress was equal to the exigency of determining its status. The proposed state included no territory east of the Allegheny Mountains. Pocahontas, Greenbrier, Monroe, Mercer, and McDowell counties were not included.

In the face of threats of violence, Willey opposed the proposed action as "most extraordinary." In this he was joined by General John J. Jackson, Francis H. Pierpont, John H. Atkinson, and other conservatives. After a heated discussion, it was decided to postpone any action with respect either to a new state or the alternative, reorganization of the Virginia government on a loyal basis. Though the results were generally conceded, it was thought best to await the referendum on the secession ordinance. In the event that it proved favorable to secession, the counties represented at Wheeling and "all others disposed to co-operate" were asked to appoint on June 4, following, delegates to a "General Convention" to meet on the eleventh of that month, at a place to be determined. A "Central Committee," composed of nine persons, headed by Carlile, was to function in the interim.

These plans and arrangements were set forth in a series of resolutions which restated the sentiments of the Clarksburg Address and urged the people of the northwest to vote against secession. The prohibition of the secession ordinance to the contrary notwithstanding, they were at the same time to elect Representatives to Congress and members of the general assembly. The Central Committee was instructed to prepare an address to "the people of Virginia," which was to be printed and circulated as "extensively as possible"; but these activities met formidable opposition from the secessionists. Among other things, they refused to permit the distribution of the United States mail; Unionists were denounced as traitors and threatened accordingly; and every effort was made to organize the militia in the Confederate interest. Thus, when election day came, "thirty thousand glittering bayonets surrounded the polls from the Chesapeake to the summit of the Alleghenies." Except in the central, southern, and eastern sections of the northwest, these acts of intimidation were ineffective, and the northwest accordingly cast about forty-four thousand votes against secession, to four thousand for it.[6]

[6] The total vote, as later proclaimed by Governor Letcher, was 125,950 for secession, to 20,373 against, but this did not include returns from 37 counties in the northwest. Smith, *Borderland,* p. 166; Hall, *Rending,* pp. 284-286; Callahan, *History of West Virginia,* Vol. I, 353.

THE SECOND WHEELING CONVENTION

(*First Session, June 11-25, 1861*)

The advance of Federal troops under General George B. McClellan permitted the election of delegates to the proposed convention to go forward. In due time, the Central Committee of the First Wheeling Convention, having meanwhile conferred with President Lincoln and taken other steps to put the northwest in a state of defense, named Wheeling as the meeting place, and on the appointed date the delegates assembled in the Federal Building of that city, in what has since been known as the "Second Wheeling Convention."[7] Its meeting place, as well as its personnel, was, of course, determined largely by the military, but to make sure of a convention in any event, the resolution authorizing it had provided that those delegates and senators elected on May 23 who approved the purposes of the convention should be entitled to seats in it.

The Second Wheeling Convention consisted of about one hundred delegates who represented thirty-four counties, five of which, Alexandria, Fairfax, Hardy, Hampshire, and Jefferson, were east of the Allegheny Mountains. Thirty-nine of the delegates were members of the general assembly, and fifteen of the forty-four Virginia counties then comprising Trans-Allegheny Virginia, or more than a third of the present area of West Virginia, were not represented. Because of disturbed internal conditions, many, if not most, of the delegates were chosen irregularly, some of them through the intervention of the military, while others were more or less self-appointed. On the second day of their session, they organized by making Arthur I. Boreman of Wood County, president, and Gibson L. Cranmer of Ohio County, secretary.

The first formal action of the convention was the adoption of resolutions, offered by Carlile, thanking Federal authorities for "the prompt manner in which they have responded to our call for protection." At the same time and in the same manner, General McClellan was thanked for having rescued northwest Virginia from "destruction and spoliation," and "the heresy sought to be inculcated by the secessionists, that it is an invasion of Virginia soil for American troops to march to the defense and protection of Virginia citizens," was repudiated. Instead, the soil of Virginia was declared to be "American soil, and free to the march of American soldiery and sojourn of American citizens from all and every portion of American territory." Then, also on motion of Carlile, a committee of thirteen was appointed "to prepare and report business for the Convention."

On June 13, this committee reported a "Declaration of Rights," which

[7] For "Journal" of this convention, see Lewis, *How West Virginia Was Made*, pp. 78-157.

was adopted four days later and in due course was signed by eighty-six delegates.[8] Reverting to the Virginia Bill of Rights of 1776, as reaffirmed in 1830 and again in 1851, this document, then considered one of the most important in the new state movement, pronounced the action of the gen-

Francis H. Pierpont, Loyal Governor of Virginia, 1861-1868

eral assembly in calling the secession convention a usurpation of the rights of the people of the state. Its subsequent acts, particularly that which attempted to force "the people of Virginia to separate from and wage war against the government of the United States and against citizens of neighboring States, with whom they have hitherto maintained friendly, social

[8] For facsimile of these signatures, see J. Marshall Hagans, *Sketch of the Formation of West Virginia* (Charleston, 1891; 1927), p. 40, and Philip M. Conley, *The West Virginia Encyclopedia* (Charleston, W. Va., 1929), p. 381.

and business relations," were therefore declared to be without authority and void. A similar declaration was made with respect to the dicta of the secession convention and the Virginia executive, whereby they had attempted to transfer the allegiance of the people of Virginia to an "illegal confederacy of rebellious states." In what amounted to a declaration of independence, the convention "imperatively demanded the reorganization of the Commonwealth."

As Governor Letcher was on June 14 announcing the results of the secession referendum and promising the northwest reforms in exchange for submission to the secession ordinance, the convention committee on business presented an ordinance for the reorganization of the state government on a loyal basis.[9] This ordinance was adopted five days later, and the next day, June 20, Francis H. Pierpont was, on motion of Daniel Lamb, unanimously elected governor of the Reorganized Government of Virginia, "until such time as an election can be properly held." At the same time and with the same tenure, Daniel H. Polsley of Mason County was elected lieutenant governor, and an executive council of five members was chosen. Later James S. Wheat of Ohio County was in a similar manner elected attorney general.

Both the legislators and the officers of the Reorganized Government were required to take an oath of loyalty to it and the Federal Government as well. The embarrassing constitutional provision which required the presence of a quorum in each house of the assembly for the legal transaction of business was met by a proviso that "a majority in each branch of the members qualified . . . shall constitute a guarantee to do business." In due time, ordinances were adopted covering such matters as the apprehension of "suspicious persons in time of war," the compensation of state officers, and the collection and disbursements of public funds. With the additional words "Liberty and Union," the seal of the Commonwealth was to be that of the Reorganized Government, but until such time as the necessary alterations could be made, Governor Pierpont was authorized to affix his private seals to such papers and documents as might require the use of a seal.

THE REORGANIZED ASSEMBLY

(July 1-26, 1861)

In pursuance of authority granted by the Second Wheeling Convention, Governor Pierpont convened the general assembly of the Reorganized

[9] The government was restored rather than reorganized, but the terminology of the *Journal* will be used in this chapter. For a pertinent comment, see W. Va. Dept. of Arch. and Hist., *Report* (1908), pp. 163-164.

Government on July 1, 1861. Though only fifteen members, three senators and twelve delegates, were present at that time, the meeting of this body was an important step in the history of the Reorganized Government. As Virginia then had a short ballot, only the governor, lieutenant governor, and attorney general being elected by the voters, the election of additional state officers was necessary, and laws had to be enacted to arrest the generally chaotic condition described in this chapter.

The most important matter for the consideration of the assembly was the election of United States Senators to fill the vacancies caused by the withdrawal and subsequent expulsion of Robert M. T. Hunter and James M. Mason. As yet the loyal Representatives elected in May, 1861, had not been seated, and as Congress had been convened in extra session on July 4, it was considered desirable to have loyal Senators present. Their reception, it was thought, would determine whether or not the Reorganized Government was republican in form.[10]

For these key positions, Waitman T. Willey was on July 9 elected for the term ending March 3, 1863, and John S. Carlile for the term ending March 3, 1865. Carlile was already in Washington and Willey hastened to join him, but for some days the course of the Senate respecting them was in doubt. On July 7, Senator Benjamin F. Wade, of Ohio, telegraphed Governor Pierpont saying: "Your senators will be admitted whenever they appear whether the old ones are vacated or not," but it was not until four days later that the seats formerly occupied by Hunter and Mason were declared vacated. On July 13, Andrew Johnson of Tennessee who represented loyal elements in that state, presented the credentials of the loyal Virginia senators. Despite Wade's assurances, their admission was questioned, but they were admitted.[11]

The assembly was being importuned meanwhile to form a new state, but pending the action of Congress with respect to its Senators and Representatives, and through deference to the plans and purposes of the leaders, it was generally agreed that any such action should have its initial authorization in a constituent assembly rather than in a legislature. Moreover, the status of any proposed new state with respect to slavery could not be determined under existing conditions. Rather than create another slave state, Abolitionists, particularly John G. Jacob, editor of the Wellsburg *Herald,* were not enthusiastic about dismemberment, but, Campbell, editor of the Wheeling *Intelligencer*, announced that "there is no one thing that our people are more bent upon."[12]

---

[10] James G. Blaine, *Twenty Years of Congress* . . . , 2 vols. (Norwich, Conn., 1884-86), Vol. I, 315.

[11] The vote was 35 for, to 5 against. See *Cong. Globe,* 37 Cong., 1 Sess., p. 109.

[12] Wheeling *Intelligencer,* July 20, 1861; Ambler, *Pierpont,* pp. 110-112.

THE SECOND WHEELING CONVENTION

(*Adjourned Session, August 6-21, 1861*)

The only important act of the adjourned session of the Second Wheeling Convention was its authorization of the initial step in the dismemberment of Virginia. Though only six weeks intervened between the two sessions of the Second Wheeling Convention, the interim events were fraught with new state possibilities. First of all, the Reorganized Government was fully represented in both branches of Congress. Of equal importance from another angle, Confederate forces had been pushed out of a large portion of the northwest as a result of the battles of Rich Mountain (July 11) and Corricks Ford (July 13), and General Wise's forced departure from the Kanawha Valley. More than anything else, perhaps, Wise's defeat quickened the new state movement. Moreover, the Battle of Bull Run (July 21) pointed to a long and bitter contest which it was feared might defeat the purpose of the Reorganized Government, the restoration of Virginia to the Union.

Under these conditions Campbell, of the Wheeling *Intelligencer,* insisted that "the time to cap the climax" has arrived. Under the aegis of such influences, the convention on the first day of its session authorized the appointment of a committee of one member for each county represented "to take the whole subject of division of this state into consideration" and report to the convention as early as possible. One week later, it reported an ordinance for the formation of the new state; but, in spite of the pronounced dismemberment sentiment, there was much opposition to this ordinance.

In the first place, delegates were not in accord with respect to the bounds of the proposed state. Carlile would have restricted it to the area west of the Alleghenies. Other delegates, notably Daniel D. T. Farnsworth of Upshur County, favored a boundary not unlike that of present West Virginia. These differences were compromised in an agreement which permitted the counties of the present Eastern Panhandle of West Virginia, together with Pocahontas and Greenbrier, to decide for themselves whether or not they would become a part of a proposed state or remain a part of Virginia.

Those favorable to preservation of the Reorganized Government were even more hesitant to go along with the new state movement. Leaders among them made a number of efforts to adjourn the convention *sine die,* but they could not command more than a third of the total number of delegates. They had a strong ally in Edward Bates, attorney general of the United States, who, in a letter to a delegate of the convention, spoke of the proposed new state as "an original, independent act of Revolution." As this was supposed to represent the President's view also, it was accepted by some delegates as final. Nevertheless, the new state movement continued to gather momentum.

The most effective opposition to the dismemberment ordinance came from those opposed to an additional slave state. In general, this element wished to preserve the Reorganized Government. "If the new state is to be a *slave state,*" John G. Jacob, of the Wellsburg *Herald,* preferred "to be a citizen of a State that at least has a history, has territory, has population, and has resources." This opposition manifested itself both in the convention and in the popular vote on the dismemberment ordinance.

Despite these opposing elements, the convention on August 20, by a vote of 48 for, to 27 against, approved "An Ordinance to Provide for the Formation of a New State out of a Portion of the Territory of this State." The proposed state was named "Kanawha" and embraced thirty-nine counties, all of them west of the Alleghenies. As previously indicated, new counties might be included later. By act of the convention, the dismemberment ordinance was submitted to the voters in a referendum set for October 24, at which time they were also to elect delegates to a convention authorized to make a constitution for the "State of Kanawha." After authorizing the printing and distributing of ten thousand copies of the "New State Ordinance," the convention adjourned *sine die.*

FINANCES AND SERVICES

The Reorganized Government was financed largely through the resourcefulness of Governor Pierpont. To meet the expenses of the Wheeling conventions, he borrowed from Wheeling banks, and on June 1, 1861, John List, acting under his orders and with the aid of General McClellan, appropriated temporarily $27,000 on deposit by the state in the Exchange Bank of Virginia at Weston, for use in building there an asylum for the insane. By authorization of the assembly, Pierpont later received a payment amounting to about $45,000 from the Federal Government. This was Virginia's share of the proceeds of public land sales under a Congressional act of 1841, which she, because of her state rights scruples, had refused to accept.[13]

Despite the war then raging, receipts of the Reorganized Government continued to be more or less regular, until its capital was on June 19, 1863

[13] House of Delegates, *Journal* (Regular Session beginning Dec. 2, 1861), pp. 23-24; W. Va. Dept. of Arch. and Hist., *Report* (1908), p. 190; Ambler, *Pierpont,* pp. 181-182, 212.

transferred to Alexandria, on the Potomac, near Washington. At that time there was a balance of $29,508.57 in the state treasury, but it had in the previous February appropriated $175,000 for the uses of West Virginia. Governor Pierpont took with him to Alexandria the balance as indicated above. The counties which recognized the authority of his government continued to contribute to its treasury almost enough to meet current expenses, so that when he went to Richmond, there was still a balance in the treasury of the Reorganized Government.

Immediately following his election, Pierpont, as "Governor of Virginia," asked President Lincoln for military aid to protect "the good people of this Commonwealth." Four days later, he was assured that his request would be granted. On June 27, General Geo. B. McClellan recognized him as the governor of Virginia and indicated that the duty of appointing regimental officers for such Federal troops as might be raised there, would fall upon him. In compliance with this notice and in cooperation with McClellan's successors, Pierpont helped to recruit, officer, and equip about twenty thousand troops. In recognition of his effectiveness, he was on May 22, 1862, elected governor to fill the unexpired term of John Letcher, which ended January 1, 1864. More than once Pierpont was at or near the front, and through trusted friends he kept in close touch with military conditions. He was a confidential friend and adviser of President Lincoln. The purposes of their several conferences are disclosed in the *Lincoln Papers* which, since 1947, have been available to the public in the Library of Congress.

Because of antislavery leanings, which in his case approached Abolitionism, and perhaps because of commitments to Lincoln, Pierpont was not at first enthusiastic over the dismemberment ordinance, but he accepted it without comment and placed no obstructions in the way of the new state makers. His was perhaps the determining influence with Lincoln in his decision to sign the West Virginia Statehood Bill. For this and similar services he is referred to as "The Father of West Virginia." With his capital at Alexandria, Pierpont continued to maintain the Reorganized Government after West Virginia became a separate state. At no time did his authority extend beyond counties bordering on the Potomac River and Chesapeake Bay, and in high places in the Union his diminutive legislature was referred to as the "Common Council of Alexandria." Pierpont had an unfortunate experience with General Benjamin F. Butler involving the respective rights of the civil and military authorities in and about Norfolk. He was, however, on December 2, 1863, re-elected without opposition to succeed himself as governor of Virginia. Early next year he sponsored a constitutional convention which abolished Negro slavery in Virginia and paved the way for reforms in the state government.

Chapter XVII

When Brother Killed Brother

THE SETTING

WHATEVER THE WAR waged throughout a large part of the United States and upon the near-by high seas in the sixties of the last century may now be called—whether the Civil War, as generally; the War Between the States, which is growing in favor; the War of the Rebellion, as in the *Official Records;* or the War of Secession, as used by Lieutenant Colonel G. F. R. Henderson in his masterly *Stonewall Jackson*—in West Virginia that conflict was a fratricidal struggle, in which brother was arrayed against brother, father against son, and neighbor against neighbor. The initial engagements were determining influences in the formation and admission of West Virginia to separate statehood and, more than is generally appreciated, in the final outcome.

In Trans-Allegheny Virginia, the 1861 conditions were not unfavorable to the Confederates. For instance, the management and control of the strategic Baltimore and Ohio Railroad had Southern leanings;[1] and, with Romney as a rendezvous, the McDonalds, the Whites, and their neighbors, almost to a man, rallied in defense of "liberty."[2] In the Kanawha Valley, as in Tennessee, the first call to arms indicated that it might be drummed and fifed out of the Union. In the northern counties, there were also many Confederates and Confederate sympathizers. Had the Confederates taken advantage of the situation by placing a large force under competent leadership in northwest Virginia, the results of their efforts there and elsewhere might have been different. The admitted reticence of local Unionists and their lack of leadership tend to confirm this conclusion.[3] Moreover, like Virginians everywhere, its residents were shocked at the

[1] Festus P. Summers, *The Baltimore and Ohio in the Civil War* (New York, 1939), pp. 45-46.

[2] William N. McDonald, *History of the Laurel Brigade* (Baltimore, 1917), pp. 17-30.

[3] Shanks, *Secession Movement in Virginia,* pp. 210-215; George E. Moore, *West Virginia and the Civil War* (Ph.D. dissertation, W. V. U., 1957).

thought of the invasion of their state by "Yankees." With notable exceptions, such as Pierpont, Campbell, Jacob, and Battelle, few of them cared for Abolitionists. As early as 1855, Thomas J. Jackson had resolved "to be on the opposite side" in any controversy with them.

Most residents of the northwest were concerned primarily with their security. In their dilemma, some of them, notably George W. Summers, of Kanawha County, sought security in neutrality, while others bided the course of events. Except officeholders, militant enthusiasts, and members of prominent families, there were few among them who could forget intrastate grievances involving taxation, internal improvements, and education. With others, their rich natural resources pointed to a manifest destiny obtainable only through the aid of Northern capital. Still others, notably members of the Methodist Episcopal Church, were indoctrinated with the principles of Abolitionism. The Union potentialities were thus strong and only awaited favorable opportunities to motivate them.

After the organization of the first volunteer companies by Colonel Benjamin F. Kelley in May, 1861, recruiting of Federals moved slowly, but with their subsequent successes at Philippi and Rich Mountain, the trend toward the Union was strong and unmistakable, even in the Kanawha Valley. In fact, hundreds of militiamen deserted the Confederate ranks. General Wise estimated that he alone lost five hundred. According to Wise, they were undependable and "utterly unfit in all respects . . . for any movement against an enemy."[4] The Emancipation Proclamation reversed this trend, but, after a short time, militant Methodists and their allies tended to dominate the situation. As a result, West Virginia exceeded by a small margin the total of the several calls made upon her for Federal troops.

FEDERALS AND CONFEDERATES

Because of re-enlistments, nonresident enlistments, and their service in other states, the exact number of West Virginia Federals cannot be determined. It has been estimated at from twenty-eight to thirty-six thousand. The Provost Marshal of the United States gave it as 31,884, but this number included re-enlistments. Including two regiments of veteran infantry, six of volunteer cavalry, and one of artillery volunteers, a total of twenty-six regiments was organized. Most of the regular volunteer regiments were organized in the summer of 1861, after the Federal successes at Rich Mountain, and in the summer of 1862, after General Lee's first invasion of the North. Most of the cavalry regiments had their beginnings

[4] *War of the Rebellion, Official Records,* I. Vol. IV, 768-771, 783.

in 1861, but they were strongly reinforced in 1863 and 1864, when Federals assumed the aggressive and determined to meet Confederates in their own way. Two hundred twelve "Colored Troops" were credited to West Virginia.[5]

The most authentic records of West Virginia Federals are the state adjutant general's reports. That for the Reorganized Government was compiled by Henry J. Samuels, its adjutant general. Those for the remaining part of 1863, and for 1864 and 1865 were compiled by Francis Perry Pierpont, nephew of Governor Pierpont and first adjutant general of West Virginia. A report of the quartermaster general of West Virginia, printed in the House of Delegates' *Journal* for the 1864 session, is a valuable source of information.

The number of West Virginia Confederates is more difficult to determine than is the number of Federals. In some cases, muster rolls were not kept, but, from such records as have been preserved and from recent researches, the number has been placed at seven thousand, which the present writers think is too low. There were twelve companies of West Virginians in the famous "Stonewall Brigade"; the Twenty-second Virginia regiment was composed entirely of West Virginians, as were also nine companies of her Thirty-first, and six of her Thirty-sixth infantry. Estimates by counties made in more recent years would bring the number to near nine thousand. A report of the adjutant general of West Virginia, made August 1, 1865, tends to confirm this estimate. During the months immediately preceding, he paroled five thousand Confederates in twenty counties in and near the Kanawha Valley. When it is recalled that the Eastern Panhandle had almost four thousand Confederates, the remaining counties would need less than one thousand to bring the total to nine thousand or more.

These numbers do not take into account hundreds of independents and scouts on each side. Whereas thousands of residents firmly resolved to be neutral, most of them took part on one side or the other before hostilities ended. With hundreds of persons, both Federals and Confederates, "bushwhacking," often disguised as squirrel hunting, was a favorite pastime, whereas others, mostly Confederate sympathizers, were sent to civilian prisons.

THE LEADERS

In a work of this character, designation of "the leaders" in the struggle must be restricted to persons who distinguished themselves by outstand-

[5] Adj. Gen., *Report,* 1865, pp. 369-373. More than three thousand West Virginia Federals lost their lives. W. Va. Dept. of Arch. and Hist., *Third Biennial Report,* pp. 217-219.

ing achievements. Among these was General Isaac H. Duval (September 1, 1824-July 10, 1902) who, after serving an apprenticeship on the Texas frontier and as a "Forty-Niner," enlisted in the First (West) Virginia infantry for three months and was elected major. When his regiment re-enlisted for three years, he retained his command. He was on September 26, 1862 appointed colonel in the Ninth (West) Virginia, with which he

General Isaac H. Duval

General Joseph A. J. Lightburn

saw most of his war service. He had a part in a total of thirty-six battles and was at or near Appomattox when Lee surrendered. Following the war he held a number of positions of honor and trust.[6]

For achievement and perseverance, General Joseph A. J. Lightburn (September 21, 1824-May 17, 1901), of Lewis County, was second to none among West Virginia Federals. A boyhood friend and companion of "Tom" Jackson, "Joe" Lightburn was denied a military education. Undaunted, he enlisted in the regular army and served for four years. When the war began, he was back on the farm working hard on weekdays and attending the Broad Run Baptist Church on Sundays. He was a member of the Second Wheeling Convention, and on August 14, 1861, was commissioned by Governor Pierpont, colonel of the Fourth (West) Virginia infantry. Following his defeat in the Kanawha Valley in 1862, he was assigned to duty with General Grant in the Mississippi Valley. He had a part in the capture of Vicksburg, and served with General Sher-

6 Atkinson and Gibbens, *Prominent Men of West Virginia,* p. 417; Wellsburg *Herald,* July 11, 1902.

man until after the fall of Atlanta. After the war, he became a minister of the Baptist Church and a circuit rider. He was known as the "Fighting Parson."[7]

General Benjamin F. Kelley (April, 1807-June 16, 1891) was largely responsible for the organization of the First (West) Virginia volunteer infantry. He planned the Battle of Philippi, where he received a wound from the effects of which he never fully recovered. In October, 1861, he succeeded Brigadier General Frederick W. Lander as commander of the Harpers Ferry-Cumberland District, organized for the defense of the Baltimore and Ohio Railroad. Thereafter most of Kelley's war service was in defense of that strategic thoroughfare. During several months he was in command of the West Virginia District.

Among other prominent West Virginia Federals were: Major Nathan Goff (February 9, 1843-April 23, 1920), of Harrison County, who kept in the limelight by his unusual experiences which, together with his fine personality, contributed later to make him a political favorite;[8] General Thomas M. Harris (June 17, 1813-September 30, 1906), of Ritchie County, who organized the Tenth (West) Virginia regiment and was a member of the military commission which tried conspirators in the assassination of President Lincoln; General Robert S. Northcott (September 30, 1818-January 21, 1906), of Harrison County, later distinguished as an editor; General Jesse L. Reno (June 20, 1823-September 14, 1862), born at Wheeling and killed in the Battle of South Mountain; General David H. Strother (September 26, 1816-March 8, 1888) who rendered valuable service in the mapmaking corps; Colonel Joseph Thoburn, of the First (West) Virginia, killed October 19, 1864, in action at Cedar Creek; Colonel George R. Latham, of the Fifth and Sixth cavalry, who later represented a West Virginia district in Congress; and numerous others whose records and achievements may be studied in the *Official Records,* the adjutant general's reports, and in county and regional histories.

Thomas J. (Stonewall) Jackson (January 21, 1824-May 10, 1863), born at Clarksburg, Harrison County, and reared in Lewis County, is the outstanding character among West Virginia Confederates. Though he had resided in Lexington for ten years before the war began, his family and traditions were inseparably associated with West Virginia. It was there that he suffered the trials and limitations of an impoverished orphanhood; it was there, as a young constable and fellow of the world, that he acquired inalienable concepts of duty and responsibility; it was there that he acquired those fundamentals of Christianity which made of him a Cromwellian warrior. As has been well said of Jackson, "His fame is no longer the exclusive property of [West] Virginia and the South; it has

[7] *Dict. of Amer. Biog.*, Vol. XI, 239; *West Va. Rev.*, Vol. XI, 72-74; Vol. XV, 240.
[8] Gerald W. Smith, *Nathan Goff, Jr., A Biography* (Ph.D. dissertation, W. V. U., 1954).

become the birthright of every man privileged to call himself an American."

Stonewall Jackson, a graduate of West Point in the class of 1846, is today recognized as one of the greatest soldiers of all time. Though he had won distinction in the Mexican War, as a professor of artillery in Virginia Military Institute he was all but forgotten when, in 1861, he cast

Thomas J. (Stonewall) Jackson, "right arm" of General R. E. Lee

Laura Jackson Arnold, "Mother" to the 32nd Ohio Infantry and other federal regiments

his lot with the Confederacy. In its service he distinguished himself as a tactician. As such he is known throughout the civilized world. His "foot cavalry," as his fast-marching infantry, numbering many West Virginians, was called, was the most famous of Confederate commands.[9]

General John McCausland (September 13, 1836-January 21, 1927), of Mason County, (West) Virginia, was born in St. Louis, Missouri, and educated in Buffalo Academy, Putnam County, (West) Virginia, and in Virginia Military Institute, where he was graduated in 1857, first in a class of twenty-three. When the war began, he was a professor of mathematics in his Alma Mater. He and Thomas J. Jackson, as officers of cadets, had witnessed the execution of John Brown. He fought from the beginning to the end of the war and until the day of his death boasted that he had never surrendered. In other words, he was an "unreconstructed and un-

[9] G. F. R. Henderson, *Stonewall Jackson and the American Civil War,* 2 vols. (New York, 1898); Thomas J. Arnold, *Early Life and Letters of General Thomas J. Jackson* (New York, 1916); Roy B. Cook, *Family and Early Life of Stonewall Jackson* (Richmond, 1924); *West Va. Review,* Vol. II, 300; Vol. X, 356; Vol. XI, 158; *Dict. Amer. Biog.,* Vol. IX, 556-559.

regenerated Rebel." At the time of his death on one of his several farms along Kanawha River, he was one of two surviving officers of high rank in the Confederate army.[10]

General Albert G. Jenkins (November 10, 1830-May 21, 1864), of Cabell County, won military distinction because of his ardor for a cause. Soon after his graduation in 1850 from Harvard Law School, he became interested in politics. This interest, together with his Virginia antecedents and the fact that his father was a large landholder and slaveholder, caused him to espouse the interests of the South. As a member of Congress during the years immediately preceding the war, he became thoroughly imbued with Southern rights and the various proposals to maintain them. From the outset he was active for the Confederacy. He died from the effects of a wound received on May 9, 1864, at Cloyd Mountain, Pulaski County, Virginia.[11]

In the initial days of the Confederacy, its most outstanding military character in the present Eastern Panhandle was Colonel Angus McDonald, Sr. (February 14, 1799-December 1, 1864). After 1856, he had resided near Winchester. With the adoption of the secession ordinance, he returned to Romney, and took an active part in rallying the fighting strength of the South Branch and neighboring valleys. He was the moving spirit in the organizations out of which grew the famous "Laurel Brigade." He was a mentor of the Ashby's, the Whites, and others who helped to make that and other Confederate commands immortal.[12]

Among other Confederate leaders were Robert White, of Hampshire County; John Hanson McNeill and his son, Jesse C. McNeill, of Hardy County; Alexander R. Boteler, of Shepherdstown, Jefferson County, an artist of distinction; John Echols, of Monroe County, who fought from the beginning to the end of the war and later became prominently identified with the Chesapeake and Ohio Railroad and higher education in Virginia; and a score or more captains and lieutenants whose activities may be studied in county and regional histories and in the *Official Records.*

Though the war interests of Laura Jackson, only sister of Stonewall Jackson, were not military, mention of her is pertinent. In 1845, she became the wife of Jonathan Arnold, an ardent Southerner and a later secessionist, and went to live in Beverly, Randolph County, where she resided during the war as an unwavering friend of the Union. Because of this loyalty, she was later the recipient of many recognitions. During her declining years, she lived at Buckhannon, where she died and was

10 *West Va. Review,* Vol. III, 221; *Dict. Amer. Biog.,* Vol. XI, 575.

11 *Dict. Amer. Biog.,* Vol. X, 43-44; *West Va. Review,* Vol. XI, 225.

12 William N. McDonald, *A History of the Laurel Brigade* (Baltimore, 1907), pp. 17-72; *Official Records,* I, Vol. II, 952-953; Vol. V, 808, 846-857.

buried. On Memorial Day, a United States flag is placed over her grave. This custom, begun by Union soldiers, was continued by the Daughters of the American Revolution, and is now preserved by the American Legion. Indicative of a changing order of things, friends and admirers of Stonewall Jackson respect and revere the memory of his sister Laura.[13]

Philippi Covered Bridge, Barbour County

MILITARY OPERATIONS, 1861

As Federal troops in superior numbers began to converge upon Grafton, Colonel George A. Porterfield moved to Philippi, which he resolved to hold until he could be reinforced and reoccupy Grafton which was seized on May 30 by Colonel Kelley. While Porterfield was waiting for reinforcements, his command was surprised on June 3, at daybreak, by two converging detachments of Federals, one under Kelley and the other under Colonel Ebenezer Dumont, who defeated him in "the first important inland engagement of the Civil War."[14] In the "Philippi Races" which followed, Porterfield retreated to Beverly, where he was on June 8 superseded by Brigadier General Robert S. Garnett.

[13] A. P. Siviter, *Recollections of War and Peace,* 1861-1868 (New York, 1938), pp. 72-73, 371n.

[14] *Official Records,* I, Vol. II, 64-74.

While General George B. McClellan's subordinates held Grafton, Clarksburg, and Philippi, and were being reinforced from day to day, General Garnett established strong defensive positions on the west side of Laurel Hill near present Belington, and in and near Rich Mountain Pass about ten miles south of Laurel Hill and five miles west of Beverly.[15] From these positions, Garnett was in striking distance of the Baltimore and Ohio Railroad, which he threatened constantly.

Taking care to announce his coming as a protector and a defender and not as an invader, George B. McClellan reached Grafton on June 23 and took personal command of Federal operations.[16] With four regiments under Brigadier General W. S. Rosecrans moving to his aid from Camp Dennison, Ohio, he decided on an aggressive policy. In pursuit of this policy, Rosecrans occupied Buckhannon on June 30, and on the same day Colonel Erastus B. Tyler occupied Weston. Brigadier General Charles W. Hill had meanwhile occupied a strong position at Rowlesburg; and Brigadier General Thomas A. Morris held Philippi.

With the Confederates enveloped on two sides and greatly outnumbered, McClellan decided to strike at once. To the surprise of the enemy, he did not move against Garnett at Laurel Hill, but centered his main attack, which he led in person, upon Rich Mountain. While Morris was advancing against Laurel Hill, McClellan contacted the enemy on July 10. On the following day, by way of a secret path and the aid of a youth named David Hart, Rosecrans came upon the rear of Colonel John Pegram's entrenchment in Rich Mountain Pass. Though Captain Julius A. De-Lagnel put up a stubborn fight for three hours, the Confederates were swept from the mountain. The following day Pegram surrendered his command at Beverly.[17]

Garnett soon learned of this disaster and, after a skirmish with advancing Federals under Morris, he evacuated his camp and retreated toward Beverly in an effort to escape by way of the Staunton and Parkersburg Turnpike. As he approached that town, he was informed that it was already occupied by Federals. He retraced his steps in an effort to gain the Northwestern Turnpike at or near present Red House. Though Morris had not pursued at once, Garnett's change of plans enabled him to keep close upon his heels all the way to present Parsons, where, at near-by Corricks Ford, Garnett was killed on July 13.[18] But for the fumbling of inexperienced Federals, his entire command, done to exhaustion by loss of sleep and forced marches, could have been captured. It escaped to Monterey by way of Greenland Gap.

---

[15] *Ibid.*, I, Vol. II, 236-242, 257.

[16] *Ibid.*, I, Vol. II, 48-49, 196; McClellan, *Report* (New York, 1864), pp. 15-16, 21-22; *George B. McClellan's Own Story* (New York, 1887), pp. 50-51.

[17] *Ibid.*, I, Vol. II, 202-205, 252-276.

[18] *Ibid.*, I, Vol. II, 204-205, 218-221.

Though McClellan had fallen short of a crushing victory, he had achieved wonders. Within three weeks after his arrival, he had all but cleared the Monongahela Valley of Confederates. Still yearning for other worlds to conquer, he on July 20 telegraphed to Governor Pierpont his intention to march his forces into the Kanawha Valley, "to complete our work and establish your authority." His achievements had attracted nation-wide attention, and two days later he was called to Washington and placed in command of the Army of the Potomac to retrieve the Federal losses of the First Battle of Bull Run.

General Rosecrans succeeded McClellan, and carried out his instructions for the fortification of Cheat Mountain Pass. He also established a reinforcing camp at Elkwater in command of General Joseph J. Reynolds. He then directed his chief attention to the Kanawha Valley, where Confederate activities had assumed threatening aspects.

With official instructions to "rely upon the arms among the people to supply the requisite armament, and upon their valor and knowledge of the country as a substitute for organization and discipline," Henry A. Wise, who, according to his own estimate, was "a civilian soldier only" and "nearly worn down in the siege of the Virginia Convention," reached Charleston on July 6 in command of the "Wise Legion," which he had recruited on the way. He was joined at once by the "Kanawha Riflemen" under command of Colonel C. Q. Tompkins and by several hundred militia, which brought his force to twenty-seven hundred men.[19] Though warned by Colonel Tompkins that the militia might not "obey a call to the field," Wise confidently expected additional recruits and planned to sweep the enemy from the Kanawha Valley and move against Wheeling, where only a few weeks before the Reorganized Government had been established.

At a time when Garnett was confident of the adequacy of the Confederate forces in the Kanawha Valley for any emergency, General Jacob D. Cox, on July 9, crossed the Ohio River at Gallipolis. With the aid of steamboats and barges, he proceeded at once up the Kanawha River. On the afternoon of July 17, his advance guard of twelve hundred men encountered eight hundred Confederates at the mouth of Scary Creek about fifteen miles west of Charleston. Despite the fact that the Confederates were outnumbered, they were, through timely reinforcements, able to turn the Federals back and to claim a victory which McClellan described as "something between a victory and a defeat."[20]

Because Cox was being reinforced, the expected recruits from the Kanawha Valley were not in sight, and all hope of reinforcements from Garnett had vanished, Wise, in keeping with a previously arranged plan,

---

19 *Official Records,* I, Vol. II, 293, 908.

20 *Ibid.,* I, Vol. II, 288-292.

beat a hasty retreat up the Kanawha Valley. This movement was accelerated by the discovery that "the grass of the soil" which he was defending was "full of copperhead traitors," who "invite the enemy, feed him, and he arms and drills them." Thus favored, Cox took Charleston on July 25 and, four days later, reached Gauley Bridge. On July 31, Wise was in Lewisburg on his way to Covington to protect the Virginia Central Railroad.[21]

At this point, Wise was diverted from his plan by a change of policy. Instead of continuing to Covington, he was ordered to co-operate with General John B. Floyd, until a short time before Secretary of War in President Buchanan's cabinet and also, like Wise, a former governor of Virginia. Floyd outranked Wise and, with contempt for him and his failures, was bent upon immediate action. On August 6, they met near White Sulphur Springs for their first conference. Five days later, Floyd formally assumed command of their forces.[22]

This marked the beginning of one of the outstanding politico-military comedies of the war. With Wise insisting that time was needed to condition his tired and neglected troops and that "the Legion" was an independent unit, Floyd continued to demand action. As Cox had not advanced beyond Gauley Bridge, where Wise, to the great disgust of the local inhabitants, had burned the bridge, Floyd had his way, and on August 18 encamped on Big Sewell Mountain. Wise reluctantly accompanied him and the following day moved farther west. During the ensuing days, he begged General Lee to separate his command from that of General Floyd.

About this time, Floyd conceived the idea of cutting the routes of intercommunication between Rosecrans and Cox by crossing Gauley River at Carnifex Ferry about thirty miles above Gauley Bridge. Wise condemned this plan as dangerous, even foolhardy. In defiance of Floyd's orders to reinforce him and center operations upon the execution of his plan, Wise continued to engage the enemy in the region of Hawks Nest. The persistence of the enemy together with the strategic importance of the James River and Kanawha Turnpike, was urged as a justification for his course. Meanwhile, Floyd on August 26 had defeated the enemy at Cross Lanes. Insisting that there was danger of his camp's being isolated at Carnifex Ferry by a Federal advance over the Wilderness Road to a strategic point on the James River and Kanawha Turnpike between the two Confederate armies, Floyd nevertheless held his ground and ordered Wise to support him.[23]

---

[21] *Ibid.*, I, Vol. II, 291, 1011-1012; Vol. V, 768.

[22] Under date of June 6, Wise had been notified that Floyd, "being senior by commission," would command the two armies in case they were for any reason combined. *Ibid.*, I, Vol. II, 909.

[23] *Ibid.*, I, Vol. V, 809, 812-816, 822-823, 831, 836-844.

As General Rosecrans was known to be advancing southward, Floyd did not occupy Cross Lanes. Instead he moved back a short distance and entrenched himself in a strong position near Carnifex Ferry, where, on the afternoon of September 10, he was discovered by Rosecrans. In the fighting which followed, the Federals had a number of casualties and failed to reach the Confederate breastworks. As soon as darkness settled upon his camp, Floyd recrossed Gauley River.[24]

In addition to being one of the most important engagements in present West Virginia, the Battle of Carnifex Ferry is notable because of the participation therein of two persons, Rutherford B. Hayes and William McKinley. Both were later elevated to the presidency of the United States.

Exaggerating the enemy losses and placing the blame for his retreat upon Wise, Floyd retired to Meadow Bluff on the James River and Kanawha Turnpike, about fifteen miles west of Lewisburg. As he had sustained only slight losses at Carnifex Ferry and his retreat was represented to be strategic, he was for some time the recipient of much praise, and Wise was, of course, pictured as the "villain." In compliance with Floyd's orders, Wise brought up the rear, but instead of joining him, encamped at Big Sewell Mountain. From their respective positions, the two commanders continued to quarrel,[25] until September 21, when General Lee rode into Floyd's camp. On that same day, the Confederate Secretary of War instructed Wise to turn over his troops to Floyd and report in person to the adjutant general in Richmond. These instructions reached Wise five days later, and after conferring with General Lee, he set out for Richmond.

Since shortly after General Garnett's defeat and death, General Lee had been in the northwest on "a tour of inspection and consultation on the plan of campaign." In this capacity he had tried to help the leaders in charge in their efforts to drive Federals from Cheat Mountain and Elkwater. They hoped thus to get within striking distance of the Baltimore and Ohio Railroad, control of which Lee considered worth an army to the Confederates. For this purpose he was given about 15,000 troops, whom he stationed along the Huttonsville-Huntersville and the Staunton-Parkersburg turnpikes east of Cheat Mountain.

Despite his superior numbers and the open avenues of approach, Lee encountered insuperable obstacles. In fact, nature seemed to conspire against him. Among other things it rained almost continuously during August and September; on the night of August 14-15, ice froze in the

24 *Ibid.*, I, Vol. V, 128-132, 146-150, 592; Jacob D. Cox, *Military Reminiscences of the Civil War*, 2 vols. (New York, 1900), Vol. I, 144-146; Whitelaw Reid, *Ohio in the War*, Vol. I (Cincinnati, 1868), 318-319; R. B. Hayes, *Diary and Letters*, Vol. II (Columbus, Ohio, 1922), 85-100.

25 *Official Records*, I, Vol. V, 854-869.

Confederate camp on Valley Mountain; and measles, which had plagued Garnett's camp at Laurel Hill, laid Lee's men low and destroyed their morale.[26]

Undaunted by these obstacles, Lee planned his campaign carefully and was rewarded on August 31 by being commissioned a general. The satisfaction and encouragement from this recognition was, however, neutralized somewhat by the necessity of dealing with General W. W. Loring, chief in command in the northwest. While Lee was a captain in the Mexican War, Loring had been a general and felt slighted by the preferment shown his former subaltern. Under the circumstances, he was indifferent and did not give wholehearted co-operation. Moreover, on the day of the Confederate attack on Cheat Mountain Pass, September 12, other subordinates bungled things, and a probable victory was turned to defeat. Furthermore, while reconnoitering Rich Mountain the following day, Lieutenant Colonel John A. Washington of Lee's staff was killed by scouts only a few miles from the Federal camp at Elkwater.[27]

Fresh from these experiences, Lee took up the rôle of inspector and consultant to Floyd and Wise. Fortunately for all, Wise's forced withdrawal cleared the situation somewhat. The defection of the leaders had, however, extended to the ranks and made co-operation difficult. Worse still, perhaps, the intractable Loring was designated to succeed Wise and was entrusted with the task of pushing the Federals out of the region about Hawks Nest. About the same time, Floyd was sent to the south side of New River. In the course of a few weeks, he established himself on Cotton Hill, from which vantage point he overlooked the Federal camp at Gauley Bridge and harassed it from time to time with shot and shell.

But for incessant rains, which on October 5, 1861 raised the Kanawha River at Charleston to a height probably never reached before or since, the contending armies might have met in the region of Hawks Nest in one of the decisive battles of the war. Capable general that he was, Rosecrans took advantage of the weather conditions to avoid battle. With the approach of winter, Lee two weeks later abandoned further movements in the direction of Gauley Bridge and ordered Loring to withdraw his forces to Lewisburg. Floyd held on for a time, but finally abandoned his position in a manner and for reasons never fully explained or understood.[28] Soon thereafter Loring was sent to Winchester and Floyd was detailed to

---

[26] Douglas S. Freeman, *R. E. Lee, A Biography*, 4 vols. (New York, 1934-1935), Vol. I, 545-578.

[27] Lee made no official report of the Battle of Cheat Mountain. The best account is in Freeman, *Lee*, Vol. I, 554-578. For Federal reports, see *Official Records*, I, Vol. V, 184-191.

[28] See Milton W. Humphreys, *Military Operations in Fayette County, West Virginia, 1861-1863* (pamphlet published privately), Fayetteville, W. Va., 1926. This pamphlet contains also an account of the Battle of Carnifex Ferry by Roy Bird Cook.

the Confederate Army in the West. The Kanawha Valley was lost to the Confederates.

With the cessation of military operations in 1861, Federals were in almost undisputed control of Trans-Allegheny Virginia. But for the effective stands of Confederates under General H. R. Jackson at Greenbrier River, October 3, and Allegheny Mountain, December 13, the Federals were in position to push toward Staunton and cut the railroads connecting Richmond, Virginia, and Chattanooga, Tennessee.

In the Eastern Panhandle the situation was scarcely more favorable to the Confederates. At the beginning of hostilities Colonel T. J. Jackson occupied Harpers Ferry, but he was on May 24 replaced by General Joseph E. Johnston, a more experienced commander. On June 13, Colonel Lew Wallace in command of Indiana troops operating out of Cumberland, Maryland, occupied Romney. Though he remained only an hour, Wallace's feat disclosed the possibility of cutting the Confederate communications between Harpers Ferry and Winchester. Meanwhile, Johnston had decided to abandon Harpers Ferry, but in doing so, the coveted "B & O" was to be made useless to the enemy. This "patriotic service" was entrusted to Jackson, who executed it with such dispatch and thoroughness as to arouse the slumbering Union sentiment in Maryland and northwest Virginia.[29]

For some time following Johnston's withdrawal from Harpers Ferry, Federals were seemingly indifferent to the importance of the railroad. Following First Bull Run, the Confederates were therefore able to repossess it and continue their work of destruction. It was not until autumn, 1861, that Federals awakened to the consequences of their neglect. To retrieve it, an independent district covering the road between Harpers Ferry and Cumberland was created, and Brigadier General Frederick W. Lander was put in command with instructions to recover and recondition the road. As Lander entered upon the execution of this assignment, he was seriously wounded in a skirmish at Edwards Ferry near Leesburg, Virginia, and the task devolved upon Brigadier General Benjamin F. Kelley. With New Creek as a base of operations, Kelley on October 26 reoccupied Romney.

THINGS MILITARY, 1862

Four days before Kelley occupied Romney, Jackson, who had been promoted in rank following Bull Run, where he received his sobriquet of

29 Festus P. Summers, *The Baltimore and Ohio in the Civil War* (New York, 1939), pp. 90-110.

"Stonewall," was placed in command of the newly formed Valley District. With headquarters at Winchester, his first task was to clear his district of enemy troops and complete the destruction of the Baltimore and Ohio. When these things had been accomplished, he planned to move swiftly across the Alleghenies, drive Federals from its passes, and recover the northwest.[30] Apprised of these purposes, Kelley ordered Colonel Samuel H. Dunning to attack the Confederate outpost at Blues Gap or Hanging Rock about thirteen miles east of Romney. Following his indifferent success there, Kelley on January 10 abandoned Romney, which was occupied three days later by Jackson.

With the advent of winter, Jackson was forced to abandon temporarily his plans with respect to the northwest, only to see them, in the course of the next two weeks, effectively nullified by the superior prestige of General Loring. After his departure from the Kanawha Valley, Loring had been sent first to Winchester, then to Romney. With Jackson in winter quarters at Winchester, Loring chafed under his comparatively insignificant assignment and set about to change it. With the aid of others, he was able to reach the ear of the Confederate War Department, which was led to believe that Jackson had made a strategic blunder in occupying Romney. Under date of January 30, he was accordingly directed to notify Loring to evacuate it and retire to Winchester.

His plans blasted, Jackson resigned and requested to be returned to his professorship. It was only through the intercession of Governor John Letcher and General Joseph E. Johnston that he was induced to reconsider.[31] Of the consequences of the withdrawal of the Confederates from Romney, it will suffice to say that the Federals on February 7 reoccupied it. Moreover, on March 30 they reopened the Baltimore and Ohio from the Ohio River to Chesapeake Bay.[32]

Wheeling had meantime become the center of military activities. During the winter of 1861-62, it was General Rosecrans's headquarters and as such was visited by many Federal officers. As they were planning for the 1862 campaign, they were astounded by the announcement of the creation of the "Mountain Department," comprising western Virginia, eastern Kentucky, and a portion of Tennessee, with John C. Frémont in command.

Frémont reached Wheeling March 28 and at once surrounded himself with a staff, composed largely of foreigners. (Rosecrans had been detailed

---

30 *Official Records,* I, Vol. V, 965-966.

31 Jackson preferred charges against Loring. See *Official Records,* I, Vol. V, 1065-1066. For Loring's answer, see *Ibid.,* I, Vol. V, 1070.

32 Summers, *Baltimore and Ohio,* p. 114. The road was closed again by Confederates at the time of Lee's first and second invasions of the North. Otherwise, except for brief periods, it was kept open during the remainder of the war. *Ibid.,* pp. 119-122. See also *Official Records,* I, Vol. V, 388.

to the Army of the Tennessee.) On the score of "pressing business" Frémont secluded himself from the public and from civilian and military officials, as well.[33] In due time, thanks to his capable wife, Jessie, he was able to move to New Creek, where his troops detrained and advanced thence through valleys and mountain passes to the region of Harrisonburg. There he met Jackson and was decisively defeated. Soon thereafter Frémont resigned his command, and, like a pebble cast into a pool, sank out of sight. Thus ended what had been heralded at Wheeling during the spring of 1862 as "the beginning of the end."

Though the long lines of marching Federals, which crossed the Alleghenies in the spring and summer of 1862, were tempting targets for Confederate bushwhackers, most of the remaining military movements of that period were raids. One of these was led by John D. Imboden to aid Lee's proposed invasion of the North. For this purpose he set out on August 14 from Franklin, Pendleton County, to destroy the Cheat River railroad bridge, but was turned back at Saint George, Tucker County.

The most important military operations of the year in present West Virginia were in the Kanawha Valley. With Lee's proposed invasion of the North, the Federal capital was thought to be in danger and all available troops were sent for its defense. Among these were troops under General Cox, who, under the direction of General Eliakim P. Scammon, a careful and methodical engineer, had built formidable entrenchments at Fayetteville and near-by points. The Federals were thus able to command the Giles-Fayetteville-Kanawha Turnpike and were within striking distance of the James River and Kanawha Turnpike. With the departure of Cox, this key to the Kanawha Valley became vulnerable, and Confederates conducted themselves accordingly. They were in desperate need of salt and still entertained the belief that the Kanawha Valley might be recovered.[34]

The possibilities were too promising to be treated lightly. General Jenkins was accordingly ordered to reconnoiter the entire situation. This he did in his now famous raid. Setting out from Salt Sulphur Springs, Monroe County, at the head of the Eighth Virginia Cavalry of five hundred fifty men, he marched through Greenbrier, Pocahontas, Randolph, Upshur, Lewis, Gilmer, Calhoun, Roane, and Jackson counties to the Ohio River, which he crossed at Ravenswood. Avoiding Federals at the mouth of the Kanawha, he rejoined his command by keeping to the south of the Kanawha River. All told, he covered a distance of more than five hundred miles. Among his reprisals were 300 prisoners, 5,000 stands of arms taken on August 30 at Buckhannon, and $5,525 taken from a Federal paymaster at Ripley, Jackson County.[35]

33 Ambler, *Pierpont,* pp. 144-147.

34 Humphreys, *Military Operations.*

35 For official report see *Official Records,* I, Vol. XII, pt. 2, 756-768.

As Jenkins found conditions favorable, General Loring attacked the Federal camp at Fayetteville. Instead of uniting his forces, General Joseph A. J. Lightburn, who had been placed in command following the withdrawal of Cox and who erroneously thought the Confederates greatly outnumbered him, concerned himself only with saving his supplies. He beat a retreat down the Kanawha without attempting even to save his magazines. Colonel Edward Siber in command of the Thirty-fourth and Thirty-seventh Ohio made a gallant stand at Fayetteville, but for some unexplained reason was permitted by Loring to evade capture and join Lightburn on his precipitate retreat. At Charleston, the Federals gained the west side of Elk River over a suspension bridge which they destroyed to prevent pursuit. Then by a circuitous route through Ripley and Ravenswood they reached Point Pleasant.

Loring occupied Charleston at once. "For many days thereafter there was a constant train of wagons hauling salt away from the Kanawha Valley." It was Lee's purpose to retain the Kanawha Valley and use it as a base of operations to recover Trans-Allegheny Virginia. To that end, Loring was ordered to destroy the railroad bridge at Cheat River and join Lee in Maryland. In these plans Lee failed, however, to reckon with the fact that in Loring he did not have a Jackson. Instead of obeying or attempting to obey Lee's orders, Loring wrote him of his intention to march by way of Lewisburg and Monterey. Before he could receive a reply, he set out according to his own plan. A week later, October 15, he was ordered to turn over his command to General John Echols and report in person to the adjutant general's office in Richmond.[36] Echols then withdrew toward Lewisburg, and the Kanawha Valley was promptly reoccupied by the Federals.

MILITARY OPERATIONS, 1863

The 1863 military operations were mostly raids and counterraids. The most important of the raids was that led by Generals William E. Jones and John D. Imboden with Jones as ranking officer. The plan of campaign originated, however, in the fertile brain of Imboden. As set forth in a letter of March 2 to General Lee, the plan contemplated: destruction of the Baltimore and Ohio Railroad from Oakland, Maryland, to Grafton, West Virginia; the defeat and capture of the enemy forces at Beverly, Philippi, and Buckhannon; enlisting "the young men of the northwest" in the Confederate Army; and the control of that section during the ensuing May elections. With General Jones making a flanking movement

---

[36] Humphreys, *Military Operations*, pp. 11-20.

in the direction of Cumberland, Imboden was to play the chief rôle in this program.[37] As modified by General Lee, it contemplated simultaneous attacks, one at Grafton, the other at Oakland.

In pursuit of his part of this plan, Imboden left Shenandoah Mountain on April 20. By forced marches his army of 3,400 men, chiefly infantry, pressed forward over the Staunton-Parkersburg Turnpike to Beverly and planned to continue at once to Buckhannon. As he came near Buckhannon, he was erroneously informed that Federals were in Philippi, and he retraced his steps to Beverly. When he learned the truth, he moved forward and on April 29 occupied Buckhannon. Here about thirty miles from Grafton, his major objective, he waited for Jones to join him. Both at Grafton and at Clarksburg the Federals had been strongly reinforced, and this; together with the impassable condition of the roads, made further action on the part of Imboden hazardous, if not impossible.

In command of three cavalry regiments, General Jones left Lacy Springs, Rockingham County, Virginia, on April 21. Five days later, he reached his chief objective, Cheat River bridge. He found it too well defended for him to repeat a futile assault, and, as he could not communicate with Imboden, he set out to find him. Subordinates, notably Colonel Asher W. Harman, had meanwhile inflicted serious but not irreparable damage on the railroad.

In his efforts to find Imboden, Jones spread terror and destruction along the route of his march. This was notably true at Morgantown and vicinity, which he visited on April 27-28. This call cost the residents of that area two lives and a number of horses and cattle. At Fairmont the new railroad bridge was destroyed, and a number of persons were made prisoners. Though encumbered by a large number of cattle and horses, Jones made his way to Bridgeport, where on April 30 he captured a company of Federals, made prisoners of sixteen civilian railroad employees, destroyed a train, and burned bridges and trestles. Avoiding Grafton, the next day he reached Philippi, where he sent a detachment to Beverly with a large number of horses and cattle. On May 2, he joined Imboden.[38]

At once the intrepid commanders planned to capture Clarksburg. For this purpose they moved the base of their operations to Weston. They then learned that Clarksburg was being strongly reinforced and changed their plans. It was decided that Imboden should move south toward Summersville with his wagon trains and livestock, and that Jones would renew his operations against the railroad. Moving in two detachments, Jones was again able to inflict great losses.

Jones left the railroad at Cairo and marched to "Oiltown," in the newly opened Burning Springs field. There on May 9 he demolished equipment

[37] *Official Records*, I, Vol. XXV, pt. 2, 652-653, 710-712.
[38] *Ibid.*, I, Vol. XXV, pt. 1, 90-105, 107-137.

and burned crude oil estimated at 150,000 barrels. In his report to General Lee, Jones described the resulting scene in these words: "By dark the oil from the tanks on the burning creek had reached the river, and the whole stream became a sheet of fire. A burning river, carrying destruction to our merciless enemy, was a scene of magnificence that might well carry joy to every patriotic heart."[39]

By way of Glenville and Sutton, Jones moved at once to Summersville, where he joined Imboden. By leisurely marches, the greatest impediment of which was short rations, the two armies crossed the Alleghenies and reached the Valley near Staunton, just as Confederates were lamenting the death of Stonewall Jackson. Though neither Jones nor Imboden had achieved his chief objective, each had served the Confederacy well.

In his report to General Lee, Jones stated that, "Although his men had killed and wounded but few of the enemy they had captured nearly seven hundred with small arms and one piece of artillery; destroyed two railway trains; sixteen railroad bridges; a tunnel; a large amount of oil field equipment, and 150,000 barrels of oil. He also reported the procurement of 1,000 head of cattle and 1,200 horses." Imboden had destroyed less enemy property, but he enlisted a few recruits and gathered a large amount of supplies, chiefly horses, cattle, grain, and forage. General Lee expressed belief that "the injury inflicted on the enemy was serious" and that the Federals would be induced "to keep troops to guard the railroad who might be otherwise employed against us."[40]

Though far removed from the main scenes of action, an incident of the Jones-Imboden Raid was important because of its subsequent bearing upon modern warfare. As a result of this raid, it was expected that troops would be withdrawn from the Kanawha Valley for the defense of the northwest, as they had been withdrawn the year before for the defense of Washington. In the event of such a shift, General McCausland was ordered to move into the Kanawha Valley and bag another supply of salt. In the execution of this order, he advanced as far as Fayetteville, where, on May 18-19, 1863, Sergeant Milton W. Humphreys of Captain Thomas A. Bryan's Battery, Kings Artillery, attempted to dislodge entrenched Federals by indirect cannon fire over an intervening forest. It is claimed that this was the first use of "indirect firing" in modern warfare.[41]

Effects of the Jones-Imboden Raid on the northwest were immediate. Among other things, regulars and home guards became more active, commands were shifted, and methods were altered. While Imboden was at Beverly and Buckhannon, General Benjamin S. Roberts, in command of

[39] *Ibid.*, I, Vol. XXV, pt. 1, p. 120.

[40] Summers, *Baltimore and Ohio*, pp. 137-138.

[41] The gun used was a 12-pound howitzer made of cast iron. See Humphreys, *Military Operations*, pp. 22-23; *Journal of U. S. Artillery*, Vol. II, No. 2; *Official Records*, I, Vol. XXV, pt. 2, 797-801, 806, 821-822, 824.

Federal troops in the northwest, was urged to rally his forces and fight, but he insisted that the roads would not permit troop movements. His critics plaguingly asked why roads good enough for "Rebels" to negotiate with some rapidity were unusable by Federals. Because of his inability to explain this and similar questions, Roberts was superseded by General William W. Averell (November 5, 1832-February 3, 1900), of New York.

Entrance to Organ Cave. In this limestone retreat, on the Greenbrier-Monroe county line about four miles from Ronceverte, Confederates made gunpowder from its saltpeter deposits. Wooden vats used for that purpose are still standing, about a quarter of a mile underground

With the turn of the tide at Gettysburg two months later, Federal commanders in West Virginia generally became aggressive. With the tables turned, destruction of the Virginia and Tennessee Railroad became one of their major objectives. In other words, this road was to the remaining part of the conflict what the Baltimore and Ohio had been before Gettysburg.

In pursuit of these objectives, Averell announced a new program. First, large numbers of infantry were changed to cavalry and were trained to a high point of efficiency. Then he announced his intention to cover and fortify the mountain passes overlooking the Appalachian Valley from the westward. Of this policy he wrote General Schenck: "It has always appeared to me that the importance of holding this mass of mountains, so full of fastnesses, . . . has never been appreciated." Then, with Beverly as a base of operations, he set about to get control of the Greenbrier Valley.

Pursuit of this policy resulted in a number of skirmishes and two important engagements. The first of these took place at Rocky Gap, Greenbrier County, where on August 26-27, 1863, Averell unsuccessfully engaged General Sam Jones in one of the important minor engagements of the war. The second battle was fought at Droop Mountain, Pocahontas County. Here on November 6, 1863, Averell met General Echols in a stubbornly fought engagement which the Federals won.

On the background of these achievements, Averell was able to render a unique service. Toward the end of 1863, General Ambrose E. Burnside was besieged in Knoxville by General James Longstreet. The only hope for the Federals lay in cutting Longstreet's line of supplies and thus forcing him to raise the siege. This Averell accomplished in one of the most brilliantly executed raids of the war. With his veteran cavalry of 2,500 men, most of whom were West Virginians, Averell left Keyser December 8. Dodging four Confederate armies, he was eight days later in Salem on the Virginia and Tennessee Railroad. Here he destroyed a large quantity of supplies and, in true Jacksonian fashion, rendered the railroad temporarily useless. As a result, Burnside was saved. With a loss of 119 men and in the face of one of the severest storms ever known in the Alleghenies, Averell reached Beverly on Christmas Eve.[42] This stroke is known as the "Big Salem Raid."

THINGS MILITARY, 1864

As in the previous years, the 1864 military operations in West Virginia were largely raids and counterraids. In retaliation for the Big Salem Raid, General Fitzhugh Lee on January 2 invaded the South Branch Valley; January 30, General Thomas L. Rosser attacked Federals near Greenland Gap, and carried off a large quantity of supplies and twenty prisoners, among them being Major Nathan Goff; May 10, the famous "Ringgold Cavalry" was defeated at Lost River, Hardy County, by Imboden; May 15, General Thomas M. Harris captured 36 "guerrillas" in Pocahontas County; June 19, Captain John Boggs, in command of the "Swamp Dragons," successfully withstood a Confederate attack at Petersburg; July 30, Generals Bradley T. Johnson and John McCausland invaded Pennsylvania and burned Chambersburg; August 7, in retaliation for Chambersburg, Averell attacked Johnson and McCausland near Moorefield and took more than four hundred prisoners; and September 28 Colonel V. A. Witcher captured Buckhannon and took one hundred prisoners, among them being Major Theodore F. Lang. There were

[42] *Official Records,* I, Vol. XXIX, pt. 1, 919-973.

literally scores of other raids and countless skirmishes, some of which were as important as any of those named in this paragraph.

The "Dublin Raid" conducted by General George Crook against the Virginia and Tennessee Railroad, was the outstanding military movement of this year. Supported by Averell, Crook on May 9 attacked and defeated Generals Jenkins and McCausland near Dublin, Pulaski County, Virginia. Here, in the Battle of Cloyd Mountain, Jenkins received a wound from the effects of which he died twelve days later. At Dublin, large quantities of Confederate supplies were taken by the Federals, who then destroyed the New River railroad bridge and set out on their return to Meadow Bluff, West Virginia, by way of Monroe County.

THE ANTICLIMAX

As the several hundred raiding and skirmishing activities in West Virginia drew to a close, they were featured by an anticlimax. In the face of about four thousand Federal troops a detachment of "McNeill Rangers" under Captain Jesse C. McNeill, early in the morning of February 21, 1865, took Generals Crook and Kelley from their hotel rooms in Cumberland, Maryland, and sent them to Richmond as prisoners of war.[43] While General Kelley tended to be solemn about the incident, General Crook was jovial and described it as "the most brilliant exploit of the war." Colonel John S. Mosby, the famous Confederate scout, said of it, "This surpasses anything I have ever done."

The McNeill Rangers were organized by Captain John Hanson McNeill (June 12, 1815-November 10, 1864). When the war began, he resided in Missouri, where he, at the first call, joined the army of the Confederacy. Soon thereafter he and his son, Jesse C. McNeill (September 22, 1841-March 4, 1912), were made prisoners of war. They escaped in 1862 and returned to the old McNeill home in Hardy County, (West) Virginia. Here the elder McNeill organized his rangers, a group of congenial fellows drawn largely from Hampshire, Hardy, and Rockingham counties, Virginia, and Allegany and Baltimore counties, Maryland. With Moorefield, Hardy County, as their chief rallying point, they belonged to the Confederate detached service and were allowed to come and go pretty much as they pleased. General Phil Sheridan regarded their leader as "the most dangerous of all the bushwhackers." After his death in action at Mount Jackson, Virginia, his son, Captain Jesse C. McNeill, continued to terrorize Federals.

---

43 *Ibid.*, I, Vol. XLVI, pt. 2, 626.

Chapter XVIII

The New State Constitution

CONVENTION PERSONNEL

THE FORMATION OF WEST VIRGINIA was the work of her First Constitutional Convention. Delegates to that body were elected on October 24, 1861, at the time that the dismemberment ordinance was ratified by a vote of 18,408 for, to 781 against.[1] It was the original intention of the new state makers to revamp the existing constitution so that it would serve their purposes until a new one could be made under favorable conditions. When they met, however, they were confronted by unexpected possibilities which involved conflicting sectional and factional interests. As a consequence, the session was prolonged, and its personnel became a matter of more than local importance.

The First Constitutional Convention of West Virginia met in the Federal Building, Wheeling, on November 26, as scheduled. A total membership of 53 in the regular session (November 26, 1861-February 18, 1862) was raised to 56 in the recalled session (February 12-20, 1863), but there was meanwhile much irregularity. Neither Webster nor Monroe county was represented in either session, and, because of disturbed internal conditions, Calhoun, Clay, Fayette, Logan, McDowell, Mercer, Nicholas, and Wyoming counties were represented through efforts of petitioning groups dominated either by the military or by Methodist Episcopal Church influences. Pendleton, Pocahontas, Greenbrier, and Morgan were repre-

---

[1] Convention, *Journal*, Doc. No. 53; Lewis, *How West Virginia Was Made*, pp. 317-318; Hall, *Rending of Virginia*, pp. 387-388; McGregor, *Disruption of Virginia*, p. 225; W. Va. Dept. of Arch. and Hist., *Report* (1908), p. 193.

Federal Building, Wheeling, 1861

sented in the recalled session only, and by irregularly chosen delegates. In the case of Pocahontas County the choice was by refugees to Upshur County.

All but fifteen of the sixty-one delegates in both the regular and the recalled sessions were native born. Of the nonnatives, six were born in Pennsylvania; three in New York; two in Ohio; two in Massachusetts; one in Maryland; and one, John Hall, the president, in Ireland. Of the sixty-one, twenty-three were farmers; fourteen were either ordained ministers or licensed exhorters; and there were four physicians, three merchants, two mechanics, two school teachers, one salt manufacturer, and one hotel keeper. Ages ranged from 24 to 66, but the average age was well over 50.[2]

The outstanding characteristic of the convention personnel was Christian piety. Almost without exception the delegates were churchmen. Seven of the fourteen minister delegates, Battelle, Brooks, Hager, Pomeroy, Powell, Ryan, and Trainer, were conspicuous by their activity.[3] But for

[2] Convention, *Bulletin*. See also, Lewis, *How West Virginia Was Made,* p. 319, and W. Va. Dept. of Arch. and Hist., *Second Biennial Report* (1908), p. 194.

[3] Other minister or exhorter delegates were Captain Richard M. Cook, "Captain" William Walker, Waitman T. Willey, David S. Pinnell, John R. McCutcheon, Richard W. Lauck, and Josiah Simmons, but they are described in the convention bulletins as farmers, lawyers, or the like.

the purposeful and practical objectives of the lawyer delegates, notably Van Winkle, the new state could and probably would have been sponsored by religious zealots. There are those who claim that "The Methodists made West Virginia."

Though ten of the fourteen minister delegates were members of the Methodist Episcopal Church, they did not dominate the convention. More than once their leader, Gordon Battelle, was outgeneraled. This does not mean, however, that their influence was not important. In fact, few of the delegates, even the Universalists, Hubbs and Soper, had escaped or cared to escape those evangelical influences which had penetrated the recesses of present West Virginia since the days of Francis Asbury and the Great Awakening. The effects were attested in numerous ways, but in none more tellingly than in the fact that five bishops of the Methodist Episcopal Church were born in present West Virginia in the sixties of the last century.[4]

"A PROPER BOUNDARY"

The convention organized on November 26 by electing John Hall, of Mason County, president; Ellery R. Hall, of Taylor County, secretary; and naming the usual committees. In the interim since the adoption of the dismemberment ordinance, the Confederates had been decisively defeated at Carnifex Ferry and Cheat Mountain Pass, and the Baltimore and Ohio Railroad had come under Federal control. Because of the possibilities thus raised, both with respect to the proposed new state and the general situation, the new state makers were dissatisfied with the restricted bounds of the "State of Kanawha." Many of them had set their hearts upon "a proper boundary."

The boundary question was referred to a select committee which made its report, whether significantly or not, on the same day that the name of the proposed state was changed from "Kanawha" to "West Virginia." Partly because of sectional differences, delegates from the northern counties objected to Kanawha, but a more general objection was found in the fact that one of the largest counties and the largest river in the proposed state bore that name. Alleghany, Augusta, and Western Virginia were suggested as preferable, but after some discussion West Virginia was selected.

[4] These bishops were William F. Anderson, born at Morgantown, 1860; Matthew Simpson Hughes (1863-1920), born at West Union; Matthew Wesley Clair, born at Union, 1865; Edwin Holt Hughes, born at Moundsville, 1866; and George R. Grose, born in Nicholas County, 1869. Other bishops of the Methodist Episcopal Church born in present West Virginia were: Thomas Asbury Morris (1794-1874), born at Charleston, and John W. Hamilton (1845-1934) born at Weston.

As stated by one of the delegates, "It is a familiar name," but more to the point was the assertion, "It is a name to speak."

In addition to the thirty-nine counties of the dismemberment ordinance, the committee on boundary recommended the inclusion of thirty-one others, and that its report be considered with respect to districts or groups of counties. The first of the proposed groups was composed of Pocahontas, Greenbrier, Monroe, Mercer, McDowell, Buchanan, and Wise counties, all west of the Alleghenies. Their inclusion was urged as necessary to make a "compact" and "well-rounded out state," but on this same score and the questioned authority of the convention, the inclusion of Wise and Buchanan counties was opposed. A sizable number of delegates desired them because of their rich natural resources and their proximity to the Virginia and Tennessee Railroad and the "Union loving portion of Tennessee." They were not included, but the other counties of this group were annexed.

The second and third groups, which will be considered together, comprised a shoestring like belt parallel and contiguous to the main ridge of the Alleghenies, together with Morgan, Berkeley, and Jefferson counties. Two of the largest counties of these groups, Hampshire and Hardy, were represented in the Constitutional Convention and the others were desired because of their strategic location with respect to transportation and defense. While annexation of the southernmost group, which began with and included Giles County, was being considered, proposals were made to include all the counties of present southwest Virginia west of the Blue Ridge Mountains. This was urged on the score that the proposed state should comprise all "Western Virginia" and not be restricted to the diminutive northwest.

The inclusion of southwest Virginia was opposed on the ground that it was "socially, economically, and traditionally inseparable from eastern Virginia." This was, however, not the determining argument causing the rejection of the counties in this group. Their inclusion was tied up closely with the proposed annexation of Alleghany County, the southernmost of the third group. In opposition Granville Parker, of Cabell County, called attention to the fact that Virginia had recently expended several million dollars on improvements in the region of Covington, county seat of Alleghany County. As the new state makers were already concerned about their proportionate part of "the state debt" and were disposed to determine their share on the basis of "benefits derived," they dropped the proposed annexation of Alleghany and neighboring counties like so many hot potatoes.

The discussion then shifted to proposals to annex counties in the present Eastern Panhandle of West Virginia, together with Frederick and a group in the Shenandoah Valley. In the course of this discussion proposals were made to extend the bounds of the proposed state to the gates of the Federal capital so as to include the tomb of Washington; but the chief purpose of this inclusion, as originally proposed, was to insure complete control of the Baltimore and Ohio Railroad. It was feared that, in case of the success of the new state, Virginia might injure, if not ruin, the railroad by oppressive taxation and unfriendly legislation. Already Henry A. Wise had deplored its alleged Abolitionist influences, and Virginia's record toward it was marked by suspicion and distrust. Provision was made, therefore, for the inclusion within the proposed new state of all the counties traversed by the Baltimore and Ohio Railroad.

THE FUNDAMENTAL LAW

Though delegates from present West Virginia had in 1829-30 and 1850-51 insisted upon the adoption of a bill of rights and kindred generalizations as bases for their subsequent work, they were more practical and took their time when given an opportunity to determine their own fundamental law. Until the very last, their "Bill of Rights" was a sort of hodgepodge. In its finished form it was remarkably free from such generalizations as "all men are by nature equally free and independent." In their moderation the new state makers were guided by Peter G. Van Winkle, the practical and experienced chairman of the "Committee on Fundamentals."

Without debate, the delegates accepted the conventional division of powers and authorized only a few changes with respect to the personnel and the functions of the divisions. Instead of a governor with a four-year term and ineligibility to succeed himself, his term in the new state was two years with eligibility to succeed himself for one or more terms. A comparatively long ballot was substituted for the short ballot then in use. As the existing judiciary was generally conceded to be "one of the best in the world," it was continued with few or no changes. All executive and judicial offices were elective by the voters.

The most important changes in the framework of the state government were in the legislative department, where a biennial session of ninety days gave way to an annual session of forty-five days. As was to be expected, representation in each branch of "the Legislature" was to be on the white population basis, and suffrage was vested in the "white male citizens of the state." The existing provision forbidding ministers of the gospel and priests to be members of either branch of the legislature was repealed, and the legislature was given power to regulate and prohibit the sale of intoxicating liquors. The legislature was forbidden to incur a state debt, except to meet casual deficits, and it was required "as soon as may be practical," to ascertain and provide for the liquidation of an equitable proportion of "the public debt of the Commonwealth" as of January 1, 1861.

According to its critics, the most objectionable thing about the new state constitution was the provision "Yankeeizing" it. In keeping with the irony of things, this was accomplished by the adoption of the "Jefferson Plan," according to which each county of the new state was divided into not less than three nor more than ten townships, and local government was vested in the voters functioning through annual "township meetings," after the manner of the New England town meeting.

With no notable exceptions, the new state makers were interested in free public schools. In the face of an undetermined state debt and the admitted need for internal improvements, the legislature was therefore required, "as soon as practicable," to establish "a thorough and efficient system of free schools." As in New England, the proposed system was to function through township meetings.

On the subject of slavery, the constitution provided that "no slaves shall be brought, or free person of color be permitted to come into this State for permanent residence." The brevity of this statement was more indicative of the time given the subject and the hushed silence which encompassed it, than of its importance. In accepting the potential extension of the bounds of the proposed state, so as to include the Eastern Panhandle of present West Virginia and increase the slave population from about 7,000 to about 18,000, those favorable to abolition were outgeneraled and all but hushed.

Early in the convention proceedings Battelle had introduced two resolutions: one, to prevent the bringing of more slaves into the state after its admission, and the other to provide for gradual abolition, beginning July 4, 1865. These resolutions were referred to the "Committee on Fundamentals," headed by Van Winkle. When they came up for consideration in the last days of the session, they were tabled "without day" by the significant vote of 24 for, to 23 against, with the minister delegates generally voting "no."

As a cloture rule restricting speeches to ten minutes had been adopted earlier in the session, and as the convention refused to rescind it at this time, Battelle was forced to appeal to the people. This he did in a notable address which was brought to the attention of Charles Sumner and others, with results to be noted later.[5] Meanwhile the new state makers compromised the slavery question by making no provision for abolition and excluding "free persons of color." This compromise was adopted with

[5] This address is printed in full in Hall, *Rending*, pp. 440-456.

only one dissenting vote, that of William W. Brumfield, of Wayne County.

The most important and difficult problems confronting the constitution makers were those having to do with taxation and finance. The state debt, variously estimated from an asset if reckoned on the basis of benefits derived, to a liability of from one to fifteen million dollars if reckoned on the basis of territory and population, hung like a millstone about their necks and cramped their plans for public buildings, education, and internal improvements. Largely because of their experiences with exemptions of slave property, the taxation problem was solved by making taxes "equal and uniform" and by taxing "all property, both real and personal, . . . in proportion to its value."

The problem of the uses of the revenues was what gave greatest trouble. Citing the experiences of New York and Ohio, a sizable group of delegates, most of them from the Kanawha Valley, insisted that internal improvements were almost, if not quite, as necessary to the progress and general welfare of the proposed state, as was education. Though assured by Van Winkle that private capital was available to build the proposed railroad between Grafton and Charleston, these delegates were not satisfied and insisted that the constitution should authorize a bonded state debt for that and other enterprises. In the ensuing discussion, Wheeling withdrew her request for a state bonded indebtedness for public buildings to be located there, and the proposal to bond the state for internal improvements was, as a result, lost by a sectional vote of 23 for, to 25 against, in what Chapman J. Stuart said was "the most fatal stab that has yet been given to the prospects of the new state."

Other proposals looking to the relief of the Kanawha Valley were defeated also by sectional votes, as a result of which the convention came to an impasse. To prevent its adjourning in disorder and abandoning the new state movement, a special committee of nine, with Henry Dering of Monongalia County as chairman, was, on the last day of the session, appointed to work out a compromise. The report of this committee, which was accepted without debate, permitted the state to subscribe to the capital stock of associations and corporations authorized for the purpose of making internal improvements, as had long been done in Virginia, but the report required that "such stocks shall be paid for at the time of subscribing," or from taxes "levied for the ensuing year, sufficient to pay the subscription in full."[6]

Though this compromise permitted the convention to adjourn with a semblance of accord and thus saved the new state movement, it did not reconcile northern and southern West Virginia. Instead, it left her divided along sectional lines not unlike those out of which she was born.

[6] Convention, *Journal*, pp. 165-167.

The later triumph of her antislavery element was another pill which the slaveowners of the Kanawha Valley and the Eastern Panhandle did not swallow readily. For some time thereafter, the antislavery element, which in due course became radical, dominated the new state to the disgust and disappointment of certain sectional, economic, cultural, and church interests. Reconciliation is only now being worked out, thanks to improved roads and other modern agencies of intercommunication.

THE VOTERS AND ASSEMBLY APPROVE

The work of the convention was approved without a dissenting voice, but, instead of adjourning *sine die* as a number of delegates wished, a commission of five was appointed to carry on in the ensuing interim and, if necessary, to reconvene the convention. In compliance with its order the commissioners caused the constitution to be published and made other necessary plans for a referendum set for April 3, 1862, at which time polls were to be opened in each township of the forty-eight counties in the proposed new state. When the time for this vote came, disturbed internal conditions prevented the execution of the referendum order in many districts, including whole counties in the central, southern, and eastern parts of the proposed state. But this condition was not discouraging to the new state makers. With them, loyalty to the Union and the nearness of their goal had superseded legal and other technicalities. So polls were taken only where conditions permitted. The total participating vote was 19,376, of which number 18,862 were for the constitution, to 514 against it.

The next step in the process of making the new state was the most doubtful and the most criticized. The Constitution of the United States provides that "no new State shall be formed or erected within the Jurisdiction of any other State . . . without the Consent of the Legislatures of the States concerned as well as of the Congress." It was, therefore, necessary to have the consent of the Virginia General Assembly to the formation of West Virginia, but there were at that time two rival functioning legislatures in Virginia.

Undaunted by this situation and imbued by the prevailing notions of loyalty, Governor Pierpont, having been officially notified of the result of the referendum on the new state constitution, convened the general assembly of the Reorganized Government at Wheeling, on May 6, following. As stated in his call, he wished to lay before the assembly the ratified constitution of the proposed state, as certified by the commissioners in charge, and ask assent to the formation and erection of West Virginia within the jurisdiction of Virginia.

In pursuance of this call, the general assembly met at the appointed time and place. It was greeted by a message from Pierpont who took advantage of the occasion to answer critics of the new state, especially those who spoke of it as "revolutionary."[7] They were reminded of the mountain barriers separating eastern and western Virginia, thus rendering the two sections "entirely dissimilar in their social relations and their institutions." Because of this fact, dismemberment had long been talked of and only awaited an opportunity, which was at hand. Without further ceremony, the assembly proceeded therefore to the business before it and, on May 13, 1862, passed an act giving the consent of "the Legislature of Virginia" to the formation and erection of the "State of West Virginia." This

Granville D. Hall

[7] Wheeling *Intelligencer*, May 7, 1862.

act named the counties comprising the new state and provided for the inclusion of Berkeley, Jefferson, and Frederick, "whenever the voters thereof shall ratify the constitution of the new State."

THE CONVENTION DEBATES

As the recalled session of the convention drew to a close, Van Winkle informed it that complete stenographic notes of the debates and proceedings of each session had been kept, and suggested that the debates be transcribed and printed in book form. In the expressed belief that they had done something worth while and of abiding interest and importance to the new state and the country at large, the delegates approved this suggestion, and a motion to make it effective was carried without a dissenting vote. But for the pressure of other matters and a shortage of funds, the debates would perhaps have been printed at that time.

Granville Davisson Hall (September 17, 1837-June 24, 1934), who had taken the notes, agreed with the delegates as to their importance. He accordingly placed them, together with copies of each and every document printed for the uses of the convention, in a trunk which he stored for safekeeping. Except for the uses made of them by Hall in the preparation of his several articles and books dealing with various phases of the dismemberment of Virginia and the formation of West Virginia, these notes reposed undisturbed where he left them for forty-four years. They were then transcribed and sold to the state of West Virginia and are today the chief source of information regarding her formation and admission to the Union. In 1942 they were published by the State in three large volumes.[8]

[8] Charles H. Ambler, Frances H. Atwood, and W. B. Matthews, eds., *Debates and Proceedings of the First Constitutional Convention of West Virginia,* 1861-1863 (3 vols., Huntington, W. Va., 1942).

Chapter XIX

Admission of the New State

CONGRESS APPROVES

FOLLOWING APPROVAL of the formation of West Virginia by the general assembly of the Reorganized Government of Virginia, those interested in completing the process turned to the Thirty-seventh Congress. The commissioners in charge presented a memorial from the proposed state, which asked for her admission to separate statehood in the Union. As this request was in due form and accompanied by documents indicating that all the necessary steps in such a procedure had been taken, Senator Willey presented, on May 29, 1862, the memorial to the Senate, which was referred to its committee on territories, of which Benjamin F. Wade, of Ohio, was chairman. Five days later, William G. Brown, of Virginia, presented copies of the memorial and accompanying documents to the House, where they, too, were referred to its committee on territories.

As Carlile, a new-state enthusiast from the outset of the movement, was then a member of the Senate Committee on Territories, everyone looked to him to draft the bill for the admission of West Virginia, but, according to Willey, his colleague, Carlile, became so engrossed in preparation of the statehood bill as to delay it unduly. It was not ready until June 23, following, and, when introduced at that time by Senator Wade as "Senate Bill No. 365," was a shock both to the friends and the foes of the proposed new state. Among other things, fifteen additional counties, Berkeley, Jefferson, Clark, Frederick, Warren, Page, Shenandoah, Rockingham, Augusta, Highland, Bath, Rockbridge, Botetourt, Craig, and Alleghany, only three of which were mentioned in the new state constitution, had been added.

More shocking still was an enabling act authorizing the proposed state, together with the counties added by Carlile, to call a convention for the purpose of making a new constitution. When this constitution had been ratified by the counties of Carlile's proposed state and been approved by the Virginia General Assembly, her loyal governor was to certify these facts to the President who was authorized, without further action of Congress, to proclaim West Virginia one of the United States, provided she had meanwhile so amended her constitution as to provide for the gradual abolition of slavery.

Undaunted by these developments, Senator Wade on June 26 called up the West Virginia Statehood Bill for amendment and debate. In the course of the latter, chief discussion centered on the proposal for the gradual abolition of slavery. Instead Charles Sumner would have incorporated the "Jeffersonian Proviso" of the Ordinance of 1787 for the Government of the Northwest Territory, which abolished slavery and involuntary servitude therein, "otherwise than in punishment of crimes whereof the party shall be duly convicted."[1]

Sumner's proposal enveloped the new state movement in doubt, and for a few days it was not discussed in the Senate. Determined to make another effort, Senator Willey, on July 1, called the bill up again. With Senators Wade, Hale, Collamer, Sumner, and Willey participating, a heated discussion ensued and culminated in the defeat of both Sumner's and Carlile's proposals. Instead a compromise, worked out by Senators Wade and Willey, was substituted and became known as the "Willey Amendment." It provided that "all slaves under twenty-one on July 4, 1863, shall be free when they arrive at the age of twenty-one."[2] With a view to winning the resulting referendum, the provision of the original constitution forbidding free persons of color to reside in the state was changed so as to apply only to additional slaves.

This compromise was not adopted without a fight. At once Carlile declared himself opposed to it and to the admission of the new state as well. His action in this matter has been explained as due to his desire to include Frederick, the county of his nativity, but that county was already included conditionally. Whatever the true explanation may be, he tried to defer action until the first Monday of the following December, but in this he was again unsuccessful. On July 14, 1862, the bill passed the Senate with 23 votes for, to 17 against. Eight senators did not vote. Among those voting "no" were Charles Sumner and Zachariah Chandler, uncompromising free state Senators. Carlile voted with them.

1 *Cong. Globe,* 37 Cong., 2 Sess., pt. 4, pp. 2941-2942.

2 *Ibid.,* pp. 3034-3036, 3307-3320.

The following day, the House was officially informed of this action and its concurrence was requested. John A. Bingham, of the Ohio district bordering West Virginia, moved the passage of the bill, but Joseph Segar, of Accomac County, Virginia, though an ardent Union man, opposed the dismemberment of his state and moved to lay the bill on the table. This the House refused to do, but on motion of Roscoe Conkling, of New York, further consideration of the measure was postponed until the second Tuesday of the following December.

When Congress reassembled, Bingham brought up the West Virginia Statehood Bill again and asked that it be voted on at once, but the ensuing debate occupied the House for the better part of two days. The opposition argument resolved itself to the contention that Virginia had not legally consented to the formation of West Virginia and that the dismemberment of Virginia would prove an insurmountable obstacle to her restoration to the Union. On the other hand, arguments favoring the bill resolved themselves to the alleged right of a loyal minority, however small, to govern a state in the presence of treason and rebellion. This view prevailed by a vote of 96 for, to 55 against.[3]

THE PRESIDENT APPROVES

It was eleven days after its passage by the House before the West Virginia Statehood Bill reached President Lincoln in form for his approval. As he took the full time allowed under the Constitution to consider the bill, the resulting uncertainty became ominous to its friends and supporters. A report which reached Wheeling, to the effect that the President was conferring with his Cabinet and others on various phases of the measure, only intensified the growing apprehension. Lincoln spent a part of New Year's Eve with friends of the bill, but they left the White House without learning his decision. Confidential information to the effect that the Cabinet was evenly divided was not assuring. But the visitors found comfort in a statement from the President to the effect that the deciding vote had not yet been cast, and in his request to see them again the next morning. In compliance with this request, Jacob B. Blair, of Parkersburg, was at the White House quite early and was greeted by the President with the question, "Do you see that signature?" It read, "Approved, Abraham Lincoln." Soon thereafter the "good news" was sent to Governor Pierpont as a New Year's gift.

As stated by Lincoln, his reasons for signing the West Virginia Statehood Bill cover two main points, that of constitutionality and that of ex-

[3] *Cong. Globe,* 37 Cong., 3 Sess., pt. 1, p. 59.

pediency.[4] On the former he regarded the legislative approval of the Reorganized Government as sufficient to cover the most controverted point. It mattered not that the action was by a body "chosen at elections in which a majority of the qualified voters did not participate." The fact remained that they had had an opportunity to vote. If, under the circumstances, their failure and neglect were countenanced, it would, according to Lincoln, have condoned "treason against the Constitution," which, in keeping with his manner of reasoning, brought the proposition to a *reductio ad absurdum*.

Though Lincoln thought the question of the expediency of the admission of West Virginia a matter for legislative rather than executive determination, he resolved this point to its effects upon the efforts then being made to restore Virginia to the Union. Although admitting that she would return "less reluctantly without the division of the old State," he was convinced that the Union would gain more by her admission than it would lose. The Emancipation Proclamation had not met with general favor in the new state, and he doubtless had in mind to raise up there a party having its strength largely in antislavery sentiments, such as was then being enlisted throughout the North. Continuing, he said:

> We can scarcely dispense with the aid of West Virginia in this struggle; much less can we afford to have her against us, in Congress and in the field. Her brave and good men regard her admission into the Union as a matter of life and death. They have been true to the Union under very severe trials. We have so acted as to justify their hopes, and we cannot fully retain their confidence, and co-operation, if we seem to break faith with them.[5]

The President's approval of the new statehood bill was, therefore, largely a war measure and was not, on that account, to be regarded as a precedent. In his own words, "Admission of the new State turns that much slave soil to free; and thus, is a certain and irrevocable encroachment upon the cause of rebellion."

THE WILLEY AMENDMENT

As the admission of West Virginia was conditional upon her acceptance of the Willey Amendment, it was necessary to refer it to the convention which had made her constitution. Fortunately, recessing the convention had provided for such a contingency, but the commissioners in charge had ceased to function. The chairman, John Hall, was in jail

[4] John G. Nicolay and John Hay, *Abraham Lincoln, A History,* 10 vols. (New York, 1890), Vol. VI, 309-311.

[5] *Ibid.,* p. 311.

charged with the murder of Lewis Wetzel, editor of the Point Pleasant *Register*,[6] and other delegates were either dead or had resigned. The resulting perplexities were relieved through an informal meeting of members of the general assembly, which, on January 30, 1863, constituted a new central committee authorized to make the necessary plans and arrangements for reassembling the convention.

By a proclamation, this committee called special elections for February 5, 1863 to fill vacancies in the convention membership and to give counties not previously represented an opportunity to elect delegates. Most of the resulting elections were uncontested, but that in Ohio County to fill the vacancy created by the death of Gordon Battelle was seized upon by Carlile and certain state rights Democrats to strike the new state a blow which it was hoped might be fatal. In this effort they found ready allies in the "liberty loving" and "nigger hating" residents of the new state, some of whom had been wrought to frenzy and disloyalty by the Emancipation Proclamation. Newly arrived German and Irish residents were equally eager to safeguard their jobs and their dignity as free white men.[7] As the result of a short but stubbornly fought contest, Professor Andrew F. Ross, principal of West Liberty Academy and an ardent friend of the new state, won in Ohio County, but by the narrow margin of about two hundred in a total vote of approximately twenty-nine hundred.[8]

With an almost complete authorized membership, the constitutional convention met at Wheeling, February 12, 1863, in recalled session. Officers of the regular session continued to function, but in the enforced absence of John Hall, president, Abraham D. Soper, of Tyler County, the oldest delegate in point of years, was made president. Then, following the seating of the newly elected delegates, the convention appointed a special committee on schedule and proceeded to the business before it. Senator Willey was present for the purpose of addressing the convention on the topic of the day, the Willey Amendment, and on the afternoon of the first day of the session it listened to "a very able address on the West Virginia statehood movement."

Prefacing his address by the statement that "Nothing has ever surprised me more than the opposition which is made to the admission of the new State of West Virginia into the Union by a portion of the people within its limits," Willey traced the various steps in her formation with special reference to the authority of the general assembly of the Reorganized Government. Next he reverted to the conditional admission of West Virginia to show that it was not unprecedented. Then he came to the crux of

[6] Point Pleasant *Register* (Point Pleasant, West Va.), November 1, 1862; Wheeling *Intelligencer*, December 12, 1862.

[7] Wheeling *Intelligencer*, February 3, 1863; February 4, 1863; Ambler, *Pierpont*, pp. 200-204.

[8] The vote was: Ross, 1,550, Richardson, 1,369. Wheeling *Intelligencer*, February 7, 1863.

the matter, which he found in the lurking fear that West Virginia, under the proposed amendment, "will become a free state." Granting that, he could not understand why the interests of two or three thousand masters should stand in the way of a body-politic of 350,000 persons.

From this point, Willey's address was given almost entirely to documentary proof to show that slavery was a dying institution in West Virginia and that it had been socially and economically harmful to Virginia. In reply to the argument then being advanced to the effect that West Virginia would be overrun with free Negroes, Willey summarized his argument in these words: "There is nothing in the soil or climate of West Virginia to attract a free Negro, but much to repel him. Besides, the kind of labor which will be required here, will not be of a character to induce his employment."

Willey could not disassociate the arguments of the new state opponents from the cry then being raised for "peace" which, as he saw it, meant simply the success of the "Rebels." In such a contingency, he predicted that "West Virginia will be dragged into the Southern Confederacy, like the captive princess chained to the triumphal car of the ancient Roman conqueror." Cut off as she was from eastern Virginia by impassable geographical and natural barriers, which no available amount of capital or skill could overcome, and wedged between "the two mighty states, Ohio and Pennsylvania," the inevitable result, as determined by the experience of the ages, would be "perpetual war or consolidation."

The effectiveness of his address was attested by a convention order authorizing the printing and distribution of ten thousand copies, eight thousand in English and two thousand in German.

Instead of determining the business before it at once and adjourning, the question of compensation for loyal masters under the Willey Amendment was raised. To avoid amending it in such a manner as to necessitate again referring its work to Congress and Lincoln, the convention named a special committee on the question of slaves emancipated, with Van Winkle as chairman. This committee was to work out a solution for this embarrassing problem. Its report recommended unqualified acceptance of the Willey Amendment, but proposed that the legislature of the new state should promise compensation for all loyal masters. As a result of this proposal, action on the Amendment was delayed five days, during which the convention engaged in the most spirited debate of this session. As worked out in the course of this debate, payments were to have been spread over a period of seventeen years, beginning four years after the adoption of the constitution. It was generally agreed that $480,000 would be sufficient for that purpose.

Although insisting that the recommendation of the special committee would not jeopardize final admission of the new state at the hands of

Lincoln, when, under the existing plan, he was called upon to proclaim the new state one of the Union, delegates favorable to the Amendment argued that compensation for possible losses under it were not only just, but also legal under the Federal Constitution. Moreover, England had set a commendable example, which, if not followed, might defeat the ratification of the amended constitution or seriously jeopardize it. More to the point were repeated assertions to the effect that confiscation of slave property would work irrevocable injury to widows and orphans whose inheritances and estates were bound up with Negro slavery.

Those opposed to the compensation proposal, for the most part preacher delegates, regarded discussion of the subject as inopportune, possibly suicidal. In proof of this, they pointed to the fact that persons in high places had their eyes upon the convention and that its action was to be submitted to a referendum. "Knowing the people of West Virginia," as they did, they expressed their inability to explain to them even an advisory recommendation which might entail increased taxes for the payment of comparatively opulent masters. They found comfort, however, in the fact that compensation was restricted to loyal masters, for, according to Joseph S. Wheat of Morgan County that simplified the matter, as there were no such persons.

Climaxing one of the ablest arguments of the session, Chapman J. Stuart called attention to the futility of guaranteeing property rights already admittedly secure under the Federal Constitution. Furthermore, he expressed in the following words the sentiments of those favorable to unqualified acceptance of the Willey Amendment: "Mr. President, I am willing to sustain this government, to fight for the suppression of the Rebellion, yet, sir, if by any act of our people we lose the new State, I will feel that I have not a great deal to fight for in Western Virginia. . . . If we lose the new State, we lose that which is of vast importance to us. It certainly surpasses any little interest I may have in a few little negroes."[9]

After trying in vain to amend the compensation resolution by substituting either a request to Congress for an appropriation to be used to compensate loyal masters or a statement of opinion to the effect that "every kind of property is secure under the Federal Constitution," the proposed advisory resolution was laid on the table by a vote of 28 for, to 26 against. By a vote of 54 for, to 0 against, and with only three delegates, Hansley, Hoback, and Robinson, not voting, the Willey Amendment was approved on February 17, 1863. On the following day the constitution, as amended, was, on motion of Van Winkle, adopted by a vote of 52 for, to 0 against.

The pro and con arguments on the compensation resolution were ammunition for the increasing number of critics of the new state. Aspersions which they cast upon her and her makers linger to this day. It mattered

[9] Convention; *Debates* (Recalled Session).

not that Van Winkle on the last day of the recalled session called attention to the fact that the unit of local government had been changed from the county to the township and that referenda were by districts and not by counties. To this day there are those who call attention to the fact that this or that county did not vote for the new state constitution.

In compliance with a schedule which accompanied the amended constitution, it was on March 26, 1863, submitted to the voters for their approval or rejection. Except for West Virginia soldiers stationed beyond the bounds of the new state, care was taken to restrict the voting to its bounds, and to have polls taken by districts rather than by counties. Inasmuch as, under the existing law, sixty days were allowed after the results of an election had been determined for contests and objections, the time for formally launching the new state was fixed at sixty days after statehood had been proclaimed by the President. Meanwhile the officers, state, county, and township, of the proposed state were to function in its name until such time as their successors could be elected and qualified. By authorizing the legislature to meet in Wheeling, the convention designated that city as the capital. To provide for a contingency such as that caused by the forced retirement of John Hall, first president of the convention, John A. Dille was, on the last day of the recalled session, elected vice-president.

Undaunted by their failure to strike the new state a death blow in the February elections of 1863, Carlile and a number of state rights leaders sought to defeat the Willey Amendment in its referendum stage. Prominent among the leaders who opposed the new state at this stage were John J. Davis, of Harrison County; General John J. Jackson, scion of a distinguished family of state rights devotees; and Sherrard Clemens, who, only a short time before, represented the Wheeling district in Congress. In a manner which did not reflect credit upon those responsible, these gentlemen were prevented from speaking in Parkersburg. Their attacks upon the amended constitution, made elsewhere, were, however, futile, but aided by the tide of "Vallandighamism" which was then sweeping the Ohio Valley and by Carlile, who remained a Republican, they then laid the foundations for a new Democratic party in West Virginia. It continued to gain in strength until 1870, when it wrested complete control from the radical Republicans.

On the other hand, friends of the new state regarded the referendum as "the crisis" which, if successfully passed, "ended the trouble in West Virginia." They accordingly took to the hustings also. As the date for the referendum drew near, Senator Willey, Peter G. Van Winkle, and Governor Pierpont addressed a mass meeting of Wheeling workingmen. Several imported speakers, among them Horace Maynard, of Tennessee, and John A. Bingham, of Ohio, were heard on various phases of the situation.[10]

The result of the referendum contest was a decisive victory for those who favored the amendment. With no reports from districts in ten of the forty-eight counties of the new state, the vote, as announced in the Wheeling *Intelligencer* for April 17, 1863, was 27,749 for, to 572 against. Of these totals 7,696 and 132, respectively, were cast by soldiers, 1,727 of whom were not at the time stationed in West Virginia. Some of them were entrenched before Vicksburg.[11]

The results were certified to President Lincoln on April 16, and four days later he issued the following proclamation, under which West Virginia, on June 20, 1863, became the thirty-fifth state in the Union:

> Whereas, by the Act of Congress approved the 31st day of December, last, the State of West Virginia was declared to be one of the United States of America, and was admitted into the Union on an equal footing with the original States in all respects whatever, upon the condition that certain changes should be duly made in the proposed Constitution for that State;
>
> And, whereas, proof of a compliance with that condition as required by the Second Section of the Act aforesaid, has been submitted to me;
>
> Now, therefore, be it known, that I, Abraham Lincoln, President of the United States, do, hereby, in pursuance of the Act of Congress aforesaid, declare and proclaim that the said act shall take effect and be in force, from and after sixty days from the date hereof.
>
> In witness whereof, I have hereunto set my hand and caused the Seal of the United States to be affixed.[12]

THE COURTS AND THE PUBLIC

The Supreme Court of the United States has rendered no opinion on the legality of the formation and admission of West Virginia to separate statehood. In the several cases coming before it involving these points, notably Virginia *v.* West Virginia to determine the territorial status of Jefferson and Berkeley counties, annexed to the latter after she had attained statehood, and in Commonwealth of Virginia *v.* West Virginia to determine the defendant's proportionate share of the Virginia debt as of January 1, 1861, the Court accepted the formation and admission of West

---

[10] Wheeling *Intelligencer,* March 16, 1863; March 23, 1863.

[11] For this vote by counties, see West Va. Dept. of Arch. and Hist., *Second Biennial Report,* p. 202.

[12] For photostatic copy of the original, see Ambler, *Pierpont,* pp. 206-207. The original is in the National Archives, Washington, D. C.

Virginia as a fact. As in the case Luther *v.* Borden, decided in 1848, West Virginia statehood was regarded as a political question to be determined solely by Congress. In formulating opinions in Commonwealth of Virginia *v.* West Virginia and in other cases, certain judges, notably the late Oliver Wendell Holmes, reviewed the steps in the formation and admission of West Virginia, but they accepted the action of Congress as final.

The liberalism of the courts with respect to the formation and admission of West Virginia was not shared to a large degree by the public, even her own. In its final stages her admission was a triumph for Abolitionists. The reaction expressed itself in Vallandighamism, which made a strong appeal to liberty-loving mountaineers and to newly arrived and job-conscious Irish and German residents. Soon thereafter the political leadership of the new state became Radical. As such, in the name of "loyalty," it treated property and other rights in such a manner as to outrage substantial elements who tended to join temporarily deposed politicians and social leaders in airing the admitted "irregularities" in the formation and admission of their state. The effects were unwholesome on the body politic which was thus denied traditions such as those which tend to immortalize the founders of Jamestown and the Pilgrim Fathers. Instead of becoming state conscious after the pattern of Virginia and Massachusetts, West Virginia tended to be sectional, sectarian, partisan, and clannish. For a long time certain sectional and family feuds were the first things thought of, when the state was mentioned among outsiders, and political contests involving "iron-headed industrialists" and "Bourbon agrarians" were scarcely more humane than family feuds and were certainly not more public spirited. West Virginia was, in fact, "a house divided"; but, thanks to modern means of transportation and communication, she is now developing a large degree of unity.

Chapter XX

West Virginia
The Thirty-Fifth State

THE LAUNCHING

IN COMPLIANCE with the "Ordinance for the Organization of the State of West Virginia" adopted by the Constitutional Convention, a nominating convention of 235 delegates of the Constitutional Union party met in Parkersburg, May 6-7, 1863, to name candidates for eight elective state offices, including three judges of the state supreme court of appeals.[1] The Constitutional Convention had set the election for the Thursday next succeeding the thirty-fifth day from the date of the President's proclamation of West Virginia's admission to statehood, which fell on May 28. Though it labored under some apprehension, due to the reported presence in the neighborhood of raiding Confederates, led by General William E. Jones, the nominating convention named Arthur I. Boreman of Wood County for governor; Samuel Crane of Randolph County for auditor; Campbell Tarr of Brooke County for treasurer; Aquilla B. Caldwell of Ohio County for attorney general; Jacob E. Boyers of Tyler County for secretary of state; and James H. Brown of Kanawha County, William A. Harrison of Harrison County, and Ralph L. Berkshire of Monongalia County for the supreme court of appeals.

Except that all but three of these nominees, Tarr, Brown, and Harrison, were members of the Methodist Episcopal Church, they were representative of all sections and factions. Four of them, Boreman, Caldwell, Berkshire, and Harrison, had been Whigs, and the others were Jackson Democrats who had voted for Douglas. By a vote ranging from about 24,000 to

[1] Wheeling *Intelligencer,* May 7, 1863; May 8, 1863.

about 26,000 for Boreman, who led the ticket, it was elected without opposition; but fifteen counties: Cabell, Calhoun, Clay, Fayette, Greenbrier, Logan, McDowell, Mercer, Monroe, Nicholas, Pocahontas, Raleigh, Tucker, Webster, and Wyoming, comprising more than one third of the entire area of the state, made no returns.[2]

Arthur I. Boreman, first governor of West Virginia

As soon as the results were determined, Pierpont, as the governor of Virginia, prepared for the installation of the officers of West Virginia. With the aid of a committee, he planned an inaugural ceremony featured by a military display and a parade. The starting point for the latter was the McLure Hotel, Wheeling, where the state officers of Virginia and those of the new state assembled preparatory to going to the tem-

[2] W. Va. Dept of Arch. and Hist., *Second Biennial Report,* p. 223.

porary capitol. Accompanied by the Fourth and Fifth regiments, West Virginia militia, they then marched to Linsly Institute, where, on June 20, 1863, the inaugural ceremonies were concluded.

Governor Pierpont's valedictory featured the inaugural exercises launching the new state government. After reviewing the legislative acts by which West Virginia had attained separate statehood, he proclaimed her "one among the United States of America." His only regret was inability to announce that the "Rebellion" against the "Stars and Stripes" was ended, but he was confident that the plain people of the United States, with the help of God, would in time triumph over her slaveholding aristocrats. Reflecting the bushwhacking practices of the belligerents, he admonished loyal West Virginians to fight "as long as a mountain presents a site for a battery or a grotto remains to serve as a rifle pit." He then introduced Governor Boreman, who was described as being "as true as steel."

Governor Boreman's inaugural address, a modest but clear-cut statement of the issues of the day, was in keeping with his character and his declared intention to make West Virginia honored and respected among the states of the Union. Then Senator Willey responded to calls for "a speech," following which thirty-five girls sang "E Pluribus Unum." With bands playing the "Star-Spangled Banner," all then stood at attention and closed the exercises which made West Virginia the thirty-fifth state in the Union.

EXTENT AND BOUNDARY

Because of the methods used, as well as the resulting legal questions, the inclusion of Berkeley and Jefferson counties in West Virginia is important.[3] Neither of these counties voted on the constitution of West Virginia at either time it was submitted, but, as it provided for their inclusion, the general assembly of the Reorganized Government, by acts of January 31, 1863, and February 4, 1863, authorized them to vote on the question of their inclusion. They each voted on May 28, following. Berkeley gave 665 votes for inclusion, to 7 against. With a total voting population of about 2,000, Jefferson County gave 238 for inclusion, to 2 against.

In official communications, dated July 22 and September 14, 1863, Governor Pierpont certified the respective results of these elections to Gov-

[3] See Boyd B. Stutler, "The Making of West Virginia: its boundaries and counties," in J. M. Hagans, *Sketch* (Reprint Charleston, 1927), pp. 82-96; Ambler, *Pierpont,* pp. 214-215; H. J. Eckenrode, *Virginia During the Reconstruction* (Baltimore, 1904), pp. 15-17; 38 Cong., 1 Sess., *House Miscellaneous Documents,* No. 12.

ernor Boreman. The new West Virginia Legislature, by acts passed August 5 and November 2, 1863, then formally included them in West Virginia. The controlling thought and purpose in these acts and the arguments sustaining them were to vest complete control of the Baltimore and Ohio Railroad in the new state. At once the question was raised as to whether or not the act of Congress admitting West Virginia, applied

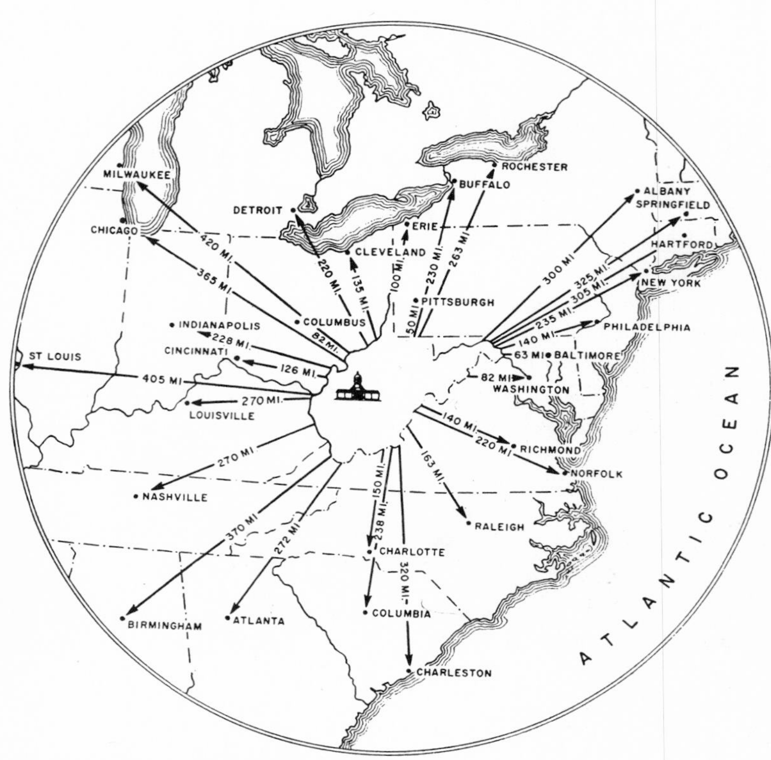

Courtesy W. Va. Dept. of Agriculture

West Virginia and her neighbors

to Berkeley and Jefferson counties. At the instance of West Virginia, the matter was carried to Congress, which on March 6, 1866, passed a joint resolution approving the inclusion.

After the cessation of hostilities, much dissatisfaction was expressed in Berkeley and Jefferson counties because of their inclusion in West Virginia. A great number of former Confederates, together with their friends and sympathizers and some Unionists, held that the transfer was null and void, because of alleged fraudulent voting and the fact that polls were opened in Jefferson County only at Shepherdstown and Harpers Ferry. In order to make sure of their status, some voters tried to vote in both states. Federal troops were in Jefferson County at the time of the election, and their presence may have influenced the results.

Unwilling to accept the action of Congress as final, Virginia took up the fight for the dissatisfied residents of Berkeley and Jefferson counties. On the second day of its session and under a suspension of rules, the first general assembly elected after Pierpont went to Richmond, repealed by a unanimous vote the several acts of the Virginia Reorganized Government authorizing the inclusion of Berkeley and Jefferson counties in West Virginia. Soon thereafter Virginia sued West Virginia to compel their return. The case was terminated five years later in favor of West Virginia, who, by implication at least, established her legal right to separate statehood.

A provision of the constitution of 1863 fixing a minimum area of 400 square miles for new counties, raised to 600 in 1872, below which existing counties could not be reduced, almost put an end to the abuse of creating new counties. As a consequence, only five have since been created. They are: Mineral and Grant, formed in 1866, from Hampshire and Hardy, respectively; Lincoln, 1867, from parts of Putnam, Kanawha, Boone, and Cabell; Summers, 1871, from parts of Monroe, Mercer, Greenbrier, and Fayette; and Mingo, in 1895, from Logan.

Beginning at Harpers Ferry and proceeding northwest, the boundary of West Virginia follows the southern bank of the Potomac River to Fairfax Stone. Then it continues with the western boundary of Maryland to the Pennsylvania line which it follows west and north to a point at low-water mark on the northern bank of the Ohio River. With low-water line of the Ohio on its northern bank, the boundary continues to a point in said line, where West Virginia and Kentucky corner at the mouth of Big Sandy River. With the north bank of Big Sandy River, the line continues to the mouth of Knox Creek. From this point, in line with and including the boundary lines of McDowell and Mercer counties, it reaches the top of East Mountain and continues with the top of that mountain, Peters Mountain, and the Alleghenies to Haystack Knob. Here it turns almost due east and follows the southern boundary of Pendleton County to the top of Shenandoah Mountain. With the top of this mountain and Branch Mountain it continues to the corner of Hardy and Rockingham counties. Then with the line of and including the counties of Hardy, Hampshire, Morgan, Berkeley, and Jefferson counties, it reaches the point of beginning.

THE FATHERS

Though Governor Pierpont is sometimes called "The Father of West Virginia," others contributed almost, if not quite, as much as did he to the paternity of that war child. Pierpont's education, wide experience, industrial interest, Abolitionist penchant, and militant reforming spirit, together with the fact that he was not of the officeholding and social elements in the old state, fitted him admirably for such a rôle. His relation to the Reorganized Government cramped his style with respect to the new state. But, insofar as it was the child of the Reorganized Government, paternity belongs to Pierpont.

As president of the Second Wheeling Convention of 1861 during its two sessions, Arthur I. Boreman (July 24, 1823-April 19, 1896) contributed effectively to the new state movement.[4] An active Methodist, Boreman had strong antislavery leanings, and, with the triumph of Abolitionists in the final stages of the admission of West Virginia, he was an outstanding leader. His selection to be her first governor was uncontested, and, unlike any of her other governors, he was twice re-elected. Though his services in the United States Senate (1869-1875) were not outstanding, they were substantial. He was a circuit judge under the Reorganized Government at the time of his first election to the governorship, and he was elected in 1888 to a similar position in the new state, an office which he held until his death.

Governor Boreman was born at Waynesburg, Pennsylvania, son of Kenner S. Boreman, a merchant of that place. Though most of his forebears were merchants, Arthur I. Boreman was a lawyer. As a result of a reading course, directed by his brother who resided at the time in Middlebourne, Tyler County, (West) Virginia, Arthur I. Boreman was in 1845 admitted to the bar and the following year began the practice of his profession in Parkersburg, Wood County, where he became prominent. From 1855 to 1861 he represented Wood County as a Whig delegate in the Virginia General Assembly.

More than any other one person, Peter G. Van Winkle (September 7, 1807-April 15, 1872) was the guiding mind in the formation of West Virginia. As chairman of the "Committee on Fundamental and General Provisions" of her First Constitutional Convention, he left unmistakable marks of his masterly hand on almost every page of its *Journal*. He was recognized by the chair twice as many times as any other delegate and he generally ended the debates on important and controversial subjects. He

---

[4] *Boreman Letters* in Dept. of Arch. and Hist., Charleston. These *Letters* have been calendared.

was not only well-versed in the law, but he had Eastern contacts and was a practical man, as determined by the fact that he promoted the Northwestern Virginia Railroad and was its president.

In politics Van Winkle was a conservative Whig, and, as such, did not become a Radical. As a Senator from West Virginia, he refused to sustain the impeachment charges against President Andrew Johnson; as a result he was bitterly assailed in the Radical press. Because of this and ill health, he declined to stand for re-election to the Senate. As a resident of Parkersburg, he was closely associated with the Jackson family, scioned by General John J. Jackson, whose son, John J. Jackson, Jr., was appointed by Abraham Lincoln to what proved to be one of the longest and most interesting careers on the Federal bench.

Archibald W. Campbell (April 4, 1833-February 13, 1899) was the free lance of the West Virginia statehood movement.[5] Too worldly to cooperate effectively with its pious supporters, his "Black Republicanism" made him taboo with old-time Whigs and Jackson Democrats. With his genius for journalism he was, however, "a voice crying in the wilderness." Both in season and out, he was for the new state, and, when the Second Wheeling Convention met in adjourned session, he announced that "the time to cap the climax has arrived."

When the Republican party became a power in West Virginia, Campbell was for years its most effective spokesman, but he recognized no boss and eschewed organizations. This independence was exemplified in his refusal to permit the Republican National Nominating Convention of 1880 to compel him, under the unit rule and a threat of expulsion, to vote for General Grant. In defiance, he gained the Convention floor and made a statement which at once became famous. "Whether in or out of this convention," said he, "I carry my sovereignty under my hat." He was not expelled.

Campbell was born in Jefferson County, Ohio, son of Dr. A. W. Campbell and nephew of Dr. Alexander Campbell, founder of Bethany College. He was graduated July 4, 1852, from his uncle's college and soon thereafter entered Hamilton College, New York, to study law. There he came under the influence of William H. Seward and became an Abolitionist and a Republican. In 1856 he became editor and part owner of the Wheeling *Intelligencer,* which, at the same time, became an organ of the newly born Republican party. As such it did the pioneering for that party in present West Virginia and was one of the most influential newspapers in the upper Ohio Valley.

Waitman T. Willey (October 18, 1811-May 2, 1900) was the orator of

---

[5] Atkinson and Gibbens, *Prominent Men of West Virginia,* pp. 507-513;Wheeling *Intelligencer,* February 14, 1899; Ambler, *Pierpont, passim;* Hall, *Rending of Virginia,* pp. 582-588.

Waitman T. Willey

Rev. Gordon Battelle

Archibald W. Campbell

the West Virginia statehood movement.[6] His best speeches were prepared and delivered with formality and effectiveness. This was notably true of his address before the recalled session of the First Constitutional Convention of West Virginia. Significant of his effectiveness is the fact that scores of persons residing in his native state bear his Christian name, which is also found in states of the West, notably Iowa and Kansas.

When Waitman was a small boy, his father moved to a site on the Monongahela River, at the mouth of Paw Paw Creek, in present Marion County. Here, beside that beautiful stream, he spent his boyhood days reveling in a background of Indian lore and pioneer adventure. Except for two or three months in a grammar school, he was self-taught. Notwithstanding, he was able to enter Madison College in Uniontown, Pennsylvania, at the age of sixteen. In college he distinguished himself as a student of Latin and Greek, and was graduated after three and one-half years of study. Meanwhile, he made many friends, among them being Matthew Simpson, who became one of the outstanding Bishops of Methodism. Willey was a member of the Reform Convention of 1850-51 and the Secession Convention, and distinguished himself in both as an orator.

Of the numerous minister, or "preacher," participants in the formation of West Virginia, Gordon Battelle (November 14, 1814-August 7, 1862) was outstanding.[7] A graduate of Allegheny College at Meadville, Pennsylvania, where he and Francis H. Pierpont "messed" together at a total cost to each of forty-five cents per week, Battelle was in 1861 presiding elder of the Wheeling district of the Methodist Episcopal Church. In the military operations in present West Virginia which followed, he was Governor Pierpont's contact man and civilian adviser. As a member of the First Constitutional Convention, he was rather too aggressive and uncompromising to be effective, but he was highly esteemed by his associates. He died of typhoid fever in line of duty, but before his fight for the abolition of slavery in the new state was crowned with success.

Though little is known of him, Abraham D. Soper (September 4, 1796-March 25, 1876), of Tyler County, stood high in the councils of the new state makers. An able lawyer with prominent Eastern connections, Soper was also a conservative and a Democrat of the Douglas type. He was president of the recalled session of the First Constitutional Convention and was offered the governorship of the new state. He declined and suggested Arthur I. Boreman.

Outstanding among a score or more other so-called "Fathers" of West Virginia were: Daniel Lamb of Ohio County, "The Code Maker"; John

---

[6] Most of his speeches were published in pamphlet form and may be found in the West Virginia University Library. See also Willey, *Diaries,* 2 volumes, also in West Virginia University Library; and Ambler, *Waitman Thomas Willey.*

[7] J. W. Hamilton, *Gordon Battelle—Preacher, Statesman, and Soldier* (1916).

List of Ohio County and Campbell Tarr of Brooke County, financiers; James H. Brown and Benjamin H. Smith, both of Kanawha County, vigilant and capable defenders of the interests of the Kanawha Valley; John J. Brown and John A. Dille, both of Preston County, Douglas Democrats whose conservative influence was felt throughout the constitution making; Rev. John M. Powell of Upshur County, who sponsored the constitutional provision forbidding the manufacture and sale of intoxicants; Chapman J. Stuart of Doddridge County, who directed the movement for the inclusion of all Virginia counties traversed by the Baltimore and Ohio Railroad; Henry Dering of Monongalia County, the compromiser; and John Hall of Mason County, who, until his unfortunate experience with his neighbor, Lewis Wetzel, ably directed the proceedings of the First Constitutional Convention. But for his defection in behalf of state rights, John S. Carlile of Harrison County would rank high among the new state makers.

THE FIRST LEGISLATURES

The first legislature of West Virginia was composed of 71 members: 20 senators and 51 delegates. The total was made up of 33 farmers, 13 merchants, five ministers, five lawyers, two physicians, two manufacturers, two carpenters, two bankers, one court clerk, one contractor, one hatter, one stage man, one land agent, one teacher, and one occupation not given. Forty-eight were native Virginians, 10 were born in Pennsylvania, six in New York, three in Maryland, two in Ohio, one in Connecticut, and one in the District of Columbia. Ages ranged from 26 to 70. The average age was slightly above 46.[8]

As the executive officers were being inaugurated, this body of legislators assembled in Wheeling and proceeded to adapt the fundamental laws of the new state to the changed conditions. In this the pertinent laws of Virginia were found to be indispensable, and it was therefore decided to codify them. For this work, Daniel Lamb of Ohio County was chosen, but, at his request, he was released in 1867 and Judge Ralph L. Berkshire and Thayer Melvin were appointed to continue it. At the session of the legislature for 1868, they reported the residue of the code, but too late for publication. Work of a revisory committee necessitated other delays and made possible the incorporation, by Judge James H. Ferguson, of the session acts of 1869 and 1870. The work is known, however, as the "Lamb Code of 1868."[9]

---

[8] W. Va. Leg., *Senate Journal,* Ex. Doc. No. 1; Lewis, *West Virginia,* pp. 425-426.

[9] "Preface," *Code of 1868,* pp. iii-iv.

August 4, 1863, the legislature proceeded to the election of United States Senators. First and almost without opposition, Waitman T. Willey, a Senator from Virginia until the preceding March 4, was chosen. Friends claimed the second place for Archibald W. Campbell, but, after several ballots, Peter G. Van Winkle was elected. As Congress was then in session, Willey and Van Winkle proceeded at once to Washington to ask admission to the Senate. As they expected, objections were made to receiving them, but these were more or less formal. After a short delay, they were duly admitted. Willey drew the term ending March 3, 1865, and Van Winkle that ending four years later.

Other notable acts of West Virginia's first legislature approved the inclusion of Jefferson and Berkeley counties; provided for the division of counties into townships; districted the state for Congressional and legislative election purposes; created a board of public works after the model of the existing board; accepted the conditions of the Morrill Act, donating public lands "for the benefit of Agricultural and Mechanical Arts"; established a system of free public schools; set up a new system of property assessment and taxation; defined the duties of state, county, and township officers; and provided for the common defense.

Like other bodies politic, the new state needed a seal for the authentication of official documents.[10] On the motion of Peter G. Van Winkle, the choice of such a device was left to a committee which availed itself of the services of J. H. Diss Debar, an artist and an expert draftsman, who was then sojourning at the state capital to contest the seat of one of the delegates in the legislature. The design submitted by him was adopted not only as the Great Seal, but also as the Lesser Seal and the state coat of arms.

The Great Seal of West Virginia is a disc, two and one-half inches in diameter, bearing upon its outer circumference the words "State of West Virginia"—the constitutional designation of the body politic—and beneath it, in a similar position the motto *Montani Semper Liberi,* meaning "Mountaineers Always Free." In the center of the disc is a rock, bearing upon its face the inscription, "June 20, 1863," the date of the entry of West Virginia to statehood. To the left of this rock stands a farmer wearing the traditional hunting shirt of the pioneer. His right hand rests upon a plow handle, and his left arm supports a woodman's ax. At his right are a sheaf of wheat and a cornstalk. To the right of the rock and in front of an anvil stands a miner with a pickax on his shoulder. On the ground in front of the rock and its accompanying figures are two hunter's rifles crossed and surmounted at their points of intersection by a Phrygian cap, which,

[10] Until a seal could be adopted and cast, the governor was authorized to use his private seal. Session, *Acts, p.* 264; W. Va. Dept. of Arch. and Hist., *First Annual Report* (Lewis, 1906), pp. 80-88.

after all, is probably the most significant emblem of the entire device. It indicates that the state won its freedom by the sword and will maintain it in the same manner. Subsequent changes in the design of this seal have not altered its essential features.

The reverse side of the seal, which is no longer used, is equally beautiful and informing. Wide wreaths of laurel and oak leaves, symbols respectively of valor and strength, intertwined with fruits and cereals, fill the outer circumference. At the right side of the seal, against a back-

Great Seal of West Virginia

ground of mountains, may be seen the famous Preston County viaduct of the Baltimore and Ohio Railroad with a train of cars passing. Industry, a feature of the design, is represented by a large building in the center of the scene. A tall smokestack, with a derrick and shed near by, rises at the left of the building; a steamboat stands in front of it; and in the foreground horses and cattle graze and rest. The background for this central design is a mountain range over which sun rays herald the words, *Libertas e fidelitate,* which means "Liberty from loyalty."

The second session of the first legislature of West Virginia was called upon by the various West Virginia regiments and other military units engaged in the defense of the Union to present battleflags. Those selected were beautiful emblems, six feet square, made of deep blue silk embroidered with golden fringe. In the center was the Great Seal, or coat of arms of the state, minus its encircling motto and name, the latter being placed instead upon a long flowing scroll below the disc. On the reverse side of these banners was a spread eagle in colors and measuring forty-four inches from tip to tip of its wings. In its right talon it carried a sheaf of arrows, and in its left an olive branch. A floating scroll held in the beak of the eagle bore the legend *E Pluribus Unum*. Some forty years ago these flags, inscribed with the names and the dates of the engagements in which they were used, were collected in the state capitol, where they now constitute one of the state's most cherished relics.

As the Emancipation Proclamation did not apply to present West Virginia, discussion incident to the ratification of the Thirteenth Amendment to the Federal Constitution brought the slavery status to the front again. With most of those favoring abolition, it was a case of getting into the band wagon. Accordingly her legislature, by an act of February 3, 1865, abolished slavery. Masters ignored the act, but the proclamation in December, 1865, of the Thirteenth Amendment made a test case useless.

LIFE AND CUSTOMS

Except for sectional and factional rivalries, which had their basis largely in conflicting economic and social interests, West Virginia was, at the time she entered the Union, a fairly homogeneous state. A white population of approximately 335,000 was augmented by 13,000 Negro slaves and 3,000 free persons of color. The subsequent incorporation of Jefferson and Berkeley counties raised the total white population to about 380,000, and the slave to about 18,000. By 1870, the total had grown to more than 442,000, which included no slaves and less than 18,000 persons of color. The foreign-born did not reach 17,000, of which number six tenths were natives of the German states and Switzerland; three tenths, of Ireland; and the remainder, of England, Scotland, Belgium, France, Denmark, and Sweden.

For some time, the inhabitants of the new state had few or no contacts with the mother state. Such contacts as there were came largely from the fact that Richmond had been a common capital. Since the days of the pack horse and stagecoach, commercial relations between eastern and western Virginia had tended to be negligible. A network of railroads in the east, constructed at state expense and having no direct connection with the west's one railroad, the Baltimore and Ohio—including a branch line between Grafton and Parkersburg, the Northwestern Virginia Railroad—only accentuated this condition and made the west dependent upon Pittsburgh, Cincinnati, Baltimore, and Philadelphia. Speaking of this condition as a reason for his opposition to a proposal, made in 1866, for the redintegration of Virginia, Senator Willey said:

> West Virginia lies on the western slope of the Alleghenies. It properly belongs to the valley of the Mississippi. All, or nearly all, of its streams flow thitherward. Its natural outlets to market, and all its available commercial connections, are diverse from Virginia—south and west with Cincinnati and the Gulf of Mexico; north with Pittsburgh and the lakes; east with Baltimore and Philadelphia. The markets in East Virginia are not our markets; and if they were, it would be difficult if not impossible to reach them from the larger part of West Virginia by any direct or convenient means of access. We are cut off from East Virginia by the almost impassable barriers of the Allegheny mountains. With the present crushing public debt of Virginia resting upon her, she would not, even if reunited with us, be able for ages to come to construct, at such heavy cost as must be necessary to accomplish it, any road or other available means of travel and transportation through those mountains into our midst, so as to connect us with the seaboard or any important place of trade or commerce within her borders. Besides, if she had both the will and the ability thus to accommodate us, any such work, when constructed, would only carry us beyond the nearer and better markets already indicated.[11]

In the absence of adequate transportation facilities, the chief economic interest of the new state continued to be agriculture, the products of which were largely for local consumption. The chief crop was Indian corn, of which about 8,000,000 bushels were grown in 1860. Other crops, in the order of their importance, were: wheat, 2,300,000 bushels; tobacco, 2,180,000 pounds; oats, 1,650,000 bushels; and potatoes, approximately 750,000 bushels. Grazing was next in importance. The census for 1860 showed, in round numbers, 85,000 horses, 100,000 cows, 210,000 oxen and other cattle, 450,000 sheep, and 425,000 swine—the total estimated value of all of which was slightly in excess of $12,000,000. From the earliest times, fruit growing had been an important enterprise.

Timbering was just in its beginnings; previous activities in that field had been confined largely to the use of forests, whose product could be marketed by rafting. However, all the saw logs, ship timber, lumber, staves, and barrels shipped from West Virginia in a single year, shortly after her admission, sold for an aggregate of more than $2,500,000. Inasmuch as more than half of the 15,500,000 acres constituting her territory were then covered with primeval forests of rare quality, there were those who saw in them a source of fabulous wealth.

As yet, the mineral resources of West Virginia were largely a source of potential wealth. Salt and iron continued to be produced, but interest was shifting to coal and oil. In the sixties, coal was mined on the Kanawha, the Coal, and the Elk rivers; at Mason City, on the Ohio; and in or near Clarksburg, Fairmont, and Tunnelton. At the same time, "oil," or

[11] W. T. Willey, "The Redintegration of Virginia," in *Pamphlet,* dated January 20, 1866.

petroleum, became an absorbing topic of conversation along the Ohio River in the vicinity of Parkersburg.[12] Although millions were invested in borings here and there, not a single paying well was found outside of a belt extending from Burning Springs, on the Little Kanawha River, in northeasterly and southwesterly directions, through Wirt, Ritchie, Wood, and Pleasants counties.

West Virginia was, in fact, an area of arrested development. Many yet living can testify to this condition. These witnesses themselves used the scythe and the grain cradle and cured meat in smokehouses long after the mowing machine and the reaper came into general use in the West and after the slaughtering of hogs and cattle on a large scale and by modern methods elsewhere became a profitable business. Indeed, West Virginians continued to ride to country gristmills on horseback astride bags of wheat, corn, and buckwheat, long after a large part of the world was using flour made by the roller process. Reluctant to yield the contest with modern progress, there are those who would even now return to the "good old days."

As might be expected, these experiences left their marks. Indeed, they helped to produce a type, the "Mountaineer," which, until recently, has been somewhat distinctive in American society. In about equal proportions, he is both admired and censured. Of his characteristics, a sympathetic contemporary wrote:

> The blending of races through several generations has resulted in a well defined Anglo-Saxon type, slightly modified by that Celtic ease of manner peculiar to the dwellers of mild and fruitful climates. The genuine rural West Virginian is not much addicted to precipitous motion, rarely loses his temper or self-possession, and beyond the acquisition of the necessaries of life, limited by almost Spartan frugality, is disposed to leave the improvement of things around him to time and chance. This unprogressive disposition is the more striking, as his native intellect and sagacity are extraordinary and susceptible of high development under proper direction or the stimulus of personal ambition. Perhaps nowhere on the continent are there such treasures of natural power buried under the rust of indolence and prejudice, and at the same time such a display of urbanity and hospitality prompted by native tact and geniality. . . . Very unlike the proverbial Jonathan, the West Virginian seldom inquires into his neighbor's business with indelicate curiosity, and no matter how strong or antagonistic his convictions, never intrudes them upon strangers in aggressive or controversial discourse.[13]

---

[12] C. A. Whiteshot, *Oil Well Driller* (Morgantown, W. Va., 1905), pp. 65-68; Festus P. Summers, *Johnson Newlon Camden: A Study in Individualism* (New York, 1937), pp. 82-194.

[13] J. H. Diss Debar, *West Virginia Hand-Book and Immigrants' Guide* (Parkersburg, W. Va., 1870), pp. 33-34.

Chapter XXI

Political Reconstruction

1865-1876

THE WAR BACKGROUND

ALTHOUGH SPARED the worst reconstruction experiences of the states which attempted to withdraw from the Union in 1861, West Virginia went through a similar transition. Separated into detached sectarian, factional, and clannish groups, as its inhabitants were, political unity was not easily attained. From the first, efforts to reach that goal were complicated also by the divided sympathies of her people with respect to the "Lost Cause." It will be recalled that they sent about one third as many soldiers to the Army of the Confederacy as they sent to the Army of the Union.[1]

To meet the resulting contingencies, a legislative act of 1863 declared forfeited to the state all property within her bounds belonging to her enemies. Although this law was somewhat of a dead letter from the first, it gave a semblance of authority to vigilant "home guards" bent upon vindicating loyalty, and to self-constituted authorities bent upon promiscuous maraudings and vengeance. Worse still, it was a constant menace to former Confederate sympathizers who were willing to accept the situation and to make the best of it.

At the same time, all officers, both state and local, were required to take

[1] Among the best secondary accounts covering this period are: W. A. Dunning, *Reconstruction, Political and Economic* (New York, 1907); J. F. Rhodes, *History of the United States,* Vols. V-VII (New York, 1900-1906); W. L. Fleming, *The Sequel of Appomattox* (New Haven, 1919), and *Documentary History of Reconstruction,* 2 vols. (Cleveland, 1906-1907); H. J. Eckenrode, *The Political History of Virginia during the Reconstruction* (Baltimore, 1904); J. G. Randall, *Constitutional Problems under Lincoln* (New York, 1926).

an oath of allegiance to the Government of the United States and to that of West Virginia. Later, the exaction of this oath from attorneys, school teachers, school trustees, and others became a favorite instrument of discrimination and persecution. Meanwhile, Confederate sympathizers were being arrested and detained for varying periods as prisoners of war. Some of them were sent to Camp Chase at Columbus, Ohio.

So long as hostilities lasted, the proscribed regarded these treatments as acts of war and repaid them in kind. In his annual message to the legislature, Governor Boreman on January 17, 1865, spoke as follows of their activities: "Recently robberies have been committed on a large scale in many parts of the State, and some of the best citizens murdered by these outlaws in the counties of Harrison and Marion. . . . One feature of this condition of things is that many of the disloyal in our midst who have remained at home, feed and harbour these marauders and murderers, knowing their purposes."[2]

Because of this situation, Governor Boreman called upon the loyal people of the state to organize themselves for their own protection. At the same time he authorized them to capture and kill "these outlaws wherever found," and promised free arms and ammunition for that purpose. Deeming these precautions inadequate, he recommended, furthermore, the enactment of additional proscriptive legislation "imposing the severest penalties, . . . but with provisions so guarded as to protect the innocent."

POLITICAL PROSCRIPTION

The "voters' test oath" of February 25, 1865, was the answer to the governor's recommendation. It gave to any voter, "present" at the polls, authority to challenge any other voter. This effectively stopped the challenged from exercising the privilege of suffrage until he had affirmed, under oath, that he had not voluntarily borne arms against the Government of the United States, the Reorganized Government of Virginia, or the State of West Virginia; that he had not at any time sought, accepted, or held an office hostile to any of these powers; that he would support the Constitution of the United States and the constitution of West Virginia; and, finally, that he took the required oath freely "without any mental reservation or purpose of evasion." As the constitution of 1863 extended suffrage to "all white male citizens"—citizens of the state being defined in the same instrument as "citizens of the United States, residing therein"—the voters' test oath was attacked in many quarters as unconstitutional, but it was justified as a war measure.

[2] Senate, *Journal* (1865), pp. 6-7.

Other acts of this legislature were equally galling to the proscribed. Excepting only those who had later volunteered into the military service of the United States, or been honorably discharged therefrom, one of these acts required an oath of allegiance, to be taken "within thirty days after notice to do so by any person." Other acts made cases at law arising in counties of strong pro-Southern leanings cognizable in neighboring counties of proved loyalty to the Union; another allowed tax collectors extra commissions not to exceed ten per cent, and otherwise provided for the collection of taxes in counties affected with secession sentiment; and still another prescribed a test oath for suitors formerly "engaged in Rebellion." Climaxing this legislation was a proposed amendment to the constitution disfranchising and "decitizening" all persons who had been active in the support of the Confederacy.

These proscriptions extended also to the judiciary and resulted in the impeachment and removal of Judge John W. Kennedy of the Tenth Circuit composed of Morgan, Berkeley, and Jefferson counties. Among other things, Judge Kennedy was charged with "huzzaing" because of a report to the effect that "Old Abe" Lincoln had deserted the Federal Capital in May, 1861. The charges against Kennedy were sustained, however, on the ground that he had appointed "rebels" to office and that he had denounced the Reorganized Government of Virginia as "an usurpation" and the government of West Virginia as a "bogus concern."

Immediately following the collapse of the Confederacy in April, 1865, this veiled warfare tended to cease for a time. Motivated by that spirit of friendship and concession extended by General Grant to General Lee at Appomattox, most West Virginia Confederates were willing to accept the situation and to make the best of it. Evidences of this attitude were abundant. For instance, the newspaper press ceased to carry accounts of maraudings and murders, and official utterances regarding them all but ceased.

In some quarters, fears were expressed lest returning Confederates would not be received in the spirit in which they came, and they were offered military protection. In some counties, notably those on the Virginia border and in the central part of the state, their presence was sorely needed to the end that local government might function effectively, and it was generally believed that state officialdom favored a modification of the existing proscriptive laws in order to make this possible.

Under these conditions, West Virginia Confederates in prison camps and in the field, together with their sympathizers at home, readily took oaths of allegiance to the Federal Government.[3] When these opportunities

[3] Under date of May 27, 1865, ninety-one Confederate officers imprisoned in Fort Delaware, most of them from West Virginia, petitioned through Senator Willey for a pardon. W. T. Willey, *Letters and Papers.*

were not extended them in the disturbed course of events, they petitioned the President for pardon and permission to go home and begin life anew. As a rule these requests were referred to the Attorney General of the United States, who in turn referred many of them to Governor Boreman. His willingness to treat them in the spirit in which they were made is evidenced by the following questions propounded by him to a loyal resident of Hardy County, regarding the request of seventeen "Rebels asking pardon":

1. What was the character of each of these applicants, before the Rebellion as to moral integrity and good citizenship?

2. What has been their position and conduct during the war, especially toward loyal people and their property?

3. Do you believe that they will be loyal and support the Government in the future, if pardoned?

4. Are they likely to be good citizens, useful and peaceable, in the future?

5. In your opinion should these applicants, or any of them, be pardoned?

But political reconstruction was not to be accomplished so easily as indicated in the above questions. About the time they were asked, Governor Boreman began to receive letters informing him that "the spirit of rebellion still reigns in the breast of these men"; that outrages were being inflicted on Negro slaves; and that loyal persons were forming committees of safety for their protection. On the other hand, Samuel Price of Greenbrier County, lieutenant governor of Virginia during the last years of the war, and Allen T. Caperton of Monroe County were arrested by a squadron of cavalry and taken to Charleston as civilian prisoners, and in the ensuing October elections, a number of former Confederates, including Samuel Price who was elected to the judgeship of his home circuit, were elected to the legislature and to county and township offices.

As in the Federal Government, the resulting conditions were more than the rapidly growing Radical element could endure, and it began to talk about making "treason odious" as a wholesome example and a necessary means to maintaining the results of the war. Under the circumstances, Governor Boreman could not be indifferent to, when he did not share, the demands of "loyal Unionists." Their sentiments were expressed by him in a message to the legislature which convened in January, 1866. in which he said:

It has seemed to me that too great anxiety is manifested on the part of those who actively engaged in the Rebellion to repossess themselves of place and power. They are too impatient under the safe-guards that it has been deemed necessary to adopt for the protection and preservation of the Government. . . . It has scarcely been nine months since their rebellious organization . . . was bidding defiance to the Government; yet now they gravely insist upon the right to immediate participation in the making and administration of the laws. . . . It must be apparent that time should be taken on this subject.[4]

In keeping with this suggestion, the governor recommended that the election law be so amended as to make it enforceable. To that end, he favored a rigid registration law. Furthermore, he asked that the disfranchising amendment to the constitution, first proposed in 1865, be concurred in and submitted to the electorate at the earliest date possible, and that all former Confederates who had been elected to office in 1865 be disqualified and removed.

A complicating factor was a decision of the state supreme court of appeals, handed down February 5, 1866, in the case of Charles J. Faulkner, an attorney who had refused to take the test oath required for his readmission to the bar. On the ground that he was not an "officer of the court," as contemplated in the act of 1863 prescribing a general test oath, he had refused to comply and was sustained by the highest court on a technicality.[5] Nevertheless, the ruling brought consternation to Union men who realized the importance of controlling lawyers and courts.

Under Radical influence, the legislature of 1866 outdid the governor in his desire for proscription. First of all, a law was enacted prescribing a test oath for lawyers similar to that required of officers under the act of 1863. The pending constitutional amendment was concurred in, and the desired registration law was enacted. With the subsequent approval of the amendment by the voters, between fifteen and twenty thousand persons were thus effectively disfranchised.

The manner of enforcing the disfranchising law was even more objectionable than the law itself. Under it the governor appointed for each county a board of registration of three members, chosen "from among the citizens most known for loyalty, firmness, and uprightness." At first the constitutionality of this act was questioned, but, in 1867, it was amended so as to meet legal objections. Henceforth, willingness to take the voters' test oath was not sufficient proof of one's right to register as a voter. Instead, the applicant was required "to make it appear" that he was qualified to take such an oath. Thus county registrars were given autocratic power to regulate suffrage. Moreover, under an act of 1867, actions for damages against registrars could be nonsuited summarily.

Resentment of these laws and practices took numerous forms, varying all the way from intimidation and control of registrars and election officials to mob violence and clandestine murder. Many of the feuds later associated with the name of West Virginia had their origin in this period. As already indicated, bitterness and factional rivalries were perpetuated in

---

4 Senate, *Journal,* January 16, 1866; Wheeling *Intelligencer,* January 17, 1866.
5 W. Va., *Reports,* Vol. I, 269-303.

the churches when controversies over the ownership of property were carried to the courts. As a result, "loyal" ministers were sometimes treated with great indignity, and ex-Confederates refused to attend religious services and social gatherings so long as proscription was continued. Some of them left the state and went to Ohio, where they could enjoy the rights of citizenship.

Meanwhile, friends of the existing order were not inactive. Many of them gave vent to their loyalty by helping "keep rebels in place" and by sustaining registration boards and election officials. In some instances, names of "rebels" were mysteriously dropped from the registration books and were refused restoration, even in the face of tactics already indicated. For the most part, the governor and officialdom dealt with the situation by the use of armed force, both state and Federal.[6]

The following summary from the governor's annual message to the legislature which met in January, 1868, tells something of the conditions, as well as of the methods of dealing with them. In Randolph and Tucker counties, "officers and Union men who took an interest in and supported the registration of voters, were threatened and menaced by open demonstrations, and also by written communications, in which they were notified to leave the county or they must suffer injury to their persons and property; in consequence of which many officers were intimidated and resigned, and it has been with much difficulty that persons could be induced to take upon themselves the execution of the law." In three townships in Barbour County, the registration officers were assaulted and driven away.

The legislative branch of the government was in complete accord with the governor. Almost unanimously Republican—the senate of 1868 containing only three Democrats out of a total of twenty-two and the house only fifteen Democrats out of a total of fifty-six members—it was at times defiant. Charges against registrars went uninvestigated, and it impeached and removed Judge William L. Hindman of Cabell County for failure to exact test oaths from persons seeking admission to the bar. At the same time, it declined to receive petitions from persons seeking restoration to the bar whose requests were not accompanied by disavowals of past conduct.

REMOVAL OF DISABILITIES

The trend of public opinion had, meanwhile, been against political proscription. When Congress, in February, 1869, submitted the Fifteenth Amendment to the state for ratification, this trend became precipitate. At

[6] Senate, *Journal* (1868), January 21, 1868.

once many Republicans either became Democrats or affiliated with the liberal wing of their own party. Almost without exception they were opposed to the enfranchisement of Negroes, as contemplated in the Fifteenth Amendment. Only six years before, they had accepted the abolition of slavery as a means to separate statehood. Ever since, most of them, for instance Campbell of the Wheeling *Intelligencer,* had denied that Negro enfranchisement was even contemplated. In defiance of these views, the Radical-dominated legislature ratified the Fifteenth Amendment with little time or opportunity for its consideration.

At once this action became the "Banquo's Ghost" of Radical Republicans in West Virginia. The conservative Republican trend to the Liberals became even more pronounced and Democrats became aggressive, in some cases belligerent. Reading the handwriting on the wall, Horace Greeley, in reply to a letter from the Wheeling *Intelligencer* stating that the West Virginia Legislature would probably enfranchise Negroes to the exclusion of ex-Confederates, gave this warning:

> Every year one thousand of your rebels die, and one thousand, or more, of their sons become of age,—you can't disfranchise them. You have now five thousand majority. The rebels will be enfranchised in spite of you. Go your way and see if the rebels don't have you under their feet. I speak from a large experience when I tell you that your house is built upon the sand. Now you can amnesty the rebels—soon the question will be, shall they amnesty you? Look at Kentucky and Maryland and read your certain fate in theirs.[7]

Greeley spoke with a view to the approaching election, which was one of the most important in West Virginia history and called forth her best talent and character. Among the members elected to the legislature at that time, October, 1869, were Francis H. Pierpont, John J. Davis, James M. Jackson, Daniel D. T. Farnsworth, Nathan Goff, Henry G. Davis, Daniel Lamb, William H. H. Flick, and George C. Sturgiss, names to conjure with in her annals. Among them were Radicals, state rights Democrats, and liberal Democrats and Republicans. The resulting legislature was liberal in both branches and committed to the "let up" policy with respect to proscription. For that purpose it submitted the "Flick Amendment" to the voters at the next ensuing election. Omitting the word "white" from the existing constitution, this amendment vested suffrage in the male citizens of voting age.

The Flick Amendment and the much discussed registration of voters were the issues in the ensuing election. Although the Radicals had, for the most part, opposed any action looking to redress for the proscribed, under the lash of Horace Greeley, Archibald W. Campbell, and James H. Ferguson, they tended to support the Flick Amendment. In other words,

---

[7] Wheeling *Intelligencer,* May 21, 1869.

they were willing to barter Negro suffrage for universal manhood suffrage, which it was claimed, would make certain about three thousand votes and arrest the popular trend against the Radical incumbents.

On the other hand, Democrats generally washed their hands of the Fifteenth Amendment and were indifferent to the Flick Amendment. Warned by the experiences of the Southern states, they were unwilling that theirs should be anything but a white man's government. In these attitudes they were sustained by subsequent events. For instance, as the session of the 1870 legislature was ending, the Fifteenth Amendment was officially proclaimed as a part of the Federal Constitution, and two months later Congress enacted a force bill to make it effective. Announcement of the latter came nine days before West Virginia Democrats met in a state nominating convention to name candidates for state offices and draft a party platform.

Planks of this platform speak for themselves. Among other things, they asserted the right of all the states to representation in Congress. Of greater appeal was their condemnation of the national Republican party for forcing the ratification of the Fifteenth Amendment, "calling to political power an alien and inferior race" and "declaring the white man incapable of self-government." The acts of Congress for carrying this amendment into effect, as well as Charles Sumner's proposal looking to the social equality of the races, also were condemned as contrary to public morals and as subversive of the rights of the states.

In state matters, the Democrats declared for a reduction in the number of officials, for the collection of delinquent taxes, for the preservation of the free public school, for the exclusion of Negroes from schools attended by whites, for the immediate repeal of all test oaths, and for protection against "outrages" being committed by registrars. The platform ended with a demand for a free ballot for all white men and a condemnation of the "injustice and disgrace incident to the disfranchisement in our midst, of 25,000 men of our own race," while "Negroes exercise the franchise without hindrance or condition." After a bitter fight, it was decided to make no mention of the Flick Amendment.

The Republicans held their convention two weeks later. Their platform mildly endorsed the Fifteenth Amendment, as in keeping with the principles of the Declaration of Independence. In the same strain, the Flick Amendment was endorsed, but the convention committed itself to the enforcement of all existing laws, as long as they were upon the statute books. A Radical platform, seeking to commit the party "to the removal of disabilities and restrictions upon the late rebels in the same measure as their spirit of loyalty will direct," was significantly defeated. The vote was 260 ayes, to 412 nays.

In the contest that followed, a determining factor was the interference of Federal officials, who caused the arrest and imprisonment of registrars who refused to allow ex-Confederates to register after taking the voters' test oath. Courts, even a Federal one, sustained the registrars, but Judge John J. Jackson, of the United States District Court, declared that the Fifteenth Amendment applied to white men as well as to black men and ordered the registration of all. Officers refusing to obey were arrested and imprisoned for contempt of court. Commenting upon the results, Governor William E. Stevenson, of West Virginia, said: "These proceedings, carried on under color of authority of the United States, were potent in preventing the registration officers from discharging their duties under the State law."[8]

As a result of "these proceedings," the number of registered voters greatly increased, and the Democrats were generally successful in the election that followed. John J. Jacob was elected governor, and the Democrats gained control of both branches of the legislature: the senate by a majority of two, and the house by a majority of twenty-five. At the same time, Democrats superseded Republicans in the lower House of Congress.

The legislature of 1871 made quick work of the removal of all disabilities. Test oaths were abolished; election officers were made elective by the voters; the registration of voters was abolished; and it was made illegal to challenge, for causes other than those set out in the constitution, the right of any person to vote. The Flick Amendment, first proposed in 1870, was concurred in and submitted to a popular referendum which approved it by a vote of 23,546 for, to 6,323 against. At the same time, the voters were asked to express their preference for, or against, a proposed constitutional convention.

THE CONSTITUTION OF 1872

The election of 1871 resulted generally in success for Democrats and liberal Republicans. The convention proposal carried by a vote of 30,220 for, to 27,638 against, and former Republican majorities in the legislature were converted into Democratic majorities: that for the senate was fourteen, and that for the house was twenty-three. In October, 1871, seventy-eight delegates were elected to a proposed constitutional convention, only a dozen of whom—humorously known as the "Twelve Apostles"—were Republicans. The Democratic majorities and accessions of strength came largely, but not wholly from former Confederate strongholds.

Simultaneously with the meeting of the legislature, January 16, the Constitutional Convention of 1872 met in Charleston. It remained in

[8] Senate, *Journal* (January, 1871), p. 23.

session eighty-four days, and, in conjunction with the legislature, effected a new order of things, savoring strongly of conservatism. Critics spoke of its work as reactionary, to which its defenders replied, "It has stood the test of time and of subsequent Republican control."[9] Together with a number of amendments, the constitution of that date is in effect today.

Preliminaries to the constructive work of the convention were amusing, but significant. For example, an invitation from Wheeling, the former capital, asking it to meet there and guaranteeing free transportation to its members, was declined by the newspaper press on the ground that nothing in the way of reform could be accomplished in that "iron hearted city." Union Democrats objected to the high-handed way in which ex-Confederates ran things in the convention and their proposal to change the names of Lincoln and Grant counties to Davis and Lee, respectively. They also opposed a resolution declaring the Constitution of the United States the supreme law of the land. It was alleged that such a course would be a repudiation of the rights of the states and the heaven-born right of revolution. Frequent jibes were made at the Baltimore and Ohio Railroad, to which paternity of the state was attributed. Reminding its critics of a time when the inhabitants of western Virginia carried deerskins on their backs all the way to Philadelphia and when they drank sassafras tea six months a year because they could not get "store" tea, friends of the Baltimore and Ohio recommended and eulogized the benefits of railroads.

A discussion precipitated by a resolution proposing to place the United States flag over the convention hall during its session degenerated into mock comedy. Some would have used, instead, "the flag of West Virginia." As there was no national flag available, delegates opposed its use on the ground of "economy." A motion permitting its use was finally adopted, but the flag again became a subject of debate when a member proposed that, whatever flag was used, it should be inscribed with the words "West Virginia Rescued from Tyranny," to which another member proposed to add "in 1861."

A way out of the difficulty was found when Henry Pike of New York, a visitor, offered to present the convention with a United States flag. The offer was accepted with thanks, and the sergeant at arms was ordered to place the emblem in position when available. It arrived February 19 and, after being embraced by each of the "Twelve Apostles," was raised, with fitting ceremony.

"Chief Executive power" in the new constitution was vested in a governor whose term was extended from two to four years and who continued to be elective by the people. Sharing the executive power were a secretary of state, a superintendent of schools, an auditor, a treasurer, and

[9] The Convention Debates were not printed. The *Kanawha Daily* (Charleston) printed a rather complete account of the proceedings. The Convention *Journal* was printed.

an attorney general. Each was given a four-year term. Except the secretary of state, all were elected by the people. Vacancies in the governorship were filled by the president of the senate and the speaker of the house, in turn. In case neither of these could qualify, the legislature was given power to appoint, provided the vacancy did not occur in the first three years of the term, in which case an election by the people was required.

Legislative power was vested in a senate and a house of delegates, to be known jointly as the "Legislature of West Virginia." The former consisted of twenty-four members and the latter of sixty-five, but provision was made for increasing these numbers by legislative enactment, but only on the basis of equal representation for equal numbers of people. A provision for proportional representation in the senate, after 1876, has been ignored. Subsequent legislatures preferred to gerrymander the state to suit the interests of dominant parties. The terms of state legislators were extended: senators to four years, one half of their number being elected biennially; and delegates to two years, all of whom were chosen at the regular October biennial elections.

Although in line with modern tendencies, the constitutional provisions limiting the importance and power of the legislature were significant Sessions were made biennial and restricted to forty-five days' duration unless extended by the concurrence of two thirds of the members elected to each house. Among other limitations were those forbidding the legislature to grant divorces, to locate highways and county seats, to form new counties—except under certain specified conditions—to authorize the sale of church property, to regulate the practice of certain courts of justice, to regulate elections, and to incorporate cities, towns, and villages of less than two thousand inhabitants.

The judiciary was completely reorganized. Judicial power was vested in one supreme court of appeals, with four judges; in circuit courts and the judges thereof; and in inferior tribunals. Terms of judges and justices filling these positions ranged from four to twelve years, and all were made elective by the voters. A distinctive feature of the whole arrangement was the autonomy of its several agencies, notably justices of the peace decisions, which were freed from supervision by circuit judges These provisions were regarded as reactionary and were condemned accordingly.

The township system of the first constitution was abandoned for modified county court system composed of commissioners elected by the voters, no two of whom could come from the same magisterial distric To these commissioners, sitting as a court, was entrusted the managemer of the fiscal and administrative affairs of the counties. The administratio of schools, the building and maintenance of roads, and poor relief wer taken away from township meetings, which were abolished, and placed in the control of elective boards and the county courts.

Other provisions of the constitution had their origin largely in former partisan rivalries and prejudices. Martial law was made unconstitutional; registration boards were forbidden; and it was made illegal to deny to any citizen the right to vote because of the fact that he was not registered. An effort was made to restrict the franchise to white men. Except for fear of the consequences, this would probably have been done. The voter was left free in his choice of an open or secret ballot.

Conservative, even reactionary, the constitution of 1872 was not without merit. A tendency to adhere to the general instead of to the particular was commendable and accounts for its longevity. Provisions for a franchise tax and for proportional representation in the senate were progressive, as were also the provisions lengthening the terms of elective officers and of members of the legislature. The majority for ratification was, however, only 4,567 in a total vote of over 80,000.[10]

UNREST AND ADJUSTMENT

At the first election under the constitution of 1872, there was a split in the Democratic party, when Governor John J. Jacob objected to the procedure of the convention that nominated the regular candidate, Johnson N. Camden. As a result, Jacob ran for re-election as an Independent. Failure to nominate a regular Republican candidate permitted Jacob to win by a bare margin, but otherwise the regular Democratic candidates prevailed. Less than one month later, General Grant, with certain liberal Republicans, notably Francis H. Pierpont, opposing him, carried the state by almost 3,000 votes.

Because of the irregularity in Governor Jacob's re-election, his second administration was featured by factional and partisan bitterness. The fact that he owed his election to repudiated Radical Republicans was accepted by the Democratic controlled legislature as a valid, if not compelling, reason for limiting his appointive powers. Accordingly the 1873 session in the first "ripper" legislation in the state, vested the board of public works with certain appointive powers usually exercised by the governor. He resented this intrusion on his prerogatives, and the board moved to test its powers by appointing William L. Bridges superintendent of the state penitentiary to succeed Thomas P. Shallcross who held the position by appointment of the governor. On May 1, 1873, the effective date of his

[10] Atkinson and Gibbens, *Prominent Men*, pp. 116-117.

appointment, Bridges presented himself at the gate of the penitentiary and demanded possession. Being refused, he threatened to use force but was informed that such action would be met in kind by order of the governor. Instead of trying to make good his threat, Bridges carried his case to the state supreme court of appeals which ruled in July, 1873 in his favor, sustaining the ripper legislation. Thus sustained, the legislative department of the state government did not hesitate thereafter to challenge the executive under similar conditions.

During this entire period, the location of the state capital was a subject of sectional and political controversy. Because of its several removals, it

Hale House, 1871, Charleston

was referred to as "the capital on wheels." The choice of Wheeling as the first capital was somewhat indefinite and, from the outset, was regarded by interested persons as temporary. It was no surprise, therefore, when the first legislature free from the dominant influences which had made the state, that of 1869, designated Charleston as the capital. The act authorizing this change was, in fact, an olive branch to the Kanawha Valley which could not forgive the action of the First Constitutional Convention with respect to internal improvements. By 1870, the Chesapeake and Ohio Railroad was in process of construction, but the act transferring the capital was, nevertheless, a gesture in the interest of greater state-wide accord.

The removal was effected April 1, 1870, and was by steamboat packet, the "Mountain Boy."

This removal gave many Charlestonians their first real interest in the new state. A state house corporation financed by Charlestonians provided a building, a three-story structure with a tower and belfry in the center, which was available in December, 1870. Dr. John P. Hale, one of the most progressive and prominent residents of Charleston and of the entire state, built the "Hale House" on the site of the present Ruffner Hotel. The Hale House was one hundred feet square and four stories high, with a basement story. "It contained one hundred bedrooms, fitted up with elegance, a splendid office, bar and billiard room, barber shop and bathroom," and was otherwise described at the time as the "largest and finest hotel in West Virginia." Except for the fact that it had only one bathroom, it compares favorably with more modern hotels.

Though the Hale House was built largely for the purpose of retaining the state capital at Charleston, and the Chesapeake and Ohio Railroad was completed to the Ohio River in 1873, the legislature authorized the return of the capital to Wheeling. At a cost of $80,000, that city had built a substantial structure, which was presented to the state. After a hard-fought legal contest, the removal was effected on May 21-23, 1875, by the "Emma Graham" for a part of the way and over the remainder by the "Chesapeake," beautiful and popular Kanawha and Ohio river packets. Transfer of the state archives was delayed by an injunction, but on September 22-25 of the same year, they were returned to Wheeling, also by the river route. While the new capitol building was being made ready, Linsly Institute was, from May 23, 1875 to December 4, 1876, again the state capitol.

The new state government was no sooner housed in Wheeling for a second sojourn than the question of a permanent seat of government was raised. Finally, following adoption of a resolution thanking Wheeling for her interest in the matter, the legislature voted to submit the choice of a permanent site to a vote of the people. This was taken on August 7, 1877, and resulted in favor of Charleston, which received a larger vote than the total of her two rivals, Clarksburg and Martinsburg. When the result of this vote was learned, Governor Henry M. Mathews proclaimed that, eight years later, Charleston would be the permanent seat of the state government. The transfer was effected in May, 1885. Assisted by the "Belle Prince" and barges, the "Chesapeake" again became temporarily a floating state capital.

Part Three

Chapter XXII

The Bourbon Democracy

1872-1897

FOR A QUARTER OF A CENTURY following the making of the constitution of 1872, West Virginia was controlled politically by Democrats. Reconstruction excesses had brought the Republican party into disfavor in most of the counties of the state, and the re-enfranchised former Confederates who swelled Democratic ranks, especially in the Potomac region and in the Kanawha Valley, were sufficient to keep the Democratic party in power. Moreover, for a generation following the Civil War, West Virginia remained ninety per cent rural, a condition that provided common ground on which Union Democrats and former Confederates could stand and work together. If another bond of unity were needed, it was provided by their common adherence to Jeffersonian principles of low taxes, economy in administration, and states' rights. Even Democrats with heavy stakes in industry remained loyal to their party, which they generally controlled through their own party machines and liberal campaign contributions.

Political leaders of this period were generally successful business men with a genius for organization. Although only a few of the records were preserved, the stories of their nominating conventions and elections constitute one of the most colorful chapters in the history of West Virginia. The period and a part of the succeeding one was featured by the old-time nominating convention. The demonstrations for candidates following the nominating speeches lasted for hours and were sometimes featured by drunken brawls, even emotional prayers. When the lights went out and there was a shift of delegates to William A. MacCorkle in the Democratic state convention at Parkersburg in 1892, it was generally agreed that the temporary darkness was not providential.[1] Small wonder that West Virginia was recognized nationally during this period for her "peculiar brand of politics."

Of the several national third party movements, only the Greenback party made headway in West Virginia in this period. A semi-agrarian organization seeking relief from economic ills through the use of cheap money, its candidates for Congress polled about 25,000 votes in the state in 1878, but no Greenback candidate was elected. In 1880 Napoleon B. French, candidate of the Greenback-Labor party for governor, received 13,027 votes in a grand total of 118,873.[2] After the manner of third party spokesmen of the period, Democratic leaders, notably E. Willis Wilson, flayed railroads and monopolies for alleged discriminations against West Virginians, and a number of reformers and dissenters followed their banners. The Greenback-Labor party preserved its organization in the state and in 1886 elected six delegates to the legislature. At the same time Colonel Robert S. Carr, Independent Republican, was elected to the senate with Greenback-Labor support.

The powers of state government lay generally dormant throughout this period. The state had few agents and it performed few services. Chief executive power was vested in the governor, who shared it with four other elective officers—the auditor, the treasurer, the attorney general, and the superintendent of free schools. The secretary of state was an appointive official and functioned as the state's chief clerk. Prior to 1891 state banks were not inspected or supervised. Beginning in 1891 there was a state bank examiner, appointed by the governor, who in 1901 became the state bank commissioner. The state superintendent of free schools performed the duties of the adjutant general and the quartermaster general from 1871 to 1877, when they were assigned to the state librarian. Finally, in 1889, the office of adjutant general was created and the governor was authorized to appoint that official. Other executive appointees included a state board of health (1881), a mine inspector and assistants (1883), and a labor commissioner (1889); but their duties were nominal. There were two *ex officio* administrative boards: the board of school finance, composed of the governor, the auditor, the treasurer, and the superintendent of free schools, which managed and invested the "School Fund"; and the board of public works, composed of all elective state executive officers.

---

[1] George W. Summers, *Pages from the Past* (Charleston, W. Va., 1935), p. 89; Festus P. Summers, *Johnson Newlon Camden: A Study in Individualism* (New York, 1937), pp. 448-449.

[2] Atkinson and Gibbens, *Prominent Men*, p. 110.

THE GOVERNORS

The governors of this period each left something rather distinct in his record, either as an objective or as an achievement. Each in his turn was handicapped in his leadership by partisanship in the legislature, by the narrow margins by which it was controlled, and by legislative deadlocks in the selection of United States Senators. Although the state in this period entered a phase of its economy featured by liberal expenditures to promote personal ambitions and the development of natural resources, the governors, in true Bourbon fashion, were generally motivated by ideas of strict economy in public expenditures, even for education. Their chief concern was for a just and equitable system of taxation, curbs on monopolies, and prevention of corrupt practices in elections.

The first of the Bourbon governors was Henry Mason Mathews (March 29, 1834-April 28, 1884) of Greenbrier County who, in 1876, defeated his Republican opponent Nathan Goff, Jr., of Harrison County by a plurality of 12,729 votes. Born in Frankford, Greenbrier County, Mathews prepared for college at the Lewisburg Academy and was graduated from the University of Virginia and from Judge John W. Brockenbrough's Law School at Lexington, Virginia. He opened a law office in Lewisburg in 1857 and in 1860 accepted a part-time professorship in Allegheny College at Blue Sulphur Springs, (West) Virginia. In the Civil War he rose to the rank of major in the Confederate army. In 1865 he was elected to the West Virginia State Senate but was unable to qualify because of his inability to subscribe to the "Test Oath," then required of former Confederates. He was a member of the Constitutional Convention of 1872 and attorney general of the state from 1873 to 1877.

Throughout his administration Governor Mathews was plagued by delinquent tax collections and industrial unrest incident to the depression of the 1870's. The great railway strike of 1877 had its beginning on the Baltimore and Ohio at Martinsburg. While regretting the consequent suffering and privation, he could, however, find no excuse for violence. To prevent it he recommended that the state militia, then maintained on a voluntary basis, be organized on a compulsory basis. Other major objectives in his policy included legislation to encourage immigration of German and Swiss settlers, to promote a cautious and farsighted internal improvement program, to assure the improvement of the Ohio and its tributaries, and to finance a geological survey of the state. His loyalty to West Virginia was perhaps best revealed in his attitude toward the Virginia Debt which had been forced into the limelight by Virginia's settlement with her bondholders and her arbitrary allocation of one third of her bonded indebtedness to West Virginia. While conceding that West Virginia should pay Virginia any debt which she might owe her, he insisted that the matter should be determined in keeping with the Dismemberment Ordinance of August 20, 1861.

Mathews' successor was Jacob Beeson Jackson (April 6, 1829-December 11, 1893) of Wood County, who in 1880 defeated his Republican opponent, George C. Sturgiss of Monongalia County, by a plurality of 16,136 votes. Jackson was born in Parkersburg and was educated there under direction of the Rev. Festus Hanks. Young Jackson read law with his distinguished father, General John J. Jackson, and, following admission to the bar in 1852, began practice in St. Marys, Pleasants County. In 1864 he returned to Parkersburg and, beginning in 1870, he served for six years as prosecuting attorney of Wood County. Near the end of his term he was elected to the house of delegates and was chairman of the judiciary committee. In 1879 he was elected mayor of Parkersburg.

Governor Jackson convened the legislature in extra session in 1882 to effect a long delayed re-codification of the state's statutes, but he is best known for his leadership in tax reforms. In compliance with demands for relief from the depression of the 1870's, the legislature had exempted salt and certain farm products from taxation, and those affected were reluctant to surrender the benefits when the depression had passed. Meanwhile the Baltimore and Ohio Railroad had paid state and local taxes under compromise arrangements and the Chesapeake and Ohio Railroad had claimed tax exemption under legislative acts of 1866 and 1867.[3] The legality of these practices and this claim was put to the test in *Miller, Auditor v. Chesapeake and Ohio Railroad,* in which the state supreme court of appeals ruled that all property, not specifically exempt in the constitution, had to be assessed for purposes of taxation. Owing to pressures exerted by farm groups and to the absence of an enforcing statute, county assessors refused for a time to make their assessments conform to the "assessment order" of the governor.

West Virginia's seventh governor was Emanuel Willis Wilson (August 11, 1844-May 28, 1905) of Kanawha County. Wilson was born at Harpers Ferry, (West) Virginia, and was practically self-educated, even professionally. He was admitted to the Jefferson County bar in 1869 and the next year was elected to the West Virginia house of delegates. Two years later he was elected to the state senate where he successfully opposed a bill to transfer control of the Kanawha River to a private corporation. He moved to Charleston in 1874 and two years later was elected to the house of delegates from Kanawha County. He was re-elected in 1880 and chosen speaker. As a legislator he denounced monopolies and trusts and was

[3] *Session Acts* (1866, 1867, and 1868); Atkinson and Gibbens, *Prominent Men,* pp. 233-234.

generally active in "the cause of the people." In a spectacular convention held at Wheeling he was nominated in 1884 by the Democrats as their candidate for governor. Although branded by opponents in his own party as "East Wind" and "Windy" Wilson, he was elected by a plurality of 5,289 over his Republican opponent, Edwin Maxwell of Harrison County.[4]

Governor Wilson won his election by attacks upon railroads and monopolies for their alleged discriminations against West Virginians. Neither the 1885 nor the 1887 legislatures heeded his requests for remedial legislation, however, and in 1887 he convened that body in extra session. After heated discussion and a tie vote on a railroad bill in the lower house, further consideration was postponed to await results of the Interstate Commerce Act, just enacted by Congress. Governor Wilson asked the 1889 legislature for a more effective corrupt practice act, including the Australian ballot system, and for laws to prevent the pollution of streams and regulate the adoption and sale of school textbooks. The legislature refused to legalize his proposed Australian ballot or to forbid the pollution of streams, but it strengthened the corrupt practice act and forbade the issuance of railroad passes to public officials. It also prohibited the revision of school textbooks in contract periods.[5]

Official returns of the gubernatorial election of 1888 indicated the election of Nathan Goff, Jr., Republican, but Judge A. Brooks Fleming, the Democratic candidate, questioned the validity of the returns and asked the legislature to determine the correct result. During the contest which followed, West Virginia was in a unique position in that she had four claimants to the governorship: Goff and Fleming, by right of election; Governor Wilson, by right of possession; and Robert S. Carr, president of the state senate, by virtue of his office under a constitutional provision which placed him in line of succession when the office became vacant. Both Goff and Fleming took the oath of office, but Governor Wilson refused to yield to the claims of either. His position was sustained by the courts in two mandamus proceedings—one brought by Goff, the other by Carr—and he continued as governor until February 6, 1890, when Judge Fleming was formally inaugurated, following election by a strictly partisan vote in the legislature which declared him the victor by a majority of 237.[6]

A. Brooks Fleming (October 15, 1839-October 13, 1923), eighth governor of West Virginia, was born in Fairmont and educated in its schools

[4] Senate, *Journal* (1883), p. 12; *ibid.* (1885), pp. 17-21; Atkinson and Gibbens, *Prominent Men*, pp. 110, 261-264.

[5] Senate and House, *Journals* (1885, 1887, 1889); William A. MacCorkle, *The Recollections of Fifty Years* (New York, 1928), pp. 98-106.

[6] James H. Jacobs, "The West Virginia Gubernatorial Contest, 1888-1890" (Master's thesis, West Virginia University, 1942); MacCorkle, *Recollections*, pp. 434-444; Gerald Wayne Smith, "Nathan Goff, Jr.: A Biography" (Doctoral dissertation, West Virginia University, 1954).

and at the University of Virginia. Beginning the practice of law in Fairmont in 1863, he was that year elected prosecuting attorney of Marion County. In 1878 he was appointed judge of the circuit court and soon thereafter became associate and legal advisor of Johnson N. Camden who was engaged in the development of the timber and coal resources of that part of the upper Monongahela region lying between Clarksburg and Fairmont. Camden was Fleming's political mentor and was chiefly responsible for his nomination and election as governor.

The Fleming administration was characterized by bitter partisanship. Republicans insisted that he had stolen the election, while Democrats accused the Republicans of having debauched the electorate by the corrupt use of money and by fraudulent voting. The bitterness thus engendered was a handicap to his effectiveness with the legislature, and only a single statute of importance was enacted in his term. Having turned thumbs down on a previous recommendation of Governor Wilson, the legislature approved Fleming's recommendation for the enactment of an Australian ballot law. His request for a registration of voters had to await the approval of a constitutional amendment which was not ratified until 1902. Governor Fleming seemed content however to give his attention to advertising West Virginia's natural resources, a work into which he threw himself with enthusiasm.

William Alexander MacCorkle (May 7, 1857-September 24, 1930) of Kanawha County, was the last of the Bourbon governors. He was born in Lexington, Virginia, and at the age of twenty-two was graduated from the Law College of Washington and Lee University. In 1879 he began the practice of law in Charleston, West Virginia, and the following year he was elected prosecuting attorney of Kanawha County. In 1892, at the age of thirty-five, he was elected governor by a plurality of 3,902 over his Republican opponent Thomas E. Davis of Ritchie County.

During the second half of MacCorkle's administration the legislatur was controlled by Republicans. He was thus denied an opportunity t sponsor effectively his political party's program. Instead, he joined th Republicans in their proposed effort to raise the standards of state in stitutions and to free them from the influence of politics. His chief serv ice was, however, continuation of the state advertising program begun b his immediate predecessor. In this he attended meetings of industrialist far and near to talk about West Virginia, and to correct misrepresentation then current about the "Mountain State" and "The Little Mountai State." The governor lost no opportunity to declare that West Virgini was not only comparatively a large state but also a potentially rich one. A the end of his administration Governor MacCorkle resumed the practic of law in Charleston, but most of his efforts were given to promoting th industrial development of West Virginia.

THE NATIONAL STAGE

Henry G. Davis

The first and perhaps the most prominent of all the Bourbons was Henry G. Davis. Born in Baltimore, Maryland, November 16, 1823, he was the first prominent West Virginia businessman to enter Democratic politics. Having served as brakeman and conductor on the Baltimore and Ohio Railroad, Davis had, while employed as station agent for the company at Piedmont, formed a partnership with his brothers and established himself in the mercantile business. When the Civil War began, Henry G. Davis and Company was the principal business concern in the Upper Potomac Valley. In the course of the war he improved his financial position through contracts with the railroad and the national government. With the close of the war, he extended his activities into farming, banking, timbering, and coal mining, and by 1871 he had become the leading figure in the business and political life of the Upper Potomac Valley.[7]

In response to a family penchant for politics, which was kept alive by intimate and frequent contacts with his politically-minded cousin, Arthur P. Gorman, long a dominant figure in Maryland Democratic politics, Davis was elected in 1868 to the West Virginia state senate. Although he had stood by the Union throughout the Civil War, he was eager to remove the restrictions which Radical Republicans had imposed upon former Confederates in West Virginia. His defeat of William H. H. Flick, author of the historic Flick Amendment which invalidated the proscription laws, brought Davis into the political limelight. Three years later he was elected to the United States Senate in succession to Waitman T. Willey. Davis was the first Democrat from West Virginia to hold that position.

Because of his limitations as a speaker and his extensive business interests, Senator Davis did not care for Senate routine. Although he occasionally crossed party lines, he generally voted with the Democrats. He was not however a partisan, as indicated by the fact that in 1877 the Republicans in the state legislature voted for his re-election, a gesture which pleased him greatly. But after twelve years in the Senate he declined in 1883 to stand for re-election, giving as his reason that business was more agreeable to him than politics.

By "politics" Davis doubtless meant Senate routine, not association with politicians; for his summer home at Deer Park, Maryland, which witnessed frequent visits by Presidents and other high government dignitaries, became a virtual summer capital of the United States. President Cleveland spent a portion of his honeymoon there in June, 1886, while

[7] Charles M. Pepper, *The Life and Times of Henry Gassaway Davis* (New York, 1920).

President Harrison and his Secretary of State, James G. Blaine, were frequent guests. Meanwhile Davis had revived a railroad project which contemplated the construction of a continuous line between northern and southern West Virginia. Because of his success as a railroad builder and his intimacy with President Harrison and Secretary of State Blaine, he was appointed in December, 1890, to membership on the Intercontinental Railway Commission and soon thereafter as chairman of the Pan-American Railway Committee.

John E. Kenna

Davis was succeeded in the Senate by John E. Kenna (April 10, 1848-January 11, 1893) of Kanawha County, who had served three terms in the House of Representatives from the Third West Virginia district. Commonly called the "Dido District" because of its striking geographical shape, this district was the largest geographically in the state. It embraced all of the counties in and south of the Kanawha Valley. More than any other one person, Kenna was responsible for making Charleston the permanent seat of the state government and for popularizing a belated movement for the improvement of navigation on the Kanawha River. These accomplishments, together with his ability as a criminal lawyer and an orator, made Kenna the idol of the Kanawha Valley. Perhaps another factor in the choice of Kenna was the desire to compensate southern West Virginia counties for the inconveniences caused by the temporary loss of the state capital to Wheeling in 1875. In any case, it was generally understood among Democrats that so long as Wheeling remained the capital of the state, one of the two United States Senators would come from the Third Congressional district, then a Democratic party stronghold.

Johnson N. Camden

Another prominent Democratic leader was Johnson N. Camden (March 6, 1828-April 25, 1908) of Wood County. Like Davis, Camden was a businessman and not an orator; but, unlike Davis, he had served two years as a cadet at West Point, had read law, and, following his admission to the Braxton County bar in 1850, had served as prosecuting attorney of Braxton and Nicholas counties. In the course of the next sixteen years he tried several business and professional ventures, becoming first a pioneer oil producer at Burning Springs, Wirt County, and finally a successful refiner of crude oil in his own plant at Parkersburg. In 1875 this plant became a part of the Standard Oil Company, and Camden became Rockefeller's chief lieutenant in West Virginia. In this capacity he served the Standard Oil Company on the legislative and congressional fronts as a lobbyist, and he also played the leading role in the drama which gave the Standard Oil monopoly almost complete control of the West Virginia oil industry. In 1878 he refused to answer a question of an investigating committee pertaining to discriminating freight rates accorded to his company by the Baltimore and Ohio Railroad and was declared in contempt of the state legislature. A letter of explanation sufficed to extricate him from this difficulty, but he was thereafter commonly regarded as "a monopolist."[8]

Twice an unsuccessful candidate for governor, first in 1868 and again in 1872, Camden remained the titular head of his party and in 1875, with the prospective retirement of Arthur I. Boreman, he became a candidate for the Senate. As yet, he had not won his "monopolist" sobriquet, and so was leading in the contest in the state legislature when a proposal was made to return the capital to Wheeling. With the approval of this proposal, Camden's hopes of becoming a Senator vanished. For with a view doubtless to placating the Kanawha Valley for its loss of the state capital, Allen T. Caperton of Monroe County, was elected Senator to succeed Boreman.

Caperton having died in office after about one year, Camden would have been a candidate in 1877 for the short term had not the understanding among Democratic leaders regarding the location of the capital and the Senatorship been considered a gentlemen's agreement and therefore binding. Moreover, had a few recalcitrant Democrats been able to prevent the re-election of Senator Davis, Camden might have entered the contest for the long term, but the Republicans prevented that by throwing their united strength to Davis, thus assuring his re-election. By the same support Frank Hereford of Monroe County was elected to fill the short-term vacancy. Though Camden was an avowed Union man, while three of his brothers fought for the Confederacy, the Republican newspaper press obliquely emphasized the fact that both Davis and Hereford had favored the Union during the Civil War.

The location of the capital having been finally fixed at Charleston in a referendum held August 7, 1877, Camden let it be known that he would be a candidate for the Senate in 1881 to succeed Hereford. With that in mind, he refused to be groomed as the Democratic candidate for governor in 1880 and directed his energy to perfecting his party's organization. He was in complete command when the legislature met in 1881 and, since that body was three to one Democratic, Camden's election to the Senate was a formality.

Camden's maiden speech in the Senate clarified the Virginia Debt ques-

[8] Summers, *Camden*, pp. 201-211.

tion and set forth the principles on which it was later settled.[9] In the subsequent debate on the tariff he made crystal clear his desire for "a tariff for revenue with incidental protection" for iron ore, coal, salt, and wool, items of special interest to his constituents. In a specially prepared article in the *North American Review* for February, 1883, he defended the practices of the Standard Oil Company as in the best interest of the country. More than any other one person he was responsible for the organization which delivered the electoral vote of West Virginia to Grover Cleveland in 1884. By sponsoring that provision of the Interstate Commerce Act of 1887 which forbade railroads charging more for a short haul than for a long one from the same point and in the same direction, Camden rendered a substantial service to West Virginia shippers and tended to neutralize the attacks that were made on himself because of his large scale business connections.

Following the election of Grover Cleveland in 1884, scores of West Virginia Democrats were eager for the spoils. As Camden could not satisfy all of them, the disappointed ones combined to prevent his reelection to the Senate. Ignoring his admitted services in explaining the Virginia Debt and solving the freight rate problems, the farmers joined with the spoils seekers and renewed their charges of "monopolist." They also charged Camden with excessive and corrupt use of campaign funds. In defense of Camden former Senator Davis declared: "You can no more run a political campaign without money than you can a church, a beneficial or temperance society, or any other organization."[10] But the appeals of the venerable Davis were unavailing and twelve Democratic members of the legislature, most of them from agricultural counties east of the Alleghenies, refused to participate in the Senatorial nominating caucus or to be bound by it either in the regular session or in the special session which followed. The deadlock was finally broken on May 4, 1887 by the election of Charles J. Faulkner, Jr., of Berkeley County, who, because of his ability and his business connections, was acceptable to Camden and his opponents.[11]

Thwarted in his desire to remain in the Senate, Camden turned his attention to railroad building and to coal mining in the Upper Monongahela Valley. But he kept an eye on the political scene. Unlike former Senator Davis, he approved President Cleveland's famous tariff message of December 6, 1887, and expressed himself as confident that its demand

---

[9] *Congressional Record, 47th Cong.*, special sess., Vol. 12, pp. 441-442; Summers, *Camden*, pp. 241-247.

[10] Quoted in *ibid.*, p. 311.

[11] On March 5, 1887 Governor Wilson appointed Daniel B. Lucas to the vacancy in the Senate and at the same time convened the legislature in extra session for the consideration of an agenda which did not include the election of a Senator. But the legislature ignored this and on its own initiative elected Charles J. Faulkner, Jr., who was seated.

for a tariff for revenue, with incidental protection, would care for West Virginia's peculiar situation with respect to coal, iron ore, and timber.

As a result of Camden's efforts Grover Cleveland won the electoral vote of West Virginia in 1888, although by the narrow margin of 506 popular votes. Aided by the unpopular McKinley Tariff Act, the Democrats carried the state by an increased majority in 1890, and Camden's friends urged him to announce his candidacy for the Senate in 1893. But he refused and in a characteristic move directed his efforts toward perfecting the Democratic organization. As in previous campaigns, it was largely owing to his efforts that Cleveland carried West Virginia in 1892 and that the legislature, elected that year, was controlled by Democrats in both branches.

Camden's position with respect to the Senatorship was unknown when the legislature met in regular session on January 10, 1893. The following day the situation was altered completely by announcement of the death of Senator Kenna. The state having been redistricted in 1882 so as to give southern West Virginia two Representatives in Congress instead of one, and Charleston having been the permanent seat of the state government since 1885, it was generally agreed that southern West Virginia had sufficient recognition and that both of the Senators might come from north of the Kanawha Valley. Faulkner was accordingly re-elected for the long term and Camden for the short one.

Charles J. Faulkner, Jr.

Charles James Faulkner, Jr. (September 21, 1847-January 13, 1929), was born at Boydville, the Faulkner family estate near Martinsburg, (West) Virginia, and received his preparatory education in the schools of that city. The son of an able, active, and considerate father, Charles J. Faulkner, Sr., who served Virginia almost continuously in various public capacities from 1829 to 1859, young Faulkner received much of his education in history and politics in the Faulkner family circle at Boydville. In 1859 his father was appointed U. S. Minister to France, and Charles J., Jr., took advantage of the opportunity to accompany him and study in Paris and Switzerland. Upon their return to the United States in August, 1861, his father was arrested by United States authorities on no specified charge and held in prison as a hostage until December, 1861, when he was exchanged for Alfred Ely, a congressman from New York. Next year, despairing of protection for his life and his property, Faulkner crossed the Confederate lines under the protective custody of Stonewall Jackson. Without enlisting or being commissioned, he accompanied Jackson on campaigns and as assistant adjutant general prepared a number of Jackson's reports of military operations. Following General Jackson's death, Faulkner resided during the remaining years of the war with his daughter, Mrs. Thomas S. Bocock, in Appomattox County, Virginia. When the war ended, he resumed the practice of his profession at Martinsburg and was a member of the West Virginia constitutional convention of 1872 and of the Forty-fourth Congress.[12]

Charles J. Faulkner, Jr., had meanwhile enrolled as a cadet in the Virginia Military Institute at Lexington. As a cadet he fought in the battle of New Market, and he later served as aid to Generals John C. Breckinridge and Henry A. Wise. He was with Wise at Appomattox. After a period of study in the office of his father, young Faulkner enrolled in the law department of the University of Virginia, from which he was graduated in 1868. He was admitted to the Martinsburg bar and soon attained distinction in the practice of his profession. From the outset he was one of the most effective and trusted of counsel for the Baltimore and Ohio Railroad Company. In 1880 Faulkner was elected judge of the Thirteenth Judicial Circuit and was serving in that capacity when he was elected Senator.

As a Senator, Faulkner opposed enactment of the Force Bill of 1890-1891, and he sponsored the first general act of the Congress forbidding the adulteration of food and drugs; but in tariff legislation, the acid test of party loyalty in the second Cleveland administration, Faulkner was found wanting. As an ally of Arthur P. Gorman, he helped emasculate the Wilson Bill which the administration sponsored and which the House of Representatives approved. In the congressional election of 1894, Faulkner may indeed have voted against his fellow West Virginian, Chairman William L. Wilson of the House Ways and Means Committee which had drafted the Wilson Bill.

Nathan Goff, Jr.

As an approach to one of the most important political contests in the history of West Virginia, we shall now review the minority leadership in this period. Following the exit of Waitman T. Willey from the political scene, Nathan Goff, Jr. (February 9, 1843-April 23, 1920), became the most prominent Republican in West Virginia.[13] When only a youth he had enlisted in the Union Army. After about four years in its service, the

---

12 See Donald R. McVeigh, "Charles J. Faulkner: Reluctant Rebel" (Doctoral dissertation, West Virginia University, 1955).

13 Gerald Wayne Smith, "Nathan Goff, Jr.: A Biography" (MS); ———, "Nathan Goff, Jr., in the Civil War," in *West Virginia History,* Vol. XIV (January, 1953), pp. 108-135; ———, "Nathan Goff, Jr., and the Solid South," in *ibid.,* Vol. XVII (October 1955), pp. 5-22.

last four months in Libby Prison, he returned to Clarksburg, West Virginia, where he had been born and reared, a hero on several counts. Among other things, he was reputed to have influenced President Lincoln in his decision to adopt a liberal policy in the exchange of war prisoners. These accomplishments, together with Major Goff's fine personality and his gift of oratory, made an effective appeal to members of the Grand Army of the Republic and their friends.

Unlike most of the political leaders of his day Goff was well educated. In 1866 he was graduated from New York University with a LL.B. degree, and the next year he was elected a delegate to the West Virginia legislature. In 1868 he was appointed United States District Attorney for the West Virginia District and by successive reappointments served in that capacity to 1881, when he was made Secretary of the Navy in the cabinet of President Hayes. Meanwhile, he had been the unsuccessful Republican candidate for governor of West Virginia in 1876. He was a delegate to the Republican National conventions from 1872 through 1880. In 1882 he was elected to Congress from the First West Virginia District and by successive re-elections served in that capacity to 1888, when he again became the Republican nominee for governor of West Virginia. As previously indicated, the returns indicated Goff's election, but Judge Fleming contested it and was seated by a partisan vote. In 1892 President Harrison appointed Goff judge of the Fourth U. S. Circuit Court composed of South Carolina, North Carolina, Virginia, Maryland, and West Virginia. As he was supposed to have an eye on the Senate, his acceptance was a surprise to all concerned. But his elevation to a judgeship removed the last obstacle to the ambitions of his closest Republican rival—Stephen B. Elkins.

Stephen B. Elkins

Stephen B. Elkins (September 26, 1841-January 4, 1911) was outstanding among the younger men who benefited by Judge Goff's elevation to the bench. Like Goff, Elkins was well educated but not primarily for either business or politics.[14] The descendant of grandparents who moved from Virginia to Ohio to emancipate their slaves, and the son of parents who moved from Ohio to southeast Missouri to become ardent pro-Southerners, Elkins was born in Ohio and educated at the University of Missouri, where he graduated with honors in mathematics, Greek, and Latin. As a school teacher in Missouri, he taught Cole "Bud" Younger, well-known member of the notorious James gang, who later saved him

14 *Biog. Direct. Amer. Cong.*, pp. 1124-1125; O. D. Lambert, *Stephen B. Elkins* (Pittsburgh, 1956).

from capture by a band of Confederate guerrillas. At the beginning of the Civil War, Elkins defied his father and his brother and enlisted in the Union Army as a captain of Missouri militia. Before the war ended he studied law and in 1864 was admitted to the bar.

In response to a spirit of adventure which later led to professional, business, and political success, Elkins left Missouri in 1864 in search of better opportunities. Because of his interest in the Spanish language and Spanish customs, he went to New Mexico Territory, where he was at once elected to the legislature as a delegate. From 1867 to 1870 he was United States District Attorney for the Territory, and in 1872 he was elected its delegate to Congress as a Republican. It was while serving in that capacity that he met and in 1875 married Hallie Davis, daughter of Henry G. Davis, Senator from West Virginia.

The marriage of Stephen B. Elkins and Hallie Davis was a determining influence in his life and in the history of West Virginia. For some time after his marriage, Elkins resided in New Mexico, but, during that time, he maintained an office and a winter residence in New York City. He was a close adviser to James G. Blaine and had an important part in his nomination for the Presidency. He first became active in West Virginia politics in 1888, when he made a scholarly address at West Virginia University and a number of political speeches in the state. In the latter he won national recognition as a spokesman of the protective tariff, and on December 17, 1891, President Harrison appointed him Secretary of War.

It was about this time that Elkins finally cast his lot with West Virginia. In 1892 he built a palatial residence in a beautiful mountain retreat of Randolph County and permitted the town which grew up around it to be named for himself. The residence is now a part of the plant of Davis and Elkins College. Elkins was already associated with his father-in-law in the construction of the present Western Maryland Railroad. Since 1890 he had been interested in coal lands in Monongalia County; consequently, in 1902 he purchased the Morgantown and Kingwood Railroad which he extended in 1907 to Rowlesburg on the Baltimore and Ohio. He was interested also in the Coal and Coke Railroad, his father-in-law's pet project for connecting northern and southern West Virginia by a continuous line. For a time the headquarters of these enterprises was 1 Broadway, New York City, the Elkins office.

A master organizer and a gracious but firm leader, Elkins developed a political machine of his own and with General Goff out of the way, he aspired to the Senate. In his planning to that end he made use of the Davis Summer House at Deer Park, Maryland, and former Senator Davis, while remaining a Democrat, placed no barriers in the way of his ambitious son-in-law. He was thus able to attain his objective with respect to the Senate and to effect a political revolution in West Virginia which excluded Democrats from power, except during brief intervals, for thirty-eight years. The contest by which these changes were effected is one of the most informing in the political history of West Virginia.

William L. Wilson

To understand this contest it will be helpful to return to the Democratic leaders of this period, particularly William Lyne Wilson (May 3, 1843-October 17, 1900), one of the best types of "the scholar in politics."[15] Wilson was born in Jefferson County, (West) Virginia, and educated at Columbian College in the District of Columbia, and at the University of Virginia. His first-hand knowledge of any considerable part of Trans-Allegheny Virginia he obtained in 1863 as a member of the Confederate cavalry force led by General William E. Jones who raided that area from the Monongahela to the Kanawha. In 1871 Wilson was admitted to the bar, and in the course of eleven years practice at Charles Town, he became widely known over a large area as an orator and a scholar. These qualities appealed to his friends among the regents of West Virginia University and in June, 1882, he was elected president of that institution; but he had scarcely entered upon his duties when he was nominated by Democrats as their candidate for Congress in the Second West Virginia District. After a spirited canvass, he was elected by a plurality of ten votes.

Wilson was re-elected regularly during the next ten years, and in the course of his service in the House he became a recognized spokesman for tariff reform. President Cleveland's tariff message of December, 1887, was entirely to his liking, and he opposed the McKinley Tariff Act of 1890 as the "paternalistic measure of the Billion Dollar Congress." He was the permanent chairman of the National Convention that renominated Cleveland for the Presidency in 1892, and he made the keynote address. Next year Wilson was appointed chairman of the House Ways and Means Committee and as such was the chief architect of the famous Wilson Tariff Bill which reduced rates generally and placed many raw materials on the free list. As a member of a conference committee, he exerted himself to the point of physical exhaustion in an unsuccessful effort to persuade the Senate to accept the House schedules. He was even reputed to have wept when informed of President Cleveland's displeasure with the bill as finally enacted. Wilson was the recognized leader of the tariff-reform forces of the entire country during the second Cleveland administration.

It was for this reason that Wilson was marked for defeat in 1894. His

[15] See Festus P. Summers, *William L. Wilson and Tariff Reform: A Biography* (New Brunswick, N. J., 1953).

opponent was Alston G. Dayton, an able but little-known Philippi lawyer, who was ably assisted in the campaign by Stephen B. Elkins, the Republican candidate for the Senate seat held by Johnson N. Camden. The contest was opened by former President Harrison in an address at Elkins. Thereafter until the day of the election, the district was crossed and recrossed by the best speakers in the Republican camp. Moreover, it was flooded with campaign funds and literature setting forth in convincing form the need for a protective tariff to develop latent natural resources and maintain a high standard of living. Democrats charged that the Second District had been "boodled."

Fully cognizant of the issue involved in the contest, John T. McGraw, Wilson's campaign manager, organized his forces and conducted the campaign on a scale "never before witnessed in the Second District." The speakers included some of the ablest campaigners in the entire country, among them being General Wade Hampton, Champ Clark, and Bourke Cochran, but the protectionist Democrats of West Virginia were apathetic. Because he was a candidate for re-election in 1895, Senator Camden contributed to Wilson's campaign fund, but former Senator Davis, for the first time perhaps in about twenty years, stood aloof and refused to make a contribution. As a consequence, Wilson's campaign was financed largely by non-residents, including President Cleveland. Probably because he thought the tariff question secondary to the money question, William J. Bryan did not speak in the district. Wilson's defeat by 2,300 votes heralded the beginning of a new period in the political history of West Virginia in which Stephen B. Elkins was to be the dominant factor.

On March 1, 1895, Wilson became Postmaster General in President Cleveland's Cabinet. As such, he inaugurated, as an experiment, the first rural free delivery mail service in the United States. Because Jefferson County, West Virginia, was a richly endowed agricultural community, and topographically representative, offices within its bounds were selected for the initial deliveries. They were made on October 1, 1896. Soon after the expiration of his services as Postmaster General, Wilson became president of Washington and Lee University, at Lexington, Virginia. There he spent the remainder of his life devoted to the work of equipping that institution for leadership in higher education in the South.

In 1896 Democrat "Gold Bugs" who could not accept the Bryan free silver program, organized a Gold Standard party in West Virginia pledged to support its standard bearer, John M. Palmer, for President. The West Virginia party was composed largely of businessmen, including Johnson N. Camden and former Governor Fleming, but it had the support also of William L. Wilson. Alarmed by the growing popularity of Bryan, as the campaign gained momentum, most of the West Virginia "Gold Bugs" threw their support to William McKinley, the Republican nominee.

Although Wilson continued to support Palmer, a number of West Virginia agrarian Democrats supported McKinley. In this some of them were influenced by the difference in the market price of wool under the McKinley Act of 1890 and the Wilson-Gorman Act of 1894. Then, too, some former Democrats, particularly young men who were being attracted to industry, believed that a protective tariff would assure them regular employment at increasing wages. The Democrats tried to forestall the trend by an alliance with the Populists; but McKinley carried West Virginia in 1896 by a plurality of 10,528 votes in a total of 202,144 and the Elkins phalanx was strengthened all along the party line.

Nathan B. Scott

Nathan B. Scott (December 18, 1842-January 2, 1924) was perhaps the most helpful of the Elkins lieutenants on the national stage. Scott was born in Gurnsey County, Ohio, where he attended the public schools. Casting his lot with the growing West, he can next be seen at the age of seventeen driving an ox team between Fort Leavenworth, Kansas, and Denver, Colorado. He was a volunteer in the Union army and following his discharge, was employed as a glass worker at Bellaire, Ohio. In 1875 he moved to Wheeling, West Virginia, where he served from 1876 to 1897 as president of the Central Glass Company. Meanwhile he had organized a bank and a trust company. He was also interested in public charities. It was he who put the Ohio Valley Hospital at Wheeling on an efficient basis. Having entered politics he served in the state senate from 1883 to 1891, as a member of the Republican National Committee from 1886 to 1912, and as collector of internal revenue in the West Virginia District during the Spanish-American War. Like other successful businessmen of his day, he was a liberal contributor to his party's campaign funds. He was the choice of his party in 1899 to succeed Charles J. Faulkner, Jr., in the U. S. Senate.

Chapter XXIII

The Beginnings of Education 1863-1910

ELEMENTARY AND SECONDARY

LARGELY BECAUSE of anti-Abolitionist sentiments, the public free school movement tended to bog down in western Virginia in the decade immediately preceding the formation of West Virginia. Movements to establish free schools after the pattern of those in Kanawha, Jefferson, and Ohio counties were generally unsuccessful in the 1850's, and there was a noticeable tendency to criticize the public free school movement as "too pro-Yankee." A newspaper editor of Charleston commented approvingly upon the tendency of east Virginia to employ only teachers "to the manor born," and disapprovingly of the influence then exerted in trans-Allegheny Virginia by "Yankee school teachers." He admonished Virginians to correct "this evil" on the score that "no education is better than bad education." In 1857 Governor Henry A. Wise charged that the Literary Fund was being robbed. Eight and one half per cent of the income from the fund went for administration, he said, and fully one fifth had been dissipated through bad investments, bad loans, and official defalcations. Large surpluses, he declared, were idle in the custody of county superintendents who had deposited them at high interest rates and appropriated the returns to their personal uses.[1] Regardless of these delin-

[1] *Kanawha Valley Star,* July 12, 1859; Ambler, *History of Education,* pp. 29-30, 61-64.

quencies, civic leaders in present West Virginia cherished the public free school as a means of alleviating the arrested development which had overtaken them.

The New System

Contrary to opinions, all too commonly held, the sponsors of free schools for West Virginia did not go to New England for guidance. Instead, the Rev. Gordon Battelle, chairman of the committee on education in the Constitutional Convention, appealed for aid to his friend, the Rev. Alexander Martin, then a professor in Allegheny College, Meadville, Pennsylvania. Like the Rev. Battelle, Martin had attained distinction as a teacher and a preacher in northwestern Virginia. Without delay he addressed himself to the task, and two weeks later Battelle was in possession of "An Outline of a System of General Education for the New State."[2]

Declaring that "the education of the people . . . is the only exhaustless mine which the states possesses" and that "there is no other subject on which the people are so entirely agreed," Martin proposed that the schools of the new state should be "as free as the air . . . and the light of Heaven." He suggested that the cost of the proposed system should be met by state aid, by income from a permanent school fund, and by local taxes equal to the total state expenditures for public school purposes. He would have vested administration of the proposed system in a state board of education, a general superintendent, county superintendents, and local officials.

As anticipated in the Martin *Outline,* the convention gave major attention to financing the proposed school system. The committee on education proposed to divert to a permanent school fund all "the revenues accruing from any stocks owned by the State in any bank or other corporation, or the proceeds of the sale of such stocks" and "the proceeds of any taxes that are now, or that may hereafter be levied on the property or revenue of any corporation." The first of these proposals contemplated an adjustment with Virginia whereby the capital stock then owned by her in banks or in railroads located in the proposed new state would become its property. The primary purpose of the second proposal was to legalize a privilege or bonus tax, in addition to the regular property tax on corporations.

These recommendations divided the convention personnel into the progressive, or public free school group, and the conservative, or internal improvement group. Professedly favorable to a permanent school fund, the

[2] Charles H. Ambler, Frances H. Atwood, and W. B. Mathews, eds., *Debates and Proceedings of the First Constitutional Convention of West Virginia, 1861-1863* (3 vols., Huntington, W. Va., 1942), I, 548; Ambler, *History of Education,* pp. 134-138.

latter wished to build slowly and to defer the establishment of a school system until the bonded indebtedness of the new state could be determined. They opposed the proposed tax on bank and railroad stocks on the ground that all such stocks, then owned by the state, were, both legally and morally, pledged to the payment of her bonded indebtedness. They opposed the proposed tax on corporations on the ground that it was double taxation and therefore both illegal and unjust. They claimed also that such a tax betrayed an "unthinkable and short-sighted hostility" toward non-resident capital.

In answer to these arguments the school group, led by Battelle, claimed that any state-owned stocks, though pledged as surety for bonded indebtedness, were, in the last analysis, no more pre-empted, either legally or morally, for that purpose than was private property subject to taxation. But the most forceful argument of the school group was to the effect that the proposed new state needed most of all an intelligent body politic which only a sound, efficient system of free public education could provide.

As finally adopted, the constitutional provisions for the creation of a permanent school fund were conservative victories. The proceeds from the sale of any stocks owned by the state in banks and other corporations were to be applied to the liquidation of the public debt, and the state was forbidden to become a stockholder in any bank or other corporation. The sources of the proposed school fund were therefore restricted to the net proceeds from the sale of delinquent and forfeited lands; to the new state's share of the Literary Fund and of moneys, stocks, and property owned by Virginia for educational purposes; to the proceeds from the sale of estates escheating to the state; to possible grants, devices, and bequests for educational purposes; and to such sums as the legislature might appropriate. Little wonder that Battelle declared that "the bottom had dropped out of the whole scheme." He therefore offered the following resolution which, as finally approved, shifted determination of the proposed school system from the convention to the state legislature:

> The Legislature shall provide, as soon as practicable, for the establishment of a thorough and efficient system of free schools. They shall provide for the support of such schools by appropriating thereto the interest of the invested school fund; the net proceeds of all forfeitures, confiscations and fines accruing to this State under the laws thereof; and by general taxation on persons and property, or otherwise. They shall also provide for raising, in each township, by the authority of the people thereof, such a proportion of the amount required for the support of free schools therein as shall be prescribed by general laws.

Like the constitutional convention, the first legislature of the new state appealed to the Rev. Alexander Martin for guidance with respect to the proposed public school system. In response Martin called attention to the

Outline and again advised that the proposed new system be adapted, "with slight amendments, to the law of the Old State." Because no state of the Union seemed to have a wholly satisfactory system, he expressed the belief that an efficient system would be a product of experience rather than of legislative enactment. He therefore advised against undue haste and suggested that, before launching a program, the legislature might well study the systems in use elsewhere in the United States and abroad.

But the legislature did not wait, and an act establishing a public free school system was approved, December 10, 1863. As drawn by A. F. Ross, former professor in Bethany College and principal of West Liberty Academy, the statute authorized a six-month term "for all the youth of the state, in such fundamental branches of learning as are indispensable to the proper discharge of their social and civic duties." In keeping with a plan proposed by Thomas Jefferson in 1779 and endorsed by Martin in 1863, the counties were to be divided into townships and the townships into sub-districts of suitable size for the determination of school affairs in mass meetings. The act also provided for the election of township commissioners and a county superintendent of schools. The commissioners reported the proceedings of the mass meetings to the county superintendent who in turn reported them to the state superintendent, certified teachers, and visited schools. Election of the general superintendent was postponed until February 16, 1864, when the Rev. William R. White of the Baltimore Conference of the Methodist Episcopal Church, then principal of the Fairmont Male and Female Seminary, was chosen for an unexpired term beginning June 1, 1864 and ending March 3, 1865. At the same time the legislature authorized a state levy for school purposes not to exceed ten cents on the $100 assessed valuation of general property.

Proposals for the education of Negro children were strongly opposed by delegates and senators from counties and districts having few or no Negro residents. Daniel Haymond of Ritchie County, which then had only 38 resident Negroes, tried to amend the school bill so as to require the approval of two thirds of the voters, before a school for Negroes could be established anywhere. Unlike most conservatives, Delegate Haymond opposed co-racial education for both social and economic reasons.[3] Regardless of the opposition, the legislature required townships having more than thirty eligible colored pupils to provide for their education, but in separate buildings from those used for white pupils.

During the next several years chief educational interest centered in putting the new system into operation. To inaugurate the program, mass meetings were held as provided in the law, but they proved ill-suited to sparsely settled and mountainous areas. Heedless of the precepts of Thomas Jefferson, the new system was erroneously branded as a Yankee

[3] *Senate Journal; Ambler, History of Education*, p. 141.

importation. To meet these difficulties and objections, the law was modified in 1866 and again in 1867, so as to vest responsibility for organizing and maintaining township schools in township boards and the immediate supervision and direction of the individual schools in trustees.

The original plans for financing the new system having failed for like reason, the 1866 legislature authorized township levies of not less than two nor more than five mills on each dollar valuation for teachers, as the voters in mass meetings might determine. The rate for buildings was fixed at seven mills. These provisions proving inadequate and unsatisfactory, the 1867 legislature reduced the legal term to four months and required all township boards of education to levy fifty cents on each hundred dollars assessed valuation for both teachers and buildings. As thus fixed, the township rates remained constant during the remainder of the period of Radical control, as did also the state rate of ten cents.

Considerable progress was made under the new system prior to 1872, when it was revised. The average term increased from 2.7 months in 1865-66 to 4.1 months in 1869-70; in 1870 there were 2,257 schools taught by 2,405 teachers (1,764 men and 641 women); there were 2,113 schoolhouses, of which number 1,104 were frame structures; the total annual expenditure for schools was about $470,000, of which about $210,000 was for building; public school property was valued at $1,060,000; and the average monthly salary for teachers was $31.79. Wheeling paid her men teachers an average of $139 per month and her "female" teachers $42 for a nine-month term. The fact that 260 of the 495 new school buildings erected in 1869-70 were log structures was regarded as a sure sign that "the free schools were gaining a foothold in the back counties."

Progress had been made meanwhile in the education of Negroes. The private school established for them at Parkersburg in 1862 was converted in 1866 into a public free school and in the following year a public free school for Negroes was established in Clarksburg. The interest manifested by them elsewhere was so appealing and assuring that the Freedmen's Bureau aided them in establishing a dozen or more private schools, most of which later became public free schools.

The Revised System

Although the Constitutional Convention of 1872 was composed largely of former Confederates and state rights Democrats, that body was friendly to public education. Most of its members were followers of Thomas Jefferson, and few possessed the means to employ private tutors for the education of their children. Besides, most of them were loyal to the new state and accepted their responsibility as constitution makers as a challenge to make their state attractive to prospective residents.

It was in this spirit that the makers of the new constitution required the legislature to provide by general law for a thorough and efficient system of free schools. Sources of the permanent and invested school fund were left practically as in the first constitution, but administration of the "School Fund" was vested in a board of the school fund composed of the governor, the superintendent of free schools, the auditor, and the treasurer. The legislature was also required to foster and encourage moral, intellectual, scientific and agricultural improvement, and to make suitable provision for the blind, mute and insane, and for the organization of such institutions of learning as the best interests of general education in the state might require. As under the first constitution, the schools were to be financed by income from the school fund, by the net proceeds of fines and forfeitures accruing to the state, by capitation taxes, by state taxes on persons and property, and by such county and district taxes as might be prescribed by law.

Additional provisions of the new constitution relating to education were determined largely by the current ideas of democracy and economy. Administration was vested in a state superintendent of free schools with duties to be prescribed by law. His compensation was not to exceed $1,500 annually, but he might be reimbursed for any expenses incurred in the performance of his official duties, provided they did not exceed $500 annually. More important still, his term was extended to four years and he was made a member of the state executive department. Unfortunately, this change made the office political and thus nullified the high hopes of educators to make it a professional one. By formal resolution the State Teachers Association objected to the change and requested that the association be permitted to designate "some able, efficient and practical educator" for the state superintendency.

Other constitutional provisions relative to education were the following: the county sheriffs were required to collect all school levies and to make annual settlements with the county courts; segregation of white and Negro youth for instructional purposes was required; teachers and public school officials, except authors, were forbidden to be interested in the sale, proceeds or profits of any book or other thing used in the public schools; the existing school districts were continued "until changed in pursuance of law"; the use of county superintendents was optional with the legislature; and, it was forbidden to make appropriations to "any state normal school, or branch thereof, not then functioning or chartered."

As under the first constitution, details of the revised system were to be determined by the legislature. Nor were some of the school laws enacted by that body without significance. Agreeable to the prevailing notions of economy, the powers and duties of the state superintendent were reduced, and in 1871 the duties of the adjutant general were assigned to his office. Important changes were also made in the county superintendency. Where the first statute had attempted to make the office professional, the revised system made it little more than clerical. The salaries of the county superintendents ranged from $75 to $300 maximum, but they were allowed three dollars a day for services as chairmen of the county board of examiners. With a view doubtless to supplementing their salaries and retaining them in the teaching profession, superintendents were permitted to teach without being certificated. Then, too, many of them taught select schools which persons desiring to be certificated were expected to attend.

On the financial side the revised public school system followed rather closely the pattern of the system established under the first constitution. The legal minimum four-month term and the maximum levy of fifty cents on the $100 assessed valuation of general property for teachers were retained, but the levy for buildings was reduced from fifty to forty cents. Additional levies of fifteen to thirty cents were authorized for graded and high schools, but their establishment was optional with the commissioners of the magisterial districts who also determined the local levies for both teacher and building purposes. The state levy of ten cents for school purposes was retained.

In the choice of textbooks, the legislature was influenced by considerations of economy and uniformity. In 1879 it vested the choice of all textbooks in a commission appointed by the governor. Texts in most general use were McGuffey's readers, Ray's arithmetics, Harvey's grammars, and Mitchell's geographies. West Virginians preferred the arithmetics and readers not only because of their superior quality but also because the author of the arithmetics had resided in Ohio County and the author of the readers was born in nearby Claysville, Pennsylvania.

Although the legislature was required to establish a thorough and efficient system of free schools, inequalities in the taxable wealth of administrative units resulted in great inequalities in educational opportunities. Ten wealthy counties with an average levy of 18.5 cents in 1873-74 had an average term of four and one half months, whereas ten poorer counties with an average levy of 39.5 cents had only three and one half months.

Teachers' organizations, publications, and institutes were important factors in the educational programs of this period. Beginning in 1872 as municipal and district affairs, teachers' institutes, though aided by the Peabody Fund, had a rather precarious history to 1879, when they were given state aid in the sum of $500. This gesture appealed to the Rev. Barnas Sears, agent of the Peabody Fund, who subsidized the program in 1880 in the sum of $3,000, and "one institute was held in every county, as required by law." Thereafter, teachers' county institutes were sources of professional fellowship and general guidance for more than a quarter century. It was there that scores of teachers first learned of the University, the state normal schools, and of educational leaders, both resident and nonresident.

The most important single innovation of the period was the development of a graduating system for country schools. The pioneer in this work was Alexander L. Wade, a county superintendent of Monongalia County, who discovered that pupils who enrolled at the age of six and re-enrolled year after year without a program lost much time. Influenced by the example of the graded schools then being established throughout the country, Wade found a remedy for the rural situation in a system of grades, promotions, and graduations.[4]

As worked out by Superintendent Wade, his "Graduation System" was brought to a degree of perfection in 1876, when his rural school promotion and graduation exercises were attended by newspaper reporters, public officials, and members of the West Virginia University faculty. Soon the "Graduation System for Country Schools" was attracting favorable attention throughout a large part of the United States; on July 30, 1879, the author explained it to the National Education Association, meeting in Philadelphia; and the resulting reports caused J. D. Philbrick, U. S. Commissioner of Education at the Paris Exposition, to accord Monongalia County "a bright spot on the educational map of the country." The system, as finally perfected by Superintendent Wade, was explained in 1881 in a sizeable volume entitled, *A Graduating System for Country Schools*.

Progress in secondary education in this period was however disappointing. Most academies closed their doors during the Civil War, and many failed to re-open. Two of the three Morgantown academies, as it will be seen, were merged in 1867 into the West Virginia Agricultural College. In keeping with plans of Superintendent White, the secondary program was directed to the training of teachers. For that purpose Marshall College, formerly Marshall Academy, was re-opened in 1868 on the secondary level as the State Normal School;[5] the Fairmont State Regency Normal, an indirect continuation of the Fairmont Male and Female Seminary, in 1869 became the Fairmont Branch Normal under the principalship of former Superintendent White; the West Liberty branch, formerly West Liberty Academy, opened its doors in May, 1870, under the principalship of F. H. Crago, and, in 1872, branch normals were established at Athens, Mercer County, Glenville, Gilmer County, and Shepherdstown, Jefferson County. As indicated by Governor Boreman in 1866, the scarcity of trained teachers was "the chief obstacle in the way of putting into success-

[4] Ambler, *History of Education*, p. 163.

[5] Robert C. Toole, "A History of Marshall College, 1850-1886," in *West Virginia History*, *XIV* (October, 1952), 28-58; *ibid., XIII* (Jan., 1952), 120-126; *ibid.* (Jan., 1953).

ful operation our free school system." There was not a single high school in the state. The Wheeling schools offering secondary work were called graded schools, and those offering a few courses on the secondary level in Fairmont, Parkersburg, and Charleston were not yet officially designated as high schools.

The Transition, 1880-1910

The cause of education advanced slowly during the period 1880-1910. State superintendents of free schools were generally lawyers and politicians; teaching was a stepping stone to other professions; teacher training was ignored; and libraries were practically non-existent. Moreover, the state levy of ten cents for school purposes was all but eliminated in 1907; property valuations having increased, the fifty and the forty cent maximum levies for teachers and buildings were at the same time reduced to twenty five and fifteen cents, respectively; in 1902 the "School Fund" was restricted to $1,000,000 by a constitutional amendment; and the legislature continued to establish independent school districts with special tax levying authority. As a result, inequalities in educational opportunities were continued and magnified, and teachers' salaries and the length of school terms remained below standard. At the end of this period the average school term in West Virginia was 125 days and the average monthly teacher's salary was $36.70. The corresponding figures for the United States were 150.3 days and $47.08.

There were however signs of progress. Use of a modified form of Superintendent Wade's Graduation System was made compulsory in 1891 on a state-wide basis; teachers' associations, institutes, and journals became important factors in the professional training of teachers; and as early as the 1880's West Virginia school teachers were being attracted by Peabody scholarships to Peabody Normal College, Nashville, Tennessee. In 1893, the state legislature made first and second grade teachers' certificates valid for four and two years, respectively. First grade certificates were renewable without examination and active teachers were required to attend teachers' institutes. In 1903, the legislature enacted a uniform teachers' examination law which put an end to much of the corruption which had attended the granting of certificates by county boards. After an experience extending from 1897 to 1909, during which county boards were given responsibility for the adoption of textbooks, that duty was entrusted to a bi-partisan state commission of nine members, including the state superintendent of free schools. Prompted by a growing conviction that crime and juvenile delinquency were directly traceable to illiteracy, the 1897 legislature passed a compulsory school attendance act applicable to all children between the ages of eight and fifteen.

The most progressive acts of the period were perhaps those pertaining to the county superintendency. Throughout the period there was an increasing desire for better supervision of school finances and teachers and for competent leadership in coordinating public opinion and action. In 1894, State Superintendent Virgil A. Lewis boldly proclaimed the county superintendent "the chief field officer of the Public School System." Two years later, the State Education Association approved a series of resolutions urging the enactment of legislation to increase the powers, qualifications, and compensation of that officer. These resolutions called for legislation which would provide an office for the county superintendent, require him to reside at the county seat, and devote full time to official duties.

Largely because of the unmistakable public sentiment back of the association requests, the 1901 legislature granted most of them. Among other things the county superintendent, whose term had been extended in 1893 from two to four years, was required to be skilled and experienced in the art of teaching and was forbidden to teach in any school, public or private, while holding the office. He was required to visit the schools under his supervision and to report under oath to the state superintendent the number of schools visited annually. At the same time an effort was made to make his salary commensurate with his increased duties and responsibilities. Under the new schedule maximum salaries ranged from $300 to $500 annually.

Although the need for high schools was officially described in 1885 as "the greatest defect in the educational system of the State," the greatest educational need in 1910 was still high schools. Throughout this entire period it required the approval of three-fifths of the voters in an election to establish them, and levies for their support and maintenance could not exceed thirty cents on the hundred dollars valuation of general property. In 1910 there were only fifty "so-called high schools" in the entire state, whereas Pennsylvania had 256 first class high schools and Ohio 474. There were however about 600 graded schools in West Virginia, a few of which offered instruction to and including the twelfth grade, but there was little uniformity in curriculums. In 1897 the State Education Association asked the legislature to correct this situation by requiring a uniform course of instruction for the first two years of all public supported high schools, but nothing was done.

Because of the advancing standards of colleges and professional schools, the academy made a temporary comeback toward the end of this period. Among the newly established institutions of academy rank were Alderson Academy (1901); Broaddus Classical and Scientific Institute (Clarksburg, 1894); Lewisburg Female Institute (1874); Greenbrier Military Academy (Lewisburg, 1890); Mt. Parvo Institute (Charles Town, 1882); West Virginia Normal and Classical Academy (Buckhannon, 1882); St. George Academy (1886), Tucker County, which was merged in 1893 into the public free school system; Elizabeth Seminary in Wirt County founded in 1900 by A. S. Lee for the purpose of training public school teachers; and Oakview Academy at Wayne, established in 1880 by Taylor B. "TB" McClure, also primarily for the training of teachers. Two preparatory schools to the University were established—one at Montgomery, Fayette County, in 1895, the other at Keyser, Mineral County, in 1901.

In southern West Virginia interest in secondary education was fostered mainly by the Presbyterian and the Christian churches. In 1891 Presbyterian missionaries converted the Pattie C. Stockdale home on Clear Fork near Colcord, Raleigh County, into the "Home School" which was the secondary school of that community prior to the erection of the Clear Fork High School. Presbyterians also pioneered the way to secondary education at Williamson, Mingo County, where they erected in 1905 the Williamson Presbyterial Academy. Members of the Christian Church were active at Beckley, Raleigh County, where they acquired Beckley Seminary and converted it into Beckley Institute. Opened in 1907 this institution remained active until 1918, when it became the Beckley high school.

Throughout this period the six state normal schools restricted their programs largely to academic courses. Because of a general lack of appreciation of the need for professional training for teachers and because of the depressed economic conditions which visited the country at large in the 1870's, the state normals were almost forced to close shop for lack of operating funds. The disfavor thus shown them continued to about 1890 when the influence of teachers trained at the Peabody Normal College began to be felt. In the movement, launched about 1880, to establish a unified state education system, the state normals were all but converted into preparatory schools to the University. In aid of that program the normal school regents declared in 1885 that it would be unwise and impracticable to develop the normals into teachers' colleges, and adopted a uniform course of study for them, which duplicated the course of the Preparatory Department of the University.

On the other hand, an increasing number of teachers, led by graduates of Peabody Normal College as well as by those who had studied at Columbia University, urged retention of all of the state normal schools and their development into first-class teacher training institutions. Consequently requests for the abolition of the normals not only ceased to be made but their use as teacher training institutions won the support of leading citizens of the state. Accordingly, the state board of regents re-established in 1901 a teacher training department at Marshall College and soon thereafter authorized the establishment of a similar department in the Branch Normal at Fairmont.

Plans were also made for the training of Negro teachers. Storer "College" had served as a training center for Negroes since its establishment in 1867. Founded by the Freedmen's Bureau with the financial aid of John Storer of Stanford, Maine, this institution remained the only one of "college grade" for Negroes in the state until 1892, when the West Virginia Colored Institute, now West Virginia State College, opened its doors at Institute, Kanawha County. For a time the program of this school was directed primarily to the training of Negro teachers, and in 1895, owing to the influx of Negroes into the coal fields of southern West Virginia, Bluefield Colored Institute was established to meet the educational needs of the growing Negro population of southern West Virginia.

Unfortunately for the educational interests of the state, the control of its industrial economy was largely non-resident. In the comparative absence of resident capital, residents generally vied with one another in making investments attractive to non-residents who, with the aid of a conservative rural public, saw to it that tax levies were kept low and that no improvements, such as roads and schools, were authorized on a large scale. In only a few instances did the leaders, either resident or non-resident, oppose public free schools; but free, tax-supported schools were a secondary consideration.

HIGHER EDUCATION

Despite the general aversion of trans-Allegheny Virginians to higher education, present West Virginia made considerable progress in it by 1860. A number of academies were then offering instruction of college grade and a number of collegiate institutes had been established. In 1856 Aracoma Polytechnic College at Aracoma, now Logan, Logan County, was incorporated for the purpose of educating "white male persons in the languages, literature, arts and sciences, and more specially in those sciences which may be deemed necessary to the skillful prosecution of farming, mining, and other useful arts"; in 1858 Marshall Academy became Marshall College, while Bethany College had since the early 1840's been one of the most progressive educational institutions in the Ohio Valley. Robert Richardson, its professor of chemistry, was closely associated with those leaders in the Middle West, who pioneered the way for the Morrill Act of 1862 authorizing the establishment of land-grant colleges in the United States.

The Civil War was as destructive of educational institutions as of educational interests in West Virginia, but there was a spirited revival of both in the Reconstruction. Bethany College then entered a "golden age," which attracted students over a wide area. In an effort to salvage traditions of Rector College (Pruntytown), Free Will Baptists established West Virginia College at nearby Flemington in 1865, which was active to the mid-nineties. In 1878 Coalsmouth High School, near present St. Albans, became Shelton College which was active to 1887. Shortly after the Civil War, Wheeling Female Seminary, founded in 1848, was reopened as Wheeling Female College and functioned as such to 1889. A few former academies were reopened as collegiate institutes, and the Agricultural College of West Virginia, established in 1867 at Morgantown, soon became West Virginia University.

In the period of transition from an agricultural to a semi-industrial economy, West Virginia made little progress in higher education. Among retarding influences were a lingering antipathy, an economy determined largely by non-resident capitalists, and a conservative rural electorate. The most important factor was, however, the comparative absence of secondary institutions of learning. As late as 1897 West Virginia was one of the very few states without a first class high school, a fact which goes far to explain why newly established "colleges" and the six state normal schools were merely high schools. The University maintained a campus preparatory department and other preparatory schools.

Moreover, as late as 1906 West Virginia contained no public collection of her own archives or of those of the Mother State, and no public collection of manuscripts and newspapers such as was then to be found in the libraries of most of the states of the Union. There was thus no incentive and no opportunity for research in history and the social sciences, and instruction on the higher educational level consisted largely of formal lectures in philosophy and metaphysics and textual recitations in English and foreign languages.

Sectarian opposition to the alleged trend of the University toward so-called materialism temporarily retarded its growth and influence. In the annual commencement exercises of 1886 President E. Marsh Turner announced publically that materialism was not then taught or even encouraged at the University, but the fact that he deemed such a denial necessary was significant. For years thereafter the University was attacked from scores of pulpits as an "ungodly institution." In the long run the attacks were however beneficial; for they led to the establishment of a number of denominational colleges which in due course divested themselves of the extremes of "fundamentalism" and, like the University, taught the sciences without offensive references to evolution. More than was generally appreciated the denominational colleges neutralized native provincialisms.

THE UNIVERSITY

In the Reconstruction

On February 7, 1867, the legislature accepted an offer from the trustees of Monongalia Academy to donate to the state their academy and the site and property of nearby Woodburn Female Seminary, representing a total value of about $51,000. The gift was made on condition that a proposed agricultural college be located permanently at or near Morgantown, site of each of the proffered institutions. On the same day the legislature established the Agricultural College of West Virginia, the name of which was changed the following year to West Virginia University. Management and control of the Agricultural College were vested in a board of visitors composed of one member from each of the eleven senatorial districts. When the name of the institution was changed, the name of the governing board was changed from "visitors" to "regents."

The University was a land-grant college established in conformity with the Morrill Act of July 2, 1862, as amended on April 19, 1864, so as to apply to the new state. Under this act, as amended, it received script for 150,000 acres of land, most of which was located in Iowa and Minnesota. As the date for the exercise of a state's right under the Morrill Act expired July 2, 1867, West Virginia sold title to her lands and invested the proceeds, amounting to about $86,000 in securities, from which only the income was available for use.

The limited funds thus available were supplemented by a small legislative appropriation and used to launch the Agricultural College. To escape the deadline the visitors met in Morgantown on April 3, 1867, at which time they elected the Rev. Alexander Martin president. The following year they sold Monongalia Academy for $15,000 which, together with a small legislative appropriation, was used to construct University Hall, now Martin Hall. It was completed in 1870, and all classes were at once transferred to the present campus which, the young women having been dispossessed, provided ample accommodations for both classrooms and residence quarters.

Despite this auspicious launching, the growth of the University was retarded in the course of the ensuing decade by conflicting plans and purposes of the pro-Southerners on the one hand and the pro-Northerners on the other. Their differences concerned such matters as co-education, relation of the Preparatory Department to the University, student discipline, and the curriculum. Generally, the pro-Northerners favored co-education, retention of the Preparatory Department, rigid discipline, and a prescribed curriculum, and as generally the pro-Southerners opposed. In 1875 their differences became irreconcilable, and President Martin was summarily discharged. Disavowing regional and partisan influences, the regents offered the presidency to Waitman T. Willey who declined it, saying, "I

West Virginia University, 1872

being a Republican and a member of the M. E. Church, as was Dr. Martin, would be obnoxious to the same objections." Willey's friend and pastor, the Rev. John R. Thompson, was elected to the presidency and retained it to March 12, 1881.

After a short interim President Thompson was succeeded by William L. Wilson who reorganized the University after the pattern of the University of Virginia. Because of their dissatisfaction with the University curriculum, particularly with respect to agriculture, pro-Southerners had meanwhile launched a movement to dismember it by diverting West Virginia's allotments for a land-grant college to a new one to be located at Lee Town, Jefferson County. Before Wilson's election to the University presidency concessions had been made to the sponsors of this move, and it had been abandoned. Thus the new president began his administration under comparatively favorable conditions, but soon thereafter he was elected to represent the Second West Virginia District in Congress, leaving the University in a somewhat chaotic condition.

In the Transition, 1880-1910

In administration this period witnessed a shift from a large degree of faculty autonomy to an equally large degree of central control. In the interest of liberty and democracy, President Wilson's successor, Robert C. Berkeley, was simply chairman of the faculty, and the eight academic schools and the two professional schools were practically autonomous. This arrangement nettled Princeton-trained President E. Marsh Turner (1885-1893), who tried to rid the University of the alleged "looseness and naiveness of the Virginia System," but at the end of eight years there were still eight more or less autonomous academic schools, the two professional schools had increased to five, and faculty relations were often strained by indirections and intrigues. As the climax of an effort to correct this situation, the janitor, acting on authority of the regents, served the president with a notice dismissing him.

Because of these experiences, the regency had some difficulty in finding a successor to President Turner, and the Vice President, Dr. P. B. Reynolds, professor of metaphysics, was made acting president. He was however reluctant to abandon his teaching, and the regents employed an auditor to control University finances. After two years the regents found a successor to President Turner in the person of Dr. James L. Goodnight who had just ended two years in study and travel abroad. Heeding an admonition of the regency to be "an executive in fact as well as in name," President Goodnight set out to convert the College into a university. With that in mind the "schools" and four special courses were grouped in 1895 into four colleges: Arts and Sciences, Engineering and Mechanic Arts, Agriculture, and Law, each with its own dean. The resulting increased enrollment led to the introduction of a student adviser system and to the appointment of a secretary to the president and a registrar. The students having meanwhile appropriated the liberties which the faculty had lost, the president proved inept in dealing with them and thus terminated his usefulness at the end of two years.

The next president, the twenty-eight year old Jerome Hall Raymond, had earned a doctorate from the University of Chicago and came highly recommended. In the presence of a number of distinguished guests, he was formally inaugurated on October 13, 1897, at which time he announced that the University faculty would have a part in determining its policies and administration. With that in view the College of Arts and Sciences and the College of Engineering were disintegrated into departments, while the deanships of these colleges having become defunct were left unfilled. Of the former schools only the Preparatory and the Commercial were retained, but a School of Music was established. As in the case of his predecessor, President Raymond was admonished by the regents to be "an executive in fact as well as in name," and he sought to attain that goal through the faculty rather than in defiance of it. In keeping with this policy administrative problems were referred to faculty committees, each of which functioned under the chairmanship of the president. At the end of two years there were twenty-three committees functioning in this manner. Thus the faculty, the bane of former presidents, was divided but far from conquered.

Although President Raymond's administrative program was designedly conciliatory, his inexperience, his "appalling puritanism," and his zealous personality made for bad faculty and public relations. Compulsory faculty leaves for study at other institutions were not always accepted kindly; differences between him and members of the faculty were personal and bitter; suspension of the granting of unearned degrees was disappointing to a number of expectant recipients; restrictions on student activities, particularly dancing, were resented by the "town crowd"; the new fangled ideas of his special lecturers and his assistant, Dr. Hannah Belle Clark, on sociology were resented in some quarters; and he was accused of discriminating against West Virginians in faculty appointments.

Under these conditions all eyes turned to the 1901 legislature, which appointed a committee to investigate and report the condition of the University. To the surprise of many, it was found to be prosperous and the report commended the zeal and the ability of the president who was, however, found to be "too young and inexperienced to deal with men." Moreover, his views and policies were described as "unsuited to West Virginia conditions." Accordingly, while the legislature increased the University appropriation for the 1901-03 biennium, it provided that no part of the appropriation for the years 1901-02 would be available "until the board of regents accepts the resignation of the present president." The board promptly resigned, and, on March 20, 1901, a new board accepted Raymond's resignation.

After a short interim during which Dr. P. B. Reynolds was again the acting president, Dr. Daniel B. Purinton, an alumnus ('73), a Baptist, a Republican, and a former acting president, who was then president of Denison University, Granville, Ohio, was elected president of the University, effective August 1, 1901. He was preferred to a younger man, as being better qualified to restore "harmony, unity, and economy." Harmony and economy were in fact to be the watchwords of his administration. There were therefore few changes in the faculty, but a number of resignations, including that of Dr. Hannah Belle Clark, were gratefully accepted.

There were a number of other developments of abiding interest and importance. Agitation for co-education, commenced in 1871 following the exit of women from Woodburn Female Seminary, increased in intensity—

dividing college faculties, the state legislature, and even the state. It was not, however, until May, 1889, when the Morgantown Female Seminary building was destroyed by fire that women were admitted to the collegiate department of the University. In 1897, they were admitted to all of its departments, except the military. The University Alumni Association, organized in 1873, took on new life in this period under the inspirational influence of Waitman Barbe who, in 1895, became field agent of the University. In 1895, in an effort to remove the University from partisan politics, its management and control were first vested in a bipartisan regency. An interest in the University Cadet Corps was aroused during the Spanish-American War and this in turn resulted in the construction of a new armory and an increase in military personnel. Although not an integral part of the University, the State Geological and Economic Survey, authorized in 1897, became closely identified with it. Inter-collegiate athletics, social fraternities, and student publications made their appearance in this period, but the most important event was perhaps the completion in 1886 of a railroad line between Fairmont and Morgantown. Soon thereafter members of the University board of regents superseded residents of Morgantown on the local executive committee of the University, and the initial step was taken in changing the "Morgantown School" to West Virginia University.

Chapter XXIV

West Virginia and Her Neighbors

A CHILD OF civil strife, West Virginia's interstate relations were not always amicable. Some of them she inherited from Virginia; others grew out of situations which involved her interests. Among the minor disputes involving the state in controversy were that with Pennsylvania regarding their common boundary line, adjusted in 1885-1886; the controversy with Virginia regarding the original records of land grants in West Virginia, adjusted in 1891-1897; and the several boundary disputes with Virginia, such as that now (1955) pending regarding the location of the line between Alleghany County, Virginia, and Monroe County, West Virginia. These questions were generally settled without recourse to the courts, but adjustment of major questions involved prolonged proceedings in law and equity. This was particularly true of the disputes affecting industrial relations, the Virginia Debt, the Maryland-West Virginia boundary, the Hatfield-McCoy feud, and Virginia's efforts to recover Berkeley and Jefferson counties.

BERKELEY AND JEFFERSON COUNTIES

The status of Berkeley and Jefferson counties gave rise to the first of West Virginia's several disputes with contiguous states. Following the Civil War, Virginia launched a movement for her redintegration.[1] When this movement failed, Virginia and West Virginia appointed commis-

[1] C. H. Ambler, *Waitman Thomas Willey* (Huntington, W. Va., 1954), p. 124.

sions authorized to adjust their common indebtedness, but before they had time to act Virginia sued West Virginia in the United States Supreme Court for the recovery of Berkeley and Jefferson counties. In support of her suit Virginia informed the court that she had on December 8, 1865 repealed her act of May 13, 1862 consenting to the formation of West Virginia, and her acts authorizing Berkeley and Jefferson counties to vote on their proposed inclusion in that state.[2] Virginia claimed therefore that the Congressional joint resolution of March 10, 1866 approving the transfer of those counties to West Virginia was null and void. Virginia claimed further that West Virginia, at the time of her admission to statehood, contained forty-eight counties designated by name and that the inclusion of additional counties was conditioned upon approval of a majority of the voters in each, a condition which had not been legally complied with. In answer to these representations counsel for West Virginia claimed that the admission of the state to the Union was a political question and thus outside the jurisdiction of the court.

The Supreme Court decided to hear the case on the ground that it was essentially a boundary dispute. After hearing evidence on both sides, the court resolved it to three questions: 1. Did Virginia give irrevocable consent to the formation of a new state within her bounds? 2. Had the Congress approved that consent in such a manner as to make it valid? and 3. Were the attending circumstances such as to nullify the legality of the results? In answer to the first two of these questions, the court ruled that the act of the Virginia General Assembly of May 13, 1862 consenting to the formation of a new state within her bounds was legal and binding and that the Congressional Act of December 31, 1862 admitting West Virginia to statehood approved informally the inclusion of additional counties. Thus the court approved indirectly essential steps in the admission of West Virginia to separate statehood. In answer to the third question, the court ruled that the authorizing act for the inclusion of additional counties gave the governor full discretion in determining the results and in certifying them. It declined therefore to question the accuracy or the legality of his acts, and Berkeley and Jefferson counties remained a part of West Virginia.

THE HATFIELD-McCOY FEUD

Governor Wilson's administration (1885-1890) featured a dispute between Kentucky and West Virginia incident to the Hatfield-McCoy feud.

[2] 11 *Wallace* 39-63.

The antagonisms engendered between the pro-Confederate Hatfields of West Virginia and the pro-Union McCoys of Kentucky during the Civil War had smouldered only to break forth in violence and bloodshed in the early 'Eighties. The immediate causes of the affair appear to have been a dispute over the ownership of a razorback hog and an ill-starred love affair between Johnson "Johnse" Hatfield and Rose Anna McCoy. In any event, beginning in 1882 the antagonists and their partisans killed each other on sight and sometimes clandestinely. So long as they confined their acts to the counties of their residence, convictions were next to impossible, and both Pike County, Kentucky, and Logan County, West Virginia, became notorious for their lack of law enforcement.[3]

These incidents reached a climax when Frank Phillips of Pike County, an agent of the governor of Kentucky, entered West Virginia with a posse, abducted members of the Hatfield clan, and imprisoned them. Because they had not been apprehended under a warrant or other legal process, Governor Wilson of West Virginia forwarded a request to Governor Simon B. Buckner of Kentucky asking for their release. The latter refused. Governor Wilson then filed a petition in the United States District Court of Kentucky for a writ of habeas corpus. The court denied the petition, and its denial was affirmed by the United States Circuit Court for Kentucky. West Virginia then appealed the case to the United States Supreme Court which handed down its decision in 1888. In *Mahon v. Justice* (jailor of Pike County), the court sustained the lower courts on the ground that no relief was provided either in the Constitution or by the laws of the United States for a person wrongfully abducted from one state to another and held by the latter for an offense against it.[4]

While the governors of West Virginia and Kentucky exchanged heated and lengthy letters and made personal appearances at court hearings, the "Border Warfare" between the Hatfields and McCoys gained nation-wide prominence, and the leaders of the feud, Anderson "Devil Anse" Hatfield and Randolph McCoy, became legendary figures. The Hatfield-McCoy feud was a favorite theme for newspaper correspondents throughout the 'Nineties, but with the coming of the railroad and industry to the Tug River Valley, passions cooled and "the feud guns were stacked."

THE MARYLAND BOUNDARIES

Another important development in interstate relations was the boundary disputes with Maryland. Inherited from Virginia, the major issue had

[3] See Virgil C. Jones, *The Hatfields and the McCoys* (Chapel Hill, 1948), pp. 17-102.

[4] 127 *U. S.* 700-716; Jones, *The Hatfields and the McCoys,* pp. 79-136.

its origin in land grants made in 1632 by the King of England to Lord Baltimore, proprietor of Maryland, and in 1669 to Lord Hopton and a group of court favorites. Each of the grants designated the "First Fountain" of the Potomac River as its western terminus, which for obvious reasons could not be located at that time. In 1688 Thomas, Lord Culpeper, purchased the shares of the patentees in the second grant and thus became the sole owner of all that vast area, familiarly known as the Virginia "Northern Neck," embracing about 2,450 square miles lying between the Potomac and the Rappahannock rivers and a line connecting their first fountains. Upon the death of Lord Culpeper ownership of the Northern Neck passed to his son-in-law, the Fifth Lord Fairfax of Denton, and in 1722, to his son, the Sixth Lord Fairfax, a familiar character in Virginia history (see pp. 38-39).

Virginians objected to the alienation of the Northern Neck, and when settlers began to push into that area, they took steps to determine its ownership and bounds. The king confirmed the Fairfax ownership on condition that those who already held patents would not be disturbed, and the Virginia Assembly in turn passed an act for "better securing the titles to lands in the Northern Neck." To aid in this a commission, in 1736, located the boundary line between the fountain springs of the North Branch of the Potomac and the Rappahannock rivers. Ten years later the line was surveyed and the first fountain of the Potomac was marked with fitting ceremony by the Fairfax Stone at the fountain spring of the North Branch.

The proprietor of Maryland objected to this line on the ground that it should have been located between the fountain springs of the Rappahannock and the South Branch of the Potomac. He also claimed that the Fairfax Stone had been erected without his knowledge or consent. Then came the French and Indian War, the Royal Proclamation of 1763, Pontiac's War, and finally the American Revolution, which halted the westward movement for a generation. However, following the Revolution, the legislature of Maryland seemed to be even more zealous of her western boundary than her colonial proprietors had been. Indeed, only by holding and perhaps enlarging her reserves west of Fort Cumberland would she be able to redeem in full her commitments to former officers and soldiers of the Indian wars and the Revolution.[5]

As a first step toward meeting these commitments Francis Deakins of Georgetown, Maryland, was employed in 1787 to "lay out" certain designated "Reserve Lands," and in December of that year he reported that 4,165 lots of fifty acres each had been surveyed. These lots were located

[5] Harold B. Fortney, "Maryland-West Virginia, Western Boundary" (MA thesis, West Virginia University, 1937); 217 *U. S.* 1-49, 577-583; 225 *U. S.* 1-32.

east of the "Meridian Line" which he had established between the Fairfax Stone and the Pennsylvania boundary. He also reported that he had found in the course of his surveys 325 families residing on 636 of the Military Lots.

Most of the Military Lots were occupied by authorized settlers in the ensuing few years, but squatters continued to push into the area intersected by the Meridian Line established by Deakins. Eventually most of these settlers secured patents for their holdings, but there were exceptions. This was especially true of those granted by Maryland which had not accepted that line as her western boundary. Virginia having confiscated the Fairfax holdings, the records of patents were moved to Richmond in 1796 (see p. 110), and Maryland took the initiative in efforts to determine her western boundary. Commissioners were appointed but could not agree as to the starting point for a survey. The formation of Preston County, Virginia, in 1818 seemed to necessitate a decision in the matter, but again the commissioners could not agree. Thereafter altercations between law enforcement officers and residents and between individuals claiming the same acreage under different patents occurred with increasing frequency.

Despairing of settlement by commissioners, Maryland proposed in 1826 a settlement by arbitration with the governor of Delaware as umpire. Virginia ignored the proposal; but residents of Maryland's newly formed county of Allegany being insistent, the arbitration offer was renewed in 1831, and a great deal of data was assembled. Finally, in 1832 Governor John Floyd of Virginia appointed Charles J. Faulkner, Sr. of Martinsburg, (West) Virginia, a special commissioner to compile data to sustain the claims of Virginia in the matter. Faulkner made a voluminous report which sustained Virginia's claims, and in 1833 her legislature again authorized the appointment of commissioners to "commence at the Fairfax Stone or at the First Fountain of . . . the North Branch of the Potomac and to run a line due north."[6]

The Maryland-Virginia boundary dispute was comparatively quiescent until the movement for the formation of Garrett County, Maryland. Even then the Maryland legislature did not press its claim regarding the starting point for determining the western boundary of the new county. Instead, in 1852, it authorized a survey to begin "at or near the Fairfax Stone on the North Branch of the Potomac." Two years later the Virginia Assembly passed a similar act and four years later the governor of Virginia appointed Colonel Angus W. McDonald of Hampshire County as a com-

---

[6] Fortney, "Western Boundary," (MS); C. J. Faulkner, "Report," in *Journal of the Virginia House of Delegates* (1832-1833, 1834).

missioner to work with a Maryland commissioner and another to be appointed by them in making the authorized survey.

To direct this work the commission employed Lieutenant N. Michler of the United States Corps of Topographical Engineers, who in 1859 surveyed an astronomically straight line from the Fairfax Stone to the Pennsylvania line. The "New," or Michler, line intersected the Pennsylvania line about three-quarters of a mile west of the intersecting point of the "Old," or Deakins, line. Because of the instrument used by Deakins and the nature of the topography, this was not surprising, and Lieutenant Michler took notice of the fact in a notation in his report to the effect that any attempt to make resident land owners conform to the New meridian would result in "great litigation." When Maryland prepared to make the most of the New line, Virginia, on the advice of her commissioner, hesitated to confirm it. Instead, she sent McDonald to England to obtain additional data. When he returned the Civil War was in progress, and, before it ended, West Virginia had taken the place of Virginia in her dispute with Maryland.

Following the Civil War little thought was given to the dispute by either state until 1886, when technical questions arising from a criminal case brought it again into the limelight. In response Governor Wilson of West Virginia included in his agenda for a special session of the legislature in 1887 a proposal to provide for establishing the boundary line between West Virginia and Maryland, and the legislature affirmed and approved the boundary line run by Lieutenant N. Michler, provided that Maryland first agreed to confirm and validate all entries, grants, patents, and titles previously made by the Commonwealth of Virginia.[7] This Maryland refused to do, and in 1890 West Virginia proposed a settlement by binding arbitration. But Maryland ignored the proposal, and on December 14, 1891 filed a suit in equity in the United States Supreme Court, charging that West Virginia exercised jurisdiction over territory that did not belong to her. West Virginia denied the charge, and the Court asked the litigants to provide it with data in support of their respective claims.

In compliance with this request both states took much time and made voluminous researches. Consequently, it took eighteen years to reach a decision and twenty-one years to make it final. Maryland rested her claims on a strict interpretation of her charter grant and the claim that she had not recognized the Fairfax Stone as the starting point for determining her western boundary. On the other hand, West Virginia asked the Court to recognize the existing situation as determined throughout the decades by the residents under conditions for which they were not responsible. But Maryland, with the help of expert engineers, established Potomac

[7] *Session Acts* (1887), p. 237; *House Journal*, p. 14.

Spring, more than a mile northwest of the spring at the Fairfax Stone, as the first fountain of the Potomac River. She then ran an astronomically straight line from Potomac Spring to the Pennsylvania line and prepared to establish her claim to a strip of territory about a mile wide along her entire western border. On the other hand, West Virginia resurveyed the Deakins line and made a house to house canvass of the persons residing along it to determine to what extent it had determined their land boundaries and their voting, roadwork, school attendance, and other customs.

Arguments in the case were made in November, 1909, and in February, 1910, the Court rendered a decision in favor of West Virginia on the ground that the Deakins line, though not astronomically correct, had been generally accepted and that it could not be disturbed without inflicting unnecessary injustices and hardships. The Court accordingly ordered that the Deakins line be resurveyed, remarked, and recognized by the contending parties as their common boundary. Moreover, their counsel was given forty days in which to employ commissioners to supervise the resurvey and the remarking. This order was complied with, and the commissioners reported on April 29, 1912, that the Old, or Deakins, line had been resurveyed and marked by 34 durable monuments. The Maryland commissioner objected to the report, but it was approved by the Court in a final order entered May 27, 1912.[8]

In the course of the land boundary hearing both states asked the Court to change their common river boundary which was then low-water mark on the south side of the North Branch of the Potomac. West Virginia asked that it be fixed at the high-water line on the north side of that stream, whereas Maryland asked that it be located at high-water on the south side. In conformity with an opinion in *Morris v. United States* and an agreement entered into by Maryland and Virginia in 1877, fixing the low-water mark on the south side of the Potomac as their common boundary, the Court ruled that it should remain there.

In this decision the Court was influenced also by a compact between Maryland and Virginia made in 1785, in which Maryland consented to the joint use of her acreage between high and the low waterlines on the south side of the Potomac. As she had not subsequently made any use of that acreage herself and Virginia had used it continuously, she had acquired ownership in keeping with well-established principles of law and equity. As West Virginia stood in the place of Virginia in this matter, her boundary was for that reason at low water mark on the south side of the Potomac. But the attorney general of Maryland ruled in 1955 that persons fishing from the south side of the Potomac above Great Falls would be required to have a Maryland license.

---

[8] 225 *U. S.* 1-32.

THE VIRGINIA DEBT

The Virginia Debt had its origin in expenditures for state purposes, mostly internal improvements, made prior to her dismemberment in 1863. As a possible condition to the success of their daring undertaking, the makers of the proposed new state took cognizance of the indebtedness of Virginia in their Dismemberment Ordinance of August 20, 1861, by agreeing to assume an equitable proportion of that indebtedness as of January 1, 1861. As stated in the ordinance, the proportion of the debt to be assumed by the proposed state was to be "ascertained by charging to it all state expenditures within the limits thereof, and just proportion of the ordinary expenses of the State government, since any part of said debt was contracted, and deducing therefrom monies paid into the treasury of the Commonwealth from the counties included within the said new state within the same period."

On October 24 following, this ordinance was approved by the loyal voters of the Reorganized Government of Virginia, and the constitution of the proposed new state required its legislature to ascertain "as soon as may be practicable," its equitable proportion of the said debt and to provide for the liquidation. This provision was approved by the voters of the proposed new state when they ratified its constitution, and by the Congress when it admitted West Virginia to statehood. The makers of West Virginia therefore regarded their agreement to assume an equitable proportion of the debt of Virginia, as well as the manner of determining it, as the law of the land.

As soon as the Civil War ended efforts were made by both states to settle the debt question, but they had scarcely got under way when Virginia sued West Virginia for the recovery of Berkeley and Jefferson counties. West Virginia, adhering to the legally approved plan of settlement which involved also the legality of her admission to separate statehood, refused to consider the matter further until her boundary was determined. Having failed in her effort to recover Berkeley and Jefferson counties, Virginia proposed in 1870 to arbitrate the debt question, but West Virginia insisted that it should be determined by commissioners in accordance with the plan set forth in the Dismemberment Ordinance.[9]

At this juncture, Virginia took the matter into her own hands. Proceeding on the basis of population and territory involved as of January 1, 1861, she agreed to pay her bondholders about two thirds of her total bonded indebtedness as of that date, or about $22,000,000, provided they would look to West Virginia for the other third. Because this proposal

[9] J. W. Mason, "The Virginia Debt," in *West Virginia Legislative Hand Book and Manual* (Charleston, 1916), pp. 756-764).

was believed to be final, the bondholders accepted it on condition that Virginia would continue efforts to collect the portion thus arbitrarily allotted to West Virginia. Thus did Virginia issue certificates of indebtedness against West Virginia for about one third of her bonded indebtedness, as of January 1, 1861. These bonds, when placed on the market, were known as the "West Virginia Certificates."

For sometime thereafter the Virginia Debt question was a political football in West Virginia. Generally Republicans agreed that a just and equitable portion should be determined and paid as quickly as possible. On the other hand, Democrats, fearing disapproval of the electorate, procrastinated. In keeping with this policy the constitution of 1872 did not mention the debt specifically but authorized the legislature to pay any state indebtedness. All agreed however that any payment should be on the basis of "benefits derived," as stated in the Dismemberment Ordinance, rather than on the basis of territory and population used by Virginia in the adjustment with her creditors. In justification of the former plan attention was called to the fact that a duly authorized West Virginia commission had found that she owed Virginia only $953,360.23, while conversely Jonathan M. Bennett, auditor of Virginia in the Civil War period, had found that Virginia owed West Virginia $525,000.

Following the airing of the Virginia Debt question in the United States Senate in 1883,[10] the market value of the West Virginia certificates declined to almost nothing; but their owners kept insisting that Virginia should aid in their collection. In response to this urging Virginia tried in vain in 1894 and again in 1900 to persuade West Virginia to accept her settlement with her creditors. Thereafter nothing more was done in the matter until February, 1906, when Virginia sued West Virginia in the United States Supreme Court to force payment of her allotted portion of the debt. The nature of the pleading was such however as to deny West Virginia an opportunity to present her case on the basis of benefits derived, and on March 6, 1911, the Court ruled that West Virginia owed Virginia $7,182,507.46 on the principal of their common indebtedness. The interest was additional, but it was not determined. Had it been allowed at the rate finally approved, the total judgment against West Virginia would have been about $20,000,000. In determining its judgment the Court rejected both the Virginia and the West Virginia proposals and based its findings on the estimated value of the property of the two states, not including slaves, at the time of their separation, June 20, 1863. On this basis West Virginia's portion of the debt was adjudged to be 23.5 per cent of the principal, as of that date.[11]

[10] *Congressional Record,* 47th Cong., special sess., Vol. 12, p. 254; Summers, *Camden,* pp. 241-248.

[11] R. E. Cushman, *Leading Constitutional Decisions,* 8th ed. (New York, 1946), pp. 228-236.

At this juncture Governor Hatfield of West Virginia entered the debt controversy by requesting the 1913 legislature to authorize the creation of a Virginia Debt Commission with power to negotiate a final settlement. This was done and the West Virginia Commission met a Virginia Commission, but they could not agree upon a settlement. In their negotiations the Virginians insisted upon adherence to the letter of the Court decision, whereas the West Virginians insisted that certain ascertainable credits should be allowed their state and used to reduce the judgment. Fortunately, the Court had ruled that, "This is no ordinary commercial suit, but, . . . a quasi-international difference," to be settled "upon the honor and constitutional obligations of the States concerned rather than upon ordinary remedies."

Thus encouraged, West Virginia requested a rehearing to permit her to present claims for credits. After some delay the request was granted, and the Court appointed a commissioner to determine the amount and the character of the claims. The outcome was a total credit allowance of $2,966,885.18 which the Court deducted from the original judgment, thus reducing the final one to $4,215,622.28. To this the Court added an interest item of $8,178,307.22, making the total judgment against West Virginia, as of July 1, 1915, $12,393,929.50, which was to bear interest at five per cent from that date.

Most West Virginians were grateful for the debt adjustment in their favor, others advised repudiation, while still others contended that the legislature of a "sovereign state" could not be compelled to make appropriations. Meanwhile, Virginia was demanding payment. In June, 1916, that state asked the Court for a writ of execution to levy upon the public property of West Virginia, but the request was denied on the ground that her legislature had not sufficient time to act. Whereupon Virginia, in February, 1917, when the West Virginia Legislature was in session, asked the Court for a writ of mandamus to compel it to levy a tax to pay the debt judgment. In response to this request the Court deferred action to April, 1918, when the writ was denied, but the Court indicated at that time that appropriate remedies could and would be found to make West Virginia perform her duty in the matter.

Unwilling to put this warning to a test and eager to establish a good name for their state in the bond market with a view to financing a road-building program, West Virginia leaders, some of whom owned West Virginia certificates, induced the legislature to satisfy the judgment in the debt case. It accordingly authorized a cash payment of $1,062,867.16 and the sale of $13,500,000 of 20-year gold bonds maturing serially and bearing interest at the rate of 3.5 per cent. In a memorable meeting, held in New York, on July 3, 1919, the cash and the bonds were delivered to the Virginia Commission. For the liquidation of the bonds the West

Virginia Legislature that year created the Virginia Debt Sinking Fund and authorized the board of public works to levy, not to exceed ten cents, on each $100 assessed valuation of general property.[12] West Virginia purchased $10,125,800 worth of the debt bonds at a price less than par and saved $800,000; she retained $439,000 on account of bonds not presented for payment; and in 1935 the outstanding portion of the debt, in the sum of $2,240,000, was refunded at an interest rate of 1.4 per cent. In 1939 the debt was liquidated.

IN INDUSTRY

For more than half a century West Virginia provided the raw materials for the growth of industrial cities in neighboring states while apparently neglecting her own. In 1955 she had no city of any kind with a population in excess of 100,000. For this situation chief responsibility rested with her own residents. Since before their separate statehood, they had welcomed non-resident capital as a chief means of developing their natural resources. In pursuit of this policy uninformed resident landowners sold their holdings—surface, mineral rights, and all—for mere pittances, while their resident leaders, in the capacity of agents and retainers, were aiding non-resident capitalists in making choice investments, in keeping tax rates low, and in thus unwittingly retarding social and cultural progress.

Alarmed by the decreasing supply of natural gas and the increasing demand for it for both domestic and industrial uses in the World War I period, the West Virginia Legislature on February 10, 1919 passed an act requiring persons furnishing natural gas for public uses within the state to provide a supply adequate for the demand, "whether domestic, industrial, or otherwise," in the district served by them. In case such persons were unable to do this from their own supplies, they were required to apply to the public service commission of the state, which on proof that the public convenience and necessity were imperiled, was authorized to order persons engaged in the same business in the same district and having gas surpluses more than enough to supply their regional demands, to divert a sufficiency of their supply to persons needing it.

Before this law became effective, Ohio and Pennsylvania jointly asked the Supreme Court of the United States to enjoin West Virginia from enforcing it. The plaintiffs claimed that enforcement of this act would withdraw a large volume of natural gas from the channels of interstate

12 For 1919-1921 the levy was ten cents, for 1922 five cents, for 1923-1932 inclusive, four cents and thereafter two cents on Class I, general property; four cents on Class II, and eight cents each on Classes III and IV.

commerce and effect irreparable injuries to individuals and industries, and that it would be an interference with interstate commerce such as was forbidden under the commerce clause of the Federal Constitution. It was further stated that West Virginia had welcomed non-resident capital and non-resident markets for her surplus resources, as a result of which non-resident consumers had developed interests that transcended state lines.

In answer to these representations counsel for West Virginia claimed that the companies engaged in the sale and distribution of natural gas within her bounds were in a quasi-public business which fittingly and legally was subject to public regulation and control in the interest of her resident and industrial consumers. More important still, natural gas was a natural product which, because of the declining supply, needed to be conserved in the interest of the people of the state. Regardless of the fact that the interstate distributing "persons" operated under the laws and regulations of West Virginia, it was claimed also that she was not subject to the jurisdiction of the Court in this matter, because the state was not engaged in the production and distribution of natural gas.

With justices Holmes, McReynolds, and Brandeis dissenting in strong opinions, the Court ruled that natural gas, "when reduced to possession," became a commodity fit for circulation in the channels of interstate commerce. As such, its distribution was subject to Congressional regulation and control in the interest of all the states as a means of enhancing their welfare by sharing their natural advantages, as intended in the commerce clause of the Federal Constitution. From this standpoint the Court considered the West Virginia case an important one, because "what may be done with one natural product may be done with others, and there are several States in which the earth yields products of great value which are carried into other States and there used." Therefore, in a decree entered on June 11, 1923, the act of the West Virginia Legislature was declared unconstitutional and void.[13]

Although *Hope Natural Gas Company v. Hall, State Tax Commissioner,* was not between states, it involved interstate relations. In 1925 the Hope Natural Gas Company, a corporation doing an extensive business in West Virginia, secured from the Circuit Court of Kanawha County an injunction to prevent the collection of a privilege or gross sales tax authorized that year on the sale of natural gas produced in West Virginia and sold in neighboring states. The injunction was granted on the ground that the tax was in conflict with the Federal Constitution because it imposed a burden on interstate commerce and deprived the plaintiff of property without due process of law since it levied a tax on a commodity

[13] 262 *U. S.* 553-624 (1923).

beyond its jurisdiction. The State Supreme Court of Appeals reversed the trial court, and the Hope Company appealed the decision to the United States Supreme Court which ruled that the tax in question was not illegal "if computed on the value of the gas at the well, before it entered interstate commerce."[14]

INTERSTATE COOPERATION

In recent years West Virginia cooperated somewhat reluctantly with neighboring states in the movement for greater uniformity in their statutes and administrative practices and in efforts to prevent the pollution of streams. For the former purpose the legislature created in 1937 the West Virginia Commission on Interstate Cooperation which worked with interim and other committees in formulating legislative programs. But the commission accomplished little because of the failure of the state to provide it with funds. To remedy its failure the 1949 legislature appropriated $8,500, of which $6,000 was earmarked for membership in the Council of State Governments. When asked to honor a requisition for that sum and that purpose, the state auditor refused on the ground that the act of 1937 creating the commission was unconstitutional in that it delegated inalienable police powers. Moreover, he claimed that the request should have been itemized as required by the constitution. In *Commission v. Sims* the state supreme court of appeals on February 6, 1951, overruled these objections, and the warrant was issued without further delay.

Of greater importance was *Dyer v. Sims,* clarifying the right of West Virginia to participate with neighboring states in efforts to prevent the pollution of the "Ohio River system." For that purpose West Virginia had entered into a compact with seven other states—New York, Pennsylvania, Ohio, Indiana, Illinois, Kentucky, and Virginia—and pledged herself to cooperate with them in maintaining the waters in the Ohio River basin in a sanitary condition through the administrative mechanism of the Ohio River Valley Sanitation Commission, consisting of three members from each of the member states and three representatives of the United States Government. The West Virginia Legislature approved this compact on March 11, 1939; Congress approved it on July 11, 1940; all the signatory states having approved, the governor of West Virginia, on June 3, 1948, formally proclaimed West Virginia's membership; and the 1949 legislature appropriated $12,500 as her share of the operating expenses of the commission for the fiscal year ending June 30, 1949.

At this juncture the functioning of the commission was threatened

[14] 274 *U. S.* 284-289 (1927); 102 *W. Va.* 272.

through the refusal of the auditor of West Virginia to honor a requisition for the payment of her appropriation. In justification of this refusal the auditor claimed that the act of March 11, 1939 ratifying the compact was unconstitutional because it committed future legislatures and delegated to other states and to the United States inalienable police powers. In answer to these objections the commission asked the state supreme court of appeals for a mandamus to compel the auditor to issue the warrant. By a vote of three to two the court refused the request, and an appeal was taken to the United States Supreme Court which ruled on April 9, 1951 that "an agreement entered into between States by those who alone have political authority to speak for a State cannot be nullified unilaterally, or given final meaning by an organ of one of the contracting States."[15]

The matter of finances having been clarified, the Ohio River Valley Water Sanitation Commission established in 1953 standards for sewage treatment in the various stretches of the Ohio River adjacent to West Virginia, and notices were sent to both municipalities and industries informing them of these standards and advising them to take appropriate action. As of January 1, 1955 all of the large cities in West Virginia had either adopted approved sewage treatment plans or had plans in process of preparation, and most of the industries were cooperating in like manner. In this both the municipalities and the industries were trying to conform to the requirements of the state water pollution control act of 1929, which, as amended in 1953, repealed the exemption of the coal industry from its operation, required municipalities and industries to secure pollution permits, and authorized, with the approval of the state water commission, persons interested in anti-pollution programs to exercise the right of eminent domain.

---

[15] 341 *U. S.* 22-36; 134 *W. Va.* 278-303.

Chapter XXV

The Shrinking of Distance

TRANSPORTATION

ONE HUNDRED YEARS AGO present West Virginia was crossed in easterly and westerly directions by four turnpikes: the Cumberland, or National, connecting Cumberland, Maryland, and Wheeling by way of Washington, Pennsylvania; the James River and Kanawha connecting Lewisburg and Guyandotte by way of "Mouth of Gauley" and Charleston; the "Old Northwestern" connecting Romney and Parkersburg via Grafton, Clarksburg, and West Union; and the Staunton and Parkersburg via Beverly, Buckhannon, and Weston. The Virginia turnpikes were built under the initial direction of Colonel Claudius Crozet, a French artillery officer who had served with Napoleon, and were masterpieces of engineering.[1] They were connected by a network of turnpikes and dirt roads which, like the main thoroughfares, spanned rivers and creeks by the use of "S-bridges" and "covered bridges." Where these were impracticable, crossings were by ferries, the sites of which grew into towns and cities. The main thoroughfares were generally macadamed, thus making them usable the year round and permitting the substitution of the stagecoach for the heavier and more cumbersome Conestoga wagon.

Trans-Allegheny Virginia was then in the stagecoach state of its transportation history. But the area served by the first roads was not destitute economically, socially, and politically. In due course, hunters' cabins and farmhouses were converted into hostelries, inns, taverns and health resorts where statesmen, scientists, authors, and travelers of both low and high estate were entertained after a fashion befitting their respective stations. Here polite greetings were exchanged, politics were discussed, the past was retold, and nuptial matches were made. The best hostelries made a

[1] Colonel William Couper, *Claudius Crozet* (Charlottesville, Va., 1936), pp. 36-67, 73-92.

point of catering to hog and cattle drivers and advertised their stables and provender rather than their sleeping and culinary accommodations.

Instead of converting the sylvan retreats of the New State into large and wealthy cities, as its leaders expected, the coming of the railroad reduced some of them to memories and others to wayside villages. Shortly after the Baltimore and Ohio Railroad reached the Ohio River in 1853, it effected connections with railroads in Ohio at Benwood and Parkersburg and before the Chesapeake and Ohio Railroad reached the Ohio, near Guyandotte in 1873, it had arranged for through connections by river. Thereafter the railway traffic through (West) Virginia scarcely halted en route, and the cattle and hog drivers who had formerly passed her way, rode to market in coaches and shipped their livestock in cattle cars.

Although the railroads crossing West Virginia stimulated the coal mining and timbering industries in an appreciable measure, by causing the great volume of traffic to pass through and around, they left her an area of comparative arrested development. This condition was prolonged by the rundown condition of her turnpikes and dirt roads due to excessive use and neglect in the Civil War and the Reconstruction and to the discriminatory practice of trunk line railroads in the 1870's and the 1880's in charging more for short hauls than for long ones over the same road and in the same direction. Thus West Virginia was left in the dirt road stage of her transportation history.

Dirt Roads

Under laws and customs inherited from Virginia, the counties of West Virginia were, until well into the present century, divided into road precincts, for each of which the county court appointed a road supervisor. Under an act of 1891, the county court was authorized to appoint a road superintendent who was charged with the duty of building and maintaining roads and bridges in their respective districts. These officials depended largely upon the labor of their neighbors performed after a fashion not unlike the corvée of feudal days. Under this system every man over twenty-one years of age and under fifty, and not a pauper, was required to work on the public roads at least two days annually, or to make payments to the county in lieu of work. In case of emergencies both the work and the pay requirements might be increased. There was also a road levy which was paid direct to the sheriff. If extensive improvements or new roads were desired, the county court might, with the approval of the voters, lay a special levy or sell bonds. Taxpayers were privileged, however, to "work-out" two-thirds of their regular or special road taxes.

The chief objection to these practices was that "road work" was rarely taken seriously. It afforded supervisors an opportunity to strengthen political fences and gave ambitious young men an opportunity to earn needed cash. To improve this system the legislature provided in 1897 for a state highway inspector who was authorized to utilize facilities of the State University in testing road building materials, to provide supervisory assistance to the several counties, and to conduct a ten-day road school at the State University. In 1909 a state road fund was established and its administration was vested in a state commission of public roads in lieu of a state highway inspector. But both the new office and the state road fund were abolished in 1911, and the county courts were again vested with responsibility for road and bridge construction and maintenance.

The public did not however sustain this policy, and in 1913 the legislature created a state road bureau of four members and authorized county courts to increase levies and use prison labor for the construction and maintenance of public roads. The results of this vacillating policy were indicated in the first report of the state road bureau, which said that the roads of West Virginia were the worst in the United States. Inasmuch as they were then largely clouds of dust in summer and streams of mud in winter, the accuracy of this statement was not questioned.

The acid test for West Virginia's roads came in areas of oil and natural gas developments. They necessitated an unprecedented use of heavy horses and heavy wagons, which "knocked the bottom out of the roads." This was notably true in the spring, following the usual freezing and thawing. At that time dirt roads in the oil fields became streams of mud and water that overflowed their beds and streaked hillsides below to their bases. Horses and mules drowned on the highways were buried in "horse graveyards."

Steamboat Days

During almost a half century following the Civil War, the Ohio River and its chief tributaries in West Virginia were important traffic thoroughfares. Contacting dirt roads and railroads were feeders, and the navigation of the Upper Ohio and tributary streams was improved by a series of locks and dams: the Monongahela from Pittsburgh to Fairmont; the Little Kanawha from Parkersburg to Creston; the Kanawha from Point Pleasant to Deepwater; and the Big Sandy to Louisa, Kentucky. Under these conditions the volume of towboat-propelled coal descending the Ohio increased annually, and packets reached Wheeling and Parkersburg more or less regularly from St. Louis and New Orleans. From St. Louis and the Tennessee River they brought iron ore and other raw materials, and from New Orleans came tropical products. Return trips consisted largely of industrial products and passengers.[2]

Largely because of failure to improve the navigation of the inland waters adequately and because of competition from railroads, the predicted exit of the steamboats became temporarily a reality. In a whole day's travel by rail along the Ohio River in 1917, one would not see a single river craft, except perhaps a ferryboat. At that time Congress was seriously considering suggestions for the abandonment of plans for the further improvement of the rivers of the Ohio Valley. But, when the railroads of the entire country officially announced their inability to meet the traffic needs of the country in World War I and were taken over by the Federal Government, industry was forced to use river transportation.

Attention was thus again diverted to the Monongahela, which had maintained its importance as a traffic stream. Old and discarded boats and barges were returned to service; new boats and barges were built; and corporations, such as the Charles Ward Engineering Works of Charleston and the Marietta Manufacturing Company of Point Pleasant, joined those of other states in supplying the increased demand for river tonnage. At first, new construction was largely of wood, but in a short time this gave way almost entirely to steel. In World War II the Point Pleasant plant built upwards of fifty ocean-going and harbor vessels for the United States Navy and Army.

The effects of the revival of river traffic were nation-wide. As already indicated, it stimulated boat building; plans for improving the navigation of the Ohio and its chief tributaries were revived; the "Lakes-to-Gulf Deep Waterways" movement was stimulated; and an "On to Cairo by 1929" movement was launched for the canalization of the Ohio by a system of locks and dams. A federal appropriation for that purpose was made in 1922, and, with President Hoover participating, the system was formally dedicated in October, 1929. This improvement provided a nine-foot stage of slack-water throughout the entire course of the Ohio. It was effected by the use of fifty locks and dams, twenty-one of which rested on West Virginia soil.

Although it did not then have a nine-foot stage throughout its entire course, the Monongahela bore the largest river traffic of any stream in the United States and one of the largest in the world, second only to that of the Rhine and larger than that of the Panama Canal. It was later provided with a nine-foot stage to and beyond Morgantown, and the volume of its traffic increased. Presently, a nine-foot stage is being projected for its entire course.

[2] Charles H. Ambler, *A History of Transportation in the Ohio Valley*, pp. 161-185, 265-319.

Motivated by the industrialization of the Kanawha Valley, attention was directed to the improved navigation of the Kanawha River. For that purpose three dams with two locks each were built: one at Winfield, one at Marmet, and a third at London. A fourth unit, Gallipolis Locks and Dam, was constructed in the Ohio about ten miles below Gallipolis. These four dams replaced ten old-type dams on the Kanawha and three on the Ohio and provided the former with a nine-foot stage to Montgomery.

Lock No. 3 (London), Kanawha River

The Kanawha thus became a part of a proposed inland navigation system, which tied in with the Great Lakes by canals connecting the upper Ohio River and Lake Erie and the Illinois River and Lake Michigan, and with the Gulf of Mexico by way of the Ohio and the Mississippi rivers. The immediate and potential results were factors in making the Kanawha Valley an industrial workshop.

Effects of these developments were revolutionary. Except a showboat or an excursion boat at rare intervals, steamboats of the passenger-packet type disappeared completely. In the place of the mammoth steam propelled towboats, came comparatively small diesel-propelled boats of the modern tug type. In perfect control of monstrous tows of fabricated steel to Mississippi and Gulf ports, they passed, without so much as a salute, former river towns along the Ohio. Most of the tonnage, including the propelling craft, was all-steel construction, and some of it was designed for use on the high seas.

Remarkable as these achievements were, they were soon outmoded.

For instance, locks 600 feet long did not accommodate, without breaking, 1,200 foot tows, and, by mid-century, some of the locks and dams were in poor repair. Moreover, a system designed to accommodate from 15 to 20 million tons of traffic annually was accommodating about 60 million tons, and the upstream traffic almost equaled the downstream. To care for the changed situation U. S. Army Engineers proposed to reduce, over a period of twenty years, the 46 locks and dams on the Ohio in 1955 to 21 and to enlarge them at a total cost of hundreds of millions of dollars. Experienced industrialists predicted that West Virginia would not come into her own industrially until this had been done.

The Railroad Era

Neither the Chesapeake and Ohio nor the Baltimore and Ohio Railroad was built for the primary purpose of developing West Virginia's natural resources. Each of them sought instead to tap the rich agricultural lands of the Midwest and its rapidly developing industrial cities. As already stated the Baltimore and Ohio Company effected through connections shortly after it reached the Ohio River, and in 1888 the Chesapeake and Ohio extended its lines to Cincinnati. Construction of railroads for the primary purpose of developing West Virginia's natural resources had to wait the lifting of the economic depression of the 1870's and the development of markets for her natural resources.

Johnson N. Camden, a pioneer in crude oil production and refining, was one of the first to seize this opportunity.[3] From profits in his oil ventures he had a major part in financing the Ohio River Railroad connecting Wheeling and Kenova. The stretch between Parkersburg and Wheeling was completed in 1884 and that between Parkersburg and Huntington in 1888. The road was extended to Kenova in 1893. Branch lines had meanwhile been built from Ravenswood to Spencer and from Millwood to Ripley.

Unlike the Baltimore and Ohio and the Chesapeake and Ohio, the Norfolk and Western Railway was built primarily to develop the Pocahontas coal fields of Virginia and West Virginia in keeping with an "act of imagination" of Frederick J. Kimball. As the guiding genius of a group of Philadelphia capitalists who had purchased in 1881 a run-down, wood-burning railroad serving South-side Virginia, Kimball conceived the idea of using it to tap the fabulously rich Pocahontas coal field and to form the nucleus of a transportation system for the primary purpose of carrying coal. With that in view the New River branch was constructed in 1881-1882, and the first shipment of Pocahontas coal thence to Norfolk

[3] Summers, *Camden*, pp. 315-415.

was made in March, 1883, and celebrated there as a municipal affair. The Flat Top Mountain extension, commenced in 1884 and completed to and through the Elkhorn Tunnel in 1886, paved the way for an extension to the Ohio River, which was completed on November 12, 1892. By use of a bridge at Kenova, an extension to Portsmouth, Ohio, and the use of lines previously purchased, through connections were at once made to both Columbus and Cincinnati, and in due course "the Ohio Extension" became "the heart of the N. & W. system."[4]

The transformation of the area traversed by the Norfolk and Western in West Virginia into populous and wealthy counties was as spectacular as it was effective. In 1888, Bluefield, "the gateway to the Pocahontas coal field," was only a flag station on the farm of John B. Higginbotham. In December, 1889, it was incorporated as a town with a population of about 600 which increased to 4,644 in 1900 and to 11,188 in 1910. The following year its post office became first class. In 1893 it forwarded 51,167 passengers over the railroad, but the number increased to 163,461 in 1912. This development was climaxed on July 12, 1924 by the friendly merging of Graham, Virginia, and Bluefield, West Virginia, into Greater Bluefield, in an occasion made notable by the presence of the governors of the two states and a telegram from the President of the United States.

The rise of Welch in McDowell County was equally spectacular. "Laid out" in 1889 on "wild lands," the coming of the railroad assured a steady growth. Land which had sold for only one dollar per acre increased rapidly in value, and the meager exports of furs and ginseng were soon supplanted by large exports of coal. The simple life of widely separated homes gave way to a community life in which Negroes and foreign-born were important elements. At an election held in September, 1891, the county seat was ordered moved from Perryville to Welch, where a substantial courthouse was erected in 1894. The rise of other towns, notably Cooper, Bramwell, Matoaka, Mayberry, North Fork, Elkhorn, Keystone, Vivian, Gary, Davy, Iaegar, Matewan, and Williamson, was equally rapid. Williamson became one of the most important coal shipping centers of the state.

Traversing the state through its most mountainous sections and in general northern and southern directions, the Western Maryland Railroad was an engineering feat. In its inception this road was one of the many dreams of Henry G. Davis. Its possibilities were conceived by him while he was yet a station agent for the Baltimore and Ohio Railroad working at Piedmont and living, for a short time, in a box car. As the West Virginia Central and Pittsburgh Railway Company, its construction was commenced in 1880. In 1883, it was completed to Gormania, Grant County. It

[4] Joseph T. Lambie, *From Mine to Market: The history of coal transportation on the Norfolk and Western Railway* (New York, 1954); Callahan, *West Virginia,* I, 483-494.

took five years more to reach Elkins, the chief objective. Later, it was extended to Beverly and Belington and still later, the line having been purchased by the Western Maryland Railroad, to Durbin, Pocahontas County, where it connected with a branch of the Chesapeake and Ohio, and finally to Webster Springs, Webster County.

With the completion, in 1906, of the Coal and Coke Railroad, first commenced in 1893 as the Charleston, Clendenin and Sutton Railway, West Virginians first realized a long-cherished desire for a railroad extending through the heart of the state from north to south. This line was 175 miles long and, together with the Western Maryland, afforded through connections from Charleston to Cumberland. It, too, was largely an achievement of Henry G. Davis who, having sold his interest in the Western Maryland, desired "to do more for West Virginia." Accordingly, he and his son-in-law, Stephen B. Elkins, built the Coal and Coke Railroad, now a part of the Baltimore and Ohio system.

At the same time branch lines to the main lines were giving inland towns and cities their first rail accommodations and tapping new coal and timber lands. Among them was the Fairmont, Morgantown, and Pittsburgh Railroad connecting Fairmont and Morgantown, completed in 1886 and extended to Uniontown, Pennsylvania, ten years later. In 1879, Johnson N. Camden built a narrow gauge road from Clarksburg to Weston, which he extended to Buckhannon in 1883 and later to Pickens. In 1890 this narrow gauge system was converted into a standard gauge line and incorporated into the West Virginia and Pittsburgh Railroad designed to connect the Baltimore and Ohio and the Chesapeake and Ohio lines. This road was completed from Weston to Camden-on-Gauley in 1891. In the late 1890's this Camden system was taken over by the Baltimore and Ohio Company under ninety-nine year leases and extended to Richwood, Nicholas County.

Among other railroads was the Kanawha and Michigan connecting Corning, Ohio, and Gauley Bridge, West Virginia, via Point Pleasant and Charleston. It was built in 1884-85 and was later taken over by the New York Central and extended to Nallen, Fayette County, and Enon, Nicholas County. The Monongahela River Railroad, built in 1889-1890 between Clarksburg and Fairmont, was a Camden device for the development of the intervening coal fields. In 1897, it too became a part of the Baltimore and Ohio system. The West Virginia Short Line, completed in 1901 to connect Clarksburg and New Martinsville, opened up a rich coal, oil, and timber area and placed a number of intervening towns on the map, among them Wallace, Smithfield, Jacksonburg, Hastings, Pine Grove, and Reeder.

Completion of the Virginian Railroad in 1909 was a feat in railroad engineering and financing. This road connected Deepwater, a point on the Chesapeake and Ohio Railroad about thirty miles east of Charleston, with Norfolk, Virginia, by a track that ignored the contour of the land and passed directly over streams and through mountains. The basic idea in its construction was to take the greatest possible advantage of gravity in transporting tonnage to the Atlantic seaboard. Unlike other railroads, the Virginian was the conception of one person, Henry H. Rogers, a Standard Oil magnate, who built the $40 million project on his own resources and credit. Like the Norfolk and Western, the Virginian was designed to be primarily a coal carrier but for the Upper Guyandot area. It thus became a formidable competitor of both the Norfolk and Western and the Chesapeake and Ohio, the largest regional coal carrier. Later a connection was made at Deepwater with the New York Central (formerly the K. & M.), thus increasing the competitive potentialities and the service opportunities of the Virginian.

The Good Roads Movement

Motor driven vehicles first made their appearance in West Virginia about 1900, but the unimproved condition of her highways discouraged their general use. As the number of car owners multiplied, the desire for better roads increased, and the legislature in 1917 codified the state highway and bridge laws. The new law created a bipartisan road commission of two members to replace a four-member state road bureau and defined the powers and duties of the commission as well as those of all state and local officers responsible for the administration of road laws. The legislature also created a connecting system of about 4,600 miles of "Class A" state highways and authorized a state road fund for distribution among the counties on the basis of their "Class A" mileage. It agreed to supplement federal aid from the income from a two per cent tax on motor vehicle licenses, authorized a county road levy of twenty-five cents on each $100 of assessed property, and established an annual good roads school at the University.

The results of the 1917 law were so satisfactory and the need was so urgent that the public demanded a larger road building program to be financed by the state and directed by the state road commission. In the absence of constitutional authority to finance such a program, the 1919 legislature asked the electorate to approve a bond issue of $50,000,000 to be used to construct a state highway system to connect "at least the various county seats of the State." In support of this proposal, the West Virginia Good Roads Federation staged a campaign of education. Under the slogan, "Help Pull West Virginia Out of the Mud," this organization, with the aid of public officials and public-spirited residents, secured the ratification of the proposed amendment and thus enabled West Virginia to take a long step toward throwing off the isolation and arrested development that overtook her when hog and cattle drivers, statesmen, and persons of various estates ceased to patronize her health resorts and places of entertainment.

The 1921 and the 1923 legislatures implemented the new program. For that purpose, the 1921 session increased the membership of the state road commission from two to three; it classified all roads either as "state" or as "county-district," instead of "Class A," and "Class B"; it formulated a program designed to provide each county seat with at least one hard-surfaced outlet and to connect main state roads with "important roads of adjoining states"; and it earmarked certain state road funds for bond and interest liquidation purposes. It also authorized the sale of $15 million worth of state road bonds, but the administrative officials experienced some difficulty in marketing them. State banks came to the rescue, and in 1923 the legislature authorized the collection of a tax of two cents per gallon on gasoline and the sale of $15 million of additional road bonds. It also authorized the commission to designate streets of municipalities as connecting parts of the state road system and to assume responsibility for the bridges on such links.

With this support the road building program moved forward. In 1925 the gasoline tax was increased to three and one half cents per gallon, and the remainder of the $50,000,000 bond issue was sold without difficulty; but it soon became apparent that the proceeds would not finance the program as outlined in 1923. Accordingly, $15 million of the $50 million bond issue authorized in 1920 was reissued in 1927, the tax on gasoline was increased to four cents per gallon, and the voters were asked to approve a $35 million non-revolving bond issue. This was done in 1928, and the new issue found a ready market. Because the program provided needed employment during the economic depression which began in 1929, road building was accelerated rather than retarded in that period.

Although the road-building program had advanced satisfactorily in 1933, it was reorganized in that year in the interest of economy and greater efficiency. The three-member commission was replaced by a single commissioner authorized to act in an executive capacity with the advice of an advisory commission of four members appointed by the governor. Perhaps even more important, practically all of the "county-district" roads were converted into a state "secondary system." The state thus became responsible for 31,166 miles of road, of which 4,560 miles were primary. The 1933 law also authorized the commissioner to designate municipal streets and bridges as a part of the primary state road system and to maintain them as such. Because the annual expenditures for the construction and maintenance of state secondary roads were only about one fifth of those made under the county court system, the change failed to win the approval of the farm element of the population, which insisted that it should have "more and better roads." Consequently the tax on gasoline was increased in 1937 to five cents per gallon, and in 1948 the voters approved a $50 million bond issue earmarked for secondary roads.

The demand for secondary roads was a primary factor in the decision of the 1953 legislature to investigate the state road commission. Moreover,

Courtesy West Virginia Industrial and Publicity Commission

Chelyan Interchange, West Virginia Turnpike

the situation led to unfavorable comparisons on the part of those who insisted that all state roads in West Virginia should be as good as those in Ohio, Pennsylvania, and Maryland. On the other hand, others saw in such comparisons the inadequacy of the available funds for a road building program in the Mountain State. This viewpoint was confirmed by the report of a statewide survey by the Automotive Foundation for the investigating committee which, in September, 1954, indicated that it would take more than a billion dollars to provide the state with an adequate road system.

Primary roads were either links in or themselves important historic highways. For instance, U. S. Route 50, the "George Washington Highway," followed the general course of the "Old Northwestern Turnpike" by way of Romney, Grafton, Clarksburg, and West Union to Parkersburg. Completion, in October, 1929, of that portion of this route in Maryland was celebrated as an event of more than local importance. For the first time in more than one hundred years, this route, which was first proposed by George Washington, came into its own as a competitor of U. S. Route 40, the Cumberland Road, to the northward.

Of the other east and west routes, U. S. Route 60, the "Midland Trail," was the most important. It followed closely the route of the former James River and Kanawha Turnpike and connected White Sulphur Springs and Huntington via Lewisburg, Ansted, and Charleston. At the north it was paralleled irregularly by U. S. Route 33, the "Blue and Gray Trail," which connected Mason City and Franklin by way of Ripley, Spencer, Glenville, Weston, Buckhannon, and Elkins. To the south of U. S. Route 60, U. S. Route 52 connected Huntington and Bluefield by way of Wayne, Williamson, and Welch.

Of greater importance perhaps were the routes crossing the state in general northern and southern directions. More than the east and west routes, they tended to break down sectional differences. Of these routes, U. S. Route 19, the "Stonewall Jackson Highway," was one of the most important. It connected Morgantown and Bluefield by way of Fairmont, Clarksburg, Weston, Sutton, Summersville, and Beckley. To the eastward it was paralleled by U. S. Route 119 from Morgantown via Grafton, Philippi, and Buckhannon, to Weston and thence westward through Glenville, Spencer, Charleston and Logan to Williamson. To the eastward was U. S. Route 219, the "Seneca Trail," which connected Princeton and Parsons by way of Union, Lewisburg, Marlinton, and Elkins.

Bridges were a factor in these routes. At the outset, small bridges were built by counties and municipalities, leaving the larger ones, such as that spanning the Ohio at Wheeling, to be built by private and corporate initiative. The toll feature of these structures having become objectionable, the state legislature created in 1929 a bridge commission authorized to purchase and build highway bridges with state funds. In the interest of economy and efficiency this commission was abolished in 1932, and its powers and duties were vested in the state road commission. Under this arrangement all the toll bridges in the state controlled by this commission, except the Steubenville, at Ohio Market Street, became toll-free, as the revenue accruing from their uses made that possible. A few toll-free bridges, including the Shadle, spanning the Kanawha at Point Pleasant, were built. By authorization of the legislature a toll bridge across the Kanawha sponsored by the city of Dunbar was opened to traffic in 1953; and that across the Ohio at Parkersburg sponsored by that city was opened to traffic on January 12, 1955.[5]

The West Virginia Turnpike, opened to traffic on November 8, 1954,

---

[5] Of the remaining toll bridges in West Virginia in 1955 all but one, the Kanawha Falls Bridge, were interstate and all were privately owned. The interstate toll bridges were the Benwood-Bellaire (Ohio), the Fort Gay-Louisa (Ky.), the Newell-East Liverpool (Ohio), the Green Springs-Old Town (Md.), and the Berkeley County-Washington County (Md.).

was heralded as "the Miracle of the Hills." A super-highway 88 miles long connecting Princeton and Charleston in generally northwesterly and southeasterly directions, it was completed at a total cost of $133,000,000. It was financed through the sale of toll bonds, and was constructed under the close supervision and control of the West Virginia Turnpike Commission, a state agency created by the 1947 legislature and constituted in 1949. The width and construction material were therefore matters of public interest. After much discussion in the state legislature and elsewhere, the commission, by authorization of the United States District Court, decided upon a two-lane highway of concrete construction designed for expansion to a forty-two foot highway, when and if the revenues from the Turnpike permit.

Starting at an elevation of 600 feet at the Charleston interchange, the Turnpike climbed an average of 43 feet per mile to 3,200 feet atop Flat Top Mountain, then descended to an elevation of 2,100 feet at Princeton. There were six interchanges en route and service areas at Bluestone, Beckley, and Morton. Of the three major bridges, the structure spanning the Kanawha was named "Yeager Bridge" for Lt. Col. Charles E. (Chuck) Yeager of Hamlin, Lincoln County, flying ace of World War II and the first person in the world to fly faster than the speed of sound. The Turnpike shortened the distance between Charleston and Princeton by 22 miles, and its dedication quickened interest in a proposed super highway connecting the North and the South. As of old, the possibilities revived sectional rivalries in the location of the northward extension in West Virginia.

Aviation

Because of topographical difficulties and the expense in constructing adequate landing fields, aviation developed slowly in West Virginia. The first airport was constructed in 1910 at Little Seven Mile, near Huntington, by Robert Shank who abandoned his enterprise and became a pilot in World War I. Although numerous "barnstorming" pilots landed in meadows to receive and discharge passengers on sightseeing rides in the 1920's, the state did not have regular aviation passenger service until October 12, 1933, when American Airlines, Inc. extended its Chicago-Cincinnati route to Washington, D. C., and established a passenger and refueling depot at Charleston. On June 10, following, that city was first provided with air mail service. The "pick-up" air mail service was however first used at Morgantown in 1939.

Although the 1931 legislature established a state bureau of aviation which became in 1937 the State Board of Aviation and, in 1947, the State

Official U.S. Air Force Photo

Lt. Col. Charles "Chuck" Yeager

Aeronautics Commission, no state appropriation was made for aeronautics before 1937. Prior thereto the financing was by the federal government: in 1933 through the Civil Works Administration; in 1934 through the Federal Emergency Relief Administration; and in 1935 through the Works Progress Administration. In 1940 Congress appropriated funds for the uses of the Civil Aeronautics Administration, and, in 1946, the Federal Airport Act made additional funds available for airport construction. As state-appropriated matching funds tended to increase meanwhile, a number of usable fields were provided. The Kanawha Airport near Charleston, opened on December 1, 1947, and completed in 1950 at a cost in excess of $9,000,000, and the Ohio County Airport were engineering masterpieces.[6]

In 1955 there were seven interstate airways communications stations in West Virginia at or near the following cities: Charleston, Martinsburg, Parkersburg, Wheeling, Morgantown, Elkins, and Princeton. They were served by planes of the American, Capital, Piedmont, Eastern, Trans-World, and Allegheny airlines. There were also thirty-three other licensed airports of sufficient size and condition to accommodate commercial aviation. Most of these ports were equipped for night landing. The entire sys-

[6] See Robert D. Stout, "Air Transportation Activity in West Virginia" (M.A. thesis, W.V.U., 1950).

tem was administered by an executive director under the supervision of a state commission of five members, including the state road commissioner.

COMMUNICATION

In colonial days and for sometime thereafter most communication was through itinerant traders, travelers, and the mail service. Post offices were first established at Morgantown and Wheeling in 1794. Many of the first roads were post roads over which mail was carried on horseback. On main-traveled routes, such as the Cumberland Road and the "Old Northwestern Turnpike," stage drivers vied with one another for mail carrying contracts. In some cases the winner was determined by his time record in a competitive contest for carrying the President's annual message to Congress between given points, such as Cumberland, Maryland, and Wheeling, (West) Virginia. In like manner keelboats and steamboats won contracts for carrying the "river mail." There was a river mail service between Wheeling and Cincinnati before either had regular mail service by post road.

The first use of the telegraph in present West Virginia was in 1847 at Wheeling, where a tap wire was run to a main line on the west side of the Ohio River. There were several telegraph lines in present West Virginia when the Civil War began. As suited the needs and the opportunities of the contending forces, these lines were used by them from time to time. This was notably true of the Baltimore and Ohio Telegraph.

Wheeling also had the first telephone line. It was installed by the Behrens brothers in 1879 for use between their two grocery stores. The next year an exchange was established in that city for the use of 52 subscribers. The first toll line in the state was established in 1883 to connect Wheeling and Pittsburgh. Between 1882 and 1895 exchanges were established in ten other West Virginia cities, and by 1910 there was a fairly extensive telephone system owned mostly by independent companies. A number of the independent companies were purchased and consolidated by the Southern Bell Company, which, in 1912, transferred its West Virginia properties to the Chesapeake and Potomac Telephone Company. The New York-St. Louis line, built in 1894, was the first long distance telephone line to traverse West Virginia. It followed closely the course of the Cumberland, or National Road. As of January 1, 1954, the Chesapeake and Potomac Telephone Company (a Bell System affiliate) had a capital investment of $81,367,191 in West Virginia. It had 121 central offices, 1,005,887 miles of lines, and 350,642 phones which processed about 1,900,-

000 calls daily. There were also 50,605 phones on connecting lines and 924 on non-connecting lines. And 21,751 state farms had telephones.

Licensed October 15, 1923, WSAZ, Huntington, was West Virginia's first radio station. WWVA, Wheeling, went on the air on December 13, 1926 followed in 1927 by Charleston's WCHS and by Bluefield's WHIS, by Fairmont's WMMN in 1928, and subsequently by a score or more others. There was also the "Personality Network" of fourteen stations covering the principal farm markets. The state department of public safety owned and operated a radio system that functioned through thirty-six police stations and a central clearings station at Charleston. Taxi-cab services in the cities also had radio systems. The police in some cities used radar techniques to determine the speed of motor vehicles.

West Virginia's first television station, WSAZ-TV, Huntington, went on the air on October 14, 1949. On August 6, 1952, its owners completed the installation of the world's first super power transmitter making it "the world's most powerful television station." On May 13, 1953, it became one of the first three members of the NBC color television network, and on July 3, 1953, it placed the first order by an independent television station for color originating television equipment. On March 5, 1954, it successfully televised the first network color television program in compatible color television in West Virginia.

WKNA-TV, Charleston, was the second television station in the state. It went on the air on October 12, 1953, and was followed twelve days later by WTRF-TV, Wheeling. In the presence of Senator M. M. Neely, Governor William C. Marland, former Representative Jennings Randolph, and others, WJPB-TV, Fairmont, went on the air, March 28, 1954. It was the first commercial outlet to use a vidicon camera chain. The installation received nation-wide publicity. With the expected use of more powerful transmitting equipment this station's Class "B" coverage was expected to include most of the Kanawha Valley. Including those at Oak Hill and Parkersburg, the state had six television outlets in 1955, and others were being projected.

Chapter XXVI

A Changing Agriculture

WITH AN AVERAGE ANNUAL RAINFALL of about 43 inches, a temperature range from 30 degrees below to 100 degrees above zero, a mean annual temperature of about 56 degrees, and an elevation range of 247 to 4,860 feet, West Virginia was adapted to a variety of crops, and accessibility to good markets made it profitable to produce them. In their natural state, enveloping forests retained moisture and soil fertility, even on hill and mountain sides, and the intervening valleys were "inexhaustibly fertile." In the course of fifty years scientific research taught valuable lessons in soil and moisture conservation. In 1950, agriculture was providing employment for about 85,000 West Virginians, and their products ranked fourth in value in the annual state production total.

In 1950 West Virginia contained 81,434 farms with a total acreage of 8,214,626, or 53.3 per cent of the grand total acreage. Farms averaged 100.9 acres in size, as compared with 194.8 for the United States, and their average value, including buildings, was $5,852, or $57.90 per acre, as compared with $7,917 and $40.63, respectively, for the country at large. There were 67,583 farms operated by their owners, 5,280 by part owners, 218 by managers, and 8,353, or 10.3 per cent, by tenants. Negroes owned 368 farms, and four were owned by other non-whites. A back-to-the-farm movement in 1930-1935 increased the total number of farms to 104,747 and the total farm population by about 114,000. Meanwhile the average farm was reduced in size to 90 acres.[1] As the state became industrialized workers tended to divide their time between industry and farming, thus developing a part-time type of farmer.

CROP AND ANIMAL HUSBANDRY, 1870-1900

Indian corn was the chief crop in 1870 but the yield per acre was tending to decrease due to excessive cropping and unscientific methods. Wheat,

[1] U. S. Census (1950), *Agriculture, Virginia and West Virginia,* pp. 376-379.

with an average yield of about ten bushels per acre, was next in importance, but threshing methods were primitive, seed was slovenly sown, and the growth was used largely as a protective crop for grasses. Buckwheat was a popular cereal well suited to mountain counties like Preston, which produced 95,000 bushels in 1860. Potatoes were grown in every part of the state but mostly for home consumption, except in a few counties bordering on or near navigable rivers. Because livestock was the basis of the state's economy, hay was of prime importance. The production for 1860 was about 156,000 tons, mostly timothy and blue grass. Because of the abolition of Negro slavery and declining soil fertility, tobacco culture declined following the Civil War. Sorghum, or Chinese sugar cane, first introduced in 1857, was converted into molasses in large quantities for home consumption. About 700,000 pounds of maple sugar and 70,000 gallons of maple syrup were produced in 1850. Although West Virginia butter sold at a premium in the Baltimore market, inadequate transportation limited the production to 4,760,000 pounds in 1860, and cheese-making was crude and limited almost entirely to home consumption. The supply of garden products and small fruits did not satisfy the local demand. Although most parts of the state were well adapted to apple and peach culture, the production of neither met the demand.[2]

"Stock farming" was aptly described by Joseph H. Diss Debar as "the pulsating artery of agricultural prosperity in West Virginia." "It is," he continued, "by her natural capacity in this line, and by no other standard, that her future *agricultural* development may be estimated with any degree of accuracy." In 1860, the livestock product of present West Virginia was valued at $12,382,680.[3] By 1870 this figure had increased by an estimated one fourth, and the livestock business was described as "never more flourishing."

As described by Diss Debar in the 1870's, West Virginia was still in the domestic stage of her economy and handicapped by lack of transportation. His emphasis upon the importance of stock farming was due not only to the natural advantages of the state for that form of economy, but also to the fact that "stock" then walked to market and to and from its food supplies. At that time and for sometime thereafter cattle were driven annually in large numbers from the South Branch and neighboring valleys over well marked "cattle trails" to the Allegheny uplands, particularly Caanan Valley, Tucker County, where they were left to graze during the spring and summer months. They were then driven direct to the Eastern markets or to their owners for wintering or further conditioning. Meanwhile the cattlemen had replenished their herds by new breed-

[2] Debar, *Hand Book* (1870), pp. 57-80; T. C. Atkeson, "Development of Agriculture in West Virginia," in J. M. Callahan, *Semi-Centennial History of West Virginia,* pp. 331-342.

[3] Debar, *Hand Book*, pp. 79, 94.

ings and by purchases of calves in Trans-Allegheny West Virginia and in southern Pennsylvania and southern Ohio. Some of the cattlemen were well known over large areas, and their annual visits were awaited as a means of disposing of surplus "springborn calves."

Deterioration of the state's agricultural economy during the decade of the 1870's was indicated by the fact that the estimated value of farm products was about $4,000,000 less in 1880 than in 1870. And that, too, despite the fact that the quantity had increased, as had also the number of farms, the acreage of improved land, and the value of farm land, the latter by $31,500,000. This condition was due to the combined effects of a number of forces: low assessments, inadequate transportation, railroad rate discriminations, prolonged effects of the economic depression of the 1870's, migrations to the Midwest, backwardness in the use of improved farm machinery, inadequate credit facilities, Midwest competition, the tightening grip of monopolies, and soil deterioration. By 1880 the once fertile Kanawha Valley had been impoverished by raising corn to feed hogs for Eastern and Cincinnati markets.

Aided by the current trend from domestic to industrial economy, by the consequent growth in population and improvements in marketing facilities, and by the betterment programs of the Patrons of Husbandry, the state's agriculture took a turn for the better toward the end of the century. The number of farms increased from 39,778, in 1870, to 92,874, in 1900. The total farm acreage for the respective years was 8,525,000 and 10,600,000, of which 2,580,254 and 5,498,980, respectively, were cultivated. Total values for all farm property for the respective years were $96,714,190 and $203,970,349, of which $17,175,000 and $30,570,000 were for livestock.

The 1930 census showed significant trends and changes. The number of farms had decreased to 82,640, but the total farm acreage had increased to 8,802,300 and the improved acreage to 6,538,800. The total value of all farm property was $411,787,500, of which $54,543,620 was for livestock. In size, the farms averaged 106.5 acres, and they had an average value of $4,138. They were operated by 66,573 owners, 15,347 tenants, and 721 managers, and 74.0 per cent of the grand total was mortgage free. There were 491 colored operators, of whom 373 were owners, 111 tenants, and seven managers.

The 1952 census data on crop and animal husbandry were equally informing. There were 988,000 tons of hay of all kinds, valued at $31,221,000, by far the most valuable crop; 8,405,000 bushels of corn at $14,793,000; 1,218,000 bushels of wheat at $2,485,000; 112,000 bushels of buckwheat at $185,000; 1,350,000 bushels of potatoes at $3,928,000; 4,653,000 pounds of tobacco at $2,592,225; 4,344,000 bushels of apples and peaches (574,000) valued at $4,361,000 (peaches, $581,000); 444,000 quarts of small fruit valued at $156,000. The products from 91,211 reporting farm gardens (1945), including both those used where produced and those sold, were valued at $13,260,000. The total cash agricultural income was $134,667,-000, of which $1,844,000 was government payments, $26,600,000 was for crops, and $106,223,000 was for livestock and livestock products. The value of products consumed on farms where produced was $45,648,000, making a gross farm income in 1952 of $180,315,000.

As predicted by Diss Debar in 1870, animal husbandry was the "pulsating artery" of the state's agricultural economy. In 1950 livestock values aggregated $80,663,000, of which, in round numbers, $6,667,000 was for 85,000 horses and colts; $60,000,000, including $15,000,000 for dairy products sold, was for 588,000 cattle and calves; $3,211,000 was for 197,000 hogs and pigs; and $7,200,000 was for 421,000 sheep and lambs, including wool. In 1952 there were 3,606,000 chickens; the gross annual income from poultry and poultry products was $40,622,000; the number of turkeys (1,799,000) and the number of broilers (19,075,000) represented an increase over the previous year of 38 and 10 per cent, respectively.

West Virginia's success in cattle raising was due largely to natural advantages and to the importation of purebreds, which began about 1870. Hereford was the favorite beef breed and constituted the bulk of the livestock herds. Other favorite beef breeds were the Shorthorn and the Aberdeen Angus. Jerseys were favored for dairy purposes, with Holsteins ranking next. Among pioneer breeders were S. W. Anderson of Greenbrier County, James K. Vandervort of Lewis County, L. D. Bond of Upshur County, C. F. Goss of Summers County, P. S. Lewis of Mason County, J. S. Arnold of Mineral County, and J. M. Ronson and Henry B. Davenport of Jefferson County. For years the Lawrence Reymann Memorial Farm of 937 acres, near Wardensville, Hardy County, was known for its prize-winning Ayrshires. Before being presented to the University, the Reymann Memorial Farm was used for raising replacement stock for the Hilltop Farms near Wheeling.

As predicted also by Diss Debar, horticulture, particularly apple culture, became an important business in West Virginia.[4] The Northern Panhandle early became an apple growing center for commercial purposes, mostly for trade with the Lower South by way of the Ohio and the Mississippi rivers. The Eastern Panhandle has been an apple growing area since pre-Revolutionary days. In 1955 it was the site of the famous Byrd Orchard of 1461 acres, said to be the largest in the world. The apple market for that area centered in the Martinsburg Apple Exchange, and Martinsburg and Inwood were storage and packing centers and the sites of apple processing plants. Favorite varieties were Stayman Winesap,

[4] See also W. H. Alderman, "Development of Horticulture in West Virginia," in Callahan, *Semi-Centennial History*, pp. 342-344.

Delicious, Golden Delicious, Rome Beauty, Grimes Golden, and York Imperial. Two of these, the Grimes Golden, first found on the farm of Thomas W. Grimes in Brooke County, and the Golden Delicious, bred from a seedling on the farm of A. H. Mullins in Clay County, were native to West Virginia. As the recognized center of the apple growing area of the Eastern Panhandle and neighboring areas, Winchester, Virginia, was the site of the annual "Apple Blossom Festival," witnessed by thousands of people. For sometime after the turn of the present century, apple culture declined due to attacks from insects and blight, but it was rehabilitated through scientific study and treatment, particularly the use of sprays.

MECHANIZATION

Mechanization was an important factor in the development of West Virginia agriculture.[5] The axe, the hoe, and the rake were the most useful tools that the pioneer settlers brought with them. Pitchforks, plows, harrows, and even riding saddles were improvised, many of them without metal, from native woods. For decades sleds, made entirely of wood, were the chief transportation devices. Corn, wheat, and buckwheat were converted into meal and flour by a wooden pestle applied in a bowl-shaped section of a tree. In time this device gave way to the hand-mill consisting of two cylindrical dressed stones placed one above the other and encased in a wooden frame. A beam was then attached to the upper stone in such a manner as to permit the use of man power to rotate it and crush the grain. In this manner was ground the meal out of which the first settlers made johnnycake, pone, and mush. In due time the hand-mill gave way to the tub-mill, which was rotated by water power. From it was developed the "up-and-down" sawmills and the grist mills which were in common use throughout West Virginia until well after the Civil War.

Harvesting and threshing processes had a similar evolution. Harvesting was first done by the use of the sickle which the "reaper" used in one hand to fell the grain in quantities large enough to be gripped by the other. The grips were then bound into sheaves which were shocked, stubble-end downward, in dozens. When dry, the sheaves were placed on a floor or on the dry hard earth and beaten with a flail until the grain was released from the chaff. The grains were then separated from the chaff by the aid of the wind and let fall on a sheet. In time these processes gave way to the grain cradle and the wind-mill, and still later horses and oxen were used to tread the grain from the chaff after the manner employed

5 West Va., *Hand Book* (1904), pp. 292-293; Atkeson, "Development of Agriculture," in Callahan, *Semi-Centennial History*, pp. 334-335.

in Palestine two thousand years ago. About 1840, the chaff-piler threshing machine came into use, and Rockaway Wind-Mills were used to separate the grain from the chaff. But these gave way in rather quick succession to the Down's Separator (1850) and the Ralston Patent Threshing and Cleaning Machine. The horse-powered reaper and the steam thresher did not come into general use in West Virginia until about 1880.

The plow and the harrow had a similar history. Prior to about 1850 most plows were wooden mould board devices, and grain-crops were "brushed-in" by the use of small tree-drags. Until shortly after the invention of the mowing machine in 1833, grass and other provender growths were cut by the scythe. Corn planters, hayrakes, and cultivators were not then in general use. With the establishment of iron furnaces and foundries, stoves came into general use, thus eliminating the cooking outfits which had adorned the open chimneys. The use of cooking stoves led to the use of coffee pots and kettles. As indicated in 1900 West Virginians spent $5,040,420 for farm utensils, implements, and household appliances in the years immediately preceding. By 1950 the wooden sled and its successor, the road wagon, had been all but eliminated by motor driven vehicles, of which there were then 21,000 trucks, 8,000 tractors, and 31,650 automobiles in use on West Virginia farms. Meanwhile all sorts of labor-saving devices, such as milk separators, patent milkers, patent feeders, improved harrows, and cultivators were being used to lighten the work of farmers and to increase the quantity and improve the quality of their products.

FARM ORGANIZATIONS

With the establishment of a lodge at Summit Point, Jefferson County, in June, 1873, the Patrons of Husbandry, generally known as the Grange, entered West Virginia. This was a secret, ritualistic organization having as its primary purpose the betterment of the social and economic conditions of farmers. The depressed economic condition of the period and the current appeal of secret societies contributed to the rapid growth of the new organization. By 1876 there were 378 lodges in the state with a total membership of 10,650, or about one eighth of the voting population.

From the outset the Grange urged the establishment of a state board of agriculture and instruction in agriculture in both the elementary and the secondary schools. The Grange was interested also in the establishment of a college of agriculture in the state in conformity with provisions of the Morrill Act of 1862. Branding the courses then offered in agriculture at the University as subterfuges, Grange leaders centered their hopes on the "Jefferson County Agricultural College," which was incorporated by the state legislature in January, 1875, with its office near Leetown. In 1877, they obtained legislative authorization to divert to the proposed college, "any public lands or land warrants, which have been, or which may hereafter be donated to the state (and not otherwise appropriated), for the purpose of endowing agricultural colleges."[6]

In 1877, Daniel B. Lucas, a leader in the movement to establish a college of agriculture in "an agricultural district of the state," was appointed to the University regency which, the following year, established a Chair of Law and Equity at the University which was proffered to Regent Lucas. Although he declined the appointment, he was instrumental in having it offered to his brother-in-law, St. George Tucker Brooke, who accepted it and thus ended, at least temporarily, efforts to detach the teaching of agriculture from the University. The movement was renewed from time to time thereafter, when the agricultural programs at the University did not satisfy the Grange. When, under the Smith-Lever Act of 1914 and the Smith-Hughes Act of 1917, they took a turn for the better, the Grange was in accord with the new programs and with the movement which resulted in the erection in 1917 of Oglebay Hall for the uses of the College of Agriculture.

The most abiding influences of the Grange were however fraternal and social. Through such influences it was a bridge between "Iron-headed Industrialists" of the Upper Ohio Valley and "Bourbon Democrats" of the Greenbrier Plateau, the South Branch Valley, and the Eastern Panhandle. More important still, its social gatherings were needed respites in the regimen of back-breaking and confining toil which featured the domestic system of economy. This was particularly true of those farm women who performed as Pomonas and Floras in Grange sponsored social affairs. With the coming of a new agriculture, facilitated by the Smith-Lever Act—particularly by its informal and non-secret extension services—the more formal, ritualistic Grange declined regionally in membership and influence. It was however functioning in 1955 with a membership of about 1,000.

The state board of agriculture, created by the legislature in 1891, was scarcely less active than the Grange. This was a four-member board, one for each congressional district, which functioned through an executive secretary with an office at the State Capital. The members held four meetings annually and helped to plan programs. Beginning in April, 1892, the board published the *West Virginia Bulletin,* which later became the *West Virginia Reporter* and still later the *Farm Review*. But the most

---

[6] W. D. Barns, "The Influence of the West Virginia Grange upon Public Agricultural Education of College Grade," in *West Virginia History,* IX, 128-155; ———, "The Influence of the West Virginia Grange upon the Public Education of Less than College Grade," in *West Virginia History,* X, 5-25.

important work of the board was organizing and conducting farmers' institutes which paved the way for the success of the later agricultural extension programs.

About 1912, state farmers began to organize bureaus, societies, and associations for the purpose of aiding extension work and to improve farm conditions generally. Representatives of these organizations who attended Farmers' Week at the University in January, 1918, became interested in a state-wide organization and as a result the State Farm Bureau was organized in the following March. As the right arm of the University Agricultural Extension Service, it enlarged the field formerly dominated by the State Grange and the state board of agriculture. In April, 1941, its Service Company, organized in October, 1925, under the cooperative marketing laws of West Virginia, was merged with the Southern States Cooperative. The Farm Bureau had a part in the organization of the West Virginia Livestock Marketing Association in 1924 and the West Virginia Wool Marketing Association in 1922. It sponsored the tax limitation amendment of 1932; a farm mutual insurance plan; and the West Virginia Congress of Agriculture, organized in 1946 to effect closer working relations among farm organizations. In 1954 the fifteen organizations comprising the Congress had a total membership of about 65,000, and there were 48 county farm bureaus with a total paid membership of about 10,000. Their press organ was the *West Virginia Farm News,* a monthly publication, founded in March, 1922, as the *West Virginia Farm Bureau News.* In 1955 it had a circulation of about 22,000.

Following the organization in 1907 of a boys' corn contest in Monroe County, more than 1,000 boys and girls were enrolled in corn clubs in West Virginia by 1911. During the next few years their projects were extended to include potatoes, pigs, chickens, and tomatoes, and their groups were generally called boys' and girls' agricultural clubs. Through contacts with the International Sunday School Association their director, William H. Kendrick, conceived the idea that their program could and should include more than improvement in farm and home practices. He therefore proposed a four-fold life program dealing with its mental, social, spiritual, and physical phases—with head, hand, heart, and health. As emblematic of these, the four-leaf clover, with an "H" on each leaf, was adopted and the groups were therefore called "4-H" clubs. In 1951 there were 1,548 4-H clubs in the state with a total membership of 31,478, including 4,880 Negro youth in 211 clubs.

Like the four-fold life program, the camping feature of the youth movement also had its origin in West Virginia. The possibilities of camping as a feature of the youth movement were first demonstrated in July, 1915, by J. Versus Shipman, county agricultural agent of Randolph County. Thereafter it became a permanent feature of the movement and culminated in a desire for a state 4-H camp. In 1920 a five-acre tract, embracing the boyhood home of Stonewall Jackson at Jackson's Mill in Lewis County was presented to the state for that purpose. The legislature accepted the gift and, in 1921, established a state 4-H camp at that point. By subsequent purchases the total acreage was increased to 523. A dining hall in the architecture of Mount Vernon was erected, a swimming pool

Jackson's Mill, Lewis County

built, and in the course of a few years thirteen counties erected cottages for the accommodation of the hundreds of boys and girls who assembled there from time to time for a course of training which was described in 1929 as the most equally balanced youth program in the United States. In 1951 fifty-two counties of the state owned 4-H camp sites, thirty of which were permanent, and on July 26, 1943, Washington Carver State 4-H Camp at Cliff Top, Fayette County, was dedicated as a camp site for Negro boys and girls. With fitting ceremony a marker was erected in August, 1940, along U. S. Route 219, a few miles south of Elkins, near the site of former Camp Good Luck, where the first youth camp was held.[7]

[7] W. Va. 4-H Clubs, "A Guide to Leaders" (1954), p. 47.

It is generally recognized as the first organized 4-H camp site in the United States.

The 4-H club had a worthy companion in the Future Farmers of America, a coordination of the several VoAg Clubs growing out of the Smith-Hughes Act of 1917. This organization was effected in Kansas City, Missouri, on November 20, 1928, and on April 20, following, the West Virginia organization was chartered.[8] The official organ of the organization since 1934 has been the *West Virginia FFA News*. The State Association, which was held annually at Jackson's Mill in July, was attended by about 500 FFA members, advisers, and visitors, and the awards —"State Farmer" and "Star Farmer"—attracted state-wide attention. In 1953 the FFA observed its twenty-fifth anniversary, at which a total white membership of 5,153, in 109 chapters, was reported. At the same time it was reported that the members had more than $1.2 million invested in farming enterprises and that they were sharing responsibility for the construction of the Youth Camp in Jackson County.

The West Virginia Future Homemakers of America was the corresponding organization for girls. It grew out of the annual conferences of Junior Homemaker representatives from high schools having homemaking departments, who met from 1930 through 1938, when the Junior Homemakers became the West Virginia Future Homemakers of America. In 1952 there were 119 chapters of this organization in the state with a total membership of 4,050. The New Farmers of America, the corresponding organization to the FFA, was organized in 1936 for Negro boys, and, in 1944, the first chapter of the New Homemakers of America, the corresponding organization to the Future Homemakers of America, was organized for Negro girls. In 1952 there were six chapters of New Farmers in the state with a total membership of 294, and 25 groups of New Homemakers with a total membership of 728.

EDUCATIONAL AND OFFICIAL PROGRAMS

Beginning in 1872 instruction in agriculture was offered in the University and in 1891 a "Chair of Agriculture" was established with Thomas C. Atkeson of Putnam County, president of the newly established state board of agriculture and a Granger, as the occupant. The program was somewhat premature, however, and after two years it was abolished. The courses in agriculture were assigned to the horticulturist of the Agricultural Experiment Station, which had been active since 1888 under di-

[8] W. A. Ross, *The Future Farmers of America Organization* (Baltimore, 1939); *West Va. Association Future Farmers of America*, "Souvenir Program" (1938).

rection of Dr. John A. Myers. Myers was elevated to the deanship of the newly created College of Agriculture in 1895, but the Grange refused to support his program, and, in 1897, Atkeson succeeded Myers as dean of the College of Agriculture. At the same time James H. Stewart, also of Putnam County and a Granger, was made director of the Agricultural Experiment Station. In cooperation with the College, the Station emphasized the teaching of agriculture on the secondary level and the promotion of farmers' institutes rather than scientific research and the publication of scientific bulletins.[9]

This regime was terminated between 1910 and 1912 by a series of important events in the history of West Virginia agriculture. Both Dean Atkeson and Director Stewart resigned in 1910 and were succeeded by E. Dwight Sanderson who, as director of the Experiment Station, made it again a research center and a source of useful bulletins. Courses of college grade were substituted for secondary offerings; and agricultural extension work, first organized in a small way in 1908, was given a definite organization, as of January 1, 1912, under the direction of C. R. Titlow.

Following the reorganization of 1910-1912, the College of Agriculture grew rapidly. In the course of ten years the faculty increased from five to fifty and the enrollment from 36 to 347, of whom 136 were in the home economics division. With a view to graduate work the curriculum was completely revised in 1931-32, giving students the choice of four courses: Agricultural economics, animal industry, plant industry, and teacher training in either vocational agriculture or home economics. A forestry curriculum was developed and, effective July 1, 1937, the name of the College was changed to the College of Agriculture, Forestry, and Home Economics. In addition to its regular collegiate and post-graduate courses, the College offered a series of annual short courses designed for farmers and others who wished to obtain instruction in certain fields.

With substantial increases in federal funds the Agricultural Experiment Station expanded its research program. In addition to work done on the campus and nearby University farms, the Station used the Reymann Memorial farms at Wardensville, Hardy County, for breeding experiments with Ayrshire cattle and for experiments in pasture improvement, erosion control, soil rebuilding, water conservation, crops, and poultry; a branch station of 150 acres established in 1921 at Point Pleasant for experiments in tobacco production and in the regional truck and field crops; a branch of 158 acres, established in 1930 near Kearneysville in Jefferson County for experimenting in fruit production, packing, and marketing; and the Reedsville Experiment Farm of 457 acres in Preston

[9] Barns, "Granger Influences," in *West Virginia History,* IX, 128-157; and *ibid.*, X, 5-25; Ambler, *History of Education,* p. 195.

County for experimentation with potatoes, small fruits, small grains, corn and legumes, livestock, and hillculture. Bulletins and biennial reports setting forth the results of experiments and investigations were published from time to time.

The Agricultural Extension Service was given legal status by the 1913 legislature, and the farmers' institute work of the defunct state board of agriculture was transferred to it. In 1914 the entire program became a part of a nation-wide system of instruction carried on by the state agricultural colleges in cooperation with the United States Department of Agriculture under authority of the Smith-Lever Act of that year. Under direction of county agents and with aid from regional chambers of commerce, national mail-order houses, and various farm groups, the state program was popularized through farmers' reading circles, correspondence courses, the college-sponsored farmers' week, and agricultural trains carrying education exhibits. As stated in 1932, "The purpose of Extension work is to increase the net income of the farm and home; to build up better homes and communities; to develop leadership among boys and girls, training them in the fundamental principles and practices of agriculture and homemaking as well as teaching them the importance of cooperation and team work.[10] The Extension Service program was further accelerated by an act of the 1915 legislature which authorized the use of public funds for the employment of county and home demonstration agents. As of September 1, 1954, the Service employed 50 county agents, three associate, and two assistant county agents; 38 home demonstration agents; and 34 4-H club agents. In addition to two Negro supervisors, the Service employed also 13 colored workers who served a total of 23 counties.

As a part of the reorganization program, the state legislature in 1911 created the office of state commissioner of agriculture, and soon thereafter the state board of agriculture voluntarily ceased to function. The law creating the new office required that the commissioner be a practical farmer with at least ten years' experience. He was to be a member of the executive department in the state government, and, beginning in 1912, was to be elected by the voters in the general election. As determined by the act of the 1913 legislature creating the University Agricultural Extension Service and prescribing the duties of the state commissioner of agriculture, all field educational work was assigned to the Extension Service of the University and all regulatory and control work in agriculture to the commissioner. In keeping with the provisions of the act the duties of his office were administered in 1955 through livestock, dairy and food, and poultry divisions; animal diseases and pest controls; fruit and vegetable inspections; farmers' marketing supervision; an agricultural

[10] Nat T. Frame, "Extension Work in Brief" (Manuscript, Morgantown, W. Va., 1933).

laboratory; and an agricultural statistics service. Since 1939 the commissioner has been chairman of the State Soil Conservation Committee, and in the course of forty years his staff personnel increased to about 100, some of whom were part-time employees of the U. S. Department of Agriculture.

In 1955 a number of West Virginia low-income farm families were receiving loans through the Farmers' Home Administration, formerly the Farm Security Administration. Beginning in 1937 these loans were made for the purchase and improvement of farms and later for the purchase of foundation herds with the hope and expectation of making the recipients self-supporting. From the outset the counties in which loans were made were selected by a state advisory committee which also exercised general supervisory control over the borrowers. For the year ending June 30, 1952, the loans totaled $1,715,989.

Under supervision of the U. S. Department of Agriculture progress had been made meanwhile in the control of tobacco and wheat production under acreage allotment and price support plans. Most of the counties of the southwestern part of the state were in the burley tobacco commercial area of the United States. As such their acreage was reduced from 6,400 in 1930 to 3,100 in 1953. The yield had meanwhile increased from 620 to 1,465 pounds per acre; the price per pound from 16.8 to 55.9 cents; and the total value of the product from $667,000 to $2,539,000. In the vote of April 28, 1955 for or against continuance of allotments and supports 95 per cent of the West Virginia commercial tobacco growers voted for continuance. All of the state was in the commercial wheat growing belt of the United States, but only a small part of the total area was affected. With a majority of the counties not participating, 80 per cent of the commercial wheat growers voted in 1954 for continuance of the allotment and support plans. Only two counties of the state, Jefferson and Berkeley, were in the commercial corn growing belt and subject to regulation and control.

Chapter XXVII

Patching the Constitution

1880-1955

THE MOST OBJECTIONABLE FEATURE of West Virginia's first constitution was the provision vesting local government in township mass meetings after the manner of New England. However compatible with Jeffersonian principles of democracy, the township system was ill-suited to large and sparsely settled counties. The township system was moreover "too Yankee" for some West Virginians. Over large areas it had not therefore been put into operation, even for the establishment of public free schools. To remedy this situation the constitution of 1872, the present one as amended, restored the county-magisterial form of government and vested responsibility for implementing it in county courts patterned after those used in Virginia to 1869.[1]

In its restored form the county court was composed of a president, elected by the voters of the county for a term of four years, and one and not more than two justices of the peace from each magisterial district. The court was required to hold six sessions annually: two for the consideration of police and fiscal matters and the others for the trial of cases, both criminal and civil, and the transaction of general business. When the court sat as a tax-levying body, the presence of a majority of all the justices of the county was required for a quorum. The court had original jurisdiction in all civil cases where the sum in controversy exceeded twenty dollars; in all cases of habeas corpus, quo warranto, mandamus, certiorari, and prohibition; in all suits in equity; and in all criminal cases below the

[1] John W. Mason, "The Origin and Development of the Judicial System of West Virginia," in Callahan, *Semi-Centennial History of West Virginia,* pp. 491-500; Burton A. Hall, "Amendments to the Constitution of West Virginia, 1872-1910" (M.A. thesis, West Va. Univ., 1938).

grade of felony. It was also the court of last appeal from decisions by the justices, and its rulings were final, except in cases involving land titles, personal liberties, and the validity of acts of the legislature and municipal ordinances. The court also had jurisdiction in matters of probate, guardianship, and apprenticeship; it was the custodian of county records and county property; it was responsible for road and bridge construction and maintenance and for poor relief administration; and it was the canvassing board of election returns.

Anticipating objections to the restored county courts, the constitution of 1872 required the legislature, upon the application of any county, to change its court to another tribunal exercising the same functions, provided such agency had been approved by a majority of the voters in an election. But these provisions did not conceal the fact that the constitution of 1872 was essentially a political document conceived, drafted, and ratified as the quickest possible way of ridding the state of a Radical regime that had tried to perpetuate itself by disfranchising former Confederates and enfranchising Negroes. The political character and purpose of the document was indicated furthermore by the fact that a complete set of officers, state and local, was elected at the same time it was ratified, August 22, 1872.

Efforts to implement the constitution of 1872 were followed at once by efforts to amend it with respect to the judicial powers of the county courts. Generally, it was claimed that the justices, though worthy men, were not trained in the law and were not capable of hearing cases involving legal questions. For the correction of these defects modified tribunals were established in 1879 by the legislature for Wood, Mason, Preston, and Pendleton counties, and the voters of Marion, Marshall, and Wetzel counties were authorized to vote on an act constituting those counties a judicial circuit with a judge elected for a term of eight years. Each magisterial district of these counties was to retain its justice of the peace, but the internal police and fiscal affairs, together with the probating of wills and canvassing of election returns, were vested in a county court composed of three commissioners elected for six-year terms, no two of them from the same magisterial district. It was thus evident that the state judicial system was on the verge of becoming hodge-podge. To prevent this the legislature on March 6, 1879 referred a constitutional amendment embodying the essential provisions of the Marion-Marshall-Wetzel county proposed circuit court bill. The amendment was ratified in 1880 by a vote of 57,941 for, to 34,270 against.

Comments incident to the ratification of the "Judicial System Amendment" indicate the low respect into which the county courts had fallen. The Parkersburg *Sentinel,* in sponsoring a change, described the county court as a "House of Refuge in every county for a lot of men too honest to steal, too lazy to work, but capable of making a good living out of the odd jobs and pickings, that are dispensed by the 'Peoples Court.'"[2] Generally, industrial areas favored the amendment and agricultural areas opposed it. Every county bordering on the Ohio River, except Wayne, voted for ratification, and every county touching Virginia, except Berkeley, voted against ratification.

THE COUNTY COURT

As reconstituted under the constitutional amendment of 1880 the county court was composed of three commissioners.[3] They were elected for six-year terms, no two of them from the same magisterial district. For that purpose the counties, as formerly, were divided into three and not more than ten districts. In their corporate capacity the county courts were vested with most of the non-judicial functions of the former justices-of-the-peace courts. They were required to hold four regular sessions each year at the courthouse, for which they were allowed two dollars per day for each day in actual attendance.

As the duties, particularly those having to do with the construction and maintenance of roads and bridges, increased, the compensation of county commissioners did not always attract capable persons. With a view to correcting this failure a constitutional amendment was voted on in 1908 and again in 1916, but in each instance it was decisively defeated. In response to insistent demands from industrialized counties for better services from their county courts, the legislature approved in 1921 an act authorizing increases in the pay of county commissioners; but the constitutionality of the act was questioned, and the 1923 legislature assigned the commissioners additional duties and retained their additional pay. Later they were relieved of most of their duties with respect to roads and bridges, but their increased compensation was retained and increased. A simultaneous movement to divest the county courts of jurisdiction in all matters of probate and vest them in circuit court judges, through a constitutional amendment, was rejected in 1930.

THE JUDICIARY

The changes of 1880 with respect to the county court necessitated a complete revision of the judiciary article of the state constitution. As thus

[2] Parkersburg *Sentinel*, Aug. 29, 30, 1879.

[3] The county court of Preston County was composed of eight commissioners; that of Jefferson County five.

revised, the judicial power of the state was vested in a supreme court of appeals, in circuit courts and the judges thereof, in such inferior courts as might be established by law, and in justices of the peace. For the purpose of electing justices of the peace each county was laid off into not less than three nor more than ten districts, each of which was required to elect one resident justice of the peace and two if its population exceeded twelve hundred. The civil jurisdiction of a justice was county-wide and extended to actions in which the sum claimed, exclusive of interest, did not exceed $300. The justices were also conservators of the peace and exercised such jurisdiction and powers in criminal cases as were prescribed by law. They also had the usual powers of a notary public. In the trial of suits at common law, where the value in controversy, exclusive of interest and costs, exceeded twenty dollars, they might, if requested by either party, use a jury of six persons, as authorized in 1880 by a constitutional amendment to the state bill of rights.

Despite the greatly curtailed powers and duties of justices of the peace, they were subjected to much criticism after 1880. After all, their decisions, when not appealed, were final and in a small way justices of the peace courts were as important as any court in the state. Because of the general lack of legal training of the justices, litigants tended to ignore them and to congest circuit court dockets. To correct this evil and the several others attributed to justices of the peace and their courts, the 1939 legislature referred a constitutional amendment authorizing the establishment of a summary court in each county of the state with jurisdiction in civil cases where the sum in controversy, exclusive of costs and interest, did not exceed $1,000. This amendment was rejected in 1940 by a vote of 133,256 for, to 300,979 against. Determining factors in this decision were the organized opposition of the justices of the peace and the popular demand for the retention of the "Peoples Court."

The state supreme court of appeals had meanwhile refused to hear cases tried by a jury in a justice's court coming to the higher court by ordinary appeal, and had ruled in 1885 that the only process of review was by writ of *certiorari*. To correct this ruling the 1887 legislature referred a constitutional amendment which was rejected in 1888 by a vote of 47,963 for, to 62,443 against. Twelve years later the court, in Richmond *v.* Henderson, reversed itself and permitted appeals, as in other cases, from justices' rulings in civil actions tried by six-men juries.[4]

Under the constitution as amended in 1880 circuit court judges were elected by the voters for eight-year terms and required to hold three terms of court annually in each county of their circuits instead of two as formerly. At the same time their salaries were reduced from $2,000 to $1,800 to offset the cost of increasing the number of circuits from nine to

[4] 48 *W. Va.*, 390.

thirteen. After 1888 the number of circuits was increased from time to time. In 1955 there were twenty-seven circuits and twenty-eight judges, the circuit comprising Hancock, Brooke, and Ohio counties having had, since 1872, two judges. But all had to wait for the ratification of the judicial amendment of 1902 for an increase in salary. Thereafter their salaries were fixed by law and varied as determined by the population of their respective circuits. Meanwhile, in certain counties circuit court judges had been relieved of some of their duties through the establishment of inferior courts presided over by judges whose salaries were also fixed by law and determined by their duties.

Except to reduce the salaries of the judges of the state supreme court of appeals from $2,250 to $2,200, the judicial amendment of 1880 made few changes in that body. It still consisted of four elected judges with twelve-year terms, and their duties were not changed. From time to time tie votes neutralized the effectiveness of the court, and efforts were made to increase the membership to five. This was accomplished in the judicial amendment of 1902, which also authorized the legislature to fix the salaries of the judges of the supreme court of appeals and of the circuit courts. In 1955 those of the highest court were increased from $12,500 to $17,500.

THE EXECUTIVE

Although the national trend was toward a short ballot, West Virginia voters in 1902 ratified a constitutional amendment making the secretary of state an elective official. The decision in this case was not due so much to political theories and practices as to a desire to rid the state of an objectionable fee system. At that time both the state auditor and the secretary of state were reputed to be collecting "enormous fees" which did not always find a way into the public treasury. As the secretary of state was an appointee of the governor, the practice subjected him to severe criticism, and leaders of the minority party insisted upon reform. When they became the leaders of the majority party, change with respect to the secretary of state's office could no longer be ignored.

Change in the method of electing the secretary of state was part of a program for abolition of the fee system on the state level. To that end the "State Officers Salary Amendment," approved in 1902, put all state elective officers on a salary basis determined by law, and they were forbidden to hold any other office during their terms of service. Moreover, they were forbidden to appropriate to their own use any fees, costs, perquisites of office, or other compensation and were required to pay all such receipts into the state treasury.

In 1918 the voters approved an amendment constituting the state elective officers a commission authorized to prepare the biennial budget for consideration of the legislature, and forbidding it to increase any item without the consent of the budgeting commission. As originally drafted by Governor John J. Cornwell in 1917, the "Budget Amendment" authorized the governor to draft the biennial budget, but interested persons succeeded in substituting the board of public works for the governor. The practice thus introduced was different from that in general use, and a movement was launched at once to change it; but amendments for that purpose were rejected in 1926, in 1930, and again in 1940, each time by increased majorities.

In 1934 the voters approved a "lame duck amendment" shifting the initial date of the beginning of the terms of the state elective officers from the fourth day of March, next after their election, to the first Monday after the second Wednesday of January. In this way their terms synchronized more nearly with regular legislative sessions, thus increasing their opportunities for leadership. But six years later the voters rejected an amendment legalizing the short ballot, then generally recognized as one of the most effective means of strengthening the executive. The proposed amendment would have restricted the state elective officers to governor, auditor, and attorney general and would have authorized the governor to appoint the heads of such executive departments as might be established by law. In 1930 the voters rejected an amendment authorizing the popular election of a lieutenant governor.

THE LEGISLATURE

Prior to the election of United States Senators by the voters, state legislatures wasted much time in electing them. Exasperated by such an experience, the legislature referred in 1887 an amendment to extend sessions from forty-five to sixty days; but there was no popular demand for such a change, and it was decisively defeated in 1888. In time however the increased volume and complexity of state legislation seemed to necessitate increased time and opportunity to study it. For that purpose a constitutional amendment was ratified in 1920 authorizing a sixty-day session in two parts: one of fifteen days, beginning on the second Wednesday in January of the odd years, for the introduction of bills; the other of forty-five days, following an interim of equal length, for the consideration and passage of bills. But the "cleft session" was a disappointment. The cost of printing bills and mailing them to legislators and their constituents tended to be prohibitive, as well as useless. The most noticeable result was an endless series of amendments intended to destroy rather than to improve measures. After six years trial the cleft session was accordingly discarded, but the sixty-day session was retained.

An amendment, approved in 1954, required the legislature to meet twice in each biennium for a possible sixty-day session in odd-numbered years for the consideration of budgetary and general legislation, and for thirty days in even-numbered years for the consideration of no other business than the annual budget bill, except such as may be stated in a proclamation issued by the governor at least ten days before the convening of the session, or such as the legislature by a two-thirds vote of the members might propose. The same amendment increased the salary of state legislators from $500 to $1,500, plus ten cents a mile for one round trip for any session going to and returning from the State Capital by the most direct route. If party caucuses for organizational purposes were held in advance of the first session, a like compensation was allowed for one round trip. Prior to 1920 the compensation had been a per diem allowance of four dollars and mileage for one round trip.

PROHIBITION

A post-Civil War prohibition movement in West Virginia was a continuation of that launched in pre-Civil War days by the Sons of Temperance. Like it, the later movement centered in the Protestant churches. When the politicians could dodge the "warriors of the Lord" no longer, they found a way out of their dilemma by referring the question to the people.[5] In the 1888 referendum the prohibition forces, though aggressive, were not well organized, and they lost by a vote of 41,668 for, to 76,555 against.

The West Virginia prohibitionists of the 1880's were successful however in effecting the enactment of a number of statutes, among them a law requiring the teaching of physiology and hygiene in the public free schools and placing emphasis on the alleged bad effects of alcohol and narcotics on the human body. Many boys and girls who came under the influence of this teaching became crusaders in the prohibition movement as it gained momentum in the early part of the present century. Generally, the rural population of the older settlement areas were prohibitionists, and the saloon, as then maintained in industrial areas, drove thousands of persons to prohibition, who otherwise would have favored temperance. As a result of these conditions the prohibition forces developed

[5] Hall, "Amendments," pp. 46-51; Ambler, *Willey*, pp. 27-28; E. Kidd Lockard, "The Temperance Movement in West Virginia," in *West Virginia History*, XVI, 273-313.

effective leadership, and a constitutional amendment forbidding the manufacture and sale of intoxicating liquors, except for medicinal and sacramental purposes, was ratified in 1912 by a vote of 164,945 for, to 72,603 against.

But "Prohibition did not prohibit"; and, in the absence of law enforcement, it tended instead to debauch the social life of the state. This was notably true in the cities. A prohibition amendment to the Federal Constitution having been repealed meanwhile, West Virginia voters in 1934 repealed their state prohibition amendment. The vote was 276,978 for, to 237,599 against. The repealing amendment authorized counties and municipalities to determine whether or not spiritous liquors would be made and sold within their bounds, but it reserved to the state a monopoly of the sales. As a result the 1935 legislature established the West Virginia Liquor Commission of three members who were required to give all their time to the discharge of their official duties.

ELECTIONS AND VOTERS

General elections of state and county officers and of members of the legislature, under the constitution of 1872, were held on the second Tuesday of October of the even years, a practice inherited from Virginia at a time when that state was "sovereign" and used various devices to demonstrate it. With a large sprinkling of state sovereignty-minded West Virginians in the electorate after 1872, it took a long time for them to find out that two elections (a state and a national) within a month of each other were confusing and expensive. The depression of the 1870's having stimulated interest in economy, the 1883 legislature asked the voters, through a constitutional amendment, to change the date of the general state election to that of the general national election. The "Election Amendment" was approved by a vote of 66,181 for, to 25,422 against.

In a partisan provision of the constitution of 1872 forbidding the legislature to "authorize or establish any board, or court of registration of voters," Democrats unwittingly laid a trap for their own political undoing. In sponsoring such a provision, they sought to prevent repetition of a practice used and abused by Radicals in the Reconstruction, but soon thereafter Negroes, foreigners, and others began to migrate to West Virginia in large numbers in search of employment in newly developed coal fields and manufacturing centers. For the most part the immigrants were Republicans who, in the absence of registration requirements, voted, sometimes repeatedly, before they had established themselves as residents.[6]

[6] James H. Jacobs, "The West Virginia Gubernatorial Election Contest, 1888-1890" (M.A. thesis, West Va. Univ., 1942).

As a result of these practices governors, irrespective of party affiliations, urged the enactment of remedial legislation. But their recommendations went unheeded, and West Virginia became notorious for her corrupt elections. Convinced of the futility of such practices and desirous of establishing a good name for their state, leaders of both major parties united in 1901 in support of a constitutional amendment requiring the legislature to enact "proper laws for the registration of all the qualified voters in this state." The amendment was ratified in 1902 by a vote of 55,196 for, to 27,379 against. Although the need was admittedly urgent, the legislature waited until 1908 to enact an effective registration law.

In 1907 Democratic legislators sponsored an amendment to disfranchise Negroes by restricting the suffrage to males who could read and write, and several attempts were made later to extend the suffrage to women. A constitutional amendment for that purpose was rejected in 1916 by a vote of 63,540 for, to 161,607 against. In March, 1920, the legislature was however convened in extra session to consider ratification of the Nineteenth Amendment to the Federal Constitution extending the suffrage, on a nation-wide basis, to women. Because West Virginia was the thirty-sixth state to ratify the Nineteenth Amendment, the action assured women throughout the entire United States the right to vote in the election of 1920. A constitutional amendment making the payment of a capitation tax a qualification for voting, was rejected in 1934 by a vote of 124,332 for, to 313,330 against.

TAXATION AND FINANCE

The Constitution of 1872 retained that provision of the Constitution of 1863 which required that "Taxation shall be equal and uniform throughout the State, and all property, both real and personal, shall be taxed in proportion to its value, to be ascertained as directed by law." The constitution further stated that, "No one species of property, from which a tax may be collected, shall be taxed higher than any other species of property of equal value." A provision, added in 1872 at the instance of the dominant agrarians, gave the legislature power to tax "all privileges and franchises of persons and corporations." The purpose of this provision was to make corporate wealth, particularly tax-exempt railroads, bear a part of the tax burden.

Prompted by a desire to protect agricultural interests in a depression of rare severity, the state legislature, in 1875, exempted certain farm products from taxation. For like reasons, it later exempted the products of mines, salt wells, and certain manufactured articles, and county assessors, imbued by the same motives, reduced assessment valuations. As a result of these acts total assessment valuations for the entire state were about $10,000,000 less in 1881 than in 1874, and administrative officers and legislators alike experienced difficulty in finding funds to meet a demand for increased government services.

To relieve this situation the governors, beginning in 1879, urged the legislature to repeal all tax exemption laws, because of their alleged illegality and the urgent need for revenue. When the legislature refused to comply with this request, Governor Jackson directed the state auditor to collect taxes from the Chesapeake and Ohio Railroad Company which claimed exemption under special acts and sought to nullify the directive order by a court injunction. In April, 1882, the state supreme court of appeals dissolved the restraining injunction, and held invalid all exemptions not specifically enumerated in the constitution.[7]

The situation being desperate, the auditor, at the instance of the governor and the attorney general, elected to use the ruling in the railroad case as a means of boosting state revenues. For that purpose Governor Jackson issued an assessment order directing compliance with the court ruling. Some assessors complied readily, but others refused and were generally sustained by the public. When the court sustained the auditor in a mandamus proceeding against the assessor of Brooke County but failed to pass specifically on the legality of the state exemption laws, the assessment order was, for some time, the most talked of topic in the entire state.

The legality of certain tax exemptions was raised from time to time to 1901, when the legislature authorized a complete revision of the tax system. Surprising as it may be, the revision was effected without a constitutional convention or even a constitutional amendment. The key statute, as enacted in 1904, simply required assessors to assess all property, both real and personal, at the true and actual value and permitted no exemptions, except for educational, religious, and like purposes. The county courts were, however, authorized to equalize and alter assessments, and the office of state tax commissioner was created and given supervisory control over the entire state tax system. The political control of the state having shifted meanwhile from Democrats to Republicans, the latter used their taxation reforms to justify their failure to call a constitutional convention, as repeatedly promised.

The only financial item dealt with under the changed political control by a constitutional amendment was that of 1902 restricting the school fund to $1,000,000 and diverting to the general school fund all moneys previously paid to the former, known thereafter as the "Irreducible School

---

[7] 19 *W. Va.,* 431, 435; W. P. Hubbard, "Development of Taxation and Finance," in Callahan, *Semi-Centennial History,* pp. 500-516.

Fund." The movement to limit it was prompted by its rapid growth, by apprehensions of possible misuse, and by increasing confidence in the ability of the future to care for itself. Those opposed to limitation were apprehensive regarding the uses of the diverted funds, and they were favorably impressed by the example of states having large permanent funds, notably Texas and Minnesota. The vote on ratification was 56,694 for, to 24,763 against.

Because the constitution forbade the state to contract a debt, except to meet casual deficits in its revenue and to redeem a previous liability (the Virginia Debt), amendments were necessary to finance road building and other programs calling for large expenditures. The good roads program calling for the expenditure of $50,000,000 was financed in that way in 1920, and, at the same time and in the same manner, the legislature was authorized to levy and collect annually a state tax to liquidate the debt within thirty years. For that purpose it authorized taxes on motor vehicles and motor fuels. The funds thus provided proving inadequate for the program, a bond issue of $35,000,000 was ratified in 1928, and like provision was made for its liquidation. To make sure that the revenues from motor vehicles and motor fuels would be used for that purpose, they were restricted to it by a constitutional amendment ratified in 1942.

Other bond issues involving large sums were those of 1948 for the construction of secondary roads and of 1950 for a veterans' bonus for West Virginia participants in World War I and World War II. The road bond issue was for $50,000,000 maturing in twenty-five years and secured by an authorized tax on real and personal property, provided other state funds were not available for the purpose. The veterans' bonus issue was not to exceed $90,000,000 and was to be paid within thirty years. Provision was made for its liquidation by imposing additional taxes on cigarettes, nonintoxicating beer, and bottled wines and liquors, as authorized in the bonus amendment.

The most important taxation amendment item was that of 1932 authorizing the classification of property and fixing maximum rates for each class. Similar amendments had been proposed previously and a long step was taken in that direction in 1926, when the legislature submitted a property qualification amendment fixing a maximum rate of fifty cents on each hundred dollars assessed value of money, notes, bonds, and accounts receivable. This amendment, which was rejected by the voters, was submitted in the belief that it would induce owners to report intangible property and thus increase the total tax receipts. The 1932 amendment was approved primarily to prevent real estate from being forfeited to the state in an economic depression of unprecedented severity and duration. It also afforded a much desired opportunity to shift a large portion of the tax burden from tangible to intangible property.

For this purpose the statute of 1904, requiring that all property should be assessed at its true and actual value, was retained and taxable property was divided into four classes: (I) All items covered in the property qualification amendment of 1926, all personal property employed exclusively in agriculture, and all products of agriculture, including livestock, owned by the producer; (II) All residential property, used and occupied by the owner, and farms occupied and cultivated by their owners or bona fide tenants; (III) All other property situated outside of municipalities; (IV) All other property situated within municipalities. The respective maximum rates were fifty cents; one dollar; one dollar and fifty cents; and two dollars; but, these rates might be increased by 50 per cent of the respective maximums, during three year periods, with the approval of 60 per cent of the voters participating in an election.

The first concern of the administration, elected at the time of the approval of the tax limitation and property classification amendment, was to implement it. It was generally expected that the amendment would be interpreted liberally so as to continue governmental functions, even in levying units having large fixed debts. Such an interpretation would have permitted levies, additional to maximums, to cover fixed debts, and the legislature acted accordingly. But the supreme court of appeals ruled that all payments from current revenues fell within the tax-limitation amendment. To comply with this ruling, the prescribed maximums were divided into two parts: 30 per cent for debt services incurred prior to the adoption of the tax limitation amendment, and 70 per cent for current operating expenses. As the result of debt liquidations, this allocation was changed in 1939 to 20 per cent for debt services and in 1949 to 10 per cent.

Because of the court's interpretation of the tax limitation amendment, practically all of the funds collected by the counties for schools were required for operation and maintenance. As the funds provided by the state were for the same purposes, school plants became outmoded and even dilapidated.[8] To remedy this situation the voters ratified in 1950 a school bond amendment which authorized county school districts to issue bonds, not exceeding 3 per cent of their total assessed valuations, for the erection of school buildings and for other school plants, which was interpreted to include play grounds, fairs, and recreation centers. With a view to further improvement of the situation, the 1955 legislature referred a constitutional amendment authorizing the voters of any county to approve a 100 per cent excess levy for schools for five years and to finance fixed debts by levies for that purpose instead of out of current expense levies, as required under the constitutional limitation amendment of 1932.

---

[8] Harold J. Shamberger and James H. Thompson, *The Operation of the Tax Limitation Amendment in West Virginia* (Morgantown, W. Va., 1950).

MISCELLANEOUS

All told, forty-eight proposed amendments to the present state constitution reached the referendum stage prior to 1955, and twenty-seven were ratified. Proposed amendments, ranging in scope all the way from exemptions on household and kitchen goods to complete revisions, were legion. There were twenty-seven in the 1905 legislature, about the same number in the 1907 session, and thirty-odd in the 1908 special session. Because of the general futility of such proposals, there were fewer of them in the succeeding years, and, more than formerly, they dealt with fundamentals.

Among amendments, not previously mentioned, which reached the approval stage was that of 1934 requiring the owner, or owners, of an individual interest in land to have evidence of such ownership recorded in the county in which it was located and to cause such land to be taxed, as required of every other owner, and subjecting it to forfeiture for failures in these matters. The "Garnishee Amendment," approved in 1936, made the salaries and wages of public officials and employees subject to the lawful claims of their creditors, in like manner as the salaries and wages of others. The "Home Rule Amendment," approved at the same time, authorized municipalities of 2,000 or more population either to change or to amend their charters in conformity with a uniform law. In 1938 stockholders in state banks were relieved of double liability for losses and the legislature was authorized to establish and regulate all such institutions. And in 1946 the state was authorized to contract with private owners for the planting, protection, and harvesting of forest lands for the conservation of natural resources.

CONVENTION PROPOSALS

Inasmuch as the Constitution of 1872 was largely a creation of conservatives, it is not strange that the creators did not welcome change. This is doubtless sufficient explanation of the fact that no constitutional amendments were referred to the voters between 1887 and 1901 and only six prior to 1887. Meanwhile, Republican leaders insisted upon sweeping changes and promised to effect them, if and when they were entrusted with that responsibility. But, when the Republicans gained control of the legislative and the executive branches of the state government in 1897, they divided into two groups in their plans for changes in the constitution. Under the leadership of Governor Atkinson, one group favored sweeping changes to be made by a constitutional convention; whereas the other, under the leadership of Senator Richard E. Fast of Monongalia County, favored a compromise objective to be attained through patchwork amendments. The compromise group prevailed in the 1897 legislature which created a bipartisan joint committee of ten delegates and six senators to make recommendations.

The joint committee report, as made to the 1899 legislature, proposed a number of constitutional amendments; but, control of the house of delegates having passed to the Democrats in 1899, they refused to concur. Under the leadership of John W. Davis of Harrison County, they proposed instead a constitutional convention, and he drafted a bill for that purpose. It was however primarily for political purposes and was not advanced to the passage stage. Thus all efforts to change the constitution in 1897 and 1899 were futile. When the 1901 session convened, the compromisers were in control and referred five amendments, all of which were, as previously indicated, ratified in 1902.

Except perhaps the voter registration amendment, none of those approved in 1902 were fundamental in nature, and the convention movement continued to grow in favor. The change from an agricultural to an industrial economy was far-reaching, even in the initial stage, and the governmental agencies and powers suited to the one were ill-suited to the other. This was especially true in matters pertaining to taxation and finance, transportation, welfare, and municipalities. Accordingly, the 1901 legislature created a state tax commission, authorized to make a thorough investigation and to report its findings. Its final report, made in October, 1902, emphasized the urgent need for a constitutional convention, and Governor White, in commenting upon the report, said, "It will require unlimited patching to get, at best, a worn-out garment with incongruous and ill-fitting patches, . . . to hold together a while longer."[9]

In presenting the report of the state tax commission to the 1903 legislature, Governor White emphasized the fact that it was "the deliberate judgment of this Commission that there can never be established in the State of West Virginia a fair and effective system of taxation under its present Constitution." The commission had therefore recommended the authorization of a constitutional convention to be assembled as quickly as possible. In support of this recommendation, Governor White said, "Our present State Constitution, . . . creaks in nearly every joint. We cannot have an efficient and ideal tax system under our present constitution with its limitations."[10]

As relief from the taxation situation was considered imperative, the leaders abandoned the convention solution and sought remedial legisla-

[9] Senate, *Journal* (1903), pp. 23-24.

[10] Albert B. White, *Public Addresses* (Charleston, 1905), pp. 118-119.

tion in a constitutional amendment dispensing with all direct taxes for state purposes, and in corrective statutes. The convention remedy was admittedly fraught with great uncertainty and with opposition from powerful corporate interests. Accordingly, the legislature was convened in extra session on July 26, 1904, to consider the altered program. It was in session eighteen days, in the course of which it rewrote the taxation code but failed to refer an amendment abolishing direct taxes for state purposes.

The tax reforms of the 1904 extra session were epoch making. Among other things, general license and inheritance taxes were increased; direct taxes for state purposes, including schools, were scaled down from thirty-five cents on the hundred dollars assessed valuation to five cents, effective in 1907; total county levies were restricted to a sixty cents maximum; and the office of state tax commissioner was created and given general supervision of the entire assessment and taxation system. Because it was then planned to eliminate by statute all direct taxes for state purposes, the proposed constitutional amendment was not referred to the voters.

The legislative reforms enacted in 1904 and in the years immediately following were so effective that leaders of the dominant party ceased to urge the need for a constitutional convention. Instead, they chose to stand on their record and generally justified it on the score of economy and the time elements and uncertainties involved in a constitutional convention. According to Governor Dawson, the recommendation of the tax commission for a constitutional convention had "unfortunately evoked the opposition of certain great interests and class of tax payers," but, fortunately, the constitution had been discovered to be more elastic than was generally supposed. While admitting the need for a new constitution, Governor Dawson saw no prospect of obtaining it in the near future. He therefore recommended that "the present one be amended in several particulars." Among other changes to be accomplished in this manner were abolition of all direct taxes for state purposes, provision for the forfeiture of land in the event of the repeal of all direct state taxes, ballot reform and a short ballot, lengthening the legislative sessions, increasing the compensation of members of the county courts, circuit court reorganization, and classification of property for purposes of taxation.

On the other hand, Governor Glasscock strongly urged the need for a constitutional convention. In support of it, he recalled the fact that the existing constitution was made for an infant state which had reached maturity, and insisted that it should not be hampered by an outmoded constitution. He urged especially the need for initiative and referendum provisions, as a means of enabling West Virginia to keep pace with her sister states in the Progressive era. His successor, Governor Hatfield, endorsed the initiative and referendum proposal but emphasized especially the need for a short ballot. He made no recommendation with respect to a constitutional convention.

But West Virginia did not keep pace with the Progressive movement, and the great interests, mentioned by Governor Dawson in 1909, continued to dominate state programs. In this they were unwittingly abetted by the resident institutions of higher learning in their failure to emphasize the social sciences. As a result, the citizenry remained indifferent to social and economic conditions and failed to develop that quality of leadership which featured the Progressive movement in the Midwest. Consequently, the state system of taxation tended to become chaotic; instead of the direct taxes for state purposes being abolished, they were increased; in response to regional demands for better roads and better schools, special legislative acts and administrative concessions produced a condition under which the total state and local tax rates on tangible property varied from $2.86 to $4.49 on the hundred dollars assessed valuation, entailing gross inequalities in the benefits; and the total average tax rate on tangible property increased from 65 cents in 1906, to $2.65 in 1929.[11]

By 1925 the state taxation situation had again become alarming. Legitimate requests for government expenditures could not be met with the available revenue, and the total taxes were increasing proportionately more rapidly than taxable property. In keeping with a practice, used increasingly since 1901, of referring difficult problems to commissions, the legislature in 1925 authorized the governor to appoint a tax commission instructed to investigate and report. But the members of this commission could not agree on a report, and, there being no expert talent available in any of the institutions of higher learning in the state, the commission employed Dr. Roy G. Blakey of the University of Minnesota to aid it in its assignment.

Blakey's report emphasized the urgent need for putting the general property tax on a sound and equitable basis; a reassessment of general property after the method proposed by Governor Dawson twenty years before; the separation of the sources of state and local revenues; the classification of all property for taxation purposes; and effective supervision of every phase of the taxation system. As these recommendations seemed to require a thorough revision of the state constitution, the 1929 legislature authorized and directed the governor to appoint a commission to study the constitution and to propose such amendments as would remove "existing barriers and restrictions" to the state's future development. If this approach did not contemplate the calling of a convention, it was not patch-work, because the commission was instructed to study the entire constitution and, if needed, to propose sweeping changes.

[11] Roy G. Blakey, *Report on Taxation in West Virginia* (Charleston, 1930), pp. 102-128; West Va. State Tax Com., *Report* (1927), pp. 183-184.

The constitution commission was appointed early in 1929 with D. J. F. Strother of Welch as chairman. In addition to short ballot, executive budget, and county treasurer amendments, it unanimously recommended a rather complete revision of the articles on the judiciary, county organization, taxation and finance, education, and land titles. Meanwhile the current difficulties confronting the legislators were alarming, some thought insurmountable. With a black depression cloud hanging over their constituents, it was no time to expose them to the delays and the uncertainties of sweeping constitutional changes. Prompt action being considered imperative, the legislature referred only one of the score or more proposed amendments. The favored amendment required the classification of all property for taxation purposes and limited the rates on each class.

Although there was much delay and uncertainty in implementing the property classification and tax limitation amendment as approved in 1932, the accompanying statutory reforms were so far-reaching and effective as again to stay the convention movement. The use, beginning in 1937, of interim legislative committees to study and draft legislation was also an arresting factor in that they enabled legislators to hurdle handicaps and restrictions that had plagued them during half a century. The most effective arresting influence was, however, the doubts and suspicions, ignorance and inertia of the voters. This, in turn, was due largely to the failure of party leaders to make issues out of constitutional questions, of the newspaper press to publicize them, and of institutions of higher learning to emphasize the social sciences.

In more recent years the constitutional handicaps and limitations on county and municipal governments, increased by the property classification and tax limitation amendment of 1932, all but made it impossible for local units to function. Then, too, changes were admittedly needed to increase the efficiency of the state executive, legislative, and judicial departments. The need for a short ballot, twice rejected; for an executive budget, thrice rejected; for increased pay for legislators, finally approved in 1954; and for a general reorganization of the judicial system, was pending in the minds of experienced legislators and informed citizens. Resolutions suggesting initial steps in a constitutional revision were introduced in the 1951, the 1953, and the 1955 legislatures, but they failed of approval. It was under these conditions that the University prepared to meet its responsibility in the matter by establishing a bureau for government research. Influenced by its publications[12] and his own experiences, Governor Patteson informed the 1951 legislature that "The matter of State Constitutional revision is most important."

---

[12] See Albert L. Sturm, *The Need for Constitutional Revision in West Virginia,* (Morgantown, W. Va., 1952).

Chapter XXVIII

The Republican Regime

1897-1933

EXCEPT DURING BRIEF INTERVALS, West Virginia was controlled by the Republicans from 1897 to 1933. However, owing to the fact that Republican administrations shared places on administrative boards and commissions with the Democratic minority, much of the partisanship of the previous period was dissipated. More than previously political spoils were economic, having to do with the location of state institutions, franchises for internal improvements, road-building projects, and industrial programs involving capital and labor. Moreover, during this period the voting public remained predominantly rural but increasingly eager to attract non-resident capital for the development of the state's natural resources. So in one election after another the electorate endorsed Republican policies, particularly the protective tariff and state economy programs.

Nor was there a voice in the state, with the possible exception of organized labor, disposed or prepared to challenge this regime. As under previous Democratic rule, institutions of higher learning, notably the University, were lacking in both the interest and the means sufficient to support a program of research in the social sciences. For example, it was not until 1929 that a department of political science was established in the University, while history, economics, and sociology were limited largely to introductory courses. Consequently, the Progressive movement, which successfully sponsored liberal expenditures and social reforms in other states, was effectively sidetracked in West Virginia. The changing situation did, however, necessitate reforms in taxation and administration, but these were, with few exceptions, effected under the compulsion of necessity rather than the promptings of reform.

THE ELKINS PHASE

From the day of his election to the Senate in 1895 to the hour of his death in 1911, Stephen B. Elkins "*was* the Republican party of West Virginia." Elkins conceived and perfected a political machine which put in leading strings Republican leaders great and small in every political unit of the state. West Virginia Representatives in Congress were known as "Elkins Orphans," and West Virginia governors were his lieutenants. Elkins also acted the role of the statesman. As chairman of the Senate Committee on Interstate Commerce, he sponsored a number of important acts, among them the Elkins Act of 1903, which increased the penalties on railroads and shippers for rebating; and he was joint author in 1910 of the Mann-Elkins Act further regulating railroad rates and rebates. Though a conservative, he used his influence to promote the tax and administrative reforms effected during the administrations of the Elkins-made governors.

Although overshadowed by their national leader, the governors of the Elkins phase left creditable records. The first of these was George Wesley Atkinson (June 29, 1845-April 4, 1925) of Kanawha County, who in 1896 defeated Cornelius C. Watts of the same county by a plurality of 12,070 votes. Born in Charleston, (West) Virginia, and educated at Ohio Wesleyan University, Atkinson was admitted to the bar at Charleston in 1875. Here he served as postmaster from 1870 to 1876 and as U. S. marshal in West Virginia from 1881 to 1885. Having moved to Wheeling, Atkinson won in 1888 a seat in the House of Representatives from the First West Virginia District, when a contest with his Democratic opponent, John O. Pendleton, was resolved in his favor. He was the author of a number of books on various phases of West Virginia life and history, and in 1876 and again in 1888, he was a lay delegate to the General Conference of the Methodist Episcopal Church. As governor, he continued the advertising program of West Virginia begun by his Democratic predecessors, Fleming and MacCorkle. Like them, he also urged the enactment of a more effective corrupt practice law, improvement of the public schools, and better highways.

Atkinson's successor in the executive chair was Albert Blakeslee White (Sept. 22, 1856-July 3, 1941) of Wood County, who defeated J. Homer Holt of Cabell County in the election of 1900 by 19,516 votes. Born in Cleveland, Ohio, and educated at Marietta College, White had been the owner and editor of a newspaper at Lafayette, Indiana, until 1883, when he acquired *The State Journal* at Parkersburg, which he edited until 1899. Meanwhile he had served as campaign manager for Senator Elkins and as collector of internal revenue for the West Virginia district. As governor, White set out to redeem his party's campaign pledges for constitutional revision and tax reform. The first was accomplished by amendments, while the legislature took the first steps toward the achievement of the second in 1901 when it authorized the appointment of a commission to make recommendations for reforms in the property assessment and taxation laws and to draft bills for that purpose.[1] The commission submitted its final report to the governor on October 20, 1902, but the legislature, which convened early in 1903, did not act on any of its recommendations.

Accordingly, Governor White convened the legislature in extra session on July 26, 1904. In an eighteen-day session that body created the office of state tax commissioner, which was given general supervisory control over county assessors who were required to assess all property, both real and personal, at its true and actual value. The legislature also fixed maximum levies on each $100 assessed valuation of general property for state and for school purposes;[2] it increased the charter tax on corporations and on inheritances and transfers; it directed the board of public works to assess public utilities; and it forbade any state institution, county court, or board of education to contract debts in excess of its available funds.

In one of the most hotly contested campaigns ever conducted in West Virginia, the Republicans carried their tax and assessment reform program to the people in 1904. Appropriately, their candidate for governor was William M. O. Dawson, the chief architect of the tax-reform program. With equal confidence the Democrats, led by Henry G. Davis, candidate for Vice-President, and John J. Cornwell, candidate for governor, assailed the Republican program as a scheme to increase taxes. The Republican candidates triumphed in the election, but the force of the Democratic arguments was indicated by the reduction of a normal Republican plurality of about 20,000 to 9,083. On the other hand, time was quick to sustain the position taken by the Republicans, for they truthfully claimed that the tax and assessment reforms of 1904, as amended in 1905, were "the most important and significant advance ever made in West Virginia finances."[3]

---

1 This commission was composed of William P. Hubbard (Chairman), Henry G. Davis, John K. Thompson, L. J. Williams, and John H. Holt. White, *Public Addresses,* pp. 110, 303, 341; and Callahan, *West Virginia,* I, 562.

2 From 1887 to 1902 the direct tax on general property for state purposes was 35 cents —25 cents for general state purposes and 10 cents for schools. Under the act of 1904, as modified in 1905, the respective rates were 16 cents and 8 cents for 1905, and 8 cents and 5 cents for 1906. Beginning with 1907 the general school fund was kept at $750,000 annually by transferring state funds, and the separate levies were abandoned. For 1907-1909 the state levy was 5 cents, for 1910, 4½ cents, for 1911, 2½ cents, and for 1912 one cent. West Virginia Tax Commission, *Report* (1927), pp. 28-29.

3 Callahan, *West Virginia,* I, 562, 616; ———, *Semi-Centennial History,* pp. 514-515.

Born at Bloomington, Maryland, William Mercer Owens Dawson (May 21, 1853-March 12, 1916) was educated in the public and private schools of that state. Soon after the Civil War he moved to Kingwood, West Virginia, and from 1873 to 1891 he was the owner and editor of the *Preston County Journal*. Prior to his election to the governorship, he had served as a state senator from 1881 to 1887; chairman of the Republican state executive committee from 1891 to 1904; clerk of the house of delegates in 1895; and as secretary of state since 1897.

Of the Dawson assessment program, it can further be said that in the ensuing seven years total assessment values increased from $278,879,659 to $1,148,006,006. The assessed value of realty was trebled and that of public utilities increased from $30,043,300 to $290,523,500.[4] To prevent local taxing units from imposing excessive burdens on the increased valuations the legislature fixed maximum rates for specific purposes. At the same time it increased the powers and duties of the state tax commissioner, and authorized the governor to remove assessors for refusal to comply with the law.

In 1909 the legislature authorized the governor to appoint a three-member bipartisan board of control charged with administrative supervision of the financial affairs of all state educational, charitable, penal and correctional institutions. Though not in line with the best administrative practices, the West Virginia board brought a large measure of efficiency into the business affairs of the state. First of all, it supplanted a myriad of smaller agencies and thus effected economies and improved the public service. Purchases of institutional supplies were made and construction contracts were let on a competitive basis; personal service costs of all kinds were carefully scrutinized and systematized; and, for the first time, supplies were purchased centrally and in large quantities.

Acts of 1909 created the office of county road engineer and a state road fund for distribution among the counties.[5] The engineers were appointed by the county courts and were required to be practical road builders. They functioned under orders from the county courts and the general supervision of the state road commissioner who that year displaced the state highway inspector. This arrangement produced a veritable storm of protests, and the office of state road commissioner was abolished in 1911; the state road fund was discontinued and complete responsibility for build-

---

[4] Items of these assessment valuations were, 1904: realty, $168,480,150; personal property, $80,356,209; and public utilities, $30,043,300; and 1911: realty, $619,156,816; personal property, $238,325,680; and public utilities, $290,523,510. In 1904 real property paid 60.1 per cent of the total taxes; personal property 29.3 per cent, and public utilities 10.6 per cent. The respective figures for 1912 were 54.8, 21.8, and 23.4 per cent. West Virginia Tax Commission, *Biennial Report,* 1911-12 and 1913-14.

[5] The state road fund was derived from a one cent direct tax on general property. West Virginia Tax Commission, *Report* (1927), p. 28.

ing and maintaining roads was returned to the county courts which were however permitted to retain their road engineers.

Other reforms concerned the removal of election abuses and the simplification of voting. A law was enacted, which provided that, beginning in 1908, identifying party emblems be placed on election ballots. Despite opposition from Democrats, who remembered all too well the proscriptive laws of Reconstruction days, the electorate had in 1902 approved a constitutional amendment which authorized the registration of voters, but Democrats were successful in preventing the enactment of a compulsory registration law before 1908. In 1904 they sponsored unsuccessfully an amendment making payment of a poll tax a prerequisite for voting.

If the Republican reform program enjoyed increasing favor in West Virginia, continued Republican success was endangered in 1908, when leaders of two rival factions of the party, Charles W. Swisher and Arnold C. Scherr, each claimed the nomination for governor. When it became apparent that neither would yield, Senator Elkins effected the withdrawal of both men. As the situation required the selection of a nominee who had not been identified with either of the rival factions, the choice went to William E. Glasscock, an Elkins attorney and lieutenant, then serving as collector of internal revenue for the West Virginia district.

Born in Monongalia County, (West) Virginia, and educated in the public schools and at West Virginia University, Governor Glasscock (December 13, 1862-April 12, 1925) had gone to Iowa at the age of eighteen, where he spent four years teaching school. Returning to his native county, he taught in the public schools until 1887, when he was elected county superintendent of free schools. He was next elected clerk of the circuit court of Monongalia County, a post he occupied without interruption until 1905, when he was appointed collector of internal revenue. Meanwhile, having studied law at West Virginia University, he was admitted to the bar in 1903. In the election of 1908, he defeated his Democratic opponent, Louis Bennett of Lewis County, by 12,133 votes. Glasscock's plurality may have been enhanced somewhat by the presence in the Democratic platform of a plank which called for the disfranchisement of Negroes and the use of "Jim Crow" cars on public conveyances.

If the Glasscock administration was launched smoothly, it was destined to enter difficult political and economic waters at midstream. In 1910 the Democrats gained control of the legislature and, by virtue of their majority on joint ballot, the right to choose a successor to Senator Nathan B. Scott, whose term expired in 1911. As if to complicate matters, Senator Stephen B. Elkins died three days after the legislature met, thereby creating an additional vacancy in the Senate from West Virginia. The battle over the choice of successors for these men attracted nation-wide attention. The probable election of two Democrats was a bitter pill for the

Republicans, and Republican members of the state senate connived with Major Charles D. Elliott, a lieutenant of the late Senator Elkins, to thwart it. For that purpose they tried to prevent the organization of the senate, which numbered fifteen Democrats and fifteen Republicans, by secreting themselves for days in the governor's office. Meanwhile, the Democratic state senators, acting under a provision of the state constitution which permitted them to meet from day to day and compel the attendance of other senators, directed James E. Mehen, their caucus nominee for sergeant-at-arms, to force his way into the governor's office and compel the attendance of at least one Republican senator. A clash was perhaps averted when Elliott sent his charges to Cincinnati, Ohio, where for two weeks they remained safe beyond West Virginia jurisdiction.[6]

With the contending forces thus widely separated, tempers soon cooled and the issue was settled by compromise. The Democrats were allowed to fill the two Senate vacancies, which was done by the election of William E. Chilton to succeed Nathan B. Scott for a full term, and Clarence W. Watson to complete the unexpired term of the late Senator Elkins which had been filled during the interim by his son, Davis Elkins, an appointee of Governor Glasscock. On the other hand the Republicans were allowed to organize the state senate, with Dr. Henry D. Hatfield of McDowell County as president.

Because of the wrangling over the vacant Senatorships, Governor Glasscock was handicapped in his efforts to go forward with his party program. Another distraction was the Paint Creek-Cabin Creek miners' strike which began in April, 1912, and continued beyond the limits of his administration. As outlined in a message to the legislature, the main points of his program called for the conservation of natural resources, restrictions upon legislative lobbying, amendments to the corrupt practice act, complete abolition of the "iniquitous" fee system, assurances to labor of "a just reward for honest effort," and a referendum on a proposed constitutional convention.

Governor Glasscock played a significant role in the Presidential election of 1912. In the campaign of 1908 the Republican plurality in West Virginia was only slightly less than in 1904, and William H. Taft received the electoral vote; but soon thereafter, the Republicans were rent into two factions by the Progressive movement which was then sweeping the country. To avert the destruction of his own party and his own leadership, former President Theodore Roosevelt entered the campaign for the nomination of the Republican party for President in 1912. Denied this, he launched the Progressive, or "Bull Moose" party, and accepted its nomination for the Presidency. Because Governor Glasscock and his associates

[6] G. W. Summers, "Pages from the Past," pp. 41-42.

urged Roosevelt to take this course, they joined the new party and named a set of Progressive electors, but made no nominations for state and county offices.

As a result of this adroit move, the Republicans recovered control of all branches of the state government in 1912. Henry D. Hatfield, the Republican candidate for governor, was elected over his Democratic opponent, William R. Thompson of Cabell County, by a plurality of 8,770 votes. In the same election, Woodrow Wilson, the Democratic candidate for President, received the electoral vote of the state by a plurality of 34,085 in a total vote of 268,828. William H. Taft, the Republican candidate, received 56,754; Roosevelt, the Progressive, 79,112; and Eugene V. Debs, the Socialist candidate, 15,248.

The legislature was Republican in 1913 in both branches, and, after a long contest, in which Davis Elkins, Isaac T. Mann, and William S. Edwards were the leading candidates for the Senatorship, Judge Nathan Goff, Jr. of the Fourth United States Circuit Court was chosen to a six-year term to succeed Senator Clarence W. Watson, Democrat. Exasperated by the persistence of corruption in the election of United States Senators, candidate Edwards rendered a distinct service in a bold effort to expose bribery. For that purpose he laid traps for bribe-seeking delegates, as a result of which five were indicted, tried, and sentenced to terms in the state penitentiary.

THE HATFIELD ADMINISTRATION

Although the Republicans were generally more interested in makin money than in social reforms, the impact of the Progressive movemen with its demand for better schools, improved highways, health protectio and security against the hazards of industrial employment, could not g unnoticed. Moreover, the people were becoming increasingly impatier with the inertia of local political units in supplying these services an were therefore looking to the state and even to the Federal Governmer for relief.

As the leader in the movement to correct this situation, Dr. Henry I Hatfield (b. September 15, 1875) earned a unique place in West Virgini history. Born on Mate Creek in present Mingo County, West Virgini and reared in the midst of an industrial development that was transforn ing southern West Virginia into a busy mining district, Hatfield studie medicine and specialized in surgery. He then became a railroad divisic surgeon and a mine physician in McDowell County with an office Eckman. As neither of Dr. Hatfield's employers would provide hospit facilities for the ever increasing number of persons who sought his services, he appealed to the state for help. The legislature responded with an appropriation of $20,000 in 1899, and a miner's hospital, the first in West Virginia, was built at Welch, McDowell County, and placed under Dr. Hatfield's supervision. In the course of his twelve years as superintendent, Dr. Hatfield supervised the care and treatment of about 18,000 patients.

In the meantime, Dr. Hatfield entered politics. Although reared in the states' rights political school, his father being a Confederate soldier, he accepted the Republican nomination for membership on the McDowell county court and was elected. As a member of the court, he stood for clean and efficient government, and he launched one of the first good roads movements in West Virginia. These activities led to his election to the state senate, of which he became the president in 1911. His fairness and ability as a presiding officer commended him to party leaders, and in 1912 he was elected governor.

Governor Hatfield's first concern was for a better health program. State agents were then providing vaccines upon request, but most of the state's population did not know when they were needed and many persons were opposed to their use. The state board of health, established in 1881, was little more than a licensing body which had just established its right to require a license of a practicing physician. The board gave little attention to public health and sanitation, despite the fact that typhoid, diphtheria, and other epidemics were common and tuberculosis continued to take its toll.

To deal with this situation the 1915 legislature established a state department of health. Consisting of a commissioner, a public health council, directors of divisions, and employees, the department was authorized to enforce the public health laws of the state, to make investigations and inquiries respecting sanitary and health conditions, to examine foods, drinks, and drugs offered for public consumption, and to make rules and regulations regarding a score or more matters affecting public health. In emergencies the state health department was authorized to take over the duties of local health officers, to establish quarantines, and to abate nuisances. In 1915 a hygienic laboratory was established at Morgantown (later moved to Charleston) for the purpose of implementing the state health program.

Other reforms were equally comprehensive. A state bureau of labor was established in 1915 and placed under the control of a commissioner who was required to visit and inspect annually every important factory in the state. For this purpose the commissioner was authorized to appoint two factory inspectors, and persons employing labor were required to assist him in making the authorized inspections. By an act of the same year, amending that of 1907, the number of mine inspectors was increased and their qualifications were prescribed; better safety precautions were required; the duties and qualifications of mine foremen were defined; and the employment of boys and girls under fourteen years of age in any coal mine was forbidden, as was also the employment of any boy between the ages of fourteen and sixteen at any time in which a free school was in session in the district in which the boy resided. A bipartisan public service commission of four members, established in 1913, was reduced to three members in 1915. These commissioners were appointed by the governor for six-year terms to act as "a court of the people" in dealing with public service corporations. By another act, administration of the workmen's compensation fund, established in 1913, was entrusted to a commissioner who was required to maintain an office at the state capitol. As this fund was primarily for the relief of persons injured in industrial accidents, industries were required to pay into it at rates determined by the hazards involved. To correct abuses in the matter of weights and measures under acts of 1882 and 1913, standards were prescribed in 1915, and the labor commissioner was made the enforcing officer.

In response to a growing interest in good roads, the legislature established in 1913 a state road bureau of four members, with the professor of railway and highway engineering in the University as temporary chairman, and the director of the experiment station at the University and two persons appointed by the governor as members. The bureau was given general supervision of road building programs; its chairman was required to give instruction in road building; county road engineers were required to visit his office once annually to receive instruction; and county courts were authorized to use prison labor. In anticipation of federal aid and to comply with an urgent demand, the 1917 legislature enacted the "Goo Roads Law." Under this law, the state road bureau became the state roa commission; roads were divided into two categories: Class A, intercounty and Class B, intracounty; the use of state and federal funds was restricte to Class A roads; county courts were required to make an additional lev of twenty-five cents on the assessed valuation of each $100 of general prop erty for use as a "county road fund" and fifteen cents additional on th property of each magisterial district for use as a "district road fund"; an the headquarters of the state road commission was moved from Morgan town to Charleston.

Other administrative functions were assigned to state elective officer notably the auditor. In 1913 enforcement of a speculative security act wa entrusted to him, and, for that purpose, he organized the "Blue Sky De partment." Other officers placed under his control were a state fire marsh charged with the duty of investigating the causes of fires and educatin the public in their prevention, and an insurance commissioner, authorize to regulate and approve companies doing business in the state.

To meet the increased cost of state services and the losses in revenue sustained with the advent of prohibition, the 1915 legislature directed the board of public works to increase the tax rate on real and personal property for state purposes from ten cents on the $100 assessed valuation, as fixed in 1913, to fourteen cents for 1915 and to maintain the levy at ten cents thereafter, if necessary. It was not necessary however, and the rate was nine cents each for 1916 and 1917, seven cents for 1918, and four cents for 1919-1920.[7] The inheritance tax was broadened, the tax on corporations was increased, and an annual excise tax of one-half of one per cent was levied on the net income from business done in the state. In 1917 this rate was increased by one fourth of one per cent and in 1919 by an equal figure.

Although there was much criticism of bosses and party nominating conventions, it was not until 1915 that the legislature passed a primary election law. The new law required that the nomination of all elective officers, except judges, candidates to fill vacancies, presidential electors, and officers in cities, towns and villages of less than 10,000 inhabitants, should be made by primary elections and under the same rules and regulations that applied to general elections. The reform was intended to destroy the "imperious and corrupt influence of bosses" who dominated the old-time nominating conventions. The direct primary achieved its purpose, but it was abused from time to time thereafter by pressure groups and the indifference of the electorate.

THE CORNWELL ADMINISTRATION

John Jacob Cornwell (July 11, 1867-September 8, 1954) was born on a Ritchie County farm near Pennsboro. In 1870 he moved with his parents to a farm in Hampshire County, where he grew to manhood. He was educated in the public schools and at Shepherd College and became a school teacher at the age of sixteen. He taught until 1890 when he and his brother, William B. Cornwell, purchased *The Hampshire Review,* a newspaper in which he retained an active interest until his death. He was admitted to the bar in 1898. He was a state senator from 1899 to 1905, a delegate to the Democratic National conventions in 1896, 1904, 1912, and 1924, and the unsuccessful candidate of his party for governor in 1904.

---

[7] Under an act of 1911 fixing the maximum rate at three cents for state purposes, the rate for 1911 was .025 cents and for 1912 one cent. Under the act of 1913 fixing the maximum rate for state purposes at ten cents, the levy for 1913 was six cents and for 1914 ten cents. West Virginia Tax Commission, *Report* (1927), p. 29.

He was however elected to that office in 1916 by a plurality of 2,755 over his Republican opponent, Judge Ira E. Robinson.[8]

The legislature elected in 1916 was Republican in both branches, and to "head off" an alleged movement for the "ruthless decapitation" of his Republican appointees, Governor Hatfield called it in session to take precautionary measures. Although Cornwell disavowed any intention of ruthlessness, the legislature placed narrow limits on the governor's removal powers. From time to time he protested against this use of "ripper" legislation, declaring that it "robbed the governor of the right to correct his own mistakes," but the limiting act was not repealed until 1921, when a Republican governor took office.

Despite the initial hostility, Governor Cornwell's relations with the legislature were generally amicable, and the 1919 session enacted a number of laws of more than passing importance. Among them was an act creating the Virginia Debt Sinking Fund and authorizing the board of public works to levy not more than ten cents on each $100 assessed valuation of general property, to meet the debt requirements. The mining code was strengthened, and the employment of children under fourteen years of age in any gainful occupation, except agriculture and domestic service, was forbidden, as was also the employment of minors under sixteen in any hazardous occupation or for night work. A state board of education was established and given control of the entire educational system, including the State University. At the same time the practice, adhered to since 1907, of supplementing the general school fund by appropriations to assure a total annual income of $750,000 was discontinued and certain state license and forfeiture taxes were channeled into it for that purpose. And the voters were asked to approve or reject three constitutional amendments: One, to make the seven state elective officials a state budgeting commission; another to extend the sessions of the state legislature to sixty days and to provide for a "cleft" session; and a third, to authorize a bond issue of $50,000,000 to "Help Pull West Virginia Out of the Mud." All were ratified by the voters.

Governor Cornwell was interested also in the enactment of a public safety law to cope with the crime and the industrial unrest which followed World War I. Instead of using the constituted police forces or the national guard or federal troops, he preferred "an all-time state department of public safety," like that of Pennsylvania and other neighboring states. The proposed bill for that purpose was bitterly opposed by organized labor, but the governor justified it on the ground that if enacted it would "eliminate the private guards and the company-paid deputy sheriffs and substitute real public officials in their stead." This reasoning

[8] Following his term as governor, Cornwell became chief of counsel for the Baltimore and Ohio Railroad Company.

prevailed and, on March 31, 1919, the public safety law was approved. This law created a state department headed by a superintendent, and provided for a force of four companies consisting of 200 officers and men. With the exception of the superintendent whose qualifications were defined by law, all were required to conform to rigid standards as determined by examinations.

THE MORGAN ADMINISTRATION

On March 4, 1921, Ephraim F. Morgan (January 16, 1869-January 15, 1949) became governor. Born in Marion County, West Virginia, he was educated at Fairmont State Normal School and West Virginia University. He began the practice of law at Fairmont in 1898 and was its city attorney in 1901-02. He was judge of the Marion County Intermediate Court from 1907 to 1912 and a member of the West Virginia Public Service Commission from 1915 to 1920. In 1920 he was elected governor by a majority of 57,565 votes over his Democratic opponent Arthur B. Koontz of Kanawha County. In this election 81,330 votes were cast for Samuel B. Montgomery of Preston County, candidate of the Non-Partisan party, and 2,695 for M. S. Holt, Socialist.

Prompted by requirements of the Virginia Debt, of a newly-launched road improvement program, and the construction of a new capitol building, both Governor Cornwell and Governor Morgan desired to improve the state's credit in the money market. For that purpose they sponsored the creation of a state sinking fund commission. This was accomplished by an act of the 1921 legislature vesting in such a commission mandatory authority to administer all the interest and sinking fund accounts of the counties, school districts, and municipalities in the state. This arrangement was effective, but not more so than the decision of the board of public works to continue the ten cent levy, additional to that for the Virginia Debt, on general property for state purposes. With a view to making this about-face of the dominant party acceptable, the state tax commissioner was given additional authority to regulate and control county assessments with instructions to eliminate "gross inequalities" then ranging from 23 to 87 per cent of true and actual values.[9] At the same time both the inheritance and the license taxes were broadened, and the annual excise tax on the net income of persons and corporations doing business in the state, enacted in 1915, was replaced by a privilege tax on persons and corporations. This tax was a varying percentage of the gross proceeds and was accordingly called "the gross sales tax."

[9] West Virginia Tax Commission, *Biennial Report* (1926-1927), p. ix.

The road laws were completely revised in 1921, and all primary roads were placed under the supervision and control of a state road commission consisting of three members appointed by the governor. Under the law, as amended, the commission was authorized to avail itself of federal funds for state road building programs; to define the offices, terms, salaries, qualifications, powers, and duties of its employees; to provide for the establishment of a state road system to connect all the county seats with the leading highways; to relieve political subdivisions of less than 2,500 population of responsibility for highway construction and maintenance; to classify and define public highways; and to sell $15 million in road bonds. Other acts of the Morgan administration had a direct bearing upon state finances. Most important of all was perhaps that of 1921 implementing the constitutional amendment of 1918 and making the board of public works a state budgeting commission. By authorization of the legislature Governor Morgan appointed in 1921 a commission, of which the governor was chairman, to build a "New Capitol" to replace the "Old Capitol" destroyed by a fire on January 3, 1921. And in 1925 a state board of finance composed of the governor (chairman), the auditor, and the treasurer, was authorized to designate active and inactive state funds and to select depository banks for each.

THE GORE ADMINISTRATION

Howard M. Gore (October 12, 1887-June 20, 1947), the first and only farmer governor of West Virginia, was born in Harrison County and educated in its public schools and at West Virginia University, where he majored in agriculture. A banker and the owner and operator of a hotel in Clarksburg, his chief interest was, however, in farming. During World War I he was assistant Food Administrator in West Virginia. He was a member of the state board of education from 1920 to 1925; Assistant Secretary of Agriculture of the United States from 1923 to 1924; and Secretary of Agriculture in President Coolidge's Cabinet from November, 1924, to March, 1925, when he became governor. He was elected by 303,587 votes, defeating Judge Jake Fisher, Democrat, of Braxton County, who received 261,846 votes, and J. W. Bosworth, Socialist, who received 7,218.

Gore's influence upon state agricultural programs was greater than the legislative acts of his administration indicated. In response to requests from rural areas for reforms in handling state funds, the board of public works was authorized to select a number of interest-paying depositories. A portion of the taxes collected from public utilities was returned to the counties and the municipalities from which they were derived. Efforts were made to control the corn borer. Agricultural credit and cooperative associations were legalized. In 1927, an additional road bond issue for $35,000,000 was submitted to the voters, and $15 million of the $50 million approved by them in 1920, were reissued. To aid the road building program the tax on gasoline was increased from two to three and one half cents per gallon in 1925 and to four cents in 1927.

Because the state then had no fixed program for taxation and the resulting unsettled economic conditions tended to discourage the proper development of industry, the legislature, in extra session (1925), requested the governor to appoint a bipartisan tax commission of seven members. In compliance, he appointed a commission which, with D. A. Burt of Ohio County, as chairman,[10] was active during a large part of 1926. Its report placed chief emphasis upon the mounting expenditures of local taxing units for roads and schools. On the theory that the people should have what they want the restraining recommendations of the tax commission went unheeded until the state was visited by an economic depression, when drastic action was taken.

THE CONLEY ADMINISTRATION

William G. Conley (January 8, 1866-October 21, 1940), who became governor in 1929, was born on a farm near Kingwood, Preston County, West Virginia, and educated in the public free schools and at West Virginia University. He was a school teacher from 1886 to 1891, when he was elected county superintendent of free schools of Preston County. While thus engaged he read law and was admitted to the bar. In 1893 he moved to Parsons, Tucker County, to practice his profession. He was prosecuting attorney of Tucker County from 1897 to 1905; mayor of Parsons from 1901 to 1903; and editor and part owner of *The Parsons Advocate* from 1896 to 1903, when he sold his Parsons interests and returned to Kingwood. He was mayor of Kingwood from 1906 to 1908. In May, 1908, he was appointed attorney general of West Virginia to fill a vacancy. In 1908 he was elected to that office and served to 1913. He was a member of the state board of education from 1924 to 1929. He was elected governor in 1928 on the Republican ticket by a vote of 345,909, to 296,673 for his Democratic opponent, J. Alfred Taylor of Fayette County.

Acts of the first legislature in the Conley administration were largely amendatory. The state labor commissioner was directed to establish and

10 The other members of this commission were E. H. Arnold, Elkins; John M. Crawford, Parkersburg; H. P. Henshaw, Bunker Hill; Virgil L. Highland, Clarksburg; J. Elwood Jones, Switchback; and J. H. Long, Huntington.

maintain a state public unemployment bureau. The state game, fish, and forestry code was completely revised, as were also the state banking code and the state prohibition law. The inheritance tax was amended, and the levy on general property was increased from fourteen to nineteen cents on the $100 assessed valuation.[11] The increase was to pay for the main unit of the New Capitol Building then under construction. New acts created a state library commission authorized to establish traveling libraries; a state bridge commission authorized to purchase, construct, and improve bridges; a state water commission authorized to regulate stream pollution; and a state athletic commission to regulate boxing, sparring, and wrestling. Still other acts established county boards of review and equalization of property assessments and regulated the drilling of oil and gas wells through coal strata. An extra session, convened in November, 1929, approved the report of a code commission, appointed in 1921, and provided for the publication, sale, and distribution of "the Revised Code," then regarded as one of the most important undertakings "that has ever confronted a West Virginia legislature."

When the 1931 legislature met in regular session, the state was experiencing a depression of unprecedented severity. For the protection of home owners, building and loan associations and credit unions were accordingly regulated; the duties of county commissioners of school lands were redefined; and county courts were authorized to provide old age pensions. When the depression failed to lift and conditions became desperate, the legislature was convened in extra session in July, 1932, to enact remedial legislation. Among measures for that purpose was a law authorizing banks and bank receivers to borrow from the Reconstruction Finance Corporation, a federal relief agency; taxes from 1933 were reduced to 85 per cent of what they had been in 1931 and permission was given to pay them semi-annually; county courts were authorized to transfer ten per cent of all regular funds under their control to their poor funds; counties of 100,000 population were authorized to employ trained investigators and dispense with the services of district supervisors of the poor; the time for the sale of real estate delinquent for the non-payment of taxes was extended three years; the compensation of sheriffs for feeding prisoners was fixed at forty-two cents per day for the unemployed and fifty-two cents for the employed; and the salaries of all public officials, including school teachers, were reduced by designated percentages for the fiscal year ending June 30, 1933. Finally, the voters were asked to approve or reject a constitutional amendment classifying taxable property and fixing maximum rates for each class.

---

[11] The ten cent levy for the Virginia Debt was used for 1919-1921, inclusive. For 1922 it was five cents and thereafter four cents to 1933. West Virginia Tax Commission, *Report* (1927), p. 30.

THE NATIONAL SCENE, 1897-1933

While new leaders were coming onto the political stage, the West Virginia Democracy attained a high point in 1904 with the nomination of Henry G. Davis, then popularly known as the "Grand Old Man of West Virginia," for the Vice Presidency as the running mate of Alton B. Parker. This nomination was not made, as was generally believed, primarily to tap a full pocketbook. It was rather a reward for a deserving Democrat of long standing. While other wealthy Democrats were deserting their party in 1896, Davis had remained loyal and active. Because he considered the money question secondary to the issue of imperialism, he was not only active but also enthusiastic in his support of Bryan in 1900.[12] Except among his immediate friends and associates, the "Grand Old Man" appeal was however unavailing, and Theodore Roosevelt carried West Virginia in 1904 by about 32,000 and Nathan B. Scott was returned to the Senate. Senator Elkins had been re-elected without Republican opposition in 1901.

During the early years of this period the outstanding Democratic leaders in West Virginia were John T. McGraw (January 12, 1856-April 29, 1920), William E. Chilton (March 17, 1858-November 7, 1939), and Clarence W. Watson (May 8, 1864-May 24, 1940). McGraw was a member of the State Executive Committee for sixteen years, national committeeman from 1896 to 1920, and the caucus nominee of his party for election to the Senate in 1899, 1901, 1905, and 1907. Generous to a fault, he was excelled by no Democrat in zeal and loyalty to his party. As previously indicated, the coveted Senatorial honor went to both Chilton and Watson in 1911. As a member of the Senate, Chilton led the fight for the confirmation of Associate Justice Brandeis and was an enthusiastic supporter of the League of Nations. He formulated and unsuccessfully sponsored a claim against the United States Government for compensation for Virginia and West Virginia for the Northwest Territory ceded to it by Virginia in 1784. Watson's desire to win the war and to continue in public service was reputed to have mellowed his attitude toward organized labor, as a result of which the operations of the Consolidation Coal Company, of which he was the key man from 1903 to 1928, were unionized in 1917. But such objectives could not withstand the vote appeal of the industrial Republicans, and both Chilton and Watson failed of re-election.

With the passing of Senator Elkins there was a dearth of leadership in the Republican party in West Virginia. Twenty years on the federal bench, together with the inertia of advancing years, incapacitated Senator

12 Pepper, *Davis,* pp. 287-288.

Goff for partisan activities. He was not therefore a candidate to succeed himself in 1918. By rallying remnants of his father's former organization Davis Elkins was elected in 1918 to succeed Senator Goff by 115,216 votes, to 97,711 for Clarence W. Watson, Democrat, and 2,288 for M. S. Holt, Socialist. With the same support Howard Sutherland, a former Elkins lieutenant and the first direct primary nominee of his party, had been elected in 1916 by 144,243 votes, to 138,585 for William E. Chilton, Democrat, and 4,881 for Gneiser, Socialist. Having successfully opposed Mrs. Izetta Jewel Brown in the 1922 primary, M. Mansfield Neely, Democrat, defeated Howard Sutherland, Republican for re-election. The vote was Neely, 198,853; Sutherland, 185,046; and M. S. Holt, Socialist, 4,895.

Shortly before 1924, Guy D. Goff, son of former Senator Goff, returned to West Virginia from a successful law practice in Milwaukee, Wisconsin, and, by reviving the Goff political traditions and taking advantage of a Republican trend, was that year elected to the Senate as the successor to Davis Elkins. The vote in the general election was Goff, Republican, 290,-004; William E. Chilton, Democrat, 271,809; and Holt, Socialist, 7,751. Despairing of effective leadership among the politicians, the Republicans drafted in 1928 Dr. Henry D. Hatfield who that year defeated Senator Neely for re-election by a vote of 327,266, to 317,620. Taking advantage of depression conditions, Neely came back in 1930 and won re-election by a vote of 342,437, to 209,427 for James Elwood Jones, Republican coal operator of McDowell County.

Of the several West Virginians who made the national political stage in this period, Neely was the only one who found a permanent place. The son of a country doctor, he was born in Doddridge County, West Virginia, and educated in the public schools and at West Virginia University. Having seen service as a volunteer in the Spanish-American War, he was admitted to the bar and in 1902 began the practice of his profession in Fairmont. He was mayor of Fairmont from 1908 to 1910; clerk of the West Virginia House of Delegates from 1911 to 1913; and a Representative in Congress from the First West Virginia District from 1913 to 1921. As a Representative, he was in complete accord with Woodrow Wilson's policies. As both a Representative and a Senator, he sponsored the objectives of organized labor.

West Virginians were meanwhile playing a part on the Presidential stage. As a national committeeman, John T. McGraw had a part in the nomination of Woodrow Wilson in 1912. In the Democratic National Convention of 1920, West Virginians first brought John W. Davis to the fore as a favorite son. From their advantageous position at the bottom of the voting list of states in 1924 they, under the leadership of Clement L. Shaver, national committeeman, controlled the balance of power and through persistence effected the nomination of Davis as the Democratic candidate for President. A gratifying feature of this accomplishment was the fact that their favorite won recognition as a result of sheer ability, as demonstrated in his ambassadorial record at the Court of St. James and in his numerous appearances before the United States Supreme Court in some of the most important cases ever heard by it. Such equipment was unavailing however against the "Normalcy" appeal of the "Golden

Courtesy Davis, Polk, Wardwell, Sunderland, and Kiendl, N.Y.

Ambassador John W. Davis

Twenties." Davis did not even carry West Virginia, her vote being Coolidge, Republican, 288,625; Davis, Democrat, 257,232. Because of the inability of the Progressive party to comply with a state law, it had no ticket in this election, and Robert M. LaFollette, its nominee for the Presidency, who ran on both the Socialist and the Farmer-Labor tickets, received 14,904 and 21,820 votes, respectively. In 1928 Alfred E. Smith received about 6,000 more votes in West Virginia than she gave Davis in 1924; but the industrial Republican appeal was still dominant, and Herbert Hoover, Republican, carried the state. The vote was Hoover, 375,551; Smith, 262,784.

Chapter XXIX

The Educational Advance 1910-1955

ELEMENTARY AND SECONDARY

BY 1910 TWO SCHOOLS OF THOUGHT had come to grips over the control of educational policy in West Virginia: the old school which clung to discipline and experience, and the new school which subscribed to the professional philosophies of Thorndike, Dewey, Giddings, Butler, Kilpatrick, and the McMurrays. The former claimed that teachers were born, the latter that they were made. One emphasized aptitude and scholarship; the other methods and professional training. Although the old school was still dominant in 1910, it stood on the defensive as it lost ground to the advancing forces of the new. Himself a former disciplinarian of the first order, Professor J. N. Deahl of the University, who had received a doctorate from Teachers College, Columbia University, was the acknowledged leader of the new educators.

Taking a cue from politics and business, the new school educators sought their objectives through control of administrative machinery. In line with this policy, the state board of education, the state board of regents, the state textbook commission, and the state vocational board were abolished in 1919 and their duties were assigned to a bipartisan state board of education of seven members, including the state superintendent of free schools. To assist this board in the performance of its duties with respect to Negroes, the act of 1919 authorized the creation of an advisory council composed of three resident Negroes, one of whom was state supervisor of Negro schools. As never before or since, the state board of education was manned and controlled by new school educators.

Accomplishments

The watchword of the new school educators was "progress." A number of surveys and studies were made on practically every phase of education; the school code was revised several times; and the certification of teachers was put on a training rather than a factual examination basis. In the interest of better administration and supervision, the 1921 legislature authorized the employment of district supervisors and an increase in the salaries of county superintendents who were also given free office space and clerical assistance. In 1915 counties, school districts, cities, and towns were authorized to establish and maintain public libraries, and, in 1917, the vocational education program was expanded.

The greatest progress was, however, in secondary education. In 1910, with only twelve fully accredited high schools in the entire state, Superintendent Morris P. Shawkey created a division of high schools in the state department of education. With aid from the Rockefeller Foundation, he employed L. L. Friend of the University to supervise the division under the slogan, "One Hundred District High Schools." Although temporarily halted by World War I, the high school movement gained momentum in the post-war years with the result that when Supervisor Friend resigned in 1925, there were 233 high schools in the state with a total enrollment of 32,075 and a total teaching staff of 1,733. The total cost had increased meanwhile from a mere pittance to $3,402,730 annually, and the old-time academies had all but ceased to function.

Throughout this period West Virginia ranked thirty-eighth among the states in educational progress. The educational needs of the state were set forth in 1929 in a four-volume report of a survey conducted by Dr. C. H. Judd of the University of Chicago and Dr. L. V. Cavins of the State Department of Education. In their report they summarized the chief needs as follows: (1) an appointive state board of education vested with entire control, both professional and financial, of the educational affairs of the state, and authorized to appoint a state superintendent of education to act as its professional adviser; (2) the retention of the existing magisterial district boards of education, with authority to direct the general affairs of the schools other than the selection of teachers; (3) the creation of a board in each county authorized to appoint a county superintendent to act as its official adviser; (4) higher qualifications for county superintendents and their assistants; (5) a closer guardianship of the personnel of teaching staffs, both at entrance into the profession and at the age of retirement; and (6) a county unit for purposes of taxation and general administration, with revenues supplemented by the state.[1]

[1] Charles H. Judd and L. V. Cavins, *Survey of Education in West Virginia,* 4 vols. (Charleston, 1928-29), I, 326-339.

The Depression and After

While educators and others were discussing the educational survey of 1927-29, the state was visited by a depression of unprecedented severity. In a short time taxable real estate, the major source of school revenue, was being forfeited to the state for the non-payment of taxes. Because of an insistent demand for economy, scores of schools were closed, school terms were shortened, and teachers went unpaid. To meet this situation the state superintendent of free schools recommended that the county be made the unit of administration, that a luxury tax be levied on cigarettes, chewing gum, and soft drinks, and that the state assume at least one-third of the total cost of elementary and secondary education. Nothing was done, however, and in 1932 the voters, chafing under the burden of an average tax rate of $2.65 on each hundred dollars assessed valuation of general property, approved a property classification and a tax limitation amendment. By this act the public schools were deprived of a large part of their revenue.

But, strangely enough, the tax limitation amendment paved the way for major reforms in the state educational system. The first of these was the adoption of the county as the unit of administration. By an act approved May 22, 1933, the legislature abolished 398 school districts, 54 of which were independent, and substituted in their stead 55 county units, each to be administered by a board of education consisting of five members. This board, which was charged with the signal duty of maintaining the schools of the county on a basis of equality, was required to maintain an office at the county seat. It was authorized to appoint and maintain a staff, including a county superintendent. The county unit system served as a compromise between those who supported local control on the one hand and those who favored state control on the other. All efforts to modify or disestablish it failed, and it attracted favorable attention throughout the country.

The tax limitation amendment of 1932 made necessary large grants of state aid to the counties. Prior to its ratification the magisterial and independent districts had borne about 95 per cent of the total expenditures for schools. Agreeable to a generally accepted belief that the entire net receipts from the tax levies under the amended constitution would be available for current uses, the legislature appropriated $5,500,000 for distribution among the fifty-five counties. This sum, together with expected additional funds and savings, was considered sufficient to finance a term of seven or eight months for 1933-34. But the state supreme court of appeals ruled that, under the tax limitation amendment, fixed indebtedness had to be paid from current revenues. To meet the resulting situation the legislature appropriated an additional $5,000,000 to be derived from an emergency consumers' sales tax. With the supplemental state aid thus provided and other funds, particularly the county tax collections, about $22,000,000 was available for 1933-34, and all the counties had a nine-month term.

In the interest of economy and a balanced budget the governor proposed a temporary reduction of the maximum school term and of teachers' salaries; but the state superintendent and the teacher lobby were persistent and the proposed reductions were not made. Instead, the state continued to guarantee an eight-month term, and teachers' salaries were restored to the 1921 basic scale. By continuing the emergency consumers' sales tax and carrying deficits from year to year, all counties maintained a nine-month term from 1934 to 1937, but the increased costs, due to increased salaries and higher maintenance, reduced the length of the term in a number of counties in the 1937-39 biennium. With an expanding economy, state treasury deficits were, however, turned to surpluses, and beginning in 1939, each county again had a nine-month term. Thereafter state aid to schools increased from biennium to biennium.

Since the adoption of the tax limitation amendment in 1932, leaders have disagreed sharply regarding the proper sources of public school revenues. One group favored placing chief dependence upon the state in the belief that funds thus derived were more readily available and more capable of distribution on an equitable basis. Another group insisted that dependence upon the state was fraught with hazards due to possible depressed economic conditions and to alleged bad effects on the democratic way of life. The 1953 "New Plan" for allocating state aid was based on the assumption that the counties should assume a larger portion of school costs. The teacher retirement act of 1939 being inadequate, that of 1941 made provision for the compulsory retirement on an actuarial basis of teachers under contract. The continuing teacher contract, effective July 1, 1940, was currently described as "well beyond first steps in the history of tenure legislation in other states." Provision for free textbooks for indigent children was made in 1939. Two years later the gradual introduction of free textbooks was authorized in all elementary grades; the nomination and election of school board members was put on a non-partisan basis; and county superintendents were authorized to nominate all teachers and assistant superintendents.

These changes led to great rejoicing among school people, particularly among officials of the West Virginia Education Association. A direct result was not only a noticeable increase in its membership but also in the West Virginia membership in the National Education Association. State interest in the national association had been stimulated by Dr. Joseph Rosier, president of Fairmont State Teachers College, who was elected in 1932 to the presidency. This interest was kept alive through the election to the same position in 1951 of Corma A. Mowrey of the administration staff of the West Virginia Education Association.

West Virginia public schools played a notable part in World War II, but their loyalty and effectiveness did not prevent an alarming teacher shortage, which necessitated the employment of thousands of emergency teachers. There was a decline in the average daily attendance totaling about 36,000 in 1943 as well as noticeable decadence of school plants due primarily to a shortage of building materials. Student and teacher morale was however unshaken. It was largely through their activities that the state exceeded its stamp sale quota for the purchase of jeeps by almost 200 per cent. With eleven chapters, West Virginia was in 1943 the Banner State in the Future Teachers of America Association. She was the third state to "go over the top" in the National Education Association War and Peace Fund drive of 1943. With 94 per cent oversubscribed, West Virginia led the states in the fifth war loan drive.

The Strayer Survey

Regardless of these achievements, post-war educational conditions were unwholesome. Thousands of youth of school age were not enrolled; juvenile delinquency had reached an alarming stage; use of emergency teachers had become general; and the administrative and financial services were out of gear. To deal with this situation the 1945 legislature constituted an interim committee, which employed Dr. George D. Strayer of Columbia University to conduct a survey. With a staff of experts to assist him, he began the survey in the summer of 1945 and submitted an elaborate report later in that year.

The Strayer Report contained full and explicit recommendations on administration, programs, and finances. The Report recommended that the state superintendent of free schools be appointed by the state board of education and that his duties be limited to service as professional adviser to and administrator for that board; that county superintendents of schools serve county boards of education in a similar capacity; that the county unit system be retained; that the counties be given a greater degree of autonomy; that care be taken to avoid the potential weaknesses of the county unit; and that control of the University by a board of governors be continued.

On the subject of programs, the Strayer Report said that West Virginia was developing in line with her needs. Segregation of the races complicated the process, as did also the prolonged use of the same textbooks in the elementary grades, the absence of free textbooks for all pupils, and limiting compulsory attendance to children between the ages of seven and fifteen. The Report therefore recommended greater latitude in the formulation of curriculums, the use of free textbooks, the establishment of compulsory kindergartens, and enactment of a law requiring the attendance of pupils from five to seventeen years of age. It also recommended the introduction of a program of adult education.

The Report also gave considerable space to vocational education, rehabilitation guidance, and practical arts education. Although the new educators had experienced much difficulty in getting the old school to accept vocational education as "a natural and inseparable part of American education," West Virginia accepted the provisions of the Smith-Hughes Act in 1917 and soon thereafter began to offer courses in vocational education on a larger scale. For some time these courses were restricted almost entirely to agriculture, home economics, and mining, but, with the enactment by Congress of supplemental legislation in the 1930's, the program was extended into other fields, notably teacher training, vocational guidance, and distributive education.

Undaunted by a shower of objections to the Strayer Report, the governor convened the legislature on March 18, 1946, and asked it to refer an amendment to the constitution for the purpose of implementing its recommendations. For that purpose the senate proposed an amendment which vested general supervision of the free schools and such colleges as the legislature might designate in a bipartisan state board of education composed of nine members appointed for overlapping terms of nine years. The amendment would also have abolished the elective office of state superintendent of free schools and substituted a state superintendent appointed by the state board of education and authorized to serve during its will and pleasure. The senate approved the amendment without debate, but it met formidable opposition in the house, which incorporated provisions retaining the state superintendent as a member of the state board of public works and requiring that "at least one member of the state board of education shall be of the Negro race." Although the proposed amendment was endorsed by a number of organizations, including the West Virginia Education Association, it was rejected by a vote of 174,156, to 181,606.

Undeterred by the voice of the people, the 1947 legislature accomplished in a measure by statute what it had failed to obtain by constitutional amendment. The most important statute was that creating a non-partisan state board of education of nine members, exclusive of the state superintendent of free schools, who was made a non-voting tenth member. This board was vested with complete control of the public free schools and the state supported institutions of higher learning, except the University and Potomac State College, which were left under control of the board of governors. Though the Strayer Report had indicated that state aid to the counties had reached the limit of sound economy and sound educational practices, the legislature appropriated for the 1947-49 biennium $69,443,-936 in state aid, an all-time high.

Beginning in 1945, the educational system of the state, except the University and Potomac State College, was administered by two semi-independent and not wholly cooperative agencies: the state board of education and the state department of education. The state board of education also directed the division of vocational rehabilitation and the division of vocational education. The latter, which was administered by a director, contained sub-divisions on vocational agriculture, home economics, business education, trade and industrial education, and guidance programs. Chief interest in the vocational agricultural program centered in the West Virginia Youth Camp, located near Ripley, Jackson County, which was completed in 1955 at a projected cost of $1,000,000 for buildings. This project was sponsored initially by the Future Farmers of America and the Future Homemakers of America (FFA-FHA) and was paid for by voluntary contributions. It was authorized by the 1947 legislature which vested responsibility for its operation in the state board of education.

In 1955 the state department of education functioned under direction of an elected superintendent who was a member of the state board of public works, and who in that capacity helped to draft the biennial budget for consideration of the legislature. He was also a member of the state board of school finance which allocated legislative appropriations of state aid to the counties and approved county school budgets. He was responsible for the following divisions: high schools, elementary schools, teacher certification, Negro schools, school transportation, school-plant planning, research and statistics, school lunch, and veterans' education and training.

For the year ending June 30, 1955, there were 3,234 elementary schools in the state with a total enrollment of 298,148, and 383 secondary schools (junior and senior) with a total enrollment of 159,600. Total receipts for the public free school program were $79,084,036, of which $47,435,828 was regular state aid; $1,671,701 was federal aid; and $28,679,100 were local collections. Public opinion was still sharply divided between those who would place greater initiative and financial responsibility on the counties, and those who would continue to rely largely on the state for leadership and financial aid. Generally, both schools of thought agreed that larger salaries must be paid teachers.

The decision of the United States Supreme Court of May 17, 1954, which declared segregation of white and colored children in the public free schools illegal, was not unexpected by most West Virginians, and it was generally accepted as the law of the land. In the course of the school year 1954-55, twelve counties were integrated; thirteen were partly integrated; eighteen waited for more definite instructions; eleven had no Negro pupils; and one rescinded an integration order when patrons protested it. Generally the public was indifferent to the desegregation program and school officials anticipated little difficulty in making it effective.

HIGHER EDUCATION

Though the University led the advance, the determining factor in the growth of higher education in West Virginia since 1910 was the expansion of the high school movement into every county of the state. From 1910 to 1955 the number of high schools increased from 12 to 382 (junior and senior). In the meantime there was a corresponding increase in total college enrollment from about 800 to almost 16,000, including part-time students. To meet the needs of a growing college population, the state normal schools were converted into state colleges, the preparatory departments in the denominational colleges and the state supported institutions of higher learning were abolished, and the curriculums and faculties, not to mention physical plants, of all were enlarged and expanded.

Between 1880 and 1927 the major educational policy had been to maintain a unified system with the University serving as the cap sheaf. But, with the establishment of a number of state colleges, sectional and personal rivalries became the controlling influences, and educators seriously considered suggestions for developing Marshall College as a co-ordinate institution with the University. The rivalries thus involved came to a head in a controversy over a proposed unifying and co-ordinating athletic program. As a result, friends of the University induced the legislature in 1927 to vest administrative control of the institution in an independent board.

Thereafter the state supported institutions of higher learning pursued somewhat independent courses. In fact, each tried to adapt its offerings to the needs of the region which it served and to justify its existence by such services. The results were described in 1945 in the Strayer Report:

> The State has assumed responsibility for a number and variety of higher institutions beyond the apparent disposition and policy of the State to provide for their adequate support and expected development.
>
> Under the conditions that have persisted for many years, each of these institutions is conducted without appreciable, cooperative reference to the plans and activities of the other state institutions; and, therefore, largely in accordance with its own immediate self-interest. Thus, at the present time there is, in this so-called "mountain locked" State, a group of higher institutions tending to be "mind locked," and serv-

ing principally local ends rather than meeting state needs. There exists no carefully drawn, state-wide pattern of higher education into which each institution may be economically fitted.[2]

Private and Denominational

Alderson-Broaddus College This institution was the result of a vote of the West Virginia Baptist Convention on October 15, 1931, merging Alderson Junior College at Alderson and Broaddus College at Philippi. The Junior College, prior to 1918 Alderson Baptist Academy and prior to 1911 Alderson Academy, was largely a creation of the pastors of the Greenbrier Baptist Church at Alderson and Emma C. Alderson, a resident of that town. The antecedents of the merged college were Broaddus Female College (1876-1885) and Broaddus College (1885-1894), each located in Clarksburg, and Broaddus Classical and Scientific Institute (1894-1918), located in Clarksburg to 1909 and at Philippi to 1918. In the latter year it again became Broaddus College and was developed to full college status in the course of the next seven years by its president, the Rev. Elkannah Hulley. Through co-operation with the Myers Clinic, Philippi, the College became in 1954 the center of a nurses' training school. Already it had pioneered the way for desegregation of the races on the undergraduate level.

Beckley College In 1955 this was an independent, non-profit, junior college with full accredited standing. It had its origin in a plan of a number of residents of Beckley to provide the youth of that town and its environs with educational opportunities at minimum cost. A primary purpose was also to train persons for immediate employment, but the college later offered pre-professional courses in medicine, law, engineering, dentistry, nursing, and dietetics. The institution was largely a creation of J. Lewis Bumgardner, president from September, 1933, to his death, September 10, 1944. On July 15, 1945, he was succeeded by Grover C. Hedrick. D. K. Shroyer, Director of Public Relations, was acting president during the interim.

Bethany College As a result of shifting from Southern to primarily Northern patronage following the Civil War, Bethany College was threatened with bankruptcy. The admission of women to full collegiate standing in 1877 did not remedy the situation, and following the death of President William H. Woolery in 1889, presidents followed each

[2] George D. Strayer, *A Report of a Survey of Public Education in the State of West Virginia* (Charleston, 1945), p. 641.

other in rapid succession to 1901, when Thomas E. Cramblet became president. With his accession, Bethany entered a new era, the watchword of which was "Build." The success was a stimulus to student life which reverted to its old time fervor for church (Christian or Disciples of Christ) and college as expressed in songs, publications, and the social life.[3]

President Cramblet was succeeded in 1919 by Cloyd Goodnight. During the "Golden Twenties," material things "flowed in upon him" increasing the endowment to almost $2,000,000 by 1932, date of his death. In 1927 the College was admitted to membership in the North Central Association of Colleges and Secondary Schools. In 1934 Dr. Wilbur H. Cramblet acceded to the presidency and retained it to September 1, 1952. His administration was featured by endowments bringing the total to more than $3,000,000; by a policy restricting the total annual enrollment to 600; by the erection of the Student Center and additional buildings, notably Alumni Field House completed in 1948; and by an adjusted program for the victory requirements of World War II. In 1953 Dr. Perry Epler Gresham, a widely known churchman, became the twelfth president.

Davis and Elkins College This institution evolved from a missionary effort launched shortly after the Civil War by the Lexington (Va.) Presbytery for the purpose of supplementing the meager educational facilities of a large mountain area of West Virginia. The movement met repeated failures until 1901, when Henry G. Davis and Stephen B. Elkins donated five acres of land and $30,000 on condition that the Lexington Presbytery raise a like sum. The condition was complied with, and Davis and Elkins College became the church school for resident West Virginia Presbyterians.

The College opened its doors to students on September 21, 1904 under the presidency of Dr. M. C. Allaben who was succeeded in 1910 by Dr. James E. Allen. During his presidency, which lasted for a quarter century, the college expanded on a wide front, with the result that the campus embraced 78 acres which were adorned by 150 species of shrubs and trees. Here the Mountain State Forest Festival has been held annually since 1937. The College participated in the Civil Aeronautics program from its inception and, following World War II, continued to offer instruction in aeronautics.

Greenbrier College This junior college for women occupies a choice site on a 26-acre tract in the suburbs of Lewisburg, Greenbrier County. Indirectly, it traced its beginnings to Lewisburg Academy (1812-1872) and directly to Lewisburg Female Institute (1875-1933). From 1892

[3] William K. Woolery, *Bethany Years; the Story of Old Bethany* (Huntington, W. Va., 1941), pp. 123-182.

to 1929 it was under the sponsorship of the Greenbrier Presbytery of the Presbyterian Church of the United States, but in the latter year, the Institute became involved in debt and was sold to a private corporation. It was chartered in 1933 as Greenbrier College, Inc. Under the presidency of the Rev. Dr. French W. Thompson from 1925 to 1952 the College adhered to "a sane and liberal arts type of education."

GREENBRIER MILITARY SCHOOL Like Greenbrier College, this junior college is located in Lewisburg and traced its origin to Lewisburg Academy. It was revived in 1890 as a secondary school for boys and was active thereafter as the Greenbrier Military Academy (1890-1897), Lee Military Academy (1897-1902), Greenbrier Presbyterial School (1902-1920), and Greenbrier Military School. Colonel H. B. Moore became the principal, and in 1908 military training was reintroduced. In 1920, Colonel Moore and his brothers purchased the school plant and changed its name to Greenbrier Military School. Under their management it grew in favor. In 1933 a freshmen year of arts and sciences work was added and in 1940 a sophomore year. In 1925 all the buildings, except the dormitory, were destroyed by fire, but they were soon replaced by modern structures of fine quality. In 1955, the curriculum was prescribed; college freshmen were required to take the "How to Study" course; and no person was granted a diploma who had not received credit for prescribed courses in the Bible. Greenbrier was a government honor school, and about 1,500 of its former students served in the armed forces in World War II. Of these, 48 were known casualties.

MORRIS HARVEY COLLEGE A number of efforts to establish an institution of higher learning under the sponsorship of the Western Virginia Conference of the Methodist Episcopal Church, South, having failed, Barboursville Seminary was opened in 1888 under its auspices. The Seminary was successful beyond expectations, and the following year it was placed under control of the sponsoring Church Conference and its name changed to Barboursville College. With a curriculum restricted almost entirely to secondary courses, the College was a struggling institution to 1901, when it received a substantial gift from Morris Harvey of Fayetteville, and its name changed to Morris Harvey College. In 1910 it ceased to grant degrees and reverted to junior college status for the purpose of training public school teachers. It retained this status to 1919 when it again returned to college grade. The change attracted a number of endowment gifts bringing the total to about $500,000, and a Greater Morris Harvey movement resulted in the construction of a number of substantial buildings.

Largely because of its building program, Morris Harvey College could not weather the financial depression which followed. Instead of purchasing the plant at the foreclosure sale, the trustees elected to approve a recommendation of President Leonard Riggleman that the College be moved to Charleston. On July 12, 1935, the sponsoring Church Conference approved this recommendation, and the College was moved to the former Capitol Annex Building. On September 1, 1939 it was officially merged with Kanawha Junior College which had been established in 1932.

Thanks to capable, inspired leadership and its many friends who never lost sight of its possibilities, Morris Harvey prospered in its new location. The College promptly accommodated itself to the Charleston community, which in turn responded with an annually increased number of students and increased financial aid. Following the unification of the three Methodist Churches in 1939, Morris Harvey College was operated by the West Virginia Conference of the Methodist Church; but, when all denominational aid was withdrawn on August 1, 1942, it became an independent institution. Soon thereafter the faculty personnel was increased to about one hundred; the College became a member of the Central Association of Colleges; and in 1945 it launched a building program. As expected, the goal was oversubscribed. The main building, bearing the legend "Morris Harvey," was dedicated in 1951. The new Morris Harvey campus, containing 22 acres, is located on the south side of the Kanawha, opposite the State Capitol.

SALEM COLLEGE In 1888, a group of Seventh Day Baptists established Salem Academy at Salem, Harrison County, which, on June 10, 1890, became Salem College. Like other colleges of the period, Salem maintained a normal department, but unlike most of them it retained an academic department to 1928. The presidency of Dr. Charles E. Clark (1908-1919) was a period of material improvements. He was succeeded by S. Orestes Bond who, at the time of his retirement in 1951, had seen more years of continuous service than any other president of a denominational institution for white students in West Virginia. President Bond's administration was featured by improvement and extension of the physical plant, by active participation in teacher training and extension work, and by strict adherence to chapel and other religious exercises. Beginning in 1934 the college offered pre-professional courses in law, medicine, engineering, dentistry, pharmacy, and agriculture. A number of Salem College graduates became prominent in the civil and political life of the state, and it had a creditable part in World War II.

Storer College Until 1900 Storer "College" at Harpers Ferry was known as "Storer Normal School," and its instruction was mostly on the elementary and secondary levels. Although situated in a region that had been divided by the slavery controversy, the school had early defied local differences and won the respect and support of whites and Negroes alike. This achievement was a product of the determination and exemplary conduct of N. C. Brackett, the first president. After a short interim, Brackett was succeeded in 1899, by Dr. H. T. McDonald who retained the presidency to July 1, 1944, when he brought to an end the longest period of continuous service of any college president in West Virginia. Beginning in 1875, the "College" pioneered the way in West Virginia by establishing a summer school. In 1909, John Brown's Fort, which had been exhibited at the Chicago Columbian Exposition, was dismantled and rebuilt on the Storer College campus for use as a museum. Since 1881, except a few years following 1892, the College was subsidized by the state for the primary purpose of training Negro school teachers. The first college degrees were awarded in 1942, but with the withdrawal of the state subsidy in 1955 the future of the institution became uncertain.

West Virginia Wesleyan College This institution, located at Buckhannon, Upshur County, was the culmination of a series of efforts, beginning in pre-Civil War days, to establish a Methodist Episcopal institution of higher learning in West Virginia. It is true, the Methodist influence was dominant during the early years of the University; but this relation was disturbed in 1875 by the dismissal of the Rev. Dr. Martin from the presidency, and the Methodists again considered the need for a seminary. Stimulated by the enthusiasm engendered by the celebration of the Centennial Anniversary of Methodism in America, and by reports that the Methodist Episcopal Church, South, would soon establish an institution of college rank in the State, the West Virginia Annual Conference of the Methodist Episcopal Church appointed trustees for the proposed seminary. In 1887, a tract of 43 acres was acquired in Buckhannon and on September 3, 1890 the Conference Seminary opened its doors to students under the presidency of the Rev. B. W. Hutchinson. It was a preparatory school to 1904, when it attained college rank as The Wesleyan University of West Virginia. Two years later the name was changed to West Virginia Wesleyan College. In the course of the next quarter century the endowment was increased, the plant enlarged, and its academic standards were raised. In 1927 the College was admitted to membership in the North Central Association of Colleges and Secondary Schools.[4]

---

[4] Thomas W. Haught, *West Virginia Wesleyan College* (Buckhannon, W. Va., 1940), p. 98.

An outstanding event in the history of West Virginia Wesleyan College was its designation on September 26, 1941, by the West Virginia Conference of the Methodist Church as its only institution of higher learning in West Virginia. The sponsoring Conference comprised a small part of Maryland and all of West Virginia, except Morgan, Berkeley, Jefferson, Brooke, and Hancock counties. The Conference, one of the largest in Methodism, was considered capable of maintaining one first-class institution of higher learning. In keeping with this program the campus was enlarged and a library, a music hall, a chapel, and dormitories for both women and men were completed in the post-World War II period.

Wheeling College Beginning in 1865 St. Vincent College, Wheeling, was active for seven years under the ownership and control of the Roman Catholic Church. Several young men who later became prominent in West Virginia were educated there. In the absence of parochial and public high schools in the Wheeling Diocese there was however no compelling need for this college. It was accordingly discontinued, and the Church directed its efforts toward the development of parochial and high schools. In 1954 there were 69 of these schools (17 secondary) with a total enrollment in excess of 11,000, and the Jesuit Fathers that year sponsored the establishment of Wheeling College at an estimated initial cost of about $2,000,000. The cornerstone of the main building of this institution was placed on November 21, 1954, with Archbishop John J. Swint, the founder, presiding. The initial operations were under direction of the president, the Very Rev. Lawrence R. McHugh, S.J.

Miscellaneous There were a number of movements to establish institutions of higher learning in the state in the post-Reconstruction period. Until about 1895, the United Brethren in Christ Church tried to develop the West Virginia Normal and Classical Academy, established in 1882 at Buckhannon, into Union College, and in the 1890's the Methodist Protestant Church sponsored a church school to be located in Harrisville, Ritchie County. Following these failures these churches joined in sponsoring Union College at Ravenswood, which was active for a short time under the presidency of Frank P. Harris. Beginning in 1900, Powhatan College, Charles Town, was active under the presidency of Dr. S. P. Hatton to 1913. In 1933 Linsly Institute became Linsly Institute of Technology. As such, it awarded college degrees to 1943, when it reverted to junior college status as a military school. Mason College of Music and Fine Arts, Charleston, founded in 1906 by Dr. W. S. Mason, became a degree granting institution.

State Supported Institutions

Bluefield State College This institution was established in 1895 as the Bluefield Colored Institute to provide the Negro population of the newly developed coal fields of the Bluefield area with educational and teacher training facilities. At the beginning, its curriculum was almost entirely elementary, but regular professional and academic courses were added in 1905. Ten years later the grades were abolished and the Institute became primarily a teacher training institution on the secondary level. In 1920 it became a junior college, and in 1928 it was authorized to offer college courses in a limited number of subjects. A class of eight was graduated in 1929, and the freshmen enrollment having increased meanwhile, the legislature in 1931 converted the Institute into a state teachers college. It was, however, little more than a normal school functioning on the secondary level. But the number of those graduating with bachelor's degrees increased annually, and in 1943 the institution was elevated to college status under the name Bluefield State College.

Concord College To appease disappointments incident to the failure of the eastern part of Mercer County to obtain the county seat, the state legislature passed an act in 1872 providing for the establishment of a Branch State Normal School at Concord Church. Three years later, May 10, 1875, the school opened its doors in an upright board structure built at a cost of $1,700. Captain James H. French, a former Confederate soldier and a graduate of Georgetown University, Washington, D. C., was the first principal.

The New Normal Building, a brick structure providing accommodations for about 300 students, was completed in 1896, yet for twenty years the institution remained a secondary school interested primarily in elementary teacher training. Subsequently a more advanced teacher training course was added, but in the absence of high schools, the Branch Normal found it necessary to devote its efforts almost exclusively to secondary work. The number of high schools having increased meanwhile, it was authorized in 1922 to grant the A.B. degree in education. In 1931 the official name was changed to Concord State Teachers College, and in the same year it was accredited by the North Central Association of Colleges and Secondary Schools. But the trend toward teacher training was soon reversed, and the college included in its offerings a variety of courses including physical education, health, home economics, journalism, commerce, and pre-professional subjects. The name was changed in 1943 to Concord College. This was followed by an enlargement of the physical plant. The Music Hall was completed in 1946, the Home Management House in 1947, and the Science Building in 1951.

FAIRMONT STATE COLLEGE From its beginnings in 1867 this institution was interested primarily in teacher training. It was a pet project of State Superintendent William R. White who, more than most administrators of his time, appreciated the need for trained teachers. His immediate successors, J. C. Gilchrist (1872-73) and the Rev. J. G. Blair (1873-78), were like-minded, and they, with timely aid from the Peabody Fund, succeeded in making the Fairmont Branch Normal primarily a teacher-training institution. Owing mainly to its teacher-training objective, not to mention the able leadership of Principal Blair, the Fairmont Branch Normal survived the meager legislative appropriations of the 1870's. As a result, Blair reported in 1878 that the school was "no longer an experiment but an established state institution."[5]

As a result of efforts, begun in the early 1880's, to unify the state educational system by making the state normals preparatory to the University, the Fairmont Branch lost some of its identity as a teacher-training institution. This was however regained when West Virginia trained educators of Peabody Normal College, Nashville, Tennessee, began to be effective in West Virginia. Soon all West Virginia state normals were aiming at "the real normal school idea," and in 1912 the normal school regents directed the head of each school to establish a full standard secondary course and a two-year professional course. In 1915 the Fairmont Branch was the only one of the six normal schools in the state that had attained that goal.

Joseph Rosier became head of the Fairmont Branch Normal in 1915, and it was he who developed it from a standard normal school into a teachers' college. The first degrees were awarded in 1924, and the name was changed to Fairmont State Teachers College in 1931. When the name was changed to Fairmont State College twelve years later, there were objections on the part of some of the faculty on the ground that there should be at least one first-class teachers' college in the state. Moreover, President Rosier, who had been on leave from January 13, 1941 to November 18, 1942, to fill an interim vacancy in the U. S. Senate, was reluctant to abandon his creation and its splendid traditions. His successor, George H. Hand, who had been trained in business administration and economics, put the new program into effect, but not without opposition.

Fairmont State College and its antecedents have occupied three sites: the Old Normal Building on Adams Street; Fairmont Avenue, dedicated in 1893; and the present site on a seventy-acre tract located in the northwest outskirts of the city, to which the Normal was moved in 1917. At that

[5] I. F. Boughter, ed., *Fairmont State Normal School: A History* (Fairmont, 1929), p. 36.

time there was only the Administration Building, but five years later Morrow Hall, a women's dormitory, was erected; Science Hall was built in 1929, the Industrial Arts building in 1946, and the Library building in 1952. The institution has worked in close cooperation with the nearby Fairmont General Hospital.

GLENVILLE STATE COLLEGE This institution traced its beginnings to a regional promotion enterprise. Because of its rural patronage and the comparative absence of high schools in the region it served, the Glenville Branch Normal, which opened its doors to students on January 14, 1873, did not readily develop into college status. For fifty years it was operated on the secondary level, and it was not until 1927 that teacher-training courses were considered important. The short-course diploma was discontinued in 1927 and the secondary in 1929. In 1930 the state board of education authorized the Glenville Normal to award A.B. degrees in education, and in 1931 its name was changed to Glenville State Teachers College. As elsewhere, there was an increasing demand for an expanded program, particularly for pre-professional courses, and the name was changed in 1943 to Glenville State College.[6]

MARSHALL COLLEGE Ownership of the building and site of former Marshall College having reverted to a private individual in the Civil War, they were purchased by Cabell County and presented to West Virginia to be used by her in establishing the West Virginia State Normal School at Marshall College, as authorized by a legislative act of February 27, 1867. But for the fact that the property was valued at from $15,000 to $20,000, the State Normal School would perhaps have been located at Fairmont, as recommended by William R. White, general superintendent of the state's public free schools, and there would perhaps have been only one such institution, as also recommended by Superintendent White.

Opened on June 15, 1869, the State Normal School remained an academy for more than a quarter century, and to 1886 it had a primary department. For the year 1873-74 the total enrollment, including that of the primary department, was only 70, and the Normal almost ceased to function in 1879-80 because of the failure of the legislature to provide adequate funds. There were no graduates in 1873. During the ensuing twenty years there were repeated suggestions that all or all but one or two of the normal schools should either be abolished or converted into secondary schools.

In 1896 administration of the State Normal School was vested in Lawrence J. Corbly who insisted that all the state normal schools should be retained and developed into first-class teachers' colleges. Upon his

[6] Patricia A. Jack, "History of Glenville State College" (M.A. thesis, West Virginia University, 1949).

recommendation a teacher training department was re-established in 1901, and Marshall began to plan for the new goal. In the process it never lost sight however of the possibility of developing both its teacher-training department and its academic department into colleges in keeping with its pre-Civil War ambitions. During the 1920's, and even later, some of its friends thought it should be expanded as a co-ordinate institution with the University. In support of this policy President Morris P. Shawkey (1923-1935) declared that the University, because of its conservatism and its location, was unable to serve the educational needs of the state and proposed that the other state supported institutions of higher learning share that responsibility.[7]

Marshall College pioneered the way in the evolution of the state normals to state colleges. Beginning in September, 1920, neither it nor the Fairmont Branch offered secondary work. In February of that year, Marshall was authorized to award A.B. degrees in education. Awarding of the first degrees in 1921 was celebrated by an elaborate pageant entitled, "The Unquenched Torch" which was participated in by more than 500 students and witnessed by about 3,000 friends of the College. Two years later Marshall was authorized to award regular A.B. degrees, and it at once established an Arts and Sciences College, in addition to a Teachers College. In 1928 Marshall College was accredited by the North Central Association of Colleges and Secondary Schools, and ten years later was authorized to award B.S. degrees in certain prescribed fields, as well as M.A. degrees in education, chemistry, history, psychology, political science, and sociology.

The Centennial Year (1937) was appropriately featured by inventories of the physical plant. Among the newer buildings were the Physical Education (1919), the James E. Morrow Library (1930), and the Shawkey Student Union (1933). In 1948 Science Hall was completed at a cost of about $2,000,000, while in 1953 the legislature appropriated $325,000 to be used toward the construction of a women's dormitory. The College had a creditable part in World War II, and it has earned nation-wide recognition in inter-collegiate athletics.

SHEPHERD COLLEGE Soon after the U. S. Supreme Court decided that Jefferson and Berkeley counties were a part of West Virginia, residents of those counties resolved to make the most of their situation from an educational standpoint. With that in mind, they organized the Classical and Scientific Institute which was incorporated on January 12, 1872 as

[7] Robert C. Toole, "The Early History of Marshall Academy 1837-1850," in *West Virginia History*, January, 1952; ———, "A History of Marshall College, 1850-1886, Part II," *loc. cit.*, October, 1952; ———, "A History of Marshall College, 1886-1915, Part III," *loc. cit.*, January, 1953.

Shepherd College.[8] Fifteen days later the state legislature approved an act establishing "a Branch of the State Normal . . . at the building known as Shepherd College," and, on April 12, 1873, the legislature placed the proposed branch normal under the jurisdiction and control of the regents of the State Normal School. In 1873 Shepherd opened its doors as a degree-granting institution and until 1884 it had collegiate, teacher-training, and academic departments.

Following 1884 the Normal at Shepherd College was little more than an academy but with the opening of the new century it, too, began to emphasize "the normal idea." Under the principalship and presidency (1909-1920) of Thomas C. Miller, the teacher-training department overshadowed all others, and, in 1931, the name of the institution was changed to Shepherd State Teachers College. Under the presidency of W. H. S. White (1920-1947) the curriculum was expanded, and in 1943 the institution again became just plain Shepherd College. Although similar changes were resented elsewhere, that at Shepherdstown was welcomed. The growth of the college was however retarded by an inadequate plant. For more than fifty years most of the buildings were improvised structures. The situation was improved by the erection of White Gymnasium in 1925, Snyder Hall in 1942, and by the expansion in 1943 of the athletic grounds, Fairfax Field.

West Liberty State College With $1,000 appropriated by the 1870 legislature and the aid of an executive committee chairmaned by General William B. Curtis of West Liberty, the West Liberty Branch Normal opened its doors to students on May 2, 1870 under the principalship of Felix H. Crago, a Civil War veteran.[9] For some time he was the only teacher, yet both teacher-training and academic courses were offered. A model school was established in 1872, and four years later prospective teachers were required to do practice teaching under observation; but chief emphasis was on the academic department which eclipsed the teacher training department. Primarily because of the location and inadequate living accommodations, attendance at the West Liberty Normal tended to be stationary. As a result, the State Survey of Education (1927-29) recommended that it be either abolished or moved to Wheeling. Already its friends had urged the construction of an adequate plant on a more suitable nearby site. With that in view a new site, about one half mile southwest of the old one, was acquired in 1915, and Shaw Hall, a women's dormitory named for Principal John C. Shaw (1908-1919) was dedicated in 1919.

---

[8] *Jefferson County Historical Society Magazine,* December, 1939; Millard K. Bushong, *History of Jefferson County, West Virginia* (Charles Town, W. Va., 1941), p. 222.

[9] C. C. Regier, ed., *West Liberty: Yesterday and Today* (Wheeling, 1939), pp. 86-93.

Although this structure was not readily accessible to the main campus, its beneficent effects could not be denied, and friends of the institution refused to agree that it was impossible to develop it into a first class teachers college. They insisted that all that was needed was an adequate physical plant, and they made common cause with other institutions to provide it. As a result, when a number of new buildings were erected on the new site the enrollment increased. In 1930 the Normal was authorized to award A.B. and B.S. degrees, and in 1931 its name was changed to West Liberty State Teachers College. Celebration of the centennial anniversary of the founding (1838) of West Liberty Academy in 1938 was a gala affair. In 1942 the College was admitted to membership in the North Central Association of Colleges and Secondary Schools, and in 1943 the name was changed to West Liberty State College.

More perhaps than any other of the state supported colleges, West Liberty launched new projects. The degree-granting Dental Hygiene School, opened in 1938, was the first in the state and one of the first fifteen in the United States; the Downtown Center, opened in Wheeling in 1938 for the use of extension classes, was successful, as was also the "West Liberty Plan," inaugurated in 1941. This plan divided the academic year into five periods of nine weeks each and required all seniors taking vocational courses to spend one of these periods in practical occupational experience.

West Virginia Institute of Technology It was primarily for political reasons that the state legislature, in February, 1895, established the Preparatory Branch of the University at Montgomery, Fayette County. Under the principalship of Josiah Keely, the school was successful, and Old Main Hall, completed in 1897, was enlarged; but, with the development of high schools in the Kanawha Valley, need for the Preparatory School was ended. Its location in a rapidly developing mining center suggested, however, its use as a center for short courses in mining. Funds were available for that purpose under the Smith-Hughes Act of 1917, and the legislature that year converted the Preparatory School into the West Virginia Trades School. It failed however to appropriate the required additional funds, and the establishment of a district high school in Montgomery seemed to put an end to the usefulness of the proposed trades school. Its principal resigned in despair, and his successor recommended that the legislature investigate the Trades School with a view to determining its future policy.

Taking advantage of a post-World War I condition fraught with an unprecedented demand for institution-earned credits, the principal of the Trades School advertised its ability to supply them, and the enrollment increased at once. The name was accordingly changed to New River

State School, and, in 1921, the principal became the president. In the face of a constitutional provision forbidding the establishment of additional normal schools, New River State School entered the field of teacher training, and to all intents and purposes became a normal school. Consequently, the Educational Survey of 1927-29 recommended that it either be abolished or converted into a public junior college to be administered by the local school authorities with the aid of a state subsidy. The president was strongly entrenched politically, and instead of accepting the recommendations of the Survey, the state board authorized the New River School to grant the baccalaureate degree. As a result, the appropriations were increased, the plant was enlarged, academic standards were raised, and the name was changed in 1931 to New River State College. In 1933 it was converted into a semi-technical institution, and Edward S. Maclin, professor of trade education in West Virginia University, was elected president. Because of accomplishments under the "Maclin Plan," alumni and others sponsored a movement to change the name to the West Virginia Institute of Technology. The 1941 legislature made the change, and the institution functioned thereafter with increasing favor. President Maclin was succeeded in 1945 by Menno J. Horsch who completed the transition from a teacher-training to a technical institution. The "Tech Golden Anniversary" which was celebrated on May 10-11, 1946, was featured by the conferring of three honorary degrees.

West Virginia State College Under the Second Morrill Act (1890) West Virginia was allotted $15,000 annually for each of the ten ensuing years, conditioned on her providing for the instruction of colored students in agriculture and mechanic arts. The grant was accepted, and on March 17, 1891, a portion of it was allocated for the education of Negroes, as required. At the same time the West Virginia Colored Institute was established and an appropriation was made for the purchase of a suitable site. For that purpose a thirty-one acre tract at Farm, now Institute, Kanawha County, was acquired, and a two-story building named Fleming Hall was dedicated in April, 1892. On May 3, 1893, an experimental term of the Institute was opened with twenty students under the principalship of J. E. Campbell.

The Institute first directed its efforts to the training of school teachers, but it admitted students of all ages—"the man of forty or fifty years undertaking elementary studies along with a child in his teens." Byrd Prillerman, born a slave in Franklin County, Virginia, became principal in October, 1909, and it was he who gave the Institute a working philosophy—that manual labor is honorable and necessary. In 1915 the name of the institution was changed to West Virginia Collegiate Institute, and Prillerman became president. Prillerman resigned in 1919 and was succeeded by John W. Davis who enlarged the plant and expanded the program. The Collegiate Institute was admitted in 1927 to membership in the North Central Association of Colleges and Secondary Schools and in 1929 the legislature changed its name to West Virginia State College.

West Virginia State College attained high rank among land-grant institutions for Negroes and became a model throughout the United States. Since 1930 specialized vocational courses have yielded ground to an enlarged program of pre-professional and cultural courses. To accommodate this trend lower division courses were offered in the social and physical sciences and in the arts; the pre-professional courses were expanded; and the teacher-training program was strengthened. The most important development in recent years at West Virginia State College was perhaps the enlargement of the physical plant. Dormitories for both men and women were completed in 1938; the Health, Physical Education, and Safety Building, completed in 1941, was one of the largest and best equipped structures of its kind in the state; the Playhouse, completed in 1942, was for classes in dramatics; and the Library, dedicated in October, 1951, contained an audio-visual room, a sound proof center for voice recording, and a microfilm department. The Science Building was completed in 1953. The campus had meanwhile increased from 31 to about 900 acres located as follows: 700 in Fayette County, used for 4-H Camp purposes; 114 at Lakin, used by the Lakin Agricultural Experiment Station; and 83 in the College campus.

WEST VIRGINIA UNIVERSITY

In the heyday of their power and influence the new educators tried with some success to determine the educational policies of the University.[10] For that purpose they sponsored the legislative act of 1909 vesting control of the financial and business affairs of all state-supported institutions of higher learning in a bi-partisan state board of control and the control of the educational policies in a bi-partisan board of regents composed of the state superintendent of free schools and four members appointed by the governor. In 1910 this board elected as president of the University Thomas E. Hodges, first treasurer of the state board of control and a professor in the University from 1896 to 1909.

While adhering to a policy of strict economy President Hodges, who assumed his duties on August 1, 1911, made a number of administrative changes. In keeping with his own notions of democracy, but against the advice of confidants, he vested University policy in the faculty, which he

[10] Ambler, *History of Education*, pp. 501-603, 843-975.

defined narrowly as consisting of all the deans, persons of professorial rank, the commandant of cadets, and the registrar. The deanships of the College of Arts and Sciences and the College of Engineering, which had become defunct in the Raymond regime, were restored, and a deanship for the School of Medicine was created. The administrative powers, exercised by the University Council from 1901 to 1911, were vested in the Council of Administration composed of the president and the five deans. Abolition of the Preparatory Department was authorized in 1909; the three-term organization was changed to the semester; the chapel hour was changed and responsibility for it was entrusted to the students; and direction and control of student affairs was vested in a faculty committee headed by Professor Robert A. Armstrong.

Student activities at the University tended to move smoothly during the Hodges administration, but it was otherwise with the external control. From the outset the new school educators, under the leadership of Superintendent Shawkey, president of the state board of regents, were dissatisfied with the entrance requirements of the University. In December, 1913, their grievances were aired before a meeting of the regents, where it became clear that Superintendent Shawkey and President Hodges did not agree on University policy. Efforts to bring the president into the camp of the new educators proved fruitless, and the *Biennial Report* of the regents for 1912-14 commented obliquely to the effect that they reserved the right to determine "the most urgent needs of the state," and indicated that they might withdraw their support from any administration when there was "due cause" to declare it a failure.

What effect, if any, this pronouncement had in the decision of President Hodges to accept the nomination of the Democratic party in 1914 as its candidate for congressman-at-large from West Virginia is not known, but it was generally believed to have been a factor. His resignation was accepted, effective September 1, 1914, and Dean Frank B. Trotter of the College of Arts and Sciences was appointed acting president, effective July 18, 1914. Two years later, Trotter was named president. During his entire presidency (1916-1928), the longest in the history of the University, the administrative organization, as determined under President Hodges, remained practically unchanged. From the beginning to the end of his administration President Trotter indicated his willingness to withdraw when the board found the "proper person" for the presidency. Friends of Superintendent Shawkey considered him a "proper person" for the presidency of the University, and, prior to 1923 when he was elected to the presidency of Marshall College and even later, he was a receptive candidate.

President Trotter retained the University presidency because of his modesty, his progressiveness, his knowledge of the state and its people, and his ability to enlist its leaders in support of his programs. Renewed efforts to move the College of Agriculture to the Eastern Panhandle were thwarted by a carefully engineered offer by Monongalia County of enough land to permit the expansion of the College there. And suggestions for removal of the University to Charleston, made frequently prior to 1921, were quieted by making common cause with her to retain the State Capitol after its destruction by fire. Without increasing the number of colleges, offerings of the University were expanded through the departmental framework, and, following World War I, the president launched a million-dollar building program. It was well received by alumni and was perhaps a determining factor in the retention of President Trotter. Substantial salary increases and annually increased enrollments were contributing factors, as was also the enthusiasm generated by a successful athletic program.

Following the appointment of Superintendent Shawkey to the presidency of Marshall College, the new school educators, then known also as the "normal school bloc," directed their efforts toward developing the normal schools, particularly Marshall College, into colleges. Generally, they favored the elevation of Marshall to co-ordinate status with the University. To friends of the University and others familiar with the financial history of the state, this was an alarming turn of events. Among other things, it meant that state support would be allocated among a number of institutions, as determined by their political influence, and that none would become first-rate and thus fit to be a center for a much needed graduate school and perhaps a medical center. Accordingly they requested that the state board of education define the respective places of each of the state supported institutions of higher learning in its proposed unified program. Its "Declaration of Policy," as made in 1927, was however unsatisfactory, particularly with respect to Marshall College and State Superintendent George M. Ford's plan to force the University to join the West Virginia Athletic Conference, and caused friends of the University to persuade the legislature to vest determination of its educational policies in a board of governors.

In turn the board of governors made known its intention to find a successor to President Trotter. In October, 1927 it elected as "President of the Faculties" Dean John Roscoe Turner of New York University, a former West Virginian. Dean Turner had held several important teaching and administrative positions, among them the post of Chief Economist and Chairman of the Advisory Board of the U. S. Tariff Commission. From July, 1928, to March, 1929, actual administration of the University was in the hands of Charles Thompson Neff, Jr., secretary to the board of governors. Thus the inauguration of the campus phase of the "Second Turner" presidency synchronized inauspiciously with the beginning of the Great Depression.

The Great Depression and After

During this entire period the educational policies of the University were determined by a board of governors. Prior to 1947 this board was composed of seven members whose tenures were dependent upon the will and the pleasure of the governor. Following some untoward incidents, the number was that year increased to nine, and they were given nine-year overlapping terms and made removable only as prescribed by law. At the same time the board of governors was given control of the business affairs of the University, but the board of public works drafted its budgets for consideration of the legislature which, in the last analysis, determined University activities by its control of the purse strings.

Influenced by lingering factional antagonisms in the faculty, President Turner dispensed with general faculty meetings and vested both the administrative and the policy determining functions in the University Council of Administration which had been enlarged in 1927 by the establishment of the College of Education. Chief reliance for initiating new programs was, however, upon a carefully selected committee of faculty members, facetiously called "the snooping committee." In keeping with its recommendations, the committee on classification and grades was dispensed with, and each college was allowed to determine its own entrance requirements.

President Turner's chief concern was, however, the establishment of a graduate school. Through the establishment of such a school he hoped to effect the long talked of unity in the state educational system and thus more effectively "build the University into the life of the State." To popularize such a program the University went on the air, and an effort was made to enlarge the extension program. In 1929 the legislature was asked to make an appropriation for the improvement of library facilities, and it promptly did so. Thus encouraged, President Turner was confident that the legislature would also provide funds for the proposed graduate school. But, when a depression of unprecedented severity settled upon the state, the funds which might otherwise have gone to the University program were diverted to the public free schools. Moreover, in July, 1932, the legislature made a general reduction of about twenty per cent in most budget items and reduced the salary of President Turner from $15,000 to $7,500.

Though President Turner accepted the crisis legislation in good faith, the failure of the graduate program, not to mention the personal equations involved, was his undoing. Preliminary to seeking a seat in the United States Senate, he was drawn into partisan politics and accepted election as a delegate-at-large from West Virginia to the Republican National Convention of 1932. He thus provoked the criticism not only of Democrats but also of leaders of his own party.

Following Turner, who relinquished the presidency December 31, 1934, University presidents and acting presidents came and went in rapid succession.[11] Under President Chauncey S. Boucher (1935-1938) members

Women's Hall, West Virginia University

of the faculty experimented with "the Chicago College Plan," and there was considerable revamping of the administrative machinery. The graduate faculty was constituted and its duties defined; the council of administration was enlarged; the committee on student affairs was revived; a committee on instructional policies and practices was constituted; and the College of Pharmacy (1936) and the School of Physical Education and Athletics (1937) were established. But the most important change was the delegation of policy-determining functions to the University Senate. This body was composed of persons of full professorial rank; all heads and acting heads of departments; the registrar; and the president of the University, who was the presiding officer.

[11] Dr Robert A. Armstrong of the University faculty was acting president from December 31, 1934, to October 1, 1935. He was aided by a faculty committee.

President Charles E. Lawall (acting Sept. 1, 1938-June 30, 1939; president July 1, 1939-Sept. 1, 1945) adhered generally to the administrative policy of his immediate predecessor and preserved his administrative organization, except the University Senate which ceased to function early in his presidency. He was embarrassed somewhat by the report of an investigating committee of the American Association of University Professors criticizing the record of the University in matters of academic tenure under the Turner and Boucher presidencies, and he sponsored a policy guaranteeing faculty tenure. An order of July 2, 1937, giving the College of Education full control of all professional teacher training, was modified so as to permit other University units to train teachers and to vest the College of Education with full responsibility for recommending them for certification. Upon his recommendation, a school of journalism was established in 1939. Anticipating heavy post-war enrollments and needed expansion, President Lawall launched a building program calling for the expenditure of $12,000,000. From its inception the Mineral Industries Building was sponsored by President Lawall, and its dedication on October 16, 1942, was heralded as a personal achievement. While pursuing a course independent of the faculty in matters of administration, he adhered to a policy of economy with respect to faculty salaries, which caused the resignation of a number of the teaching staff. In 1944, following an unsuccessful effort by the board of governors to dismiss President Lawall, the faculty effected an organization which served in a quasi-administrative capacity pending the outcome of court action. After a successful defense of his legal right to the office, President Lawall resigned, but not until attention had been focused on conditions which exposed the University to attack from without as well as from within.

At the end of an interim extending from August 31, 1945 to July 1, 1946, during which Charles Thompson Neff, Jr., was acting president of the University, Dr. Irvin Stewart, Deputy Director of the Office of Scientific Research and Development, Washington, D. C., became its president at a salary of $17,500. At the time of his election state leaders were engrossed in consideration of recommendations of the Strayer *Report,* as they applied to higher education. In 1947 the legislature vested the board of governors with the entire control of the business and educational affairs of the University. The fact that the salary of President Stewart was later increased to $20,000, without provoking comment, was significant of something more than an increase in living costs.

Under the Stewart presidency the several colleges and schools were given a large degree of autonomy. An important step toward making the University a cooperative undertaking was taken when the University Senate was revived and enlarged. The new regime enlarged the Council of Administration by the inclusion of a vice-president (appointed in

1946),[12] the deans of the newly established College of Commerce (1952) and the School of Dentistry (1953), and other administrative officers subject to call. The office of dean of the graduate school was created in 1949 and the graduate program expanded. The extension graduate program was likewise enlarged and implemented on a state-wide basis. The forward march of the University was further reflected by professional accreditation in music, forestry, social work, commerce and in certain fields of engineering. Since 1948 the University has maintained close contact with the high schools of the state through visits made annually by selected members of the faculty and administrative staff. Despite the policy of the state budgeting commission to divert surplus revenues accumulated in World War II to capital expenditures, substantial advances were made in University salaries.

With the increased post-war enrollments came material expansion of the University. In 1948 the Krepps and Dille farms (260 acres) were acquired and converted into the "Evansdale Campus," and the plant was enlarged by the erection of a number of modern buildings on the "Old Campus." Armstrong Hall, a classroom building, was completed in 1950, Brooks Hall, a biological science building in 1951, the Physics Building in 1952, and the Music Building in 1954. Four stack levels were added to the Library in 1951. In the meantime, temporary cafeteria and student union buildings, as well as scores of barrack and trailer units for student housing, were erected from surplus property donated by the Federal Government. The most important expansion was however that of the two-year Medical School into a four-year School of Medicine, Dentistry, and Nursing, as authorized by the 1951 legislature. For twenty years or more the West Virginia Medical Association had urged the establishment of a four-year College of Medicine, but the public was divided with respect to its location. By authorization of the 1951 legislature, Governor Patteson decided that it should be at Morgantown.

As the proposed medical school was to have been established and maintained "in the University," regardless of the location of the school, University authorities had given much thought to its requirements. They thus expedited its construction, which had been provided for by an excise tax on soft drinks and soft-drink syrups. In a gala occasion ground was broken for the Medical Center on December 9, 1952. As the Mechanical Plant was nearing completion in September, 1954, the contract was let for the 1,000-room Basic Sciences Building at a cost of $10,675,000. Already a hospital building, with 400 beds, had reached the advance planning stage. Revenues remaining constant and sufficient, the Basic Sciences Building was scheduled for completion in the fall of 1957. With the completion

12 Following the death of Vice-President Neff in 1953, the office was allowed to lapse.

of the Medical Center, it was confidently expected that it would become a health center for the entire state. That was perhaps the decisive influence in locating it at the University, a land-grant institution whose extension services reached every nook and corner of the state and whose experiment stations kept its people abreast of social and scientific progress.

Chapter XXX

The Industrial Revolution

AS PREDICTED BY THE FOUNDERS of West Virginia, development of her natural resources converted her into a great industrial state. The possibilities of such a development had been foreseen before the Civil War; but, owing to unsettled conditions during the War and the Reconstruction, little progress was made, except in the petroleum and iron industries. Other developments had to wait improved transportation and adequate financing. The New State was thus left in the domestic stage of economy. In this stage each county had its gristmills, sawmills, and carding machines; woolen mills made cloth, jeans, linseys, and flannels; and more than $1,000,000 worth of these goods, including blankets, hosiery, and carpets, were produced in homes. Except the carding, every operation from the shearing of the wool to its conversion by the loom was performed within the family circle. Cities and towns were few and far between, and each village or community had its tannery, blacksmith shop, livery stable, and general store. Farmers slaughtered their own hogs, sheep, and cattle; cured and preserved their own meats; and fabricated their own tools and farm implements. From maple sap and sorghum juice they produced syrup and molasses, while their wives were equally efficient in soap making, baking, knitting, weaving, and tailoring. Granaries bulged with grain; barns were filled with hay and fodder; and cellars were storage places for canned fruits and vegetables. Money for taxes was usually secured through the sale of farm products, particularly cattle, hogs, and sheep, and, in the more remote parts, through the sale of ginseng, poultry, and peltry.

MANUFACTURING

By 1870 West Virginia had made a beginning in manufacturing. In that year the state had 2,444 industrial establishments employing more than 11,600 persons. In round numbers, the capital invested was $11,000,000; wages totaled $4,325,000; materials were worth about $14,500,000; and the finished products, almost two fifths of which were accredited to Ohio County, sold for more than $24,000,000. Other counties, in the order of their industrial importance, were Mason, Marshall, Jefferson, Berkeley, Kanawha, and Wood. Neither Raleigh nor McDowell reported manufactures, and in at least half of the other counties their total value did not exceed $10,000 each.[1]

Because of the tendency to shift from man and horse to steam power, the number of industrial establishments in West Virginia declined between 1870 and 1900; but the capital increased to $49,000,000, the number of wage earners to 33,000, the total wages paid annually to $12,640,000, and the value of the product to $67,000,000. In this period the state moved from thirty-first to twenty-eighth in industrial production. Wheeling, called the "Nail City," was the leading manufacturing center. In 1885 more than half of its population of about 30,000 was dependent upon industry. It had long been known for its wood manufacturing, its bronze and brass fabricating, its textiles and meat packing, and the fine quality of its pottery. It was also the home of "Mail Pouch Tobacco" and "Wheeling Tobies." Here, steel was first substituted for iron in the making of nails, and, for ten years or more prior to 1900, scores of iron products were shipped from its factories to world markets.

Other West Virginia towns and cities also had important industrial establishments. Parkersburg was long the chief oil-refining center. In 1886 about 300,000 barrels of petroleum were refined there, and the kerosene and by-products were valued at $1,500,000. New Cumberland had brickyards and potteries; Wellsburg had paper, glass, cotton, and woolen mills; and iron and nails were made in Benwood. Every town had one or more flour mills, and they were located also at country crossroads and at favorable sites on creeks and rivers. Salt and bromine were extracted at Hartford and Mason City along the Ohio, as well as in the Kanawha Valley. Practically every town on a railroad or a navigable river shipped farm products, livestock, lumber, cross-ties, hoop poles, and tanbark. With the coming of the railroad, repair shops and car shops were established at Bluefield and Hinton. Already Parkersburg, Grafton, and Martinsburg were centers for these enterprises.

Until about 1890 the state's industry was confined almost entirely to river and railroad towns. Large rural areas were still in the domestic stage of economy and overpopulated. The state was thus ready for an

[1] The sources for this chapter were the U. S. Census (1870-1950); the W. Va. Commissioner of Labor, biennial reports, and "Directory of West Virginia Business and Industry" (1953); James H. Thompson, "The Manufacturing Industries of West Virginia," W.V.U. *Bulletin,* series 52, No. 12-4, June, 1952; and bulletins of the West Virginia Industrial and Publicity Commission.

other migration movement. The West having temporarily lost its attractiveness, industry provided an outlet. The movement to it was facilitated by the extension of railroads into undeveloped areas and by the investment of non-resident capital on a grand scale. It was for these reasons, intensified by the economic depression of the 1890's, that West Virginians left their farms in large numbers to find employment in mines, mills, and factories. Women found employment in the new cities as clerks, stenographers, and teachers.

On the eve of World War I West Virginia had 2,749 industrial establishments representing a total investment of $175,000,000. This investment produced annually wealth estimated at $194,000,000 and afforded employment for 71,000 laborers who received a total annual wage of about $44,000,000. The chief enterprises, as determined by the value of their products, were iron and steel, $21,000,000; tin plate and terneplate, $15,000,000; glass, $14,500,000; leather, $11,000,000; and flour and grist mills, $7,000,000. In 1914, West Virginia ranked second among the states in the production of glass, tin plate, terneplate, and clay products. Of these the glass industry ranked first, with almost 9,000 employees; car and general repair work second, with 8,500; iron and steel third, with more than 5,300; and pottery came fourth with slightly more than 3,300 employees.

It was not until World War I that West Virginia took the high road to industrialization. As supplies of German-produced chemicals were cut off, American producers set out to meet the challenge not only with large-scale production but also with the discovery and production of new by-products. Thanks to its rich deposits of coal, oil, gas, rock salts, and salt brines, the state early attracted the attention of promoters of the new American chemical industry. As a result, the Kanawha Valley became an industrial workshop and Charleston a large manufacturing center. Belle, located about ten miles east of Charleston, became the site of an extensive plant, established in 1926, which produced more than 100 industrial chemicals; and 20 miles farther eastward at Alloy was located the largest ferro-alloy plant in the world. It produced more than 50 of the alloys used in the production of fine grades of steel.

Prior to 1914 small chemical plants had been built at Clarksburg, Moundsville, and Huntington, but the new development ignored municipal boundaries and expanded into suburban developments which in time became cities. The chemical industry made increasing use of the salt-brine and rock-salt deposits along the Ohio River, with the result that the Ohio Valley from Wheeling to Huntington became an important industrial area. In 1954 West Virginia chemical and related industries employed 38,000 persons with a total annual payroll in excess of $156,000,000.

Most of the new steel mills which came to West Virginia following World War I were located in the Northern Panhandle. They were in fact an extension of the Pittsburgh-Youngstown-Akron area, widely known for its heavy industry. From their furnaces and foundries belched clouds of smoke and steam by day, while their streams of molten steel poured out at night to light up the shadows against darkened skies. Small boats and freight trains supplied the plants with fuel and raw materials, and towboats carried the finished product to Gulf ports and Eastern markets. Other plants producing steel were located at Parkersburg, Clarksburg, Huntington and Charleston. In 1954 the iron and steel industry of the state employed about 39,000 persons whose annual payroll totaled about $174,000,000.

Of all the state industries, the iron and steel had the oldest continuous history. Iron furnaces still standing in 1955 here and there throughout the northern part of the state from Hancock to Clay counties were reminders of a time, beginning shortly after the American Revolution, when charcoal was used for fuel to convert native ore into the iron that was used to make farm tools and household utensils.[2] But the Wheeling Steel Corporation traced its beginnings to 1715 at Principio, Maryland. Moreover, this corporation illustrated the three stages in the development of the iron and steel industry: the individual furnace to 1885; the transition, 1885-1920; and the integrated corporation stage since 1920.[3] In West Virginia, as elsewhere, the demand for steel products has long been the economic barometer.

The post-World War I period also witnessed a steady growth of West Virginia textile industries. For about 100 years the Stifel mills in Wheeling produced choice calicoes, much of which found markets in Latin America; Martinsburg and Berkeley Springs specialized in hosiery on a grand scale; Charleston produced blankets; both Huntington and Wheeling were known for the superior quality of their upholstery and mens' working clothes, particularly overalls; and there were a number of other plants in widely scattered centers. Among the important new industries was the manufacture of rayon yarn, a material made by chemically processing raw cotton and wood pulp. For this purpose plants were established at Nitro and Parkersburg which, in 1954, employed 4,200 workers and produced about 90,000,000 pounds of yarn.

The glass industry had a phenomenal growth in West Virginia after World War I. As in the past, the location of new plants was determined largely by proximity to natural gas for fuel and to lime and silica, the chief raw materials of the industry. Important manufacturing centers included Morgantown and vicinity which produced cut glass, table glass-

[2] The first iron furnace in present Trans-Allegheny West Virginia was built by Peter Tarr on King's Creek in present Hancock County in 1790. Soon thereafter a number of iron furnaces were erected in Monongalia County near Morgantown.

[3] Earl C. May, *Principio to Wheeling, 1715-1945* (New York, 1945), pp. xiii, 172-173, 294-299.

ware, hand-blown tableware, pressed prism plate, bottles, globes, shades, illuminating and stationary glass, and novelties; Huntington, flint glass, optical elements, novelties, reflectors, lenses, lamp parts, and hand-blown communion glasses; Parkersburg, tubing, vials, technical and fiber glass; Clarksburg, flat, drawn-sheet, plate-window, tumblers, balls, toys, marbles, signal lenses, and specialties; Weston, handmade crystal and hand-blown ware, cut glass, and decorated ware; Fairmont, opal jars, shaving mugs, fluorescent lamps, and sealed beam headlamps for automobiles; Moundsville, Fostoria hand-made table glassware; Milton, stained-glass windows; and St. Marys, marbles. A dozen or more other towns had one or more glass plants, some of which employed several hundred persons. Invention of a bottlemaking machine in 1903 by Michael J. Owens revolutionized that phase of the industry, and the Owens-Illinois Glass Company, with plants at Charleston, Huntington, and Fairmont, employed more than 4,000 workers and produced more than 5,000,000 glass containers a year. In 1954 there were 67 glass plants in the state employing about 19,000 persons, and the glass and kindred industries had about 28,000 employees and a total payroll of $98,557,510.

Of the several important West Virginia industries, the electrical was the most rapidly growing. In 1950 West Virginia ranked second among the South Atlantic states in the production of electricity. About eight billion kilowatt hours of energy were produced that year, six billion of which were generated by public utilities. The remainder was produced by industrial plants for their own uses. Dedication, in May, 1953, of the $36,000,000 Albright Power Station was an interstate affair featured by the presence of the governors of Maryland and West Virginia. Like the other large power systems in the state, this one was interconnected with those of surrounding states, thus providing a pool of electrical energy for any contingency. In 1952 there were 517,000 pay customers in the state using electricity, and West Virginia was 14th among the states producing that commodity.

Whatever can be said of the vast potentialities for the development of hydro-electric power, most of the current generated in West Virginia in 1955 was produced in steam plants using coal, such as those located at Beech Bottom, Graham Station, Rivesville, Cabin Creek, Albright, Willow Island, Logan, and Kenova. The largest water-power plants were at Lake Lynn, Monongalia County, and Hawks Nest, Fayette County. For the latter a tunnel three and one half miles long, with its intake at the base of Hawks Nest, was drilled through Gauley Mountain. The Tygart Valley Dam near Grafton and the Bluestone Dam near Hinton, which were built primarily for flood control, each has power generating possibilities.

New impetus was given to West Virginia manufacturing during World

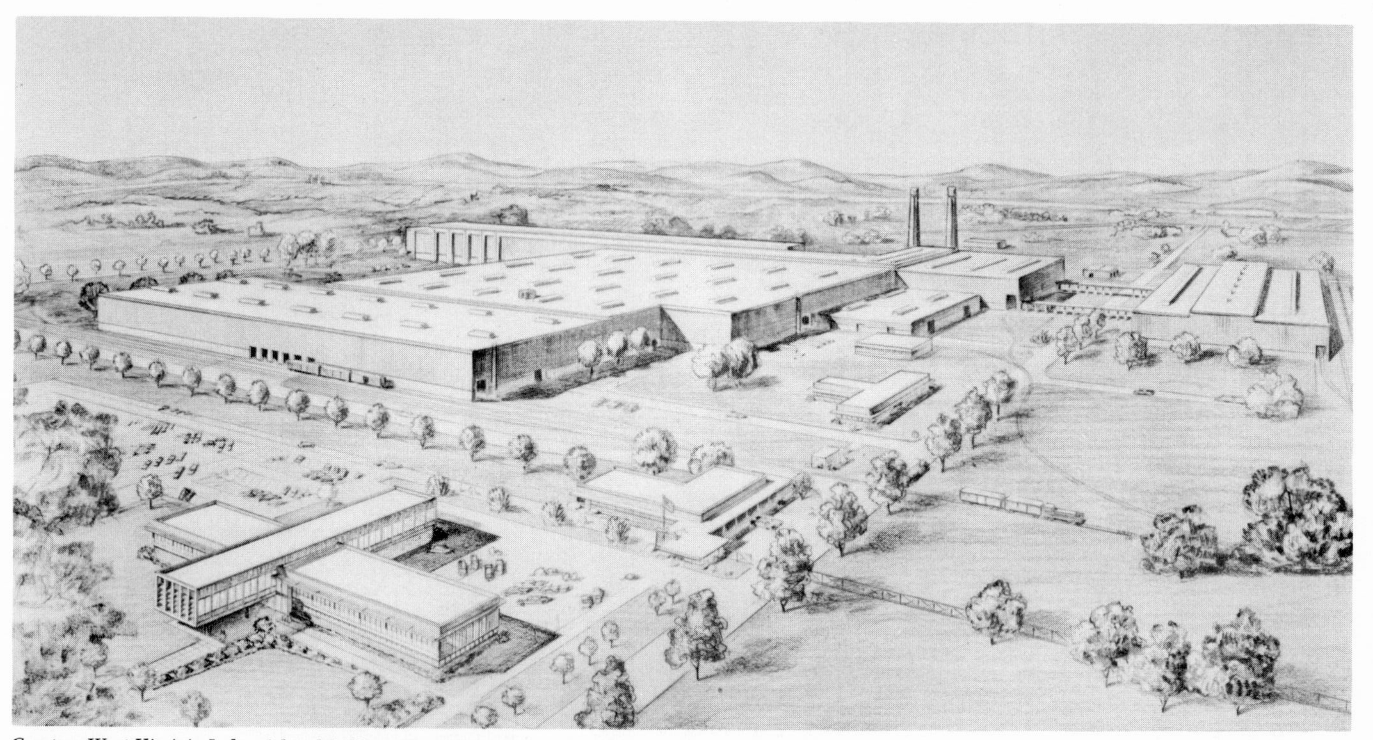

Courtesy West Virginia Industrial and Publicity Commission

Artist's sketch of the Kaiser Aluminum plant at Ravenswood, West Virginia

War II. When the war began the total employed averaged about 105,000 monthly, and the total value of the annual product was $688,000,000. When the war ended the number of employees averaged about 130,000 monthly, and the total value of the annual output was $1,465,000,000. Except during brief recessions, both the number of employees and the value of their product increased to 1955, when the respective totals were 125,000 and $2,106,500,000. The demand for industrial employment was not however great enough to attract the entire labor supply and the surplus sought employment elsewhere. West Virginians were therefore seeking new industries and for that reason welcomed the establishment of the new metal and chemical industries mentioned above. As indicated in the report of a survey of its industrial potential, made by the Arthur D. Little Company of Cambridge, Massachusetts, in 1954-55, they had every reason to be encouraged: the manufacturing "labor climate" of West Virginia was better than the average for some of the neighboring states; the historic metal and chemical industries had latent possibilities; and woodworking and apparel-making afforded "growth opportunities" that seemed adequate to check the migration of workers, particularly of former coal miners.[4]

THE EXTRACTIVE INDUSTRIES

In 1955 West Virginia was still rich in natural resources. Her hills were underlaid with untapped mineral wealth; she had water power in abundance; and her mountains and hills were being reforested. Thanks to her geographic location and transportation facilities, markets were conveniently close and accessible.

Coal Mining

Throughout her entire history, coal has been West Virginia's basic resource. Before she was admitted to separate statehood, bituminous mines were opened along navigable rivers and the Baltimore and Ohio Railroad, and cannel coal was mined in Kanawha, Marion, and Preston counties. The number of new operations increased with the coming of peace in 1865, with the result that five years later there were 185 mining operations, including "quarrying, oil-boring, and peat-cutting." These were however small, employing 1,527 wage earners, only 646 of whom, including 69 boys, worked underground. In 1870 the total capital invested in coal min-

[4] The Little survey was made at the instance of Governor Marland.

ing exceeded $2,500,000; the wages totaled $825,000; and the 600,000-ton production was valued at $1,000,000. In the absence of investment capital and transportation facilities, there was little change in coal production during the 1870's. A total of 1,568,000 tons, valued at about $2,000,000, was however produced in 1880 for commercial purposes.[5]

With the coming of new railroads to West Virginia in the eighties and nineties, there came also a revolution in her coal mining industry. By 1890 production had reached 6,321,218 tons, which was more than doubled in 1897. In both the quality of their product and in mining costs the West Virginia operators had advantages which enabled them to undersell their competitors in Pennsylvania, Ohio, Indiana, and Illinois. As a result, the West Virginia output jumped from 16,000,000 in 1898 to 66,730,000 tons in 1912, only ten per cent of which was consumed in the state.[6]

Meanwhile, mining towns with their painful monotony of architecture and color, sprang up, as if by magic; while coal tipples and the refuse which accumulated around them disfigured primeval landscapes. If scores of residents sold their mineral rights for pittances, their sons became mine foremen, business executives, and successful operators. Some became millionaires. Accompanying this boom was the inevitable conflict between capital and labor, and it was not long until the press was reporting industrial unrest in the West Virginia coal fields, notably in Kanawha, Logan, and Mingo counties.[7]

Operators and miners united to increase production and to stabilize coal mining in World War I. It was during this period that most of the West Virginia fields were unionized. The war was no sooner ended, however, than strikes were resumed with a view to unionizing the southern West Virginia operations, particularly those in Mingo and Logan counties. As it will be seen, this attempt featured such incidents as the "Matewan Massacre," the "Assassination of 'Sid' Hatfield," and the "Battle of Blair Mountain." By the repudiation of contracts with miners' unions, reductions in wages, use of court injunctions, and employment of armed guards, West Virginia operators were a law unto themselves during the "Golden Twenties." Accordingly, practically all of them followed the Smokeless Field operators in their refusal to recognize union labor. On the other hand, the coal industry prospered, owing to the steady market and the increased use of mechanical devices, and the total annual output reached 146,088,121 tons in 1927, when West Virginia took first place in the nation

5 U. S. Dept. of Commerce and Labor, *Mines and Quarries* (1902), p. 338; *West Virginia Blue Book* (1954), p. 785.

6 U. S. Senate, *Report No. 321*, 63rd. Cong., 2nd Sess.

7 U. S. Coal Commission, *Report*, 68th Cong., 2nd Sess., Doc. No. 195, p. 169.

as a coal-producing state. This heyday came to an end, however, in the economic depression of the 1930's, when the total production dropped in 1932 to 86,114,506 tons and the total number of men employed from 117,781 to 82,930.

Thus operators and miners alike were willing, the latter eager, to take

Coal shipping center, Williamson, Mingo County

advantage of the National Industrial Recovery Act (NIRA) of 1933 and of the National Labor Relations Act (1935), to stabilize the coal mining industry. For West Virginia this was accomplished through contracts between operators and miners' unions made in conformity with the Appalachian Agreement, as formulated in October, 1933. In the course of the next few years about 98 per cent of the operations were unionized. Strikes occurred from time to time thereafter, but with few exceptions they were settled by negotiation. In 1947, the peak year, 173,653,816 tons were mined. This was affected by the use of increased mechanization which, by 1950, had displaced about 40 per cent of the employees.

The increasing use of residual oil, the consolidation of companies, deeper mines, and high labor costs, combined to reduce the total West Virginia bituminous output to 131,872,563 tons in 1953. As a result, scores of operations were closed, and thousands of miners were unemployed. The West Virginia coal industry had in fact entered a transitional stage, from which it was confidently predicted that the increased demands of new industrial establishments and of electrical energy producing plants would lift coal to higher levels. Thus students of West Virginia economy were not discouraged, for they saw a bright future in coal and its by-products.[8]

The evolution of mining in the state was reflected in its safety legislation and administration setup. Appointment of a mine inspector was first authorized in 1883, another was added in 1887, and a third in 1893. The office of chief mine inspector was created in 1897, and by 1905 there were seven assistants. The department of mines was created in 1907, when the number of district inspectors was increased to twelve. By 1925 there were 25. In 1950 the inspection force comprised, in addition to a chief and the usual staff, seven inspectors at large in as many districts, and a total of forty-seven other inspectors and assistants, including three mine-foremen examiners, an accident prevention commission of four members, a safety director and six assistants, and a rock dust inspector and four assistants.

Defying safety precautions, coal mining in West Virginia, as elsewhere, was plagued by numerous accidents, some of them of disaster proportions. This was notably true of "the Nation's worst," the Monongah explosion of December 6, 1907, which took 361 lives. Other "horrible disasters," to mention only a few, were: Eccles, April 28, 1914, with 183 fatalities; Layland, March 2, 1915, with 112; Benwood, April 28, 1924, with 119, and Everettville, April 30, 1927, with 97.[9] Also appalling were the average annual totals of deaths and accidents which for the period 1941-1951 were 306 and 21,829, respectively. Equally distressing was the official conclusion that these death-dealing and incapacitating incidents could not be prevented. Statements to that effect were made following an explosion in Jamison Mine No. 9 near Farmington, where 16 men lost their lives on November 13, 1954, in what was then officially regarded as one of the safest and best kept mines in the state.

---

8 Although of decreasing importance since about 1918 when new methods began to be used in the fabrication of steel, coke was, until that time, an important by-product of West Virginia coal. Coke reached peak production in 1910 with a total of 4,217,381 tons. Since then it declined rapidly but somewhat regularly to 1953, when the total production was only 93,991 tons. *West Virginia Blue Book* (1954), p. 785; *U. S. Census* (1880), Vol. X.

9 Department of Mines, *Annual Report* (1953), pp. 131-132.

Petroleum and Natural Gas

The use of both oil and gas in West Virginia antedated the coming of the white man. Long before his arrival, Indians were tapping seepages for petroleum which they used as a medicine; and the Burning Spring at present Malden was regarded by them as one of the mysteries of creation. Other burning springs, notably those on the Big Sandy, the Elk, and the Little Kanawha rivers, had already been used by Indians. Oil development remained obscure however until 1810, when Bushrod Creel collected "bank oil" from seepages on his farm on Hughes River and carried it to Marietta, Ohio, where it was sold as "Seneca oil." From this simple beginning the demand for this strange substance increased to the point where Creel made the "Creel Sand Diggings" to supply it. In 1836 these diggings (wells) produced from fifty to one hundred barrels of oil, which was dipped from the wells by buckets and hauled to market on oxcarts. Such was the beginning of one of West Virginia's most important industries.[10]

Salt makers on both of the Kanawha rivers were meanwhile experiencing difficulty from "devil's grease" and natural gas. Learning of these "nuisances" Charles H. Shattuck of Tarentum, Pennsylvania, decided to put them to practical uses, particularly the oil, so he purchased ten acres of land adjoining the Creel farm on Hughes River and drilled the first well for oil in West Virginia. It was completed on October 26, 1859, less than two months after the completion of the famous Drake Well at Titusville, Pennsylvania, but, unlike the Drake Well, the Shattuck Well was a dry hole. This would perhaps have ended temporarily the oil development in West Virginia, had not General Samuel D. Karnes then been in the process of drilling deeper the "old greasy waterhole," near Burning Springs, Wirt County. It was this well, completed in the spring of 1860 with a daily output of only seven barrels, that launched the first oil boom in (West) Virginia.

The rush to the Burning Springs oil field, which began immediately, was not unlike that of the 'Forty-Niners to California. Within two years some six thousand people were quartered in shacks and tents on the banks of the Little Kanawha River. Everywhere along the Ohio, in the region of Parkersburg, oil and leases were chief subjects of conversation, even surpassing the Civil War then in progress. Nor was this the whole story. In the course of two years the development extended to Horseneck, Pleasants County, where, for a short time, the first well produced at the rate of one thousand barrels a day. By 1869 the annual production of the

[10] See S. F. Peckham, "Report on the Production, Technology and Uses of Petroleum and Its Products," in *U. S. Census* (1880), X, 1-301; Debar, *Hand Book*, pp. 139-144.

West Virginia "Oil Break" had become somewhat settled at about 300,000 barrels, of which 25,000 was pure lubricating oil.[11]

Meanwhile operators had become interested in solidified oil, or grahamite, found near MacFarlan, Ritchie County. To all appearance a freak of nature, this substance was formed by the accumulation of crude oil in an open rock fissure. Under these conditions the lighter parts evaporated, leaving the oil in a hardened condition, not unlike coal. It was found to be rich in oil of fine qualities for lubricating purposes. Beginning in 1859 the deposit was operated intermittently as the "Ritchie Mines" for about fifty years.[12]

If production of crude oil in West Virginia in the seventies was restricted to shallow sands, the time was not far off when borings went deeper; for Dr. Israel C. White of West Virginia University, in cooperation with Pennsylvania and Ohio geologists, William A. Earseman and Edward Orton, was soon able to persuade operators to make practical use of the anticlinal theory of oil and gas bearing stratas. As a result a test, made in 1889 near Mannington, brought in a "gusher," and soon other prospectors, mostly New Yorkers and Pennsylvanians, joined resourceful natives in search of oil leases. Except in the immediate vicinity of a gusher, these leases cost little and were taken with a view to their sale to *bona fide* operators.

Sparked by the discovery of the rich Mannington field, West Virginia became in a short time one of the most important oil producing regions in the world. In 1890-91 other fields were opened in the Northern Panhandle and in Doddridge and Wetzel counties, while at the same time large producing wells were drilled in Ritchie, Pleasants, Harrison, and Monongalia counties. Of all the new fields, the one at Sistersville in Tyler County was however the most productive. Opened in 1892, this field became within a year the "greatest oil producing region in the world," only to lose first place to Lewis County by 1900. There the famous Copley well was brought in with a yield of some 7,000 barrels daily. Thus did the West Virginia oil production grow from 120,000 barrels in 1888 to an annual output of 16,195,675 barrels in 1900, the peak year.

West Virginians and Pennsylvanians had meanwhile developed techniques of their own for well drilling. "Major Billy" Morris of Kanawha County, West Virginia, invented a deep-drilling device called "the slips" which was used by the Ruffner Brothers and other salt makers in reaching the more concentrated salt brines. This and other devices such as "bits," "jars," "stems," and "derricks" used by the salt makers, were used

---

11 As indicated by Professor E. B. Andrews of Marietta, Ohio, in the *American Journal of Science* (May 20, 1861), the (West) Virginia "Oil Break" was confined to a well defined anticlinal formation. Debar, *Hand Book*, pp. 139-144.

12 West Va. Geological Survey, *County Reports: Pleasants, Wood and Ritchie*, pp. 244-252.

Producing oil well with modern steel derrick, Blue Creek

later in the extraction of petroleum and natural gas in all parts of the world. In their use Michael L. Benedum, "The Great Wildcatter," born and reared at Bridgeport, Harrison County, was fabulously successful.[13]

After 1900 the West Virginia oil industry declined steadily at an average rate of about 200,000 barrels per year. In 1912 the total yield was 12,129,000 barrels; in 1952 it was 2,602,000 barrels. For some time natural gas pressure was used to stimulate production, and the legislature in 1953 authorized the use of water pressure for that purpose, as a result of which the production for 1953 was increased to 3,038,000 barrels. Nevertheless, oil production in West Virginia was a declining industry and abandoned

[13] Sam T. Mallison, *The Great Wildcatter* (Charleston, W. Va., 1953).

wells were being used as storage reservoirs for natural gas. Oil towns, which fifty years ago were not unlike western mining camps, had long since disappeared, and nature was reconverting former oil fields into forest lands. On the other hand, oil was still a factor in the lives of those West Virginians who continued to receive royalties and to live upon the incomes of those received in the "boom days."

Until the 1890's, when natural gas first began to be used in a large way for the manufacture of glassware, drilling operations were primarily for oil. Unwelcomed gas flows were left uncontrolled for months to discharge into the air with thundering sounds that could be heard miles away. When, by accident or otherwise, the flow was ignited, it destroyed the drilling equipment and the vegetation over considerable distances and illuminated the hillsides, thus enabling farmers to dispense temporarily with their lanterns. One of these giant flambeaus was "Big Moses," located on the Moses Spencer farm on Indian Creek in Tyler County. This well was "drilled in" on September 6, 1894, and discharged gas into the air for more than a year at an estimated initial flow of 100 million cubic feet a day. When ignited, it illuminated the landscape over a radius of about twenty miles.

With the construction of pipelines to supply the growing needs of industrial and domestic consumers and with the increasing concern of producers, the production of natural gas in West Virginia reached 120,000 million cubic feet in 1906, when she took the lead among the states in its production. The "wet" gas was converted into casinghead gasoline, in the production of which West Virginia led all the states until 1914, when she yielded first place to Oklahoma. She retained first place in total production of natural gas to well beyond 1917, the peak year, when it totaled 308,000 million cubic feet valued in excess of $57,000,000. At that time most of her production was sold in neighboring states, but it later failed to supply intrastate needs which were met by importations from the Southwest.

From 1917 to 1932 gas production declined to 100,000 million cubic feet, but by 1943 the production had risen to 252,000 million cubic feet, most of it from Oriskany sands in Jackson and Kanawha counties. Thereafter the production declined gradually, and the total for 1950 was only 197,000 million cubic feet. However, successful "wildcat" developments in the Terra Alta (Preston County) and the Canaan Valley (Tucker County) fields then indicated a sustained and even an increased production.[14] The use of depleted gas wells as underground storage reservoirs tended to assure adequate supplies of gas during periods of maximum con-

[14] Frank Reeves and Paul H. Price, "Early Devonian Gas in Northern West Virginia and Pre-Devonian Oil Prospects," *Bulletin,* Amer. Asso. of Petroleum Geologists, Vol. 34, No. 11 (November, 1950).

sumption. In 1955 the chief scientific interest in natural gas was, however, in the possible reclamation of additional by-products by new methods of processing and manufacture.

Timber Industries

Of all West Virginia natural resources, none was so directly available and so evenly distributed as her forests. In 1870 these covered 14,000,000 acres, or seven eighths of her surface; ten million acres were still in the full vigor and freshness of the forest primeval; and, not including ample allowances for domestic uses, the value of her forest growth was estimated at $500,000,000. The largest and most valuable trees were oaks and poplars; walnut, cherry, sycamore, ash, chestnut, chestnut oak, and locusts were found in less abundance. If the region could be described as "emphatically the home of deciduous timber," there were also white pines, hemlocks, and spruces of remarkable size and faultless growth.

Too well is it known how these resources were exploited in a most reckless and prodigal manner. Generally, tillable land was considered valueless except for agriculture. To condition it for that use trees were girdled and left to die. They were then felled and burned, and the resulting fields were enclosed by rail fences made from priceless black walnut, cherry, and chestnut logs. Thousands of choice trees were converted into ship timber for Atlantic coast shipyards and the English markets; thousands of staves were shipped annually to Baltimore, Pittsburgh, Cincinnati, and Wheeling; millions of hoop-poles were marketed in towns and cities in the Ohio Valley; while the markets for West Virginia tanbark expanded at home and abroad.

However exhilarating the effect, "timbering" produced overtones of exploitation rather than development. As stated by J. H. Diss Debar in 1869, "An occasional survey of the railroad depot at Parkersburg, when filled with tons of wagons, carriages, ploughbeams, furniture and twenty other articles of wooden ware, manufactured from West Virginia timber, *outside of the State,* and westward bound, gives but a faint idea of what is continually being lost through our lack of manufacturing enterprise."[15] He estimated the total value of the sawlogs, ship timber, lumber, staves, and barrels then produced annually in West Virginia at $2,500,000 and the number of persons employed in the timber industry at 1,600.

In 1870 there were twenty to thirty "first class mills" along the Baltimore and Ohio Railroad, each cutting on an average of 3,000 lumber feet a day. The Baltimore and Ohio also served barrel factories which produced from 150 to 200 barrels per day, and shipped large quantities of dressed

[15] Debar, *Hand Book,* pp. 103-113, 116.

and seasoned staves to Baltimore and to New England cities. There were also lumber mills and factories on the Ohio River and its tributaries. In 1880 there were 472 sawmills, most of them first class and steam driven, operating in West Virginia, or 124 more than in 1870, when more than half of the sawmills were operated by water power. Except along the Baltimore and Ohio Railroad, the chief method of transportation in the area westward of a line extending from Valley Falls, Taylor County, to the Kentucky state line, by way of Bulltown and Kanawha Falls, was by rafting sawlogs and crossties and floating lumber, staves, tanbark, and hoop-poles in small barges on the larger streams. Middle Island Creek and the Little Kanawha, Elk, Guyandot, and Big Sandy rivers were the most used.

The boom was a device for marketing timber. During the eighties and nineties and for sometime thereafter, the boom, with its impounded "catch" of millions of crossties and sawlogs, was a familiar sight on the lower courses of streams flowing into the Ohio from the south. When booms broke, the waters below were covered with crossties and sawlogs, and dwellers in shanty boats and other denizens of the rivers reaped small fortunes as salvagers. Arrived at the Ohio and its navigable tributaries, the contents of these booms were either assembled into rafts or loaded into barges, and thus carried to market. Booms were generally owned and operated by stock companies, and some of them, such as the Elk River Land, Improvement, Manufacturing and Boom Company, enjoyed exclusive privileges.

With the introduction of the bandsaw and the extension of railroads into remote areas of the state, the timber industry entered a new phase in the early 1880's. As already mentioned, it had been confined largely to the Baltimore and Ohio Railroad and to the tributaries of the Ohio River; but now the industry pushed into the mountainous areas of the interior. There choice timber lands were purchased at prices ranging from two to five dollars per acre by lumber companies, mostly residents of New York, Pennsylvania, Michigan, and Wisconsin, which erected bandsaw mills and literally swept the forests before them. In his *History of Nicholas County, West Virginia,* William G. Brown, a resident of that county during the heyday of the lumbermen, tells how their agents fleeced uninformed resident landowners out of "mineral lands that would never be of any possible use to them" and out of "wild" lands that were represented as equally valueless. When they could not acquire lands in fee, they were generally able to purchase the mineral and timber rights. Having acquired ownership in whatever form, "Great yellow poplars producing fifteen hundred to two thousand feet of lumber that had cost from fifty cents to a dollar a tree," said Brown, "were cut into export boards two inches thick and twenty-four to thirty-six inches wide, and sold in the export trade for as much as $80 to $100 a thousand feet."[16]

The year 1909 marked the peak of the lumber and timber industry in West Virginia. In that year the greatest output, 1,473 million board feet, valued at $28,758,000, was manufactured. During the ten years which followed the average annual production was about 900 million board feet,

Hardwood forest, Nicholas County

and in 1919 West Virginia ranked third in the production of hardwood lumber and seventeenth in lumber of all grades. She led the country in the production of chestnut and yellow poplar lumber. Oak, chestnut, hemlock, yellow poplar, maple, and spruce, in the order named, made up the bulk of her timber products.

After World War I the West Virginia lumber industry declined steadily. In 1953 the total output was 382 million board feet, which was only slightly more than one fourth of the production in 1909, the peak year. Bandsaw mills were in production in 1955 at Bluefield (three), Clarksburg, Kenova, Charleston, Williamson, Rainelle, Richwood, Pineville, Camden-on-Gauley, Swandale (Clay County), Dixie (Nicholas County), and Riverton (Pendleton County). Tanneries at Frank and Marlinton, Pocahontas County; Petersburg, Grant County; and Parsons, Tucker County, used West Virginia-produced tanbark, and West Virginia-produced pulpwood was exported in considerable quantities.

16 William G. Brown, *History of Nicholas County, West Virginia* (Richmond, Va., 1954), p. 182.

Despite the declining importance of her timber industry, West Virginia in 1950 ranked seventh among the states in the production of hardwood lumber, her total for that year being 411 million board feet. The use of pipelines, metallic storage tanks, tank cars and drums had long since destroyed the demand for staves and headings. Her hardwoods were then being converted into building materials, furniture, tool handles, children's toys, trays, and scores of other articles. Clothespins, butter bowls, and drinking cups were made at Richwood, while four million heels for women's shoes were made annually at Rainelle. In 1955 several lumber companies in the state were building kilns to be used for the conversion of slabwoods into "hard-sapwood" charcoal to supply an expanding market for outdoor and indoor fireplaces. But this search for by-products only emphasized the fact that the rough-and-ready days of lumberjacks were ended, and the forest lands of the state had been reduced to a mere shadow of their former magnificence.

Stone and Clay Products

Limestone and sandstone were the basis of other important West Virginia industries. Sandstone was found in all parts of the state, but most abundantly in the Trans-Allegheny region north of the Kanawha River. If traces of limestone were found here and there in the same region, it occurred in unlimited quantities in certain southern counties and in the eastern part of the state. A great deposit of Mississippian age was exposed throughout the length of the Alleghenies; older large deposits of the Devonian and Silurian ages occurred farther east along Allegheny Front, upper tributaries of South Branch River, and along and near Cacapon River; and vast stores of high grade limestone and dolomite of the Cambrian and Ordovician ages were found in Berkeley and Jefferson counties.

In 1950 limestone, in large quantities, was used in West Virginia to make Portland cement, chemical and metallurgical limestone, rock-wool, agricultural lime, road ballast, and aggregates. Limestone of high purity was then being conditioned for use as flux for glass making and for various chemical uses near Martinsburg, Berkeley County, and near Fort Spring, Greenbrier County. Many kinds of insulating materials were then made from limestone, most important among them being rock-wool. In 1950 West Virginia producers sold and used 6,011,120 tons of crushed and broken limestone, valued at $6,747,575, for riprap, fluxing stone, crushed stone, agricultural, and miscellaneous uses. At the same time dolomite, a close relative to limestone, was being quarried in Jefferson County for use in the open hearth process of making steel and for making mineral wool.

West Virginia was well supplied with shales and clays suitable for the manufacture of face brick, paving tile, drainage tile, and similar products. Here and there were residences built with "brick made on the site." In 1955 there were a number of brick-and-tile making establishments in the state, and fire brick, glass pots, and furnace linings were being made in Mineral, Hancock, Taylor, and Kanawha counties. In 1948 the production of fire clay reached 314,084 tons, valued at $756,627, and miscellaneous clay products, not including pottery, totaled 276, 395 tons, valued at $220,049.

From simple beginnings at Morgantown in 1785 the pottery industry extended over a wide area of present West Virginia. In 1955 earthenware plants were located at Wheeling, Mannington, Paden City, Huntington, Ravenswood, Grafton, and Parkersburg. The Bowers plant at Mannington was one of the largest sanitary potteries in the world, and Moundsville was the site of one of the largest enamelware industries in America. The industry centered however in Hancock County which had been known for its fine quality chinaware. To develop further the statewide possibilities of these industries, courses in ceramics were offered at the University and in a number of high schools.

Sand and Gravel Products

As already stated, the presence of silica in West Virginia was one of the chief factors which gave her high ranking among the glass producing states. Deposits of silica, of 98 to 100 per cent purity, occurred in Morgan, Preston, Monongalia, Randolph, Taylor, and Upshur counties. Silica was also found in the flood plains of the Big Sandy and the Ohio rivers. In 1950 West Virginia producers sold 473,574 tons of sand, valued at $708,928, for glass making and molding purposes. Silica was also used in the manufacture of aircraft engines, steel castings, armour plate, silicate of soda, electrical porcelain, and refrigerators. Construction of improved highways, modern bridges and buildings boosted the sand and gravel business. Most of the materials for these purposes came from the larger streams of the state, particularly the Ohio, and was of glacial origin. During the last half century the total value of these products tended to increase annually. In 1950 it was $6,241,057 for 3,613,046 tons, while the respective totals for the country at large were $295,040,000 and 370,455,000 tons.

Salt and Salt Brines

Owing to the expansion of production after 1849 in Mason County, (West) Virginia, and in contiguous counties of Ohio, the salt industry on the Kanawha declined rapidly after 1850. There the manufacturer enjoyed not only superior facilities but also a higher quality of brine. Consequently the Kanawha operators joined in 1854 in the organization of the Ohio River Salt Company and diverted their production into a common stock which was sold on a pro rata basis. Under this arrangement the Ohio River production increased rapidly, while that on the Kanawha decreased. Their respective outputs for 1875 were 2,500,000 and 967,465 bushels. Owing to competition from rock-salt operations in New York and Michigan, salt making declined rapidly in West Virginia after 1880. In 1907 only four plants, the Dickinson at Malden and three in Mason County remained active. In that year the Malden plant produced daily from 125 to 150 barrels of salt, 150 pounds of bromine, and four tons of calcium, while the corresponding daily output for the Mason County Works was 500 barrels, 500 pounds, and eight tons.[17]

In 1876 Dr. John P. Hale of Charleston predicted that the day was not far off when the most important use of West Virginia salt brines would be in the manufacture of alkalies and chemicals. This prophecy came true with the coming of the chemical industry to the Kanawha Valley in World War I. Either directly or indirectly this industry made extensive use of salt brine, and the salt works in both Kanawha and Mason counties were all but converted into chemical plants. In 1937 the Dickinson plant at Malden, employing about 85 men, produced 500 tons of salt, 3,000 pounds of bromine, and 100 tons of mixed calcium and manganese chlorides each month. Meanwhile, the two plants in Mason County, employing about 90 persons, produced 392,519 tons of salt a year, or a little more than two per cent of that for the entire country. At the same time the state ranked second in the production of calcium magnesium chloride and fourth in the production of bromine.

Beds of rock of the Upper Silurian age occurred beneath an area of about 2,400 square miles in the northwestern part of West Virginia, including most of the following counties: Hancock, Brooke, Ohio, Marshall, Wetzel, Tyler, Pleasants, Ritchie, Doddridge, Harrison, Marion, and Monongalia. The depth of these deposits ranged from about 5,000 feet at Chester, Hancock County, to more than 10,000 feet in parts of Monongalia County. The salt was thus too deep to be mined, but it was obtained by forcing water into the strata and pumping the saturation to the surface in the form of artificial brine. For example, a chemical plant, established in 1941 at Natrium, Marshall County, used brine from five wells

---

[17] James H. C. Martens, "Rock Salt Deposits in West Virginia," *Bulletin No. 7*, West Va. Geol. Survey; Paul H. Price, "Natural Resources of West Virginia," *Bulletin*, Geological Survey Commission (1952).

drilled to the rock salt bed, about 6,700 feet below the earth's surface, and thence through a salt strata 110 to 120 feet thick. Artificial brines of this kind were superior in many respects to natural brines for industrial purposes. As the reserve of this resource was estimated to be 188 million tons per square mile, a great industrial future was predicted for West Virginia.

Chapter XXXI

Labor Moves Forward

THE INDUSTRIALIZATION of West Virginia brought in its wake the organized labor movement, which steadily gained ground after the Civil War. There, as elsewhere, workers sought to obtain through unity rights, privileges, and advantages which were beyond their power to obtain individually. Despite the inevitableness of the result, their objective was not attained without a struggle. In West Virginia it was featured by bitterness, violence, and tragedy. The rapid industrialization of a predominantly rural area, the nature of its major industries, the uneven growth and distribution of its population, and the individualistic traditions of its inhabitants made it difficult to reconcile differences and objectives. The struggle was climaxed, however, by general agreement to the effect that employees had a right to organize, to bargain collectively, and to participate in making the laws and rules governing capital and labor relations.

Following minor clashes between capital and labor in the Wheeling area,[1] resident employees of the Baltimore and Ohio Railroad in Martinsburg, on July 17, 1877, precipitated a strike that soon assumed national scope and importance. Out of resentment of a reduction in wages, members of the Trainmen's Union of that city left their posts and were joined at once by other trainmen and workers over a wide area. Since the strike was featured by rioting, burning, and plundering, Governor Mathews called out the state militia only to find it unable to cope with the situation. He thereupon requested President Hayes to send federal troops. These were promptly sent and the strikers dispersed; but their action did not retard the labor movement in the state, which was then being sparked by the Knights of Labor.[2]

1 The Wheeling *Intelligencer* for January 4, 1873, said, "All the coal miners are out on a strike for 3¾ cents per bushel—a half cent advance on the price they have been receiving."

2 Wheeling *Intelligencer,* July 18, 24, 26, 1877; *Calendar of the Henry Mason Mathews Letters and Papers in the State Department of Archives and History* (Charleston, W. Va., 1941).

THE UNITED MINE WORKERS

With the organization of the United Mine Workers of America in 1890, they soon became the dominant influence in the labor movement in West Virginia. This organization was an affiliate of the American Federation of Labor which, at the instance of Samuel Gompers, the president, called an organizing meeting at Wheeling on April 21, 1890, at which time and place the State Union of the United Mine Workers was organized as District 17 with M. F. Moran as president at a salary of $40 per month. Under direction of Gompers, Moran and his associates proceeded at once to implement their organization by unionizing the miners in West Virginia. With the aid of the Knights of Labor they achieved some success in 1894 and were thus prepared to carry on more effectively in an enlarged program formulated in 1897.

The year 1897 was indeed an important one in the history of the United Mine Workers of America in West Virginia, as elsewhere. Alarmed by the increasing shipments of superior and cheaper coal that were then reaching Midwest and Great Lakes markets from West Virginia, operators of western Pennsylvania, Ohio, Indiana, and Illinois, comprising the "Central Competitive Field," agreed to permit the unionization of their mines on a standard wage and dues check-off basis, provided the United Mine Workers would organize the mines in West Virginia and Kentucky on the same basis.

This offer was accepted and Gompers called an outdoor meeting at Wheeling for July 27, 1897, to launch the organization campaign in West Virginia. This meeting was attended by Gompers, M. D. Ratchford, president of the United Mine Workers, and James Sovereign of the Knights of Labor, each of whom addressed the meeting of about 17,000 persons in what was officially described as "one of the most important gatherings of its kind in the history of the country." It voted to divide West Virginia into three organization districts and to send its leaders to Governor Atkinson to protest against the use of injunctions in labor disputes.[3]

The first of these injunctions in West Virginia was issued on July 26, 1897, by Judge John W. Mason of the Marion County Circuit Court. It forbade employees of designated mines in that county to use threats, intimidation, or violence to induce fellow employees to strike. The injunction was not enforced, but on August 15, 1897, Judge John J. Jackson of the United States District Court enjoined Ratchford and Eugene V.

[3] Charles P. Anson, "A History of the Labor Movement in West Virginia" (Doctoral dissertation, University of North Carolina, Chapel Hill, 1940); Governor Atkinson, *Public Addresses,* p. 73; West Virginia Labor Commission, *Report* (1898), p. 69.

Debs from interfering in any manner with the operations of three designated mines in Harrison County. Three days later 200 miners moved over the public highway near one of these mines, and two of them were arrested. They were tried before Judge Nathan Goff, Jr. in the United States Circuit Court, who ruled that such use of a public highway was contempt of court within the meaning of the injunction.[4]

It was about this time that the operators began to employ special police, mine guards, and detectives to thwart the efforts of organizers. Because of the vigilance of these agents, it was not always safe even for disinterested parties to come within range of coal mine operations. In a special message to the legislature in 1907 concerning "Cases of Peonage and Labor Conditions," Governor Dawson said of the company agents: "They are used by some collieries to protect the property of the owners, to prevent trespassing, and especially to prohibit labor agitators and organizers of the miners' union from gaining access to the miners. . . . Many outrages have been committed by these guards, many of whom appear to be vicious and dare-devil men who seem to aim to add to their viciousness by bull-dozing and terrorizing people."[5]

It was by such methods that the operators defeated the union movement launched in 1897. Of the 23,262 miners then employed in the state 5,314 participated in the strike and 4,507 of them returned to work. Of these only 758 returned at the wage scale paid in the Central Competitive Field, and only 1,402 received an increase in wages. The total union membership in the state was however increased from 206 to 3,693 and the number of union locals from six to forty.[6]

The labor movement was, however, gaining in popular favor, as indicated by an act of the 1899 legislature including Labor Day among the legal holidays in West Virginia. The first observance was held on September 4, 1899.[7] It had, however, been a national holiday since 1894, when President Cleveland approved an act of Congress setting aside the first Monday in September as "An annual legal holiday in honor of the men and women of the nation who toil and produce."

Spurred on by the operators of the Central Competitive Field, the union organizing movement in West Virginia was resumed by a general strike called on June 7, 1902. It covered fifteen counties, involved about 16,000 miners, and closed 108 of the 408 active mines. Although the results were not all that was desired, the movement made appreciable

---

4 Smith, "Nathan Goff, Jr."

5 "Message," January 17, 1907, p. 34; Writers' Program of the Works Projects Administration, comp., *West Virginia: A Guide to the Mountain State* (New York, 1941), p. 90.

6 Anson, "Labor Movement" (MS); West Va., *A Guide*, pp. 88-96.

7 See Atkinson, "Proclamation," in *Public Addresses*, p. 323. The idea of Labor Day was first suggested in 1882 by Peter J. McGuire at a meeting of the New York City Central Labor Union (New York *Times*, Sept. 6, 1954).

gains. It lost ground in the smokeless coal fields of the southern part of the state, but largely through the efforts of "Mother" Jones, the "Angel of the Miners," the mines in the Central Kanawha field were almost completely organized at that time. Union organization movements were successful also in the northern part of the state, particularly in the Panhandle counties.

The union movement was however far from complete, and it was revived in 1906 on a grand scale by the use of the strike, only again to fall far short of its objective. This failure was generally attributed to the practice of bargaining by sections and districts instead of by and for the industry as a whole. The resulting lack of uniformity defeated the purposes of the union even within the bounds of the Central Competitive Field. Consequently it was the chief topic of discussion in the International Convention of the United Mine Workers of America held at Indianapolis in January, 1907. In the course of the discussion delegates stated that great quantities of West Virginia coal had passed through the towns and cities of Ohio in 1906 before the eyes of striking miners, and their delegates demanded that something be done about it.[8]

After "earnest and prolonged discussion" and after assurances of financial aid from operators, the delegates voted to abandon the sectional or district practice of bargaining and to unionize the coal fields of the entire Ohio Valley on a uniform wage and check-off basis. West Virginia operators charged conspiracy, but the organizers went forward with their program. For that purpose John Mitchell, president of the United Mine Workers, took personal charge and upon his arrival in Charleston, West Virginia, in February, 1907, announced that he had come to stay; but his efforts were soon thwarted by court injunctions and company guards. As a result the union could claim a membership of only about 7,000 in District 17 after three years of intensive effort.

Although about $1,000,000 had been spent by organizers in West Virginia by 1911, she was then described as "A dagger in the heart of the United Mine Workers of America." Non-union mined coal from her mines was then being "put on the docks in Lake Michigan at $1.70 and $1.80 f.o.b.," and her total production had increased from about 5,000,000 tons in 1888 to about 60,000,000 tons, only 10 per cent of which was then consumed within the state. Both the Central Competitive Field operators and its miners pronounced the competition prohibitive and, with the operators providing the "sinews of war," they again made concerted plans "to wipe out cheap coal from West Virginia" by unionizing her mines on the same wage scale and check-off basis as those in force in the Central Competitive Field.[9]

---

[8] 245 *U. S.* 229-274.

[9] *Ibid.*; Anson, "Labor Movement."

With the operators resting their case on the court opinion in the Hitchman case, to be noted presently, and on a state pride and patriotism not unlike that which had defied "Northern invaders" in 1861, a struggle was precipitated in 1912 when the operators on Paint Creek, Kanawha County, refused to renew their contracts with the union. The miners struck on April 1, and were soon joined by those in the Cabin Creek area. Most of them were discharged at once and evicted from their houses. They then established themselves in tents where they assembled large quantities of ammunition, pistols, shotguns, rifles, and machine guns for the avowed purpose of giving the mine guards some of their own medicine. In July, 1912, an armed force of miners, in a retaliatory move, marched toward Mucklow, where they were met by a posse of mine guards which had, a few days before, fired upon their tented residence colony. In the "battle" which followed twelve miners and four guards were killed. Soon thereafter Governor Glasscock established martial law over both the Paint Creek and the Cabin Creek districts.[10]

Due to the intercession of "Mother" Jones, the strike situation cleared somewhat, and on October 15, 1912 martial law was discontinued. As it was the first use of such force in the mining history of the state, the governor had hesitated to use it and he embraced the first possible opportunity to discontinue it. But violence broke out again, and on November 15, 1912, martial law was restored and remained in force during another month. It was again restored on February 12, 1913, and remained in force to the end of the strike. During this unrest approximately a hundred persons, including Mother Jones, were tried by military courts and sentenced to prison. Mother Jones got twenty years, but she was pardoned after spending considerable time in jail.[11] Soon after Henry D. Hatfield became governor he suggested that the operators concede to the miners the right to organize, adopt a nine-hour day, grant the right to trade at other than company stores, agree to semi-monthly pay days, and cease their discrimination against union men. The operators accepted the "Hatfield Contract," and the strike ended on April 28, 1913. The results were generally favorable to the union which had, temporarily at least, become the bargaining agent for the miners of the whole Kanawha Valley.

The "lawlessness of Paint Creek, West Virginia," and the remedies, particularly the use of martial law, had meanwhile attracted nation-wide attention, and in May, 1913, the United States Senate directed its Committee on Education and Labor to make an investigation and a report. The

---

10 U. S. Senate, "Investigation of the Paint Creek Coal Fields of West Virginia," in *Report No. 43,* 63rd Cong. 1st sess.; *ibid., Report No. 321,* 63rd Cong. 2nd sess.; Governor Glasscock, "Message," Jan. 2, 1913, pp. 49-50.

11 Mary (Harris) Jones, *Autobiography of Mother Jones* (Chicago, 1925); West Virginia, *A Guide,* pp. 88-96; Charleston *Gazette,* Dec. 3, 1912; *ibid.,* Dec. 24, 1912.

Committee was specifically instructed to determine whether or not there was a system of peonage in the West Virginia coal fields; whether or not the postal system had been obstructed; and whether or not the disturbed conditions were due in any measure to unlawful combinations in restraint of trade. For these purposes the Senate Committee appointed a subcommittee consisting of Claude A. Swanson of Virginia, chairman, William S. Kenyon of Iowa, John K. Shields of Tennessee, James E. Martine of New Jersey, and William E. Borah of Idaho.

Generally, the Committee found the lawlessness as bad as represented, but it found no peonage. The mails had not been tampered with; the coal operators had not violated the immigration laws; but employment agencies had imposed upon innocent immigrants. As a federal court was then considering the Hitchman case involving an alleged illegal combination in restraint of trade, the Committee made no recommendation on that point; but Senator Borah emphasized the fact that martial law had been abused, because it had been invoked on the "mere assumption" that the civil authorities could not have preserved law and order, and because persons had been tried and sentenced under it for crimes not committed in the geographic area to which it applied.[12]

THE HITCHMAN CASE

The union movement in District 5, which embraced the Northern Panhandle of West Virginia, was meanwhile making labor history. Encouraged by the successful use of injunctions elsewhere in the state, the operators of the Hitchman Coal and Coke Company mines near Benwood, Marshall County, on October 24, 1907, asked Judge A. G. Dayton of the United States District Court for West Virginia for a restraining order to prevent union organizers from interfering in any way with the operation of their mines. In support of their request they alleged that the United Mine Workers' union was an illegal organization under the laws of West Virginia and under the Federal Anti-Trust Act; that the union had conspired with the operators of the Central Competitive Field to force the operators of West Virginia to approve a destructive wage scale; and that their experiences with a union mine during the three years immediately preceding had demonstrated the impossibility of dealing with it on a peaceful, just, and profitable basis.

The request was granted by the District Court and continued by it as a temporary injunction until it was dismissed by the United States Circuit Court. The case was then heard on its merits as an equity proceed-

[12] U. S. Senate, "Investigation," in *Report No. 43,* 63rd Cong., 1st Sess.

ing by the District Court, which issued an injunction forbidding interference with the non-union status of the Hitchman Mine. This order was reversed by the United States Circuit Court but under a stay of execution to permit an appeal to the United States Supreme Court. With Justices Brandeis, Harlan, and Clarke dissenting, the Supreme Court sustained the District Court in an opinion handed down on December 10, 1917, which became widely known as the "Hitchman Case." Briefly, this opinion was to the effect that the operators of the Hitchman mines had a legal right to operate them under their own rules and regulations and without interference from the union.[13]

However, the effectiveness of the Hitchman opinion was temporarily nullified by the demands of World War I, then in progress. To meet these demands President Wilson, in April, 1918, created the War Labor Policy Board and authorized it to enforce a mandatory industrial code designed to assure continuity of production in maximum quantities. In the face of this order the coal operators did not claim their rights under the Hitchman Case opinion but consented instead to the unionization of their mines on a "closed shop" basis. As a result practically all the mines in West Virginia, except those in the smokeless field and in Clay County, were unionized, and the membership of the United Mine Workers increased from about 7,000 to about 50,000. But the Court opinion in the Hitchman Case remained the law of the land and available for use when the emergency had passed.

The importance of this case can be best understood in the light of the events which caused it to be heard and determined. Strange as it may seem, the issue centered about efforts to organize the Colliers Mine near Wellsburg, Brooke County, rather than about the Hitchman Mine near Benwood. As in the case of the latter, Judge Dayton issued an injunction to restrain organizers from interfering in any manner with the operation of the Colliers Mine, but the enforcement of this order was accompanied by the destruction of property and by personal encounters. The offenders were hauled before the Court on contempt charges, but the Court was in turn accused of unjudicial conduct. It was widely criticized in labor circles for meting out a sixty-day jail sentence to a private citizen for renting lots to the United Mine Workers to be used by them as a headquarters site, and for imposing a jail sentence on an organizer for advising a man in search of employment to return to Pennsylvania.

Because of these and like actions, resentment was widespread among the miners. Therefore, with the support of about 3,000 miners from the state at large, some 6,000 of those in West Virginia's First Congressional District petitioned President Wilson to order an investigation of the official conduct of Judge Dayton. This request was referred to Representa-

[13] 245 *U. S.* 229-274.

tive M. Mansfield Neely of the First West Virginia District, who, on February 9, 1915, offered a resolution directing the House Committee on the Judiciary to investigate the official conduct of Judge Dayton and to report whether or not it was of such a nature as to warrant impeachment.

The resolution was approved and a subcommittee of three was appointed to make the investigation. The substance of the report, as it pertained to striking miners and labor leaders, was to the effect that the judge had issued, under somewhat extenuating circumstances, "very drastic and comprehensive" orders and that his conduct on the bench at times had been "that of one who had prejudged the cases before him." But, "a careful consideration of all the evidence and the attendant circumstances" convinced the Committee that there should be no further proceedings.[14]

An aftermath to the industrial unrest in the Northern Panhandle came on July 17, 1922, when non-union employees of the Richland Coal Company, near Clifton, Brooke County, who had refused to heed the general strike order of April 22, 1922, were attacked by about 1,200 men from across the Pennsylvania line. In the course of the encounter seven union men, thirteen strike breakers, and H. H. Duval, sheriff of Brooke County, were killed. Governor Morgan attributed the attack to the lax morals that usually follow periods of prolonged warfare,[15] but it was nevertheless an effort to force the complete unionization of District 5 with headquarters at Pittsburgh.

TRADE UNIONS

Trade unionism had meanwhile made notable advances in West Virginia. The diversity of industry incident to the rise of towns and cities and to the extension of transportation facilities in the 1880's and the 1890's brought a variety of skills and labor functions. Consequently, the "one big union" idea of the Knights of Labor gave way to federated groups each in charge of its own affairs. In compliance with this policy railroaders, glass, iron, and steel workers were especially active. By 1902 the number of locals had increased to 152 and the total membership to 9,535. Of these the largest membership group was that of six locals of the Amalgamated Association of Iron, Steel, and Tin Workers with 1,142. With 2,476 members and 36 locals the Railroad Brotherhoods was the largest group classification. Other large groups included 1,215 glass work-

[14] U. S. House of Representatives, *Report No. 1381*, 63rd Cong., 3rd sess.; ———, *Report No. 1490*, 63rd Cong., 3rd sess.

[15] Ephraim F. Morgan, *State Papers and Addresses* (Charleston, W. Va., 1925), pp. 23-24.

ers, 778 carpenters, 490 stogie makers, 364 potters, 275 tobacco workers, 194 musicians, 172 machinists, 150 blacksmiths' helpers, 149 painters, 137 typographical unionists, and 133 clerks. With 42 locals and 3,926 union members, Wheeling was well in the lead. Of the 65 strikes in West Virginia in the 1887-1894 period, 37 were by trade unions. Of all these the most effective was perhaps that of 1899 by the employees of the Wheeling Electric Railway Company.[16]

In the period 1902-1914, the number of craft unions increased from 152 to 270 and the total membership from 9,525 to 31,315. Of the latter 12,880 were members of Railroad Brotherhoods, 2,320 were glass workers, 1,605 carpenters, 1,200 machinists, 900 iron and steel workers, 865 musicians, 770 maintenance-of-way employees, 755 boiler makers, 667 bricklayers, 665 federal unions, 550 painters, and 520 potters. With a total of 6,420, Wheeling led all the cities in trade-union membership. Huntington, with 2,217, was in second place.[17]

Trade unionism made rapid progress in West Virginia during World War I. In the early years of that conflict organizers claimed that the wages of members of craft unions were almost double those paid employees who relied upon "the generosity of their employers." The number of state locals affiliated with the American Federation of Labor increased from 527 in 1917, to 548 in 1918, and those affiliated with the State Federation of Labor increased to 438 in 1920 with a total membership of 45,000. Indicative of the strength of the trade union movement in West Virginia was the appearance at Wheeling in 1916 of *The Majority,* a journal established under sponsorship of the West Virginia Federation of Labor and the Ohio Valley Trades and Labor Assembly. This journal proposed to set a pace for the newspapers of Wheeling by using only the highest class metropolitan newspaper features and by adding comic strips.[18]

The history of craft unions in West Virginia was also reflected through that of the West Virginia Federation of Labor. This organization, the twenty-fifth of its kind in the United States, was formed April 30, 1903, at Huntington. At the outset there were only 600 members, but these increased to 6,000 in 1906, when *The Labor Argus,* edited by Frank W. Snyder, was established at Charleston. Because of an impasse in a struggle for control, the State Federation was almost defunct by 1908, but it was reorganized under auspices of the American Federation of Labor. The revived State Federation was sponsored by the craft unions of Huntington and by the Ohio Valley Trades and Labor Assembly with headquarters in Wheeling. The primary purpose in reviving it was to sponsor

16 West Va., Labor Bureau, *Biennial Report* (1902), pp. 68-75; West Va. Com. of Labor, *Report* (1896), Appendix; Anson, "Labor Movement."

17 West Va. Labor Bureau, *Report* (1914), pp. 71-84.

18 *The Majority,* June 5, 1920.

organization, education, and progressive legislation. Prior to 1915 the membership of the State Federation did not exceed 11,200 for 141 affiliates, but in 1920 it rose to 45,000 from 438 affiliates.

THE RETURN TO NORMALCY

With the return of peace following World War I, the labor movement in West Virginia entered a sensational and tragic phase. Determined "not to lose in peace what they had gained in war," the rank and file of labor joined the leaders, not only to preserve their own improved social and economic status but also to carry the banners of unionism into unorganized fields. In this effort the miners in particular presented a solid front. With one accord they claimed that they had a right and a moral duty to organize; that their problem in West Virginia was not one of union versus non-union but one involving their allegiance to fundamental principles and practices; that unionization would stabilize the coal mining industry and put an end to industrial warfare; that the United Mine Workers of America was a lawful organization cooperating with operators of the Central Competitive Field for mutual advantages that assured miners in the bituminous coal fields of the Ohio Valley better living standards; and finally some of them charged that non-union operations in West Virginia, particularly the "captive mines," were engaged in a conspiracy with the United States Steel Company and affiliated interests to destroy industrial unions.[19]

On the other hand, the operators demanded a free hand in conducting "their own business" and claimed it was legally theirs under the court opinion in the Hitchman Case. Therefore, they continued to arraign the United Mine Workers union as an illegal organization engaged in a conspiracy with operators of the Central Competitive Field to destroy the non-union operations in West Virginia, and to insist that unionization meant a continuation of industrial strife with incalculable losses to both employers and employees. The operators had a tremendous advantage because they generally owned the mining towns as well as the plants, and, under authority of the court, sustained the relation to their employees of master and servant and not that of landlord and tenant. They could therefore legally evict an employee when he quit work regardless of the cause.

Confronted by increasing living costs and the failure of the Federal Government to take positive action in their behalf, the miners went on general strike in 1919 and through government arbitration won a 14 per

[19] U. S. Coal Commission, *Report* (1923), pp. 168-169.

cent advance in wages. In the meantime word came that unionization was being prevented in Logan County by mine guards and deputy sheriffs under the direction of Sheriff Don Chafin. As official redress seemed remote, an army of miners assembled at the mouth of Lens Creek in Kanawha County near Charleston, prepared "to get Don Chafin" and the operator-paid guards. To prevent possible bloodshed Governor Cornwell asked officers of District 17, United Mine Workers, to intervene. Refusing the advice of their leaders, the miners asked instead to hear the governor in person.[20]

Accordingly, Governor Cornwell visited the miners on September 6, 1919, and was greeted by about 5,000 guns and an explosion of dynamite. In the course of his address he assured the miners that the conditions complained of in Logan County would be investigated. This announcement was greeted by a salvo of guns, which the governor tactfully chose to accept as a salute rather than as a warning. Thereafter most of the would-be-invaders dispersed, but a number of them persisted and were turned back only by a falsified assurance from their officials to the effect that the atrocity reports from Logan County were false.

This turn of events, together with the results of the investigation promised by the governor, produced friction among labor leaders. As a result some of them resolved to organize the Logan County coal fields at once and not wait on "political maneuverings of the Governor." For that purpose about fifty organizers left Charleston on October 15, 1919, by train for Logan County. As it approached its destination, it was boarded increasingly by armed guards and deputy sheriffs who warned the organizers not to let their feet touch the soil of Logan County. Thus was the invasion turned back.

Following the Logan debacle related above, organizing activity shifted to Mingo County, where union sentiment was crystalizing. By mid-May, 1920, twenty-two locals had been organized there, and many evictions of miners from company-owned houses had followed. This work was performed by Baldwin-Felts detectives sent out from agency headquarters in Bluefield. When, on May 19, 1920, a number of them arrived in Matewan to catch a train after completing an eviction job, an altercation took place with the result that not only their leader and the mayor, but six other Baldwin-Felts detectives and two union men, were shot to death in a few seconds. Responsibility for starting the shooting could not be determined, but "Two Gun" Sidney "Sid" Hatfield and some twenty codefendants were later tried and acquitted on a murder charge.

Following this clash, since known as the "Matewan Massacre," the union membership in the Mingo field increased rapidly. By July 1, 1920,

[20] Anson, "Labor Movement"; Governor Morgan, "Statement on Armed March," in *State Papers*, pp. 230-236.

it was about 6,000, of whom about 3,000 had been discharged and evicted from company houses. As the situation of the union men grew desperate, some 4,000 of them held a mass meeting and called a strike; but the operators refused to negotiate on any basis of compromise and instead resorted to the use of imported Negro and foreign-born "transports," as strike breakers. Meanwhile there was much firing of guns back and forth across Tug Fork, and personal encounters, some of them fatal, occurred almost daily. On August 21, 1920, a three-hour battle was fought in which six men were killed and a score wounded. Little wonder that the county was currently described as "Bloody Mingo"!

As the state police had not yet been effectively organized, Governor Cornwell asked for federal troops to deal with the Mingo situation. They were sent at once, and the county was forthwith placed in a state of siege. That the civil law had all but broken down was indicated by the fact that military police disarmed spectators, witnesses, and officials alike in Judge R. D. Bailey's court so that the trial of "Sid" Hatfield and his codefendants under indictment for the murder of Baldwin-Felts detectives could proceed with a degree of safety. Strikers claimed however that the soldiers acted in the interest of the operators, and President C. Frank Keeney of District 17, threatened to call a general strike of all the union miners in West Virginia, if the federal troops were not withdrawn. The governor consented to their withdrawal, provided the sheriff of Mingo County would appoint enough deputy sheriffs, approved by the presiding judge, to assure the maintenance of law and order.[21]

The sheriff promised to comply with this condition and the troops were withdrawn; but they had scarcely departed when, on October 6, 1920, a deputy sheriff was killed and three other deputies and two miners were wounded. The troops were accordingly returned, and the governor announced with regret the failure of the county authorities to maintain law and order.

During the winter of 1920-21 and the spring of 1921, most of the striking miners in the Mingo field lived in tents with the largest concentration on Lick Creek near Williamson. Most of their food and other supplies were provided by the United Mine Workers at a cost in excess of $1,000,000, but the strikers' movements were restricted by the police, who forbade all public assemblies, except church gatherings, and all unauthorized demonstrations and parades. Those carrying food and supplies to storage places in tented colonies were required to walk single file. Under such discipline the relations between strikers and officers became tense. To relieve their resentment the strikers resorted to sniping. On January 31, 1921, they caused "a veritable hail of bullets" to fall on Williamson. They also poured shots into Merrimac, Rawl, Sprigg, and

[21] Anson, "Labor Movement."

Matewan in Mingo County, and into McCarr, Kentucky. The shooting ended on the third day, but not until word went over the grapevine that President Harding, at the request of Governor Morgan, was preparing again to send federal troops into the affected area. On May 19, Governor Morgan proclaimed the existence of "a state of war, insurrection, and riot in the County of Mingo."

Because of its electrifying effect upon the miners, the "Assassination of 'Sid' Hatfield" (August 1) was of more than regional importance. While in Washington, D. C., testifying before the Senate Committee on Education and Labor, Hatfield was summoned to Welch, McDowell County, to stand trial for the alleged "shooting up" of Mohawk, a small mining camp. Although he felt that he was being framed by persons bent on vengeance for his alleged part in the Matewan affair more than a year before, Hatfield answered the summons. As a result he and his companion, Edward Chambers, paid with their lives as they ascended the courthouse steps in Welch.

Incensed by this series of events and by the resort to martial law, about 3,000 miners from the unionized Paint Creek and the Cabin Creek fields in Kanawha County, mobilized at Marmet near Charleston in the summer of 1921 for the purpose of joining forces with their compatriots in Mingo County. By August 23 the valley below Marmet was "teeming with armed miners and their varied vehicles." On that day, Mother Jones, age ninety-one, arrived on the scene and informed the miners that she had in her possession a telegram from President Harding promising to investigate the mining situation in West Virginia. When this information could not be verified, the assembled miners took up the line of march toward Logan and Mingo counties with the zeal and determination of crusaders.

Because of the presence in their ranks of a number of veterans of World War I, the "March on Logan" assumed features of a military movement. There were sentries, patrols, passwords, and marching chants, a favorite being, "John Brown's Body." Some of the marchers declared also their intention "to hang Don Chafin on a sour apple tree." Uniforms of nonveterans were blue denim overalls, and most of the marchers wore red bandanna handkerchiefs. Enroute they commandeered automobiles and freight trains, one of which was labeled the "Blue Steel Special," another the "Smith & Wesson Special."[22]

Alarmed by this unauthorized movement, Governor Morgan appealed to the President for military aid. At the same time he alerted the militia

---

22 Governor Morgan, "Biennial Message" (1923), pp. 21-25; ———, "Statement"; Anson, "Labor Movement"; John M. Barb, "Strikes in the Southern West Virginia Coal Fields," *1912-1922* (M.A. thesis, West Virginia University, 1949); *Labor's Daily,* Jan. 23, 1953-Feb. 10, 1953.

and the state police. In response to the governor's appeal to the President, General Harry H. Bandholtz arrived in Charleston at 3:05 a.m. on August 26 and proceeded to the "Pasteboard Capitol," where Governor Morgan was waiting.[23] At once officials of the United Mine Workers were summoned and directed to recall the marchers. As a result of the combined efforts of the governor, the general, and union officials, the marchers were persuaded to turn back and the crisis was pronounced at an end.

To all appearances, the affair would have been history at this juncture but for an ill-timed action on the part of the state police, who were operating in conjunction with the Logan County authorities. With about 130 men Captain J. R. Brockus set out from Logan for Sharples in Logan County to arrest 42 men charged with having, on the previous August 12, held up and disarmed a number of state police. On the way this force arrested a number of union miners and, it was alleged, used them as hostages. When the detachment reached Sharples other arrests were attempted, but the officers were resisted and two miners were killed and three wounded. This clash, called the "Sharples Massacre," sounded a new battle cry for the miners and next day the march on Logan was resumed.

On August 31, when the marching miners reached the crest of the watershed separating Coal and Guyandot rivers, they were met by a force of some 1,200, consisting of state police, deputy sheriffs, armed guards, and others who were identified only as "volunteers." There a four-day battle was waged along a twenty-five mile front. The severest fighting was known as the "Battle of Blair Mountain." Both sides had patrols, physicians, nurses, and chaplains, and the defenders employed aviators of World War I to make observations and to drop bombs. Of the defending forces three were killed and some forty wounded, but the number of casualties suffered by the miners was never known. The hostilities were terminated on September 4 by the arrival of a detachment of federal troops from Ft. Thomas, Kentucky, and a squadron of Martin Bombers from Langley Field, Virginia.

For alleged participation in the "March on Logan" 543 persons were indicted by the Logan County grand jury, 54 of them for treason against the State of West Virginia. Oddly enough, through a change of venue, the trials were held in Jefferson County in the same courthouse where John Brown had been tried for murder and treason sixty-three years before. Because of the great issues at stake, both the prosecution and defense were not indifferent to public opinion. Through the aid of a generally friendly press, the operators made much of the charge that the United Mine Workers of America had made war on the state, which its constitution defined

[23] The Capitol had burned on January 3, 1921, and the temporary one was called the "Pasteboard Capitol."

as treason. On the other hand, representatives of the accused, led by John L. Lewis, insisted that they had no quarrel with the state but only with an industrial autocracy which had usurped both civil and military power and used it for its own selfish purposes and in a most arrogant and brutal manner. Thus the trials resolved themselves largely to contests in generalship between the mine operators and their attorneys and John L. Lewis and his attorneys.[24]

The first contingent of the accused, numbering about 200, arrived at Charles Town on April 22, 1922, with their witnesses and attorneys. Each wore a pink ribbon labeled "United Mine Worker of America Defendant." On the next day a special train brought Governor Morgan and about 250 coal operators, attorneys, and witnesses. The same train brought nine of the accused who had not been bonded. Completely surrounded by armed guards, hand-cuffed, locked in pairs, and chained together, they were marched from the train to the jail through lines of curious spectators, some of whom resented the fact that Negroes and whites were chained together.[25]

With Judge J. M. Woods of Martinsburg presiding, William Blizzard, the alleged generalissimo of the invaders, was put on trial for treason. As his conviction on the charge would be equivalent to conviction of the United Mine Workers of America and their possible dissolution in West Virginia by court order, the verdict involved more than the fate of one person. As the "March on Logan" had all the aspects of an insurrection in that all the available state forces, together with federal troops, were required to suppress it, the prosecution tried only to prove that Blizzard was its leader and that his alleged treasonable acts had been seen by two witnesses.

On the other hand, the defense contended that the miners had no grievance against the state but only against an industrial autocracy which had arrogated to itself the military power of the state and used it for its own advantages. In support of this contention much was made of the admission that prosecuting lawyers were paid by coal operators and that they had to all intents and purposes superseded the legally constituted authorities. Moreover, the two witnesses used to prove overt acts on the part of Blizzard were completely discredited, since it was not proved that he was with the marchers at the time alleged. Despite instructions from the court which seemed to make conviction imperative, the trial jury acquitted Blizzard.

As a result of other trials held in the ensuing summer and autumn,

---

24 The prosecuting counsel included A. M. Belcher, Charles W. Osenton, and John Chafin. Harold W. Houston and Thomas C. Townsend headed the defense counsel.

25 *Labor's Daily*, Feb. 10, 1953.

the Rev. James E. Wilburn and his son John were found guilty of the murder of a Logan County deputy sheriff and sentenced to serve eleven years each in the state penitentiary. Walter Allen who was found guilty of treason, was sentenced to ten years. The trials of C. Frank Keeney and William Blizzard for murder were moved first to Berkeley Springs, Morgan County, then to Lewisburg, Greenbrier County, where the trial of Blizzard resulted in a jury deadlock. The trial of Keeney was then ordered removed to Fayette County, where the charge was dropped from the docket. Blizzard was not retried. Moreover, when feeling in the industrial warfare had subsided, Governor Morgan commuted the sentences of the Wilburns to five years each, and they were later pardoned by Governor Gore. Allen "jumped his bail" while his case was pending in the state supreme court of appeals and was never apprehended.

From the beginning to the end of this troubled period in her coal fields, West Virginia received unfavorable nationwide publicity. Indeed, reporters with a penchant for the sensational had a field day. Overlooking social and economic forces, they said much about the "Matewan Massacre," the "Assassination of 'Sid' Hatfield," "Bloody Mingo," "the Sharples Massacre," the "March on Logan," and the trials for murder and treason, but little about the issues in an industrial conflict which involved principles as fundamental as those of the Civil War of which John Brown was a harbinger.

The U. S. Senate, having meanwhile taken notice of the industrial warfare along the West Virginia-Kentucky border, passed a resolution on June 21, 1921, authorizing its Committee on Education and Labor to make an investigation. Accordingly, a sub-committee, chaired by Senator William S. Kenyon, interrogated a number of persons and submitted a report. It was to the effect that the coal operators would not employ men belonging to labor unions and that they claimed a constitutional right to discharge anyone who belonged to a union. On the other hand, the miners claimed a constitutional right to join a union, to assemble freely, and to defend their actions by free speech. In their struggle to maintain their respective rights each side had however been equally forgetful of "the great third party, the public."

The Committee reported furthermore that the operators constituted an "industrial autocracy" which, through the use of armed guards, kept organizers and suspected organizers from coming onto or near their operations, and, through the use of deputy sheriffs and policemen in the employ of the operators, assumed complete control of the county and municipal governments. Of these practices Senator Kenyon said, "The system of paying deputy sheriffs out of funds contributed by operators, and not out of the public treasury, is a vicious and un-American policy and a practice that should cease."[26] On the other hand, acts of organizers and strikers were described by the Kenyon Committee as "absolutely indefensible." This was true of their clandestine murders, their ruthless destruction of property, their tapping of telegraph and telephone lines, their commandeering railroad trains and crews, and their armed marches bordering on insurrections. He concluded however that if miners had a right to organize and to bargain collectively under the National War Labor Board Code, they should be protected in the exercise of that right.

THE NADIR OF LABOR

In the course of five or six years following World War I industry entered the "normalcy" of the "Golden Twenties," but for the coal mining industry in West Virginia it was the normalcy of the pre-war period. In the war period production for the entire state had expanded 25 per cent, but that of Logan County had expanded 95 per cent and neighboring counties in the non-union smokeless coal field had been almost equally prosperous. Much of this advantage was the result of increased mechanization which had been installed at considerable expense, and the determination of operators to maintain their advantage by operating on a non-union basis.[27] In the interest of industrial peace E. T. England, the attorney general of the state, secured a court order in 1924 restraining the sheriff of Logan County from using public funds to employ deputies to guard private property,[28] but little attention was paid to the order. As before the war, court injunctions were used freely and effectively to thwart unionization, thereby making the Hitchman opinion again the law of the land.

Under the circumstances most of the other operators in the state felt constrained to cancel their contracts with the union. Thus the future of organized labor in West Virginia suddenly became precarious. The membership of District 17, United Mine Workers, declined from about 42,000 in 1921 to about 21,000 in 1924, when, in the interest of economy and efficiency, the officers were, at their request, deposed, and District 17 lost its autonomy and became provisional. For like reasons District 31, comprising northern West Virginia except the Northern Panhandle, was established at that time and given provisional status with the main office at Fairmont. In 1929 the secretary-treasurer of the State Federation of

[26] Senator Kenyon, "Personal Views," in U. S. Senate, *Report No. 457,* 67th Cong. 2nd Sess., pp. 4-6.

[27] West Va. Department of Mines, *Report* (1934), p. 135.

[28] This injunction was based on the legislative act of 1913 forbidding such practices.

Labor reported that, "within the last three or four years, the coal companies have been successful in wiping out the last vestige of collective bargaining in the coal mines of West Virginia." In 1932 there were only a few hundred dues-paying members, and both the craft unions and the affiliated unions of the State Federation of Labor were near extinction. In 1932 there were only 65 craft affiliates, with a total membership of about 3,000, while about 600 union affiliates were asking to be exonerated from the payment of membership assessments. At that time the total dues-paying membership of the State Federation of Labor was less than 3,000.[29]

This state of impotency does not however mean that the union spirit was dead. Here and there throughout the entire state through 1923-1933 there were groups of union sympathizers who were "on strike." From time to time, as their means and opportunities permitted, they picketed non-union operations and lost no opportunity to brand the employees as "yellow dogs" and "scabs." From the beginning to the end, the union sympathizers were shadowed by detectives, known as "Pinks," a contraction from the Pinkerton agency. Mindful of previous experiences, a number of operators installed arsenals for the defense of their properties and searchlights to illuminate them. But their chief reliance was on court injunctions which, in most cases, were drastic and detailed in their prohibitions.

The period was not however unfruitful for labor. Although the courts held that industrial activity was the business of the owners and operators, neither could escape a social responsibility, the need for which was emphasized in the reports of the several investigations made in this period. Thus industry was challenged, and some operators met it through more generous programs and through check-off arrangements with their employees. As never before company owned stores were put on a competitive basis; nurses and physicians were assigned to mining camps; mine workers were aided in the establishment of recreation centers, gardens, and canning clubs; miners' hospitals were established; sickness and death insurance benefit plans were sponsored; and some operators even bargained with independent unions. As indicated in the report of an investigation of the medical and sanitary conditions of the bituminous coal field, made in 1929, conditions were however far from satisfactory.

THE LABOR ZENITH

These efforts at reform prepared the way for a cordial reception by West Virginians of the National Industrial Recovery Act (NIRA) of

[29] "Proceedings," p. 6.

June, 1933, enacted for the purpose of stabilizing industry in a period of unprecedented economic depression. The eight hour day and minimum wage provisions were to absorb surplus labor, but "Section (7a), . . . the magna carta of labor," guaranteed employees the right to bargain collectively through representatives of their own choosing, and outlawed the yellow dog contract under which an employee agreed not to join a labor union. Before the NIRA was declared unconstitutional in 1935, most of the industries in West Virginia had thus been unionized. In the fiscal year 1933-34 there were 641 new affiliates with the State Federation of Labor which, during the same period, increased its membership by 106,175. The miners in Logan County organized, and in commemoration of the event, the State Federation of Labor held an annual meeting there.

Beginning in 1935 the changed attitude of employers and the public in general toward labor was reflected in acts of the state legislature. In 1935 it abolished the mine-guard system; approved a prevailing wage-rate law; amended the workmen's compensation law; and provided compensation for workmen suffering disability or death from silicosis. In 1936 it implemented the Federal Social Security Act of 1935, passed a comprehensive unemployment compensation act, and liberalized the workmen's compensation fund. Acts of 1939 prevented the employment of children under 16 and 18 in certain hazardous occupations, regulated industrial homework, eased the collection of wage claims, simplified the unemployment compensation law, and clarified and broadened the workmen's compensation act.

Meanwhile labor was being recognized in various administrative capacities. Governors made a point of appointing active trade unionists to various administrative boards, to conference commissions, and to positions in state departments. Labor was represented on the advisory board of the department of public assistance and on the staff of the department of unemployment. Each year the governor appointed two trade unionists to represent the state at the National Conference on Labor Legislation, held in Washington, D. C.

A movement launched in 1935 by John L. Lewis made labor history in West Virginia and in the country at large. Because of his conviction that craft unionism, under conditions of mass production, did not contribute effectively to the labor organizing program, Lewis organized the Committee on Industrial Organizations which soon thereafter became the Congress of Industrial Organizations (CIO). When this was repudiated by the AFL, it became an independent organization.

In 1937, when the West Virginia State Federation of Labor, under the presidency of John B. Easton since 1924, refused to "disassociate" affiliated unions belonging to the new CIO and notified President Green of the AFL of its policy to associate unions regardless of whether they were chartered by the CIO or the AFL, Green declared the State Federation insubordinate and revoked its charter. It applied for membership in the new CIO and was chartered on September 9, 1937 as the West Virginia Industrial Union Council.[30] As in the old organization, the bulk of the membership in the new one consisted of the United Mine Workers. In 1955 the membership totaled about 50,000.

Meanwhile the West Virginia State Federation of Labor (AFL) was reorganized. On March 12, 1938, a meeting attended by more than 200 delegates, was held in Charleston. President William Green of the AFL and Senator Rush D. Holt were the speakers; Thomas Cairns, a veteran unionist, was elected president; and Volney Andrews was appointed secretary-treasurer. Five months later there were 152 affiliates. Following the withdrawal in 1942 of the United Mine Workers from the CIO, the membership of the State Federation tended to increase and in 1955 it claimed a membership of about 50,000.

Fresh from victories in "Big Steel" and "Little Steel," the CIO undertook to organize the employees of the Weirton Steel Company at Weirton, West Virginia, and Steubenville, Ohio. In this the organizing committee encountered opposition from the Employees Security League formed in 1933 and modeled after the plan then used in Eastern mills. Their rivalry continued until the National Industrial Relations Act was invalidated, leaving the Security League in control. Later the CIO-Steelworkers Union, with assistance from the National Labor Relations Board, renewed its efforts to organize the Weirton plants. This was contested during a number of years and was finally resolved in October, 1950, when the employees of the Weirton Steel Company chose the Employees Security League to represent them as their bargaining agency. The National Labor Relations Board then recognized it as the bargaining agency for the Weirton employees. It was then the largest independent union in the steel industry.[31]

The United Mine Workers of America had meanwhile made several attempts to supplant the Employees League of Widen Miners as the bargaining agency of the Elk River Coal and Lumber Company of Widen, Clay County. When the last of these attempts had failed by a narrow margin vote, the United Mine Workers, in September, 1952, accepted an invitation from striking members of the Employees League to help them to attain their objective. In the course of the unrest which followed much property, some of it public, was destroyed; a number of persons were injured, one fatally; one striker was sentenced to a term in the state penitentiary for manslaughter; officials in high places were accused of abetting lawlessness for political purposes; the situation was aired in the 1953 legis-

[30] Convention, "Proceedings" (1936), I, 59-66; *ibid.*, (1942), I, 188-194.
[31] *American Metal Market*, Nov. 1, 1950; West Va., *A Guide*, p. 93.

lature;[32] the state was given much unfavorable publicity; and the Federal Government was unofficially asked to intervene to punish violators of federal laws. In December, 1953, the striking members of the Employees League abandoned their objectives, and the United Mine Workers ceased to aid them. The determining factor in the situation was the advantage afforded the operator, Joseph G. Bradley, in his ownership of a large area surrounding the mine operations, which was occupied by his employees and used in small farming operations.

Having withdrawn from the CIO, John L. Lewis, as president of the United Mine Workers of America, had meanwhile taken drastic action with respect to the administrative setup of the union in West Virginia. On July 14, 1942, he established District 29, with George R. Titler as president and headquarters in Beckley. This district embraced practically the entire smokeless coal field. It was created in the interest of economy and the convenience of those miners who objected to making long and expensive trips to headquarters of District 17 in Charleston. In 1955 the United Mine Workers of America functioned also through District 31 with headquarters at Fairmont, through a part of District 6 with headquarters in Columbus, Ohio, and a part of District 16 with headquarters at Cumberland, Maryland. All the districts lying wholly within West Virginia were provisional and, as such, did not elect their own officers.[33]

Following the stabilizing results of the NIRA of 1933 and the Wagner Labor Relations Act of 1935, industrial relations were comparatively peaceful in West Virginia until after World War II. Then and later intermittent efforts to organize strip mining operations in Preston, Braxton, and Webster counties resulted in the destruction of much property and in a few fatalities. In the Appalachian shutdown in 1939 Governor Holt urged the reopening of certain mines pending negotiations, but the miners elected to wait renewal of their contract which, since September, 1933, had been determined in conformity with the blanket provisions of the Appalachian Agreement. Contracts affecting the several districts and associations in West Virginia were determined in conformity with that agreement until April, 1945, when it was superseded by the National Bituminous Coal Wage Agreement. In the strike that followed, President Truman, on May 21, 1946, seized the mines covered in this agreement which was adhered to, with modifications, in the contract signed on May 29 of that year by the Secretary of the Interior and John L. Lewis.

Among the provisions of the 1946 contract was the famous Welfare and Retirement Fund clause, under which the government agreed to pay into

[32] West Va. Legislature, *House Journal* (1953), pp. 1436-1619.

[33] Convention (1942) "Proceedings," pp. 19, 177-195, 233-242; Beckley *Post-Herald,* August 26, 1950.

a miners' welfare and retirement fund five cents on each ton of coal mined. After the mines were returned to their owners tonnage increases in the Miners' Welfare and Retirement Fund were the chief topics of bargaining contention in contract renewals. Through the persistence of Lewis the fund was, in the course of six years, increased to ten, twenty, thirty, and finally to forty cents on each ton. As a result hundreds of miners in West Virginia and elsewhere, who had attained the age of sixty, were in good standing, and otherwise qualified, were retired on pensions of $100 per month. This allowance, together with their social security payments, kept the retired miner from becoming a public charge and an object of charity.

Since about 1900 politically-minded West Virginians have watched "the labor vote" with concern, and the gubernatorial election of 1940 resulted in a triumph for organized labor. Since then labor leaders have been increasingly prominent in political party councils, particularly the Democratic, and the labor lobby has been as powerful in legislative halls as that of "the interests." Exigencies of possible wars and economic depressions excepted, it was generally conceded in 1956 that the gains of labor in West Virginia during the previous half century were substantial and permanent. It was indeed a far cry from a condition in which miners worked from twelve to fourteen hours daily in unsanitary and hazardous conditions for an average annual wage of $554.26, as they did during 1905-1911, to a condition under which they worked only seven hours a day five days a week for an average annual wage of $3,476, as they did during 1946-1951.[34] It may be noted also that children of tender ages were, prior to 1900, employed in factories and a few of them in coal mines for mere pittances. Apropos of this fact it is recalled that West Virginia had in November, 1954, the lowest juvenile employment record of any state in the Union.[35]

---

[34] West Va. Dept. of Labor, *Bien. Report* (1950-52), pp. 36, 76; Paint Creek Investigation, U. S. Senate, *Report No. 321*, 63rd Cong., 2nd Sess.

[35] National Child Labor Committee, *Report*.

Chapter XXXII

The Vogue of Conservation

ONLY ABOUT 2,500,000 ACRES, or about one sixth of the total area of West Virginia, had been cleared for cropping and pasturage in 1870. The remaining acres were for the most part forest primeval. The cleared land, mostly valley, was supposedly rich beyond the possibility of exhaustion. Most of the acreage was known to be underlaid with coal which, together with a matchless water power, was depended upon to convert the New State into an industrial empire. Both petroleum and natural gas had been discovered, but neither their extent nor their uses had been visualized. In the absence of scientific direction and of social and governmental restraint, possible use of other resources were lightly considered. Before the turn of the century, hard-working and well-meaning landowners were ruthlessly destroying choice trees which would today be worth many times the original value of the land and the trees, and robbing the land of its natural fertility. At the same time scores of persons were dying annually from diseases contracted from stream pollution; fire and the "lumber kings" were completing the depletion of the forests; lower strata of coal were being mined before upper strata, leaving the latter valueless; and coal was being converted into coke and natural gas into lamp black on grand scales without so much as a thought of by-products. In 1908, Dr. I. C. White, the State Geologist, estimated the daily wastage of natural gas at 250 million feet, the equivalent of 10,000 tons of coal.[1]

The record of this prodigality is one of the most shameful chapters in West Virginia annals. The fact that the practices were somewhat general did not justify them. Rather, they raise the question of whether or not the guilty parties were capable of carrying on indefinitely, had these practices continued. Then, too, one cannot dismiss lightly the fact that West Virginia did not share in a large way in the exploitation of her natural re-

[1] Conservation Commission, *Report* (1908), pp. 5-8, 19.

sources. To make matters worse, attempted remedial measures were thwarted by an "unseen power . . . greater than her governors or legislatures." During ten years prior to 1908 this power "thwarted and palsied" the appeals of Dr. White to the state legislature "to do something to save to the state and to the nation this priceless heritage [natural gas]."

Because of lack of precautions in the use of railroad locomotives and steam propelled sawmills and the carelessness and ignorance of farmers and hunters, losses due to forest fires were even greater than those due to the waste of natural gas. The "great fire" of 1899 was reputed to have "burned a hole in the sky," and that of 1908 covered 1,703,850 acres and effected a loss estimated at about $6,000,000. Because of the losses and destruction of this fire, the 1909 legislature appropriated $5,000 to finance the first study of the forest and wood industries of the state. This study was made by A. B. Brooks and published in 1910 as a volume of the West Virginia Geological and Economic Survey series.[2]

Unpleasant as additional details of these phases of West Virginia history are, they should be known as a means of preventing their repetition and of sustaining corrective programs. The best approach is perhaps through a review of the legislative and the administrative history. Only as the need for it became evident and the ability to finance it became possible did the state government take notice of conservation. The interest aroused by President Roosevelt's Conservation Conference of 1908 and by Dr. White's participation and able presentation of the conditions in West Virginia was fleeting. In its wake Governor Dawson appointed a state conservation commission, but it ceased to function after making a single report.

The exit of the last wild elk (1820) and of the last buffalo (1825) from western Virginia caused the general assembly to enact a law to protect "certain kinds of game." The first legislature of West Virginia re-enacted this law and, at the request of Governor Stevenson, it was amended in 1869 so as to include "certain species of birds." In 1877 the legislature created a fish commission, to be composed of three "discreet and proper persons" appointed by the governor for four-year terms and authorized to establish hatching houses and pools, to erect fish ladders, to remove obstructions in the passage of fish, and to stock waters of the state with food fishes. The commissioners served without compensation other than their actual expenses; their office expenditures were limited to $3,000 annually; and there was no provision for enforcing their authority. Under such conditions they exercised only supervisory control, and the destruction of mammals, birds, and fish went ruthlessly on. An act of 1891 attempted to remedy these practices with respect to deer and the sale of game, but

[2] *West Virginia Wild Life*, June, 1923, p. 4; West Va., *Legislative Hand Book and Manual* (1916), pp. 521-527; West Va., State Forest, Game and Fish Warden, *Bien. Report* (1915-16), p. 39.

violations were accelerated by the rapid industrialization of the state, which brought into it persons who did not hesitate to dynamite streams and kill insectivorous birds. They habitually used double-barreled shotguns, which were then rapidly displacing old-time rifles.

THE WARDEN SYSTEM

To remedy the above described situation the 1897 legislature strengthened the game and fish law and created the office of game and fish warden with an annual salary of $1,200, provided collections from fines equaled that sum. One warden found it impossible, however, to police the entire state. His compensation was accordingly reduced in 1901 to $1,000 annually, plus such expenses as the governor might approve, and he was required to appoint deputy wardens who received the fines imposed in prosecutions which they instituted. But violations continued on an increasing scale; mine and industrial wastes killed the fish in the larger streams; log and lumber rafts damaged tributaries; mill dams and other artificial obstructions prevented fish from reaching spawning retreats; and sportsmen continued the ruthless use of shotguns.

The enormous and appalling destruction of the forest fires in 1908 was largely responsible for the West Virginia Reform Law of 1909. This law made the office of fish and game warden responsible for forest protection and authorized the governor to appoint a forest, game, and fish warden to a four-year term at a salary of $1,800, to be paid quarterly by the state. He was allowed also an expense account not to exceed $500 annually. The warden was required to appoint two chief deputies, at salaries of $900 each and with expense allowances not to exceed $400 annually, and as many county deputy wardens as might be required. County deputies served without salaries, but they were allowed one half of the fines imposed for violations which they detected and prosecuted. As all sheriffs, deputy sheriffs, constables, and chiefs of police in the state were wardens *ex officio,* it was confidently expected that the amended warden system would be effective.

Under the reform law all hunters and fishermen, except those on their own lands, were, for the first time, required to have a license, for which residents paid seventy-five cents each and non-residents fifteen dollars. The law made the dynamiting of fish a felony; forbade the sale and shipment of game; designated game animals and game fish; prescribed open seasons and bag limits; forbade chasing deer with dogs; made it unlawful to kill a doe at any time; outlawed the use of bird plumages for decorative purposes; and banned hunting and fishing on Sundays. To aid in fire protection, wardens and their deputies might require private individuals to fight fires, and persons convicted of setting forest fires, whether carelessly or intentionally, were subject to fine and imprisonment. Railroads, sawmills, and industrial establishments came under this provision, and most of them provided corrective measures.

As the forest, game, and fish warden of the state from 1909 to 1917, Jules A. Viquesney took the first important steps toward making his office effective. In the course of his first year of service he appointed about 250 county deputies, most of whom were "good and respectable" persons and effective in counties where public sentiment was favorable to law enforcement. License fees for the first year netted about $21,500 and fines for violations about $5,000. But the restrictions on resident hunters and fishermen produced a storm of protests, and the 1911 legislature repealed them, leaving the warden's office all but helpless for lack of funds. Influenced by the Weeks Act of 1911, authorizing the Federal Government to cooperate with the states in forest conservation, the reform trend was resumed in West Virgina, and in 1915 her legislature required all hunters to have a state license. There was, however, no fee charge for county resident hunters. The fee for state-wide resident hunter's license was three dollars, for non-resident hunters sixteen dollars, and for all fishing licenses, five dollars.

Again the total receipts exceeded $21,000 annually, and the warden's office resumed its progressive program. On October 16, 1913, it had signed a contract with the federal government, under authority of the Weeks Act of 1911, in which it agreed to match dollar for dollar state funds for the construction of forest lookout stations, then generally regarded as the key to the solution of the forest fire problem. With $5,000 saved from license collections in 1909-1910, and with federal aid, thirteen wooden lookout stations were built at a total cost of about $10,000, and law enforcement was strengthened. The Allegheny Sportsmen's Association having pointed the way to the rehabilitation of "big game" by the importation of fifteen elk to stock private lands in Pocahontas County, Warden Viquesney imported a whole carload for restocking purposes.

The impelling force behind these achievements was the increasingly favorable attitude of the public, which was being educated by such agencies as the West Virginia Fish and Game Protective Association, organized in November, 1906; the West Virginia Audubon Society, organized in October, 1911; the Central West Virginia Fire Protective Association, organized in March, 1914; the Southern West Virginia Forest Fire Protective Association, organized in June, 1916; and by private individuals who cooperated in establishing game refuges and in the propagation and protection of game, insectivorous birds, and other animals. Public interest was however far behind that in neighboring states. The county wardens were admittedly not all "good and respectable" persons; the need for forest protection was not appreciated, especially by hunters and fishermen; and the staff of the warden's office was inadequate for law enforcement and the education of the public.

THE COMMISSION SYSTEM, 1921-1933

With a view to improving the warden system in the light of experience, the legislature in 1921 vested administration of the forest, game, and fish laws in a three-member body called the "Game and Fish Commission of West Virginia." Appointed by the governor, this commission was authorized in turn to appoint a chief game protector at a salary not to exceed $3,000, exclusive of expenses, and additional game protectors. The commission was required to maintain an office at the State Capital and to hold meetings there in January, April, July, and October of each year. Residents hunting and fishing on their own lands were not required to have a license, but they were required to conform to the rules and regulations applied to others in such matters as open and closed seasons and bag limits. The license fee for residents was one dollar and that for non-residents fifteen dollars. All collections were diverted to the "Game and Fish Fund," which was administered by the commission. In its corporate capacity the commission was authorized to establish game, fish, bird, and frog refuges; to survey certain designated streams so as to determine what lands were suitable for parks and game preserves; to offer bounties for the destruction of animals and birds of prey; and to protect forests from destruction by fire. Furthermore, the act of 1921 forbade killing elk at any time within a ten-year period; open seasons for deer, wild turkey, quail, ruffed grouse, frogs, rabbits, squirrels, skunks, and several species of fish were fixed; and persons and corporations were forbidden to obstruct and pollute streams.

In 1921, the commission appointed as game protector A. B. Brooks, a pioneer in the conservation movement, particularly those phases of it having to do with forests and wildlife. With an annual income from hunting and fishing licenses of about $81,000, which was augmented from year to year by federal allotments under the Clarke-McNary Act of 1924, grants from private land owners, and by the active support of the West Virginia Wildlife League, the conservation program made steady progress. Sixteen poorly equipped wooden lookout stations were converted into modern steel structures and additional modern towers were built; the commission participated in studies and discussions which resulted in the establishment of the Monongahela National Forest; it purchased, at

French Creek, Upshur County, the first state-owned game reserve, the first state-owned park, Watoga, in Pocahontas County, and the first state forest, Seneca, also in Pocahontas County. The commission also participated in the construction of experimental filtration plants; it noted with protective approval the voluntary return of beavers to the Hampshire County area; and from the U. S. Hatchery at White Sulphur Springs it stocked a number of streams.

But there were rival factions in the conservation camp. Because hunters and fishermen supplied most of the state funds, they insisted upon the greater part of the benefits and were hostile to large expenditures for forest protection. On the other hand, those who favored the latter insisted that they were indispensable to the success of the conservation movement.[3] The resulting differences were contributing influences to the resignation of Chief Brooks at the end of five years, to accept a position at Oglebay Park, Ohio County. The interest thus aroused was however a contributing factor in the enactment by the legislature in 1927 of a law creating the state forest and park commission. When the state was visited in the spring of 1928 by the most destructive forest fires in twenty years, the legislature responded in 1929 by changing the name of the game and fish commission to the "West Virginia Game, Fish and Forestry Commission" and by emphasizing the need for forest conservation and protection by additional legislation.

The economic depression which settled upon the country in 1929, proved to be a blessing in disguise for the West Virginia conservation movement. As the depression refused to lift, it became necessary to find employment for many persons to keep them out of bread lines. Among the most helpful devices for that purpose was the federal Civilian Conservation Corps (CCC), in which hundreds of young men were employed to fight forest fires and to man conservation projects. Governor Kump seized upon this agency as an opportunity to "make our mountains, streams and forests the beautiful and inviting resorts to which they are so wonderfully adapted." In response to his vision and enthusiasm the legislature, in extra session in 1933, created the conservation commission. At the same time the powers and duties of the game, fish and forestry commission were transferred to the new conservation commission, and the license fees were changed to one dollar for county resident hunting and fishing, three dollars for state-wide resident, and fifteen dollars for non-resident.[4]

---

[3] For statement of the forestry side, see West Va. Game and Fish Com., *Eighth Annual Report* (1928), p. 16.

[4] Beginning in 1937 aliens were permitted to hunt and fish in the state, provided they paid a $15 license fee. In 1949 the fee for a non-resident hunting and fishing license was increased to $25, but it was reduced to $20 in 1953.

THE CONSERVATION COMMISSION SINCE 1933

As originally constituted the conservation commission consisted of fiv members. In 1943 the number was increased to seven, one from each con gressional district and one at large, but the membership was reduced i 1945 to six, one for each congressional district. At the outset the adminis trative staff consisted of four members: a director, an executive secretary a director of game and fish propagation, and a chief game protector; an the staff was soon enlarged by the addition of directors of law enforce ment, parks, forestry, and education. The number of employees wa subsequently increased to more than two hundred, including engineers, b ologists, foresters, protectors, superintendents, managers, deputies, cler cal workers, and custodians. Beginning in 1948 tenures were under con trol of the merit system.[5]

From the outset the conservation commission was interested primaril in "renewable natural resources": forests, soils, water, and wildlife. I 1955 it administered nineteen state parks as follows: Watoga, 10,052 acre Pocahontas County; Babcock, 3,231 acres, Fayette County; Cacapo 5,812 acres, Morgan County; Lost River, 3,841 acres, Hardy Count Holly River, 7,592 acres, Webster County; Tomlinson Run, 1,351 acre Hancock County; Blackwater Falls, 935 acres, Tucker County; Gran view, 878 acres, Raleigh County; Tygart Lake, 1,849 acres, Barbour ar Taylor counties; Cedar Creek, 2,037 acres, Gilmer County; North Ben 1,369 acres, Ritchie County; Droop Mountain, 265 acres, Pocahont County; Hawks Nest, 148 acres, Fayette County; Pinnacle Rock, 32 acr Mercer County; Carnifex Ferry Battle Field, 275 acres, Nicholas Count Cathedral, 126 acres, Preston County; Audra, 315 acres, Barbour Count Watters Smith Memorial, 270 acres, Harrison County; and Booker Washington Park of 7.43 acres, located near Institute, Kanawha Coun In 1951 the West Virginia legislature appropriated $350,000 for the p chase of 514.96 acres of land which in turn was transferred to the Natio Park Service as a part of the "Harpers Ferry National Monument."

Park visitations met expectations. In 1939 there were only 320, visitors, but by 1953 the number had increased to 1,528,789. Hawks N with more than half a million guests each in 1952 and in 1953 was most popular, followed by Tomlinson Run, Blackwater Falls, and Ca pon, in the order named. Watoga entertained the most night guests. cause it was the site of one of the few primeval forests left in West V ginia, Cathedral Park was the most interesting. The total park acre in 1954 was 40,387.74.

[5] The law enforcement and the forestry division were first placed under the merit sys in 1945.

In 1954 there were ten state forests with a total acreage of 78,255 and an additional tract, Sleepy Creek, of about 20,000 acres in Morgan and Berkeley counties, which had been purchased for future development. The forests were maintained primarily for timber production, recreation, hunting and fishing management, demonstration purposes, watershed protection, and fire control. The largest ones were equipped with vacation cabins, playgrounds, picnic areas, and swimming facilities. In cooperation with the State Department of Agriculture and the University College of Agriculture, Forestry, and Home Economics, they were used in efforts to locate and control oak wilt and white pine blister rust. Trees on a tract of 200 acres in Cabwaylingo Forest were marked for "selective cutting" for demonstration purposes. Together with their respective acreage and county location, the state forests were Cabwaylingo, 7,418, Wayne; Cooper's Rock, 13,030, Monongalia and Preston; Greenbrier, 5,004, Greenbrier; Kanawha, 6,858, Kanawha; Kumbrabow, 9,534, Randolph; Seneca, 11,016, Pocahontas; Panther, 7,724, McDowell; Forest Tree Nursery, 25, Cabell; Camp Creek, 6,870, Mercer, and Calvin Price, 10,776, Pocahontas.

The chief interest in forests was to preserve and restore them. With more than 9,000,000 acres of forest land in the state, an enlightened forestry policy was increasingly regarded as essential to the success of any conservation program. Forest management therefore received increased attention. The forest tree nursery at Lesage proving inadequate, the federal nursery at Parsons, of much greater capacity, was taken over by the state on a lease arrangement. Increasingly, Boy Scouts, 4-H Club members, and members of other youth organizations put into practice what they learned at their Camp Caesar annual outings, by themselves planting seedlings on a large scale. For the first time a mechanical tree planter was used in 1953 and was credited with 46,000 plantings.[6] The total number of seedlings planted increased from 780,000 in 1945 to 2,884,000 in 1953.

In addition to the ten state forests all of the Monongahela and 97,419 acres of the George Washington, formerly the Shenandoah, national forests were in West Virginia. Both of the national forests were acquired under the Weeks Act of March 1, 1911, and both were proclaimed by President Woodrow Wilson—the Shenandoah on May 16, 1918, and the Monongahela on April 28, 1920. The George Washington National Forest was proclaimed on June 28, 1932 by President Herbert Hoover. In 1953 the boundaries of the Monongahela inclosed 1,673,747 acres of which 805,903 had been acquired by the United States. These forests were established primarily for flood protection in the Potomac and Ohio valleys, and for timber production.

---

[6] *West Va. Conservation*, Feb., 1951, p. 17; *ibid.*, May, 1952, p. 21; *ibid.*, Jan., 1954, pp. 14-15, 26; *ibid.*, Feb., 1954, p. 3; *ibid.*, Oct., 1954.

Control and prevention of forest fires was perhaps the most bafflin problem of conservation. Such fires were ruthlessly destructive of tre growth, wildlife, and game fish. By removal of soil coverings of fores areas fires also contributed to land erosion and to soil leaching. In one o the worst seasons since 1908, the autumn of 1952 had a total of 3,048 fire which covered about 650,000 acres and wrought damages estimated i excess of $2,500,000. The forest fires of 1947 and 1950 were scarcely les destructive. Causes were officially attributed to carelessness, 75 per cent incendiaries, 24 per cent; and less than one per cent to natural phenomena Because of these disclosures, the 1953 legislature extended the fire sea sons from March 1 to May 31 and from October 1 to December 31 o each year. In emergencies the conservation director was authorized t close any forest land and to exclude any person or persons, except bon fide users.

For the prevention and control of forest fires the conservation con mission, in 1954, maintained 55 modern steel fire towers, strategically l cated and adequately equipped with telephones, field glasses, radios, an loud speakers. It also used an airplane and "pumper fire wagons." The were fourteen similarly equipped fire stations in the national forests, an their officers cooperated with the state service in numerous ways in fi prevention and control. The state department maintained regular schoo for training full time employees who were charged with directing abo 3,000 local forest protectors and the thousands of volunteers and recrui who were paid small hourly wages for time actually spent in fire fightin After the departure of the Civilian Conservation Corps, studied effor were made to make Boy Scouts, Future Farmers, and other youth grou as well as the general public, more forest-fire conscious.

In 1954 the commission administered five fish hatcheries. Together wi their acreages and county locations, they were Ridge bass and trout, 31. Morgan; Palestine bass, 127.40, Wirt; Edray trout, 28.61, Pocahonta Petersburg trout, 9.00, Grant; and Spring Run trout, 41.03, Grant. Fro these sources and the federal hatcheries at Leetown and White Sulph Springs almost 1,000,000 fish, more than half of them of legal size, we distributed in the year ending in 1951 to farm ponds, artificial lakes, a to scores of running streams. Fish management was given increased tention; artificial lakes were constructed in state forests; and under sup vision of the Soil Conservation Districts about 8,000 farm ponds we constructed. From funds derived from the National Forest Stamp, rep senting a one dollar additional license charge for hunting or fishing in National Forest, the U. S. Forest Service cooperated with the state co mission on June 6, 1953 in dedicating Spruce Knob Lake, a 25-acre i poundment designed for trout.[7] In 1954 a number of artificial lakes were being planned for similar purposes in state forests.

With about 1,000,000 acres of state and federal owned land, West Virginia offered suitable retreats for wildlife, particularly turkey, white-tailed deer, ruffed grouse, gray squirrels, cottontail rabbits, snowshoe hare, and fur-bearing animals. For any and all of these some state parks and forests and the national forests were natural propagating areas. On November 14, 1945, the State Conservation Commission entered into a cooperative arrangement with the U. S. Forest Service whereby funds for the propagation of wildlife were made available to the state under the Pittman-Robertson Act. Under this arrangement eleven areas of the Monongahela National Forest, with a total acreage of 301,452, were designated and later developed into wildlife refuges. In 1950 a number of ponds were constructed on the state owned Game Farm Area near Point Pleasant for refuges for waterfowl, bobwhites, chuckar partridges, and fur-bearing animals. These ponds proved surprisingly attractive to waterfowl. This migratory population increased from about 200 in 1950 to 2,000 in 1952, when the commission established there the state's first duck-banding station.[8]

In the field of wildlife, conservation effectiveness was demonstrated with respect to deer. As the result of unrestricted slaughtering, primarily for commercial purposes, deer became almost exterminated in West Virginia by 1900. Accordingly, the 1909 legislature forbade the sale and shipment of game from the state and the killing of does. The results were not satisfactory however, and in 1923 the game and fish commission began to import deer for stocking purposes. This was continued to 1947 when the conservation commission discovered to its surprise that some parts of the state were overstocked. This condition was the result of prolonged closed seasons, of improved law enforcement, and of cooperation on the part of sportsmen and landowners. Consequently, the open season on bucks was lengthened, but the deer herd continued to grow and to extend to all parts of the state north of the Kanawha River, as well as to Raleigh, Mercer, Wyoming, and McDowell counties south of it. Estimates of its size varied from 150,000 to 200,000. The 1951 season was therefore opened on a "hunter's-choice" basis and resulted in 21,951 kills, an all-time record. The respective kills for 1952, 1953, and 1954 were 17,140, 19,844, and 16,652,[9] but wildlife biologists reckoned that the size of the herd in the

[7] West Va. Con. Com., *Report* (1951-52), pp. 20-25; *ibid.* (1950-51), pp. 38-54; *West Va. Conservation* (July, 1954), p. 2; *ibid.* (July, 1952), p. 5; *ibid.* (Oct., 1953), p. 3.

[8] *West Va. Conservation* (June, 1951), pp. 25-27; *ibid.* (Sept., 1953), p. 6.

[9] *West Va. Conservation* (Dec., 1953), pp. 8-23; (Feb., 1953), pp. 34-37; (Aug., 1952), p. 18; West Va. Con. Com., "West Virginia's Deer Problem" (Pamphlet, 1951).

future would be determined by the food supply rather than by hunting regulations.

In 1954 uses of non-renewable resources were still on a somewhat exploitative basis. This was notably true of coal, in that only slightly more than fifty per cent of the content of mineable strata was recovered, and the removal of lower before the upper strata was not forbidden. The practice of storing natural gas in abandoned oil and gas wells created other problems. Strip-mining admittedly contributed to soil erosion, stream pollution, and destruction of wildlife. Performance bonds for the reconditioning of such lands proving ineffective, a correctional program was inaugurated in 1954 through cooperative efforts of the state department of mines, the state's Soil Conservation Districts, and the Agricultural Experiment Station of the University.

The situation with respect to oil and gas operations was more satisfactory. Since 1903 "gas drives" in secondary recovery operations for oil were generally successful. For some time prior to 1953, when the use of water pressure for that purpose was legalized, it had been used with phenomenal success by a few operators. In fact some of them found the secondary operation more productive than the first. The drilling of oil and gas wells through mineable coal strata was regulated by law, as was also the plugging of abandoned oil and gas wells.

In the conservation of water chief dependence was upon the Federal Government. By the use of fifty locks and dams, it provided in 1929 a nine-foot stage of slack water in the Ohio River from Pittsburgh to Cairo. In like manner the Kanawha was made navigable from its mouth to Boomer, and the Monongahela was improved beyond Morgantown. When it was found during the drought season of 1953 that 80 per cent of the total daily river flow in the Monongahela above McKeesport, Pennsylvania, came from the Tygart River Reservoir, a movement was launched for additional reservoirs in the Monongahela watershed. After careful study Army engineers recommended the construction of a 3,200 acre reservoir on the West Fork River at Brownsville about five miles above Weston.

Prior to 1948 prevention of water pollution in West Virginia was vested in a state water commission of five members, which was ineffective because polluted streams, described as "open sewers," continued to interfere with projected industrial developments. The solution was obviously an interstate problem. With leading industrialists pointing the way, West Virginia accordingly became a member of the eight-state Ohio River Valley Water Sanitation Commission, organized July 30, 1948. The West Virginia commission continued however to function as the directing agency for industry and municipalities in sewage disposal and treatment facilities in the state.

Under this arrangement considerable progress was made by 1953, when nine per cent of the population of the state served by sewer facilities had been provided with treatment works; treatment works were under process of construction for 10 per cent; and plans had been approved for additional facilities to serve 30 per cent more. To accelerate the movement, the 1953 legislature enacted "one of the strongest pollution-control measures to be found among the states." Among other things, it authorized the right of eminent domain in the acquisition of sewage disposal sites and authorized county courts to create public-service districts for the purpose of financing sewage disposal facilities in unincorporated areas.

Because of a growing belief that the health, safety, and general welfare of West Virginians bear a direct relation to the fertility of the soil, the state legislature made a declaration to that effect in its soil conservation district act of 1939. This act authorized the establishment of soil conservation districts and provided the administrative machinery for implementing them. The key agency for this purpose was the state soil conservation committee, composed of three representative citizens and four ex officio members: the state commissioners of agriculture and of conservation and the directors of state agricultural extension and of the state agricultural experiment station. In September, 1939, this committee was organized, and in 1955 there were fourteen soil conservation districts, embracing about 98 per cent of the entire area of the state. Grants in aid under the Congressional Soil Conservation and Domestic Allotment Act of 1936, as amended in 1938 and 1942, were an essential part of the conservation program. These grants were made to farmers who followed certain duly recognized agricultural practices.

Chapter XXXIII

The New Democracy

ON THE EVE of the "Great Depression," beginning in 1929, many West Virginians were speculating upon current suggestions to the effect that they were then on the verge of an era of scientifically ordered economy, in which it would no longer be necessary for them to earn their bread by the sweat of their brows. In pursuit of this utopia they spent much time in the stock markets which had sprung up in every important city of the state, and here and there day laborers found their way to the "ticker" and talked about fewer hours and more pay. When these utopias were dispelled by a depression of unprecedented severity, all parties looked to the Federal and the state governments for relief.

It was under these conditions that Franklin D. Roosevelt was elected President of the United States in 1932 by an unprecedented popular vote, West Virginia giving Roosevelt, Democrat, 405,128; Hoover, Republican, 330,731. The minority party candidates and votes were Thomas, Socialist, 5,133; Upshaw, Prohibitionist, 2,342; and Foster, Communist, 444. The outstanding problem for the victor was to make the best possible use of governmental agencies to avert further economic and social disaster and to preserve for men and women their traditional liberties and dignity. During the years immediately following this was accomplished measurably through the "New Deal" which, for present purposes, is called "The New Democracy."

President Roosevelt's personality and his programs gave him a longer tenure than any of his predecessors. West Virginia's accord with this approval was indicated by her popular vote in his three re-elections: 1936, Roosevelt, 502,582, Landon, Republican, 325,388; 1940, Roosevelt, 496,530, Willkie, Republican, 373,238; 1944, Roosevelt, 392,777, Dewey, Republican, 322,819. Roosevelt's popular vote in 1936 was the largest ever given any candidate by West Virginia for President. More significant still, perhaps, the New Deal having been expanded to include "The Fair Deal," in 1948 West Virginia cast 429,188 votes for Harry S. Truman, Democrat, for

President, to 316,251 for Thomas E. Dewey, Republican. And the Republicans having in 1952 named a winning candidate in the person of Dwight D. Eisenhower and with the country at large clamoring for "a change," West Virginia cast 453,578 votes for Adlai E. Stevenson, Democrat, to 419,970 for Eisenhower. Except Kentucky, West Virginia was the only one of the Middle Atlantic states that remained in the Democratic column.

In the choice of United States Senators in this period, West Virginia was influenced largely by the New Democracy as endorsed by organized labor. Except Chapman Revercomb, elected to a six-year term in 1942, and Hugh Ike Shott, elected at the same time to an interim term extending from November 18, 1942 to January 13, 1943, the West Virginia Senators were all Democrats. Because of their general accord with the objectives of the New Democracy, the Democratic Senators supported the administration programs, except when they affected adversely West Virginia's coal mining and glass manufacturing industries. In keeping with an inherited tendency to independence, Senator Rush D. Holt broke with the Roosevelt administration and was defeated in 1940 for renomination by Harley M. Kilgore.

Throughout this period West Virginia's Representatives in Congress were generally Democrats. In the seventy-two election contests for full terms only ten resulted in victories for Republicans. Three Republicans were elected in 1942 and four in 1946. Without notable exceptions, the Democratic Representatives supported the Roosevelt-Truman programs, except the reciprocal trade arrangements permitting the importation of residual oils and cheap glassware.

Except Senators and Representatives in Congress, few West Virginians made the national political stage in the New Democracy. A notable exception was Louis A. Johnson of Clarksburg, who was National Commander of the American Legion, 1932-33; Assistant Secretary of War from June 28, 1937, to July 25, 1940; personal representative of the President in India, March 16-December 17, 1942; and Secretary of Defense in President Truman's Cabinet from March, 1949 to July, 1950.

THE KUMP-HOLT REFORMS

Responsibility for executive leadership in the worst crisis in West Virginia's political and economic history fell to Governor H. Guy Kump, Democrat, who was elected in 1932 by 402,325 votes, to 342,660 for Thomas C. Townsend, Republican; 2,788 for J. N. Snider, Socialist; and 452 for Mike Stone, Communist. Governor Kump was born October 31, 1877, at

Capon Springs, Hampshire County, West Virginia, and was educated in its public schools and at the University of Virginia. As a lawyer, farmer, and banker, he was interested in the civic affairs of Randolph, his adopted county, and served it as prosecuting attorney for two terms. He was also mayor of Elkins. He was an army captain in World War I and in 1920 a delegate to the Democratic National Convention. He was elected judge of the Twelfth Judicial Circuit in 1928 and resigned in 1932 to become a candidate for governor. As such, he pursued an independent course and thus won the respect and confidence of the public generally.

When Governor Kump was inaugurated, there was a deficit in the state treasury in excess of $4,000,000, and its creditors had refused a renewal. Enamored by the delusion that the industrial prosperity of the "Golden Twenties" would last indefinitely, the board of the school fund had taken chances with a part of its trust and lost. In practically every county of the state real estate was being advertised in a wholesale fashion for sale for the non-payment of taxes, and, in the absence of purchasers, it was being forfeited to the state. And here and there in the industrial centers scores of persons were in breadlines. Or, as stated by Governor Kump four years later, "Thousands were destitute. Public revenues were falling. Public credit was falling. Schools were closing. Home, farm, and business were vanishing from the inexorable pressure of the taxgatherer. It was the darkest period of our Statehood."[1] In dealing with it the Forty-first legislature spent 240 days, the longest period of such service by a single legislature in the history of the state.

The first and greatest need of the state in this crisis was revenue. In addition to the deficit, interest and sinking fund requirements had to be met, and a minimum of public service had to be maintained. Ratification of a constitutional amendment limiting the tax rates on general property in 1932 had reduced local revenues to such points that state supplemental aid was required to keep schools open, to relieve the destitute, and to keep highways usable. The court's insistence upon a literal interpretation of the tax limitation amendment delayed and handicapped efforts of the leaders to find a way out of this appalling situation.

To relieve this situation the legislature in 1933 widened the base of the gross sales taxes, increased the rates, imposed a fifty per cent emergency surtax on the latter, and increased the capitation tax from one to two dollars, the additional dollar being for roads. At the same time and for the same purpose the legislature authorized a number of new taxes, the most important of which was an emergency consumers sales tax of two per cent of retail sales earmarked for schools, and a personal income tax of one per cent on gross incomes.[2] Other new taxes included those on chain

[1] Herman G. Kump, *State Papers and Public Addresses* (Charleston, W. Va., 1937), p. 143.

[2] In 1935 the personal income tax was changed from a gross to a net income basis.

stores; on manufacturers, distributors and retailers of nonintoxicating beer, wines, and spirituous liquors; and on horse racing. Although some of these taxes were emergency, all, except the personal income tax, were retained with later downward reductions. The only reduction in 1933 was in the general property tax which was adjusted to meet the requirements of the property classification and tax limitation amendment of 1932 and the requirements of the Virginia Debt and the State Debt Refunding bonds.[3]

The revised tax program called for the greatest economy and efficiency. Among legislative acts for that purpose was that making the county the unit of administration for the public schools of the entire state, and that authorizing the state to assume control of about 31,000 miles of secondary roads and placing the entire system under supervision of a single commissioner to replace the three member commission established in 1921. At the same time the biennial budget was simplified and placed under a director; a central mailing system was provided for the accommodation of Capitol-centered officials; the board of control was relieved from responsibility for the central purchasing of commodities and equipment for the institutions under its control and this responsibility was vested in a department of purchases headed by a director; and the board of public works was directed to classify state employees and to make a quarterly audit of all requisitions drawn on the state.

Through economies effected by the above and other programs state finances compared favorably in 1937 with those of any other state in the Union. A deficit had been converted into a small surplus; for the fiscal year ending in 1936 state aid to public free schools exceeded $13,000,000; state welfare aid totaled $5,500,000; and, in addition to fixed charges, $4,000,000 had been diverted from surpluses to primary and secondary roads. More significant still, the total net income, state and local, was about $10,000,000 less in 1936 than in 1929, the last pre-depression year.

Differences between state and federal authorities over the administration of Works Progress Administration (WPA) funds deprived West Virginia of a proportionate share of federal emergency relief. By depriving local political units of required matching funds for participating in Public Works Administration (PWA) programs, the tax limitation amendment of 1932 greatly curtailed the sums which could otherwise have been used locally. Thus West Virginia did not share equally with

[3] For these purposes and the State Capitol Building Fund the direct levies for 1933 and 1934 were two cents on class one property, four cents on class two, and eight cents each on class three and class four. These rates were continued to 1939 when, the Virginia Debt having been liquidated, the rates were fixed at one fourth of one cent on class one property, one half cent on class two, and one cent each on classes three and four. West Va., *Annual Financial Report* (1933-34), p. 24; *ibid.* (1939-40), p. 31. State Debt Funding Bonds were sold in 1933 to meet a current deficit incident to declining revenues.

sister states in either of these relief programs. Her financial status having improved, she did better under the Federal Social Security Act of 1935 providing matching funds for the states to be used for assistance to the aged, the blind, and dependent children. Through the Public Welfare Law of 1936 the legislature authorized participation in such grants and made the necessary appropriation which was increased biennially thereafter. As a counterpart to the Public Welfare Act of 1936, the legislature, that year, passed an unemployment compensation law which Governor Kump described as "the greatest movement in our history to protect those who toil from the hazards and the punishments of the economic cycle."

Other acts passed at this time helped to effect a complete change in the administrative setup. The department of public safety was rehabilitated and provision was made for the compensated retirement of its personnel; supervision of conservation programs and a number of newly established state forests and parks was vested in a director; the powers and duties of the state banking commissioner were increased; administration of the workmen's compensation fund was liberalized; the public service commission was authorized to make investigations on its own initiative; and local political units were authorized to control the distribution of alcoholic beverages; but the state retained a monopoly of their sale.

Although West Virginia leaders went along with the paternalistic programs of the New Democracy, they did so with misgivings, as indicated in Governor Kump's last biennial message to the legislature, in which he said: "We must raise our guard against placing a penalty upon industry or a premium upon indolence. We must cut off special privilege and governmental concession, but we must neither shackle individual initiative, nor stifle honest enterprise. We must not permit our people to believe that the government will do for them what they should do for themselves and thus foster a race of weaklings where strong men should stand."[4]

As the first governor of West Virginia under a constitutional amendment which shifted the inauguration date from March 4, next after his election to the first Monday after the second Wednesday of January next after his election, on January 18, 1937, Homer A. Holt became the twentieth governor. Holt was born at Lewisburg, Greenbrier County West Virginia, on March 1, 1898, and educated at Greenbrier Presbyterial School and at Washington and Lee University, from which he was graduated in 1918 with an A.B. degree and in 1923 with a law degree. He was a professor in the Law School of his alma mater from 1923 to 1925 when he opened an office for the practice of his profession in Fayetteville West Virginia. In 1932 he was elected attorney general and was serving in that capacity when he was elected governor by 492,333 votes, to 338,50[illegible]

[4] Kump, *State Papers*, p. 153.

for his Republican opponent, Judge Summers H. Sharp of Pocahontas County.

As governor, Holt attempted no basic changes in the state's governmental structure. His chief concern was to adapt the existing functions and services, particularly the administrative and the fiscal, to normal conditions. Because the state finances were closely geared to an expanding economy, it was possible to meet the demands for increased revenues for schools and relief without increasing taxes. By increasing the gasoline tax from four to five cents per gallon in 1937 additional funds were provided for secondary roads, while the resale of bonds, authorized in 1920, helped the primary road program. Throughout a rigid budgetary control was maintained.

On the legislative side the Holt administration was featured by acts implementing the home rule amendment to the state constitution permitting municipalities of more than 2,000 population to adopt and amend their charters in conformity with a general law, and the amendment permitting creditors to garnishee the wages of public officials for the nonpayment of debts. Other legislative acts established a joint legislative-executive commission on inter-state cooperation; created an ex-officio state publicity commission which, in 1945, became the West Virginia Industrial and Publicity Commission headed by an executive director; initiated the use of free text books in the public free schools; prescribed a new formula for the distribution of state aid for public school programs; authorized the governor to appoint a director of probation and parole for convicts; required three days' notice, in writing, before a marriage license could be issued to a couple planning marriage; established a medium security prison farm at Huttonsville, Randolph County, and authorized the acceptance of federal funds in aid thereof.

A concurrent resolution, first approved in 1937, establishing a legislative interim committee to study proposed legislation and to draft bills for its enactment, was a significant innovation. It was a product of the constructive work done previously by an interim legislative committee appointed to study and report on legislation for the sale of nonintoxicating beer. It had a background also in the academic experiences of Governor Holt and in the effective services of specialists, humorously called "brain trusters," who aided the Kump and Holt administrations in the formulation of the details of their programs.

Through economies and efficiency the Holt administration was largely responsible for a building program which improved the physical plant of practically every institution in the state. The Medium Security Prison at Huttonsville, Randolph County, relieved the over-crowded condition at the state penitentiary and attracted favorable comment beyond the state. A merit system council was established in 1940 by executive order to meet requirements of the Federal Security Act of 1935, but the council did not attain legal status in West Virginia until 1947.[5]

During this entire administration there was an ever widening rift between Governor Holt and the senior Senator from West Virginia, M. Mansfield Neely. It became impassable, when the governor, to avoid a threatened depletion of state revenues by a prolonged strike of coal miners, urged them to return to work, indicated that they were being imposed upon by "selfish totalitarian" leaders, and offered to assist them to return by force. As labor leaders then controlled the balance of political power in West Virginia, they made an issue of this situation. After sifting all the available candidates for governor and finding them wanting, they drafted their "tried and trusted friend," Senator Neely. "At the greatest political sacrifice of his life," involving, as it did, loss of seniority in the Senate, Neely accepted the leadership and launched one of the most colorful primary contests in the history of the state. He won the primary by a plurality exceeding 48,000 over his nearest competitor, R. Carl Andrews, and the election by a vote of 496,028, to 383,608 for D. Boone Dawson, the Republican candidate.

THE SENATOR GOVERNOR

The first legislature in the Neely administration passed a number of acts of general interest. Among them were those establishing a court of claims (repealed in 1953); providing for the permanent registration of voters; exempting certain food articles from the consumers' sales tax; requiring miners to have certificates of competence; creating a council of defense establishing a planning board authorized to prepare master plans for the physical, social, and economic development of the state; providing for the non-partisan nomination and election of county boards of education and creating a teacher retirement fund and the administrative machinery to activate it.

Having unsuccessfully attempted to recover his seat in the Senate in 1942 in an election which increased the Republican membership in the state legislature, Governor Neely was not on the most amicable working relations with it. His attitude toward it was perhaps best revealed in his vetoes. This was particularly true of vetoes of bills repealing the personal income tax law of 1933, as amended in 1935, and reducing the gross sales tax and surtax by ten per cent.[6] Governor Neely claimed that these mea-

[5] Homer A. Holt, *State Papers and Public Addresses* (Charleston, W. Va., 1942), p. 497-507.

[6] In 1937 the emergency surtax was reduced to thirty per cent and made permanent.

ures had passed at the behest of a "blind, heartless and heedless plutocracy" at a time when the state was sorely in need of hospital care for the needy and of funds for penal, correctional, and educational institutions, schools, and highways. Both of these bills were passed over the Governor's veto, as was also that restricting the right of the governor to fill vacancies in public office. At his request the legislature did, however, re-enact the law exempting certain foods from the consumers' sales tax (repealed in 1945), and it sustained his veto of an act for the relief of bondholders on account of the University Stadium. It also approved arrangements for a four-year medical school at the University and increased substantially appropriations for welfare and teachers' salaries.

The administration was handicapped in this period by a war situation. There were, however, important developments, particularly with respect to the charitable and correctional institutions. Administration of the industrial schools was changed both in method and objective, and improved facilities were provided for the care and the treatment of tuberculars. An abortive effort on the part of Governor Neely to make the University more attractive and serviceable to West Virginians was halted by a court injunction, but the interest thus aroused led to corrective reforms soon thereafter. Care and efficiency reduced mining fatalities, and the feeling among miners that they had a friend at the helm of state may have increased their production which mounted constantly during the war period to the unprecedented total of 164,954,000 tons for 1944. The Inter-Racial Commission, later named the Human Relations Commission, established in 1943 by executive order, was a step in advance.

THE MEADOWS-PATTESON ADMINISTRATIONS

On January 16, 1945 Clarence W. Meadows became the twenty-second governor of West Virginia. Meadows was born in Beckley, Raleigh County, West Virginia on February 11, 1904, and educated in its public schools, at Georgia Military Academy, Washington and Lee University, and the University of Alabama. In 1928 he began the practice of law in Beckley. He represented Raleigh County in the house of delegates during 1931-32 and was its prosecuting attorney from 1933 to 1936, when he resigned to become a candidate for attorney general of West Virginia. He served in that position by re-election from 1937 to May 16, 1942, when he was appointed judge of the Tenth Judicial Circuit and, by election in 1942, served until elected governor. For that position he received 395,122 votes, to 330,649 for D. Boone Dawson, Republican.

In the appointment of Okey L. Patteson to be his executive assistant,

Governor Meadows inaugurated an innovation which did not have specific legislative authorization. Creation of the position was generally approved, however, as an effective way to facilitate the work of the governor's office. More than any of his predecessors, Governor Meadows carried his programs to the people in radio broadcasts. As a successful mediator, he had a part in a number of industrial disputes. After the return of peace, he participated in more than the usual number of dedicatory and public affairs. He carried to successful conclusion the controversial purchase by the state of Old Sweet Springs which the legislature converted into a home for aged men and women. He helped to divert wartime surpluses in the state treasury to peacetime educational, construction, and relief programs.

Like some of the administrative problems of the Meadows administration, legislative problems were inherited. This was notably true in the field of education, where both salaries and administrative techniques were inadequate. In their eagerness to correct their grievances teachers unsuccessfully pressured the 1945 legislature for salary increases. The formula for the distribution of state aid was revised in 1947 and again in 1949, and teacher retirement benefits were extended. As no one knew the answer to the other pending educational problems, an interim committee was constituted and given $75,000 to use in finding expert guidance, but most of the resulting Strayer Report was rejected.

Most of the other legislative acts of the Meadows administration were amendatory in an effort to adjust wartime to peacetime conditions. This was notably true of acts dealing with salaries of county and state officials, taxation, unemployment, workmen's compensation, conservation, agriculture, highways, motor vehicles, and the sale of nonintoxicating beer and spirituous liquors. Among significant new laws was that of 1945 detaching the divisions of vocational rehabilitation and vocational education from the state department of education and vesting their control in the state board of education. Standardization and certification of nurses was required; and in 1947 the office of state insurance commissioner was created and vested with the enforcement of all laws dealing with insurance and fire prevention. Because the court nullified an act of 1941 authorizing the sale of lands delinquent and forfeited for the non-payment of taxes, other acts for that purpose were approved. In 1947 the "ubiquitous" fee system of sheriff-fed prisoners was abolished, and sole responsibility for such service was vested in the county courts on a strictly cost basis. In an extra session, convened on June 23, 1947, cities and municipalities were authorized to levy gross sales taxes to replenish their depleted funds.

Okey L. Patteson, the businessman governor, was born in Mingo County, West Virginia, September 14, 1898. He was educated in public free schools, at West Virginia Wesleyan College, and the Carnegie Institute of Technology. For years he was a successful automobile and real estate dealer in Mount Hope, Fayette County, West Virginia. He was president of the county court of Fayette County from 1935 to 1941; sheriff of Fayette County from 1941 to 1945; and state campaign manager for the Democratic party in the 1944 general election. He was assistant to Governor Meadows from January 15, 1945 to January 1, 1948, when he resigned to become a candidate for governor. He was elected by 438,752 votes, to 329,309 for Herbert S. Boreman, Republican. Governor Patteson was not an arbitrary executive, rarely vetoing an act of the legislature. His decision to locate the School of Medicine, Dentistry, and Nursing at Morgantown was made after careful study and in compliance with expert advice.[7]

Acts of the 1949 legislature continued the adjusting process. This was notably true of those dealing with education, elections, public health, conservation, insurance, and municipalities. Among significant new acts was one requiring the teaching of regular courses in United States and West Virginia history; the state board of education was authorized to establish and receive gifts for a camp and conference center for the use of Future Farmers of America and Future Homemakers of America organizations; the continuing contract for teachers was legalized; the use of voting machines in primary and general elections was authorized; county school districts and municipalities were permitted to issue bonds to finance self-liquidating recreation centers; the state government was authorized to cooperate with the federal government in making available to state and subdivision employees the privileges accorded them under federal social security acts; and game, fish, and forestry laws were completely revised, as were also those dealing with the national guard.

Much of the time of the 1951 legislature was consumed in amending the motor vehicle laws in such matters as registration, certification of title, speed restrictions, driving regulations, inspection, size, weight, loads, and driver responsibility for safety. A constitutional amendment, approved in 1950, authorizing the sale of a bond issue of $90,000,000 to be used for veterans bonuses was implemented by creating the necessary machinery and levying additional taxes on nonintoxicating beer, cigarettes, and spirituous liquors to meet interest and sinking fund requirements. The four year School of Medicine, Dentistry, and Nursing, established at Morgantown in 1951, was financed by a tax of one cent on each sixteen fluid ounces, or fraction thereof, of bottled soft drink, and eighty cents on each gallon of soft drink syrup, and in like ratio on each part thereof, and on each ounce of mixture used in making soft drinks. Other significant

[7] By an act of the 1951 legislature the governor was required to designate a location for the School on or before July 1, 1951.

legislation included a two per cent use tax on tangible personal property purchased outside the state and used in it; a civilian defense act to meet possible exigencies of atomic warfare; an act authorizing the establishment and maintenance of vocational rehabilitation centers; and an act authorizing the director of conservation to convey lands purchased by West Virginia to the Harpers Ferry National Monument.

THE MARLAND ADMINISTRATION

Governor Patteson took an active part in the selection of his successor, William C. Marland, the twenty-fourth and the youngest governor of West Virginia. Marland was born March 26, 1918 in Johnson City, Illinois, and moved with his parents to Wyoming County, West Virginia, while he was yet a small boy. He was educated in the public schools of that county, in the University of Alabama, and in West Virginia University, from which he was graduated in 1947 with a law degree. Meanwhile, he had worked in and around coal mines in Wyoming County as a member of the United Mine Workers of America, and seen four years service in the Navy as a lieutenant. Following his graduation from the University, he was clerk to the judge of the Federal District Court of Southern West Virginia until he was appointed assistant attorney general. By election he was serving as attorney general, when he became a candidate for governor, to which office he was elected in 1952 by 454,898 votes, to 427,629 for his Republican opponent, Rush D. Holt. Governor Marland inaugurated regular press conferences and launched a program for "selling the state" to non-resident industrialists.

The regular session of the 1953 legislature was featured by an impasse between the governor and the state senate, that had its origin in conflicting ambitions and in opposition to executive proposed severance and gasoline taxes to finance road building and public school betterment programs. Instead of levying the proposed taxes, the legislature appropriated $150,000 to be used by a joint committee of its two houses to investigate the state road commission and to suggest a road building program. Differences between the executive and the state senate were responsible also for the enactment of a budget that failed to meet approval of the court, and the legislature was convened (June 4) in extra session to approve a valid budget, which was done in one day. Acceptance of the "New Plan for the Allocation of State Aid for Schools" aimed at greater fairness, but it did not guarantee a minimum foundation program or satisfy all of the counties.[8]

[8] Charleston *Gazette*, Feb. 5, 1954.

In the first annual budget since 1872 the state board of public works handed the 1955 legislature a budget about $6,700,000 out of balance. As the public was unwilling to forgo the proposed services and additional funds were needed for schools and roads, it was therefore necessary for the legislature either to deny them or to find additional revenues. In a special message the governor suggested that funds for schools could be raised from an individual income tax of 3 per cent on income tax payments to the Federal Government. Because the state had in 1933 "undertaken more than it could do," he suggested that part of the responsibility for financing roads be returned to local units and recommended that the legislature raise the necessary revenue by equalizing property valuations and by increasing taxes on automobiles, gasoline, and certain fringes. He suggested that the budget could be balanced by widening the base and increasing the rates of the gross sales tax, by increasing the pari-mutuel racing fees, and by extending the corporation license tax to insurance companies.

Instead of accepting the governor's suggestions for schools the senate voted to increase the consumers sales tax from two to three per cent, but the house refused to concur and formulated its own program. Both houses refused, however, to do anything for roads in a financial way until their widely divergent proposals for the reorganization of the state road commission had been determined. The resulting stalemate continued to the last day of the session, leaving the schools without additional funds. The gasoline tax was increased from five to six cents a gallon. By following generally the recommendations of the governor the budget was balanced, but he vetoed a road commission reorganization bill vesting control in ten executive appointed members with four year terms and removable only for cause.

Of the 715 bills introduced in the legislature in 1955, it approved 216. Acts of general interest clarified and strengthened both the consumers sales and the gross sales tax; provided for the annual inspection of all motor vehicles; named November 11 Veterans' Day and made it a legal holiday; deleted the names of presidential electors from election ballots; increased the salary of the governor from $12,500 to $17,500; authorized the West Virginia Turnpike Commission to survey and construct Crozet Superhighway; forbade state legislators, state officials, and their near relatives holding liquor and wine accounts; made it possible for persons threatened with injunctions to be heard in court; increased the penalties for second and third drunken driving offenses; and required the annual vaccination of dogs against rabies. Three enabling acts would, if approved by the voters in 1956, make women eligible for jury service; extend the direct property tax 100 per cent for schools over five year periods, when approved by 60 per cent of the participating voters in an election; and make Korean war veterans eligible for the same bonuses paid veterans of World War I and World War II.

In a five-day (May 9-13) extra session of the 1955 legislature the senate and the house failed to reconcile their differences regarding the consumers sales tax and to provide otherwise for an increase in teachers' salaries. By using the tax survey made in 1952 instead of the incomplete one for 1954, the extra session reallocated state aid for schools for 1955-56. It also created a state commission of 21 members to study all phases of public school finance and report by January, 1956, and required counties to keep property assessments at 50 per cent of actual values after 1959 or suffer a proportionate loss in state aid.

In recent years state government in West Virginia was featured by differences between the legislative and the executive departments regarding the control of executive appointed officials. Generally, the executive department claimed that they should be immediately and continuously responsible to it, whereas the legislature tended increasingly to make exceptions. And that, too, despite the fact that the governor was admittedly a weak official, in that only the "chief executive power" was vested in his office. This weakness was responsible for much of the muddling through in times of crises and the creation of topheavy and somewhat chaotic administrative machinery. Most of the six vetoes of acts of the 1955 session were in the interest of a more effective executive. The need for such an official had been repeatedly indicated in scholarly monographs,[9] but, as already indicated short ballot proposals were three times rejected, each time by an increased majority. A phase of this controversy was brought into focus when the state supreme court of appeals, in State *ex rel* Wayne *v.* Sims (1955), decided that the governor must submit his appointments to the state senate at its next session after they are made, whether the session be regular or extra.

---

[9] Albert L. Sturm, "The Need for Constitutional Revision in West Virginia," *Publication No. I* (1950) Bureau of Govt. Research, West Va. Univ.; ——————, "State Administrative Organization in West Virginia," *Bulletin No. 7,* 1952, Bureau of Govt. Research of West Va. University.

Chapter XXXIV

The Churches, Professions, and the Fine Arts

FROM GENERAL PRACTICES of extreme individualism West Virginians, in the course of less than a century, became collective minded. In the outset secret organizations were opposed by such leaders as Waitman T. Willey and by the public generally.[1] As this attitude tended to vanish, the Masons, the Odd Fellows, and other secret orders grew in favor, and their influence extended across church, partisan, and regional barriers in a truly fraternal manner. Later the Maccabees, the Woodmen, and other groups featured insurance benefits, and still later the Moose, the Elks, and the Owls placed increased emphasis on things social. All were benevolent. For instance, the Odd Fellows maintained a home at Elkins for aged persons and orphans; the Masons had a similar institution in Parkersburg; and the Moose made contributions to Mooseheart, a boys' home and school at Mooseheart, Illinois.

In the corporate ownership and control of industry, capital had meanwhile made it necessary for labor to find bargaining strength in unity. As a result West Virginia became an effectively unionized state. The West Virginia Chamber of Commerce and forty-two regional chambers, with a state junior chamber and twenty-seven regional junior chambers, were meanwhile promoting various phases of the life of the state. These organizations had counterparts in practically every phase of its life. In unconscious preparation for such a society high school and college fraternities, though purportedly social, were also political and economic. Consequently individualism, except in rare cases, was submerged, and leaders spoke through and for organizations. In 1955, it required fifty pages of the state *Blue Book* to list their names and their officers.

[1] Ambler, *Willey*, p. 188.

A number of these organizations were civic and patriotic. Among civic clubs were Kiwanis with 48 clubs; Rotary International with 58 clubs functioning in three districts; and Lions International with 140 clubs functioning in three districts. In 1955 the American Legion had state officials and commanders of ten districts. Beginning in 1936 it sponsored the Mountaineer Boys' State for white youths and in 1941 the West Virginia Boys' State for Negro youths. Later it sponsored the Rhododendron Girls' State for white youths and a comparable program for Negro girls. In 1955 the West Virginia Department of the Veterans of Foreign Wars had ten district commanders and 108 active post commanders. Sons of the Revolution, Sons of the American Revolution, and Sons of Confederate Veterans also had active chapters.

These organizations had counterparts in women's groups. Among their civic clubs were the West Virginia Federation of Women's Clubs, organized April 22, 1904; the West Virginia Federation of Business and Professional Women's Clubs, organized in May, 1921; and the Quota Club International, organized in 1922. The West Virginia League of Women Voters was active. The West Virginia Division, United Daughters of the Confederacy, was organized in 1898; the National Society, Daughters of the American Revolution in 1899; the National Society of Colonial Dames of America in 1900; and the Society, Daughters of 1812, in 1907. There were women auxiliaries to both the American Legion and the Veterans of Foreign Wars. In 1954, the former was functioning through a full set of state departmental officers and six district presidents; the latter, in a like manner, on the state level with officials of ten districts and presidents of sixty-three auxiliary posts.

THE CHURCHES

Of all the organizations churches were the oldest and most stable. But a temporary wave of skepticism resulted in a decline in both the number of churches and their total membership for the decade ending in 1936, the last for which church census data were available.[2] The Methodist bodies sustained the largest losses, but those of the Presbyterians, the Churches of Christ, and the United Brethren were considerable. The largest gains were by the Baptists, the Catholics, and the Churches of God. Total expenditures of all churches in 1936 were $4,726,486, which was little more than half that for 1926.

Among the newer denominations was the Eastern Orthodox, composed of two bodies—Greek and Russian—whose membership increased

[2] U. S. Census Bureau, *Religious Bodies* (1936), I, 58-60.

from zero in 1906, date of the first special church census, to 3,875 and 1,947, respectively, in 1926, only to decline to 3,565 and 953 in 1936. Jewish congregations abandoned one church in the 1926-1936 decade, and their membership tended to be stationary, as did also that of the Churches of Christ (Scientist) and that of four Adventist bodies. The Latter Day Saints had 15 churches with 2,020 members. The total church membership of Negroes for 1926 and 1936 was 28,102 and 34,121, respectively. Salvation Army citadels remained stationary at eighteen, but the total membership increased from 984 to 1,635.[3]

As shown in the 1955 *Yearbook of American Churches* the increase in church membership during the period 1940-1955 was about 30,000,000. Numerically, this increase was three times greater than that of the comparable fifteen-year period ending in 1940. Of the grand total (1954), 94,842,845, there were 31,476,261 Catholics, an increase of 4 per cent, whereas that for all Protestant bodies was only 3 per cent. As these figures covered the general situation, they doubtless applied to West Virginia.

PROFESSIONS

Doctors

The West Virginia State Medical Association, prior to 1902 the Medical Society of West Virginia, was organized at Fairmont on April 10, 1867, in pursuance of a call issued on February 28, 1867 by Dr. William J. Bates of Wheeling. There were twenty-one participants in the organization meeting. Their purposes in organizing were to elevate the standard of practice of medicine and surgery, "to render quackery odious," and to assure representation from West Virginia in the American Medical Association meetings.[4] Dr. Bates was the first president of the organization, and in the elections held annually no president was re-elected. In keeping with its purposes, the organization was largely responsible for the legislation of 1881 creating a state board of health and regulating the practice of medicine and surgery, and for subsequent amendatory statutes. The association was actively interested in health and welfare programs of the Hatfield administration. Subsequently, the work of the association increased, and in 1925 it employed a full-time executive secretary with an office in Charleston.

---

[3] U. S. Census Bureau, *Religious Bodies* (Selected Statistics, 1936), pp. 158-160.

[4] Woman's Auxiliary, *Past Presidents of the West Virginia Medical Association, 1867-1942* (Charleston, W. Va., 1942), p. x; Charles A. Wingerter, "Development of Medical Practice and Public Health," in Callahan, *Semi-Centennial History,* pp. 538-555.

In more recent years, the association, in cooperation with various groups and committees and the Women's Auxiliary, had an increasingly important part in shaping the welfare policy of the state. Among other things, it sponsored bills requiring the immunization of school children and tests for syphilis prior to the granting of marriage licenses, establishing tuberculosis sanitariums, and raising the standard of medical care in state institutions. Members of the association rendered valuable aid to physical rehabilitation programs; they were largely instrumental in maintaining the standards of the two-year medical school at the University, and, more than any other agency, the State Medical Association was responsible for the conversion of the latter into a four-year school.

Pharmacists

At the instance of the Pharmacy Board, created by an act of the 1881 legislature, a group of pharmacists, meeting in Wheeling on June 1-2, 1881, under the guidance of Edmund Bocking of that city, organized the West Virginia Pharmaceutical Association for the purpose of uniting "the reputable druggists of this state for mutual assistance and improvement." After five years, the organization ceased to function, and the only cooperative action among the state pharmacists during the next twenty-one years was through the State Board of Pharmacy. Through efforts of Dean James H. Beal of Scio College, Scio, Ohio, the advantages of organization were brought to the attention of West Virginia pharmacists who, in a meeting held at Parkersburg, October 16, 1906, re-organized the West Virginia Pharmaceutical Association. This organization held meetings annually thereafter, except in a few war years.[5]

The guiding spirit in the new association was its first president Stephen Alfred Walker who also served as secretary of the state pharmacy board from May, 1902, until his death, March 21, 1932. Walker did more perhaps than any other one person to put his profession on an effective and respectable basis. In 1907 he sponsored a legislative act which restricted the sale of drugs and the filling of prescriptions to qualified druggists, increased the membership of the state pharmacy board to one for each Congressional district, and made them appointive by the governor. Walker was likewise chiefly responsible for the standards and the plans which resulted in 1914 in the establishment of a department of pharmacy in the School of Medicine of West Virginia University, and the order of July 1, 1936 converting the department into a college. Dr. Roy Bird Cook succeeded Walker as secretary of the State Board of Pharmacy and carried on after his pattern. In 1955 Dr. Cook was awarded the Remington

[5] Roy Bird Cook, *The Annals of Pharmacy in West Virginia* (Charleston, W. Va., 1946).

Honor Medal, the highest honor that can come to a pharmacist in the United States in recognition of professional services.

Nurses

The West Virginia Nurses Association was organized in 1906 and incorporated in 1933 for the purpose of promoting professional and educational advancement, of establishing and maintaining a code of ethics, of assuring interstate reciprocity among nurses, and of advancing their post-graduate education through a scholarship loan fund. Those who contributed most in the initial years to these objectives were Mrs. Harriet Camp Loundsberry, president of the association from 1907 to 1915, and Mary E. Reid who came to Charleston in 1898, opened the first hospital school of nursing in that city, and was active to her retirement in 1933. State headquarters were opened in Charleston in 1935. The association held annual meetings and, since 1932, functioned through ten regional districts. In the course of its history the West Virginia Nurses Association successfully sponsored a permissive licensing law, developed and sponsored the Hupp Scholarship Loan Fund and a service fund for the benefit of needy nurses, and maintained professional nurse registries: one in Charleston, one in Huntington, and a third in Parkersburg.[6]

Dentists

Although "The Father of Modern Oral Surgery," Dr. Simon P. Hullihen (1810-1854), was a resident dentist in Wheeling, and Dr. Abraham Robertson, author of *A Manual on Extracting Teeth,* 1863, practiced there, most of the dentists in present West Virginia before the turn of the present century, were itinerants who visited its several cities and towns by appointment. In 1881 the legislature took cognizance of their activities by the enactment of a law establishing adequate standards of education and experience for the practice of their profession and creating examining boards in each of the three congressional districts. This law was amended in 1883, rewritten in 1897, and amended several times thereafter with a view to strengthening the authority of the West Virginia Board of Dental Examiners.

The West Virginia State Dental Society, organized in Wheeling on January 7, 1892, having become defunct after about eight years, was reorganized in Clarksburg on May 27, 1907 with Dr. H. H. Harrison of

[6] Mary E. Reid, comp., *Thirty Five Years of the West Virginia State Nurses Association* (Charleston, W. Va., 1941).

Wheeling, who was president of the first organization, as president of the new one. From its reorganization this society was interested in improving the oral health of the people of the state. Among other things, it sponsored the establishment of dental clinics for the care of school children, and, in 1920, it made efforts to secure the appointment of a dentist as a member of the West Virginia Board of Health. In 1933 Dr. W. E. Minghini received such an appointment, and in 1940 Dr. Russell Smith became the first director of the bureau of dental hygiene in the state department of health. Beginning in 1926 the West Virginia Dental Society sponsored the *West Virginia State Dental Bulletin,* a quarterly publication, the name of which was changed in 1935 to *The West Virginia Dental Journal.*

The West Virginia State Dental Society was largely responsible for the establishment of a school of dentistry in conjunction with the schools of medicine, pharmacy, and nursing located at Morgantown in 1951. During 1952 Dr. J. Ben Robinson (a native of Harrison County), former dean of the Baltimore College of Dental Surgery, Dental School, University of Maryland, was the consultant for dentistry in developing plans for the new Medical Center. On May 1, 1953, he was installed as the first dean of the West Virginia School of Dentistry.

Lawyers

In response to a movement launched by Joseph Sprigg of Hardy County, fifty-seven lawyers met at Grafton on July 8, 1886, and organized the West Virginia Bar Association. This organization was largely responsible for a new code, for raising the standards for graduation from college and for admission to the bar; for defining the property rights of married women; and for clarifying land titles. In 1917, *The Bar* (1894), the organ of the association, was taken over and converted into a faculty and a student publication, sponsored by the College of Law of West Virginia University and renamed *The West Virginia Law Quarterly.* Since 1938, the Bar Association has had a full-time secretary-treasurer. In the early years, Parkersburg was a favorite meeting place, but in later years it was White Sulphur Springs.

Despairing of the ability of a voluntary association to come to grips with the problems of the profession, particularly the increasing tendency of persons to turn to non-professionals for legal advice, resident lawyers, in the early 1930's, began to plan an "integrated service." In 1945, their plans took form in an act of the legislature, which created the West Virginia State Bar, to which all persons practicing law in West Virginia were required to belong and to be in good financial standing.

Engineers

The West Virginia Section of the American Society of Mechanical Engineers was organized in 1925. With two meetings annually—one in the southern and the other in the northern part of the state—it was active until 1929, when it became dormant because of depression conditions. It was revived in 1936 and grew steadily particularly in the Kanawha Valley. In recent years it held monthly meetings, except in the summer season.

In response to a call issued by C. P. Fortney, president of the Charleston Chapter of Professional Engineers, thirty engineers met in Charleston on July 28, 1934, and organized the West Virginia Society of Professional Engineers. They purposed to perfect and enforce the registration laws governing engineers, to stimulate public works, to educate the public in the use of engineering service, to develop a fraternal spirit among engineers, and to adopt a code of ethics and fair practices. Since its organization the society has had a continuous existence and has held annual conventions. Beginning in July, 1939, *The West Virginia Engineer* was the official organ, and since 1941 the society has had a full-time executive secretary.

Teachers

Having previously organized, teachers of Wheeling, Clarksburg, and Fairmont sent delegates in August, 1865, to a meeting in Fairmont, where they organized The State Teachers Association with William R. White, the first state superintendent of free schools, as the president. In 1874 the name was changed to The State Education Association and in 1909 to the West Virginia Education Association.

Prior to World War I the membership and the attendance at the annual conventions of the association were comparatively negligible, the respective numbers for 1917 being 1,362 and 262. Under the leadership of W. W. Trent, on a part-time compensated basis beginning in 1919, the membership totaled 6,912 in 1923. As this was too large an organization for the administration and control of one person, on a part-time basis, administration was vested in the executive committee and policy determining in an assembly composed of delegates elected annually by county teachers' associations and by regional round-tables.

In 1923 the association purchased *The School Journal and Educator* and changed its name to *The West Virginia School Journal,* which then became the official organ. In 1926 Trent was made full-time secretary-editor, and, in 1929, the membership of the association passed the 12,000 mark. In 1938 Rumsey B. Marston became full-time executive-secretary and the membership continued to grow. Because of transportation restrictions, the attendance at the annual conventions was greatly reduced in World War II. Fearful of the results, the executive committee in 1944 substituted six regional for the regular annual convention, but it was restored in 1947. One year later, the attendance again exceeded 12,000, and the membership continued to increase. A number of counties boasted a one hundred per cent membership in both the state and the national associations. Following World War II, the association sponsored a number of educational conferences, notably those at Camp Caesar on Gauley River, near Webster Springs. In January, 1955, the association occupied its own headquarters at 1558 Quarrier Street, Charleston, near the state Capitol.[7]

Prior to 1923 the Negro teachers had two organizations: The West Virginia Teachers Association (1891) and the Northern Teachers Association (1905). Following the adoption in 1919 of a policy to make Negroes increasingly responsible for their educational programs, these organizations were merged in 1923 under the name of the older one. For years thereafter William W. Sanders, State Supervisor of Negro Schools, was the moving spirit in the new organization. As a recognition of his leadership and the success of the regional education programs of the colored race, the American Teachers Association held its annual meeting for 1941 at West Virginia State College. In a memorable ceremony the West Virginia Teachers Association was merged on October 15, 1954 with the West Virginia Education Association as a part of a desegregation program to conform with the epoch making ruling of the United States Supreme Court of May 17, 1954.

Historical Societies and Collections

In keeping with the importance of their achievement, the makers of West Virginia early turned their attention to the task of preserving the records of the state and its traditions. It was primarily for this purpose that they organized the West Virginia Historical Society. This organization was effected on September 30, 1869 at Morgantown at the instance of Waitman T. Willey and with help from Dr. Alexander Martin, president of West Virginia University. The Society sponsored a number of publications, among them Willey's "Sketch of the Life of Philip Doddridge," 1875, and held fourteen annual meetings, the last one on June 11,

7 *West Virginia School Journal,* April, 1955. The association had previously owned two other headquarters.

1884. For a like reason Richard E. Fast and Hu Maxwell revived the defunct West Virginia Historical Society, but as the Trans-Allegheny Historical Society. In the course of its brief existence (1901-02) this society published seven numbers of *The Trans-Allegheny Historical Magazine*. With the death of Fast and Maxwell's removal from the state, the society ceased to function.[8]

The West Virginia Historical and Antiquarian Society was organized in Charleston in 1890 by Virgil A. Lewis for the primary purpose of collecting the archives, books, relics, etc., pertaining to West Virginia. The society was accordingly financed by a legislative appropriation. It was however a historical society and as such published in 1901-05 four and one half volumes of *The West Virginia Historical Magazine,* edited in turn by John P. Hale and William S. Laidley. With their passing the Society became defunct and the magazine ceased publication, but beginning in 1905 the main purpose of the organization was continued by the Bureau of State Archives and History. Since then it has functioned as a department of the state government and has increased its original collections. The head of this department is called the State Historian and Archivist.

Following the exit of the West Virginia Historical and Antiquarian and the Trans-Allegheny Historical societies, there was no like organization until 1925, when the governor, in pursuance of an act of the legislature, established the West Virginia Historical Society by appointing a member from each county for the purpose of publishing and preserving the state's written history. As there were no funds available for that purpose, the society was given space in the *Legislative Handbook* (Blue Book), and a number of articles by Andrew Price, the president, and John D. Sutton were published in the 1926-1929 issues. With the death of President Price, the society functioned nominally for a time and then went the way of its antecedents.

The State Historical Society having ceased to function, Governor Kump, in 1934, appointed twelve persons to constitute an unofficial commission on Historical and Scenic Markers. This commission was instructed to cooperate with the state road commissioner, the state conservation commissioner, and the state historian and archivist in locating and marking historical and scenic points of interest in the state. In the course of the ensuing half decade many sites were located and marked. Largely because of the interest thus aroused, a small group of persons issued in October, 1939, the first number of *West Virginia History: A Quarterly Magazine* under the auspices of the West Virginia Department of Archives and History, with Roy Bird Cook editor and Innis C. Davis man-

[8] West Virginia, Dept. of Archives and History, *First Biennial Report* (1904-06), pp. 13-32; Ambler, *Willey,* p. 172.

aging editor. When a new West Virginia Historical Society was organized on October 5, 1940 it sponsored the new magazine and, beginning with the July, 1941, issue, Cecile R. Goodall became the editor.

Because of interest aroused by Delf Norona of Moundsville, through his *Upper Ohio Valley Pioneer: A Historical Quarterly,* established March, 1946, the West Virginia Archeological Society, Inc. was organized on January 29, 1949, with Joseph H. Essington of Moundsville, as president and Norona as secretary-treasurer. The organization purposed "to encourage and promote the study of and to disseminate information concerning the archeology of West Virginia," and it adopted rules and regulations to guide its members and others in the scientific pursuit of its purpose. The society published *The West Virginia Archeologist* and sponsored the Grave Creek Mound Museum on the site of "Mammoth Mound" at Moundsville.

The most effective work of the state historians was perhaps the collection of source materials in the form of newspaper files, manuscripts (private and public), and rare books. The acquisitions begun by Virgil A. Lewis, first State Historian and Archivist, were enlarged by his successors and made available to the public. Charles H. Ambler, beginning in 1929 on his own initiative and at his own expense, collected a number of newspaper files, manuscripts, and books and deposited them in the University Library. Prompted by the possibilities, the University Board of Governors established in 1933 the division of documents in the University Library, and the next year the state legislature authorized the removal of inactive county records to it. As a result its contents were enlarged by about 15,000 volumes, several hundred newspaper files, and upwards of 2,000,000 manuscript items. Under direction of Festus P. Summers as chairman of the West Virginia War History Commission, upwards of 500,000 additional documents were deposited in the University Library. Later the collections were enlarged by Oscar D. Lambert in the capacity of Archival Consultant, and in 1950 a beginning was made in making them available to students and the public through the aid of a University curator.

THE FINE ARTS

Architects

In 1953 there were 77 licensed resident architects in West Virginia. Of this number 35 were located in Charleston, and the others were concentrated in the large cities. Forty-two of the 55 counties had no resident architect, but there were 102 non-residents who practiced in the state. All were required to be licensed, but there was reciprocity with other states. All licenses and approvals were made by the state board of architects, a non-partisan, executive appointed board of five members. Sixty-three of the resident architects were members of the West Virginia Chapter of the American Institute of Architects. Three of the members: James L. Montgomery, Cyrus E. Silling, and Walter F. Martens, all of Charleston, were fellows of the National Institute, and Silling was a director.

Artists

When the West Virginia Artists Association was organized in Charleston in 1928, it had splendid traditions. The skill and imagination of native craftsmen, as preserved in their chairs, tables, bedstands, and utensils, and of their housewives, as preserved in their coverlets and quilts, defied reproduction and were prized as antiques. Joseph H. Diss Debar, designer of the West Virginia Seal and Coat-of-Arms, had made unique sketches of prominent persons and important places in the Civil War period. Frank Holme, artist and newspaper cartoonist born in 1868 near Terra Alta, Preston County, had left abiding reminders of historical events and personages in his *Picturesque Street Types.* Eleazer H. Miller (1831-1921), born at Shepherdstown, was famous as an etcher and illustrator of such books as *Tam O'Shanter* and *Songs of the Sea.* Elliott Daingerfield (1859-1932) was famous both at home and abroad for his landscapes, especially *The Lost Sheep, Planting,* and *My Lady Rhododendron.* The drawings of butterflies by William H. Edwards were contributions to art as well as to science. And William R. Leigh, born in Berkeley County, had won abiding fame and numerous prizes for his oils, particularly *The Poisoned Pool,* the *Maya Historian,* and *The Stampede.*[9]

Among other artists who attained distinction were William C. Estler of Huntington, who, in 1938, was awarded the Allied Artists' first prize for the best three paintings by a West Virginian; Miss Randolph Venable won first prize in landscape watercolor for her *Perce Rock from North Beach;* and Mrs. Nell Hayden of Huntington took first place in figure composition in oils with her *Composition for a Dream.* Annie Campbell of Charleston, and Virginia B. Evans of Moundsville, participated in the exhibition program of the Studio Guild, national art organization, New York City. Etchings of the West Virginia coal fields by Jesse F. Reed of Davis and Elkins College, were exhibited in art museums and school libraries throughout the country. Their contempo-

[9] *West Va., A Guide to the Mountain State,* pp. 152-154.

raries included Naomi S. Hosterman of Charleston, the state's ranking still-life, flower-composition and portrait artist whose portrait of Charles E. "Chuck" Yeager adorns a wall of Kanawha Airport; Clara E. Wiltse of Huntington, whose etching, *West Virginia Capitol from Kanawha River,* was widely exhibited; Joseph S. Jablonski, director of the art department, Marshall College, known for his water colors; Alice Kershaw of Huntington, a portrait artist; Samuel C. Malone of Smithtown, an artist penman and handwriting expert; Roger Price of Lewisburg, an artist, an author, and the inventor of "droodles"; William Pflock of Monongah, whose photographs won several national prizes; Henrietta Murdock of Kingwood, for many years, beginning in 1937, interior decoration editor of the *Ladies Home Journal;* and Arthur H. Rhead, craftsman in ceramics and architectural decorations of Newell.

Practically all the institutions of higher learning in the state offered courses in art, and the University and Marshall College had well-developed art departments. During more than thirty years the art department of Marshall College was directed by Edwin E. Myers, dean of West Virginia landscape artists. Mason College of Music and Fine Arts, Charleston, specialized in art, and many secondary schools of the state did creditable work in it. The Daywood Art Gallery at Lewisburg, founded and maintained by Ruth Woods Dayton, as a memorial to her husband, the late Arthur S. Dayton, was a tribute to her energy and cultural background. Under direction of Fred L. Messersmith the Strawberry Festival at Buckhannon featured the best products of the state's artists the Clarksburg Art Center featured paintings and also ceramics and photography; and through April 23-May 1, 1955, the West Virginia Division, American Association of University Women, sponsored in Charleston the first Creative Art Festival in West Virginia.

Musicians

The West Virginia Federation of Music Clubs, organized at Clark burg in 1917 to stimulate interest in good music and to educate nativ talent, was a product of the latter purpose. "Since the era of the hom made fiddle and buckskin banjo, the mountain ridges and steep-walle valleys of West Virginia have echoed to ballads and jigs, set to scores a simple and direct as the hill folk who originated them."[10] To such a folk incidents of the American Revolution, of the Civil War and the Recon struction, and of the Industrial Revolution made lasting impressions tha found expression in unique ballads and songs such as "John Brown Body Lies A'mouldering in the Grave," which originated in Martinsbur

[10] *Ibid.*, p. 154.

Among native musicians who owed much to their West Virginia backgrounds were Susanne Fisher of Sutton and Eleanor Steber of Wheeling of the Metropolitan Opera Company. Still others included George F. Gillespie of Mason College of Music and Fine Arts, Charleston, who composed the *Scherzo* for piano, which, in 1939, won the State Composition Contest; J. Henry Francis, Sr. of Charleston, author of a number of

Eleanor Steber

songs and popularizer of public school music in West Virginia; Paul Mason of Moundsville, a talented clarinetist, who starred in Radio City; Ralph Federer of Morgantown, a pianist and composer of note; Clarence E. Haworth of Marshall College, whose *Te Deum* and *Jubilate* were used widely in Protestant Episcopal church services; and Everett Lee, born in Wheeling and presently conductor of the City Center of Music and Drama in New York City. During a considerable period Al G. Field (Alfred Griffith Hatfield), "Dean of American Minstrelsy," resided at Morgantown.

The interest in music was not confined to the masters. Most of the leading cities had music festivals and concert orchestras, and the Wheeling Symphony, organized in 1929 and conducted successively by Enrico Tamborini, the late Antonio Modarelli, and, currently, by Henry Mazer, was perhaps the most popular. Under the direction of Modarelli from 1943 to 1954 and presently of Geoffrey Hobday, the Charleston Symphony Orchestra was scarcely less popular. Under direction of John Hiersoux, the Charleston Chamber Music Players opened its first session in 1942. Charleston was also headquarters of the American Symphony Orchestra League, organized in 1942, as a clearinghouse for the orchestras of the United States. The musical tone of Huntington was set by Marshall College which sponsored the Marshall Symphonette conducted by Alfred Lanegger. Raymond Schoewe of Huntington, Albert Albinger of Wheeling, and George Secrist of Parkersburg, each achieved success as conductors. Almost every high school in the state had a band, and the State Band Festival, held annually at Huntington since 1926, became a state institution. In 1954 there were about 100 regional members of the State Federation of Music Clubs with a total membership of about 3,000; every institution of higher learning had a department of music; and the University School of Music, established in 1897, was one of the oldest in the United States.

The abiding interest of West Virginians in good music was responsible for a number of gala occasions. This was notably true of the appearance of Jenny Lind, the "Swedish Nightingale," in Wheeling, in June, 1851, under the management of Phineas T. Barnum, the great showman. His request for a $5,000 guarantee was readily met, 2,000 Wheeling auditors heard a "soul-stirring program," and the guarantors divided the profits. On March 5, 1868, Wheeling music lovers were equally delighted with Ole Bull, another great Scandinavian artist, who on that day gave a violin concert in Washington Hall. A long-remembered feature of this appearance was the participation of Mrs. Joseph Dorsey DuBois, a resident of Leatherwood Lane, Wheeling, who, without rehearsal, took the part of the regular accompanist and faultlessly executed it.[11]

Actors

Although the theater did not attain guild status in West Virginia, the state made notable contributions to that field of art and experienced notable reactions to its various phases. Wheeling was a stopping place for the numerous actors who, in troupes and individually, toured the Ohio Valley in the heyday of the passenger packet. The commercial theater was introduced about 1870, and West Virginians had an opportunity to see and

[11] May, *Principio to Wheeling*, pp. 300-301; Ambler, *History of Transportation*, p. 174.

hear Maude Adams, Sarah Bernhardt, Raymond Hitchcock, Frank Bacon, Guy Bates Post, and a host of others. To accommodate them, the Burlew Opera House was built in Charleston, the Camden Theater in Parkersburg, the Fifth Avenue in Huntington, and the Court in Wheeling. At the turn of the century, a college course was considered incomplete without some attention to grand opera, and a number of stars were brought to the University campus in an effort to give students a well-rounded education.

Circuses and showboats were contemporaries of the theaters. Taking advantage of the popularity of John Robinson's Circus, John E. Kenna and Romeo H. Freer, two of the state's most gifted orators, told voters in 1877 why their Capitol should be in Charleston. Their efforts and tactics, aided by John Lowlow, a popular clown, were reputed to have been the determining influence in locating it there permanently. Residents of river towns and of the surrounding areas, in range of the beckoning call of a calliope, were meanwhile listening to such heart-rending repertoires as *Ten Nights in a Barroom, Nellie the Switchman's Daughter,* and *Over the Hill to the Poor House,* as presented by players on the "Cotton Blossom," the "Valley Bell," the "River Queen," and "Markle's Floating Palace." It was out of such an environment that West Virginia gave to the theater world Henrietta Crosman, born in Wheeling, and Pare Lorentz, born in Upshur County, who achieved success with his documentary films: *The Plow That Broke the Plains,* 1935, *The River,* 1938, and *The Fight for Life,* 1940.[12]

With the passing of the commercial theater in the first quarter of the present century, came the little theater, staged by amateurs and semi-professionals. All of the important cities of the state and the institutions of higher learning sponsored such institutions, and, in 1932, Sara Spencer established the Children's Theater in Charleston. The membership of sponsoring organizations ran well into the hundreds, and their performers played to even larger audiences. Wheeling's Little Theater attracted favorable comment for its open-air performances in Oglebay Park.

---

[12] *West Va., Guide,* p. 184.

Chapter XXXV

The Literary Scene

FICTION

WEST VIRGINIA FICTION had its beginnings in the writings of Rebecca Harding Davis (1831-1910), whose novels dealt with labor and the beginnings of modern industry. While a resident of Wheeling, Mrs. Davis wrote "Life in the Iron Mills," which was published in the *Atlantic Monthly* in 1861 and reprinted in 1866 in a collection titled *Atlantic Tales.* In *Margaret Howth,* 1862, Mrs. Davis dramatized certain ethical and social problems incident to the rise of industry in an agricultural community. In *David Gaunt,* 1862, she portrayed hardships of West Virginia small farmers. She was the author of a number of other books, dealing with various phases of American life, and for several years, she was an editorial writer for the New York *Tribune.*

Mrs. Davis had a worthy peer in Francis (Frank) R. Stockton (1834-1902) who, when he moved to Claymont, Jefferson County, West Virginia, in 1899, had long been a master of the art of short story writing. In this field his *The Lady or the Tiger,* 1884, attracted international attention. While a resident of West Virginia, he wrote a number of stories, some of which, including *Tales Out of School,* were reproduced in book form. Of his passing William Dean Howells said, "eternity seems the richer and time the poorer."

The non-fiction "Coin Series" of William Hope Harvey, born and reared in Putnam County, West Virginia, was read perhaps more extensively in the United States than any other book except the Bible at the turn of the century, but Melville Davisson Post (April 19, 1871-June 23, 1930) was then generally recognized as the most gifted West Virginia author of the period. The pros and cons of his detective stories attracted much attention. While admitting its literary merit, critics of *The Strange Schemes of Randolph Mason,* 1896, claimed that it showed criminals how to beat the law. In reply, Post admitted their claims but insisted that public appreciation of the weakness of the law would help strengthen it. He, too, was a master of the art of short story writing. His *The Mountain School Teacher,* an allegorical story of the life of Christ, was regarded by many as his best contribution to literature. Other works included *The Man of*

Melville Davisson Post

Last Resort, 1896; *Dwellers in the Hills,* 1901; *The Gilded Chair,* 1910; *Uncle Abner, Master of Mysteries,* 1918; *Walker of the Secret Service,* 1924; *The Man Hunters,* 1926; and *The Silent Witness,* 1930, which was published posthumously.

Like Post, Margaret Prescott Montague (Nov. 29, 1878-Sept. 26, 1955) was a master of the short story. Few West Virginia authors have used local color more effectively. She was born at White Sulphur Springs, and the heroine of her first published story, *The Poet, Miss Kate and I,* 1905, was a West Virginia girl. *The Sowing of Alderson Cree,* 1907, *In Calvert's*

Valley, 1908, and *Linda,* 1912, were stories of West Virginia mountaineer life. Some of Miss Montague's best works deal with issues of World War I. In *England to America,* 1920, winner of the O. Henry prize, she sought to bring about a better understanding between the two countries, and *Uncle Sam of Freedom Ridge,* 1920, praised by President Woodrow Wilson, was a plea for a league of nations. While her brother, R. Cary Montague, was superintendent of the schools for the deaf and the blind at Romney, West Virginia, Miss Montague became deeply interested in its students and wrote *Closed Doors,* 1915, describing their life in a state institution. Other works included *Home to Hims Muvver,* 1916; *The Great Expectancy,* 1918; *The Gift,* 1919; *Deep Channel,* 1923; *The Man from God's Country,* 1923; *Up Eel River,* 1928; and *Lucky Lady,* 1934. Her essay, "20 Minutes of Reality," was widely translated.

Since about 1930 Pearl Buck, formerly Pearl Sydenstricker, born (June 26, 1892) at Hillsboro, West Virginia, was West Virginia's most eminent native author. She was the daughter of a missionary, and, as a child, spent much time in China. In 1917 she married Dr. John Lossing Buck, an agricultural missionary, and went with him to China to live. As an interpreter of an awakening China to the Western World, as set forth in *The Good Earth,* 1931, her fame became international, and she was awarded both the Pulitzer and the Nobel prizes and many other honors. *The Good Earth* was followed in rapid succession by a half score or more other books, most of which dealt with social conditions in China.

A number of other West Virginia authors were meanwhile attaining distinction. Granville Davisson Hall's *Daughter of the Elm,* 1899, was a vivid picture of rural life in the area of present Shinnston. Albert Benjamin Cunningham's ability to depict nature was demonstrated in *The Manse of Barron Rocks,* 1918; in *Singing Mountain,* 1919; in *Old Black Bass,* 1922; and in *Animal Tales of the Rockies,* 1925. And William Perry Brown of Glenville wrote a number of books for boys including *A Sea Island Romance,* 1888; *Ralph Grangers Fortunes,* 1902; *Our Sammies in the Trenches,* 1918; and *Our Jackies in the Fleet,* 1918. In the course of a twelve-year residence at Coolfront, Morgan County, Herbert Quick wrote *On Board the Good Ship Earth,* 1913; *The Brown Mouse,* 1916; *The Fairview Idea,* 1916, and other volumes dealing with rural social life. In 1903 Anna Pierpont Siviter, daughter of Francis H. Pierpont, Union War Governor of Virginia, published *Nehe, A Tale of the Time of Artaxerxe[s]* which was republished in 1932 under the title, *Within the Palace Gates*

In her *The Cross Roads Meetin' House,* 1918; *The Good Old Days* 1922; *The Woman on the Farm,* 1924; *The Shining Hours,* 1927; and he[r] studies in literature, Mary Meek Atkeson left abiding pictures of th[e] state's rural life. Although Henry Sydnor Harrison's *Queed,* 1911, hi[s] *V.V.'s Eyes,* 1913, and his *Angela's Business,* 1915, were written while h[e] was a temporary resident, they breathed the West Virginia spirit. Fanny Kemble Johnson's (Mrs. Vincent Costello's) *Beloved Son,* 1916, was well received, and her "The Strange Looking Man," was included in a selection of the best short stories of 1917. Oren F. Morton was the author of *Winning or Losing,* 1901, and the *Land of the Laurel; A Story of the Alleghenies,* 1903.

From time to time a number of West Virginia authors, beginning with William Leighton (1833-1911), a glass maker of Wheeling, were interested in Shakespearean scholarship. His *A Sketch of Shakespeare,* 1879, *Shakespeare's Dream and Other Poems,* 1881; and *Subjection of Hamlet,* 1882, were notable books. The work begun by Leighton was continued by C. F. Tucker Brooke and John W. Draper. As a professor of English in Yale from 1909 to 1946, Brooke, a graduate of West Virginia University, attained wide recognition as a Shakespearean scholar and an authority on Elizabethan literature. Beginning in 1929 Draper was professor of English in West Virginia University, from which vantage point he tried to keep alive Shakespearean traditions in the face of a defiant materialism. Among his several published works were *A Century of Broadside Elegies,* 1928; *The Funeral Elegy and the Rise of English Romanticism,* 1929; and *The Hamlet of Shakespeare's Audience,* 1938.

In the field of the novel, a new generation of authors maintained high standards. Among them were the Skidmores—Hubert and Hobert D.—born April 11, 1911, in Webster County. Hubert's *I Will Lift Up Mine Eyes,* 1936, won the Hopwood Prize. His later works included *Heaven Came So Near,* 1938; *River Rising,* 1939; *Hill Doctor,* 1940; *Hawks Nest,* 1941; and *Hill Lawyer,* 1942. On February 2, 1946, he met a tragic death in his cabin while on terminal leave from the U. S. Signal Corps service. Hobert's published works included *Valley of the Sky,* 1944; *More Lives Than One,* 1945; *Disturb Not Our Dreams,* 1947; *O Careless Love,* 1949; and *The Years Are Even,* 1952. They were stories of bomber crews in the South Pacific and of life in the hill country of West Virginia.

The writings of Alberta Pierson Hannum of Moundsville were widely acclaimed. Through contacts with Berea College, Kentucky, she became interested in the life of the Appalachian mountain country and formed attachments which found vent in her writings. Her first novels: *Thursday April,* 1931; *The Hills Step Lightly,* 1934; *The Gods and One,* 1941; and *The Mountain People in the Great Smokies and the Blue Ridge,* 1943, each had a background in the Appalachian Mountains. In *Spin A Silver Dollar,* 1946, the locale shifted to the Navajo desert; but in 1947 she returned to the mountain theme and wrote her captivating *Roseanna McCoy.* She was also the author of a number of short stories.

Other novelists of merit included Mr. and Mrs. George Evans of Old Hemlock Farm, Preston County, who, under the pseudonym "Brandon

Bird," were joint authors of intriguing mystery stories. Among their published works were *Death in Four Colors,* 1950; *Never Wake A Dead Man,* 1950; *Downbeat for A Dirge,* 1952; and *Hawk Watch,* 1954. Alice E. Franklin, born and reared at Moundsville, wrote *A Wreath of Evergreen* depicting the quietude of forest-protected highways in horse and buggy days. Davis Grubb's *The Night of the Hunter,* 1954, a poetic and terrifying melodrama dealing with Ohio Valley scenes, and his *A Dream of Kings,* 1955, a love story of the Civil War, had a wide market. In his *American Nabob,* 1939, Holmes Alexander depicted post-Civil War days in West Virginia in a style and with a viewpoint that prepared him for success as a newspaper columnist. In *Again the River,* 1939, Stella E. Morgan, Fairmont, portrayed the indomitable struggle of the Ohio Valley farmer against ruinous floods. John Peale Bishop of Charles Town, preserved Shenandoah Valley traditions in his *Many Thousands Gone,* 1931, while he recalled phases of the Virginia Debt in his *Act of Darkness,* 1935. Mary Lee Settle (Mrs. Douglas Newton), born and reared in Charleston, wrote *The Love Eaters,* 1954, and *The Kiss of Kin,* 1955, which were published in both England and the United States.

Eleanor Carroll Chilton (Mrs. Herbert Agar), born and reared in Charleston, was best known for *Shadows Waiting,* 1927; *The Garment of Praise,* 1929; and *Follow the Furies,* 1935. *The Country Lass,* 1953, by Regina and Roy D'Ariano of Monongah, co-authors, dealt with peasant life in their native Italy. In his short stories in the *Atlantic Monthly,* 1931-1933, Louis E. Reed, son of a native who lost his life in a mountain feud, preserved much of the color of remote regions of the Kanawha Valley. In her several novels, particularly *The Enchanted Cup,* 1953, Dorothy James Roberts, born in Elizabeth, Wirt County, emphasized the importance of the individual as a factor in human achievements. Anne Chamberlain's *The Tall Dark Man,* 1955, a mystery story, was published in both the United States and in England. W. E. Blackhursts' *Riders of the Flood,* 1954, was a story of lumbering on Greenbrier River. Muriel Early Sheppard's *Cloud by Day,* 1947, depicted life in the West Virginia coal fields. Much of the humor and the wit peculiar to native West Virginians, was preserved by the late William E. "Cousin Riley" Wilson in his waggish *From Philadelphia, Pa., to Charleston, W. Va., via Nome, Alaska.*

A belated, but important, development of recent years was the study of folk literature, ballads, rhymes, songs, and jingles, many of which had their origin in foreign lands. The originals of these stories were carried to America and transmitted by word of mouth from generation to generation. In the course of six summers tramping the highways and byways of Marshall, Wetzel, Marion, and Monongalia counties a Harvard student "re-found practically all the traditional British ballads current in the more widely publicized southern states." A beginning at collecting and preserving this literary heritage was made by Professor John H. Cox of West Virginia University, in *Folk Songs of the South,* 1925. Among the old-time favorites thus preserved were: "Barbara Allen," "Johnny Armstrong," and "The Jew's Daughter." Among the newer folk songs included in the collection, some of them of local origin, were "John Hardy," "The Battle of Point Pleasant," and "The Wreck of the C & O." In *John Henry: A Folk-Lore Study,* 1933, Louis W. Chappel of West Virginia University, enlarged these collections, as did also Professor Cox in his *Folk-Lore, Mainly West Virginia,* 1939. In 1954, Capitol Recordings released "Folk Songs of the Allegheny Mountains," by Patrick W. Gainer, also of West Virginia University.[1]

WEST VIRGINIA POETS

West Virginia poets and would-be poets tend to be legion. Something in the mountain retreats seemed to stir the poetic Muse, and those who came under her spell burst into rhythmic song after the manner of the authors of folk songs through the ages. Others were more academic. This was notably true of William Leighton whose *The Sons of Godwin,* 1877, *At the Court of King Edwin,* 1878, and numerous sonnets were the products of an academically cultivated genius for rhythmic expression. In like manner, Daniel Bedinger Lucas kept alive traditions of the Lost Cause in his *The Land Where We Were Dreaming,* 1865, in *The Wreath of Eglantine and Other Poems,* 1869, and in *The Maid of Northumberland,* 1879. Following five years (1852-1857) as a resident practicing physician in Logan County, William Dunn English (1819-1902), author of *Ben Bolt* (1843), one of the most popular love songs in the English language, drew heavily upon his Trans-Allegheny Virginia experience in his *American Ballads,* 1880, his *Select Poems,* 1894, and his several plays.

At the turn of the century Dr. Waitman Barbe (Nov. 19, 1864-Oct. 30, 1925), a member of the faculty of West Virginia University, was West Virginia's most popular poet. His "Song of the Centuries," 1888, was classic, but *Ashes and Incense,* 1892, established his reputation. His several studies including *Famous Poems Explained,* 1909, and *Great Poems Interpreted,* 1914, plus his fine teaching personality, did much to interest

[1] For additional listings see Ella May Turner, *Stories and Verse of West Virginia* (Revised, Scottdale, Pa., 1940); Mary Meek Atkeson, "West Virginia Writers and West Virginia Literature and Literary Writers," in Callahan, *History of West Virginia,* I, 679-696; West Virginia Writers' Project, *West Virginia: A Guide to the Mountain State,* pp. 144-150; Conley, *West Virginia Encyclopedia,* pp. 499-506; and Mrs. Mary V. Harris, *Poetic Pictures of West Virginia* (M.A. thesis, W.V.U., 1952).

young West Virginians in good literature. "Stars of Gold," a memorial ode to University students who lost their lives in World War I, was one of his last and best poems.

Among resident poets of the next generation, together with their works, were John Peale Bishop of Charles Town, sometime staff and managing editor of *Vanity Fair,* who wrote *Green Fruit,* 1917, *The Undertaker's Garland,* 1922, *Now With His Love,* 1933, *Minute Particles,* 1936, and *Collected Poems,* 1944, reproductions from which were translated into foreign languages; Gertie Stewart Howard (Mrs. Harry C. Howard) of Weston, *Blown Leaves and Petals,* 1934, *Lonely Apples,* 1942, and a number of poems in several magazines; Charles G. Stater of Huntington, *Buckwheat Fields and Brush Fences,* 1935, and *Life's Loveliness,* 1939, excerpts from which had wide publicity; J. Herbert Bean of Hinton, *A Pilgrim Harp,* 1923; Lawrence M. Brile of Fairmont, *Israel and Other Poems,* 1939, and *Fresh Leaves,* 1947; Thomas B. Sweeney of Wheeling, *Horizon Flames,* 1931, *Legend of Leonardo,* 1936, *Sunward,* 1933, *Flight to Erin,* 1948, and *Makers of War,* 1950; Warren B. Hornor of Shepherd College, *Lichen,* 1935, and *Hill Saga,* 1936; Elizabeth Davis Richards of Morgantown, *Leaves of Laurel,* 1925, *The Peddler of Dreams,* 1928, and poems published in English and American anthologies; Anna Louise Price of Marlinton, *The Old Church and Other Poems,* 1921; and St. John Byer of Shepherdstown, editor of *The Art Journal* (New York) and author of *Stories in Rhymes,* 1915, and *Pickled Chestnuts,* 1923.

Present day West Virginia poets generally accord first place to Louise McNeill (Mrs. Roger W. Pease) of Morgantown, whose *Mountain White,* 1939, *Gauley Mountain,* 1942, *Time Is Our House,* 1951, and currently published poems were of "the highest quality." Her "Mountain Corn Song" won an *Atlantic Monthly* prize and scholarship in 1938. Prominent also in the list of later West Virginia poets was Constance Rinehart of Huntington. Her *Autographed Copy,* 1951, and individual poems were prize winners. Among her contemporaries, together with their products of more than transient merit, were Vera Andrea Harvey (Mrs. John Speed Harvey) of Huntington, *Touching the Stars,* 1954; Mrs. Mary Virginia Harris of Hinton, *Songs of Redeeming Love,* 1941, *Messages in Melody,* 1949, and *Echoes from the Hills,* 1946; Mrs. Lena Hall Day of Hinton, *The Clearer View,* 1945, and *The Signal Light,* 1947; Columbus J. Meade of Davy, *Pit Skyline,* 1950, voicing the sentimental life of West Virginia coal mines; William Russell Ames LeGrand of Huntington, *From the Embers Glow,* 1953, a Poetry Book of the Month Club, and "The Defenders of Bataan"; Grace Yoke White of Morgantown, *Unhoarded Gold,* 1953; Mrs. Gertrude Thompson Miller of Huntington, *Aeolian Harps,* 1954; and Lillian Beinkampen of Huntington, *The Heart Overflows,* 1954.

By appointment of the governor, Karl Myers of Parsons became the poet laureate of West Virginia on June 9, 1927. His *The Quick Years,* 1926, contained poetry of fine quality, and his "Memorial Ode on Corrick's Ford" was included in the *North American Book of Verse* for 1939. On March 11, 1937 he was succeeded by Roy Lee Harmon, a journalist, who was sometimes referred to as "the Will Rogers of West Virginia." As Poet Laureate, Harmon published *Hillbilly Ballads,* 1938, *Around the Mountain,* 1941, and *Up the Creek,* 1948. In response to the growing interest in poetry in West Virginia he founded on July 13, 1950 the West Virginia Poetry Society, and the governor proclaimed the period October 7-15, 1952, Poetry Week in the state. It has since been observed as such, and the poet laureate has spoken officially through the Poet Laureate's Page of *Echoes of West Virginia.*

Echoes of West Virginia, A Magazine of Verse, was founded on April 18, 1949 by Doris Enfield Hicks of Charleston, for the purpose of stimulating the writing of poetry and as a means of preserving the works of West Virginia born poets. In 1951, Doris C. Miller (Mrs. John Hawes Miller) of Huntington, became the editor and Miss Hicks continued as co-publisher. Miss Hicks was the author of *Rambling Thoughts,* 1941, *Bright Through the Flames,* 1944, and a number of poems published from time to time in magazines, but her major interest was promotion of the works of others. Mrs. Miller was the author of *Who Burnishes the Lamp,* 1952, and the editor of "The Poetry Corner," a regular feature of the Huntington *Herald-Advertiser.* The newest and most active of these groups was the Appalachian Poetry Guild organized on November 18, 1950 at Kermit by Mrs. Amanda Meade Brewer. Membership was drawn largely from Tug Fork Valley. Beginning in 1952 this guild published the *Appalachian Poets Year Book* which contained a number of poems by Mrs. Brewer and her co-workers.

THE NEWSPAPER GUILD

In 1860 there were 43 newspaper publications in present West Virginia, distributed among nineteen counties.[2] They included three dailies, two tri-weeklies, thirty-six weeklies, and two monthlies. The *Millenial Harbinger,* a monthly edited by Alexander Campbell, President of Bethany College, had a circulation of 8,500 copies. Prior to about 1875 most of the political news sheets adhered rather closely to pre-Civil War patterns. In the eighties old-time printing techniques began to give way to modern

[2] Col. John E. Day, "Development of Journalism," in Callahan, *Semi-Centennial History,* 551-555; ———, *History of West Virginia,* I, 298-314.

appliances, particularly the linotype, thus greatly reducing the cost of printing. As a result the 43 newspaper publications of 1860 increased to 223 by 1912 and each county of the state boasted a newspaper. By 1930 the total number of newspapers had decreased to 164, the decrease being confined almost entirely to the weeklies, many of which were not, as formerly, printed locally, and the Republican sponsored dailies outnumbered those sponsored by the Democrats.

Professional journalism was an important factor in preserving the newspaper press against encroachments of the radio and television. As a subject for academic instruction journalism had its beginnings in the state in 1915 in a single course offered at the University. By 1927 this course had expanded into a department which, in 1939, became the University School of Journalism. Beginning in 1950, the school offered the standard curriculum in journalism. Marshall College also had a highly developed department of journalism. Every institution of higher learning in the state and most of the secondary schools had meanwhile offered instruction in that subject. The Intercollegiate Press Association, organized in 1921, stimulated professional journalism on a state-wide basis; the West Virginia Newspaper Council, organized in 1924, united editors and publishers on a professional basis; and the West Virginia High School Press Association, organized in 1939, met annually under the sponsorship of Marshall College. In 1953, the West Virginia Newspaper Council and the State Publishers' Association were merged into the West Virginia Press Association.

Achievements of distinguished journalists were commemorated in the West Virginia Journalism Hall of Fame and in the Fifty-Year Club. The Journalism Hall of Fame was created in 1935 by the State Newspaper Council as a means of recognizing the achievements of deceased editors and publishers. The Fifty-Year Club created in 1950, recognized those who had served the profession long and well. Elections to the Hall of Fame were made in odd-numbered years and were limited to two for each election year.

HISTORY AND BIOGRAPHY

Interest in the history of the Trans-Allegheny in the post-Civil War period was stimulated by Lyman C. Draper who collected its source materials for pioneer days and deposited them in the Library of the Wisconsin Historical Society at Madison. With the aid of this source, scores of authors, in the course of the ensuing decades, wrote on various phases of West Virginia history, and Reuben Gold Thwaites of the Wisconsin

Historical Society published in 1895 a revised edition of Alexander Scott Withers, *Chronicles of Border Warfare.*

In the quality of his writings, John P. Hale, a salt manufacturer and a hotel owner of Charleston, was first among West Virginia historians of the post-Civil War period. His *Trans-Allegheny Pioneers,* 1877, and his *History of the Great Kanawha Valley,* 1891, were followed by *Some Local Archaeology,* 1898, and by *Scraps of Tradition, History, and Facts,* 1899. Hale had a productive co-worker in George Wesley Atkinson, also of Charleston. His *History of Kanawha County,* 1876; *Among the Moonshiners,* 1881; *The West Virginia Pulpit,* 1882; and *Prominent Men of West Virginia* (in collaboration with Alvaro F. Gibbens), 1890, were storehouses of information. At the same time Virgil A. Lewis of Mason County, was producing his *A General History of West Virginia,* 1889; *The Life and Times of Anne Bailey, Pioneer Heroine of the Great Kanawha Valley,* 1891; and *The Original Indiana Territory,* 1895.

The regional historical outlook widened appreciably in 1902 when Dr. James Morton Callahan became head of the department of history in the University. Under direction of Herbert B. Adams of Johns Hopkins University, he had already made notable contributions in the field of American Diplomatic history. Because of inaccessibility to source materials in his chosen field, he was temporarily diverted to the regional field and in 1913 wrote his *Semi-Centennial History of West Virginia.* In 1903, he was given an assistant in the person of Associate Professor Walter L. Fleming who, in the course of a four-year tenure, edited his well-known *Documentary History of Reconstruction.* In 1902, Granville Davisson Hall, published *The Rending of Virginia* and, in 1915, *The Two Virginias, Genesis of Old and New.* Warren Wood was meanwhile producing *The Tragedy of the Deserted Isle,* 1909, and *When Virginia Was Rent in Twain,* 1914. In 1910 Charles H. Ambler published *Sectionalism in Virginia, 1776-1861,* and in 1913 *Thomas Ritchie, A Study in Virginia Politics.* James C. McGregor of Wheeling wrote *The Disruption of Virginia* in 1922, while Edward C. Smith of Lewis County, published *A History of Lewis County* in 1920, and *The Borderland in the Civil War* in 1927.

Contemporaneous writings by Booker T. Washington (April 5, 1856-Nov. 14, 1915), Negro educator born in Franklin County, Virginia, and reared at Malden, West Virginia, were contributions to history. His *Up from Slavery,* 1901, was translated into many languages. He was the author also of *The Future of the American Negro,* 1899; *Sowing and Reaping,* 1900; and *The Story of the Negro,* 1909.

Passing of the frontier, preoccupation in industry, and entrance of the United States into world affairs tended to shift regional historical interests from pioneer days to national and even international affairs, and West

Virginia historians followed the trend. James Morton Callahan returned to his first love and produced a volume on *American Foreign Policy in Mexican Relations,* 1932, and another on *American Foreign Policy in Canadian Relations,* 1937. Oliver P. Chitwood, Professor in West Virginia University from 1907 to 1946, was the author of *A History of Colonial America,* 1931, which was widely used as a college textbook, and

Home of Booker T. Washington, Malden, West Virginia

John Tyler: Champion of the Old South, 1939. He collaborated on *A Short History of the American People,* in two volumes, which was also used as a college text. *Johnson Newlon Camden: A Study in Individualism,* 1937, and *The Baltimore and Ohio in the Civil War,* 1939, by Professor Festus P. Summers of the University, were well received, as was also his *William L. Wilson and Tariff Reform,* 1953. His colleague, Professor Thomas E. Ennis, had meanwhile published *French Policy and Development in Indo-china,* 1936, and *Eastern Asia,* 1946, and Benjamin Keen, also of the University faculty, was the author of *David Curtis De-Forest and the Revolution of Buenos Aires,* 1947, and the editor of *Readings in Latin American Civilization, 1492 to the Present,* 1955. John Anthony Caruso of the University extension faculty was the author of *The Liberators of Mexico,* published in 1954. From the pen of O. D. Lambert came *Pioneer Leaders of Western Virginia,* 1935, *Campfires and Firesides West of the Alleghenies, 1941, West Virginia and Its Government,*

1951, and *Stephen Benton Elkins,* 1955. Charles H. Ambler published his *History of Transportation in the Ohio Valley with Special Reference to Waterways,* 1932, *A History of West Virginia,* 1933, *George Washington and the West,* 1936, and *Francis H. Pierpont: Union War Governor of Virginia,* 1937. His later works included *A History of Education in West Virginia from Early Colonial Times to 1949,* 1951; and *Waitman Thomas Willey,* 1954.

Among notable historical works of non-academic origin, were *The Family and Early Life of Stonewall Jackson,* 1924, by Dr. Roy Bird Cook, which had several printings; *Lewis County in the Civil War,* 1924; *Washington's Western Lands,* 1930; and *The Annals of Fort Lee,* 1935. *Lee of Virginia, A Biography,* 1932, and *Grant of Appomattox: A Study of the Man,* 1942, by William E. Brooks, pastor of the First Presbyterian Church, Morgantown, were well received. In his *Virginia, the Old Dominion,* 1937, Matthew Page Andrews of Shepherdstown, produced one of the best one-volume histories of Virginia. Ruth Woods Dayton's *Greenbrier Pioneers and Their Homes,* 1942, and her *Pioneers and Their Homes on the Upper Kanawha,* 1947, were intimate portrayals. *The West Virginia Encyclopedia,* 1929, by Philip M. Conley was a storehouse of historical information, and Sam T. Mallison's *The Great Wildcatter,* 1953, a life of Michael L. Benedum, was widely circulated and read. In *Pageant of the Packets,* 1929, and *Salt: The Fifth Element,* 1948, Garnett Laidlaw Eskew condensed into readable form stories of steamboat days and industries of the Kanawha Valley. Julia Davis (Mrs. Paul West) wrote a number of books on historical subjects for children. Among them were *Swords of the Vikings,* 1927; *Mountaineers Are Free,* 1930; *Stonewall,* 1931; *No Other White Men,* 1937; and *Peter Hale,* 1937. She was also the author of *The Shenandoah,* 1945, a volume of the Rivers of America series. Without peer in the field of children's literature was Jean Lee Latham of Buckhannon whose *Story of Eli Whitney,* published in 1953, was followed by *Medals for Morse,* 1954, and *Trail Blazer of the Seas,* 1956. In 1956 Miss Latham won the Newberry Award with her *Carry On, Mr. Bowditch,* published in 1955.

SCIENCE

In response to the interest aroused by the opening of new coal fields, the timber industry, and newly projected railroads, West Virginians tended to bury political and social differences incident to the Civil War and the Reconstruction and to revive plans for the development of their state's natural resources. Their interests were accordingly directed to the sciences which were enriched by *The Butterflies of North America,* 1879-1897, in three volumes by William H. Edwards of Coalburg, Kanawha County, a pioneer work recognized by both Agassiz and Darwin. *Medical Botany of West Virginia,* 1875, by Dr. Augustus E. Hildreth; *Birds of West Virginia,* 1888, by William D. Doane; *Flora of West Virginia,* 1892, by Charles F. Millspaugh; *Coals and Cokes of West Virginia,* 1892, by William S. Edwards; and the "Report" on the cause of unhealthy conditions of the spruce and pine by Professor Andrew D. Hopkins of West Virginia University, 1899, made contributions in their respective fields. The Appleton and Company *Reprint of the Annual Reports and Other Papers on the Geology of the Virginias,* 1884, by William Barton Rogers (Dec. 7, 1804-May 30, 1882), state geologist of Virginia from 1835 to 1841, had meanwhile found a place in many private libraries.[3]

Among these pioneer scientists, Professor Israel C. White (Nov. 1, 1848-Nov. 25, 1927) of West Virginia University, was the most productive. In "Notes on the Geology of West Virginia" he paved the way for implementing the several suggestions, made increasingly since the formation of the state, for a geological and economic survey. His practical application of the anticlinal theory of oil and gas accumulations was described by his co-worker, Edward Orton of Ohio, as "an epochal work."[4] The resulting demands drew Professor White into commercial geology, in which field he attained international distinction. His work in the University was continued by Samuel B. Brown who published in 1901 his *Bibliography of Works upon the Geology and Natural Resources of West Virginia.* When, in February, 1897, the legislature established the West Virginia Geological and Economic Survey, Dr. White served it as state geologist, a post which he held after 1899 without salary, until his death. Under the general direction of Dr. Paul H. Price, state geologist since October 1 1934, the program of the Survey was designed to examine more specifically the geology and the physical and chemical properties of the state's natural resources. Notable among monographs by Dr. Price were "Evolution of Geologic Thought in Prospecting for Oil and Gas" and "The Anticlinal Theory and Later Developments in West Virginia."

The Agricultural and Engineering Experiment stations of the University were meanwhile increasing both the scope and the number of their research projects and publications. Among contributions of general interest by University staff members included *West Virginia Grasses* 1944, an Agricultural Experiment Station bulletin, by Earl L. Core, and

---

[3] Most of these reports and papers, including maps of mountains in present West Virginia were reprinted in *The Virginias* (Staunton, Va., 1880-1884).

[4] Paul H. Price, "Evolution of Geologic Thought in Prospecting for Oil and Gas," in American Association of Petroleum Geologists, *Bulletin,* Vol. 31, No. 4 (April, 1947).

associates; *Spring Wild Flowers,* 1948, a State Conservation Commission bulletin by Earl L. Core; *Shrubs of West Virginia,* 1950, a University bulletin, by Nelle Ammons; and *Flora of West Virginia,* Part I, 1952, and Part II, 1953, by P. D. Strausbaugh and Earl L. Core. Noteworthy among West Virginians who have achieved eminence in the field of science were William J. Humphreys, Alpheus W. Smith, Douglas W.

Dr. I. C. White, noted geologist

Johnson, Karl S. Lashley, and Charles T. Brues. Humphreys, a United States Weather Bureau physicist, was born at Gap Mills, Monroe County, February 3, 1862. In addition to a number of publications in his field, he was associate editor of the *Journal of the Franklin Institute.* Dr. Smith was born at Philippi, Barbour County, January 15, 1876. For 35 years he was a member of the faculty of Ohio State University and was the author of a number of research projects in physics. Dr. Johnson, geologist and geographer, was born at Parkersburg, Wood County, November 30, 1878. In addition to a half score or more books in his field, beginning in 1938, he was editor of the *Journal of Geomorphology.* Dr. Lashley, psychologist and zoologist, was born at Davis, Tucker County. He attended West Virginia University, where he came under the inspiring influence of Dr. Albert M. Reese, a noted zoologist. Beginning in 1942, Dr. Lashley was director of the Yerkes Laboratories of Primate Biology. Dr. Brues, a zoologist, was born in Wheeling and educated at the University of Texas and Columbia University. Before he became Associate Curator of Insects in the Museum of Comparative Zoology of Columbia University, he was successively Field Agent of the U. S. Department of Agriculture and Curator of Invertebrate Zoology of the Milwaukee Public Museum.

Chapter XXXVI

With the Colors

THE NATIONAL GUARD

THE WEST VIRGINIA NATIONAL GUARD has a long and creditable military history. In various units Company D, 201st Infantry, West Virginia National Guard, had practically a continuous existence since it was first organized by Morgan Morgan on February 17, 1735, in present Berkeley County, then a part of Orange County, Virginia. The 150th Infantry, West Virginia National Guard, traced its antecedents to a militia company organized in 1777 in Greenbrier County, (West) Virginia. In various organizations these units had a part in every war in which the United States participated. Units of the 201st Infantry fought in both the Union and the Confederate armies.[1]

War-weary and distraught, West Virginia disbanded its militia after the Civil War and in 1867 the offices of adjutant general and quartermaster general were combined. In 1871 both of these offices were abolished, and their duties were assigned to the state superintendent of free schools. This arrangement continued to 1877, when the offices were revived and their duties assigned to the state librarian. Because of unrest incident to the railroad strike of 1877, several volunteer companies were organized in the state but no provision was made for training and equipping them.

In compliance with an act of Congress of 1887, the 1889 legislature authorized the establishment of the West Virginia National Guard and separated the office of the adjutant general from that of the state librarian; but the adjutant general was required to perform the duties of quartermaster general. It was under this arrangement that a brigade organization was effected in 1890. The first military code was published in 1905.

In compliance with the National Defense Act of June, 1916, the West Virginia National Guard became a part of the U. S. Expeditionary Forces

[1] West Virginia, *Historical Annual National Guard* (1938), pp. 1, 99.

in World War I. Following the war, it was demobilized to await the outcome of Governor Cornwell's efforts to have the state legislature establish a department of public safety. Reorganization was effected under a legislative act of 1921, which, as amended in 1949, determined the present organization. As thus constituted, the National Guard was a reserve component of the Army of the United States, composed of officers and enlisted men who volunteered for duty and qualified in accordance with federal and state regulations. It was equipped and paid by the United States.

Except when in the active military service of the United States, the National Guard is commanded by the governor. As commander-in-chief he issues orders through the adjutant general who disburses state and federal funds, serves as custodian of equipment, and supervises and directs training. In case of war, insurrection, rebellion, and the failure of local police authorities to preserve law and order, the governor may order the national guard, or any part of it, into the active service of the state. Martial law, a temporary suspension of the civil courts, was used only twice in West Virginia: first in dealing with the Paint Creek-Cabin Creek strike situation of 1912-13, and second in dealing with a similar situation in Mingo County in 1921-22. In *Ex Parte Jones* and related cases, the state supreme court of appeals sustained the use of martial law in 1913 on the ground that it was "incident to sovereignty." In strong overtones of *Ex parte Milligan* (1866), it over-ruled its use in Mingo County in 1921 on the ground that martial law cannot obtain in the absence of military operations; nor could the governor enforce martial law by means of civil authority.[2]

THE SPANISH-AMERICAN WAR

On February 15, 1898, the Battleship *Maine* was destroyed in Havana harbor, and two officers and 258 members of the crew lost their lives. Spaniards in high places were generally thought to have been responsible for these acts, and at once residents of the United States, under the slogan "Remember the *Maine*," prepared for military action. When the resulting investigation failed to remove suspicions of guilt from the suspected parties, the United States declared war, and the President asked West Virginia to provide one regiment immediately and another later.

In response to this request Governor Atkinson ordered the mobilization of the West Virginia National Guard. At once eighteen companies pitched camp on the site of Kanawha City, now a part of Charleston, and twelve of them were organized into the First West Virginia Volunteer Infantry regiment under command of Colonel B. D. Spillman. Volunteers from

[2] 71 *W.Va.*, 567-625; 88 *W.Va.*, 714-721.

many parts of the state formed the second regiment which mobilized on the west side of Elk River in present Charleston under command of Colonel D. T. E. Casteel, as the Second West Virginia Volunteer Infantry.

Andrew Summers Rowan, who carried the message to Garcia

Four additional companies: E and G of the Fourth Regiment United States Volunteer Infantry, and L and M of the Eighth Regiment United States Colored Volunteer Infantry, were raised in the state and accepted by the government. Many West Virginians enlisted in other commands and saw service in Cuba, Puerto Rico, and the Philippines. The number credited to West Virginia units totaled 3,004, and the state adjutant general estimated that 10,000 had been ready to volunteer.[3]

Rear Admiral French Ensor Chadwick of Morgantown served with distinction in this war as chief-of-staff of Rear Admiral William T. Sampson. He commanded the *New York*, the flagship of Rear Admiral Sampson's fleet, at the battle of Santiago. Later he was the author of several historical works on Spanish-United States relations. The reception given him in 1899 by Morgantown in recognition of his service in the Spanish-American War was an event in the history of the state.

It was in this war also that Lieutenant Andrew Summers Rowan won fame. Born in Monroe County, (West) Virginia in 1857, and graduated from the United States Military Academy, Rowan had entered the Army in 1881. At the beginning of the war President McKinley wished to communicate with Garcia, commander of Cuban insurgents, who was virtually marooned in the interior of Cuba by a cordon of Spanish troops. Lieutenant Rowan volunteered for the hazardous task which was successfully executed. Later his feat was made the subject of a story by Elbert Hubbard in the classical "A Message to Garcia," which was translated into several languages.

Although the war with Spain lasted only 112 days, it had lasting effects in West Virginia. The University Cadet Corps which had trained a number of the officers and privates was for the first time put on a permanent and creditable basis. The corps was enlarged and provided with an Armory, dedicated in 1902, and the West Virginia National Guard was reorganized in 1899. Nor was this all. Young West Virginians took initial steps toward participation in world affairs, as they accepted service as soldiers, sailors, teachers, and other employment in our island possessions, especially the Philippines. On the other hand, there was strong opposition to the acquisition of the Philippine Islands in West Virginia. In truth, the Republicans all but lost the state election in 1898 on the issue of imperialism.

WORLD WAR I

When, on April 6, 1917, the United States entered the war against Germany, West Virginia had but two regiments of national guard infantry—the First and the Second—ready for active service. Only two weeks before the declaration of war the Second had been released from national service on the Mexican border, but when war seemed imminent both regiments were reassigned to duty in the national service. Meanwhile a preliminary council of defense of twenty-one representative citizens had been organ-

[3] West Virginia, *Public Documents* (1897-1899).

ized in response to a request from the Council of National Defense, which had been created in August, 1916, by an act of Congress.

Governor John J. Cornwell convened the state legislature in special session, May 14, 1917, to deal with problems incident to the war, and the legislature responded with an act which replaced the preliminary council by a state executive council of defense composed of the state board of public works. To this council was assigned responsibility for keeping the state on an effective war basis. Under its direction additional revenues were provided; a watchful eye was kept on speculation in fuel, foodstuffs, and other necessities; and additional protection for life and property was authorized. The council of defense also made a survey of state institutions to determine their capacity and fitness for the care of tubercular and wounded soldiers. In its efforts to prevent idleness, it caused a census to be taken, which resulted in the enactment of a law requiring all able-bodied men to work at least thirty-six hours each week. Under this law 811 persons were arrested and about 5,000 of the voluntary unemployed became workers.

Before either a state or a Federal food administrator had been appointed, the state executive council of defense adopted the slogan, "Help West Virginia Feed Herself." Under this slogan patriotic citizens organized boys and girls into farming and canning clubs, induced farmers to plant on a large scale, and inculcated generally lessons in thrift and conservation. To conserve construction materials, the council of defense censored all applications for private building permits. It cooperated wholeheartedly with E. W. Oglebay, state food administrator; with James R. Trotter, state food distributor; and with J. Walter Barnes, the state fuel distributor. An auxiliary council of defense performed like services among the Negro population. As never before, the entire state was mobilized for all-out war.

West Virginia schools were also active in the war effort. They were especially helpful in spreading and popularizing practices of thrift and conservation. Under direction of the secretary of the state board of education, the first food-pledge campaign was carried on almost entirely by the public schools. The schools were used also to raise funds for welfare organizations; many high schools gave draftee courses in mechanics; and the University became an institution of applied arts. By 1918, the University was also a military camp. Student army training corps were also organized at Bethany, Davis and Elkins, and West Virginia Wesleyan colleges. The chief war service of the institutions of higher learning was however their contributions to war morale.

War morale was being kept alive meanwhile by the "Four Minute Men." With a total personnel of about one thousand members, including men, women, and children, they presented the purposes of the war in short addresses, whenever opportunities offered, and sometimes they made them. With the aid of professional and business men and women, the "Four Minute Men" conducted speaking campaigns that reached the entire population and helped to sustain the fighting edge by discussions of facts and conditions. More than anything else, perhaps, this democratic method of presentation contributed to the sustained state interest in the war and to the fact that it left few sores in its wake. It also explains why the state over-subscribed its allotments in each Liberty Loan Drive as well as the final Victory Loan Drive.

While doing their part in the various service organizations, women of the state rendered still other war services. Their Red Cross work was notable; they made bandages, sweaters, and other garments; they successfully solicited contributions for their own organizations and for others; and, finest of all, they served as nurses both on the battlefields of Europe and in the training camps at home. In the latter capacity, their work during the influenza epidemic of 1918 was heroic.

It should also be noted that many young West Virginians volunteered for service in the Canadian, the English, and the French armies; and West Virginia was one of the first states in the Union to complete its registration for war purposes. In the first registration 64.7 per cent of her registrants qualified for service as compared with 58.7 per cent for North Dakota with the next highest rating. In the four registrations a total of 323,383 West Virginians were registered, and 45,648 were called into service under the Selective Service Act of May 18, 1917. There were also 177 women from West Virginia who served in the Army Nurse Corps.

Meanwhile the West Virginia National Guard was being readied for foreign duty. With headquarters at Camp Cornwell, Fairmont, the First Regiment of West Virginia Infantry was called into the service of the United States on March 28, 1917, and, on April 4, the Second Regiment of West Virginia National Guard began mobilization at Kanawha City. In August both regiments were sent to Camp Shelby, Mississippi, where they were reorganized and assigned to the Thirty-eighth Division. The First Regiment was then immobilized and its personnel was assigned as replacement troops to the 113th Engineers, the 137th Machine Gun Battalion, the 113th Ammunition Train, and to the 150th Infantry, all parts of the Thirty-eighth Division. The Second Regiment sailed with that division for overseas duty in October, 1918, and during the remainder of the war was stationed at Le Mans. During the war, 26,677 West Virginians went to England, France, Belgium, and Siberia. They fought at Catigny, at Chateau-Thierry, on the St. Mihiel Salient, and in the Meuse-Argonne. Eleven hundred and twenty were killed in action, while 691 died in training camps. Other casualties, including those lost at sea, died of accidents, missing in action, captured by the enemy, and the wounded, raised the total of West Virginia casualties to about 5,000.

Among West Virginians who attained high rank in the uniformed services were John L. Hines of White Sulphur Springs, who rose to the rank of major general and succeeded General John J. Pershing as Chief of Staff of the United States Army; Mason M. Patrick of Lewisburg, who became a major general and the first Chief of the United States Air Service; and Julian Lane Latimer of Shepherdstown, who commanded the battleship *Rhode Island* during the war and who later attained the rank of rear admiral. Newton D. Baker (December 3, 1871–December 25, 1937), Secretary of War in President Wilson's Cabinet, was born and reared in Martinsburg, West Virginia.[4]

WORLD WAR II

The Armed Forces

Responsibility for administration of the Federal Selective Training and Service Act of September 16, 1940, as amended in August, 1941, was vested in the governors of the states. Accordingly, the governor of West Virginia constituted a local draft board for each 30,000 of the general population and determined the jurisdiction of the several boards. The boards were composed of male civilians who were at least 36 years of age and residents of the counties which they served. They served without pay but were authorized to employ clerical assistance. In the course of their service in West Virginia the local draft boards were assisted by 438 examining physicians and 98 dentists. For the review of the decisions of the draft boards there were four state appeal boards created by the governor on the basis of one for each 70,000 registrants and selected on the basis of occupational representation: one from labor, one from industry, one from the medical profession, one from the legal profession, and one from farmers. Because of international tensions after 1945 this organization was retained for channeling draftees and volunteers into the peace-time Army and finally into the Korean War service.

The first West Virginians to enter the Federal armed service in World War II were 155 volunteers who left the state in October, 1940, at the time of the first registration under the Selective Training and Service Act. Their departure marked the beginning of a soldier-sailor exodus that at one time totaled 6,500 in a single month. The volunteers were soon followed by the West Virginia National Guard which was among the first units called into the national service. In January, 1941, the 150th Infantry,

[4] O. P. Chitwood, "West Virginia and the World War," in Callahan, *History of West Virginia,* Vol. I, pp. 697-710; West Va. Leg., *Hand Book and Manual* (1923), pp. 442-649.

under command of Colonel William E. Eubank, moved to Camp Shelby, Mississippi, and in December, 1941, to the Canal Zone, where it remained during the greater part of the war. After a short training period at Fort Benjamin Harrison, Indiana, the 201st Infantry was assigned to security duty in Alaska. There, under command of Colonel James M. O'Reilly, its three battalions spent 31 months guarding posts in the Aleutians.

There were 66,716 West Virginia volunteers for the armed services in World War II, and 465,668 registered for service in six registrations extending from October 16, 1940, to September 1, 1945. The rejection rate per 100 of white registrants was 32.8, or 2.2 more than the national average, whereas the rejection rate of the state's Negro registrants was 38.3 per 100, or 8.1 less than the national average for that race. Of the 465,668 registrants, 151,949 were inducted into the armed forces. Of the 218,665 who joined the colors, 160,234 served in the Army, 49,090, in the Navy, 7,653, in the Marines, and 1,688 in the Coast Guard. West Virginia women saw service in the Women's Army Corps (WAC), in the Women's Marine Corps, in the WAVES, and in the SPARS. The casualties, other than wounded, were 4,865, Army; 654, Navy; 302, Marine Corps; and nine, Coast Guard.

Thousands of soldiers received their tactical training in the West Virginia Maneuver Area, a rugged mountain expanse of about 2,000,000 acres located near Elkins. Because of the striking resemblance of the terrain of this area to that of northern Italy, it was used as a training ground for combat and service troops for assignment to the Italian front. From early 1943 until mid-year 1944, infantry, artillery, and signal corps units shuttled into the area for seasoning and training in mountain warfare. Headquarters were located on the campus of Davis and Elkins College at Elkins, while camps were established in the field in Randolph, Pendleton, Grant, and Tucker counties. Assault climbing was taught at Seneca Rocks and at crossings on the Blackwater, while training looking toward the co-ordination of all arms went forward elsewhere on the Allegheny slopes.

At a camp site in the same area known as the "Huckleberry Plain," combat teams of infantry and artillery learned to operate as a unit on steep, wooded mountainsides. For that purpose guns of practically every caliber up to 105 millimeters were fired from various angles and elevations. Early in the summer of 1944, a unit of the Office of Scientific Research and Development was established on Bear Rock Range atop Allegheny Mountain, near Petersburg, for testing new types of explosives and firing devices. At the same time the Army Evacuation Hospital Training Unit was receiving intensive training at Stuart Recreation Area, near Elkins. The delivery of supplies to these various camps was a part of the war training program. Generally, it was effected by the use of heavily-loaded trucks operating with dimmed headlights over tree-canopied mountain trails. At the peak of the program the West Virginia Maneuver Area trained about 16,000 troops every eight weeks.[5]

Civilian Defense

Long before the Japanese struck at Pearl Harbor on December 7, 1941, the West Virginia legislature had created a state defense council with the governor as chairman, and authorized the appointment by the governor of local defense councils. On March 22, 1941 Governor Neely constituted the state council with Louis A. Johnson of Clarksburg, as vice-chairman. With the beginning of hostilities this organization was, however, found to be inadequate, and the governor appointed an executive advisory committee composed of the heads of six state departments, with Carl G. Bachman of Ohio County as state coordinator. Acting upon the advice of this committee, the defense council at once began rationing automobiles, tires, tubes, gasoline, typewriters, and sugar—a task later enlarged and assigned to the Office of Price Administrator. The council also took jurisdiction in the matter of forest fire protection, first aid relief, and the establishment of a statewide protective system against enemy air attacks.

With the Weirton Steel Company pointing the way on May 11, 1942 with a complete blackout that did not stop its mills, West Virginia staged on November 10, 1942, one of the first successful blackouts in the entire country, a performance that brought merit citations to more than a score of participating units. Determining factors in the success of this blackout were the radio; station-wide coverage by *Mountaineer Defense,* a bimonthly publication of the civilian defense organization; cooperation of the department of public safety; and the wholehearted cooperation of civilians generally. Although civilian defense was maintained primarily for the protection of industrial centers, it was also a means for mobilizing the people for all-out war.[6]

And West Virginia made substantial contributions to the United States Civil Air Patrol, an agency established in May, 1943, to provide a backlog for the air branches of the Army, the Navy, and the Marine Corps. For the purpose of administration the state was divided into five districts, each with a headquarters and a commander and hometown squadrons. Each was formed with private or borrowed planes and operated at private expense, and all were readied for search for lost aircraft and for emergencies, such as flood and fire disasters. Indicative of the importance of this service was the fact that approximately 350 Army Air Force pilots

[5] James Gay Jones, "West Virginia in World War II" (Doctoral dissertation, West Virginia University, 1952); Adjutant General, *Reports,* 1943-44 and 1945-46.

[6] Jones, "World War II."

were trained by the West Virginia Civilian Air Patrol before the end of 1944. The quota of West Virginia cadets for the period beginning January 1, 1945 was set at 3,800.[7]

In the absence of the National Guard, the 1941 legislature authorized the creation of a State Guard. Two regiments, one in the southern and one in the northern part of the state, were recruited and organized under direction of the state adjutant general. Also mustered into the State Guard were two companies of Negroes—one at Charleston and one at Welch. The State Guard, consisting of 1,200 men, was provided with uniforms made in WPA sewing rooms from cloth provided by the Federal government. Except as forest-fire fighters, flood-relief aids, and guards for Army and Navy planes crossing the state, no detachments of the State Guard were called to active duty, and, beginning in 1946, it was progressively disbanded as the National Guard was reorganized. The last State Guard unit was disbanded on June 30, 1947.

Civilian Services

West Virginia civilians contributed substantially toward financing World War II. By February 1, 1942, they had purchased more than one billion dollars' worth of defense bonds and forty-one million in defense stamps. In each of seven campaigns they exceeded their quotas by percentages ranging from 68 to 109.[8] In five of them West Virginia was one of the ten leading states of the Union; while in the third and the fifth, she exceeded all of the states in the percentage of over-purchased quotas. At the end of the fifth campaign West Virginia was the only state that had twice won the distinction of over-purchasing its quota.

Meanwhile the school children were doing their part through the sale of war bonds and stamps. In the "jeep" campaign of the third bond sale drive, conducted in 1943, they exceeded their quota many times. In this campaign the pupils and teachers of Wood County alone sold enough bonds and stamps to finance the purchase of 153 jeeps. So outstanding was the work of the schools in this drive that the state superintendent of free schools was awarded a silver medal in recognition of their services.

Extending to the authorities their whole-hearted cooperation, citizens of the state were largely responsible for the enforcement of the Emergency Price Control Act of January 30, 1942, and for the success of the rationing program administered by the Office of Price Administration. Rubber, gasoline, sugar, meats, fats, oils, typewriters, and automobiles were among the essential war goods and materials included in the provisions of the

---

7 West Va., *Blue Book* (1944), p. 640.

8 There was no quota in the first campaign.

rationing and price laws. In foregoing the use of such things, residents generally regarded their sacrifices as a patriotic service. In this spirit they made a number of suggestions leading to conservation economies. This was notably true of the bakers who proposed that they be permitted to eliminate delivery service one day each week. The proposal was approved, and West Virginia was first among the states to receive high official approval for a conservation program.

In like manner county salvage units formed the basis of a state salvage organization interested in recovering waste paper, metals, rubber, and other discarded materials useful for war purposes. So efficient were these organizations that 2,500 tons of "scrap" were moving out of the state weekly by April, 1942. Much of it came from "auto graveyards," while defunct street-car companies made contributions of steel rails and other equipment idled by the competition of motor vehicles. Old cannons from previous wars were commandeered from courthouse grounds, and the 3,000 pound bell from the State House, destroyed by fire in 1921, went into a Charleston scrap pile "to aid the war."

Educational Programs

Following a statewide conference of school people held at Charleston in January, 1942, the state superintendent of free schools appointed a commission authorized to serve as a clearing-house for problems arising at all levels of the public school system. This commission recommended that all teachers take the twenty-four-hour course in first aid, as prescribed by the American Red Cross; that first aid be taught in the public schools, beginning in the sixth grade; that increased emphasis be placed on physical education and health and that salaries be increased as a means of retaining competent teachers. Recognizing the merits of these recommendations, the state board of education approved them and made a number of curricular changes with a view to increased emphasis on mathematics, physics, vocational education, physical education, and health studies.

In keeping with the awakened interest, the schools had a part in scrap drives; in the collection of milkweed floss school youths doubled their 15,000 bag quota; classes in vocational agriculture and the Future Farmers of America stimulated the production of farm crops; trade and industrial teachers trained high school boys for a part in industry and for service in the armed forces; and teachers of distributive education trained replacements for employees called into the armed forces and war-time work. The public schools were also an effective medium for keeping the home fires burning and for maintaining the fighting edge.

But the schools had problems of their own. The decline in pupil enrollments was more than balanced by teacher resignations. Although the total enrollment in September, 1942, was 15,000 less than in September, 1941, it was necessary to issue 2,512 emergency certificates in 1943 to recruit the teaching force. Early in the war an issue arose over the enforcement of a state law requiring teachers and pupils on stated occasions to salute the United States flag. Parent-Teachers' Associations, Boys' and Girls' Scout clubs, American Red Cross organizations, and Federations of Women's clubs objected to the requirement as too Nazi-like, and some modifications were made. On the other hand, members of Jehovah's Witnesses, a religious sect, objected on religious grounds and refused to comply under any and all circumstances. As a result a few children were expelled from school for insubordination, and the parents of others were fined for violation of the attendance laws. Finally, in *West Virginia State Board of Education et al vs. Barnette et al* a case reached the United States Supreme Court which ruled on June 14, 1943, that the West Virginia requirement was unconstitutional.[9]

On the other hand civilian mobilization on the higher educational level encountered little or no opposition. Prior to the beginning of hostilities, the University had adjusted its program to the national defense effort through training courses in engineering and agriculture. With the beginning of hostilities, it adopted an accelerated program and placed its facilities at the disposal of the national government. In like manner, the state board of education, on January 9, 1942, placed the institutions under its control at the disposal of state and Federal authorities and authorized schedules in conformity with acceleration programs of the Wartime Commission of the United States Bureau of Education. Practically all of the institutions of higher learning offered additional courses and placed new emphasis upon those that contributed directly to the war effort. Science, mathematics, physical education, commercial subjects, and courses designed to meet military and naval needs were stressed. Holidays and vacations were limited and work-days and work-weeks were lengthened, thereby reducing the time of attendance commonly required for the completion of curricular courses. The campuses were practically given over to students taking pre-induction courses, to air cadets for pre-flight instruction, to Army specialists, and to the large group detached from the Army under the Army Specialized Training Program (ASTP).

In these activities the University pointed the way. For example, its two-year School of Medicine was placed on a quarter system. In addition to its work with pre-professional trainees for the Army and the Navy, the school hospitalized trainees for the Army and the Navy as well as for the University Health Center. It also cooperated with the United States Public Health Service and the Monongalia County Hospital in training nurses

[9] 319 *U.S.*, 624-671.

who agreed to remain in their profession for the duration of the war. Beginning in January, 1941, the University offered courses in the engineering, science, and management war training program for in-service and pre-employment men and women. Pre-radar courses, begun in October, 1942, and ended in September, 1943, were a part of this program, which, under the general direction of the University College of Engineering, trained more than 12,000 persons for war jobs.

With some of its colleges practically defunct, the University campus was converted into a semi-military camp. Most of the students wore uniforms and marched to and from classes under section leaders; for the first time in the history of the institution the women matriculates in civilian courses outnumbered the men; the Men's Residence Hall, the Law College building, four fraternity houses, and Newman Hall were occupied by trainees. Terrace and Men's Residence halls were converted into military mess halls. Moreover, at the end of 1943, eighty-eight members of the University faculty and administrative staff were absent on leave, most of them for war service; and more than 2,500 alumni and former students were in the armed services.

Distinguished Personnel

A number of West Virginians attained high rank in World War II. Richard K. Sutherland, Elkins, served as a lieutenant general, and there were five major generals: Delos C. Emmons, Huntington; Walter C. Sweeney, Jr., Wheeling; John Y. York, Yorkville; John P. Lucas, Kearneysville; and Philip E. Brown, Morgantown. Brigadier generals included George S. Eyster of Jefferson County; Herschel Middleswarts of Bluefield; James M. Lewis of Moundsville; Robert T. Wylie of Huntington; and Charles T. Myers of Mannington. There were also three rear admirals from West Virginia; Claud A. Jones and C. Philip Snyder of Charleston; and Felix B. Stump of Parkersburg.

At the beginning of hostilities General Emmons was in charge of the Air Force Fighter Command. Following the attack upon Pearl Harbor, he replaced General Walter C. Short as Army Commander and Military Governor of the Hawaiian Department. His part in the defense of the Hawaiian Islands and in the planning for the battle of Midway won high praise. Lieutenant General Sutherland was Chief of Staff to General MacArthur from 1939 to 1945. As such, he received the surrender papers of the Japanese at Manila. Brigadier General Charles T. Myers was for a time commanding general of the Italian Theater Air Force; Colonel Walter C. Sweeney, Jr. led the first flight of Army B-17 bombers in the attack on the Japanese fleet and later received two star rank, as had his father before him; Admiral Snyder was the first Naval Inspector General; and Admiral Jones was in charge of the Naval Engineering Experiment Station during the same period.

Among other West Virginians who won distinction in the war were Lieutenant Commander Frederick B. Warder of Grafton, who commanded the submarine *Seawolf* which, in a daring raid off the coast of Java, sank a Japanese light cruiser, a destroyer, and a transport, and damaged four other vessels; Colonel Frank Allen of Charleston, who planned and led the first military shuttle mission from the United States to Soviet Russia; Captain Jimmy Van Pelt of Oak Hill, who, as navigator of a B-29, dropped the atomic bomb on Nagasaki; Lieutenant Leonard J. O'Dell, Charleston, who served for a time as co-pilot on the private plane of Generalissimo Chiang Kai-shek; Captain James B. Johnson of Keyser, the physician who attended General Hideki Tojo following his unsuccessful attempt to commit suicide; and Lieutenant Lewis Arthur Edwards of Charleston, who was credited by Brigadier General Carlos P. Romulo of the Philippines with saving his life.

Of the 429 persons awarded the Congressional Medal of Honor in World War II, eleven were West Virginians. They were Sergeant Stanley Bender of Scarbro; Sergeant Bernard P. Bell, Grantsville; Lieutenant Robert E. Fremoyer, Huntington; Sergeant Clinton M. Hedrick, Riverton; Staff Sergeant Jonah E. Kelley, Keyser; Corporal Melvin Mayfield, Salem; Sergeant Junior J. Spurrier, Bluefield; Sergeant Herbert J. Thomas, Huntington; Private First Class Walter C. Wetzel, Huntington; Corporal Hershel W. Williams, Quiet Dell; and Colonel Justice M. Chambers, Huntington. Sergeant Spurrier, mentioned above, was "the most decorated Army Ground Force enlistee of World War II." In addition to the Congressional Medal of Honor, he was awarded the Distinguished Service Cross, Bronze Star, French Croix de Guerre, eight clusters on a Purple Heart, and numerous ribbons, battle stars, and other decorations. He was credited with having single-handedly captured more than 250 Germans.[10]

Among prominent West Virginia newspaper correspondents who served with distinction in the war, Larry Allen of Charleston had perhaps the most unique experiences. During the first years he traveled some 75,000 miles with the British Mediterranean fleet; he was on the sinking carrier *Illustrious;* and for his story of the event he was awarded a Pulitzer prize in 1942. Witt Hancock of Bluefield was in charge of the Moscow Bureau of the Associated Press at the beginning of the war, and moved to India shortly after Pearl Harbor in time to witness the invasion by the Japanese of Batavia and the Dutch East Indies. In the meantime Roy Cronin of Huntington, who was in charge of the Manila Bureau of the

[10] Jones, "World War II"; Charleston *Gazette,* April 18, 1954.

Associated Press, was captured by the Japanese and interned for two years. Correspondents who reported from the European theater included Ernest Agnew and Leo S. Disher in London; Edward Kennedy, bureau chief in Rome; and Howard Chernoff, managing director of radio station WCHS, Charleston, who interviewed hundreds of West Virginians in the service and reported to the home folk regarding them. Boyd B. Stutler of Charleston, a veteran of World War I, was a war correspondent and managing editor of the *American Legion* magazine and its affiliated publications. Willard C. Hess, former West Virginia newspaper reporter, was the first Office of War Information employee to be awarded the Purple Heart in World War II.

Post-War Developments

In keeping with the War Department policy to expand the National Guard after World War II, West Virginia was allotted almost three times the force formerly authorized. As accepted by Governor Meadows on July 13, 1946, the allotment had a total strength of 5,906 men in 55 units. By June 30, 1949, fifty of these had been organized and federally recognized. Subsequently, the former 201st Infantry became the 201st Armored Field Artillery battalion, and the 197th Tank Battalion was organized.[11]

As thus constituted the West Virginia National Guard was, as formerly, a part of the National Guard of the United States, but it was a state organization in compliance with a legislative act of 1921, as amended in 1949. The governor was the commander-in-chief, functioning through the state adjutant general, and he could use the state National Guard, or any part of it, to preserve the peace, suppress insurrections and rebellions, and to deal with disasters, such as floods and forest fires.

In 1950 three West Virginia Army National Guard battalions and the 167th Fighter-Bomber Squadron of the Air National Guard were ordered into active federal service to assist in stemming the tide of Communism in Germany and Korea. After a period of training at Fort Campbell, Kentucky, the 1092nd Engineer Combat Battalion saw active service at Pusan and Inchon under the command of Lieutenant Colonel Wrene J. Smith of Parkersburg; from Fort Benning, Georgia, the 201st Armored Field Artillery Battalion was assigned to duty with the Seventh Army at Dachau, Germany; and two companies of the 126th Transportation Truck battalion were detached for overseas duty in Germany. After a short period of training at Fort Knox, Kentucky, 26 officers and 75 enlisted airmen had meanwhile been transferred from the West Virginia 167th Fighter-Bomber Squadron for replacement personnel with U. S. Air Force

[11] Adjutant General, Reports (1945-46), p. 3; (1947-48), p. 5.

units in Korea, Europe, and the United States. On April 8, 1951, tragedy struck this squadron when eight officers and twelve men were killed in the crash of a C-47 plane near Kanawha Airport, Charleston, while on a flight from Godman Air Force Base, Kentucky, to Charleston to serve as honor guard at the funeral of their commanding officer, Major Woodford W. Sutherland.

In compliance with a request of the Federal Civil Defense Administration, Governor Okey L. Patteson appointed Brigadier General Charles R. Fox, the adjutant general, as Director of Civil Defense, and he in turn organized the West Virginia Council of Civil Defense. For that purpose the state director, with the aid of his deputy, Lieutenant Colonel Edgar M. Sites, had already made a minute study of civil defense organizations in England, Germany, Japan, and the United States and formulated a plan suitable to the needs of West Virginia. This plan provided for the establishment of nineteen divisions covering practically every phase of civilian life that would be useful in meeting emergencies. The plan provided also for county units organized on the state pattern.

The state director and his staff had meanwhile continued their study of civil defense requirements. In this they were aided by the Eastern Conference of State Civil Defense Directors, organized in New York City on August 13, 1950, and by conferences with state and Federal officials. Out of these conferences and studies came the Model State Civil Defense Act which, with minor changes, was approved by the 1951 legislature. Primarily for the purpose of facilitating cooperation with Federal authorities and of increasing the emergency powers of the governor, the "Model Act" was amended in 1953, and $25,500 was appropriated for civil defense for each year of the 1953-55 biennium. However, in 1952 only 835 persons (ten full time) of the estimated 1,500 needed for administrative positions in civil defense, and only 28,680 of the 172,287 required to provide a full program, were enrolled.[12]

The 290-bed Veterans' Administration Hospital at Huntington being inadequate for the care and rehabilitation of servicemen, the Greenbrier Hotel at White Sulphur Springs was commandeered by the Army in 1942 and converted into a 2,200-bed hospital. Renamed the "Ashford General Hospital," it became a center for vascular surgery, neurosurgery, and general medicine. It was later converted into a replacement pool for the training of medical officers. Patients from practically every battle front were placed under their care. By November, 1945, about 20,000 of them had been admitted to Ashford General.

The Newton D. Baker General Hospital, located four miles east of Martinsburg, was an even more pretentious effort in the care and rehabilitation of sick and disabled servicemen. This installation consisted of

[12] West Virginia, Department of Civil Defense, *Report* (1950-52).

100 buildings, mostly one story and connected by corridors, with a floor space of about thirty acres. Built under direction of U. S. Army engineers at a cost of about $5,000,000 it was opened early in 1944. As at Ashford General, this hospital gave medical treatment and care to thousands of sick and wounded veterans and provided facilities for their rehabilitation. It was however inadequate and a 200-bed Veterans' Administration Hospital for general, medical, and surgical cases was opened in Beckley in 1951, and another at Clarksburg in 1952.

Chapter XXXVII

Life in the Mountain State

THE CALL FOR IMMIGRANTS

IMPELLED by the possibility of diverting to West Virginia a goodly number of the thousands of immigrants who were then moving into the Midwest annually, her legislature, on March 2, 1864, authorized the governor to appoint a commissioner of immigration to aid him in inducing settlers to make homes in the state. For the position Governor Boreman chose Joseph H. Diss Debar, an immigrant and a member of the legislature. Debar accepted the appointment with the understanding that he would serve without pay until the state was able to provide a salary.

Born March 6, 1820, at Strasbourg, Alsace, of German-French parents, Debar came to the United States in 1842 on the same ship that brought Charles Dickens as a visitor. For a time he resided in Cincinnati, Ohio, where, in 1848, he married Clara Julia Levassor. In April, 1846, he came to Doddridge County, (West) Virginia, as the agent of John Peter Dumas, trustee of the James Swan interests in about 10,000 acres of land located on Cove Creek, which he was trying to settle with immigrants from Central Europe.[1] With his ready command of English, German, and French, Debar was well equipped for such an undertaking. For about three years he resided in Parkersburg, where, on April 23, 1849, his wife died. Soon thereafter he established a residence on Cove Creek which became the center of a German-Swiss settlement which he named Santa Clara in honor of his deceased wife.[2]

---

[1] The "Swan Lands" comprised about one sixth of present West Virginia and were located mostly south of the Kanawha River. The nucleus of these lands was a tract of 500,000 acres which Robert Morris of Philadelphia, sold in 1796 to James Swan who spent most of his life trying to colonize them on a large scale with immigrants from Continental Europe. Following his death (1831) the conveyance previously made by him became the subjects of extensive litigation as the "Swan Land Cases."

[2] Boyd B. Stutler, "Joseph H. Diss Debar—Prophet, Colonizer," in *The West Virginia Review,* IX, 154-156, 171.

According to Debar, his first step as commissioner of immigration was "to write and publish a pamphlet of eight pages in 8 vo. descriptive of the State, in English and German, of which 3,000 copies were circulated on both sides of the Atlantic." He distributed thousands of documents in Europe and in the Northern states designed to inform immigrants about West Virginia. In 1865, he appointed C. Lautenschlager, an officer in the Department of Interior of Wurtemberg, to be his agent in Southern Germany and in Switzerland. It was perhaps through him that Debar recruited settlers for the Helvitia and Alpena settlements in Randolph County and for several small ones in Doddridge, Lewis, and Wood counties.

Most of the appropriation made in 1866 for Debar's uses was used by him to make a display of West Virginia products at the World's Universal Exposition, held at Paris in 1867. Finding the state funds inadequate for that purpose, Debar took it upon himself to gather, classify, label, pack, and ship specimens of West Virginia products. The lubricating oil display from Parkersburg was awarded a bronze medal, and he received many inquiries regarding West Virginia from prospective immigrants. Thus encouraged Debar entertained for a time a notion that his dreams of large scale immigrations from Europe to West Virginia might come true. With that in mind he negotiated with the Swiss Emigration Society; he secured concessions from the Baltimore and Ohio Railroad on fare rates to immigrants; he received assurances that the New York Immigration Commission would cease to discriminate against West Virginia in routing immigrants; and he wrote to the governors of all the states to determine what they were doing to attract them. But West Virginia was sparing of funds for the uses of its commissioner and did not seriously consider making gratuities, such as were then used elsewhere, to attract immigrants.[3]

Under these conditions Debar seriously considered resigning his office. Fortunately, he was dissuaded from this, and, in 1869, he compiled the *West Virginia Hand Book and Immigrant's Guide*. This publication was designed not only to inform prospective immigrants but also to correct certain misrepresentations of West Virginia, some of which were regarded as malicious. The following year Democrats gained control of the legislature and vested control of immigration matters in the state board of public works which appointed a Democrat and thus superseded Debar; but economies incident to the financial depression of the 1870's terminated temporarily the state's efforts to attract immigrants. Meanwhile they continued to pour into the Midwest, bypassing stores of natural wealth in the Mountain State for that more readily available in plain and prairie

[3] Roberta Stevenson Turney, "The Encouragement of Immigration in West Virginia, 1863-1871," in *West Virginia History,* XII, 46-60.

farm lands. In the comparative absence of capital and transportation to develop their natural resources, hundreds of West Virginians joined them.

POPULATION GROWTH AND TRENDS, 1870-1950

In 1870 West Virginia had a population of 442,014 including 17,980 Negroes and one Indian. The bulk of it was native whites residing along or near navigable rivers, turnpikes, and the Baltimore and Ohio railroad. The bulk of the Negro population was in the following counties: Jefferson, 3,488; Kanawha, 2,234; Berkeley, 1,672; Greenbrier, 1,103; Monroe, 1,003; Harrison, 655; Hampshire, 640; Hardy, 616; and Mason, 534. Only McDowell and Webster counties had no Negro residents. There were 17,091 foreign-born, of whom 6,020, or more than one-third, resided in Ohio County. Other counties with large foreign-born populations were: Wood, 1,287; Mason, 953; Marshall, 909; Preston, 717; Kanawha, 687; Berkeley, 629; Lewis, 522; Taylor, 484; Mineral, 426; and Harrison, 422. Only Clay County had no foreign-born residents. McDowell and Wyoming had three each; Webster four; Pendleton six; and Logan seven.

Prior to about 1900 most of the population increase in West Virginia was native-born whites, but the beginning of her industrialization brought Negroes and foreign-born whites in large numbers. By 1930 the Negro population had increased to 114,893, and McDowell county had 22,000. Other counties with large Negro populations were Kanawha, Fayette, Raleigh, Mercer, and Logan. At the same time there were 51,520 foreign-born whites, or about 10,000 less than in 1920; but more significant perhaps were the 152,390 residents of "foreign white stock," one fifth of whom were Italians. Government restrictions following World War I had limited the immigrant flow, but coal operators continued to import Southern Negroes in large numbers.

The effects of industrialization were reflected in population shifts from rural to urban and suburban. For instance, the rural farm population declined from 491,700, or 51.3 per cent of the total, in 1900, to 447,750, or 25.9 per cent, in 1930. More significant, the rural non-farm population for the corresponding dates increased from 341,635, or 35.6 per cent of the total, to 789,951, or 45.7 per cent. Consequently counties in former agricultural, oil producing, and timbering areas lost population, whereas those in industrial and mining areas gained. Gains for a single decade, as in the case of Logan, Hancock, Raleigh and Boone counties, ranged from 60.5 to 183.3 per cent.

A back-to-the farm movement which began early in the depression of the 1930's added 114,000 persons to the farm group in five years. Most of them were young people who could not find employment elsewhere. At the same time the birth rate tended to decline causing predictions to the effect that it would be stationary by 1960. In the accompanying interstate shift, there was a net loss of about 50,000 whites in the total state population and a gain of about the same number of Negroes, most of it in the coal mining areas.[4]

A unique movement was launched in 1933 by Mrs. Franklin D. Roosevelt for the rehabilitation of stranded industrial workers. For that purpose large tracts of land were purchased at Arthurdale, Preston County; in Tygart Valley, Randolph County; and near Redhouse, Putnam County. These tracts were subdivided into lots of varying sizes, upon fifty or more of which at each location the Federal Government built residences. These, including the lots, were then sold to approved purchasers, who agreed to pay over a period of years. To make this possible, it was planned to combine industrial and agricultural employment. But efforts to provide employment fell short of expectations and the settlement projects were liquidated after serving their initial purposes.

THE 1950 CENSUS

With a total of 2,005,552, West Virginia was twenty-ninth among the states in population in 1950 and thirty-second in per cent of increase since the census of 1940. Her increase was however only 103,578, or 5.4 per cent, whereas that for the United States was 14.5 per cent. The comparatively poor showing of the state was officially attributed to migrations of persons in search of industrial employment. The only notable increase was in the "five and under" age group which was higher than that for the country at large. The numerical increase was smallest since 1870, and the rate of increase was the smallest in the history of the state.

In 1940 native-born whites constituted 91.6 per cent of the total, foreign-born whites 2.2 per cent, and Negroes 6.2 per cent. The respective figures for the country at large were 81.5, 8.7, and 9.8. Most of the state's foreign-born population was in the northern counties with heaviest concentration in the Northern Panhandle. In 1950 the median age for the state was 24.3 years, whereas that for the country at large was 29.0 years, a condition explained by the high birth rate in World War II and the subsequent migration of those in the employment groups. This movement caused

---

[4] West Virginia State Planning Board, "A Study of the People of West Virginia" (Charleston, W. Va., 1937).

concern throughout the state and led to concerted efforts to attract new industries to it.[5]

According to a new census plan for determining urban populations that of West Virginia for 1950 included the following: (1) The 644,443 inhabitants of the 55 incorporated places of 2,500 or more; (2) the 29,506 inhabitants of the seven specially delineated unincorporated places of 2,500 inhabitants or more; and (3) the 24,375 persons living in the "urbanized fringes" of Charleston, Huntington, and Wheeling. Including the second and third groups, the urban population was 53,881 more than it would have been otherwise. Including it, the total was 698,324, or 34.8 per cent of the total for the state. If however the new method had not been used, only 32.1 per cent of the total would have been urban, which would have been an increase of only 4 per cent for the two decades ending in 1950. On the other hand, the rural population of the state declined from 86.9 to 65.2 per cent between 1900 and 1950. Between 1940 and 1950 there was a numerical loss of 6,573, the first in the history of the state.

On a percentage basis neither the urban nor the rural population kept pace with the non-farm rural which increased from 341,635, or 35.6 per cent in 1900, to 900,143, or 44.9 per cent of the total in 1950. But for the change in the method of reporting, it would have been even greater. The suburban migration was influenced by a desire for industrial employment, for lower taxes, for greater security against possible atomic attacks, and for the conveniences and attractions of city life. In 1950 large areas of the state were being converted into "urbanized fringes" and "specially delineated unincorporated places," and population, business, and industry were spreading into the country-side along improved highways far beyond city limits.

Traces of two-type small communities: the trade town, or village, and the coal mining town, featured West Virginia landscapes in 1950. The trade towns served the needs of limited agricultural and grazing areas; many of them were older than the state; and some of them had changed little in appearance in the course of a hundred years. But they were the centers of its conservative and stabilizing forces, both socially and economically. Most of the coal-mining towns were in the southern part of the state. They were mushroom growths, exploitive in appearance and, until recently, coal-operator owned and controlled.

At the same time West Virginia counties ranged in population size from Wirt, with 5,119 inhabitants, to Kanawha with 239,629. Between 1940 and 1950, 27 of the 55 counties gained in population. The highest rate of growth, 26.1 per cent, was registered by Wyoming County which also had the highest rate in the previous decade. In both the decades ending

[5] James H. Thompson, "The Manufacturing Industries of West Virginia," in Business and Economic Studies of West Virginia University, Vol. II, No. I, p. 7.

in 1940 and 1950, the largest numerical increase was in Kanawha County which was credited with more than two fifths of that for the entire state in the 1940-50 decade. The counties which lost in population in that decade were those which had been losing since 1920. Those with the highest rate of loss were Wirt, 20.9 per cent; Tucker, 19.5; Gilmer, 19.1; Ritchie, 18.5; Calhoun, 17.6; Doddridge, 17.4; Braxton, 16.5; Tyler, 16.1; Pendleton, 14.4; and Roane, 11.4.

The foreign-born white population of West Virginia declined in 1950 to 33,640 of which number more than 20,000 were in the 45 to 70 age groups. Practically all this population was either urban or rural non-farm. Only 1,665 foreign-born whites resided on farms.

From a peak of 117,754 in 1940, West Virginia's Negro population declined to 113,735 in 1950. Of the total in the latter date 64,230 were classed as rural non-farm, 46,650 as urban, and 2,855 as farm residents. As in the previous reports, since 1900, the bulk of this population was in the coal mining areas. It included 33,375 native West Virginians. Of the others, 8,825 were born in Virginia, 4,850 in Alabama, 2,350 in North Carolina, 1,125 in Kentucky, 935 in Georgia, 825 in Tennessee, 805 in Ohio, 795 in South Carolina, 650 in Pennsylvania. More than half of the total Negro population was concentrated in Kanawha, McDowell, Raleigh, and Fayette counties.

In 1950 forty-seven per cent of the "fourteen year old or older" population of West Virginia was in the "labor force," as compared with 53.5 per cent for the entire country. Of the 692,105 males in that age group 516,520, or 74.6 per cent were in the labor force, but only 490,185 were gainfully employed. Of the 707,775 females in the same age group only 139,000, or 19.6 per cent, were in the labor force and only 133,375 were employed.

In 1950 West Virginia had a total dwelling resident population of 1,963,114. They lived in 544,075 units of 4.6 rooms average capacity, or the same as that for the entire United States. The units housed an average of 3.4 persons each; 22.6 per cent of them housed an average of one or more persons per room; 5.3 per cent were occupied by non-whites; 55.0 per cent were owner occupied; 25.1 per cent were provided with central heating; and 74.2 per cent had mechanical refrigeration. The corresponding figures for the country at large were 3.1 residents per unit; 15.7 housing one or more persons; 8.8 occupied by non-whites; 55.0 owner occupied; 50.4 centrally heated; and 80.2 with mechanical refrigeration. Of the total number of dwelling units in the state, 44.6 had hot water, private toilet, and bath; 19.1 per cent were built in or since 1940; and 1.2 per cent were for rent. The corresponding figures for the United States were 20.7 with hot water, private bath, and toilet; 63.1 built since 1940; and 1.6 for rent. The median value of owner-occupied non-farm dwellings was $5,473, and 32.5 per cent of that value was mortgaged. The corresponding figures for the whole country were $7,354 and 44.0 per cent.

The illiteracy census for 1950 showed West Virginia above the average for the United States in essential items. In a total state population of 1,039,555, aged twenty-five or over, 13.7 per cent had completed less than five years of schooling; 2.5 per cent had completed no schooling; 11.2 per cent had completed from one to four years; and the median school years completed was 8.5. The corresponding figures for the country at large were 11.0 less than five years; 2.6 no schooling; 8.4 one to four years; and 9.3 median years. Although much of the poor showing of West Virginia was due to her Negro population, particularly newly arrived immigrants, it attracted state-wide attention. The failure of 21.8 per cent of her sons to qualify for military service in 1950-1951, was attributed, in part, to illiteracy. Together with that of the country at large, it was thus brought into the limelight as a menace to the potential manpower of the nation. It thus became a national problem, and Senator Harley M. Kilgore of West Virginia, began a campaign in an effort to have the National Government assist the states in the removal of this blot.

THE CHANGING ORDER

Agrarian economy was still practiced in 1955 in remote parts of West Virginia and even in suburban areas. On the other hand, West Virginia was being industrialized more rapidly than the percentage of her urban population (34.8) would indicate. Because of improved transportation and modern utilities, industry attracted many to suburban areas. Indeed, it was confidently predicted that the valleys of her navigable rivers would, in the not distant future, be the sites of more or less continuous industrial areas. Because of the shortened work day, residents of these areas practiced a diversified agriculture after the fashion of the old-time small farmer. This trend was revealed in the 1950 federal census which indicated a small percentage growth in the urban population, a rapid decline in the rural, and an equally rapid increase in the suburban. Presently, a number of suburban areas are establishing public service districts for the purpose of supplying themselves with utilities under a permissive act of the 1953 legislature.

URBAN LIFE

Each West Virginia city has an individuality that is reflected in its population. Though an industrial center, Huntington, the largest in 1955, was in keeping with the plans of its founder, Collis P. Huntington, more commercial than industrial. The ethnic groupings common to other urban areas were absent there, and the population, which was 95 per cent white, native born, and mostly of Southern origin, was socially homogeneous. The city was noted for its broad streets, fine churches, and religious activity. Accessibility made Huntington an ideal educational center.

Prior to World War I Charleston, the capital and the second largest city, was a quiet, rustic Southern town whose repose was disturbed only by the arrival and departure of numerous trains on the Chesapeake and Ohio, the Kanawha and Michigan, and the Coal and Coke railroads. Biennially, from January to March in the odd-numbered years, the city welcomed the state legislature and its coteries of lobbyists. Charleston was the center of a large area rich in natural resources capable of sustaining a metropolitan population. The requirements of World War I directed attention to this fact, and in the course of a few years Charleston became a trade center for a large industrial area. Consequently its old-time buildings gave way to modern structures ranging in height from three to twenty stories; legislators were lost in the hustle of industrialists, salesmen, and clerks; transportation facilities adapted themselves to the changed situation; and Kanawha Street, paralleling the Kanawha River on the north side through the entire length of the city, was converted into one of the most beautiful boulevards in America. Despite these changes, Charleston retained its Southern flavor.

The tempo of Wheeling, a manufacturing and commercial center of the Northern Panhandle and the third largest city in the state, was more akin to that of neighboring cities in Ohio and Pennsylvania than to the more leisurely-paced cities of West Virginia. More than any other city in the state, Wheeling, with its parks and orchestras, had the atmosphere of a long-settled metropolitan area. An industrial center for more than one hundred years, it had attracted foreign-born groups including Germans, Irish, Italians, Poles, and Greeks, most of whom had their own churches and fraternal societies. As the birthplace of the state and twice its capital, Wheeling had a sentimental appeal that lingered in defiance of the effacing influence of the years.

Other cities had distinguishing characteristics. Weirton, eighth largest, was, prior to being incorporated in 1947 with Holliday's Cove, the largest unincorporated and company-owned city in the world. From the date of its establishment, it measured progress by the millions of dollars spent for civic, recreational, and municipal purposes. Clarksburg was an industrial and transportation center of a large surrounding area occupied by farmers, cattlemen, coal miners, and oil and gas production employees. Fairmont retained some of the characteristics of a country town, but it has long been an educational center. For years it was the center of the coal mining industry of northern West Virginia. A glass manufacturing and mining center for about fifty years, Morgantown was primarily an educational center. Its industrial and commercial growth was retarded somewhat by the comparative lack of transportation facilities, but that handicap was overcome by the improved navigation of the Monongahela River. Although an industrial center, Parkersburg was spared the smoke, disorder, and congestion common to manufacturing centers by grouping her industries along the Little Kanawha and the Ohio Rivers. She owed her importance to her location, her transportation facilities, and her oil and gas operations.

Life in the smaller cities was as varied as the cities themselves. Weston, site of the oldest institution for the mentally ill in the state, was both a farming and an industrial center. Grafton, the rail hub of northern West Virginia, was still remembered as a strategic point in the Civil War. Buckhannon, a college town with shady streets unblemished by factory soot, was the center of a rich farming area noted for its strawberries. Elkins, gateway to the Monongahela National Forest, a college town, and a railroad center situated in a bowl-shaped valley of the Alleghenies, kept alive incidents in the life of its founder and namesake. Kingwood, county seat of Preston County and site of an annual buckwheat festival, was a somewhat unique product of agricultural, mining, and timbering activities. Richwood, Nicholas County, where ramps, as well as robins and crocuses, were the harbinger of spring, was trying to escape oblivion by fabricating the products of its sawmills instead of exporting them as lumber. And Rainelle, Greenbrier County, a common meeting place of farmers, miners, and lumbermen, was at mid-century the chief lumber producing center of the state.

To the eastward municipal varieties were even more pronounced. Martinsburg, gateway to the Shenandoah Valley, had an industrial atmosphere not unlike that of Wheeling but, unlike Wheeling, reverted to her easy-going Southern ways with the close of the work day. Keyser, Mineral County, a strategic point on the Baltimore and Ohio Railroad in the Civil War, has, since 1902, become increasingly important as an educational center. Centers of rich agricultural areas, Romney and Moorefield kept their Civil War memories greener than other cities in the state, while their neighbor, Petersburg, Grant County, located in a mountain retreat surrounded by ardent state rights devotees, continued to adhere to nationalistic traditions. While reveling in her Rumseyan steamboat traditions, Shepherdstown was prouder of achievements in higher education. Charles Town, site of noted treason trials, was more interested in race horses than in John Brown of Osawatomie. Twice annually she assumed a gala air to welcome the thousands of racing fans who visited her Jockey Club. And war-battered, flood damaged, neglected Harpers Ferry was living in anticipation of becoming the center of activity of the National Monument being projected by the National Park Service.

A score or more comparatively new developments in the southern part of the state were rapidly assuming an individuality of their own. Bluefield, the nature air-conditioned city that treated the public to lemonade each day of the year the thermometer reached ninety degrees Fahrenheit, was the "Gateway to the Pocahontas coal fields." Williamson, site of a cornfield in 1891, was by 1900 a transportation point in the "Billion Dollar Coal field." Logan's importance as a mining center had virtually eclipsed her Indian traditions. Bramwell was featured by large houses and wide lawns, remnants of its millionaire glory in the pre-depression days of the 1920's. Welch had solved its perennial parking problem by the erection of the first municipally owned parking building in the state. Fayetteville, an agricultural center with many reminders of the Lost Cause, was noted for its weekly newspapers. Rapidly growing Beckley rejoiced in the distinction of being the "Smokeless Coal Capital of the World" and was confidently contemplating the advantages of becoming the axis of a superhighway system. Practically all of the coal field cities contained large Negro populations, and in a few the Negro population exceeded the white.

There was little social life in the mining towns, where the economic life revolved around the magic phrase, "pay day at the mines." In response to this appeal, the streets were thronged, the stores crowded, the movies jammed. Women in shiny rayon dresses shopped with a sharp eye for bargains, as they anxiously shepherded numerous children of varying sizes. The bustle subsided as suddenly as it began, and pay day was followed by thirteen days of almost rural quiet. On the other hand, the larger cities of the area displayed a degree of culture with their symphony orchestras, their poetry guilds, and their little theaters, while life in the smaller intervening towns followed the periphery of a specialized industry or a well established state institution.

PUBLIC WELFARE

As West Virginia failed to respond to the impulses of the Progressive Movement, social reform did not get under way in the state until the return of peace at the end of World War I. It was in 1919 that the legislature created a state board of children's guardians authorized to receive dependent and unfortunate children by court commitments. Such children were wards of the state until they became of age. A number of charitable institutions cared for dependent children until they were placed in private homes. An act of 1925 created a crippled children's council authorized to inquire into and make provisions for promoting the care, treatment, and general welfare of crippled children, and four years later this council opened diagnostic clinics.

The program as applied to adults was perhaps even more progressive. If aid to the poor had been meager and unscientifically administered prior to 1921, under an act of that year more than half of the counties of the state granted pensions to widows in 1930. These grants were made by

State Capitol, Charleston

county courts upon the recommendation of an examining representative, the guiding purpose being to maintain home conditions wherever possible. An act of 1923 authorized the establishment of county welfare boards, or county welfare secretaries, where boards were not needed. Through the use of these agencies it was possible for counties to break away from the old-time method of administering poor relief through overseers of the poor. Immediately several counties appointed welfare secretaries and otherwise prepared for a more scientific administration of matters pertaining to dependents. An act of 1927 established a veterans' service office to assist and advise veterans of any war in which the United States had participated.

In response to demands for greater efficiency in the expenditure of funds for public welfare, the legislature in 1931 consolidated the Veterans' Service Office, the Board of Children's Guardians, and the Crippled Children's Council into a department of public welfare administered by a director under supervision of an advisory council of ten ex officio members. Because of the current depression the department had no funds, and from 1932 to 1934 welfare work in the state was financed by federal funds and by limited grants by the county courts. To meet an emergency $250,000 was diverted in 1934 from the state road fund, and shortly thereafter the legislature, meeting in extra session, appropriated $1,000,000 for the remainder of that year. At the next regular session, the appropriation was increased to $3,000,000 for each year of the 1935-1937 biennium.

West Virginia state flower, rhododendron maximum, or "big laurel"

The Federal Government had meanwhile entered the picture with the Social Security Act of 1935. To comply with its requirement the legislature enacted in June, 1936, a comprehensive public welfare law which abolished the department of public welfare and vested its duties in a department of public assistance. This agency was authorized to examine and integrate the state welfare services under supervision of a director and an advisory board of five members appointed by the governor. The duties of the department were to administer old-age assistance, to aid dependent children and the blind, and to grant relief. It was responsible for the distribution of commodities to needy persons and of funds allocated for child welfare and medical care. For most of these services the Federal Government matched the state dollar for dollar, but general relief funds were supplied entirely by the state and the counties and were administered through county councils.

Civilian rehabilitation, first authorized in 1921 and financed with state and federal funds in approximately equal amounts, was administered through the state department of education until 1945. That year the legislature approved the federal State Rehabilitation Act and designated the state board of education as the West Virginia Board of Vocational Education, which was authorized and directed to cooperate with the Federal Government in an effort to provide vocational rehabilitation for disabled persons. A division of vocational rehabilitation was then established and placed under the administration of a director. In the year ending June 30, 1953, this division served 7,126 persons and rehabilitated 1,655 at an average cost for the latter of $466.27, of which the state paid 32.47 per cent.

The West Virginia Department of Veterans Affairs was established in 1945 with duties similar to those of the former veterans' office. The new department was administered by a director, appointed by the governor, who functioned under the supervision and control of a veterans' council composed of five members, each of whom held an honorable discharge from the armed services. In 1955 there were four United States veterans' hospitals in the state: The Baker Veterans Administration Center at Martinsburg, with its 900 hospital beds and 500 domiciliary beds; and three administration hospitals—one each in Huntington, Clarksburg, and Beckley—with a total of 690 beds. There was also a veterans' employment service in Charleston.

Despite the efforts to deal with veterans and dependents constructively, problems remained and some facts were discouraging. For instance, 67 in each 1,000 of the school population of West Virginia in 1954 were on relief, as compared with only 28 in each 1,000 for the country at large. Chief contributing causes were officially attributed to deaths and unemployment of the family wage earner in the coal fields. Also disturbing was the fact that three in each 100 of the adult population were alcoholics. While the percentage rate of resident alcoholics was lower than that of neighboring states, an interim committee of the 1953 legislature recommended that funds from state liquor and beer revenues be used to finance a West Virginia commission on alcoholism authorized to formulate and direct a program for its treatment.

But West Virginia's welfare situation was not entirely hopeless. Thirty other states had more persons over sixty-five years of age on relief; by the use of "ice pick" surgery West Virginia was rehabilitating a large number of her hospitalized mentally ill; an act of 1937 permitted, under certain conditions, the sterilization of inmates of charitable and correctional institutions; and a somewhat concerted effort was being made to hospitalize the sick and the afflicted. For the year ending in 1953, eighty-five per cent of the 46,652 live births occurred in hospitals, as compared with only thirty per cent in 1933; and 98.3 per cent of the births in 1953 were attended by a doctor. Whereas hospitals had been few and far between at the turn of the century, every city in the state and many of the towns had at least one such institution.

WELFARE INSTITUTIONS

These institutions were classed officially in 1955 as charitable, correctional, penal, and as hospitals and sanitariums. The Children's Home at Elkins, established in 1899 and formally opened in 1911, provided training in domestic work for children between the ages of six and fourteen until they could be placed in foster homes. The West Virginia Colored Children's Home at Huntington, was incorporated in 1900 for use as a home for Negro orphans and neglected children under the age of nineteen, until such time as they could be placed in homes. The West Virginia Training School at St. Marys was established in 1921 for the treatment, training, and readjustment of mentally defective children. And the West Virginia Home for Aged and Infirm Colored Men and Women, was established in Charleston in 1923, moved to Huntington in 1928, and to its present location at McKendree, Fayette County, in 1941. In 1954 there were 371 inmates in the state charitable institutions.

Because of a belief that major crimes were increasingly due to juvenile delinquency, the 1889 legislature established a reform school for boys. Located at Pruntytown, Taylor County, and later renamed the Industrial School, the reform school was devoted to the care and training of wayward boys. For some time it adhered to a policy of strict discipline, but, thanks to a better knowledge of the social and the medical sciences, this gave way to corrective and reformative measures provided by the elementary and the secondary schools, sports, 4-H clubs, Boy Scout troop activities, and religious services. The West Virginia Industrial Home for Girls at Industrial, near Salem, established in 1897 and formally opened on May 5, 1899; the West Virginia Industrial School for Colored Boys at Lakin, established in 1921 and opened in 1924; and the West Virginia Industrial Home for Colored Girls at Huntington, established in 1921 and opened in 1926, experienced a transformation similar to that of the Pruntytown School but with greater emphasis upon corrective and reformative programs.

In 1955 the state maintained three penal institutions: the West Virginia Penitentiary at Moundsville, established in 1866; the Medium Security

Prison at Huttonsville, Randolph County, established in 1937; and the West Virginia State Prison for Women at Pence Springs, Summers County, established in 1947. In the 1870's officials were criticized for building a larger and more expensive penal structure at Moundsville than the state would ever need, but its overcrowded condition has long been a state problem complicated at times by a lack of permissible employment for the inmates. Establishment of the Medium Security Prison helped to solve that problem, as did also the policy of using convict labor on state road projects and in the manufacture of goods used by the state. The Medium Security Prison was a part of the Penitentiary at Moundsville and subject to the same rules and regulations until 1947, when it became a separate institution. For the confinement of female prisoners from 1924 to 1947, the state used facilities of the Federal Reformatory for Women at Alderson. In 1954, eighty-two inmates were confined in the West Virginia State Prison for Women at Pence Springs, and the total confined in the two state penal institutions for men numbered 2,674.

In 1955 West Virginia had five sanitariums—three tubercular, one home, and one memorial. The sanitariums were Denmar, near Marlinton, established in 1917 for Negro tuberculars; Hopemont Tubercular, established in 1913 at Hopemont, near Terra Alta; and Pinecrest Tubercular, near Beckley, established in 1927 and opened on March 18, 1930; the Andrew S. Rowan Memorial Home at Sweet Springs, established in 1945 for aged men and women; and the Berkeley Springs Sanitarium in Morgan County, leased in 1939 by the state to private individuals in an effort to restore something of the popularity these springs enjoyed during a hundred years prior to the Civil War. The state also operated seven hospitals. The surgical hospitals were the Fairmont Emergency and the Welch Emergency established in 1899 for the free treatment of emergency occupational cases. In 1955 the Fairmont Emergency Hospital was the surgical clinic for the state charitable and correctional institutions. The mental hospitals were Weston State, authorized by the Virginia General Assembly in 1858 and opened to patients in 1864 as the oldest state institution in West Virginia; Spencer State, established in 1887 and opened in 1893; Huntington State established in 1897 as the "Home for Incurables" and changed in 1901 to the "West Virginia Asylum" and in 1916 to its present name; Lakin State at Lakin, near Point Pleasant, established in 1923 and opened in 1926 to Negro patients; and Barboursville State established in 1942 in former dormitories of Morris Harvey College as a branch of the Weston State Hospital. In 1947 this institution became the Barboursville Unit of the Huntington State Hospital and in 1949 the Barboursville State Hospital. In 1954 the population of the state mental hospitals totaled 4,500.

FAIRS AND FESTIVALS

Even before West Virginia became a separate state, county and regional fairs depicted industrial and agricultural life. In 1955 many counties sponsored one or more annual fairs, some of which were county-wide in their appeal. From 1880 to 1921 the State Fair on Wheeling Island eclipsed them all. With its exit, the Greenbrier Valley Fair at Lewisburg became the State Fair. As if in preparation for it, chief interest had already shifted from the awe-inspiring Howe sewing machine, the McCormick mower and reaper, and the squeaking Edison phonograph to the prize-winning steers and steeds for which the Greenbrier area was famous. Held annually since 1923 during the last week of August, the Lewisburg State Fair featured farm exhibits, purebred horses and cattle, canned goods, needle work of all kinds, wood carving, basket weaving, baking, health exhibits, horseshoe pitching, sack races, croquet matches, trotting races, band concerts, children's day, and fireworks. Chief interest was however in the horse show and the races. For a number of years the estimated annual attendance exceeded 100,000.

The Ritchie County Fair, held regularly since 1887 near Pennsboro, was first among the county fairs. On the opening day all chores were completed before daylight; lunches were carefully packed; before sun-up the finest cattle, pigs, sheep, chickens, and farm products were loaded into the farm truck; and the family was off for a week of excitement and fun-making. At the Fair the children gravitated to the midway to spend their treasured nickels and dimes on Ferris wheels and merry-go-rounds, while their mothers inspected needle work, canned fruits, choice baking, and potted plants and their fathers visited the stock pens, watched the races, and inspected agricultural exhibits. As the day faded one or two members of the family went home to do the evening chores, but all returned to witness the events of the evening—midway displays, concession activities, and a final display of fireworks.

In some parts of the state the fair gave way to the festival. Through this agency an ever increasing number of persons sought to revive interest in folklore traditions and to find meaning in them. The West Virginia Folklore Society, organized in 1925, held annual meetings and featured expert as well as amateur ballad singers who made contributions to the history and folklore of the state. The West Virginia Folk Festival, held annually at Glenville State College since 1950, was a product of this interest and was organized for the purpose of acquainting West Virginians with the origin of their cultural traditions as symbolized in native ballads such as "John Henry," "Barbara Allen," and "Sourwood Mountain."

The Spud and Splinter Festival, "Spud" for potato and "Splinter" for the wood working industry, held annually in August at Richwood during three days, revived memories and traditions of the once-thriving timber industry. When Cherry River was not dry, this festival was featured by maneuvers of the "Cherry River Navy" and its flagship, *The Clothespin*. This ship was "manned by one deckhand and a dozen admirals chosen from an honorary roll of 1,500 names of former governors, state and local officials, business men, and old time lumberjacks. The admirals wore cocked hats of black paper with gold insignia in the shape of crossed clothespins; epaulets of gilded cardboard with rope fringe; lapel insignia of gold in the shape of clothespins; and Sam Browne belts of white clotheslines and side arms of white maple in the form of giant clothespins. The festival was concluded with a parade by the admirals and crew, followed by a banquet and a ball."

The Mountain State Forest Festival, held annually in peacetime on the campus of Davis and Elkins College at Elkins since 1930, was a tribute to the sylvan glory of West Virginia. The main events were the coronation of "Queen Sylvia," the reception of forest princesses representing the Congressional and the state senatorial districts, the queen's ball, and an elaborate parade of floats. The program included also contests in horseback tilting at rings, wood chopping, and marksmanship with muzzle-loading rifles by mountaineers who had attained the age of sixty. The number of persons witnessing these exercises reached well into the thousands and included hundreds of non-residents.

In like manner the Preston County Buckwheat Festival, held annually at Kingwood since 1941, attracted thousands of persons, including many non-residents. With participants from Maryland, Pennsylvania, and Ohio, it was, in fact, an interstate affair. In 1954 the festival was featured by a dozen or more scenes from Alice in Wonderland, as depicted from floats staged by the school children of Preston County. Other features included the "Buckwheat Bowl" football game, the crowning of "King Fireman" by the state fire marshal; a free aerial act by "Kayletta, the Girl in the Sky"; a farmers' day parade; a firemen's parade; a display of fireworks; a public school community day; and finally the crowning of "Queen Ceres." Scabbard and Blade, honorary military fraternity at West Virginia University, was the honor guard for the queen and her princesses. The Preston County high school bands provided entertainment for the entire program, and the various women's organizations of the county served buckwheat cakes, sausages, syrup, apple sauce, and coffee.

The Central West Virginia Strawberry Festival, held annually in peacetime for two days at Buckhannon in the first week of June since 1926, attracted 53,000 persons in 1952 and was featured by the crowning of the "Strawberry Queen" by the late Senator Robert A. Taft of Ohio. This affair was conducted by an association of central West Virginia counties. In 1954, there were nine participating counties, each of which sent five princesses. Most of the exercises centered about West Virginia Wesleyan College and were featured by competitive contests, an art exhibit, a chicken exhibit, square dancing, a parade, and finally the "Queen's Ball." Music for the occasions was furnished by the high school bands of the participating counties. In 1954 their mass concert of 500 participants was directed by Paul Yoder of Chicago, a distinguished composer of school band numbers.

Other festivals of more than local interest included the Berkeley Springs Tomato, held annually for three days in September in honor of the tomato, chief crop of the surrounding area. The producer of the best bushel of tomatoes was crowned "King of Morgan County Tomato Growers," and the entertainment program was featured by appearances of the "Tomato Queen," a pageant, a parade, a musical concert, a baby show, a drum-corps drill, a candlelight vesper and choral service, and a display of fireworks. At the Tobacco Festival held annually in November at Huntington, center of the tobacco growing area of the state, growers of choice burley tobacco exhibited their products and were awarded prizes for superior entries. On November 4-5, 1955, Spencer, Roane County, staged her first Black Walnut Festival, and still other cities were seeking ways and means to exploit their distinctive features through festive affairs.

Other festivities were the Upshur County Singers Convention, held in August of each year; the Petersburg Tri-County Fair; and the Bluefield Coal Show. The Singers Convention was composed of soloists, quartettes, and choirs from the central mountain region of the state, who assembled annually at Jackson Grove, near Buckhannon, to "promote social fellowship among the people of Upshur County, and to create more interest in vocal music." Some came as listeners, others to renew acquaintances, but the active participants came to sing "sacred songs in keeping with the day." All participated in the huge basket-lunches spread under the trees. The Tri-County Fair (Petersburg) was featured by rodeos, riding tournaments, and other riding contests. Uniformed horsemen, bearing titles such as "Knight of the South Branch Valley" and "Knight of Middle Mountain," imparted a medieval air to the occasion. The knight who collected the most rings was permitted to name the "Queen of the Tournament." The Bluefield Coal Show, the Southern Appalachian Industrial Exhibit, was held in alternate years as a companion event to the American Mining Congress exhibit held in Cleveland, Ohio. The Bluefield exhibit was held in May of the even-numbered years and was featured by the latest improvements in mining machinery and by sidelights, such as the Pioneer Miners' Reunion, the Miners' Gadget Contest, and finally, the crowning of "Queen Bituminous."

FAMILY REUNIONS

Since late in the last century the family reunion, a product of the clannishness of Mountaineers, was increasingly popular in West Virginia. Tradition has it that this institution had its origin in the Fleming Family Reunion held in Fairmont, in August, 1891, but credit for its launching was claimed by several other families. A chief purpose of these gatherings was the collection and preservation of family history. Although the reunions were sometimes disappointing from the standpoint of history, a number of creditable volumes, notably those on the Fleming, the Barns, and the Nuzum families, were indebted to them. In recent years these affairs were not so well attended as in the 1920's, but they were still magnets attracting thousands of persons suffering from homesickness for the West Virginia hills.

Of the numerous family gatherings, the Lilly Family Reunion, sponsored for twenty years by A. A. Lilly ("Cousin Abe") was the largest in West Virginia and one of the largest in the United States. From a small beginning in 1930 the attendance at this affair sometimes exceeded 75,000 persons. To accommodate them a rolling hillside on Flat Top Mountain was equipped with a grandstand, a stage, and frame booths for the sale of refreshments and souvenirs. Most of the participants were either the descendants or the kinfolk of Robert Lilly, son of an associate of Cecil Calvert, Second Lord Baltimore, who came to Maryland in 1640.

SPORTS AND AMUSEMENTS

At the beginning of the present century amusements in West Virginia conformed rather closely to puritanical patterns. Dancing, card playing, even theater going, were banned by "good" people generally, and amusements for young people consisted almost entirely of carefully chaperoned parties. Authors and Rook took the place of cards. In higher educational institutions, including the State University, all forms of vice, a most comprehensive term, were taboo, and students were expelled for attending dances and theaters and even for smoking. To be sure, all this has since changed.

As elsewhere, entertainment was affected most by mechanical inventions. In 1955 approximately one half of the homes were equipped with radio and television sets; there were about 400,000 privately owned passenger motor vehicles; and most homes were equipped with labor-saving devices. With the populace thus emancipated from back-breaking toil, its activities took a wider range, and the old fashioned Sunday School picnics and annual tournaments gave way to carnivals with their new-fangled dances and machine-produced music. Outdoor life was fostered by municipal parks and swimming pools and by state-owned and supervised parks, and, more than before, West Virginians tended to see the world through auto and bus excursions to the Pacific coast and winter sojourns in Florida.

Close proximity to large metropolitan areas, plus a perennial interest in horses caused the 1933 state legislature to legalize horse racing on a pari-mutuel basis. By this law horse racing was placed under the supervision of a racing commission consisting of three members appointed by the governor. Since 1933 three race tracks have been opened: the Charles Town, Wheeling Downs, and Waterford Park. 1955 was the fifth year for the Waterford Park Club, located in Hancock County, the nineteenth for the Wheeling Downs Club, and the twenty-third for the Charles Town Club. For a dozen years the state received only one per cent of the daily net collections, but in 1947 the state's part was increased to three per cent and in 1955 to four per cent.

The daily attendance at these races reached well into the thousands, and the interest developed, plus the financial benefits to the state and the promoters, led to movements to establish race tracks in other metropolitan areas, notably the Charleston-Huntington. But the movement encountered stiff opposition from ministerial and other organizations, and the 1953 legislature forbade the state racing commission to authorize the construction of a race track for pari-mutuel wagering in any county where a majority of the voters opposed such action.

To a degree somewhat out of proportion to their non-urban population, West Virginians shared the twentieth century enthusiasm for athletic sports, but for a quarter of a century interest was limited generally to baseball and football. In 1922 the University reached "the pinnacle of football fame in West Virginia" when its team was unbeaten and it was the winner of a post-season game played with Gonzaga College at San Diego, California. The football enthusiasm of West Virginians reached another peak in 1953, when at the end of a brilliant season, the University team met Georgia Tech at New Orleans on New Year's Day, 1954, in the Twentieth Annual Sugar Bowl contest, but only to be beaten. Meanwhile, successful coaches and star football players eclipsed college and university presidents and professors in popularity. In 1925 the director of athletics at the University carried to successful completion a football stadium and in 1929 a fieldhouse, thereby paving the way for the expansion of basketball, the introduction of other sports, and the establishment of a West Virginia Sports Hall of Fame.

The West Virginia Sports Hall of Fame was established in 1950 by the West Virginia Sports Writers Association. The first persons elected to membership were Ira Errett "Rat" Rodgers, West Virginia's only All-American inter-collegiate football player prior to 1955; Fielding H. "Hurry-up" Yost, a former football player at West Virginia University and later coach and athletic director at the University of Michigan; A. Earle "Greasy" Neale, athlete at West Virginia Wesleyan College and subsequently a member of the Cincinnati Reds baseball team and a college and professional football coach; Cliff "Gyp" Battles, star halfback at West Virginia Wesleyan and later a professional football player; and Rocco J. Gorman of Charleston, who for many years was active in the promotion of high school athletics. In January, 1953, Harry A. Stansbury who, as Director of Athletics at West Virginia Wesleyan and later at West Virginia University, placed those institutions on the athletic map, and Cecil Byron "Cebe" Ross, for years a successful coach and athletic director at West Virginia Wesleyan, were added to the roll of "West Virginia athlete immortals." In 1954 the honor went to Roy M. "Legs" Hawley, who served as director of intercollegiate athletics at West Virginia University from 1938 to 1954, and to Joseph F. Stydahar, a star University football tackle and basketball center and an All-American professional football star and coach. In 1955 the honorees were Cameron "Cam" Henderson and Lewis R. "Hack" Wilson. As the coach of both football and basketball at Davis and Elkins College from 1923 to 1935 and of football from 1935 to 1949 and basketball from 1935 to 1955 at Marshall College, Henderson kept both of those institutions in the intercollegiate athletic limelight during his tenures. In December, 1947, a quintet coached by him won the Los Angeles Invitational. As a Chicago Cub, Wilson set a record in 1930 in the National League for home runs and runs batted in.

A favorite place for conventions, both state and national, White Sulphur Springs was also a popular sports center. Since 1884, when the first organized golf club in America was formed there, it was a favorite rallying point for the rapidly growing tribe of golfers. In 1955 it had three golf courses, two of eighteen holes each. Two of these courses were designed by Charles Blair MacDonald, the first amateur golf champion of the United States. The West Virginia Annual Golf Tournament, organized in 1932, was held on the White Sulphur courses, as were also contests of national and international interest; "Slamming Sammy" Snead, a resident of White Sulphur Springs, won many major tournaments at home and abroad. With one of the largest and most beautiful pools in the United States, swimming was one of the most popular of White Sulphur sports; polo was introduced in 1932; its tennis courts were frequented by the country's ranking stars; and skeet shooting was introduced in 1935.

Of West Virginia sports, skiing was perhaps the newest in 1955. Beginning about 1950 the Oglebay Park Skiing Club maintained a quarter-mile run at Oglebay Park, near Wheeling. Since 1950 also the Ski Club of Washington, D. C. has owned and operated a skiing area on Cabin Mountain near Davis. Unlike the Oglebay run, the Davis course was usable during most of the winter and spring seasons.

The state, as a whole, had meanwhile become sports-minded with respect to golf, hunting, and fishing. Practically every city and even some of the small towns had a golf course; the state forests were created and maintained largely to accommodate hunters; and streams were stocked and artificial lakes and ponds were built for the use of fishermen. The open season on deer was an unofficial holiday attracting thousands of hunters with a total annual kill in recent years of about 20,000; thousands of fishermen eagerly awaited the opening of the trout and the bass seasons; and the total receipts from the sale of hunting and fishing licenses were almost sufficient to enlarge and maintain an extensive state forest and park program. The changed order of living thus reflected was as significant and perhaps as far reaching as that by which the Industrial Revolution changed the agrarian to an industrial economy.

West Virginians were equally successful in sports on a national and even an international scale. In 1924 Martha Norelius, trained at White Sulphur Springs, won the 400-meter Olympic swim at Paris. She repeated the feat in 1928 at Amsterdam, and in 1929 she won the ten-mile Wrigley Marathon in Toronto, Canada. In 1917, a West Virginia rifle team, true to 1776 traditions, won the world record for consecutive hits. Five out of six of the contestants made perfect scores. In 1928 and again in 1932, Don Gwinn of St. Marys, won Olympic honors as a hammer thrower. For three quarters of a century West Virginia has been represented on one or more of the major league baseball teams.

STATE PRIDE

The common statehood of the Virginias denied to West Virginia exclusive claim to those frontier events and conditions, within her bounds, out of which state pride is born. But, in the course of almost a century, the daughter state developed traditions which were pride inspiring. The beauty of her hills, her mountains and her streams is not the least of her natural resources. Meanwhile, residents were slowly awakening to the fact that their state was becoming increasingly attractive to tourists. Relying upon its natural beauty and its location at the crossroads of the eastern part of the United States, they have taken steps toward making it one of the choice tourist spots of the country. This possibility was the motive force in the cooperative movement of the West Virginia Department of Mines, the State Soil Conservation districts, and the Agricultural Experiment Station to prevent mutilation of the West Virginia landscape through strip-mining operations as well as to correct that already committed. There was also a growing sentiment on the part of residents of the state against marring the scenic beauty of their highways by advertising billboards and other commercial devices.

Among still other things making for pride in the Mountain State was the system of locks and dams assuring a year-round stage of navigable water on the Ohio River and its Monongahela and Kanawha tributaries; the Tygart Valley and the Bluestone reservoirs making possible a measure of flood control, fishing and recreation centers, and year-round water supplies for a number of municipalities; a system of state and national parks and forests for the preservation of historic sites and as an aid to conservation; and last, but not least, the State Capitol with its gold-gilded dome visible by day and by night over considerable distances. The Capitol was located in East Charleston on an elevation overlooking the Kanawha River. Here, under direction of Cass Gilbert, famous designer of public buildings, was erected one of the most beautiful state houses in the United States. Including the ground and the architect's fee, it cost $9,310,-677.19. The first unit was occupied in 1925, and the finished Capitol was dedicated on June 20, 1932, the state's sixty-ninth birthday.

White Sulphur was not only a sports center, but also a shrine. Here General Robert E. Lee spent the last three summers of his life, and his affection for the place was memorialized by a famous mural of his post-Civil War meeting with General Grant. Here visited Presidents of the United States, including Van Buren, Tyler, Fillmore, Grant, Arthur, Benjamin Harrison, Taft, and Wilson, as well as Senators and Representatives in Congress, governors, and state legislators. Here the Prince of Wales, later King Edward VII of England, visited in 1860, and here, in 1919, West Virginia girls danced with another Prince of Wales, later Edward VIII, now the Duke of Windsor. Thus, while ceasing to be "the Valhalla of the Old South . . . the Old White . . . opened its wide portals to welcome alike the people of every section of our beloved country." For their accommodation the Greenbrier Hotel, an eight-story Georgian structure, was erected in 1913.

State pride was a factor also in the deference paid to the state official symbols—the state seal and coat of arms, the state flower, the state flag, the state bird, and the state tree. Largely because of the beauty of the design and motto, *Montani Semper Liberi* (Mountaineers are always free), the state seal, adopted in 1863 did not lose appeal. As the choice of the school children of the state in a legislative authorized referendum (1903), the state flower (the *Rhododendron Maximum,* or "big laurel") was increasingly popular. Although adopted belatedly (1905), the state flag was generally accorded a place alongside of the national flag. The state flag is composed of a field of pure white carrying in its center the state seal bearing the state motto and the date of its admission to the Union. Above the coat of arms is a ribbon lettered "State of West Virginia" and beneath it is a wreath of rhododendron. A blue border surrounds the white field on all four sides. Civic clubs, garden clubs, and sports organizations participated with the school children and their teachers in a referendum authorized by the legislature in 1949 in the choice of the cardinal as the state bird and the sugar maple as the state tree.

West Virginia's greatest pride, however, was her native and adopted sons and daughters who distinguished themselves by their achievements. In addition to the persons already mentioned were Dwight W. Morrow (Jan. 11, 1873-Oct. 5, 1931), born in Huntington, Cabell County, who, as Ambassador to Mexico, restored friendly relations between that country and the United States following an interim of threatening friction; John Barton Payne (Jan. 26, 1855-Jan. 24, 1935), born at Pruntytown, Taylor County, who was a confidential adviser of President Wilson in World War I and, at the time of his death, Chairman of the Central Committee of the American Red Cross; Anna Jarvis, born at Grafton, Taylor County, founder of Mother's Day; Harry Flood Byrd (b. June 10, 1887) and A. Willis Robertson (b. May 28, 1887), the present United States Senators from Virginia, both of whom were born in Martinsburg, West Virginia; James Hubert Price (Sept. 7, 1878-Nov. 22, 1943), born in Greenbrier County and governor of Virginia from 1938 to 1942; Frederic William Boatright (b. Jan. 28, 1868), born at White Sulphur Springs, who was president of the University of Richmond from 1894 to 1946; Walter P. Reuther, president of the Congress of Industrial Organizations (CIO), who was born (1908) and reared in Wheeling; Charles Byron Jolliffe (b. Nov. 13, 1894), a radio engineer, born at Mannington, who developed frequency standards for measuring operating frequencies of radio stations and who in 1945 became vice-president in charge of laboratories of the RCA corporation; Lt. Col. Frank K. "Pete" Everest of Fairmont, the second person in the world to travel faster than the speed of sound; Lewis L. Strauss, Chairman of the Atomic Energy Commission and director of the Radio Corporation of America, who was born (1896) in Charleston; and James E. Allen, Jr., Commissioner of Education for the State of New York and president of the University of the State of New York comprising the largest educational program in the United States, who was born (1911) and reared in Elkins.

Bibliographical Note

"A Bibliography of West Virginia in Two Parts," in West Virginia Department of Archives and History, *Biennial Report* (Charleston, 1939) is the most complete in print. Part I, of 140 pages, is "A Subject Arrangement of Books which relate to West Virginia and West Virginians; the Title of Books written by West Virginians and Those Printed in West Virginia." Part II, of 369 pages, gives "The Titles of Printed Official Documents of the State, 1861-1939, and the Documents (Printed and Manuscript) Preceding and Relating to the Erection of the State." For additional listings of West Virginiana see James M. Callahan, *Semi-Centennial History of West Virginia* (Charleston, 1913); West Virginia Department of Archives and History, *Third Biennial Report* (Charleston, 1911); Virgil A. Lewis, *Hand Book of West Virginia* (Charleston, 1904); Warren Wood, *Representative Authors of West Virginia* (Ravenswood, W. Va., 1926). The following are helpful: Earl G. Swem, "A Bibliography of Virginia, Part I," in Virginia State Library, *Bulletin,* Vol. 8, nos. 2-4 (Richmond, 1916), being the title of books in the Virginia State Library which relate to Virginia and Virginians; ——————, "A Bibliography of Virginia, Part II," in Virginia State Library, *Bulletin,* Vol. 10, nos. 1-4 (Richmond, 1917), being the titles of the printed official documents of the Commonwealth, 1776-1916; ——————, *Virginia Historical Index,* 2 vols. (Roanoke, Va., 1934-1936), being an analysis of the information that relates to Virginia and Virginians in the *Virginia Magazine of History and Biography* (38 vols.), *William and Mary College Quarterly Historical Magazine* (37 vols.), *Tyler's Quarterly Historical Magazine and Genealogical Magazine* (10 vols.), *Virginia Historical Register and Advertiser* (6 vols.), Hening, *Statutes at Large* (13 vols.), and *The Calendar of Virginia State Papers* (11 vols.).

Journals and diaries of the first explorations of the English beyond the Blue Ridge Mountains include Clarence W. Alvord and Lee Bidgood, *The First Explorations of the Trans-Allegheny Region by the English, 1650-1674* (Cleveland, 1912); Alexander Spotswood, "Official Letters," in Virginia Historical Society, *Collections,* New Series, Vol. VII (Richmond, 1882); Rev. James Fontaine, *Memoirs of a Huguenot Family* (New York, 1853, 1872); "Diaries of Moravian Missionaries," in *Virginia Magazine of History and Biography,* vols. XI and XII (Richmond, 1903-1905); Donegal Presbytery, *Minutes,* in

Witherspoon Library, Philadelphia, Pa.; J. Stoddard Johnston, "First Explorations in Kentucky," being the journals of Thomas Walker and Christopher Gist, in *Filson Club Publication,* no. 13 (Louisville, Ky., 1898); William M. Darlington, ed., *Christopher Gist's Journals* (Pittsburgh, 1893); Thomas Lewis, *Journal, September 10, 1746-February, 1747* (New Market, Va., 1925); Lois Mulkearn, ed., *George Mercer Papers Relating to the Ohio Company* (Pittsburgh, 1954); Delf Norona, ed., "Joshua Fry's Report on the Back Settlements of Virginia," in *Virginia Magazine of History and Biography,* Vol. LVI (Richmond); J. C. Fitzpatrick, ed., *Diaries of George Washington,* 4 vols. (Boston, 1925); and the writings of public men, such as George Washington, George Mason, Thomas Jefferson, Benjamin Franklin, and Sir William Johnson. For additional listings, see Abernethy, *Western Lands;* Alvord, *Mississippi Valley;* Ambler, *George Washington and the West;* Bailey, *Ohio Company;* Buck, *Planting of Civilization;* Pease, *Anglo-French Boundary Dispute in the West;* Saville, *George Morgan;* and Volwiler, *George Croghan.*

The following are useful for the study of the American Revolutionary and the post-Revolutionary periods of West Virginia history: the Boone, George Rogers Clark, Pittsburgh and Northwest Virginia, and Virginia MSS in the *Draper Collection* in the Library of the Wisconsin Historical Society, Madison, Wis. See also Louise P. Kellogg, "West Virginia Material in the Draper Manuscripts," in *West Virginia History,* Vol. II (Charleston, 1940); ———, *Frontier Advance on the Upper Ohio, 1778-1779* (Madison, Wis., 1916); ———, *Frontier Retreat on the Upper Ohio, 1779-1781* (Madison, Wis., 1917); Reuben G. Thwaites and Louise P. Kellogg, *Documentary History of Dunmore's War, 1774* (Madison, Wis., 1905); ———, *Revolution on the Upper Ohio, 1775-1777* (Madison, Wis., 1908); ———, *Frontier Defense on the Upper Ohio, 1777-1778* (Madison, Wis., 1912); Consul W. Butterfield, ed., *Washington-Crawford Letters* (Cincinnati, 1877); U. S. Congress, *Annals, 1789-1824;* Gaillard Hunt and Worthington C. Ford, eds., Continental Congress, *Journals, 1774-1789,* 27 vols. (Washington, 1904-1928); Virginia General Assembly, *Session Acts;* Virginia, *Revised Code,* 2 vols. (Richmond, 1819).

Primary sources for the period of West Virginia history preceding the Civil War include public documents, newspapers, and debates and proceedings. *Debates of the Virginia State Convention of 1829-1830* is indispensable. The debates of the constitutional convention of 1850-1851 were not printed, but speeches were published in pamphlet form and in Richmond newspapers, as were also most of the speeches in the slavery debate in the Virginia General Assembly of 1831-1832. An *Address to the People of West Virginia Showing that Slavery is Injurious to the Public Welfare,* otherwise known as the "Ruffner Pamphlet," first published at Lexington, Virginia, in 1847, was reprinted in Wheeling in 1862, and at Bridgewater, Virginia, 1933. The Virginia codes of 1849 and 1860 are useful, and journals of the general assembly contain much data. John W. Williams, *The Index to the Enrolled Bills of the General Assembly, 1776-1862* (Richmond, 1908) is a convenient guide to the contents of session acts.

The best primary source for the formative period of West Virginia is the *Debates and Proceedings of the First Constitutional Convention of West Virginia, 1861-1863,* 3 vols. (Huntington, 1942). *The War of the Rebellion, Official Records,* 70 vols. in 128 books, contain the most authentic information on military movements. Public and private letters of individuals and soldier memoirs, such as *Diary and Letters of Rutherford Birchard Hayes,* Vol. II, ed. by Charles R. Williams (Columbus, Ohio, 1922), and Jacob Dolson Cox, *Military Reminiscences of the Civil War,* 2 vols. (New York, 1900) contain data. The story of the formation and admission of West Virginia is told in the *Congressional Globe,* Thirty-seventh Congress, Second and Third Sessions, and in the *Lincoln Papers,* now available in the Library of Congress. Newspapers, notably the Wheeling *Intelligencer,* the Wellsburg *Herald,* the Point Pleasant *Register,* and other files, available in the West Virginia University Library, in the Department of Archives and History at Charleston, and in the Library of Congress, give local color as well as facts.

Primary sources for West Virginia history covering the period since the Civil War are the public archives, including codes, session acts of the legislature, executive papers, and reports of boards and commissions. The newspapers are useful, and private papers, mostly letters, aggregating about 2,500,000 items in the West Virginia University Library, are relatively unexplored fields. Brief listings of manuscripts and archival accessions are contained in five reports of the Division of Documents, West Virginia University Library (Morgantown, 1936-1953). The State Department of Archives and History has, since 1948, prepared a "Short Title Check-List of West Virginia State Publications." The Virginia and West Virginia reels of the microfilm collection of *Early State Records,* compiled by the Library of Congress and the University of North Carolina, are available in the West Virginia University Library.

In addition to the guides and sources cited above, many of the titles mentioned in Chapters XIII and XXXV, and in footnotes throughout the book, are rich in bibliographical data.

Appendix A

Roster of West Virginia Governors and U. S. Senators

1863-1957

GOVERNORS

NAME	RESIDENCE	POLITICS	FROM	TO
Arthur Ingram Boreman	Wood	Republican	June 20, 1863	Feb. 26, 1869
*Daniel D. T. Farnsworth	Upshur	Republican	Feb. 27, 1869	March 3, 1869
William Erskine Stevenson	Wood	Republican	March 4, 1869	March 3, 1871
John Jeremiah Jacob	Hampshire	Democrat	March 4, 1871	March 3, 1877
Henry Mason Mathews	Greenbrier	Democrat	March 4, 1877	March 3, 1881
Jacob Beeson Jackson	Wood	Democrat	March 4, 1881	March 3, 1885
Emanuel Willis Wilson	Kanawha	Democrat	March 4, 1885	Feb. 5, 1890
Aretas Brooks Fleming	Marion	Democrat	Feb. 6, 1890	March 3, 1893
William Alexander MacCorkle	Kanawha	Democrat	March 4, 1893	March 3, 1897
George Wesley Atkinson	Ohio	Republican	March 4, 1897	March 3, 1901
Albert Blakeslee White	Wood	Republican	March 4, 1901	March 3, 1905
William M. O. Dawson	Preston	Republican	March 4, 1905	March 3, 1909
William Ellsworth Glasscock	Monongalia	Republican	March 4, 1909	March 3, 1913
Henry Drury Hatfield	McDowell	Republican	March 4, 1913	March 3, 1917
John Jacob Cornwell	Hampshire	Democrat	March 4, 1917	March 3, 1921
Ephraim Franklin Morgan	Marion	Republican	March 4, 1921	March 3, 1925
Howard Mason Gore	Harrison	Republican	March 4, 1925	March 3, 1929
William Gustavus Conley	Kanawha	Republican	March 4, 1929	March 3, 1933
Herman Guy Kump	Randolph	Democrat	March 4, 1933	Jan. 18, 1937
Homer A. Holt	Fayette	Democrat	Jan. 18, 1937	Jan. 13, 1941
Matthew Mansfield Neely	Marion	Democrat	Jan. 13, 1941	Jan. 15, 1945
Clarence W. Meadows	Raleigh	Democrat	Jan. 16, 1945	Jan. 16, 1949
Okey L. Patteson	Fayette	Democrat	Jan. 17, 1949	Jan. 18, 1953
William C. Marland	Wyoming	Democrat	Jan. 19, 1953	Jan. 13, 1957
Cecil H. Underwood	Tyler	Republican	Jan. 14, 1957	....

* President of the state senate. Served as governor for the unexpired term of Governor Boreman, who was elected to the United States Senate in 1869.

SENATORS, 1863-1956

Name	County	Politics	From	To
Peter G. Van Winkle	Wood	Republican	1863	1869
Waitman T. Willey	Monongalia	Republican	1863	1871
Arthur I. Boreman	Wood	Republican	1869	1875
Henry G. Davis	Mineral	Democrat	1871	1883
Allen T. Caperton	Monroe	Democrat	1875	1876
Samuel Price	Greenbrier	Democrat	1876	1877
Frank Hereford	Monroe	Democrat	1877	1881
Johnson N. Camden	Wood	Democrat	1881	1887
John E. Kenna	Kanawha	Democrat	1883	1893
Charles J. Faulkner	Berkeley	Democrat	1887	1899
Johnson N. Camden	Wood	Democrat	1893	1895
Stephen B. Elkins	Randolph	Republican	1895	1911
Nathan B. Scott	Ohio	Republican	1899	1911
Davis Elkins	Randolph	Republican	1911	1911
Clarence W. Watson	Marion	Democrat	1911	1913
William E. Chilton	Kanawha	Democrat	1911	1917
Nathan Goff	Harrison	Republican	1913	1919
Howard Sutherland	Randolph	Republican	1917	1923
Davis Elkins	Monongalia	Republican	1919	1925
M. Mansfield Neely	Marion	Democrat	1923	1929
Guy D. Goff	Harrison	Republican	1925	1931
Henry D. Hatfield	Cabell	Republican	1929	1935
M. Mansfield Neely	Marion	Democrat	1931	1941
Rush D. Holt	Lewis	Democrat	1935	1941
Harley M. Kilgore	Raleigh	Democrat	1941	1956
Joseph Rosier	Marion	Democrat	1941	1942
Hugh Ike Shott, Sr.	Mercer	Republican	1942	1943
Chapman J. Revercomb	Kanawha	Republican	1943	1949
M. Mansfield Neely	Marion	Democrat	1949	....
William R. Laird, III	Fayette	Democrat	1956	1956
Chapman J. Revercomb	Kanawha	Republican	1956	....

Appendix B

West Virginia Counties

Name	County Seat	When Formed	Area	Population (1950)	Named For
Barbour	Philippi	1843	345.41	19,745	Philip P. Barbour
Berkeley	Martinsburg	1772	324.78	30,359	Norborne Berkeley (Baron Botetourt)
Boone	Madison	1847	506	33,173	Daniel Boone
Braxton	Sutton	1836	519.70	18,082	Carter Braxton
Brooke	Wellsburg	1797	92.50	26,904	Robert Brooke, Governor of Virginia
Cabell	Huntington	1809	285.95	108,035	William H. Cabell, Governor of Virginia
Calhoun	Grantsville	1856	280.20	10,259	John C. Calhoun
Clay	Clay	1858	346.61	14,961	Henry Clay
Doddridge	West Union	1845	321.61	9,026	Philip Doddridge
Fayette	Fayetteville	1831	666.50	82,443	General LaFayette
Gilmer	Glenville	1845	342.40	9,746	Thomas W. Gilmer, Governor of Virginia
Grant	Petersburg	1866	478	8,756	General U. S. Grant
Greenbrier	Lewisburg	1778	1,022.80	39,295	Greenbrier River
Hampshire	Romney	1754	641.44	12,577	Hampshire, England
Hancock	New Cumberland	1848	88.55	34,388	John Hancock
Hardy	Moorefield	1786	575.52	10,032	Samuel Hardy, A Virginian
Harrison	Clarksburg	1784	417.85	85,296	Benjamin Harrison, Governor of Virginia
Jackson	Ripley	1831	471.98	15,299	Andrew Jackson
Jefferson	Charles Town	1801	212.41	17,184	Thomas Jefferson
Kanawha	Charleston	1788	913.38	239,629	Kanawha River
Lewis	Weston	1816	391.35	21,074	Colonel Charles Lewis
Lincoln	Hamlin	1867	437.04	22,466	Abraham Lincoln
Logan	Logan	1824	455.82	77,391	Indian Chieftain Logan
Marion	Fairmont	1842	313.55	98,887	General Francis Marion
Marshall	Moundsville	1835	315.26	71,521	John Marshall
Mason	Point Pleasant	1804	445.75	36,893	George Mason
McDowell	Welch	1858	538.40	98,887	James McDowell, Governor of Virginia
Mercer	Princeton	1837	423.91	23,537	General Hugh Mercer
Mineral	Keyser	1866	330	75,013	Its mineral resources
Mingo	Williamson	1895	423.50	22,333	Mingo Indian Tribe
Monongalia	Morgantown	1776	368.82	47,409	Monongahela River

Name	County Seat	When Formed	Area	Population (1950)	Named For
Monroe	Union	1799	473.80	60,797	James Monroe
Morgan	Berkeley Springs ..	1820	231.26	8,276	General Daniel Morgan
Nicholas	Summersville	1818	656.77	27,696	Wilson C. Nicholas, Governor of Virginia
Ohio	Wheeling	1776	109	71,672	Ohio River
Pendleton ...	Franklin	1788	696.88	9,313	Edmund Pendleton
Pleasants ...	St. Marys	1851	134.65	6,369	James Pleasants, Governor of Virginia
Pocahontas ..	Marlinton	1821	942.61	12,480	Indian Princess Pocahontas
Preston	Kingwood	1818	653.88	31,399	James P. Preston, Governor of Virginia
Putnam	Winfield	1848	350.57	21,021	General Israel Putnam
Raleigh	Beckley	1850	610.15	96,273	Sir Walter Raleigh
Randolph ...	Elkins	1787	1,046.34	30,558	Edmund Randolph, Governor of Virginia
Ritchie	Harrisville	1843	455.27	12,535	Thomas Ritchie
Roane	Spencer	1856	486.20	18,408	Judge Spencer Roane
Summers ...	Hinton	1871	367.76	19,183	Judge George W. Summers
Taylor	Grafton	1844	177.10	18,422	John Taylor
Tucker	Parsons	1856	421.67	10,600	Judge St. George Tucker
Tyler	Middlebourne	1814	260.12	10,535	John Tyler
Upshur	Buckhannon	1851	354.86	19,242	Judge Abel P. Upshur
Wayne	Wayne	1842	517.88	38,696	General Anthony Wayne
Webster	Webster Springs ..	1860	558.60	17,888	Daniel Webster
Wetzel	New Martinsville ..	1846	360.47	20,154	Lewis Wetzel
Wirt	Elizabeth	1848	234.41	5,119	William Wirt of Maryland
Wood	Parkersburg	1798	377.82	66,540	James Wood, Governor of Virginia
Wyoming ...	Pineville	1850	507.30	37,540	Wyoming Indian tribe
	Totals	....	24,282.45	2,005,552	

Index

D

I

M

N

X

Y

Z